W9-CBJ-902

Wines and Vineyards of Character and Charm in France

Published in the United States by Fodor's Travel Publications, Inc.
Published in France by Payot/Rivages

Fodor's is a registered trademark of Fodor's Travel Publications, Inc.

ISBN 0-679-00205-7
First Edition

Wines and Vineyards of Character and Charm in France

Translators: Anne Norris, James Lawther MW, Craig Baker
Layout: Marie Gastaut
Cover design: Fabrizio La Rocca
Front cover photograph: Château de Chaintres, photo by François Tissier

Special Sales

Printed in Italy by Printer-Trento
10 9 8 7 6 5 4 3 2 1

Fodor's RIVAGES

WINES AND VINEYARDS of Character and Charm IN FRANCE

Project editors

Antoine Gerbelle and Dominique Couvreur

Fodor's Travel Publications, Inc.

New York • Toronto • London • Sydney • Auckland

www.fodors.com/

FOREWORD

First published in Paris, Rivages' *Guide to the Wines and Vineyards of France* contains descriptions of 514 vineyards, including 111 which appear here for the first time; most are privately owned vineyards but we have also included *négociants* and cooperative cellars, all selected for their practice of selling wines directly from the property.

Meant for the traveler, the Guide is designed for wine lovers who enjoy tasting in the company of charming winemakers, joining in the atmosphere of their cellar, as well as seeing the beautiful French countryside on the way.

Selective, it is the result of the authors' many annual tastings and visits to fifteen vineyard regions in France, finally choosing the outstanding winemakers in each region. They have been selected for the quality, the regularity, and the availability of their wines.

Independent, the Guide is not supported by any advertising or financial backing from the winemakers, and it is not affiliated with any press organization using such advertising.

Practical, it offers you all the information you need, including road maps, to drive to the vineyard with a precise idea of the winery, the wines, and the owner who will greet you. We have also indicated the best hotels and bed-and-breakfasts in each vineyard region; restaurants notable for their cuisine or their prices; and wine museums and points of interest along the way.

Up to date, it mentions only wines which can actually be bought and, most importantly, those which will be made available during the year. You can thus look forward to them and reserve them in advance.

The prices given in this Guide are indicated in French francs for one bottle, based on a minimum purchase of twelve bottles shipped from the vineyard (shipping costs not included). It is always possible that prices may change during the year, notably when the new vintage is made available.

HOW TO USE THIS GUIDE

At the beginning of each region you will find an introduction to the wines and the appellations as well as recommended hotels and restaurants, preceded by a road map on which each vineyard is indicated by its page number. In the second part, the vineyard regions are presented in alphabetical order. Within each region, the wines are classified by alphabetical order of the appellation. The Loire Valley region has been divided into four sub-regions: Muscadet, Anjou-Saumur, Touraine, and the Center; that of the Rhône Valley, into two: North and South.
At the end of the book, two alphabetical indexes are given for the vineyards and the vineyard owners.

With our thanks in advance, please send your comments and/or suggestions to:

Guide de Charme des Vins et Vignobles en France
Dominique Couvreur et Antoine Gerbelle
Éditions Payot et Rivages
106, boulevard Saint-Germain
75006 Paris - France.

TABLE OF CONTENTS

Recommended Hotels, Restaurants, and Places of Interest are given throughout the Guide, region by region. They are numbered and indicated on the road maps by their number on a purple flag. The vineyards which follow this part of the Guide are indicated on the map by their page number on a red flag.

CORSICA

JURA

LANGUEDOC

PROVENCE

ROUSSILLON

SAVOIE

SOUTH-WEST

LOIRE VALLEY

NORTHERN RHONE

SOUTHERN RHONE

KEY TO THE MAPS

Scale : 1:900,000

maps 15 to 17 : scale 1:920,000

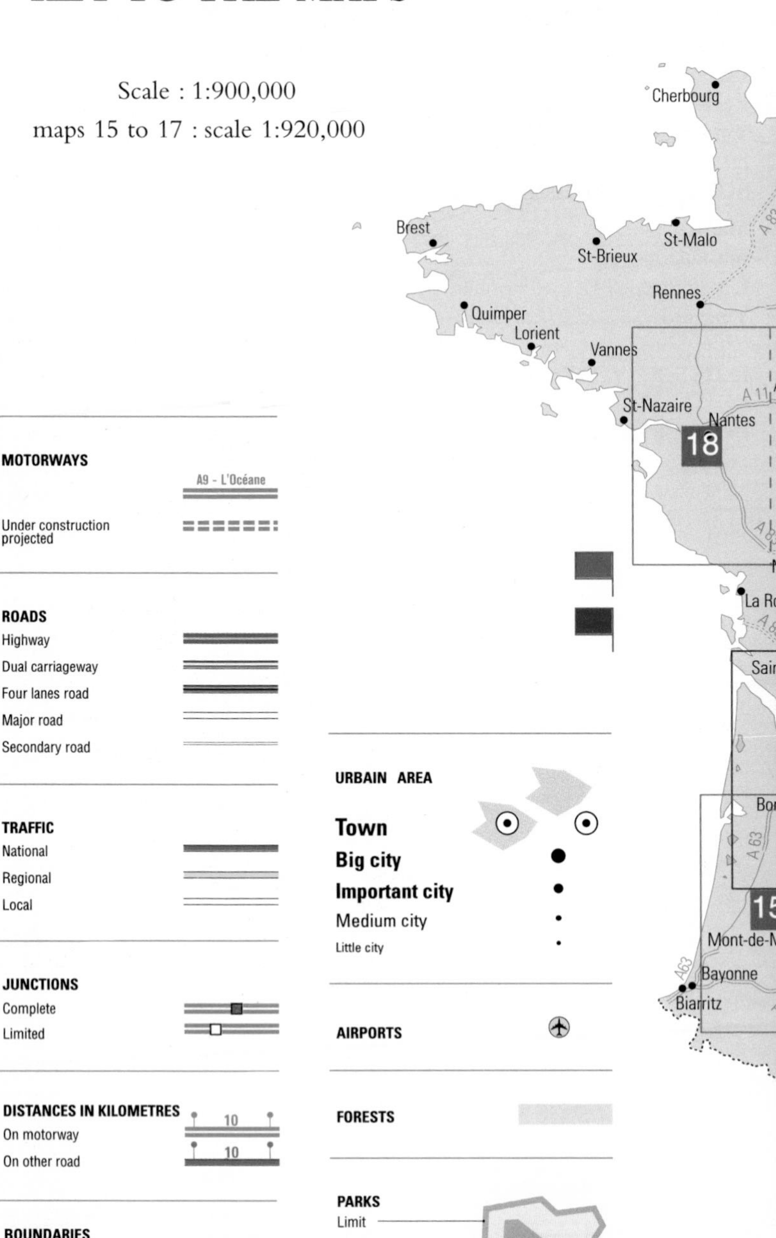
Cherbourg
Brest
St-Malo
St-Brieux
Rennes
Quimper
Lorient
Vannes
St-Nazaire
Nantes
A 11
A 83
18
Bayonne
Biarritz
Mont-de-Ma
15
A 63
MOTORWAYS
A9 - L'Océane
Under construction projected
ROADS
Highway
Dual carriageway
Four lanes road
Major road
Secondary road
TRAFFIC
National
Regional
Local
JUNCTIONS
Complete
Limited
DISTANCES IN KILOMETRES
On motorway
On other road
10
10
BOUNDARIES
National boundary
Region area
Department area
URBAIN AREA
Town
Big city
Important city
Medium city
Little city
AIRPORTS
FORESTS
PARKS
Limit
Center of the park

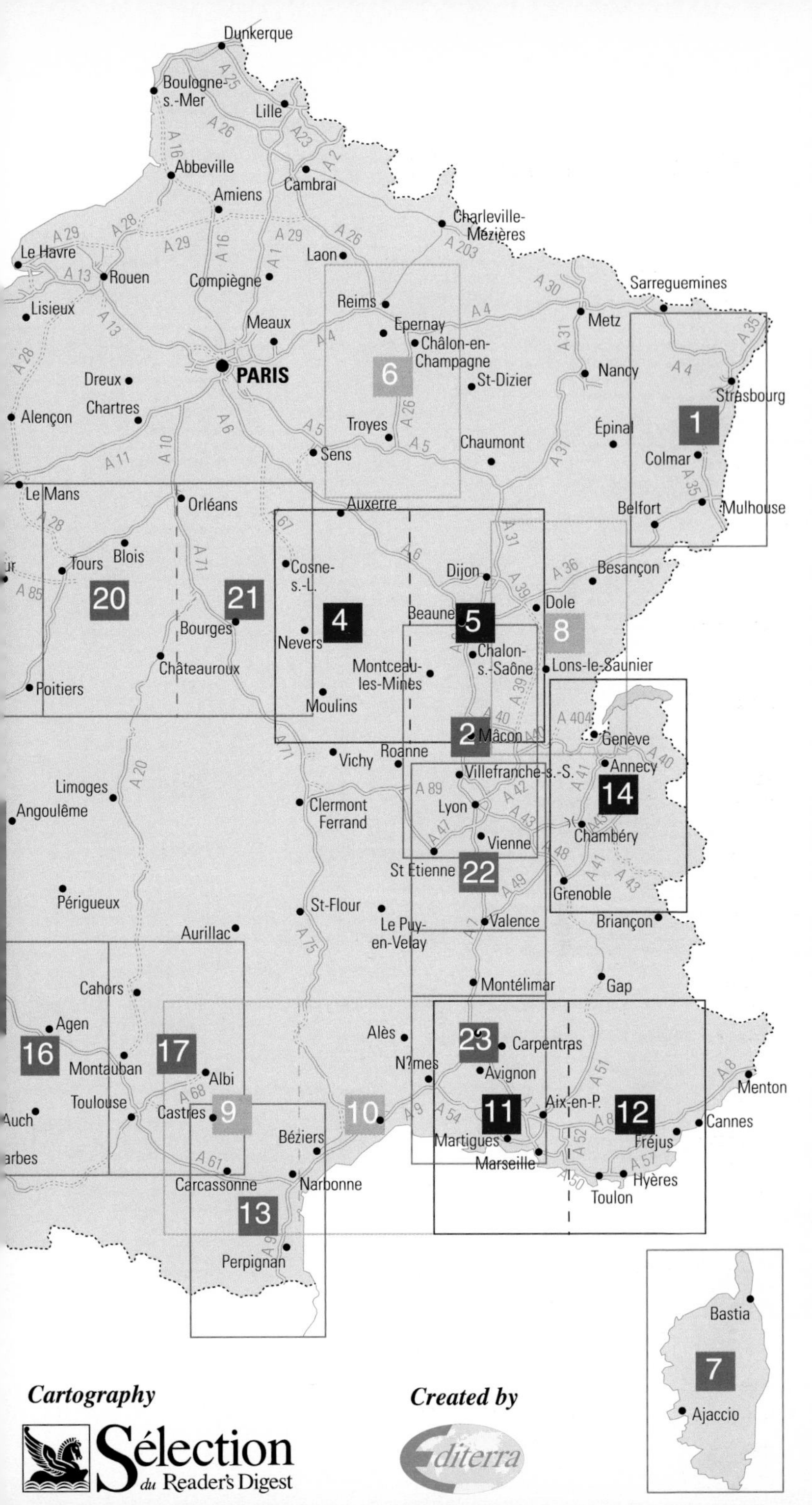
Dunkerque
Boulogne-s.-Mer
Lille
Abbeville
Cambrai
Amiens
Charleville-Mézières
Le Havre
Rouen
Laon
Compiègne
Lisieux
Reims
Sarreguemines
Metz
Epernay
Meaux
Châlon-en-Champagne
PARIS
Nancy
Dreux
St-Dizier
Strasbourg
Chartres
Alençon
Troyes
Épinal
Colmar
Sens
Chaumont
Le Mans
Belfort
Mulhouse
Orléans
Auxerre
Tours
Blois
Cosne-s.-L.
Dijon
Besançon
Dole
Beaune
Bourges
Nevers
Châteauroux
Chalon-s.-Saône
Lons-le-Saunier
Montceau-les-Mines
Poitiers
Moulins
Mâcon
Genève
Vichy
Roanne
Annecy
Villefranche-s.-S.
Limoges
Angoulême
Clermont Ferrand
Lyon
Chambéry
Vienne
St Etienne
Grenoble
Périgueux
St-Flour
Le Puy-en-Velay
Valence
Briançon
Aurillac
Montélimar
Gap
Cahors
Agen
Alès
Carpentras
Montauban
Albi
N?mes
Avignon
Menton
Toulouse
Aix-en-P.
Auch
Castres
Cannes
Béziers
Fréjus
Martigues
Marseille
Carcassonne
Narbonne
Hyères
Toulon
Perpignan
Bastia
Ajaccio
A 25
A 26
A 16
A 23
A 2
A 28
A 29
A 16
A 1
A 29
A 26
A 13
A 203
A 30
A 4
A 31
A 35
A 4
A 6
A 5
A 26
A 5
A 31
A 10
A 11
A 28
A 71
A 85
A 31
A 36
A 39
A 6
A 40
A 404
A 40
A 77
A 89
A 42
A 43
A 41
A 47
A 48
A 41
A 43
A 49
A 20
A 75
A 7
A 51
A 68
A 9
A 54
A 8
A 52
A 57
A 61
A 50
A 9
A 8
20
21
4
5
8
6
1
2
14
22
16
17
9
10
23
11
12
13
7
Cartography
Sélection du Reader's Digest
Created by
Editerra

C O N T E N T S

A L S A C E

B E A U J O L A I S

B O R D E A U X

B O U R G O G N E

C H A M P A G N E

C O R S I C A

J U R A

LANGUEDOC

P R O V E N C E

R O U S S I L L O N

S A V O I E

S O U T H - W E S T

L O I R E V A L L E Y

SOUTHERN RHONE

ALSACE

1
Sarreguemines
Bitche
Sturzelbronn
Wissembourg
Rohrbach-lès-Bitche
Lembach
Lauterbourg
Hellimer
Sarralbe
Lemberg
Niederbronn-les-B.
Woerth
Soultz-s/s-Forêt
Sarre-Union
Lorentzen
Tieffenbach
Rothbach
Reichshoffen
Seltz
Drulingen
La Petite-Pierre
Ingwiller
Moder
Sauer
Soufflenheim
Mittersheim
Fénétrange
Bouxwiller
Haguenau
Rauwiller
Phalsbourg
Drusenheim
Bischwiller
Hochfelden
Brumath
Sarrebourg
Azoudange
Saverne
Bühl
Ottersweier
Rheinau
Maizières-lès-Vic
Héming
Marmoutier
Truchtersheim
Dabo
La Wantzenau
Schiltigheim
Lorquin
Bas-Rhin
Wasselonne
Abreschviller
Achern
Lafrimbolle
Kehl
Strasbourg
Blâmont
Cirey-s.-V.
Niederhaslach
Mutzig
Molsheim
Oberkirch
Domèvre-s.-V.
Montigny
Rosheim
Offenburg
Allarmont
Schirmeck
Obernai
Badonviller
Baccarat
Erstein
Gengenbach
Raon-l'Étape
Le Hohwald
Barr
Senones
Benfeld
Friesenheim
Moyenmoûtier
Villé
Dambach-la-Ville
Boofzheim
Lahr
Biberach
La Salle
Provenchères-s.-Fave
St-Dié
Liepvre
Sélestat
Ettenheim
Haslach-im-Kinzigtal
Ste-Marie-aux-Mines
Herbolzheim
Brouvelieures
Bruyères
Anould
Ribeauvillé
Marckolsheim
Kenzingen
Elzach
Emmendingen
Corcieux
Fraize
Kaysersberg
Endigen
Waldkirch
Granges-s.-V.
Xonrupt-Longemer
Orbey
Colmar
Ihringen
Breisach-am-Rhein
Freiburg-im-Breisgau
Le Tholy
Wintzenheim
Gérardmer
Kirchzarten
Vagney
La Bresse
Munster
Neuf-Brisach
Metzeral
Rhin
Cornimont
Lautenbach
Rouffach
Fessenheim
Kruth
Regulsheim
Hirtzfelden
Bad-Krozingen
Saulxures-s.-M.
Buhl
Guebwiller
Staufen-im-Breisgau
Le Thillot
Bussang
Soultz-Haut-Rhin
St-Amarin
Ensisheim
Chalampé
Todtnau
Müllheim
Sewen
Cernay
Ottmarsheim
Bernau
Servance
Thann
Illzach
Schönau-im-Schwarzw.
Masevaux
Schliengen
Todtmoos
Rougemont-le-Ch.
Mulhouse
Kandern
Zell-im-Wiesental
Haut-Rhin
Kembs
Balschwiller
Schopfheim
Valdoie
Sierentz
Lörrach
Altkirch
Wehr
Belfort
Dannemarie
St-Louis
Rheinfelden
Hirsingue
Basel
Waldighofen
Héricourt
Montbéliard
Grandvillars
Seppois
Werentzhouse
Reinach
Delle
Liestal
Gelterkinden
Sochaux
Audincourt
Ferrette
Sissach

INTRODUCTION

Travellers about to visit Alsace for the first time are lucky, for they are about to discover a region of unique charm: quaint cottages nestling in the heart of vineyards, brightly colored half-timbered houses; intriguing wrought-iron signs above the shops; Romanesque churches whose sculptures invariably evoke the world of wine; winemakers' footpaths winding through the vineyards like so many lanes in a lovely park; flaming tarts brightening bistrot tables where, on Saturday, a guest often serenades with his accordion; gastronomic restaurants not too grand to honor traditional Alsatian recipes; farmhouse/inns which keep alive the taste of ancient dishes; wine festivals like so many Flemish bazaars, travelling from village to village; the winemakers themselves, so different in character--the Protestant inevitably more austere than his wine, the Rabelaisian Catholic--and the innumerable wines that constantly display their different facets. Lucky, too, are those who return: They know Alsace well, and yet they will never tire of her.

ALSATIAN APPELLATIONS AND CRUS

The most common appellation is the AOC Alsace *(Appellation d'Origine Contrôlée)*, followed by the name of the grape variety and possibly a mention of the wine village. Fifty villages are entitled to mention Grand Cru on the label. For them, production standards are more severe, requiring lower yields (65 hectoliters per hectare as opposed to 80 hectolitres for the simple Alsace appellation), and a higher minimum degree of potential alcohol in the must, or unfermented grape juice. Wines made from only four grape varieties are entitled to the Grand Cru mention: Riesling, Pinot Gris, Muscat, and Gewürztraminer.

VARIETALS AND BLENDS

As opposed to the other French AOC vineyards, the grape variety takes primacy in Alsace over the *terroir,* the vineyard region. It must be mentioned on the label, including Grand Cru labels (elsewhere in France, this mention is generally forbidden).
Such was not the case before the phylloxera scourge, when grape varieties were often planted together in the vineyards (*en foule*, crowded), then harvested and

vinified together.

But to emphasize the outstanding quality of certain *terroirs,* a few rare winemakers mention the *terroir* on the label before that of the grape variety, while respecting the Alsatian tradition of making their wines from a single grape, called varietals.

However, Alsace does make wines blended from several grape varieties, but these are generally disparaged (sometimes wrongly so). First, there is Edelzwicker (often called *Edel* for short), often sold by the liter or, in restaurants, by the carafe. Sylvaner, Pinot, and Chasselas usually make up the Edelzwicker blend, which is most often made from wines left over in vats which had been used for vinifying those varietals. The wine thus earned its pejorative name, "the cellar garbage can." Several winemakers make especially good "Edel", adding so-called "noble" grape varieties--Riesling, Muscat, or Gewürztraminer--to the usual blend. In the vineyard descriptions that follow, we have indicated several remarkable Edelzwickers whose reasonable price make them a pleasant wine for every day.

Gentil is a special kind of Edelzwicker, designating the wine from parcels where vines are planted together, as in the past. By extension, the term Gentil can occasionally refer to a cellar-blended wine made from grapes from different parcels, and blended from noble grapes.

ALSATIAN *CEPAGES,* GRAPE VARIETIES

Officially, there are eight *cépages,* mostly white grapes, but with several more or less distant cousins also invited to the table.

Chasselas (or *Gutedel*) is the poor cousin, representing about 4% of the vineyards, but these are being dug up and replanted with more popular grapes. Cool and light, it is found mainly in Edelzwicker blends.

Sylvaner, introduced into Alsace from Austria and perhaps Transylvaia at the end of the 18th century, is the principal Alsatian *cépage,* even if it is considered at the bottom of the quality scale. It is planted mainly in the northern Bas Rhin *département,* which accounts for about 22% of Alsatian vineyards. Also an Edelzwicker base wine, refreshing and firm, Sylvaner can be of fine quality when it comes from old vines with low yields or from a great *terroir.* Some winemakers, particularly those of the Zotzenberg vineyard site in Mittelbergheim, make astonishingly good Sylvaner.

Pinot Blanc is a Burgundian grape originally from Northern Italy, while the Auxerrois (not to be confused with the red grape of Cahors) apparently came from Lorraine or Luxembourg. These two grape varieties are widely cultivated (in about 17% of Alsatian vineyards) and are often blended under the generic name of Pinot Blanc. Pinot Blanc itself is often fresh and lively, the Auxerrois more round. As they are not recognized as noble grape varieties, wines from these *cépages* are not entitled to the Grand Cru mention. Several winemakers persist, however, and rightly so, in keeping their old vines planted on Grand Cru *terroirs* despite the law (this is the case with André Kientzler's "K" Auxerrois planted in his Kirchberg vineyard.)

Muscat is planted in only about 4% of the vineyards but it is known for its fruitiness and musky aroma. There are two varieties: Alsatian Muscat, which is full-bodied; and the more delicate Ottonel Muscat, most often blended to produce very aromatic dry wines and rare Late Harvest wines.

A L S A C E

INTRODUCTION

Riesling, the great Rhine grape, is widely planted in over 18% of Alsatian vineyards. A delicate wine of great breeding, fruity when young and often developing distinctly mineral notes (tasters often describe old Rieslings as having "petroleum" or "hydrocarbon" notes), it continues to mature even in relatively low temperatures, making it the king of late-harvest and *Sélection de Grains Nobles* wines.

Pinot Gris Tokay is becoming highly fashionable but it is grown in only about 4.5% of the vineyards. The word *tokay* is said to be Hungarian, but the grape is in fact of Burgundian origin and has been known in Alsace since the 17th century. It makes a rich, luscious wine with very typical smoky aromas, often marked by a trace of residual sugar. A healthy wine, it matures well in cold temperatures. While it doesn't easily acquire *pourriture noble*, it is magnificent when it does, yielding great *Vendanges Tardives* and *Sélections de Grains Nobles* bottlings.

Gewürztraminer, one of the main white grapes of Alsace and planted in 21% of the vineyards, is an especially aromatic clone of the Traminer or Savagnin Rose grape; the latter is found in its pure form in the Klevner appellation from the Heiligenstein vineyard site. Gewürztraminer produces open wines, very round, with a fragrance of rose water and cloves, and often with a hint of residual sugar. Gewürztraminer easily acquires *pourriture noble*: it thus is often found in *Vendange Tardive* and *Sélection de Grains Nobles* wines.

Pinot Noir, the only red grape variety in Alsace, has only limited success in the region, even though some vineyards--Ottrott, Marlenheim, Rodern--make a specialty of it. You should be careful in selecting Alsatian Pinot Noir, but there are some brilliant exceptions, which we have indicated.

SPECIAL VINIFICATIONS

The majority of Alsatian wines are dry, even though they are unfortunately often marked by some residual sugar. On the other hand, Alsace stands out with two great specialties, the late-picked *Vendanges Tardive* (or VT) wines, and its *Sélection de Grains Nobles* (SGN) sweet wines.

Vendage Tardive wines are made with overripe grapes rich in natural sugar; they are more robust than wines with the simple Alsace appellation, and they have more residual sugar. *Sélections de Grains Nobles* wines are vinified from individually sorted grapes which have acquired *pourriture noble,* or the famous *botrytis cinerea,* which accounts for most of the world's great sweet wines. For both of these specialties, chaptalization is forbidden and the minimum sugar content is set by law.

Alsace also makes *crémants,* slightly sparkling, literally "creaming" wines which are sometimes well made, although from less expressive grape varieties. The best are the *crémants* of surprising taste, those made with the Muscat grape, for example.

BUYING ALSATIAN WINES

Alsatian wines are greatly diverse because of its array of different grape varieties, *lieux-dits,* Grands Crus, sweet wines, and often highly splintered domaines, thus complicating the wine buyer's choices. Furthering complicating matters, each cellar offers not only a great number of wines but several different vintages of each, and a broad price range: from less than 30 F to about 800 F a bottle. It isn't rare to find estates selling some fifty different wines.

If you are buying wines to cellar, it's best to choose the three most recent vintages; and--if they are still available or if they are being offered following long ageing--the '88, '89, and '90 vintages. For wines intended to be drunk now, '91 and '93 are good, average vintages which open out more quickly. With rare exceptions, '92 is a weak vintage, generally too diluted.

A TABLE WITH ALSATIAN WINES

Before suggesting several dishes to accompany the great Alsatian wines, note that as a rule of thumb, Sylvaner and Pinot Blanc are good as an apéritif and with shellfish, quiche lorraine, sausages and pâtés, flamed tarts; Muscat as an apéritif and with asparagus; Riesling goes well with delicate fish, grilled or sauced; chicken, veal, and pork; and fish pâtés. Pinot Gris is best with preserved duck and goose; foie gras; game birds, or delicate pâtés. Finally, Gewürztraminer is enjoyed with exotic dishes, spicy or very aromatic, or with strong cheeses like münster; while Pinot Noir, the good ones at least, should be served with red meat in a sauce or with game.

WITH RIESLING

With a young, very dry Riesling: baked oysters with leeks, but also smoked meat. With dry Riesling: smoked meat or fish pâté; with a dry, highly structured Riesling from a great year, try salmon cooked in a clay pot. With a minerally Riesling: fish cooked in foil or steamed. A full-bodied, powerful Riesling of average bottle age, from the Rangen or Brand vineyards, calls for a large hen, but a young Riesling is good with chicken baked with pineapple. Enjoy a Grand Cru Riesling with lobster; fish in a cream sauce with a Grand Cru Riesling already opened; a Grand Cru Riesling from a good vintage, dry and minerally (but not excessively so), a Schlossberg type, calls for sweetbreads baked with honey. And finally, hot smoked salmon is magnificent with a Grand Cru Riesling from a great vintage at its peak (or a Pinot Gris, depending on the garnish).

GEWÜRTZTRAMINER

Gewürztraminer is excellent with sea bream à l'orange, curried lamb, and strong cheeses. Baked potatoes with munster go well with a Gewürztraminer at its peak ('91 or '92), while a Grand Cru Gewürztraminer is best with marinated game.

PINOT GRIS

Sautéed perch calls for Pinot Noir, but watch out for residual sugar; hen stuffed with foie gras for a Pinot Gris *Sélection de Grains Nobles*; and spiced guinea fowl for the same wine or for a *Vendange Tardive*. Baked figs are marvelous with an old Pinot Gris *Sélection de Grains Nobles*.

AMMERSCHWIHR

1 - HOTEL-RESTAURANT - **Aux Armes de France**: 1 Grand' Rue, 68770 Ammerschwihr. *Tel. 03.89.47.10.12 Fax 03.89.47.38.12. Closed Wed. and Thurs. noon.* Rooms: 360 to 460 F. Breakfast: 50 F. Menus: 360 to 510 F. A la carte: around 600 F. The cuisine, well-prepared, hasn't evolved as quickly as prices have skyrocketed. The wine list is staggering (for its selection... and prices).

ANDLAU

2 - RESTAURANT - **Au Bœuf Rouge**: *6 rue Dr-Stoltz, 67140 Andlau. Tel. 03.88. 08.96.26 Fax 03.88.08.99.29. Closed Wed. evening and Thurs.* Menus: 98 to 128 F. A la carte: around 200 F. Traditional cuisine and a good cellar centered on Andlau vintners.

3 - HOTEL - **Zinck-Hôtel**: *13 rue de la Marne, 67140 Andlau. Tel. 03.88.08. 27.30 Fax 03.88.08.42.50. Closed from 12/10 to 20 and 1 week in February.* In a mill decorated with numerous collector's pieces. Rooms are all very different, sometimes quite fanciful (choose " la Baroque ") from 300 to 600 F. Breakfast: 40 F.

AVOLSHEIM

4 - BED & BREAKFAST - **Le Relais du Dompeter**: *2 rue du Dompeter, 67120 Avolsheim. Tel. 03.88.49.89.30, 03.88.38.49.41 and 03.88.38.43.96.* This large farm has been rebuilt in the traditional style to house a horse farm (riding). Essentially a rural vacation house, but one can rent by night depending on availability (250 F).

BERGHEIM

5 - RESTAURANT - **Winstub du Sommelier**: *51 Grand' Rue, 68750 Bergheim. Tel. 03.89.73.69.99. Closed Sunday, noon Monday (except holidays and holiday eves), and during February vacation.* Spacious winstub, good cuisine, and above all a splendid wine list with a hundred entries. A la carte: around 180 F.

6 - HOTEL-RESTAURANT - **Chez Norbert**: *9 Grand'Rue, 68750 Bergheim. Tel. 03.89.73.31.15 Fax 03.89.73.60.65.* Well-restored buildings and pretty rooms: 320 or 350 F, depending on

dates. Sumptuous wine list in the restaurant (closed Tues. noon and Thurs.) : 200 entries, with many collector's wines. Menus: 180 to 250 F (dinner). Reduced menu at lunchtime.

COLMAR

7 - RESTAURANT - **Le Fer Rouge**: *52 Grande-Rue, 68000 Colmar. Tel. 03.89.41.37.24. Closed Sunday evening and Monday.* Serious cooking. Good selection of wines (Alsace and Bourgogne), with many old Alsatian vintages from excellent years. Menus: 295 to 480 F. A la carte: around 500 F.

DACHSTEIN

8 - RESTAURANT - **L'Auberge de la Bruche**: *1 rue Principale, 67120 Dachstein. Tel. 03.88.38.14.90.* Menus: 150 to 250 F. A la carte: around 280 F. Next to the beautiful entry to the old village, a decidedly modern cuisine featuring fish dishes. Good wine list.

DAHLENHEIM

9 - RESTAURANT - **Au Tilleul**: *55 rue Principale, 67310 Dahlenheim. Tel. 03.88.50.66.23. Closed Wed.* 10 km west of Strasbourg. People from all around come a good distance to savor the tartes flambées on Thursdays, Fridays, Saturdays and Sunday evenings.

EGUISHEIM

10 - RESTAURANT - **Le caveau**: *3 place du château Saint Léon IX, 68420 Eguisheim. Tel. 03.89.41.08.89.* Menus: 145 (Alsatian) to 455 F. A respectable table offering traditional dishes and other more personal creations. The wine list, limited to the Eguisheim growers associated with the cellar, must be sorted through.

Caveau d'Eguisheim

11 - HOTEL - **Hostellerie du château**: *2 place du Château Saint Léon IX, 68420 Eguisheim. Tel. 03.89.23.72.00 Fax 03.89.23.68.80.* A very beautiful modern hotel with large rooms, from 350 to 750 F. Breakfast: 55 F.

GUEMAR-ILLHAEUSERN

12 - HOTEL - **La Clairière**: *50 route d'Illhaeusern, 68970 Guemar-Illhaeusern.*

Tel. 03.89.71.80.80 Fax 03.89.71.86.22. Unattractive surroundings compensated by the splendor of the vast, well-decorated rooms. An amusing maze of nooks. Very good breakfast: 75 F. Rooms: 580 to 1,600 F.

ILLHAEUSERN

13 - HOTEL-RESTAURANT - **Auberge de l'Ill**: *2 rue de Collonges au Mont d'Or, 68970 Illhaeusern. Restaurant: Tel. 03.89.71.89.00 Fax 03.89.71.82.83. Hotel: Tel. 03.89.71.87.87 Fax 03.89.71.87.88. Closed Mon. (except lunchtime in high-season) Tues., and in February.* Immense rooms which marry perfectly the old and the new, from 1,300 to 2,500 F (for the fisherman's house). Exemplary breakfast: 130 F. Menus: 520 (lunch weekdays) to 720 F. A la carte: around 750 F. Legendary cuisine, attentive to preserving tradition, discovering new harmonies or rehabilitating forgotten products- always extremely tasteful. Perfect wine list with over one hundred entries from Alsace, well chosen and classed, with some very old vintages. Good selection of Bordeaux and Côtes-du-Rhône.

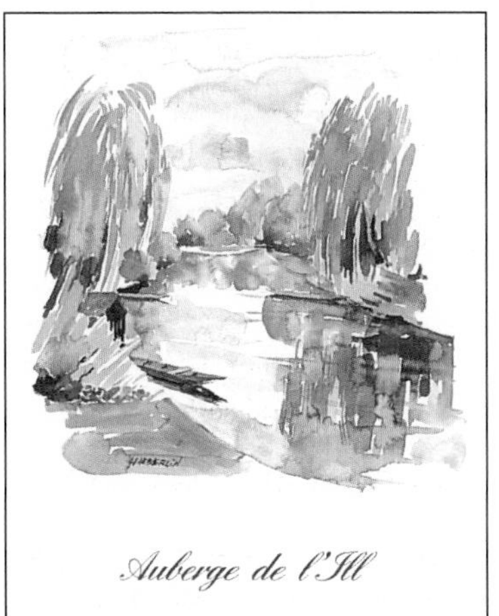

Auberge de l'Ill

KAYSERSBERG

14 - HOTEL-RESTAURANT - **Chambard**: *9 rue du Général-de-Gaulle, 68240 Kaysersberg. Tel. 03.89.47.10.17 Fax 03.89.47.35.03. Closed Mon. and Tues.* Menus: 250 to 450 F. A la carte: around 500 F. Lovely rooms overlooking the vineyard or the garden from 650 to 750 F. Very good breakfast: 60 F. Conservative but faultless cuisine whose limited offerings guarantee the freshness of products. Remarkable wine list. Pierre Irrmann also offers a bistro service (closed Mon.) at moderate prices (menu: 120 F) with a more traditional but extremely palatable menu.

15 - RESTAURANT - **L'Arbre Vert**: *1 rue Haut-du-Rempart, 68240 Kaysersberg. Tel. 03.89.47.11.51. Closed Mon., Sun. evening in low-season and January.* Unchanging but ever-classic. Good wine list favoring local products. Menus: 138 to 250 F.

16 - HOTEL - **Hôtel Constantin**: *10 rue du Père-Kohlmann, 68240 Kaysersberg. Tel. 03.89.47.19.90 Fax 03.89.47.37.82.* A beautiful winegrower's house, perfectly restored and furnished. Rooms: 320 to 370 F. Breakfast: 39 F.

KIENTZHEIM

17 - HOTEL - **Hostellerie de l'Abbaye d'Alpach**: *24 rue Foch, 68240 Kientzheim. Tel. 03.89.47.16.00 Fax 03.89.78.29.73.* A vast and ancient

dwelling, full of nooks and recesses. Spacious, comfortable rooms, from 340 to 440 F. Breakfast: 48 F.

KINTZHEIM

18 - RESTAURANT - **Auberge Saint-Martin**: *80 rue de la Liberté, 67600 Kintzheim. Tel. 03.88.82.04.78. Closed Wed., noon Thurs. from October to April, from 12/25 to 1/01 and 10 days in early July.* A pleasant winstub where traditional cuisine rhymes with fine wine. Menus: 75 (lunch weekdays) to 140 F. A la carte: around 150 F.

LAPOUTROIE

19 - RESTAURANT - **Les Alisiers**: *5 rue Faudé, 68650 Lapoutroie. Tel. 03.89. 47.52.82. Closed Mon. evenings, Tues., and in January.* No-smoking restaurant. Splendid view of the mountains and forest. Mild prices for

a fine cuisine full of character. Attractive selection of wines. Menus: 80 to 200 F. A la carte: around 200 F. Pretty little rooms, some with view of the valley, from 250 to 450 F.

LA WANTZENAU

20 - HOTEL - **Hôtel le Moulin**: *3 impasse du Moulin, 67610 La Wantzenau. Tel. 03.88.59.22.22 Fax 03.88.59.22.00.* An old, perfectly renovated mill accomodating bright, modern rooms from 345 to 460 F.

21 - RESTAURANT - **À la Barrière**: *3 route de Strasbourg, 67610 La Wantzenau. Tel. 03.88.96.20.23. Closed Tues. evening and Wed.* Rustic decor but very refined dining. Attractive wine list. Menus: 150 (lunch weekdays) to 260 F. A la carte: around 400 F.

MARLENHEIM

22 - RESTAURANT - **Le Cerf**: *30 rue du Général-de-Gaulle, 67520 Marlenheim. Tel. 03.88.87.73.73. Closed Tues. Wed. Service until 9:15pm.* Alsatian culinary tradition in all its glory. Don't miss the Clin d'œil au terroir alsacien menu at 395 F. Remarkable wine list, offering the classics and

some refreshing finds: a hundred Alsatian wines classed by communes that form a guard of honor for a succulent cuisine. Menus: 250 (lunch) to 500 F. A la carte: around 500 F.

MOLSHEIM

23 - HOTEL-RESTAURANT - **Hôtel Diana**:

14 rue Sainte-Odile, 67120 Molsheim. Tel. 03.88.38.51.59 Fax 03.88.38.87.11. Service until 9:15pm. Refreshing cuisine with a good selection of wines from Alsace and the Bordelais. Menus: from 185 F (beverages included). Spacious, modern rooms: 405 to 435 F. Breakfast: 50 F.

OBERNAI

24 - RESTAURANT - **La winstub de Bruno Sohn**: *6 rue de la Gare, 67210 Obernai. Tel. 03.88.48.33.38. Closed Sun. evening and Mon.* Menus: 130 F (lunch weekdays), 195 F. We fell head over heels for this find of the year: a cuisine deep-rooted in tradi-

tion, copious and refined, that melts in your mouth. Remarkable wine list (which shares most of our preferences, including those in other wine-producing regions), without excessive prices.

OTTROTT

25 - HOTEL-RESTAURANT - **Hostellerie des Châteaux**: *11 rue des Châteaux, 67530 Ottrott. Tel. 03.88.48.14.14 Fax 03.88.95.95.20. Restaurant closed Sun. evening (and noon Mon. in low-season).* A large mansion full of recesses offering spacious rooms decorated with reproductions of miniatures from the Sainte-Odile manuscript, the famous Hortus Deliciarum. Dazzling, exuberant cuisine. Good wine list. Menus: 160 to 450 F. Rooms: 470 to 1,500 F.

RIBEAUVILLÉ

26 - RESTAURANT - **Zum Pfifferhus**: *14 Grande Rue, 68150 Ribeauvillé. Tel. 03.89.73.62.28. Closed Wed. and*

Thurs from October to June; closed in March and the first 10 days of July. An historic façade and excellent traditional cuisine. A la carte: around 250 F.

RIQUEWIHR

27 - BED & BREAKFAST - **La Maison Dissler**: *6 rue de la Couronne, 68340 Riquewihr. Tel. 03.89.47.87.31. Fax 03.89.49.06.53.* Four guest rooms amidst flamboyant disarray. The one with the façade's bay window is splendid (300 F for 2 pers.).

28 - RESTAURANT - **Le Sarment d'or**: *4 rue du Cerf, 68340 Riquewihr. Tel.*

03.89.47.9.85. Menus: 110 to 290 F. The most consistent of the village's restaurants. Attractive game menu in season. Sixty well-chosen Alsation wines on the list, with good attention paid to the Grands Crus.

ROSHEIM

29 - HOTEL-RESTAURANT - **Hostellerie du Rosenmeer**: *45 Avenue de la Gare, 67560 Rosheim. Tel. 03.88.50.43.29 Fax 03.88.49.20.57. Restaurant closed Sunday evening and Monday from November to Easter, hotel open every day.* Comfortable rooms from 340 to 480 F. Menus: 99 to 385 F. We love this " sea of roses " (an allusion to the gardens irrigated by this little stream) for the warm welcome and the cuisine full of inventivity, as skillful with tradition as with innovation. On the wine list, a hundred

Alsatian wines, generally well-chosen, from enticing vintage years (90, 89, 85 and 83) even if varietal wines are prefered to the Grands Crus. Good forays into Côtes-du-Rhône, Burgundy and especially the Bordelais. Large selection of half bottles and reasonable prices. Excellent winstub next to the restaurant offering the best of popular Alsatian cuisine.

ROUFFACH

30 - RESTAURANT - **A la ville de Lyon**: *1 rue Poincaré, 68250 Rouffach. Tel. 03.89. 49.62.49. Closed Monday and late February-early March.* Local tradition rediscovered, reinterpreted and transformed. Attractive wine list. Menus: 120 (except Sundays), 180 and 385F A la carte: around 300F.

31 - HOTEL-RESTAURANT - **Château d'Isenbourg**: *68250 Rouffach. Tel. 03.89. 78.58.50 Fax 03.89.78.53.70.* Luxurious rooms and apartments from 865 to 1580 F (690 to 1265 F in low-season). Menus: 270 to 700 F. A la carte: around 450 F. A very appealing cuisine firmly anchored in regional tradition. Fabulous wine list owing to the choice of owners and vintages whose prices are far from excessive, fifty old collector's bottles, some wines served by the glass. The presentation is irreproachable. Very good choice of Bordeaux and some sly incursions into other regions.

SCHARRACHBERGHEIM

32 - BED & BREAKFAST - **Lauth**: *67310 Scharrachbergheim. Tel 03.88.50. 66.05.* Spacious rooms, modern and brand new, in the heart of the Bas-Rhin vineyard. 240 to 270 F.

SÉLESTAT

33 - HOTEL-RESTAURANT - **Abbaye la Pommeraie**: *8 avenue du Maréchal-*

Foch, 67600 Sélestat. Tel. 03.88.92.07.84 Fax 03.88.92.08.71. Restaurant closed Sunday evenings. Large rooms (700 to 1,800 F), some of which are mansarded, in the old 17th-century Cistertian abbey, offering a view of the garden or the old city. Breakfast: 60 and 90 F. Menus: 290 to 450 F. A la carte: around 350 F. In the restaurant, a classic cuisine with some charming variations. Excellent welcome. Good wine list with fifty wines from Alsace, favouring, however, varietal wines over the Grands Crus. Notable selection of half bottles.

SOULTZ-LES-BAINS

34 - BED & BREAKFAST - **Le Biblenhof**: *67120 Soultz-les-bains. Tel. 03.88.38.21.09 Fax 03.88.48.81.99.* Guest rooms in a large farm from 220 to 260 F. Meals at a communal table in the evening by reservation: 80 F not including beverages.

SOULTZMATT

35 - HOTEL-RESTAURANT - **Klein**: *44 rue de la vallée, 68570 Soultzmatt. Tel. 03.89.47.00.10. Fax 03.89.47.65.03. Closed Monday and from January 15 to 31.* Menus: 95 to 250 F. Rooms (acceptable): 250 to 350 F. Good home-style cooking but which is continually losing its regional and seasonal marks. On the other hand, sumptuous wine list with 120 entries from Alsace and a quite intriguing selection from other appellations, whether prestigious or not (wines from Savoie, Jura, Midi and Côtes-du-Rhône are particularly well-chosen).

STRASBOURG

36 - RESTAURANT - **Buerehiesel**: *4 parc de l'Orangerie, 67000 Strasbourg. Tel. 03.88.61.62.24 Fax 03.88.61.32.00. Closed Tuesday and Wednesday* Amidst the trees, an ascetic but terribly tasty cuisine. Attractive wine list. Menus: 290 (lunch weekdays) to 690 F. A la carte: around 600 F.

37 - RESTAURANT - **Au Crocodile**: *10 rue de l'Outre, 67000 Strasbourg. Tel. 03.88.32.13.02 Fax 03.88.75.72.01. Closed Sunday and Monday, and from 12/24 to 1/04 (open for lunch*

Easter, Pentecost, Mother's day and 2 Sundays in December). Sumptuous wine list. Menus: 295 to 640 F (lunch), 420 to 640 F (evening).

38 - RESTAURANT - **La Vieille Enseigne**: *9 rue Tonneliers, 67000 Strasbourg. Tel. 03.88.32.58.50. Closed Saturday noon and Sunday.* Good wine list, some served by the glass. Menus: 168 to 305 F.

39 - RESTAURANT - **Le Rathsamhausen**: *9 rue des Dentelles, 67000 Strasbourg. Tel. 03.88.23.51.61. Closed noon Saturday and Monday.* 400 wines on the list - and among the best - from Alsace, all of France and elsewhere. Some are offered in the cellar at near cost price. A model address.

Menus: 70 (lunch weekdays), 125 and 230F.

40 - HOTEL - **Le Dragon**: *2 rue Ecarlate, 67000 Strasbourg. Tel. 03.88.35. 79.80 Fax 03.88.25.78.95. Closed for Christmas.* Close to Petite-France. Lovely rooms in a simple and contemporary decor, from 430 to 655 F.

TRAENHEIM

41 - RESTAURANT - **Le Loejelgucker**: *17 rue Principale, 67310 Traenheim. Tel. 03.88.50.38.19. Closed Mon. and Tues.* Menus: 105 and 240 F. A la carte: around 200 F. A beautiful Alsatian house, judicious cuisine and prices. Decent wine list.

TURCKHEIM

42 - RESTAURANT - **Le Caveau du Vigneron**: *5 Grand'-Rue. Tel. 03.89.27. 06.85. Open evenings, except Mon. Closed 1 week in early July and late August, and from 12/25 to 1/1.* Historic winstub. A la carte: around 150 F.

VAL-DE-VILLÉ

43 - RESTAURANT - **Au Valet de Cœur**: *24 route de Villé, 67730 Val-de-Villé. Tel. 03.88.85.67.51 Fax 03.88.85. 67.84. Closed Sun. evenings and Mon.* Innovative cuisine. The wine list wagers on local productions, unfortunately not unforgettable. Menus: 180 to 420 F. A la carte: around 400 F.

WESTHALTEN

44 - HOTEL-RESTAURANT - **Auberge du Cheval Blanc**: *20 rue de Rouffach, 68250 Westhalten. Tel. 03.89.47. 01.16. Fax 03.89. 47.64.40. Closed Sun. evenings and Mon.* Well-prepared cuisine in the Alsatian tradition, but felicitously livened up. Good selection of wines that favors the village winegrowers, but somewhat neglects the Grand Cru Zinnkoepflé. Menus: 153 to 410 F (children's menu at 75 F). A la carte: around 300 F. Comfortable rooms: 310 to 450 F.

WINTZFELDEN

45 - HOTEL-RESTAURANT - **Arbre vert**: *2 route de Soultzmatt, 68570 Wintzfelden. Tel. 03.89.47.02.13. Fax 03.89.47.60.83. Closed in February.* Pleasant rooms: 235 and 285 F. Within two paces of Soultzmatt, up towards the forest: a pleasant country inn whose cuisine respects local tradition; the wine list, however, could do with revision.

ZELLENBERG

46 - RESTAURANT - **Maximilien**: *19 route d'Ostheim, 68340 Zellemberg. Tel. 03.89.47.99.69 Fax 03.89.47.99.85.*

Closed Sun. evenings and Mon. Right along the rows of vines. Tradition revised and tickled with a felicitous modern touch. Good selection of Alsatian wines, generic as well as old vintages from good years (130 entries). Menus: 175 (lunch weekdays) to 415 F. A la carte: around 400 F.

TO SEE

AMMERSCHWIHR

OUTING - Situated near the porte haute tower, the old site of the vintner's guild, is a beautiful house from 1613, with corner beams and sculpted windows.

ANDLAU

OUTING - The Romanesque sculptures in the portal of the abbatial church magnify the grapevine: facing the dessicated fig tree, the dove of Faith happily pecks a lush vine.

COLMAR

MUSEUM - **Unterlinden Museum**: *1 rue d'Unterlinden, 68000 Colmar. Tel. 03.89.20.15.50. Open every day from 4/1 to 10/31, 9 am to 6 pm; from 11/1 to 3/31, 9 to 12 and 2 to 5 except Tuesdays.* In addition to the famous

Issenheim retable, one can see the capstan wine presses and sculpted casks in the cellar recreated on the ground floor, the collections of inn signs, waffle- (and Host-) irons, anise-bread molds, objects from Munster valley farms and vinedresser's tools in the second-floor hall.

DAMBACH-LA-VILLE

OUTING - The Renaissance fountain on the market square is crowned by the town emblem: a grape-loving bear. Rue des Tonneliers: beautiful 16th and 17th-century houses.

DANGOLSHEIM

OUTING - A pretty village in the Strasbourgeois wine belt whose ancient

houses display pediment sculptures evoking viticulture and cooperage.

HEILIGENSTEIN

OUTING - The bear fountain whose coat of arms is decked with a bunch of grapes and a vinedresser's pruning knife.

HUNAWIHR

OUTING - The fortified church that emerges from an ocean of vines.

KIENTZHEIM

MUSEUM - **Alsatian Wine Museum**: *68240 Kaysersberg. Tel. 03.89.78. 21.36. Open from June to the end of October, from 10 to 12 and 2 to 6.* For a comprehensive vision of the work and daily life of a winegrower. Some beautiful pieces, including an impressive wine press.

MITTELBERGHEIM

OUTING - Among the village's numerous polychromatic wrought iron signs

(including that of Albert Seltz), one of the oldest, known as " the bouquet " (Maikrug), depicts the vine tulip that flowers in Spring.

OBERNAI

OUTING - Next to the famous six-bucket well is the hôtel de la Cloche, one of whose rooms, decorated by the renowned inlayer Spindler, recreates the " stove " (meeting place) of the winegrowers and coopers with its painted vine arbours and dancers.

RIQUEWIHR

OUTING - One of the vineyard's most beautiful villages with its old houses, their sculpted façades and the poly-

chromatic wrought iron signs (some signed by Hansi). At number 7 rue Saint-Nicolas, a surprising open-air vinedresser's museum beneath the loggia.

SAINT-HIPPOLYTE

OUTING - Go to nearby Haut-Koenigsbourg castle (decor to Jean Renoir's La grande illusion) for its view over the vineyard.

SIGOLSHEIM

OUTING - The wine-evoking church of Saint-Pierre and Saint-Paul: on the tympany, a vintner offers a cask of wine, while birds peck at grapes on the frieze.

STRASBOURG

MUSEUM - **The Alsatian Museum**: *23 quai Saint-Nicolas, 67000 Strasbourg. Tel. 03.88.52.50.01. Hours: 10 to 12 and 1:30 to 6 (5pm on Sun.). Closed Tues. and holidays.* Admission: 20 F; children: 10 F. A superb

museum of 17th to 19th-century popular traditions where room 25 is devoted to viticulture and cooperage.

UNGERSHEIM

MUSEUM - **The Ecomuseum**: *Tel. 03.89.74. 44.74. Open in January, February, November and December from 10:30 to 4:30; in March, April, September and October from 10 to 6; May through August from 9 to 6.* On a large open-air site, traditional houses destined to be demolished have been taken down and rebuilt. A vast evocation of vines and vineyard work, with a Sungau winegrower's house erected over a cellar from 1540.

WANGEN

OUTING - A pretty village in the Strasbourgeois wine belt whose ancient houses display pediment sculptures evoking viticulture and cooperage.

WESTHOFFEN

OUTING - A pretty village in the Strasbourgeois wine belt whose ancient houses display pediment sculptures evoking viticulture and cooperage. One will observe that winegrowers' fears didn't begin just yesterday: at 90 rue Traversière, among the sculptures on a cooper's house from 1601, there is a fantastic animal devouring vine leaves.

FETES

JULY
The wine flows in the Wangen fountain on the first Sunday in July to commemorate the suppression of an old tax.

AUGUST
Most villages organize friendly wine festivals each weekend.

SEPTEMBER
During Ribeauvillé's wine festival, on the first Sunday in September, the riesling flows in the fountain on the market square.

OCTOBER-NOVEMBER
In most villages, harvest and vin nouveau celebrations, that are always very festive.

DECEMBER
The Christmas markets: above all, choose those in Strasbourg and Keysersberg - irresistible.

Cabaret scene on a cask lock.

Maison Martin Schaetzel

Owners Jean and Béa Schaetzel. **Address** 3 rue de la 5e Division Blindée, 68770 Ammerschwihr - Tel. 03.89.47.11.39 Fax 03.89.78.29.77. **Open** By appointment. **Spoken** German.

"Whoever has had to pacify remorse, awaken a memory, drown sadness, build a chateau in Spain...": Béa and Jean Schaetzel chose Baudelaire as the guiding spirit of their vineyard.

Previously, their vines were planted in the Kaefferkopf site, a *terroir* whose geological disparity made it unacceptable for Grands Cru status. The Schaetzels have now bought vines in the Rangen and Schlossberg vineyards: the heart of the great names.

Jean Schaetzel vinifies individual parcels in small *cuvées,* seeking very dry wines with no residual sugar. His prices are especially attractive. Like those from all good Alsatian winemakers, his least expensive wines are very well made, such as his Sylvaner Vieilles Vignes '95 (29 F), delicate and lingering; the Pinot Blanc Réserve '95 (29 f), beautifully round and fruity; and his Riesling Réserve '95 (36 F), plump with vitality and fruit.

Our choice: The Riesling Kaefferkopf in all forms. The '95 Granit (55), still aromatically closed, is already lovely, full-bodied and intense. The Vendange Tardive (VT) '95 (about 110 F), from limestone soil and thus more open, is already a charmer. Its '94 vintage (110 F) is simply luscious.

Reception: In the cellar, among the casks, some of which have beautifully sculpted locks.

***How to get there** (Map 1): NW of Colmar via N415 towards Kayssersberg. At the tower along the Route Nationale, turn left, go back up the main street a short distance, first turn on left. The cellar is on the left, after the Place du Marché.*

The tasting room.

André et Rémy Gresser

Owner Rémy Gresser. **Address** 2 rue de l'école, 67140 Andlau - Tel. 03.88.08.95.88 Fax 03.88.08.55.99. **Open** From Monday to Saturday 9:00-12:00 and 14:00-19:00. **Spoken** German, English.

The bottom line is brilliant: there are three Grand Cru vineyard sites in Andlau –Moenchberg, Wiebelsberg, and Kastelberg– and Rémy Gresser's vines are in all three. An impassioned promoter of this rich *terroir,* he mentions the Grand Cru first on his labels, followed by the name of the site or the simple communal appellation, and finally that of the grape variety. A tasting in his company is like an understandable lesson in geology as he explains how each kind of soil affects the way the grape expresses itself. Of the twenty-seven wines currently on offer, you will find '89 Rieslings from the Wiebelsberg Grand Cru vineyard: The dry Riesling (75 F) has an intense, slightly botrytized nose; in the mouth, it is splendid, full, rigorous, combining fruit, nuts, and mineral notes. The VT (125 F) is full-bodied, unctuous, with sweet overtones. For a Gewürztraminer, choose the Andlau '94 (60 F) for its concentration, finesse, and notes of roses and almonds.

Our Choice A variation on the Riesling '92 (58 F). From the sandstone soil of the Wiebelsberg vineyard, yielding an agile style "like a handful of sand flowing through your fingers", says Rémy Gresser. From the limestone Muenchberg soil, a round, full-bodied Riesling, its body well balanced by good acid structure. The Steig schist soil of the third vineyard, Kastelberg, yields a very powerful, floral Riesling with a mineral overtone. (To be cellared).

Reception In a large cellar decorated with antique objects.

How to get there *(Map 1): From Strasbourg to Barr (to the southwest) via N422. Continue to Andlau via the Route des Vins (4 km). The cellar is in the center of Andlau, behind the post office (signposted).*

Guy Wach.

Domaine des Marronniers

Owner Guy Wach. **Address** 5 rue de la Commanderie, 67140 Andlau - Tel. 03.88.08.93.20 Fax 03.88.08.45.59. **Open** From Monday to Saturday 9:00-12:00 and 14:30-19:00. **Spoken** German.

The 1996 vintage from this domaine yielded wines of great diversity: the Sylvaner (26 F) is straighforward and lively, while the Clevner (27 F) is a round, balanced wine, a thoroughly agreeable Pinot Blanc; the Pinot Gris Vieilles Vignes (55 F) is still a heavyweight until its residual sugar softens. Guy Wach's Gewürztraminer Vieilles Vignes (60 F), is sleek, powerful, well balanced, its hints of spice cake soaring gloriously.

Two splendid VTs are available. A Gewürztraminer '92 (120 F), its nose of violets with mineral hints (from damp chalk); concentrated and well structured in the mouth, with a layer of delightful freshness. For Guy Wach, wine is essentially linked to the table, and he isn't stingy with advice, even when we teased him about the trace of residual sugar that often is present in his wines.

Our choice The '94 Grand Cru Rieslings. Moenchberg (52 F): nose discreet at first, becoming more mineral in the air; always reserved in the mouth, but with power in reserve, especially in the very spicy finish. A more crystalline style for the Kastelberg (53 F), very lingering in the mouth, delicate, discreetly spicy. (To keep).

Reception In a working cellar.

How to get there *(Map 1): From Strasbourg to Barr.*

Liliane Hering in her kingdom, the tasting room.

Pierre Hering

Owner Pierre Hering. **Address** 6 rue du Docteur-Sultzer, 67140 Barr - Tel. 03.88.08.90.07 Fax 03.88.08.08.54. **Open** From Monday to Saturday 9:00-19:00, Sunday by appointment. **Spoken** German, English. **Credit cards** Visa, Eurocard, MasterCard.

Emile-Gustave, Edouard, Louis, and now Pierre: four generations of Herings have tended the vines around the Folie Marco, a building that sent its owner into bankruptcy and is today a museum.

Wines from the estate are invariably very dry, with the Rieslings quickly becoming strongly mineral. In the first price category, we found a delightful Klevner '94 (about 25 F), all roundness and harmony. For just a few more francs, try the Riesling from Barr (about 35 F), whose aroma is reminiscent of Gewürztraminer, yielding a taste of pineapples and nuts, and a smoky finish.

Our choice Three wines from the Kirchberg Grand Cru appellation. Riesling '95 (about 44 F), spicy, fresh, very lingering and persistent in the mouth. Gewürztraminer '95 (about 45 F), its nose of roses, raisins, spices, nuts, which develops in the air; full-bodied on the palate. The Pinot Gris VT '94 (105 F): well-balanced in the mouth, beginning with caramel and finishing with raisins and figs. (Cellar for several years, especially the Gewürz).

Reception Usually by Madame Hering, who is helpful and competent. In one of the beautiful old houses of the town. Charge for tasting if wine is not purchased.

How to get there *(Map 1): The cellar is between the Folie Marco Museum and the Hôtel de Ville, on the right, in front of the beautiful sign of the Le Brochet Restaurant.*

Charles Stoeffler and his son Vincent.

Domaine Charles Stoeffler

Owners Vincent and Martine Stoeffler. **Address** 4 rue des Jardins, 67140 Barr - Tel. 03.88.08.52.50 Fax 03.88.08.17.09. **Open** From Monday to Saturday 8:00-12:00 and 13:40-18:30. **Spoken** German, English. **Credit cards** Visa, Eurocard, MasterCard.

These two enologists belie the proverb that cobblers wear the worst shoes of all. For the Stoefflers' wines are exemplary, concentrated and clean, unconcealed by residual sugar. Father and son cultivate ten hectares, including one and a half on the Kirchberg Grand Cru vineyard at Barr, whose limestone soil gives very fine wines, but they take quite a long time to develop. Of the lowest priced wines, note the Sylvaner '95 (19 F), full-bodied and mellow; the Pinot Blanc '94, with a honeyed finish; the Muhlforst Riesling '94 (36 F), its finish both graceful and powerful; the Pinot Gris '95 (28.50 F), with a lovely smoky edge. But first take special note of the wines from the Kirchberg Grand Cru vineyard in Barr, at very attractive prices. A Pinot Gris '95 (48 F), its very delicate nose of figs and quince; a lingering taste, very fresh and straightforward, with slight residual sugar well-balanced by acidity. A Gewürztraminer '94 (48 F), spicy, explosive with power, which continues to develop in the air. The same grape from the same *terroir* gives a good, very mellow VT (90 F), but you should wait for it to fully develop.

Our choice The Kirchberg Riesling '95 (48 f). Very ripe on the nose, with even a hint of *botrytis.* In the mouth, delicate, intense, full, with traces of caramel. A lingering, persistent wine, well structured by magnificent acidity. (To keep).

Reception Open and helpful.

How to get there *(Map 1): From Strasbourg to Barr, southwest voia N 422. Go through the town. The Rue des Jardins is at the exit, just before the Hôtel Le Manoir on the left.*

Anne-Marie Schmitt, *con brio.*

Domaine Roland Schmitt

Owner Anne-Marie Schmitt. **Address** 35 rue des Vosges, 67310 Bergbieten - Tel. 03.88.38.20.72 Fax 03.88.38.75.84. **Open** By appointment. **Spoken** Italian. **Credit cards** Visa, Eurocard, MasterCard.

An "Alsatian in heart and soul" but Neopolitan by birth (her father came to France to work as a crane operator), Anne-Marie Schmitt diligently tends her eight-hectares of vines, two hectares of which lie in the Altenberg Grand Cru appellation at Bergbieten. Riesling flourishes on the mix of limestone and clay there, which enhance the wine's delicacy while emphazing its mineral nature.

The '95s are lean, very dry, their acidity conferring fine structure without being sharp: their backbone is beautifully fleshy, producing a lovely group of Rieslings: fruity Glintzbergs (32 F), silky Glintzberg Vieilles Vignes (38 F), linden-like Altenberg Grands Crus from Bergbienten (52 F). The Gewürztraminers can hold their own: licorice and dry flowers for the Glintzberg (40 F); melon from the Vieilles Vignes (45 F). And take a look at the lower-priced wines! Anne-Marie's Edelzweicker hints of Muscat (30 F per liter); her Auxerrois is stylish (30 F); the Sylvaner (27 F) exceptionally lingering on the palate, with hints of ripe apricot.

Our choice The '95 Altenberg Riesling Vieilles Vignes (65 F). From 60- and 48-year-old vines, yielding a wine of great delicacy. The extract is silky, intense, with perfect overall balance and great distinction. (To be kept so as to allow mineral character to develop).

Reception With southern hospitality (Anne-Marie Schmitt is Neopolitan).

How to get there *(Map 1): From Strasbourg to Molsheim (southwest). Drive towards Saverne (N4). After 6kms, turn left and continue to Bergbieten. The cellar is in the center of the village, on the road to Barbon (D275), on the left.*

Clarisse and Jean-Michel Deiss.

Domaine Marcel Deiss

Supervisor Jean-Michel Deiss. **Address** 15 route du vin, 68750 Bergheim - Tel. 03.89.73.63.37 Fax 03.89.73.32.67. **Open** From Monday to Saturday 8:00-12:00 and 14:00-18:00, but closed Saturday in January and February, Sunday by appointment. **Spoken** German, English. **Credit cards** Visa, Eurocard, MasterCard.

"The '93s have a damned good framework, distance, restriction. They aren't wines that throw themselves around in your mouth!" Jean-Michel Deiss describes his wines with his hands, raises his eyebrows, clenches his fists. He takes them to heart, throws his whole body into making them, launches them in life in the hope that they will realize some of the ambition he has for them. In a sense, they are like his children whose secrets he hasn't entirely discovered. Even his most versatile wines should be kept until they attain their peak even though, like all great wines, they can be drunk young. You have to go into Deiss' cellar with uncertainty in your heart, taste all his wines, or simply a few. All are heady experiences.

Our choice The Altenberg Grand Cru Riesling '93 (139 F). Still very closed, but with enormous power to come. Extremely intense in the mouth, full-bodied and generous. A monumental wine, very well balanced. A Riesling? In any case, the expression of a *terroir,* and of the winemaker's knowhow. You could drink it now with enormous pleasure, but you risk regretting that you missed its potential greatness. It's best to buy several bottles and then watch them grow up "like a child". The subsequent vintage is sure to be as outstanding.

Reception Usually by Clarisse Deiss, happy to let you taste almost every wine.

How to get there *(Map 1): From Strasbourg to Colmar. 6 km after Sélestat, turn right towards Bergheim, go into the village. After going under the monumental porch, turn left. The cellar is 100 meters farther on, on the left.*

The painted wardrobe in the tasting room.

Domaine Spielmann

Supervisor Sylvie Spielmann. **Address** 2 route de Thannenkirch, 68750 Bergheim - Tel. 03.89.73.35.95 Fax 03.89.73.22.49. **Open** By appointment. **Spoken** German, English. **Credit cards** Visa, Eurocard, MasterCard.

For wines that are intended to be cellared, Sylvie Spielmann aims at very mature, intense qualities, wines that are quite dry but are good reflections of the vintage: her price list specifies whether the wines are dry, contain residual sugar, sweet *(moelleux)*, or *liquoreux*. Your patience will be rewarded with Sylvie Spielmann's Riesling Réserve '95 maturing in your cellar. Much too young now, its extract and its structure nevertheless promise a marvelous wine. At its price (38 F), the Réserve will appear in several years as the outstanding buy of the vintage. More impatient drinkers should opt for the Blosenberg Pinot Gris '94 (44 F), with delicate smoky overtones, or the Kanzlerberg Gewürz '92 for its spicy taste. Those who enjoy sweet wines can choose from several. If you are looking for full-bodied richness, your wine is the SGN '90 Altenberg Gewürztraminer from Bergheim (90 F for 50 cl bottle). If you prefer Vendanges Tardives whose richness is firmly balanced by acidity, you will enjoy the Kanzlerberg Riesling VT '94 (135 F). Both have similar toastiness and need further bottle ageing.

Our choice The Kanzlerberg Grand Cru Riesling '94 (54 F). Delicate nose, hint of aniseed; wonderfully lingering on the palate, with layers of fruit kernels and minerals; excellent acid structure gives good balance for slight residual sugar. (Keep at least 5 years.)

Reception In a rustic tasting room decorated with a beautiful painted wardrobe.

How to get there *(Map 1): From Strasbourg towards Colmar. 6kms after Sélestat, turn right toward Bergheim, go into village. Go under the monumental porch, straight ahead towards Thannenkirch. After 2kms the Domaine is on the right.*

Jean-Pierre Dirler at the prow of his beautiful pale-wood tasting room.

Domaine Dirler

Owner Jean-Pierre Dirler. **Address** 13 rue d'Issenheim, 68500 Bergholtz - Tel. 03.89.76.91.00 Fax 03.89.76.85.97 **Open** From Monday to Saturday 8:00-12:00 and 14:00-18:00. **Spoken** German, English. **Credit cards** Visa, Eurocard, MasterCard.

Jean-Pierre Dirler and his wife await you in their beautiful pale-wood cellar soberly decorated with a few antique glasses and documents recalling Jean Dirler, who founded the estate. A teacher who refused to give his classes in German, he decided to become a "gourmet", as Alsatians call wine brokers. Here, the visitor quickly becomes the gourmet. The estate has good parcels of vines on the Grand Cru vineyards Sacring, Kessler, and Spiegel, whose soils are very different (limestone or sandy gravel), and the grapes are planted accordingly. Among the generic wines, take special note of the Sylvaner Vieilles Vignes '95 (35 F): part of the blend comes from very ripe grapes on the Kessler vineyard, yielding a great amount of extract, and a full-bodied, lingering taste. The wine is worlds away from the common notion of Sylvaner. For the wines from great *terroirs,* taste the powerful '95 Kessler Rieslings (80 F), to be kept for ten years; or the Saering (62 F), a Riesling of élan (cellar 5 years); the Spiegel Muscat (55 F), powerful with mineral traces: cellar 3 years. There are splendid, honeyed '94 Gewürztraminer SGNs from the Saering vineyard (280 F); and especially the Spiegel (300 F), a monumental Gewürztraminer on the palate.

Our choice The Saering '95 Saering Gewürztraminer (about 62 F), rich, powerful, vigorous. (To be cellared).

Reception In a large, simply decorated tasting room with pale-wood panelling.

How to get there *(Map 1): From Colmar towards Guebwiller (south). 5kms after Rouffach, turn right towards Bergholtz. The cellar is in the center, on the right. (Signposted).*

"Love me", says the poster. Well, we do love them!

Éric Rominger

Owner Éric Rominger. **Address** 6 rue de l'Église, 68500 Bergholtz - Tel. 03.89.76.14.71 Fax 03.89.74. 81.44. **Open** By appointment. **Spoken** German, English. **Credit cards** Visa, Eurocard, MasterCard.

The elder Rominger used to concentrate on varietals from the sandy soils of Bergholtz. Today, his son emphasizes the *terroir* with a terraced 3 1/2-hectare vineyard on the Zinnkoepflé appellation. His wines could be criticized as being the product of an overly zealous winemaker (the vines are still much too young), but with each passing year they are gaining in intensity. Rominger himself can sometimes be impatient, as when he puts a dozen harvesters to work for half a day picking...one hundred liters of Sélection de Grains Nobles, but this is the new generation of Alsatian winemakers, who should be discovered and encouraged. In the spring, the first '96 wines from sandy soils will be out, full of fruit. Take special note of the Pinot Blanc Vieilles Vignes (about 40 F), harmonious and well built; and the dry, full-bodied Schwarzsberg Pinot Gris (about 35 F). Of the ambitious wines, try the '95 Zinnkoepflé Sinneles Riesling (about 60 F), for its richness with good acid structure balancing the sugar; or the Zinnkoepflé '95 VT (about 115 F) for its finesse and toasty hints.

Our choice The cellar is bringing out a great number of old and great bottles. In VT: Riesling '90 (90 F); Gewürz '85 (130 F), '89 (140 F), and Zinnkoepflé Gewürz '93 (115 F). In SGN: Pinot Gris '89 and '90 (175 F), Gewürz '89 (175 F), Zinnkoepflé Gewürz (185 F). We chose the Gewürz VT '85 for its nose of litchi, and its powerful, well-structured taste finishing with hints of lichen. Drink now.

Reception Open.

How to get there *(Map 1): From Colmar towards Guebwiller in south. 5 kms after Rouffach, turn right towards Bergholz. Go right at crossroads in middle of village. Cellar on the right.*

An old gargantuan lock.

André Pfister

Owner André Pfister. **Address** 53 rue Principale, 67310 Dahlenheim - Tel. 03.88.50.66.32 Fax 03.88.50.67.49. **Open** From Monday to Thursday by appointment, Friday and Saturday 9:00-12:00 and 13:00-19:00. **Spoken** German, English.

Angel or silver? André Pfister cultivates his vines on the Engelberg Grand Cru vineyard, the "Mountain of the Angel", and on the Silberberg site, the "Mountain of Silver". The marl-limestone and pebbly soils give vigorous, lean Rieslings which need bottle age to mature because in their youth they are more austere than angelic. It is interesting to notice the effect of the *terroir* on the same grape in the same vintage.

The Silberberg Riesling '94 (37 F) is already speaking loudly, changing in a mineral direction, while the Engelberg (48 F) is hardly murmuring, hiding its intensity beneath its youth. It is a vertical, tense wine. At least two years' bottle age "will make it speak up," says André Pfister. Both are perfectly dry, without cosmetic effects. In SGN, try the Pinot Gris '92 (145 F a 50 cl bottle), for its honeyed richness.

Our choice For the pleasure of thumbing our nose at the incontestable fame of the Engelberg Rieslings (but the angels will approve), we invite you to discover the astounding Engelberg Gewürz '93 (50 F). A still discreet nose, a restrained taste, which is more one of finesse and potential than aromatic explosiveness. It is a dry wine, perfect with meals. (Three years' bottle age).

Reception Very cordial, alongside a few beautiful casks with sculptured locks and old tools.

How to get there *(Map 1): From Strasbourg to Ittenheim and Furdenheim (N4, west). At the Furdenheim intersection, turn left for 4 kms, then right to Dalhenheim. The cellar is in the center, on the right, next to the Le Tilleul Restaurant.*

Suzanne Arnold.

Pierre Arnold

Owners Pierre and Suzanne Arnold. **Address** 16 rue de la Paix, 67650 Dambach-la-Ville - Tel. 03.88.92.41.70 Fax 03.88.92.62.95. **Open** By appointment. **Spoken** German.

"People like to touch and look at the cellar." Suzanne Arnold wouldn't think of not receiving her customers in the cellar, where they can get close to the winemaker's work. And when she "talks wine," she means "the pleasure of talking wine with you."

The small, seven-hectare vineyard lies on the granite Frankstein Grand Cru site, which favors Riesling and Gewürztraminer. The wines open up quickly, revealing charm and fruit, but they have further development potential. From two different but recent vintages (31 F), Pierre Arnold's Riesling typifies the rapid development of granite-soil wines. The 1995 is already open, natural, a good friend. For the 1993, the nose is becoming minerally, the palate startles the senses with its spiciness. Don't overlook the Arnolds' first-price wines, the '95 Sylvaner (about 21 F) and the '95 Auxerrois (about 24 F), both totally charming.

Our choice The Frankstein Grand Cru Riesling (45 F). The '95 is intense, fruity, and lingering. The '94 revealed a fresh nose with some aniseed; silky extract, spicy (pepper and mint) on the palate. The '93 was outstanding: smooth and straightforward, with a hint of development; firm and very dry. (Some bottle age).

Reception Passionate discussion with Pierre, more reserved but just as competent with Suzanne. The tasting room is being renovated.

How to get there *(Map 1): From Strasbourg towards Sélestat via Obernai and Barr. In Barr, take the Route des Vins. Dambach is 13kms away. Go through the town. The cellar is signposted on the right, just before leaving the town and its monumental gateway.*

The sales room overlooks the beautiful village square.

Maison Léon Beyer

Responsable Marc Beyer **Address** Office: 2 rue de la 1ère Armée, 68420 Eguisheim, Tasting room: place du château - Tel. 03.89.41.41.05 (office) and 03.89.23.16.16 (tasting room) Fax 03.89.23.93.63 – web: www.vinternet.fr/leonbeyer **Open** In the tasting room, every days, from April to November, except Monday 10:00-12:00 and 14:00-19:00. The rest of the time at the office. **Spoken** German, English.

A third of the wines sold by this shipper come from its own vineyard of twelve hectares on the Grands Crus sites. But they are not mentioned on the labels. Marc Beyer explains that "we prefer to put our name on a *cuvée* rather than hide behind the notion of *cru* which is sometimes overworked."

The Beyer name on the bottle is synonymous with very dry wines with long bottle age. Don't neglect the lowest priced wines. The '96 Pinot Blanc, smooth and round, has "good cheeks without sugar", says Monsieur Beyer, while the '96 Riesling is vigorous and dry. A good Riesling tip: take the Cuvée Ecaillers '95. The name, "shellfish platters", sounds like a local Alsatian *brasserie,* but it is actually a blend of un-named Grands Crus. Perfectly dry, it is a sumptuous, gastronomic wine, clean and graceful (about 79 F). Of Beyer's sweet wines, try mainly the '89 Pinot Gris VT (160 F) for its spice; or better still the SGN (450 F) for its finesse, outstanding lingering flavor and aromatic hints.

Our choice The '85 Pinot Gris Cuvée Comtes (95F). Refreshing nose, crisp and steely; generous on the palate, a wine made to defy time. Smoothness and acidity balance each other. Very alcoholic (14.5%), no residual sugar and yet the result is an extremely supple, soft wine. (Drink now or bottle age).

Reception The tasting room overlooks the theatrical decor of the village square.

How to get there *(Map 1): 4kms south of Colmar via N83, turn right towards Eguisheim and go to the Place du Château. Cellar on left.*

Installation design in the brand-new reception room.

André Ostertag

Supervisor André Ostertag. **Address** 87 rue Finckwiller, 67680 Epfig - Tel. 03.88.85.51.34 Fax 03.88.85.58.95. **Open** By appointment. **Spoken** German, English.

"Fruity wines, stony wines, mature wines...". André Ostertag has charming (and correct) expressions to classify his wines: "those which take X-rays of their grape variety, those which dig into their *terroir* to show it off, and those which ask you to describe them and then see what you come up with".

We started with the '95 Sylvaner Vieilles Vignes (33 F), ripe but refreshing; the Pinot Blanc (38 F), silky with a hazelnut taste. Next, the Franholz Riesling (75 F), very generous and rich (an unusual trace of residual sugar, but the winemaker didn't want to "horsewhip" his wine); the Pinot Gris (about 70 F), vinified in barrels but the oak has softened, preserving the wine's laciness; and the Muscat (55 F), very clean and crisp.

Those who enjoy sweet wines would make a big mistake in passing up the '94s: the Fronholz Gewürz VT (150 F), intense and honeyed; and above all, the Muenchberg SGN (160 F the half bottle), with hints of candied fruits and quince.

Our choice: The Muenchberg Riesling Vieilles Vignes '94 (106 F). Nose still discreet, very delicate on the palate, becoming increasingly powerful. Very lingering, persistent finish. (Bottle age).

Reception In a bright, brand-new room, reflecting André Ostertag's taste in modern art.

How to get there *(Map 1): From Strasbourg to Barr via N 422. Epfig is 6 kms south. At the intersection upon entering the village, turn right. Cellar 1 km ahead on left.*

Charles Brand.

Domaine Lucien Brand

Supervisor Charles Brand. **Address** 71 rue de Wolxheim, 67120 Ergersheim - Tel. 03.88.38.17.71 Fax 03.88.38.72.85. **Open** From Monday to Saturday 9:00-19:00. **Spoken** German, English. **Credit cards** Visa, Eurocard, MasterCard.

Charles Brand has no calling card full of Grand Cru names to give you. The Kefferberg parcel where most of his vines are planted is a commoner even though they are planted on aristocratic limestone-marl soil. But the winemaker has several golden rules of his own: no residual sugar but very crisp wines, including Gewürz and Pinot Gris; low alcohol which he doesn't boost with beet sugar; and the reintroduction of dessert wines.

And he sets the example. With an amazing '89 Sylvaner Cuvée Sainte-Cécile (60 F), which combines impressions of chalk on the nose and hints of mint on the palate; a Muscat Vieilles Vignes '96 (30 F), musky and then mineral on the palate, very crisp; a Kefferberg Gewürztraminer '94 (35 F), mellow yet dry, a gastronomic wine. On the sweet side, the price is sweet, too (61 F the half-bottle) for the Kefferberg Riesling '90 (lots of sugar, but so light!) or the very lingering Gewürz '89 VT (115 F).

Our choice The '94 Kefferberg Riesling (32 F) for its power and structure on the palate. A crisp wine, but fleshy, muscular, and vigorous. (Bottle age). It is also offered in '88 (52 F), now developed: the nose has become intense and mineral, it is stil generous, refreshing, and sprightly on the palate, mellow and minty. (Drink now).

Reception In the old 18th-century cellar.

How to get there *(Map 1): West of Strasbourg via D 45 towards Molsheim. The cellar is in the center of the village on left (large porch).*

The legend of Saint Imer sculpted on a lock.

Domaine Ernest Burn

Owners Joseph and Francis Burn. **Address** 8 rue Basse, 68420 Gueberschwihr - Tel. 03.89.49.20.68 Fax 03.89.49.28.56. **Open** From Monday to Saturday 9:00-12:00 and 14:00-18:00 **Spoken** German. **Credit cards** Visa, Eurocard, MasterCard.

Of this estate's nine hectares, seven are in the Goldert Grand Cru site. But only the vines from the Clos Saint-Imer are declared Grand Cru and a small parcel of vines on more limestony soil is vinified separately under the name of Cuvée de la Chapelle. It often has somewhat more finesse.

Burn's wines are inevitably very ripe, with residual sugar in their youth which is gracefully balanced by strong acidity. Bottle ageing will complete the balance. Two beautiful Cuvées de la Chapelle are available. The '95 Riesling (about 65 F) with a smoky nose and rich palate will be very elegant when it develops. The '94 Gewürz (about 70 F) for its unctuous palate, emphasizing complexity rather than aroma. The Muscat vines are beginning to be old enough to yield interesting wines: the '94 Clos Saint-Imer (40 F) combines power with freshness.

Our choice The SGN from the Clos. Either the Gewürz (350 F) for its brilliant color, its intensity, its *botrytis*. Or better still, the Pinot Gris (300 F) for honey, toasty layers, and remarkable freshness which balances the sugar. (Bottle age).

Reception In the cellar with very beautiful casks. Don't miss a look at the spiral staircase next to the cellar.

How to get there *(Map 1): 10km south of Colmar via the Route des Vins. The Rue Basse overlooks the Place de l'Eglise; the cellar is indicated by a beautiful copy of a dolphin sign; (the original, in the Colmar Museum, dates from 1791).*

The Kitterlé terraced vineyards.

Domaine Schlumberger

Owner Family Schlumberger. **Address** 100 rue Théodore-Deck, 68500 Guebwiller - Tel. 03.89.74.27.00 Fax 03.89.74.85.75. **Open** From Monday to Friday 8:00-12:00 and 14:00-18:00. **Spoken** German, English. **Credit cards** Visa, Eurocard, MasterCard.

Schlumberger is a very large estate of 140 hectares owned by a single winemaker and planted on the Searing, Kessler, and Kitterlé Grand Cru sites. Kitterlé is especially spectacular, its hillside very steep and its vineyard firmly enclosed by one hundred kilometers (sixty miles) of walls. Wines from the estate are typically well aged but dry and intended for drinking with meals. Among the Rieslings, we hesitated between the Saering '93 (79.50 F), very mineral but fruity; and the more luscious Kitterlé '93 (100 F). For a Pinot Gris, try the Kitterlé '94 (135 F) for its toasty nose. If you enjoy dramatic wines, note the full-bodied '94 Princes Abbés Muscat (44.50 F). There is a beautiful choice of sweet Gewürztraminers: the '94 VT Cuvée Christine (200 F), a very ripe, balanced VT with hints of mandarin; and the '89 SGN Cuvée Anne (320 F), generous and spicy on the palate.

Our choice The highly elegant Gewürz, whose richness is balanced by fine acidity. The Kessler '94 (104.50 F), with layers of coffee and spice, firm flesh without rigidity. The '94 Kitterlé (151 F) is more open, perhaps finer still; generous, rich and fresh. (Both should be bottle aged).

Reception At the very top of the Kitterlé slope, don't miss the Wine Museum where winegrowing methods -from planting to pruning the vines- are demonstrated in the actual vineyard. There is a beautiful tasting cellar for groups.

How to get there *(Map 1): Follow the Route des Vins from Colmar and the river at the entrance to Guebwiller. At the third small bridge, turn left (signposted) and follow the arrows.*

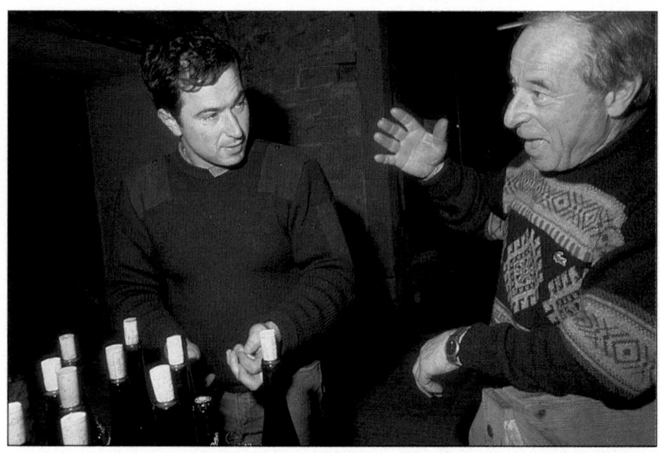

Gérard Schueller enthusiastically recounts the saga of his vintages.

Gérard Schueller

Owner Gérard Schueller. **Address** 1 rue des Trois-Châteaux, 68420 Husseren-les-Châteaux - Tel. 03.89.49.31.54 Fax 03.89.49.36.63. **Open** By appointment. **Spoken** German, italien, English.

This is old-fashioned viticulture, from working the soil to solid vinification: ageing on the lees in oak barrels. The Schuellers always start with very ripe grapes, rich in sugar, but fermentations are long in order to obtain very dry wines. Those which come from the heavy soils of the Eichberg Grand Cru are especially powerful and remain somewhat cloudy when young, becoming all the more charming with bottle age.

The first-price wines are astounding: the '95 Sylvaner (25 F) is beautifully golden, balanced, full-bodied, with low acid; amazingly lingering on the palate. The Pinot Blanc '95 (28 F) is very toasty, full-bodied, and dry. With a luscious '95 Muscat (32 F); a powerful Pfersigberg Riesling in its '94 version (60 F), decidedly more mineral in the '93 vintage (65 F), we could well understand Gérard Schueller's enthusiasm for his vintages.

Our choice Gérard and Bruno Schueller concentrated on Alsatian "specialties", its sweet wines, well before they became fashionable. 1994 was a great year in Alsace for *liquoreux* wines: the Riesling VT (110 F), powerful and well structured; Pinot Gris VT (120 F), elegant, fruity, and smoky; the Pinot Gris SGN (200 F), luscious, smoky, toasty; Gewürz VT (150 F), flowers and honey. Both should be bottle aged.

Reception In the cellar, amid the casks.

How to get there *(Map 1): From Colmar to Guebwiller. After 8kms, turn right towards Husseren, go into village. The cellar is next to the church, indicated on the door bell.*

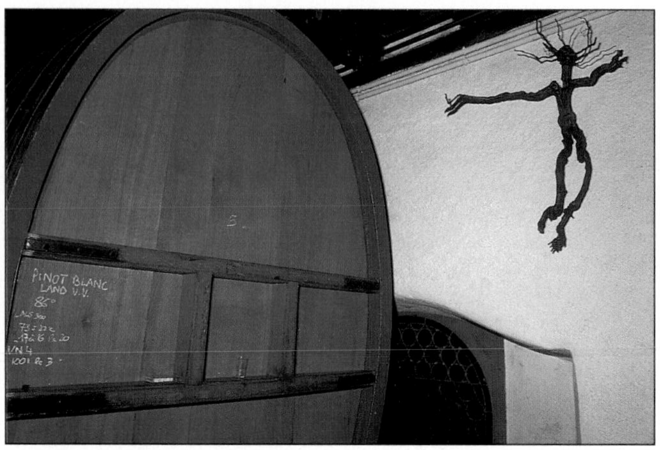

A crucifix? No, a vine, found as is.

Domaine Meyer-Fonné

Owner Family Meyer-Fonné. **Address** 24 Grand-Rue, 68230 Katzenthal - Tel. 03.89.27.16.50 Fax 03.89.27.34.17 **Open** By appointment. **Spoken** German, English.

This estate had long been renowned for its blended wines (Edelzwickers) when they weren't yet fashionable in Alsace. The 1995 Edelwzicker (21.50 F) perpetuates that reputation with a nose hinting of Muscat and a full-bodied, refreshing palate, without the weight of residual sugar. The other first-price wines in the cellar are also interesting: the Sylvaner '94 (22.50 F), powerful and very different from those of the Bas Rhin *département;* and the Pinot Blanc Vieilles Vignes '95 (22.50 F), balanced and delicious.

But we are increasingly interested in Meyer-Fonné's efforts to express his *terroirs.* The old vines of his Wineck-Schlossberg vineyard yield a '95 Riesling (60 F) which is lovely, combining fruit and minerals without undue richness, remaining elegant and thirst-quenching. In Gewürztraminer, we would take both the 1995s: a Réserve Saint-Urbain (47 F), floral and spicy; and the Kaefferkopf (75 F), rich and botrytized, with hints of tobacco. These are surprises in a vintage which was not kind to Gewürztraminers.

Our choice The Hinterburg Pinot Gris, a terraced parcel where all the work is done by hand. The '95 has an amazing roasted-coffee finish. The VT '94 (125 F) offers a full-bodied wine on the palate, candied fruits, and distinct hints of peat at the finish.

Reception A tasting corner in the cellar, whose casks are decorated with beautiful locks.

How to get there *(Map 1): From Colmar to Kaysersberg via N415. After 2 kms, turn left towards Katzenthal, go through village, turn right at the junction.*

Visitors love the automated storks in the cellar.

Domaine Paul Blanck

Owners Paul Blanck and son. **Address** 32 Grand-Rue, 68240 Kientzheim - Tel. 03.89.78.23.56 Fax 03.89.47.16.45. **Open** From Monday to Saturday 10:00-12:00 and 14:00-18:00. **Spoken** German, English. **Credit cards** Visa, Eurocard, MasterCard.

The Domaine Paul Blanck carries on the family tradition. After Paul and then his sons Marcel and Bernard, today it's cousins Philippe and Frédéric's turn to till the thirty-one hectares of the estate, of which three are on the Schlossberg Grand Cru site and six on the Furstentum appellation.

Of the 1996 Classiques, fruity wines which will be offered as of Easter, first try the Pinot Blancs (especially the Rosenbourg Auxerrois, very lingering on the palate); the Patergarten Pinot Gris; the lemony Patergarten Riesling; and an outstanding Sylvaner Vieilles Vignes, with a full-bodied, lingering, persistent flavor.

Of the cuvées which highlight their terroir, taste the Schlossberg Rieslings: the '95 for its finesse and fruit, the Vieilles Vignes '94, with spicy hints; or the minerally, silky extract of the '93 (87 F). In Vendanges Tardives, note the Furstentum Gewürz '94 (about 148 F) for its generous style.

Our choice Two wines from the Frustentum Grand Cru: the Pinot Gris '93: powerful nose, mouth-filling and crisp, almost dry, minty finish; it will be ready to drink quite soon. The Gewürz Vieilles Vignes '95 (76 F), sustained by its terroir, expresses its structure, round and balanced, rather than its aromas. Quite dry, it will make a great gastronomic wine. (Bottle age for several years).

Reception Excellent, in a cellar where automated storks--traditional in Alsace--chase bottles of wine.

How to get there *(Map 1): From Colmar to Strasbourg. After 4kms, left in the direction of Kaysersberg. Kientzheim is 6kms away on D4. The cellar is just before the church on the left, indicated by an automated swan.*

The beautiful sign of the Seltz estate.

Albert Seltz

Owner Albert Seltz. **Address** 21 rue Principale, 67140 Mittelbergheim - Tel. 03.88.08.91.77 Fax 03.88.08.52.72. **Open** By appointment. **Spoken** German, English. **Credit cards** Visa, Eurocard, MasterCard.

"In 1892, it snowed on October 28, while during the summer, the temperature had gone up to 122°F: the grapes had begun ripening on August 3," recounts the *Weinschlagbuch*, the Book of Wine Prices kept by the town of Mittelbergheim since 1456. On the occasion of the last wine festival there, Pierre Seltz noted his observations for 1995 in the book: "We should point out that a harvesting machine is being used in a local vineyard."

Pierre Seltz became the champion of Sylvaner. The grape variety has been denigrated as being "like a pretty young girl from a poor family who doesn't interest boys from a good family," Seltz' son Albert recounts. Albert has taken up the torch, continuing to bring out marvelous Sylvaners from the Zotzenberg vineyard, even if "the poor girl" is not entitled to the Grand Cru appellation there. He has also developed a passion for Pinot Auxerrois, from which he plans to make Vendanges Tardives vinified in oak barrels. We tasted an outstanding Auxerrois '95 (45 F), 70% botrytized and opulent on the palate; but also classic wines, including a lovely Brandluft Riesling '95 (55 F), meaty and intense.

Our choice The '96 Zotzenberg Sylvaner (about 50 F). From old vines; high alcoholic content (more than 14%) gives firm structure, which is balanced by its delicate extract; fruity (quince) and spicy (pepper). Formidable! Drink now.

Reception Beautiful cellars and tasting room hewn out of the limestone beneath the old winery.

How to get there *(Map 1): 2km south of Barr via the Route des Vins. The cellar is in the center of the village.*

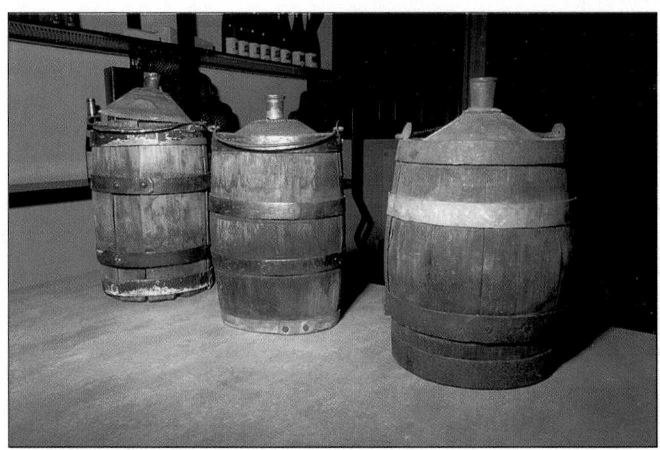

Gérard Neumeyer's *loejeles.*

Gérard Neumeyer

Owner Gérard Neumeyer. **Address** 29 rue Ettore Bugatti, 67120 Molsheim - Tel. 03.88.38.12.45 Fax 03.88.38.11.27. **Open** From Monday to Saturday 9:00-12:00 and 14:00-18:00. **Spoken** German, English. **Credit cards** Visa, Eurocard, MasterCard.

Gérard Neumeyer is a "coffee drinker", as the inhabitants of Molsheim are known. But their town is above all associated with Ettore Bugatti.

Neumeyer's '94 Finkenberg Riesling (34.60 F) is as cheerful as a chaffinch (*finken* in German), mixing hints of spice cake and fruit on the nose. The '95 vintage from the Bruderthal Grand Cru (57 F) is of rare purity on the nose, very elegant, with hints of citrus fruit on the palate (both should have 2 to 3 years' bottle age). If the Muscat is available when you visit, don't hesitate (the production is small). It is invariably of great quality (34.10 F for the '94), powerful and complex, mixing musky traces, almonds, and dry fruits.

You will still find a beautiful '90 Riesling VT (125 F), with hints of toast, spice cake, and dried orange rind; and a sumptuous '94 Gewürz SGN (235 F for 50 cl), allying power and extreme finesse, very honeyed but tempered by its fine acidity.

Our choice The '95 Bruderthal Pinot Gris (65 F). Smoky nose, palate firmly structured by alcohol, but well balanced by the extract and acididity, with some residual sugar. Very lingering finish, with hazelnuts. (Bottle age).

Reception In a new cellar, decorated with a collection of *loejeles,* small Alsatian kegs filled with cheap wine, *trinkwein,* which the old winemakers used to take into the vines.

How to get there *The cellar is at the exit from Molsheim (west of Strasbourg), on the left coming from the town center (signposted).*

Bernard Weber.

Bernard Weber

Owner Bernard Weber. **Address** 49 route de Saverne, 67120 Molsheim - Tel. 03.88.38.52.67 Fax 03.88.38.58.81. **Open** By appointment. **Spoken** German, English. **Credit cards** Visa, Eurocard, MasterCard.

Well before the Bruderthal vineyard was classified as a Grand Cru, Bernard Weber had already planted the largest part of his vineyard there: three hectares of the 5.5 hectares of the estate. Most of his wines open up less easily than their garrulous winemaker. You should thus choose them depending on your cellar capacity; or else select older vintages, which Bernard Weber regularly offers, as well as the several wines which are already good for drinking now.

Among these, the '94 Sylvaner (25 F), a flowery wine with a powerful palate; and the '94 Pinot Blanc (27 F), with a praline finish. Of the older vintages, the very minerally '93 Bruderthal Riesling (50 F); the '91 Bruderthal Gewürz (55 F), with hints of cinnamon; and the '90 Pinot Gris (95 F), rich and elegant. Other outstanding choices include the '94 Bruderthal Muscat (45 F), honeyed and dense; and the '94 Pinot Gris (65 F), very rich.

Our choice The '89 Bruderthal Muscat VT, very rare because this grape variety is not often vinifed in Vendange Tardive (150 F). Intense nose; generous on the palate, spicy at first, opening out with musk and hazelnuts; fruity again at finish. Lingering and intense. (Drink now or bottle age longer).

Reception An enthusiastic discussion in a cellar whose glassed-in timbered walls afford a view of the cellar.

How to get there *(Map 1): The cellar is at the exit from Molsheim (west of Strasbourg), on the road to Saverne, on the right coming from the town center.*

Jean Albrecht.

Maison Lucien Albrecht

Supervisor Jean Albrecht. **Address** 9 Grand-Rue, 68500 Orschwihr - Tel. 03.89.76.95.18 Fax 03.89.76.20.22. **Open** From Monday to Friday 8:00-12:00 and 14:00-19:00, Saturday 9:00-12:30 and 14:00-18:30. **Spoken** German, English. **Credit cards** Visa, Eurocard, MasterCard.

This wine brokerage also has a foot in Paradise: Of its thirty hectares of vines, including seven on the Pfingstberg Grand Cru vineyards, one parcel is called the Clos Himmelreich, "Paradise". Take special note of the wines from the Pfingstberg vines on the Pentecôte slope (68 F for the '94s), such as a powerful, intense Riesling and particularly a generous, full-bodied Pinot Gris. In ageing, the latter becomes extraordinary. The '95 Cuvée Martine Gewürz (47 F), delicately spiced, is also a Pfingstberg non-declared as such. The '94 vintage was remarkable in Albrecht's sweet specialties. For VT, try the generous Pinot Gris (150 F); and the luscious Gewürz (150 F). (Both should be bottle aged for two years to allow the sugar to soften, but the structure is clearly there.) Of the SGNs, we preferred the Riesling (250 F), for its honey and toast; the Gewürz (130 F for half-bottle), very *liquoreux;* and especially the Pinot Gris (285 F), its nose smoky, its palate generous and soft, markedly botrytized.

Our choice The '94 Himmelreich Riesling (49 F). This "wine from Paradise" deserves the name for its purity and ethereal, downy style lingering on the palate: great music of the spheres. (Bottle age). Between Christmas and Easter, Albrecht brings out a remarkable choice of old wines in great vintages for reasonable prices. He who hesitates will be lost!

Reception Around a beautiful marquetry table, in a tasting room dating from the 18th century.

How to get there *(Map 1): From Colmar to Guebwiller. After Rouffach, turn right towards Soultzmatt, then left to Orschwihr. The cellar is in the center: left and then right turns (signposted).*

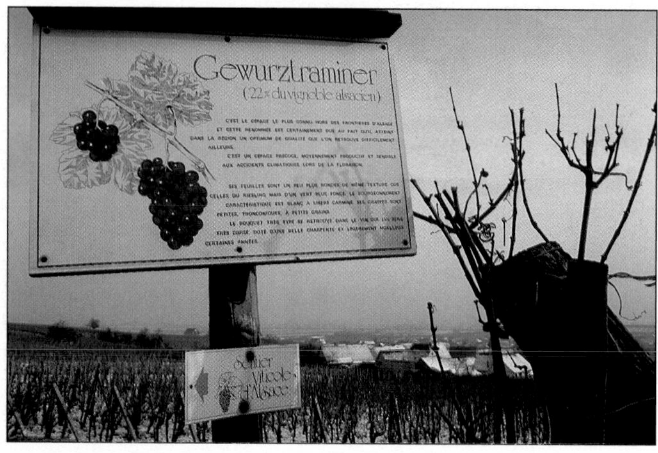

The Pfaffenheim Wine Route.

Cave vinicole

Manager Alex Heinrich. **Winemaker** Michel Kueny. **Address** 5 rue du Chai, 68250 Pfaffenheim - Tel. 03.89.78.08.08 Fax 03.89.49.71.65. **Open** From Monday to Saturday 9:00-12:00 and 14:00-18:00 (non-stop to 19:00 from May to October), Sunday open from 10:00. **Spoken** German, English. **Credit cards** Visa, Eurocard, MasterCard.

The leading Cave Coopérative in Alsace includes 220 producers on 240 hectares. It is well represented on four prestigious *terroirs*: the Goldert, Steinert, Hatschbourg, and Zinnkoepflé vineyards. Because of its large size, the Cave can make clearly distinctive wines. It also makes a policy of stocking large quantities of wines from the great vintage years.

As an introduction to the Cave, taste a wine from an Alsatian grape variety which is becoming extinct: the '95 Cuvée Lafayette Chasselas (30 F), bright silver in color. Try a blind tasting with the '94 Schneckenberg Pinot Blanc (35 F) with its honeyed nose, rich palate, with a trace of botrytis while remaining dry: you'll fool everyone! Keep your eye on the '93 Steinert Pinot Gris (69 F): aroma of peanuts, taste of dried citrus fruits. There is a spectrum of styles among the Gewürz: roses with the '94 Bergweingarten (48 F); hay and flowers from the '94 Steinert (65 F); spices with the '94 Hatschbourg (65 F); power from the '93 Goldert (65 F); and dried flowers with vanilla from the '93 Steinert (65 F).

Our choice The Rieslings (69 F). '89 Steinert: intense aroma, extremely delicate on the palate, typical of a limestone-soil Riesling. (Ready to be drunk). For bottle ageing: the '95 Zinnkoepflé for its nose of orange blossom, maturity on the palate, delicate structure.

Reception In a tasting room for the sale.

How to get there *(Map 1): From Colmar towards Guebwiller. Pfaffenheim is 12kms farther along. Follow signs from the exit on N 83.*

Daily fermentation notes on the casks.

André Kientzler

Owner André Kientzler. **Address** 50 route de Bergheim, 68150 Ribeauvillé - Tel. 03.89.73.67.10 Fax 03.89.73.35.81. **Open** By appointment.

André Kientzler's vines are extensively planted on Ribeauvillé's three Grand Cru sites at Kirchberg, Geisberg, and Osterberg, producing great Rieslings and Muscats, as well as charming fruity wines to be enjoyed young.

The cellar isn't stingy with reasonably priced pleasures among the '95 wines: the Chasselas (about 29 F) and the Pinot Blanc (about 38 F) are rare delights that can hold their own with the great names: for example, the '95 Kirchberg Pinot Gris (about 100 F), silky and delicate.

The two '94 Rieslings available allow us to see how the *terroir* put its stamp on the grape. The Osterberg (about 77 F) is an austere wine, but it should open beautifully. On the other hand, the Geisberg (about 97 F) is more open, fruity, full of fresh almonds in taste.

Our choice The '95 "K" Auxerrois (about 56 F). From old Pinot Auxerrois vines planted on the Kirchberg Grand Cru vineyard. But as Auxerrois is not recognized as a noble grape, the wine is not entitled to the Grand Cru label. The aroma is brilliant, very ripe; full-bodied, intense taste with a hint of toast, almonds, and apricot. Long and persistent finish. (Some bottle age).

Reception Excellent, in a cellar overlooking the vines.

How to get there *(Map 1): From Strasbourg towards Colmar. 8kms after Sélestat, turn right towards Ribeauvillé. Take in the direction of Bergheim. The cellar is isolated, midway between Ribeauvillé and Bergheim on the right.*

Made in 1717, this cask is still in service.

Domaine Trimbach

Owner Family Trimbach. **Address** 15 route de Bergheim, 68150 Ribeauvillé - Tel. 03.89.73.60.30 Fax 03.89.73.89.04. **Open** From Monday to Friday 9:00-12:00 and 14:00-18:00. **Spoken** German, English.

The Trimbachs prefer not to put their *terroirs* in the spotlight because they feel that the boundaries of Grand Cru vineyards are determined too vaguely. And yet this wine broker owns vines in the Geisberg and Osterberg Grand Cru sites, whose wines are blended in the Cuvée Frédéric-Emile.

There is a Trimbach style: their very crisp wines are more remarkable for their fine structure than for their aromatic charm. They are bottled quickly but then left to mature at length, until their aromas finally "speak out".

From the '95 Pinot Blanc (40.50 F), unctuous without being heavy; to the '90 Vendange Tardive, full-flavored and balanced, Trimbach's wines are simply excellent.

Our Choice The '83 Riesling Cuvée Frédéric-Emile (150 F). Very intense aroma, first sligtly sweet and toasty, its fruitiness opening up in the air. It is concentrated on the palate, with an aromatic trace of mint and fern balancing the fresh acidity. Long, straightforward finish, toasty again with a hint of orange. Very persistent, still young, but you can drink it without regret.

Reception In a large, new tasting room at the foot of the hillside.

How to get there *(Map 1): From Strasbourg towards Colmar. 5kms after Sélestat, turn right to Ribeauvillé. In the center, towards Bergheim on right. The cellar is somewhat farther on, on left (the tower at foot of hillside).*

François Lehmann.

François Lehmann

Owner François Lehmann. **Address** 12 rue Jacques Preiss, 68340 Riquewihr - Tel. 03.89.47.95.16 Fax 03.89.47.87.93. **Open** By appointment. **Spoken** German, English.

François Lehmann tends his small estate like a garden: three hectares in Riquewihr, including an even smaller parcel of 29 ares on the Schoenenbourg vineyard, with Riesling vines more than 50 years old. Convinced that "wine begins with the vine", he takes loving care of his vines, "shaping the plant, watching the leaves grow, smelling the flower."

Even when the wines have the power of a Grand Cru, they are invariably delicate and above all, very crisp: wines for gastronomy. Of the good, deliciously priced first-price wines in the cellar, we tasted the '95 Pinot Blanc (28 F), fine and toasty; the '95 Riesling (32 F), already "eloquent", smooth, crisp, and vigorous on the palate; and the '95 Muscat (32 F), full-bodied, also crisp, with a beautiful raisin finish. For a lovely price (150 F), we also found a splendid '89 Riesling VT, with a concentrated, mineral aroma, full-bodied taste, very long with marvelous candied traces.

Our choice The '95 Schoenenbourg Riesling (52 F). A fine aroma mixing fruit and minerals. Splendid flavor, graceful and elegant, with obvious but fine extract. Good structure, rich, and above all, very beautiful acidity, long and persistent, very crisp. (Bottle age).

Reception Simple, in the cellar.

How to get there *(Map 1): Colmar towards Strasbourg. At Houssen, towards Kaysersberg, then on the right, towards Riquewihr. The cellar is on the road leading to the village, on left (signposted).*

Monsieur and Madame Mittnacht-Klack.

Domaine Mittnacht-Klack

Owner Family Mittnacht-Klack. **Address** 8 rue des Tuileries, 68340 Riquewihr - Tel. 03.89.47.92.54 Fax 03.89.47.89.50. **Open** From Monday to Saturday 9:00-12:00 and 13:30-19:00 (18:00 the Saturday). **Spoken** German. **Credit cards** Visa, Eurocard, MasterCard.

This estate includes nine hectares, almost three of which lie on three famous Grand Cru vineyards: the Schoenenbourg, its Rieslings of superb maturity; the Sporen and the Rosacker, known for their opulent Gewürztraminers. Also, there are two parcels with well earned reputations: the Muhlforst and the Clos Saint-Ulrich. Selecting wines from their different *terroirs,* Mittnacht-Klack offers a broad range of expressions in each grape variety, including 12 Rieslings, 17 Gewürztraminers, and 5 Pinots Gris.

We also tasted vintages with long bottle-age before being made available: the estate is just now selling its '93s and '94s, and its 1990s are still on offer. Those who like dry wines will enjoy the '93s: the Schoenenbourg Riesling (54 F), full and mineral in taste; and the Sporen Gewürz (57 F). For a *Sélection des Grains Nobles*, try the '92 Pinot Gris (235 F) for its plummy, smoky sweetness; or the '94 Gewürz (230 F) for its ample flavor. Both are long, persistent, and remarkably well balanced.

Our choice The Gewürztraminers. '94 Sporen (65 F), intense nose, full, mellow taste. '93 Sporen (57 F), typical of the *terroir,* powerful, spicy, vigorous. '94 Schoenenbourg Gewürz (70 F): intense aroma, very full flavor with hints of hazelnut and mint. All should be kept several more years.

Reception Simple, helpful.

How to get there *(Map 1): From Colmar towards Strasbourg. At Houssen, towards Kaysersberg, then on the right, towards Riquewihr. In front of the village sign, turn left, then sign on left.*

Christian Koehly has kept his father's old sign.

Domaine Charles Koehly

Owner Christian Koehly. **Address** Rodern, 68590 Saint-Hippolyte - Tel. 03.89.73.00.61 Fax 03.89.73.05.38. **Open** Every day 9:00-12:00 and 14:00-19:00. **Spoken** German, English. **Credit cards** Visa, Eurocard, MasterCard.

Charles Koehly's vines cover eight hectares, of which 2.3 lie on the Gloeckelberg Grand Cru site at Rodern, a complex geological formation whose Gewürztraminers and Pinots Gris open out slowly; and 1.2 hectares on Bergheim's Altenberg, a limestone-clay vineyard which is favorable to Riesling and Gewürztraminer.

Christian Koehly aims at highlighting the influence of each *terroir* on the grape variety. He likes--and we don't disagree--crisp, dry wines without the cosmetic effects of residual sugar.

Of the many wines whose availability is not always certain, take special note of the often delightful Pinot Blanc (28.50 F for the '95); the '93 Bergheim Altenberg (65 F), its aroma well balanced and its taste very delicate, slightly mineral; and the '95 Saint-Hippolyte Gewürz (about 48 F), straightforward, crisp, a wine to drink with meals.

Our choice The '95 Gloeckelberg Gewürz (about 70 F). The aroma is still trying to open out; fine, concentrated, expressive on the palate (spice, rose water), with its structure more obvious than its aromas. (Bottle-ageing will develop its potential).

Reception Simple, in the cellar.

How to get there *(Map 1): From Colmar towards Strasbourg. After 8 kms, turn towards Ribeauvillé and follow the Route des Vins on the right via Bergheim. After 5 kms, take a left to Rodern. Go up main street; the cellar is on the right, with sign.*

The dragons in the cellar prefer spitting grapes rather than fire.

Maison René Muré

Owner René Muré. **Address** Clos Saint-Landelin, route du vin, 68250 Rouffach - Tel. 03.89.78.58.00 Fax 03.89.78.58.01 – e-mail : rene.mure@hrnet.fr – web : http://www.hrnet.fr/rene.mure/ **Open** From Monday to Saturday 9:00-12:00 and 14:00-18:00. **Spoken** German, English, Italian. **Credit cards** Visa, Eurocard, MasterCard.

Maison René Muré divides its activities between its brokerage house, whose wines, along with those from its own vines, go into the Côtes-de-Rouffach *cuvées*; and its own 21-hectare vineyard, of which 16 are in the Clos Saint-Landelin on the Vorbourg Grand Cru appellation. Be sure to see, or better still, stroll through the vines, which are cultivated on impressive terraces sustained by high walls. Of the '95 Côtes-de-Rouffach wines, you will find a lovely Muscat (48 F), powerful and fine; and a fruity, elegant Riesling (56 F). Of the wines from the Clos, taste the '95 Riesling (98 F), its smoothness due to mature grapes aged on the lees. Capable of great maturity, this “monk's wine”, as René Muré calls it, will not remain ascetic for long, one day developing into a veritable Rabelaisian gourmet. For a Vendange Tardive, try the beautiful '95 Riesling (about 207 F) for its freshness, length, and persistence, with hints of violets and almonds. The estate also offers a whole series of 1990s: you should take special note of the Riesling (186 F for a half-bottle) and the Pinot Gris (457 F).

Our choice The '95 Muscat VT (about 227 F). A quite rare varietal in Vendange Tardive, thus a wine to discover for its intense, typically Muscat aroma, full-bodied and generous palate, very ripe, fresh, long, and persistent. (Bottle age).

Reception In the cellar with view over the vines, protected by a small Bacchus.

How to get there *(Map 1): 16kms south of Colmar via N83. Soultzmatt exit, turn right on leaving the interchange.*

The 18th-century door of woven straw in the cellar.

Domaine Léon Boesch

Owner Gérard Boesch. **Address** 4 rue du Bois, 68570 Soultzmatt and CD 18 bis westhalten - Tel. 03.89.47.01.83 Fax 03.89.47.64.95. **Open** From Monday to Saturday 8:00-12:00 and 14:00-18:00, Sunday by appointment. **Spoken** German, English. **Credit cards** Visa, Eurocard, MasterCard.

In order to obtain the aromatic expression of the grape at Léon Boesch, Pinot Gris, Gewürz, and Muscat undergo slight maceration before the grapes are pressed: With a trace of carbon dioxide, young wines are often lighter. The wines are fully fermented, leaving no residual sugar.

The crisp '95 Sylvaner (24 F) made us think of tobacco leaves just beginning to dry; the '95 Pinot Blanc (28 F), very dry, spice-cake aroma. A versatile grape, the Riesling is a good portrait of the various *terroirs* in the '95 vintage: the generic wine, grown on sandy gravel, is a delicious Riesling, all legs and balance; while the Vallée Noble (38 F), from grapes of the same maturity grown on a limestone-clay parcel, is a Riesling of great finesse, long, with hints of lime. The limestone soils of the Zinnkoepflé Grand Cru confer the varietal with greater power, concentration, and élan.

Our choice The '94 Zinnkoepflé Gewürz (61 F). It is trying to close up, but the taste is there, with the finesse of a fine grape, unctuous, alcoholic, but perfectly balanced. Needs three to four years' bottle age to make its comeback.

Reception See the door of woven rye straw, dating from the 13th century (original in the cellar, copy in the tasting room).

How to get there *(Map 1): 18kms south of Colmar via N83, in the direction of Soultzmatt (on right). The tasting room is at the entrance to village, on left.*

Myriam and Jean-Marie Haag.

Domaine Haag

Owners Jean-Marie and Myriam Haag. **Address** 17 rue des Chèvres, 68570 Soultzmatt - Tel. 03.89.47.02.38 Fax 03.89.47.64.79. **Open** From Monday to Saturday 9:00-12:00 and 14:00-19:00, Sunday by appointment. **Spoken** German, English. **Credit cards** Visa, Eurocard, MasterCard.

The Zinnkoepflé Grand Cru vineyard doesn't have the reputation it deserves. Perhaps because many winemakers in Zoultzmatt attach little importance to the notion of the prestigious vineyard, declaring only a tiny part of their harvest as Grand Cru so as not to be restricted by the more severe requirements of the appellation.

Not so with Jean-Marie and Myriam Haag. They staunchly defend their *terroirs* because all their wines are Grand Crus, including their special sweet wines. The wines are very characteristic of their vineyard, very crisp (except for the VTs or SGNs), thus wines to be enjoyed with meals. The generic '95s are excellent; fruity Sylvaner (20.50 F); very round Pinot Blanc (21 F); stylish Muscat (27 F). The cellar's treasures are to be found among the Grand Cru Gewürztraminers, long and well balanced: '93 (56 F), full flavored and rich; and the '94 Cuvée Marie (60 F), concentrated and spicy.

Our choice The Zinnkoepflé Grand Cru SGN Gewürztraminers. The '94 (168 F/50 cl): intense aroma, full-bodied, very botrytized while remaining fruity and fresh. (Bottle age). The '89 (195 F) is concentrated, with hints of verbena and moss, intact freshness. (Drink or cellar). Both have a beautiful, persistent finish with hints of roasted coffee beans.

Reception Very friendly, in the tasting room.

How to get there *(Map 1): 18kms south of Colmar via N 83. Take towards Soultzmatt on the right. Go up main street and turn left in front of the statue of Saint Grégoire (arrow). Go up Rue des Chèvres: the cellar is on the left (signposted).*

Martin Klein.

Raymond et Martin Klein

Owners Raymond and Martin Klein. **Address** 81 rue de la Vallée, 68570 Soultzmatt - Tel. 03.89.47.01.76/03.89.47.09.70 Fax 03.89.47.64.53. **Open** From Monday to Saturday 9:00-12:00 and 14:00-19:00, Sunday by appointment. **Spoken** German.

The Kleins, father Raymond and son Martin, remained attached to their vines on the Zinnkoepflé site when it wasn't yet classed as a Grand Cru, while many winemakers from their village preferred to plant on less steep hillsides which are easier to cultivate. Today, their four hectares of vines have been promoted to Grand Cru status, including 80% old Gewürztraminer vines.

Like the best winemakers in the village, who raise high the colors of their Grand Cru, the Kleins declare the Grand Cru appellation on all their Zinnkoepflé wines, accepting the more severe production criteria, particularly concerning yields per hectare.

Don't overlook the '95 generic wines: the flowery, charming Sylvaner (16 F); and especially the Muscat (25 F).

Our choice The Zinnkoepflé Grand Cru Gewürztraminers. All softness and spice in '96 (40 F), but fruity in the '94 VT (85 F): very full, rich flavor and smooth extract, with lovely hints of mint in the '89 SGN (160 F). (All need further bottle ageing). The '95 VT was brought out in early 1998. Don't miss it: fine acidity gives it exceptional balance, long and spicy.

Reception By a member of the family in the wine-tasting room. The Kleins are also beekeepers and their spruce honey is delicious.

How to get there *(Map 1): 18kms south of Colmar via N 83. Take towards Soultzmatt on the right. The cellar is in the center of the village, on the right.*

Seppi Landmann, bard of the Zinnkoepflé.

Seppi Landmann

Owner Seppi Landmann. **Address** 20 rue de la Vallée, 68570 Soultzmatt - Tel. 03.89.47.09.33 Fax 03.89.47.06.99. **Open** From Monday to Saturday 9:00-12:00 and 14:00-18:00. **Spoken** German, English. **Credit cards** Visa, Eurocard, MasterCard.

The 1996 *crémant* from this cellar is a splendid, un-dosed half-sparkling wine (69 F), frothy and graceful. A booming Rabelaisian winemaker, Seppi Landmann is the poet of the Zinnkoepflé Grand Cru vineyard, where he makes glorious Gewürztraminers, especially in VT and SGN. But don't overlook his '95 Zinnkoepflé Riesling, with its elegant mineral taste and touches of grapefruit (75 F), nor his '93 of the same wine (95 F), with hints of hay and menthol.

Landmann's Gewürztraminers are often beautifully aromatic (licorice), like the '82 VT (450 F), with little sugar, light, spicy; and the Cuvée Vallée Noble '92 (59.50 F), spicy with an orange finish. Each year, Seppi Landmann offers wines from the latest harvest at very attractive prices. For 1188 Francs, you can reserve 24 bottles of Gewürz Grand Crus (49.50 F a bottle); 12 bottles of Vendange Tardive (99 F a bottle); or 6 bottles of Sélection des Grains Nobles (198 F a bottle). The offer is usually valid until December 15 following the harvest.

Our choice The '94 Zinnkoepflé Gewürz (125 F). Its over-ripeness is obvious in the bouquet but it is well-balanced on the palate, smooth, firmly structured, spicy, and very long. (Bottle age).

Reception Gregarious, booming, impassioned.

How to get there *(Map 1): 18kms south of Colmar via N 83. Take towards Soultzmatt on the right. The cellar is in the center of the town, on the left.*

Born in 1872, two sirens in full form.

Frédéric Mochel

Owner Frédéric Mochel. **Address** 56 rue Principale, 67310 Traenheim - Tel. 03.88.50.38.67 Fax 03.88.50.56.19. **Open** From Monday to Saturday 8:00-12:00 and 13:30-18:00. **Spoken** German. **Credit cards** Visa, Eurocard, MasterCard.

Alsace honors the old, especially when they are vineyard slopes: Altenberg, "old slope" in German, accordingly enjoys three Grand Cru vineyards: Wolxheim, Bergheim, and Bergbieten. The most northerly of the Alsatian vineyards, Bergbieten introduces the visitor to the region's fifty Grands Crus that slowly unfold to the south. Its heavy, marly soils are especially hospitable to the Riesling and Muscat grapes, of which Frédéric Mochel has made a specialty. His *terroir* keeps firm check on the Muscat's aromatic exuberance, calling more attention to its structural finesse and its long finish.

The wines mature quickly but can age well in bottle because of their structural acidity. You might try an unusual wine, the '95 Klevner (33.80 F), a blend of the Pinots Auxerrois and Blanc, for its charmingly smoky overtone. Reliable bets are the Altenberg Gewürz at 56.70 F: a fine vintage in '94, and already more full-bodied and complex in '93, with traces of coffee and dry moss.

Our choice The '95 Altenberg Riesling Cuvée Henriette (65.10 F); from old vines, it yields a distinct, complex aroma; fine and elegant on the palate; very persistent, somewhat more powerful finish. (Bottle age for several years).

Reception A tranquil winery with an 18th-century grape press in the paved courtyard. Lovely tasting room competently run by Madame Mochel.

How to get there *(Map 1): West of Strasbourg via N4, then D422 to Marlenheim (on the left), towards Molsheim. After 4kms, right on D225. The cellar is in the center of the village, next to the "Mairie".*

One of the oldest locks in Léonard Humbrecht's collection.

Domaine Zind-Humbrecht

Owners Léonard and Olivier Humbrecht. **Address** 2 route de Colmar, 68230 Turckheim - Tel. 03.89.27.02.05 Fax 03.89.27.22.58. **Open** From Monday to Friday 8:00-12:00 and 14:00-18:00. **Spoken** German, English. **Credit cards** Visa, Eurocard, MasterCard.

A legendary figure in the Alsatian vineyards, Léonard Humbrecht has always had a reputation for reclaiming abandoned vineyards and replanting them, favoring vines on the plains for their greater ease of cultivation. His wines are fermented slowly, aged on the lees, yielding body with the fine acidity that softens residual sugar. Of some fifty wines currently available, we tasted the fruity '95 Pinot Blanc (69.50 F), the elegant Riesling Clos Windsbuhl (139 F); the Pinot Gris from the same Clos (149 F), noting its concentration and finesse; and the '94 Gewürz Clos Windsbuhl (149 F), well-balanced, the "pretty girl whose breasts and thighs aren't too big," in Léonard Humbrecht's analogy. In the '95 VT camp, try the Riesling from the Brand vineyard (275 F). And for a '94 SGN, ask your bank to mortgage the Heimbourg Pinot Gris (540 F), very sweet, rich, and botrytized; or the Rangen Gewürz (730 F), a monument of intensity and *pourriture noble*.

Our choice The '95s from the Rangen vineyard. The Riesling (198 F), which is still searching its style but will become amazingly smooth; the Pinot Gris (198 F), with sumptuous density and finesse, solidly built though delicate; the enormous Gewürztraminer (198 F), sweet, very long. (Drinking it now would be a crime).

Reception Two tasting areas, by appointment only. With view over the vines or, better, over the cellar. Beautiful collection of old locks.

How to get there *(Map 1): West of Colmar. The cellar is located just before entering Turckheim, on the left, clearly indicated.*

Francis Muré.

Francis Muré

Owner Francis Muré. **Address** 30 rue de Rouffach, 68250 Westhalten - Tel. 03.89.47.64.20 Fax 03.89.47.09.39. **Open** By appointment. **Spoken** German, English. **Credit cards** Visa, Eurocard, MasterCard.

A computer scientist formerly with a *cave coopérative*, Françis Muré has had his own estate since 1991: two and a half hectares including 50 ares on the Zinnkoepflé Grand Cru site, equally divided between Gewürztraminer and Pinot Gris. Some of his vines are almost 70 years old. Muré's wines are fresh, distinct, dry... and appealing. In their style as well as their price: the '96 Sylvaner (about 21 F), ripe, bursting with energy and fruit; the '94 Pinot Blanc (23 F), vigorous, smooth and fine; the '95 Riesling (29 F), a round wine that still must lose its small touch of residual sugar; the '95 Pinot Gris (29 F), with an expressive, toasty aroma. He will offer a lovely '96 Gewürz (about 34 F), fine, well structured, very spicy. The Zinnkoepflé Grand Cru is on the most elevated site of the Alsatian vineyards, protected from rain by the two Ballons d'Alsace peaks in the Vosges Mountains. It is especially well suited to Alsatian specialties, as its sweet wines are called. You will find a beautiful '94 Gewürz Sélection des Grains Nobles (150 F), with an intense, distinct, pure aroma; very fine on the palate, rich without being heavy, elegant and persistent. The wine should develop further with bottle age, but it already "spoke to us" amiably.

Our choice The '95 Muscat (29 F). A true marriage of love between 1/3 Alsatian Muscat, affirming presence on the palate; and 2/3 Muscat d'Ottonel for finesse. The wine is very fresh and crisp: a festival of tastes.

Reception Friendly, in the tasting room.

How to get there *(Map 1): 18kms south of Colmar via N 83. Turn right towards Soultzmatt, then right again to Westhalten. It's in the center of the village, on the left.*

The Barthelmé brothers, Maurice and Jacky.

Domaine Albert Mann

Owners Maurice and Jacky Barthelmé. **Address** 13 rue du Château, 68920 Wettolsheim - Tel. 03.89.80.62.00 Fax 03.89.80.34.23. **Open** From Monday to Saturday 8:00-12:00 and 13:00-18:00. **Spoken** German, English, Spanish. **Credit cards** Visa, Eurocard, MasterCard.

There are no miracles here! We're not referring to the life-size replica of the Lourdes Grotto for which Wettolsheim is famous, but to the marvelous wines made in this cellar. Their quality starts with that of the estate's 19 hectares of *terroirs*, five of which are classed as Grands Crus-- Schlossberg, Furstentum, Hengst, Pfersigberg, and Steingrubler--and the talent of the two Barthelmé brothers.

1995 was an outstanding vintage, yielding wines of great maturity. You can taste the results with an elegant Schlossberg Riesling (60 F); a Hengst Pinot Gris (72 F), full-bodied, with alluring hints of apricot and orange, and the most beautiful Pinot Noir of Alsace (50 F), dense and fruity (black currants, cranberries). For sweet wines, take special note of the '94s. Either in VT, with the Rosenberg Riesling (95 F for 50 cl), with an intense linden bouquet; or the Furstentum Gewürz SGN (280 F), delicate and graceful on the palate, "like a ballerina in the air", says Maurice Barthelmé.

Our choice The '95 Furstentum Gewürz (65 F). Very fine bouquet, with layers of mandarin; floral (violets) on the palate, with smooth extract; finish marked by a small suggestion of *pourriture noble.* A very long, persistent wine, fresh and balanced. (Some bottle age).

Reception In a charming rustic tasting room.

How to get there *(Map 1): In the southwestern outskirts of Colmar via N83. Wettolsheim is on the right. Go into the village to the main square, turn left, go to the front of the life-size replica of the Lourdes Grotto; first left, portal immediately on left.*

BEAUJOLAIS

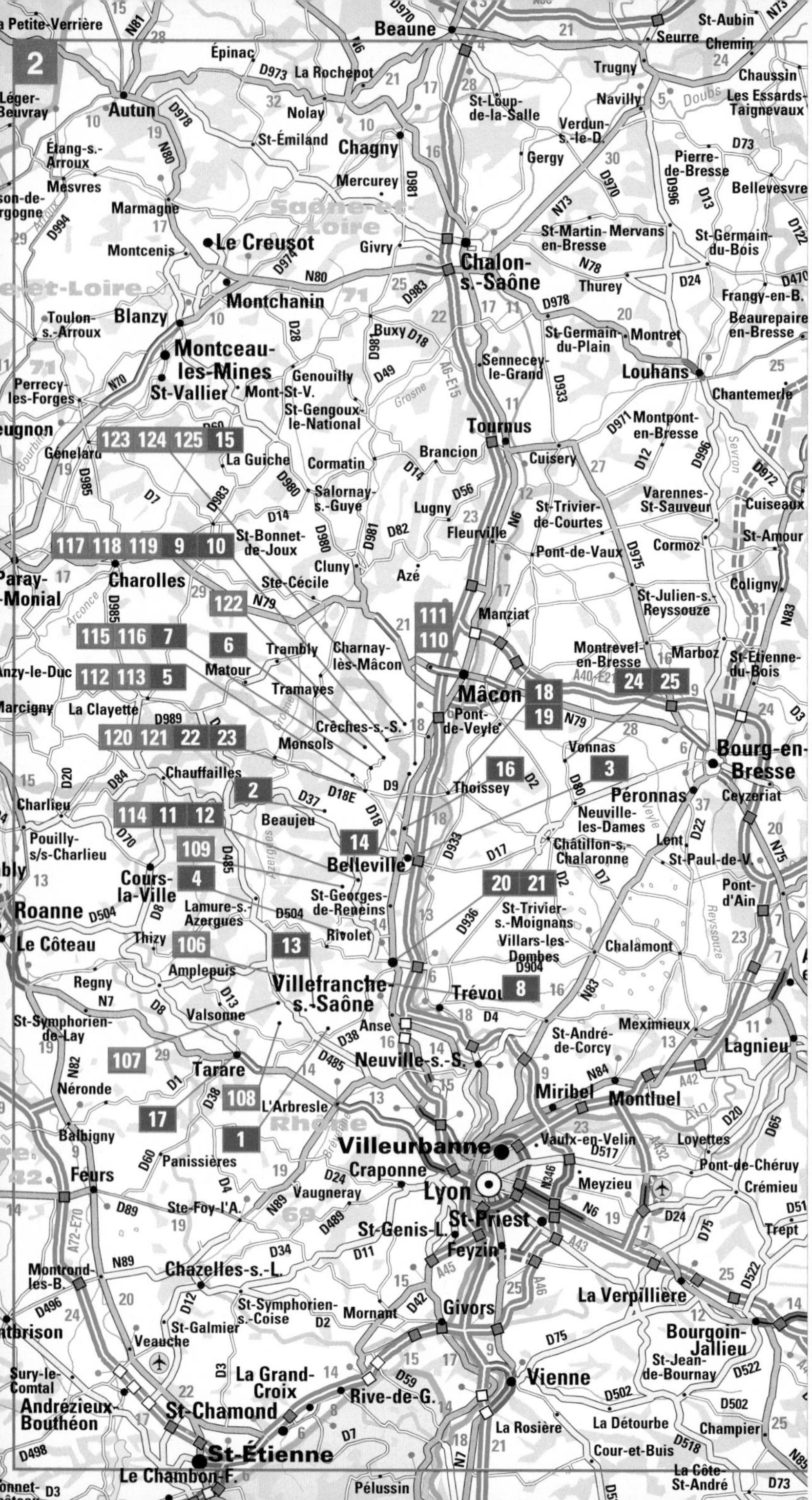
2
Beaune
St-Aubin
Seurre
Chemin
Petite-Verrière
Épinac
D973
La Rochepot
Trugny
Chaussin
Léger-Beuvray
Autun
D978
Nolay
St-Loup-de-la-Salle
Navilly
Doubs
Les Essards-Taignevaux
St-Émiland
Chagny
Verdun-s.-le-D.
Étang-s.-Arroux
N80
Gergy
D970
Pierre-de-Bresse
Mesvres
Mercurey
D981
D996
D13
Bellevesvre
Marmagne
Saône-et-Loire
N73
D994
Le Creusot
Givry
St-Martin-en-Bresse
Mervans
St-Germain-du-Bois
D122
Montcenis
D974
Chalon-s.-Saône
N78
Thurey
D24
D470
Montchanin
D983
D978
Frangy-en-B.
Toulon-s.-Arroux
Blanzy
D28
Buxy
D18
St-Germain-du-Plain
Montret
Beaurepaire-en-Bresse
Montceau-les-Mines
Genouilly
D49
Sennecey-le-Grand
D933
Louhans
Perrecy-les-Forges
St-Vallier
N70
Mont-St-V.
Grosne
A6-E15
Chantemerle
St-Gengoux-le-National
D971
Montpont-en-Bresse
Génelard
Tournus
123
124
125
15
La Guiche
Cormatin
Brancion
Cuisery
D12
D996
D985
D14
D56
D972
D7
D983
D980
Salornay-s.-Guye
Lugny
St-Trivier-de-Courtes
Varennes-St-Sauveur
Cuiseaux
D14
D82
N6
Fleurville
St-Bonnet-de-Joux
D981
117
118
119
9
10
D980
Pont-de-Vaux
D975
Cormoz
St-Amour
Cluny
Charolles
Paray-Monial
Azé
Ste-Cécile
Coligny
122
N79
Manziat
St-Julien-s.-Reyssouze
Arconce
111
110
N83
115
116
7
6
Trambly
Charnay-lès-Mâcon
Montrevel-en-Bresse
Marboz
St-Étienne-du-Bois
Anzy-le-Duc
112
113
5
Matour
Mâcon
18
19
A40-E21
24
25
Marcigny
La Clayette
Tramayes
Pont-de-Veyle
D989
N79
Crêches-s.-S.
120
121
22
23
Monsols
Vonnas
Bourg-en-Bresse
D20
Chauffailles
16
D2
3
D84
2
D37
D18E
D9
Thoissey
Péronnas
Ceyzériat
Charlieu
D80
Beaujeu
D18
114
11
12
Neuville-les-Dames
D22
D70
14
D933
Lent
N75
Pouilly-s/s-Charlieu
109
D485
Azergues
Belleville
D17
Châtillon-s.-Chalaronne
St-Paul-de-V.
Cours-la-Ville
4
20
21
D2
D7
St-Georges-de-Reneins
Pont-d'Ain
Roanne
D504
D8
Lamure-s.-Azergues
D504
D936
St-Trivier-s.-Moignans
Reyssouze
Rivolet
Le Côteau
Thizy
106
13
Villars-les-Dombes
Chalamont
Amplepuis
D904
Regny
Villefranche-s.-Saône
Trévoux
8
N83
N7
D13
D8
Valsonne
D4
St-Symphorien-de-Lay
Anse
St-André-de-Corcy
Meximieux
Lagnieu
D38
107
N82
Tarare
D485
Neuville-s.-S.
D1
D38
108
Miribel
N84
Montluel
A42
Néronde
L'Arbresle
Ain
D20
17
1
Rhône
Villeurbanne
Vaulx-en-Velin
D517
A432
Loyettes
D65
Balbigny
D60
Panissières
Craponne
Pont-de-Chéruy
Feurs
D24
Lyon
N346
Meyzieu
Crémieu
Vaugneray
D89
Ste-Foy-l'A.
N89
D489
St-Priest
N6
D24
D51
D75
Trept
A72-E70
St-Genis-L.
D34
D11
Feyzin
A43
Montrond-les-B.
N89
Chazelles-s.-L.
A45
A46
D522
D496
D12
St-Symphorien-s.-Coise
Mornant
D42
Givors
La Verpillière
D2
Montbrison
St-Galmier
Veauche
D75
Bourgoin-Jallieu
St-Jean-de-Bournay
D522
Sury-le-Comtal
D3
La Grand-Croix
D59
Vienne
Andrézieux-Bouthéon
St-Chamond
Rive-de-G.
D502
D502
La Rosière
La Détourbe
Champier
D7
D518
D498
St-Étienne
Cour-et-Buis
N7
Le Chambon-F.
Pélussin
La Côte-St-André
D73
D3
N85

INTRODUCTION

For administrative purposes, the Beaujolais region has been considered part of "greater Burgundy" since 1930, but as a vineyard region it is quite independent, with its own strong identity and observable unity. The southern prolongation of the Mâconnais, its vines spread over eleven communes in the Saône-et-Loire *département* and seventy-nine communes in that of the Rhône, extending all the way to the Lyonnais mountains. Almost a thousand square kilometers of vines are sheltered from the west winds by the foothills of the Massif Central, thus enjoying a temperate climate and the gentle weather of the Rhône Valley. The northern Beaujolais is home to the "united states" of the ten Appellation d'Origine Contrôlée (AOC) *crus*, whose vines cover 6280 hectares. To the west and south of these élite vineyards are the vast appellations Beaujolais-Villages, with 6020 hectares, and Beaujolais, covering 9700 hectares in the "land of the golden stones". The Beaujolais is like a roof with a double slope, with one slanting toward the Loire and the other toward the Saône; the latter flank is the kingdom of the Gamay grape variety. Seen from Route Nationale 6, this hillside, as it slips down toward Villefranche-sur-Saône, appears as gentle as the tannins of the Beaujolais Primeur that is made here. It is only when we turn onto the Route des Crus, from Saint-Amour in the north to Odenas in the south, that our first impression changes as we come upon sinuous turns that wind around jagged hillsides and a succession of steep slopes and deep valleys. On clear days you will discover breathtaking views, sometimes as far as the Alps. The Beaujolais is less densely populated than northern Burgundy, with its hillside towns scattering out into a string of small hamlets and isolated houses. While Beaujolais *vignerons* have a marked community spirit, they are first and foremost sons and daughters of a village, and of a wine. You might call them "stubbornly Gallic", but that accounts for much of the charm of the Beaujolais, whose hospitality is legendary. Is it because the winemakers here are so charming that their wines are equally so, or could it be the other way around? Offering a piece of bread and a slice of sausage as you taste wine is an instinctive reflex. Keeping the Beaujolais tasting room tidy and welcoming customers hospitably is a regional duty. The customer soon becomes a friend, his annual visit a joy to be celebrated.

Such is the reason why the Beaujolais is invariably a formidable vineyard region for the initiate: partly because of its Beaujolais Nouveau, a delightful wine for arousing the oenophile's first tasting sensation, but mainly because a good Beaujolais goes right to what wine is all about: pleasure.

VINIFICATION IN THE BEAUJOLAIS

The Gamay is a grape with a black skin and white juice. It is *the* grape variety in the Beaujolais, representing 98% of the vines planted (the remaining 2% being Chardonnay for making white Beaujolais.) To further ensure its reputation for producing a soft, aromatic wine, the Gamay undergoes natural, semi-carbonic maceration, the traditional Beaujolais fermentation technique: Grapes must be picked by hand so that they can be put whole into the fermentation vats: Beaujolais and Champagne are the only two French vineyard regions in which harvesting machines are outlawed. The grapes are then poured into the vats without being crushed *(foulé)*; their stems, to which the grapes are attached, are left on. Weighted down by the grapes in the vat, those at the bottom burst, their juice running out and beginning to ferment. Fermentation slowly makes its way throughout the vat, finally reaching the whole grapes and initiating fermentation inside them; this promotes the extraction of their aromatic substances. Carbon dioxide is released during carbonic maceration, keeping the fermenting grapes from oxydizing and preserving their aromas. Some winemakers keep the *marc* (the skins, pips, and stems) immersed in the juice by means of horizontal bars attached inside the vat--a technique called *grillage*--in order to concentrate the color and the tannins. Once the fermentation has transformed all the grape sugar into alcohol, the juice is run off from the vat, the *marc* is pressed, and this "press wine" is kept. The second fermentation, called malolactic, now takes place. The wine is then quickly bottled, producing Beaujolais Nouveau; or it is aged in vats or barrels during the winter and bottled the following spring, which is the case with generic Beaujolais and the ten élite *crus*.

THE BEAUJOLAIS APPELLATIONS

The region's most famous ambassador is, of course, Beaujolais Nouveau. An ephemeral wine, it is made in two months and drunk in the same lapse of time beginning on the third Thursday of November. An undisputed success in marketing terms, it began simply as a lovely, light wine to be enjoyed around a bar counter before it became a drink of renown, its *arrivé* awaited expectantly around the world: more than 55% of Beaujolais Nouveau is exported. Bistrot owners in Lyon buy it "raw" from the vineyards, finishing the fermentation themselves and then putting it into traditional Beaujolais *pots*, round-bottomed bottles of 46 centiliters, a little more than half a bottle. The legal birth date of Beaujolais Nouveau goes back to 1951, but it wasn't instantly marketed the way it is today by *négociants* and skillful promoters: scarcely 40,000 hectoliters were sold in 1960, as against more than 500,000 today. The new wine represents more than three-fourths of the production in the Beaujolais appellation, covering the entire southern part of the region, and one-fourth of the Beaujolais-Villages wines.

Overshadowed by this hegemony of the *primeurs*, the true Beaujolais and Beaujolais-Villages, those that we drink in April after they have "celebrated Easter", are experiencing grave difficulties. While quaffable Beaujolais can be enjoyed young in the spring and summer, wines with the little-known Beaujolais-Villages appellation on their label are more substantial wines, some almost as long-lived as the famous-name *crus*. They are soft, full-bodied wines with backbone and ripe, grapy aromas that are a far cry from the Beaujolais Nouveau stereotype.

But most importantly, there are the ten Beaujolais *crus*, each named after a village or a group of villages in the northern Beaujolais between Chânes and Belleville. Their vines are planted in predominantly granite-based soils with, depending on the location of the vineyard, various adjuncts of schist. The crus are wines of a stronger perfumed bouquet, greater concentration, and fuller taste than a simple Beaujolais.

THE *CRUS*

Planted on 1200 hectares of predominantly granite sub-soil, Brouilly is the largest vineyard region of the ten *crus*. Actually, it is too vast to call it a true entity. Often disappointing, Brouilly, when it is well made, is a charmingly soft wine with an incomparable bouquet of fresh grapes.

The next door neighbor of Moulin-à-Vent, Chenas covers 280 hectares of vines in granite soil topped with clay and sand. It yields a wine with a certain resemblance to its neighbor but Chenas suffers from its small size. Vigorous, solid, rustic, Chenas keeps well (from two to six years) but it can lack elegance and distinction. It nevertheless offers good quality for the price.

Chiroubles comprises 365 hectares of vineyards clinging to quite high slopes, with shallow top-soil on a heavy granite base and late-ripening grapes. Some enthusiasts love Chiroubles' lightness and aromatic richness, while others criticize its lack of body or its acidity. An alluring, ethereal wine (light in color and tannin), thirst-quenching, it slips down easily and charms with its pronounced aromas of flowers and red berries.

On the southern slopes of Mont Brouilly (290 hectares on hard volcanic rock, called "Brouilly blue stone"), the Côtes-de-Brouilly appellation furnishes red wines of deeper color, richer, more alcoholic and more concentrated than those of its cousin, while retaining the family finesse. It is much more recommendable than Brouilly itself and can be drunk between one and four years of bottle age.

With 825 hectares planted in granite sub-soil, Fleurie is a large Beaujolais appellation whose exposures, *terroirs*, and thus wines are varied but of homogenous quality. The Fleurie vineyards close to Moulin-à-Vent (Roilette, Point-du-Jour) are close to it in taste, also. Less tannic than Moulin-à-Vent, Fleurie can be enjoyed younger and has a more typical Beaujolais identity: fruity, charming, and aromatic. It is best after two to eight years' ageing in the bottle. The supply far exceeds the demand and thus the prices of Fleurie are quite high.

The best Juliénas wines (600 hectares on clay-schist and granite) are fruity and fresh but full-bodied and have a high alcoholic content; they are more robust than the majority of the *crus*. Reminiscent of Moulin-à-Vent and Morgon, Juliénas can be enjoyed after one year of bottle age.

The Morgon appellation is vast, with vines planted on 1100 hectares of crumbly granite schist. There is therefore a real difference between the large-backboned Morgons from the Côte-de-Py and the lighter wines from the flat vineyards. The most typical Morgon is that from the Côte-de-Py, which can be kept from two to eight years, yielding a powerful wine with a characteristic mouth-filling quality--so characteristic, in fact, that a verb has been devised, *morgoner,* to qualify its firm fleshiness.

Moulin-à-Vent (650 hectares on manganese-rich granite) is "the most Burgundian of the Beaujolais *crus*" because of its richness, its imposing structure, and its ability to age four to ten years. Many winegrowers vinify and age Moulin-à-Vent in oak barrels, which conceals the traditional fruity character imparted by the Gamay grape, making it a gastronomic wine and one which improves with age.

With 660 hectares of vineyards on sandy granite, Régnié is the newborn of the ten *crus*, having been promoted in 1989. Previously it had been one of the most sought-after wines in the Beaujolais-Villages appellation. Therefore, what was the point of transforming it into a *cru*? The present commercial difficulties of Régnié make us wonder. A wine of fruity aromas, it is quite restrained in taste, a kind of less full-bodied Morgon. It needs two to four years in the bottle to mature properly.

Saint-Amour, the most northerly *cru* with 310 hectares on sandy clay, is as sought after as Fleurie and Moulin-à-Vent. The style is different, however, because Saint-Amour is supple, quite lively and fruity, suggesting raspberries and black currants in those sold in the spring (the autumn bottlings are fuller in body.)

BUYING IN THE BEAUJOLAIS

Beaujolais Nouveau is mainly made by *négociants* and distributed through traditional retail stores, although private winemakers do bottle a small quantity for their customers. The Beaujolais buyer should come here in spring, just following the first bottlings around March or April. Beaujolais and Beaujolais-Villages are summer wines, to be drunk fresh and cool. The *crus* can also be enjoyed young (Brouilly, Régié, Saint-Amour) or laid down for one to two years (Chiroubles, Fleurie, Juliénas, Côtes-de-Brouilly) or even longer in the case of Chenas, Morgon, and Moulin-à-Vent.

A year of record yields, and thus of diluted wine, 1996 was saved by a north wind, making it possible for most grapes to ripen at the last minute, one week before the harvest. 1996 Beaujolais and Beaujolais-Villages are perfumed and quite acid, wines to be drunk quickly. The ten *crus* defended themselves well, offering average cellaring potential, but less than in 1995. They aromatic, open up quickly on the palate, and can be drunk now. The prices are quite stable, with one of the best price-quality ratios in France: 25 F for a classic Beaujolais; between 30 F and 45 F for the *crus* (50 F for the *cuvées* aged in oak barrels).

A TABLE WITH BEAUJOLAIS WINES

Wines of the Beaujolais have two great advantages: They can be drunk cool (at cellar temperatures of 50°F to 54°F) and they are good with simple, rustic cuisine. With the young wines, the best dishes are traditional cold cuts (avoid excessive fat, which makes the wine "thin"): dry sausages, lean ham, parsleyed Burgundy ham, and densely textured dishes. With wines two to four years old, good choices are farm-raised chickens and meats in simple dishes or more refined preparations. Avoid heavy sauces, fatty dishes, and overly sweet desserts.

BAGNOLS

1 - HOTEL-RESTAURANT - **Château de Bagnols**: *69620 Bagnols. Tel. 04.74. 71.40.00 Fax 04.74.71.40.49. Closed in November and December. Restaurant closed from 11/2 to Easter.* 12 km southwest of Villefranche, a genuine medieval fortress with drawbridge and moat, restored at great expense. A sober and majestic site for a descreet billionaire's getaway. Surely France's best in terms of historic palaces. In the restaurant, a traditional cuisine enhanced by felicitous personal touches. Menus: 195 (lunch weekdays) to 450 F. A la carte: around 450 F. Each room in the castle is a museum in and of itself. Prices correspond to the luxury. 12 rooms: 2,600 to 5,000 F. 4 suites: 4,000 to 5,000 F. 8 rooms in the main house: 2,200 to 3,000 F and 1 suite: 3,000 F.

BEAUJEU

2 - HOTEL-RESTAURANT - **Anne de Beaujeu**: *28 rue de la République, 69430 Beaujeu. Tel. 04.74.04.87.58 Fax*

04.74.69.22.13. An inviting family house offering good regional cuisine accompanied by a selection of over 20 Beaujolais. Menus: 112 to 279 F. 7 rooms: 290 to 368 F.

BELLEVILLE

3 - RESTAURANT - **Le Buffet de la Gare**: *Place de la Gare, 69220 Belleville. Tel. 04.74.66.07.36 Fax 04.74.69. 69.49. Always open for lunch. Closed weekends.* A friendly address for bistro-style cuisine (pumpkin au gratin, wine sausage, homemade cakes) and very pleasant service. Only one Beaujolais supplier, but quite good. Menu: 89 F.

BLACE

4 - HOTEL-RESTAURANT - **Le Savigny**: *69460 Blacé. Tel. 04.74.67.52.07 Fax 04.74. 60.51.54. Closed in December.* A perfectly quiet family hotel. Comfortable rooms appointed in a former vatting room and winegrower's house. Kind and curteous welcome. Inconsistent restaurant. 14 rooms: 360 to 480 F.

CHIROUBLES

5 - BED & BREAKFAST - **Domaine de la Grosse Pierre**: *Véronique and Alain Passot, La Grosse Pierre, 69115 Chiroubles. Tel. 04.74.69.12.17 Fax 04.74.69.13.52. Closed in December and January.* Five guest rooms arranged in 1995 in a large Beaujolais dwelling set amidst the vines; peaceful, with a view as pleasant as the welcome (see Chiroubles address). Rooms are not big, but offer 3-star hotel comfort. 280 F per

night with homemade breakfast (2 pers.). 300 F with large bed. Pool.

ÉMERINGES

6 - RESTAURANT - **Auberge des Vignerons**: *69840 Émeringes. Tel. 04.74. 04.45.72 Fax 04.74.04.48.96. Closed Sun. evenings and Mon.* Spry and inventive market-based cuisine. Large selection of wines and not only of Beaujolais. Pleasant surprises at wise prices. Menu: 250 F.

FLEURIE

7 - RESTAURANT - **Auberge du Cep**: *Place de l'Église, 69820 Fleurie. Tel. 04.74.04.10.77 Fax 04.74.04.10.28 Closed Sun. evenings and Mon. and early December to late January.* Refined Beaujolais gastronomy, currently the best table in the vineyard. Large selection of Beaujolais with a preference for the Fleurie (count on 150 F a bottle). Very solicitous welcome. Menus: 200 to 350 F. Menu dégustation: 575 F.

JARNIOUX

8 - BED & BREAKFAST - **Château de Bois Franc**: *69640 Jarnioux. Tel. 04.74. 68.20.91 Fax 04.74.65.10.03.* 7 km west of Villefranche-sur-Saône, within two paces of " Golden rock " country, a beautiful residence offering two suites for 2 to 6 persons. The most attractive, the " suite jaune ", is very nicely furnished. From 400 to 900 F depending on the number of persons, breakfast included. No meal service.

JULIÉNAS

9 - RESTAURANT - **Le Coq au Vin**: *Place du Marché, 69840 Juliénas. Tel. 04.74.04.41.98 Fax 04.74.04.41.44. Closed Wed. and mid-December to mid-January.* A chic address, colorful and bright. Very good bistro-style cuisine, nimble and inventive. Ten vintages from good owners (80 to 120 F). Menus: 98 (weekdays) to 230 F.

10 - HOTEL - **Hôtel des Vignes**: *69840 Juliénas. Tel. 04.74.04.43.70 Fax 04.74.04.41.95.* 1 km from Juliénas on the Saint-Amour route, a new hotel (sans restaurant) amidst the vineyard, with good 2-star comfort. 22 rooms: 200 to 275 F. Breakfast: 35 F.

ODENAS

11 - RESTAURANT - **Christian Mabeau**: *La jardinière, 69460 Odenas. Tel. 04.74.03.41.79 Fax 04.74.03.49.40. Closed Sun. evenings and Mon.* Good market-based cuisine. Catch-all wine list with the best Brouillys at accessible prices. View of the vineyard from the terrace. Menus: 105 (except Sunday) to 265 F.

12 - RESTAURANT - **Restaurant du Col de Brouilly**: *La Poyebade, 69460 Odenas. Tel. 04.74.03.40.55. Closed from 12/23 to 1/10, Wednesdays and*

evenings from September to June. Good, hearty regional cuisine and good value (frog's legs, Bressan poultry). Menus: 90 to 162 F.

OINGT

13 - RESTAURANT - **Le Donjon**: *Place du Marché, 69620 Oingt. Tel. 04.74.71.20.24 Fax 04.74.71.10.91. Closed Tues. evenings and Wed.* Unrestricted view over the south Beaujolais vineyard. One will enjoy the good regional cuisine and the chilled Beaujolais at cool prices. Menus: 98 to 210 F. A la carte: around 200 F.

ROMANÈCHE-THORINS

14 - HOTEL-RESTAURANT - **Les Maritonnes**: *route de Fleurie, 71570 Romanèche-Thorins. Tel. 03.85.35.51.70 Fax 03.85.35.58.14. Closed Sun. evenings (low-season), Mon., Tues. noon and from mid-December to late January.* A prosperous family house covered with Virginia creeper, well kept, with a pleasant park. Good, straightforward, genuine cuisine, and above all a perfect selection of Beaujolais and Mâconnais. A classic stop in the Beaujolais vineyard. Menus: 160 (lunch weekdays) to 420 F. A la carte: around 350 F. 20 rooms (400 F to 560 F), well-insulated from noise given the proximity of the train tracks. Breakfast: 60 F.

SAINT-AMOUR-BELLEVUE

15 - RESTAURANT - **Auberge du Paradis**: *Le platre Durand, 71570 Saint-Amour-Bellevue. Tel. 03.85.37.10.26 Fax 03.85.37.47.92. Closed Mon. evenings and Tues.* A village inn refurbished in spring of 97. In the bright new bistro decor, a young new chef with a fondness for spices and contrasting flavors. Wine list in the

making at the time of our visit. To be continued. Menus: 80 (lunch weekdays) to 140 F.

SAINT-JEAN-D'ARDIÈRES

16 - HOTEL-RESTAURANT - **Château de Pizay**: *69220 Saint-Jean-d'Ardières. Tel. 04.74.66.51.41 Fax 04.74.69.65.63. Closed for the Christmas holidays.* Imposing, magnificent castle of the 14th and 17th centuries surrounded by a vineyard and French gardens. Spacious, comfortable new rooms in the annexes. Pool. Menus: 200 to 395 F. 62 rooms: 575 to 1,900 F.

TARARE

17 - RESTAURANT - **Jean Brouilly**: *3 ter rue de Paris, 69170 Tarare. Tel. 04.74.63.24.56 Fax 04.74.05.05.48. Closed Sun. (except for lunch on holidays) and Mon.* At the southern tip of the Beaujolais vineyard, in a contemporary setting, a cuisine founded on regional tradition that judiciously

brings together products from the sea and those from the countryside. An attractive selection of Beaujolais (at ever-reasonable prices) and an equally commendable choice of Burgundies. Menus: 160 to 370 F. A la carte: around 350 F.

THOISSEY

18 - RESTAURANT - **La Guinguette**: *01140 Thoissey. Tel. 04.74.04.02.03 Fax 04.74.04.94.67.* Above the Saône, on the left bank in the port of Thoissey, a guinguette for a family lunch on the waterside. Simple family cooking. Some good Beaujolais vintners on the list. 3 menus from 128 to 230 F.

19 - HOTEL-RESTAURANT - **Paul Blanc - Au chapon fin**: *Rue Paul Blanc, 01140 Thoissey. Tel. 04.74.04.04.74 Fax 04.74.04.94.51. Closed Tues. and Wed. noon.* Brisk Bressan cuisine whose clacissism reassures the local regulars. Remarkable selection of Beaujolais. Menus: 160 to 520 F. 20 very comfortable, partly refurbished rooms that look onto a park. From 250 to 700 F. Breakfast: 55 F.

VILLEFRANCHE-SUR-SAÔNE

20 - RESTAURANT - **L'Épicerie**: *55 rue de Thizy, 69400 Villefranche-sur-Saône. Tel. 04.74.62.04.04 Fax 04.74.68. 86.60. Closed Sat. noon and Sun. and the week of 8/15.* In Villefranche's old city, a friendly bistrot-bouchon lyonnais (excellent traditional French cuisine) offering the classics: tablier de sapeur (tripe), hot sausage steamed potatos, pike quenelles accompanied by the traditional jug of Beaujolais-Villages. Menus: 89 to 119 F. A la carte: around 120 F.

21 - RESTAURANT - **Le Juliénas**: *236 rue d'Anse, 69400 Villefranche-sur-Saône. Tel. 04.74.09.16.55.* Still in the bistro style, but with a more stylish decor than l'Épicerie (see above). The cuisine is generous, regionally characteristic (Lyonnais sausage and salad, Beaujolais chitterling-sausage, fromage blanc crème fraîche) and not costly. A pity that the list of Beaujolais and estate bottled wines isn't more complete. Menus: 85 to 150 F.

VILLIÉ-MORGON

22 - HOTEL-RESTAURANT - **Le Villon**: *69910 Villié-Morgon. Tel. 04.74.69.16.16 Fax 04.74.69.16.81. Closed Sun. evenings and Mon. from 10/1 to 4/30, and from 12/19 to 1/22.* Modern with standard comfort. Small rooms looking out on the Beaujolais peaks. Menus: 110 to 235 F. 45 rooms: 270 to 330 F.

23 - RESTAURANT - **Le Morgon**: *69910 Villié-Morgon. Tel. 04.74.69.16.03 Fax 04.74.69.12.77. Closed Wed., Sun. evening.* Very good regional cuisine and a near exhaustive list of Morgons. Menus: 80 to 200 F.

VONNAS

24 - HOTEL-RESTAURANT - **Georges Blanc**: *01540 Vonnas. Tel. 04.74.50.90.90 Fax 04.74.50.08.80. Closed Mon. year-round, Tues. from 9/15 to 6/15 and closed in January.* 20 km southeast of Mâcon. The international renown of Georges Blanc's cuisine and magnificent hostelry (Relais & Châteaux) speaks for itself. As is proper, an eloquent and majestic wine list that gives

a boost to the Azé estate, the owner's Mâconnais property. Menus: 470 to

850 F. A la carte: around 700 F. 32 rooms: 800 to 1,500 F. 6 apartments: 1,750 to 3,000 F. Pool.

25 - HOTEL-RESTAURANT - **L'Ancienne Auberge-Résidence des Saules**: *01540 Vonnas. Tel. 04.74.50.90.50 Fax 04.74.50.08.80. Closed in January.* A real beginning-of-the-century inn, recreated by Georges and Frédéric Blanc. Retro decor, regional cuisine (sautéed frog's legs, Bresse chicken with cream sauce), and a wine list (mostly Mâcon, Beaujolais) that offers simplicity and reasonable prices. Very pleasant. Menus: 98 F (weekdays) to 210 F. A la carte: around 250 F. 8 rooms and 2 apartments: 550 to 700 F with the possibility of participating in the open-air activities of the main house.

TO SEE

BEAUJEU

OUTING - **Beaujolais oil-mill**: *29 rue des Echarmeaux, 69430 Beaujeu. Tel. 04.74.69.28.06/06.80.30. 96.93 Fax 04.74.04.87.09. Open Mon.-Sat. from 8am to 8pm.* A well-known oil-mill where numerous chefs come to stock up.

ROMANÈCHE-THORINS

MUSEUM - **Le Hameau du vin (Georges Dubœuf)**: *71570 Romanèche-Thorins. Tel. 03.85.35.22.22 Fax 03.85.35. 21.18. Every day from 9 to 6 (closed in January).* Admission: 70 F; 8-16 years old: 50 F; under 8: free. A fascinating museum on wine in general and Beaujolais in particular. A dozen rooms devoted to transportation, aging cellars, ampelography, vinification, cooperage, etc. Everything is illustrated by projections and lighting effects (very well done in the viticultural museum) and by automaton scenes. Plan on an hour and a half for the visit which ends with a mini-tasting of Dubœuf's wines.

VITICULTURAL FESTIVITIES

OCTOBER
Fête Raclet: late October in Romanèche-Thorins, a presentation of Mâconnais-Beaujolais wines and the Beaujolais Nouveau fête.

DECEMBER
The " Two Bottle " contest, the first weekend in December in Villefranche-sur-Saône. Information: Tel. 04.74.65.46.20. Giant wine tasting to which all Beaujolais vintners can bring their wines (most recent vintage).

Jean Joyet "goblet-pruning" his Gamays.

Coteaux de la Roche

Owner Jean Joyet. **Address** La Roche, 69620 Létra - Tel. 04.74.71.32.77 Fax 04.74.71.32.77. **Open** Every day, 9:00-12:00 and 14:00-19:00, preferably by appointment.

At the foot of the Létra hillsides, the small, winding road that leads to Jean Joyet's cellar puts you in the picture. Gamay vines cling to violent grey- and black-granite slopes exposed to the south and southwest that call to mind certain lunar landscapes around Banyuls in Languedoc. A winemaker needs tremendous courage to cultivate this soil and these vines pruned like goblets--which the harvesting machine couldn't touch--to produce simple Beaujolais. Joyet's Beaujolais has no *cru* status, not even that of Beaujolais-Villages, but what his wines do have is a solid build, character, and ruggedness. Of 10 1/2 hectares of vines, 45 years old on the average (Jean is 52), he makes three wines: some Beaujolais Nouveau (25 F); a Beaujolais, charming, fruity, and quite lively in 1996: (26 F); and a Beaujolais Vieilles Vignes (our choice). "In this part of the Beaujolais, the *terroir* isn't right for the new wines. Our wines have too much body." Vinified in vats and casks, the wines are sold in the spring following the harvest.

Our choice The '96 Beaujolais Vieilles Vignes (28 F). This isn't a soul-less Beaujolais that we often see in the supermarkets. It has the characteristic fruitiness of the Gamay; solid tannins, still sharp, and quite powerful extract, with a *goût de terroir*, earthy and smoky, very typical of Létra. Drink now.

Reception Jean and his wife take care of everything on the property, from the vines to marketing; but they always find time to greet their many private customers.

How to get there *(Map 2): On D485 coming from Lozanne, turn right towards Létra (D130), then right again towards the hamlet La Roche. Signs.*

Bernard Perrin, a former student at the Music Conservatory, winemaker and jazz musician.

Domaine de Milhomme

Owners Robert and Bernard Perrin. **Address** 69620 Ternand - Tel. 04.74.71.33.13 Fax 04.74.71.30.87. **Open** Every day, 9:00-12:00 and 14:00-19:00, preferably by appointment. **Spoken** English.

There are those who think that clever marketing has put Beaujolais on the map, just a drink that people feel obliged to gulp down on the third Thursday of November every year. Those people should pay a visit to the Perrin brothers' Domaine de Milhomme in Ternand. Robert, 44, is in charge of their 13 hectares of vines, and Bernard, 36, handles vinification and sales. Their grapes are grown on poor granite soil, that of the "anti-Beaujolais nouveaux" wines *par excellence.* Currently, they are still offering the '93 and '94 vintages, and have just recently brought out their '95s and '96s: generous wines with the accent of their famous cousins, the Beaujolais *crus* to the north. "We have no complexes about the *crus.* We are proud to produce Beaujolais, and a Beaujolais made to be kept," explains Bernard. "It's painful to hear our region denigrated. People should come and see our old vines before judging us." The truth is at the bottom of the glass: we were not disappointed.

Our choice The '95 Beaujolais Villages Centenaires (34 F). From a 109-year-old Gamay vine! The yield was ridiculously low, giving fine, dense extract, amazing length on the palate, with suggestions of cherry pits, prunes, humus. Open in two years and be sure to decant it before serving.

Reception Very friendly, in a large tasting cellar decorated with drawings by the drummer in the jazz group in which Bernard plays the trombone.

How to get there *(Map 2): On D485 coming from Lozanne, turn left direction Ternand. Go towards the village, turn left, follow signs to the cellar (2kms).*

Pierre-Marie Chermette.

Domaine du Vissoux

Owners Martine and Pierre-Marie Chermette. **Address** Le Vissoux, 69620 Saint-Vérand - Tel. 04.74.71.79.42 Fax 04.74.71.84.26. **Open** From Monday to Saturday, 8:00-12:00 and 14:00-19:00, by appointment.

Several knowledgeable wine merchants, wine bars, and *sommeliers* made the reputation of this southern Beaujolais estate, one which it has upheld for twelve years. Pierre-Marie Chermette believes in keeping chemical fertilizers to the minimum, plowing the soil constantly, and using sulphur moderately, thus reinstating Beaujolais as a straightforward, natural wine. In 1994, he enlarged his estate with five hectares in Fleurie and one hectare in Moulin-à-Vent. But the heart of Chermette's production still beats in Saint-Vérand, with 15 hectares on a granite enclave, including one hectare of Chardonnay for white Beaujolais . From the small new vines, hats off to the excellent Fleurie Les Garants (42 F): distinctly aromatic, very floral, lively, lacy; and a Moulin-à-Vent Rochegrès, with silky, dense tannins marked by its barrel ageing, with hints of roasted coffee. Among the classics, the simple '96 Beaujolais (24 F), is deliciously fruity in the mouth, distinct, forthcoming, a faultless wine.

Our choice One of the best '96 Beaujolais Blancs we've tasted (30 F), its intense aroma of citrus fruit; a soft, fruity, full-bodied taste, above all, fresh and young. Of the reds, the '96 Beaujolais Tradition Vieilles Vignes (29 F), with little filtration, is still meaty and marked by red berries.

Reception In the large barrel-vaulted cellar filled with casks, Pierre-Marie, seconded by his wife, Martine, takes pleasure in explaining his winemaking techniques.

How to get there *(Map 2): On D485 coming from Lyon, turn left towards Saint-Vérand. On the village square, go down the street left of the church for 50 meters, then left again towards Le Vissoux.*

Béatrice and Laurent Martray with their son, Corentin.

Domaine Laurent Martray

Owners Béatrice and Laurent Martray. **Address** La Chaize, Combiaty, 69460 Saint-Étienne-la-Varenne - Tel. 04.74.03.51.03 Fax 04.74.03.50.92. **Open** From Monday to Saturday, 9:00-12:00 and 14:00-19:00, by appointment.

Young Laurent Martray grows nine hectares of Brouilly on the Combiaty hillsides, sharecropping with the Château de la Chaize. He keeps half of the harvest, which he vinifies under his own name, thus producing only a small volume. In close collaboration with his brother Christian, the *sommelier* at the prestigious *Ermitage* Restaurant in Vufflens-le-Château, Switzerland, Laurent makes two Brouillys. The Vieilles Vignes *cuvée* (35 F), comes from a selection of Gamay vines more than 60 years old and yielding 30 hl/ha; it is a full, smooth, structured wine with mineral tastes, from a good volume in 1996. The same selection is also barrel-aged for the Cuvée Corentin (our choice). This ageing technique was refined in 1996, almost tripling the volume from two *barriques* in 1994 to five in 1995: inflation! It is at its peak with this non-filtered *cuvée*. When you visit the Domaine, don't miss seeing the impressive cellars of the Château de la Chaize, which is owned and run by Laurent's mother.

Our choice The '96 Cuvée Corentin Brouilly (45 F; sold by 6-bottle case). The oaky edge is still quite present when young (mocha, toast) but doesn't mask the intense cherry taste characteristic of Brouilly. The extract is dense, still firm, and forthcoming. It will mature more quickly than the '95. Drink it as of 1998. Careful: the vintage was limited.

Reception Informal, in a small tasting cellar, beneath the Martrays' home.

How to get there *(Map 2): On leaving Odenas, direction Saint-Etienne-des-Ouillières, turn right to Château de la Chaize. Go into the château property, then go up the hillside via a small road: signs for "Combiaty".*

Will you dare to taste the Spécial Santé (Health Special) marc with a snake?

Domaine Santé

Owners Bernard and Françoise Santé. **Address** Les Blémonts, Route de Juliénas, 71570 La Chapelle-de-Guinchay - Tel. 03.85.33.82.81 and 03.85.36.79.32 (cellars) Fax 03.85.33.84.46. **Open** From Monday to Saturday, 9:00-12:00 and 14:00-19:00. **Spoken** English. **Credit cards** Visa, Eurocard, MasterCard.

Following in the footsteps of his grandfather and his father, Jean-Louis, who is still active on the estate, Bernard Santé cultivates 8 1/2 hectares in Moulin-à-Vent, Juliénas, and Chenas. *(Santé* means "health": what a name for a winemaker!) He is one of a small group of winemakers who are fighting to bring the Chenas appellation out of obscurity. During blind tastings of three vintages, Chenas was precisely the *cru* that we found delightful. The traditional '96 Chenas (35 F) has a very fruity, open bouquet; on the palate, it is soft, round, quiet light (the 1996 hallmark). You can begin drinking it now. Santé's '96 Juliénas (35 F) is also a beautiful bottle. Grapier, with a touch of acidity, an aroma of peonies and a lively finish, "it slips down easily."

Our choice The '94 Fut de Chêne Chenas (41 F). From a selection of old vines half-vinified in hogshead barrels. Raspberries and wild strawberries, spices and resin on the palate, it is soft and somewhat granular, with a layer of cocoa tastes. You can enjoy it now.

Reception Friendly, family-style in the winery or in the cellar 200 meters away, where you can admire (while scaring the wits out of children) Bernard's small Beaujolais snakes, dried and embalmed in marc brandy. It appears that the harvesters drink it. We didn't have the courage.

How to get there *(Map 2): On N6, in Pontanevaux, direction Juliénas via RN95. In 3kms, the estate is on the right in Les Blémonts.*

Hubert Lapierre, President of the Chenas *cru.*

Domaine Lapierre

Owners Denise and Hubert Lapierre. **Address** Les Gandelins, 71570 La Chapelle-de-Guinchay - Tel. 03.85.36.74.89 Fax 03.85.36.79.69. **Open** Every day 9:00-12:00 and 14:00-19:00, preferably by appointment.

Chenas is a small *cru* -about 280 hectares in all- which suffers from wine brokers' lack of interest in it as well as the fact it lies in the shadow of its illustrious neighbor, Moulin-à-Vent. The wines are not all worth writing home about, but the best are definitely writing material: solid wines that keep well. Beginning with those of Hubert Lapierre, the President of the Chenas *Cru.* Like many winemakers here, he also has vines in Moulin-à-Vent, on an estate of 7 1/2 acres. But those who are not heading straight for Moulin-à-Vent should discover Lapierre's Chenas. In 1996, a high-yield vintage with marked acidity, Hubert severely selected and ran off great quantities of the fermenting must. His first '96 Chenas is especially supple and lively. The Vieilles Vignes (35 F) is more austere, powerful in taste, while retaining a certain charm. The Moulin-à-Vent (37 F), fresh and grapy, combines hints of prunes, spices, and a touch of acidity. The Vieilles Vignes version is firmer, with tight tannins. These wines are at their best with three to five years' bottle age.

Our choice The '95 Chenas Vieilles Vignes (90 F for magnum). Still fermenting when we tasted it, the wine retained generous extract, very ripe, with solid tannins for ageing potential. Cellar for three years. The '93 Fût de Chêne version (36 F) is arriving at its peak, with soft, velvety tannins, a trace of cocoa and cherries. Drink now.

Reception Hospitable, usually by Denise, Hubert's wife, in the basement of the Domaine.

How to get there *(Map 2): On N6, in Pontanevaux, didrection La Chapelle-de-Guinchy, then straight ahead towards Les Deschamps. The estate is on the right (signs).*

The estate also offers bed-and-breakfast... in the midst of the vines, as you would expect.

Domaine de la Grosse Pierre

Owners Véronique and Alain Passot. **Address** La Grosse Pierre, 69115 Chiroubles - Tel. 04.74.69.12.17 Fax 04.74.69.13.52. **Open** Every day 9:00-12:00 and 14:00-19:00. **Credit cards** Visa, Eurocard, MasterCard.

Alain Passot's father was a sharecropper for thirty years on this estate high above the surrounding hillsides of Chiroubles, Fleurie, Morgon and, as far as the eye can see, Mont Blanc, Beaujolais weather permitting. "The vines were put up for sale in 1982," recounts Alain Passot. "As my father already owned vines elsewhere, we bought the six hectares here." Ten years later, Alain and his wife, Véronique, also bought the big, abandoned farmhouse, dating from the late 19th century. They restored it and opened five guest rooms in the summer of 1995 (see *Recommended Hotels and Restaurants*). "At the beginning, we did this out of necessity, to make ends meet. Today, it's become a pleasure. We work seven days a week, but we don't regret a thing." The Passots' Chiroubles is of the solid, vigorous breed, especially the second bottling in March. They produce some Fleurie, with a bouquet of strawberries, well structured in 1996.

Our choice The '96 Chiroubles (37.50 F). In this especially high-yielding year, Alain drew off some 30% of the fermenting wine, thus concentrating the extract. Its aroma is still closed, the palate round, full, very up-front in attack, with good softness, tannins still sharp; and a slight vegetal finish. Drinkable now.

Reception Generous, in a small tasting cellar. Panoramic view. The Passots are used to guests from the bed-and-breakfast rooms coming to taste.

How to get there *(Map 2): On N6, at La Maison Blanche, take direction Lancié, then Chiroubles. 500 meters before Chiroubles, on the left, small road indicating Grosse Pierre. You can see the name of the estate painted on the hillside.*

The Chiroubles vineyards: highly protected.

Domaine de la Combe au Loup

Owners Gérard and David Méziat. **Address** Le Bourg, 69115 Chiroubles - Tel. 04.74.04.24.02 Fax 04.74.69.14.07. **Open** Every day except Sunday, 9:00-12:00 and 14:00-19:00. **Spoken** English, Spanish, Portuguese. **Credit cards** Visa, Eurocard, MasterCard.

La Combe is one of the best sites of Chiroubles, where the Méziats have two parcels. As for the Loup ("wolf"), the story goes that he used to enjoy prowling around here: did he enjoy the grapes? There are many Méziats in Chiroubles. Gérard and Marie-Claude, their son David and his wife, Nathalie, own ten hectares in three Beaujolais *crus* and in Beaujolais-Villages, many parcels, and a large number of old vines. Their very aromatic wines have been temperature-controlled during vinfication since 1990, in order to extract more fruit and color. We tasted a very good 1996 Beaujolais-Villages, Cuvée de l'Oisillon (27 F); from old vines, it is aromatic, its palate full-bodied and generous. The '96 Régnié (32.50 F) is a big, muscular wine in its family, powerful and spicy in taste. The '96 Morgon (from vines in Corcelle), which we tasted from the barrel, had more finesse. You will always find two vintages here, and you can rely on them.

Our choice The '95 Chiroubles (36.50 F). Attack round and powerful, with great structure on the palate (the tannins are still rustic), tasting distinctly of ripe cherries and wet earth. A wine of character. Bottle age for three years. The '96, with greater acidity and fruit, is very solid for the vintage.

Reception Friendly, warm, and family-style, in a village cellar.

How to get there *(Map 2): On N6 at La Maison Blanche, direction Lancié, then Chiroubles. In the town, direction Beaujeu, on the right. Signs.*

Évelyne and Claude Geoffray, heirs of a line of winemakers in Thivin since 1879.

Château Thivin

Owners Évelyne and Claude Geoffray. **Address** 69460 Odenas - Tel. 04.74.03.47.53 Fax 04.74.03.52.87. **Open** From Monday to Saturday, 9:00-12:00 and 14:00-19:00. **Spoken** English.

Few estates are as harmonious as the Château Thivin. In this beautiful old residence, clinging to the southern hillside of Mount Brouilly and spreading over 18 1/2 hectares, the Côte-de-Brouilly appellation acquired its *lettres de noblesse* thanks to the pugnacity of the Geoffray family. This too unfamiliar appellation, if you compare it to that of simple Brouilly (four times larger), deserves to be the leading *cru* of the Brouilly vineyards. Grown on blue volcanic soils, Côte de Brouilly has the characteristic fruit and finesse of Brouilly but is richer and more vigorous as it ages (the '91 is superb at the moment). Thivin is "the" name in Côte-de-Brouilly, but you should also taste the estate's excellent Beaujolais-Villages Manoir du Pavé 1996 (27 F), fruity, well structured, and firm in its category; the '96 Beaujolais Rosé (25 F), with a distinct aroma of strawberries, is soft on the palate, with a touch of acidity; and the '96 Brouilly (36.50 F), its flavor of acidulated fruits, is a silky, delightful wine to be drunk now.

Our choice The '96 Côte-de-Brouilly (39 F). Slow to open up, well structured, full but soft, it has a lingering taste of strawberries and acidulated cherries. A classic. Three bottlings are carried out in succession.The May bottling from old vines in La Chapelle invariably takes two years to mature.

Reception By Claude or Evelyne Geoffray, impassioned, very amiable, in the entrance to the cellar where there is an old vertical wooden grape press from the 19th century.

How to get there *(Map 2): On N6 in Belleville, direction Beaujeu on D37. In Cercié, turn left toward Odenas, then right onto D43E toward Brouilly. On this road on the side of Mont Brouilly, the house is on the left.*

Michel Chignard, a happy producer of Fleurie, one of the most sought-after *crus* of the Beaujolais.

Domaine Michel Chignard

Owner Michel Chignard. **Address** Le Point du Jour, 69820 Fleurie - Tel. 04.74.04.11.87 Fax 04.74.69.81.97. **Open** From Monday to Saturday, by appointment.

With Saint-Amour and Brouilly, Fleurie today is the *cru* most popular with wine brokers, and the demand from Switzerland keeps the prices high. As rich as a Moulin-à-Vent but with finer tannins, Fleurie can be enjoyed younger; more like a Beaujolais, it is fruity, floral, and aromatic, especially the 1996. Michel Chignard, 51, the third generation on the estate, cultivates 8 1/2 hectares entirely in Fleurie, bordering on Moulin-à-Vent (with parcels in Le Point-du-Jour and Les Moriers); many of his vines are 40 to 80 years old, and thus produce low yields. Two very regular *cuvées* are available, having been aged in casks and *barriques,* or hogshead barrels. "This method of ageing is not very traditional in Beaujolais," Chignard explains, "but some customers have enjoyed it very much since we launched the technique in 1981." The '96 Fleurie Les Moriers (43 F), with forthcoming aromas, a silky texture and persistent tannins, is ready to be drunk now.

Our choice The '95 Fleurie Cuvée Spéciale (53 F). A generous wine in the mouth, a fine oaky taste without masking its distinctive traces of ripe red berries. Well structured. Needs some bottle age. Open beginning winter 1998.

Reception Informal, in the tasting cellar beneath the Chignards' house, facing the small casks and hogshead barrels.

How to get there *(Map 2): On N6, at La Maison Blanche, direction Fleurie. Entering Fleurie, turn right to Le Point-du-Jour.*

Alain Coudert, winemaker and volunteer fireman.

Clos de la Roilette

Owners Alain and Fernand Coudert. **Address** La Roilette 69820 Fleurie - Tel. 04.74.69.84.37/ 04.74.04.12.12 Fax 04.76.69.81.26. **Open** Every day except Sunday afternoon 9:00-12:00 and 14:00-19:00. **Spoken** English. **Credit cards** Visa, Eurocard, MasterCard.

La Roilette owns two parcels in Fleurie and Le Point du Jour facing Moulin-à-Vent: the two finest *terroirs* for Fleuries that keep well. With an eastern exposure facing the Savoie mountains and a sub-soil of clay and manganese, the Clos de la Roilette is an historic estate among the Beaujolais *crus*. Its former owners, the Crozet family, began bottling the wine in the 1920s, with a horse as their hallmark to symbolize their stable of race horses. Alain Coudert took over from his father, Fernand, who had bought the Clos in 1968. Coudert has 9 1/2 hectares of vines. His vinifications are classic, with quite long fermentation (12 days); he adds no yeast and ages wines in casks. The Fleuries from the Clos are full-bodied but velvety wines which need two to three years' bottle age to develop. If you find a '95 in a restaurant of the region, *carpe diem*!

Our choice The '96 Fleurie Classique (39 F), dark and deep in color, with an intense bouquet, full-bodied, soft, unaggressive texture, simply delicious. Drinkable now. The Cuvée Tardive (45 F), from selected vines on more clayey soil, yielding a more concentrated wine, a fruitier bouquet (blackberries, stewed raspberries), more tannin at the finish. For 1999. When the *cuvée* of 1500 bottles is finished, you can enjoy it at the *Cep* Restaurant in Fleurie.

Reception Friendly and helpful, in the cellar with the casks, at a large bar.

How to get there *(Map 2): On N6, at La Maison Blanche, drive towards Fleurie. Entering Fleurie, turn right to Le Point-du-Jour and Roilette. Follow the signs for "Coudert".*

Michel Tête, a sense of humor and solid Juliénas.

Domaine du Clos du Fief

Owners Françoise and Michel Tête. **Address** Les Gonnards, 69840 Juliénas - Tel. 04.74.04.41.62 Fax 04.74.04.47.09. **Open** From Monday to Saturday, 8:00-12:00 and 14:00-19:00, preferably by appointment.

Wines from Juliénas invariably have the fruity freshness characteristic of Beaujolais, but they also have much more body and quite a high alcoholic content. They are above all dinner wines, quite powerful (similar to Moulin-à-Vent and Morgon), more robust than most of the Beaujolais *crus.* They should be drunk at least a year after bottling. Michel Tête, 41, is an ace when it comes to Juliénas. His wines, as big as he is, always stand out at tastings. Especially his Prestige *cuvée,* which he barrel ages and bottles fairly young depending on the structure of the wine."I like oakiness in a wine, harmony, a velvety texture," says Michel. We could only agree as we tasted his '96 (our choice). In addition to his seven hectares in Juliénas, well-exposed on the middle of the slope, Michel has a hectare of Saint-Amour (39 F) and two hectares of Beaujolais-Villages (27 F). In both cases, the wines are meatier and more tannic than the average, and thus they keep longer. It's a question of yield and *terroir.*

Our choice The '96 Juliénas Prestige (48 F). From selected old vines in Les Gonnard and Les Berthets. Good balance between lively fruit and roasted coffee hints imparted by the oak. Charming, youthful extract, soft texture, opens up well on the palate. Enjoy it in two to three years.

Reception By Michel, a *bon vivant,* or his wife, Françoise, at a bistrot bar in the spacious cellar beneath their renovated house.

How to get there *(Map 2): On N6 in Pontanevaux, direction Juliénas. Entering the village, first street on right, in front of the Total station.Green door immediately on left.*

Thierry Descombes, a small producer in Jullié, one of the four *communes* entitled to the Juliénas appellation.

Domaine Thierry Descombes

Owner Thierry Descombes. **Address** Les Vignes, Jullié, 69840 Juliénas - Tel. 04.74.04.42.03. **Open** Every day by appointment.

Thierry Descombes is a winegrower with 8 1/2 hectares in Juliénas, his vines on a slope there, and in the Beaujolais-Villages appellation. Jullié, with its schistous-granite *terroir,* is known for yielding long-lived Beaujolais-Villages. Some are so well structured that it is often difficult to distinguish them from a *cru.* In 1995, this was very much the case with bottles from this small, ever impeccably kept cellar. In 1996, the harvest yielded wines with less structure, more youthful and more vigorous. Descombes' '96 Beaujolais-Villages Jullié Vieilles Vignes (27.50 F) is a firm wine from old vines, much more reluctant to open than the Juliénas, all fruit and finesse. The '96 *cuvée* Beaujolais-Villages Jeunes Vignes (24.50 F), from young vines, is quite delicious with its aroma of red berries and its delicate tannins, a *cru* that slips down with beautiful ease. Drinkable now.

Our choice The '96 Juliénas (33 F). Still lovely aromatic intensity (blackberries, cherries, blackcurrants), youthful and fresh taste, delicate, balanced, young but controlled tannins. It is very good young, with hot sausage. Good value for the money, too.

Reception As the cellar is so isolated, visitors are rare. But if you telephone in advance, Thierry will happy to welcome you between stints in the vineyard.

How to get there *(Map 2): On N6 in Pontanevaux, direction Juliénas, then Jullié (5kms). Entering the village, turn right direction Les Vignes. In 1km, the house is on the edge of the street, on the left. No sign, but the name is on the mailbox.*

Paul, Vincent, and Jacques Audras.

Clos de Haute-Combe

Owners Vincent and Jacques Audras. **Address** Haute-Combe, 69840 Juliénas - Tel. 04.74.04.41.09 Fax 04.74.04.47.69. **Open** From Monday to Saturday 9:00-12:00 and 14:00- 19:00.

Climbing up the steep hillside towards Haute-Combe brings you a double reward: a majestic view over the southern Beaujolais and the excellent Juliénas made by the Audras family. Following in the footsteps of their father, Paul, sons Vincent and Jacques till thirteen hectares on the Clos de Haute-Combe. Vinifications are totally traditional: no yeast is added, grapes are pressed vertically, vinified in oak vats, and aged in casks. Half of the production always goes to the *Cave Coopérative*. The first bottling of '96 Juliénas (36 F) from selected young vines is a fresh, fruity wine, charmingly delicate and elegant to drink. Superb. The following bottlings will have more backbone. Try the good '96 Bourgogne Blanc (35 F), from Chardonnay grown on the granite soils of Juliénas: full-bodied, soft, with overtones of mint and licorice.

Our choice The '95 Juliénas Cuvée Prestige (45 F). From old vines, aged two years in casks. Discreet oaky aroma, very mellow taste, balanced and full, with solid tannins, spices; ages well. Keep away from a cork screw for five years. In the rare-wine department: the '96 La Lyre red *vin de table* (25 F), from young experimental Gamay vines cultivated *en lyre*, pruned in a lyre shape, a method forbidden in the Beaujolais and thus its classification as a *vin de table*. A delightful wine, balanced and mellow, with a purity of fruit that should give plenty of Beaujolais winegrowers food for thought.

Reception Family-style, with typical Beaujolais generosity, in an old cellar.

How to get there *(Map 2): On N6 in Pontanevaux, direction Juliénas. Enter the village, in front of the restaurant "Le Coq au Vin", direction Pruzilly. In 2kms, follow signs.*

Jean Calot, right, is in charge of vinifying wines, while his brother, François, maintains his nursery and wicker brokerage.

Domaine Calot

Owners François and Jean Calot. **Address** Le Bourg, 69910 Villié-Morgon - Tel. 04.74.04.20.55 Fax 04.74.69.12.93. **Open** From Monday to Friday 8:00-12:00 and 14:00-19:00. Weekend by appointment.

The Calot brothers own ten hectares of vines in Morgon, with granite and sandy soils on the Corcelette side near Chiroubles; and in Doulby, on the Fleurie boundary. These *terroirs* characteristically give an elegant and very fruity Morgon, "which makes longer fermentations possible in order to yield more extract without running up against hard wines," Jean indicated. Very eclectic when it comes to vinification, he constantly experiments with different containers--vats, barrels, *foudres,* casks of 150 liters; temperatures (heating the fermenting wine, cold maceration)....But the customer isn't taken for a guinea pig because Calot's wines are faultless. We tasted four Morgons: the Tradition (32 F), a standard Morgon representative of his cellar, with typical meatiness and an aroma of black berries; the Tête de Cuvée (37 F), the most aromatic and fresh, to be drunk young; the Vieilles Vignes (37 F), aged in casks and barrels: cherry pits, full, firm, complete; and the *cuvée* Jeanne (our choice).

Our choice The '96 Morgon Cuvée Jeanne (39 F). The second edition of this *cuvée,* created in homage to Madame Calot *mère,* from a selected parcel of grapes aged in casks. Its fruit invariably is a touch more vivacious than the others; a generous wine with dense extract; the tannins will soften by the spring of 1998.

Reception Informal, in the vat room, usually by Jean, who speaks passionately of his wines.

How to get there *(Map 2): On N6, between Maison Blanche and Saint-Jean-d'Ardière, direction villié-Morgon. In the center of town, in front of the "Mairie", the cellar is at the back of a dead-end.*

Dominique Piron and his spirited Magnum and Bacchus.

Domaine Dominique Piron

Owner Dominique Piron. **Address** Morgon, 69910 Villié-Morgon - Tel. 04.74.69.10.20 Fax 04.74.69.16. 65. **Open** From Mon. to Fri., 9:00-12:00 and 14:00-19:00. Weekend by appointment. **Spoken** English.

With 17 hectares of family holdings, essentially in Morgon, Dominique Piron has built up a kind of contemporary *négoce* by buying grapes directly from winegrowers (the equivalent of 23 hectares in 1996). Throughout the year, he follows the selected parcels, evaluates their potential, and vinifies them as if they were his own grapes, mentioning the parcel, *lieu-dit*, on the label. The 1996 vintage confirmed the increasing quality of wines made in this way, whether we're talking about the '96 Beaujolais Blanc Vigne de Roche Noire (32 F)--beautifully fruity extract, mouth filling--or his Mâcon Chardonnay Vigne de Beauvois (35 F), a more delicate, vigorous wine vinified without malolactic fermentation. Of the reds, the Beaujolais-Villages from Pierreux is a big, plummy tasting wine; and the Nouveau Brouilly Château du Prieuré (35 F), bursting with fruit and full-bodied, is superior to the Domaine de Combiaty, which he has replaced. As for the Morgons from the Domaine de la Chanaise, they are still the leaders in the appellation. The '96 Classique (36 F) has a charming taste, delicate, straightforward, long for the year, all prunes, violets, and cocoa.

Our choice The '96 Morgon Domaine de la Chanaise Les Pierres de La Chanaise (39 F). From selected old vines at the bottom of the Côte du Py (the equivalent of a *premier cru* in Morgon). Magnificent fullness, with an aroma of cherries, a backbone of tight but soft tannins, spicy extract, powerful finish. Keep for two to three years.

Reception Positive, helpful, informal, at a bistrot bar.

How to get there *(Map 2): On N6 at Saint-Jean-d'Ardières, direction Pizay, then Morgon. On leaving Morgon, direction Villié-Morgon, last house on left.*

Bernard Méziat: follow the arrow.

Domaine du Pourpre

Owners Bernard and Véronique Méziat. **Address** Les Pinchon 69840 Chenas - Tel. 04.74.04.48.81 Fax 04.74.04.49.22. **Open** From Monday to Saturday, 9:00-12:00 and 14:00-19:00, preferably by appointment.

For the old winemakers in the Moulin-à-Vent appellation, the best vineyards are those "which can see the mill, *(moulin)*", those which encircle the last remaining windmill in the region, perched on a gentle hillside covered with Gamay, which gave its name to the *cru.* For this quite large appellation of 640 hectares, divided between the *communes* of Romanèche-Thorins and Chénas, has its privileged *terroirs.* Bernard and Véronique Méziat's ten hectares, mainly in Moulin-à-Vent and some in Chénas, attest to the old winemakers' wisdom with each new harvest. For their vines are indeed next to the windmill, yielding a full, meaty wine, but with the extra backbone that you don't always find in Moulin-à-Vent from the other parcels. At the instigation of Georges Duboeuf, who buys wines from him regularly, Bernard made his sixteenth vintage in 1996, yielding Moulin-à-Vents to be cellared, the fruit of long maceration. His '96 Chénas (30 F), a big, broad-shouldered wine, will develop with two to three years in bottle.

Our choice The '95 Moulin-à-Vent (40 F). The generous maturity of this vintage gave a Moulin of solid, meaty texture, with characteristic overtones of black fruit and moist earth, a sweetish touch, and a long, firm finish. Should be cellared for two years.

Reception Bernard is not overly gregarious but he will receive you courteously.

How to get there *(Map 2): On N6 in Pontanevaux, direction La Chapelle-de-Guinchay, Les Deschamps, then left towards Chénas. On this road, in the hamlet Les Pinchons, the cellar is on the left, at the back of a courtyard.*

A former graphic artist in Paris, Denis Barbelet took over the family estate in Saint-Amour in the mid-1980s.

Domaine Barbelet

Owners Hélène and Denis Barbelet. **Address** Les Billards, 71570 Saint-Amour-Bellevue - Tel. 03.85.36.51.36 Fax 03.85.37.19.74. **Open** Everydays 9:00-12:00 and 14:00-18:00, preferably by appointment.

Having spent the first part of their lives in a design studio in Paris, Denis Barbelet and his wife, Hélène, a teacher, took over this family estate of 6 1/2 hectares entirely in the Saint-Amour appellation. In this very popular *cru* (every Valentine's Day, the cellars run dry), which has the reputation for making delightful wines, there are two schools of winemaking: those who favor the "delightfully drinkable" Saint-Amour, which is not unlike a good but simple Beaujolais; and those who pursue the identity of a real *cru,* to be drunk in two to three years. Denis Barbelet belongs to the latter. His Saint-Amours invariably have a *goût de terroir* very much like that of next-door Juliénas and a fullness that you don't find in the other cellars. There were two bottlings for the '96 Saint-Amour: one in the spring, yielding a very flowery bouquet of cherries, soft and elegant in taste; the other (our choice), has more backbone and will come into its own fully in 1998.

Our choice The '96 Saint-Amour. Fruity, round flavor, the finish balanced by structured, delicate tannins and a velvety texture. Better still served in a carafe just before you drink it.

Reception In a small tasting cellar with delightful Denis Barbelet.

How to get there *(Map 2): On N6, in Crêches-sur-Saône (south of Mâcon), direction Chânes, then left towards Saint-Amour. Leaving the village, direction Juliénas, turn left to Les Billards (signs).*

Monsieur le Maire in his vineyard.

Domaine de la Cave Lamartine

Owners Bernadette, Paul and Christophe Spay. **Address** Vers l'Église, 71570 Saint-Amour - Tel. 03.85.37.12.88 Fax 03.85.37.45.19. **Open** Every day 9:00-12:00 and 14:00-19:00. **Spoken** English. **Credit Cards** Visa, Eurocard, Mastercard.

This beautiful old estate was once the property of the Lamartine family, that of the great French poet and politician, Alphonse de Lamartine. Could it be destined to produce politicians? Perhaps, because today the domain is the home of the Mayor of Saint-Amour, Paul Spay, and his family. But Mayor Spay, a garrulous, friendly man, is first and foremost a winemaker and the cause he fervently champions when you visit him is that of his Saint-Amour *cru.* On his twenty hectares, which he cultivates with his son, Christophe, the Mayor makes wines which have the regularity of a metronome. It's true that the vintages add their touch to the wine (a tender touch in '90, '92, '94, '96; firmness in '91, '93, '95), but we have always found his wines to be a straightforward, direct lesson in the *cru.* He also makes a good Beaujolais Blanc (38 F), from old Chardonnay vines; and a little Juliénas.

Our choice The '96 Saint-Amour "Vers l'Eglise" (40 F). Like many neighbors, the estate does three bottlings per year. Our choice is that of the spring. Its fleeting fruitiness and soft, liquid taste conceal reserved extract and a dense, well-built finish.It will be perfect in the spring of 1998.

Reception With great enthusiasm, usually by Bernadette Spay, a native of Bresse.

How to get there *(Map 2): On N6, in Crêches-sur-Saône (south of Mâcon), direction Chânes, then left towards Saint-Amour. On the main square, turn right towards the top of the village. The entrance to the estate is on the left, in front o the church.*

Saint-Amour.

Domaine des Duc

Owners Marie-Jo, Jacques, Claude and Laurent Duc and Lucien Blanchard. **Address** La Piat, 71570 Saint-Amour-Bellevue - Tel. 03.85.37.10.08 Fax 03.85.36.55.75. **Open** From Monday to Saturday 9:00-12:00 and 14:00-19:00, preferably by appointment. **Credit cards** Visa, Eurocard, MasterCard.

The whole Duc family, and Lucien Blanchard, their neighbor and associate since 1984, hold sway over a vineyard of twenty-eight hectares. It is a large property for the northern Beaujolais, comprising two *crus -Saint-Amour* and Chénas- and Beaujolais-Villages, with some vines in Beaujolais Blanc (a lovely '96, citrus fruit, floral, fluid) and in Pouilly-Loché ('95, 40 F). In the spacious, recently enlarged cellar, we tasted the '96 Beaujolais Villages (26 F), to be drunk young for its soft, flowery aroma and light tannins, its taste of strawberries and raspberries. The Saint-Amour is something else, a big, fleshy wine. The Chénas is partially aged in barrels, which flatters the wine even though its oakiness needs to mature. The '89 we tasted (out of stock) was evidence of this: it was just beginning to open up.

Our choice The '96 Saint-Amour (39 F): an intense, open aroma of small red and black berries. It is generous on the palate, mouth-filling; its tannins will soften by 1998. Even in this liquid vintage of average concentration, it is a wine of character. The '95 Chénas (38 F): cherry and prune aroma, full-bodied, powerful taste (should be kept two to three years) with a finish hesitating between cherries and cocoa.

Reception Family-style, in the office and cellar.

How to get there *(Map 2): On N6, in Crêches-sur-Saône (south of Mâcon), direction Chânes, then left towards Saint-Amour. On the main square, in front of the Auberge du Pardis, turn left towards La Chapelle-de-Guinchay. 600 meters on right.*

BORDEAUX

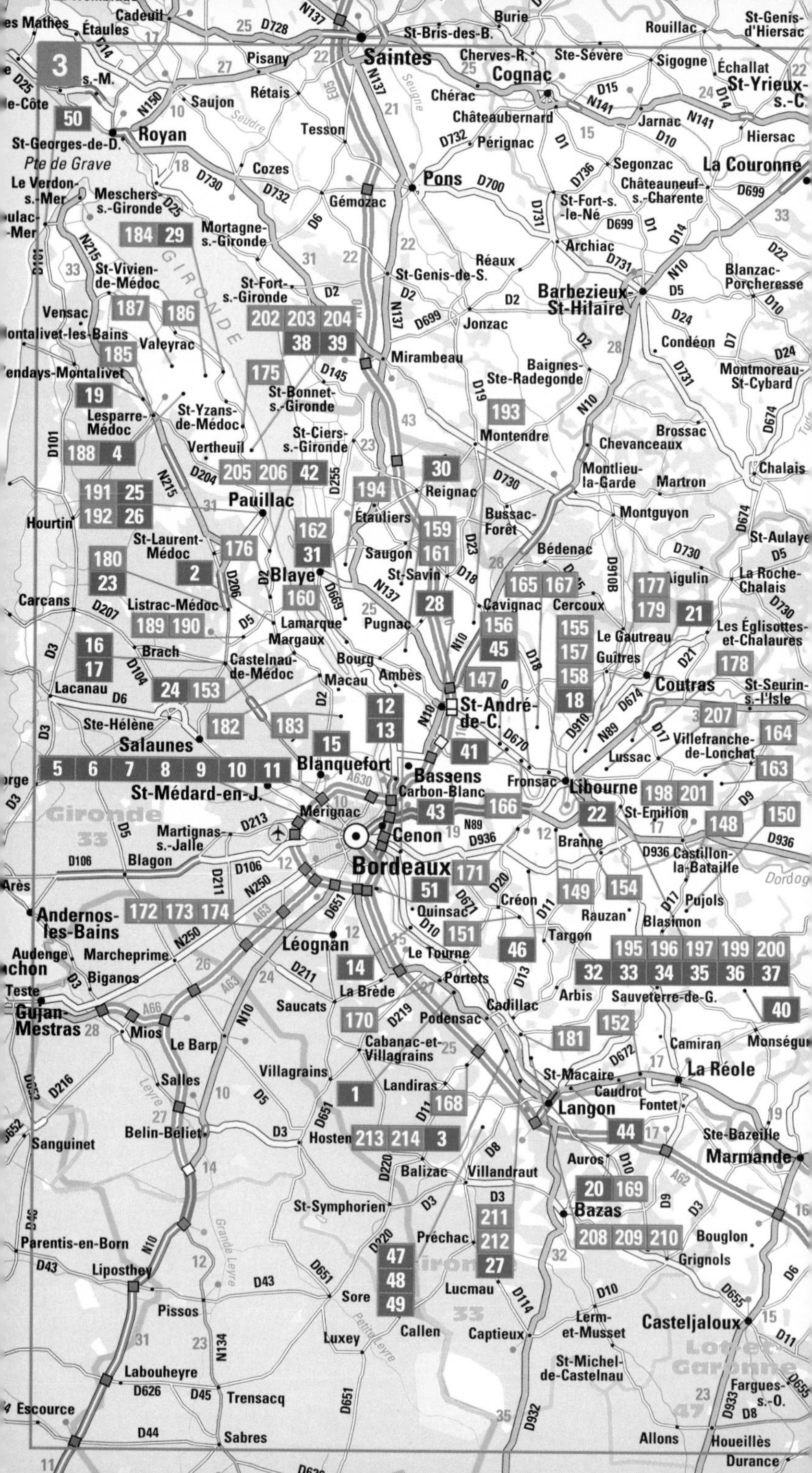
3
50
Cadeuil
Étaules
Burie
Rouillac
St-Genis-d'Hiersac
St-Bris-des-B.
Saintes
Pisany
Cherves-R.
Ste-Sévère
Sigogne
Échallat
Cognac
St-Yrieux-s.-C.
Saujon
Rétais
Chérac
Jarnac
Royan
Tesson
Châteaubernard
Hiersac
St-Georges-de-D.
Pte de Grave
Pérignac
Segonzac
La Couronne
Cozes
Pons
Châteauneuf-s.-Charente
Le Verdon-s.-Mer
Meschers-s.-Gironde
Gémozac
St-Fort-s.-le-Né
Mortagne-s.-Gironde
Archiac
Réaux
St-Genis-de-S.
Blanzac-Porcheresse
St-Vivien-de-Médoc
St-Fort-s.-Gironde
Barbezieux-St-Hilaire
Vensac
Jonzac
Montalivet-les-Bains
Valeyrac
Condéon
Mirambeau
Baignes-Ste-Radegonde
Montmoreau-St-Cybard
St-Bonnet-s.-Gironde
Lesparre-Médoc
St-Yzans-de-Médoc
Brossac
Montendre
Chevanceaux
St-Ciers-s.-Gironde
Vertheuil
Chalais
Montlieu-la-Garde
Martron
Reignac
Pauillac
Hourtin
Étauliers
Bussac-Forêt
Montguyon
St-Laurent-Médoc
Saugon
St-Aulaye
Bédenac
St-Savin
Blaye
La Roche-Chalais
Carcans
Cavignac
Cercoux
Listrac-Médoc
Lamarque
Pugnac
Margaux
Les Églisottes-et-Chalaures
Le Gautreau
Brach
Bourg
Guîtres
Castelnau-de-Médoc
Ambès
Coutras
Macau
Lacanau
St-Seurin-s.-l'Isle
St-André-de-C.
Ste-Hélène
Villefranche-de-Lonchat
Salaunes
Lussac
Blanquefort
Bassens
Fronsac
Libourne
St-Médard-en-J.
Carbon-Blanc
Mérignac
St-Émilion
Gironde
Cenon
Martignas-s.-Jalle
Branne
Castillon-la-Bataille
Blagon
Bordeaux
Arès
Créon
Pujols
Andernos-les-Bains
Quinsac
Rauzan
Blasimon
Léognan
Targon
Audenge
Marcheprime
Le Tourne
Biganos
Portets
Arbis
Sauveterre-de-G.
Teste
La Brède
Saucats
Cadillac
Gujan-Mestras
Podensac
Mios
Camiran
Monségur
Le Barp
Cabanac-et-Villagrains
St-Macaire
La Réole
Villagrains
Caudrot
Salles
Landiras
Fontet
Langon
Belin-Béliet
Hosten
Ste-Bazeille
Sanguinet
Marmande
Aurós
Balizac
Villandraut
Bazas
St-Symphorien
Bouglon
Parentis-en-Born
Préchac
Grignols
Liposthey
Sore
Lucmau
Pissos
Callen
Captieux
Lerm-et-Musset
Casteljaloux
Luxey
St-Michel-de-Castelnau
Labouheyre
Trensacq
Fargues-s.-O.
Escource
Sabres
Allons
Houeillès
Durance
Dordogne
Seugne
Seudre
Leyre
Grande Leyre
Petite Leyre
Lot-et-Garonne
184 29
187 186
202 203 204
38 39
185
175
19
193
188 4
205 206 42
30
194
191 25
192 26
162
31
159
161
176
180
23
2
160
28
165 167
177
179
21
189 190
156
45
155
157
158
18
16
17
24 153
147
178
182
183
12
13
207
164
15
41
5 6 7 8 9 10 11
163
198 201
43
166
22
148
150
171
51
149
154
172 173 174
151
46
195 196 197 199 200
32 33 34 35 36 37
14
40
170
152
181
1
168
44
213 214 3
20 169
211
212
27
208 209 210
47
48
49

B O R D E A U X

INTRODUCTION

Bordeaux is a mix of glittering châteaux and discreet *chartreuses,* of privileged and simple country people, and of merchants and wine growers. Passing by the 45th parallel, the visitor can be as charmed by the elegance of the orderly countryside, moving with the rhythm of the streams and rivers, as irritated by the sometimes arrogant and brusque welcome.

On the right bank of the Dordogne, in the Libournais, one can be surprised by the dullness and austerity of Pomerol and enthuse over Saint-Emilion (preferably out of season), the tiny hillside town whose glowing architecture reveals the past and which conceals its vinous treasures in the rock. Hidden between the Dordogne and Garonne rivers, baptized as "seas" as they ebb and flow with the rhythm of the tide, is the most beautiful countryside in the Gironde. Red and white grape varieties are concealed behind woods, lording over fields of cereal crops. Plateaus succeed valleys with the perfect harmony of an English garden, sprinkled with quiet, authentic market-towns and abounding with true wine growers and gems from Aquitaine's rich heritage (châteaux, abbeys, menhirs and megaliths). On the left bank of the Garonne, the Graves extends for more than 100 kilometers. In the north are the aristocrats of Pessac and Léognan, an historic vineyard area of Bordeaux eaten away by urbanization, and alongside them the mixed farmers from the south with their vineyards in open glades. In the middle, the austere, Middle Age strongholds of Sauternes, including Château d'Yquem, defend the tradition of sweet wines armed with "noble rot" and the magic of autumnal mists. Beyond Bordeaux, then Blanquefort, the explorer of the 45th parallel has to come to terms with another world. The insular and fascinating countryside of the Médoc comprises a series of gentle slopes that gaze at the Gironde estuary, the muddy Mississippi of the French Southwest. The monotonous landscape is enlivened by tiny harbours, the "tree-house" huts of the *palombe* (pigeon) hunters, and the picture-postcard châteaux of the celebrated villages of Margaux, Saint-Julien, Pauillac and Saint-Estèphe. Farther north, the horizon opens onto a cinematic sky-line highlighted by a countryside of undulating hills. The appellation Médoc, the final vineyard area, basks in the glow of Atlantic light.

INTRODUCTION

The Bordelais have rules and codes. Here, everyone has a château (a synonym for a viticultural property without necessarily the physical building), recognition is given by a classification (not by *terroir*, as in Burgundy, but by "château") and for more than 150 years commercial activity has been handled by the *negociants*. Bordeaux properties have for a long time existed behind closed doors but over the last few years attitudes have changed. New owners and institutional investors are now more than willing to organize guided visits to their châteaux and open their parks to the public. However, at most of the Médoc *Crus Classés*, several of the châteaux in the Graves and Sauternes, and the most high profile of the properties in Pomerol and Saint-Emilion, direct selling to the public does not exist. Owing to this, and even if we consider the quality of the wines excellent, they do not figure in this guide.

BORDEAUX APPELLATIONS

Twice the size of Australia's vineyard area, the same as that of Germany and a little smaller than that of Chile or California, Bordeaux comprises 113 000 hectares of vines and 57 appellations. The total vineyard area falls within the Gironde *département* and is arranged around an axis of three rivers: the Garonne, which arrives from the Pyrenees, the Dordogne, which descends from the Massif Central, and their common estuary, the Gironde.

The majority of the surface area dedicted to red wine is planted with Merlot (dominant in the Libournais), Cabernet Sauvignon (king of the Médoc and Graves), and Cabernet Franc. In sweet and dry white wines, the trilogy Semillon-Sauvignon-Muscadelle conclude the grape varieties found in Bordeaux. Contrary to the single grape varieties found in the wines of Burgundy, the wines of Bordeaux are usually made from a blend of varieties. The ageing of wines in oak barrels (225 liter *barriques*) is a religion here. They usually spend from 10 to 18 months in oak having completed the alcoholic fermentation and generally the malolactic fermentation in vat. Sometimes, this last fermentation is conducted in new oak barrels which adds more "fat" and mellowness to the wine in the initial years.

The appellations Bordeaux and Bordeaux Supérieur provide the volume of wines in the region. They can be produced throughout the Gironde but the principal zone of production is in the Entre-Deux-Mers. A Bordeaux and Bordeaux "Sup" vary according to yields and minimum alcohol content. For Bordeaux Supérieur there is also a more rigorous tasting to obtain the *agrément* or label (in the month of March following the vintage) taking into account the wine's aptitude for ageing which should, theoretically, be "Supérieur."

On the right bank of the Gironde, the Côtes-de-Blaye produces agreeable dry, white wines, often based on Sauvignon. There are several very successful red wines from the Premières Côtes-de-Blaye at reasonable prices. The same applies in the Côtes-de-Bourg, the neighboring picturesque region which borders the Dordogne and Gironde and which is delimited by some rather abrupt limestone hills. The wines are full, powerful, long ageing and gain in finesse after four years.

The Libournais embraces 15 of the most well-known appellations in the Bordelais. This is the realm of Merlot and round, supple, generous wines. Opposite Libourne, between the meandering Isle and Dordogne, the vineyards of Fronsac benefit from two excellent appellations, Fronsac and Canon Fronsac. The wines, on ageing, are similar to those of Pomerol but with a little more rusticity. North of Libourne,

Pomerol covers 732 hectares situated on a clay plateau mixed with gravel and planted to 70% with Merlot. The reputation of Pomerol is extremely high (like the price), thanks in part to the Libournais *negociants* who own more than 30% of the surface area. Certainly the least austere of the *Grands Vins* from Bordeaux with a polished style, Pomerol has no official classification. The soils of the neighboring appellation of Lalande-de-Pomerol are not quite at the same quality-level (a lot less fine), so don't, therefore, confuse the two wines.

Saint-Emilion is the largest regional appellation in Bordeaux, delimited to Saint-Emilion, seven neighboring communes, and a tiny part of Libourne. The soils are clay-limestone (sometimes very calcareous) and sandy-clay. The Merlot is in its element here but the Cabernet Franc also provides some spectacular results (particularly at Château Cheval Blanc). You find everything in Saint-Emilion as the appellation can be claimed throughout the delimited region. The appellation, Sain-Emilion Grand Cru, however, obeys a stricter set of directives (an *ad hoc* tasting committee controls, judges and accords or refuses the appellation). Saint-Emilion has its own classification which is of interest to the wine lover as it is revised every ten years.

To the northeast of Saint-Emilion, four so-called "satellite" communes (Saint-Georges, Montagne, Puisseguin and Lussac) have the right to add their name to that of Saint-Emilion. One can unearth some good-value wines as there has been clear progress made over the last ten years. Direct sales to the public are well-developed. There are also some attractive wines to be discovered in the appellations Bordeaux Côtes-de-Francs and Côtes-de-Castillon to the east of Puisseguin and Lussac, close to the border with the Dordogne *département.*

Forty kilometers southeast of Bordeaux, on both sides of the Garonne, six appellations defend the honor of Bordeaux's sweet white wines: Sainte-Croix-du-Mont, Loupiac, and Cadillac on the right bank and Cérons, Sauternes and Barsac on the left bank. Due to the variability of the onset of the famous "noble rot" harvesting should be done in successive sweeps through the vineyard with severe manual selection. Less esteemed than their neighbors on the left bank, Sainte-Croix-du-Mont, Loupiac and Cadillac continue to cultivate, harvest and vinify in a traditional manner. Their price-pleasure value is often interesting.

Divided in two by the zone for sweet wines, the Graves carries the name of its soil, which is a mix of pebbles, stones, and sand brought by the swell of the river Garonne. The best Graves are situated in the north (AOC Pessac-Léognan) where all the *Crus Classés* are to be found (with Château Haut-Brion at the head). The southern Graves, courageous but still under-valued, always appear as outsiders but there is an undeniable value-for-money aspect (particularly for the whites).

The Medoc extends for 80 kilometers from Bordeaux through to the Pointe de Grave in the north. Known throughout the world, the Médoc peninsula, between the ocean and the right bank of the Gironde, includes (from north to south) the appellations Médoc (in the north), Haut-Médoc (in the south) and the six communal appellations: Saint-Estèphe, Pauillac, Saint-Julien, Margaux (included within these four are the 60 *Crus Classés* from the 1855 classification), Listrac and Moulis. Margaux, the most southerly of these appellations, extends over five communes and 1150 hectares. The wines combine structure and finesse. A third of the *Crus Classés* are found in Margaux; nevertheless, today this is the most heterogenuous of the great appellations of the Médoc. Moulis and Listrac are located to the northeast and inland from Margaux. Owing to the climate and geology the red wines are powerful but generally have less finesse than Saint-Julien and Margaux. There are no *Crus Classés* but some excellent *Crus Bourgeois*. Further north but still close to the Gironde, Saint-Julien (the communes of Saint-Laurent, Cussac and Saint-Julien) registers 11 *Crus Classés* and a total of 744 hectares. The wines are perhaps the most perfectly balanced in the Médoc. In Pauillac (1022 hectares in five communes) the wines gain in structure and depth. There are 21 *Crus Classés* including the three First Growths that have promoted Pauillac's world reputation. Saint-Estèphe (1270 hectares), the last of the communal appellations, has made amazing progress over the last 15 years, combining vigor and charm ("iron fist in a velvet glove"). Saint-Estèphe has only five *Crus Classés* but lists an amazing number of successful *Crus Bourgeois*.

THE CLASSIFICATIONS, FROM 1855 TO 1996.

The yearly production of Bordeaux wines approaches 700 million bottles, which is a quarter of the production of French appellation wines! From the trickle of *Grands Crus* (approximately 2% of the production of red wines), which have provided a world reputation, to the flood of well-priced *petits châteaux,* the strength of this viticultural region is its ability to offer a wide range of wines to wine lovers. For this reason Bordeaux formulated a number of classifications which have virtually become "Tables of Law." But be careful, there is no single classification that covers all the wines of the Gironde, each one only concerns the wines of a particular appellation. In reality, all these "awards" have principally an historical significance and the wine lover does well not to take the indications on the label as the gospel truth.

The most famous classification is that of the red wines of the Médoc established in 1855 for the *Exposition* Universelle in Paris by the *negociants* and wine brokers of Bordeaux. Their opinion was not founded on a tasting but on the notoriety of the *terroir* and the prestige and sales price of the wines at the time. In this classification there are 61 *Grands Crus Classés* in five categories including four *crus* listed as First Growths. Since then, this hierarchy has seen only one change, in 1973, the five First Growths remaining the famous châteaux Lafite-Rothschild, Latour, Margaux, Haut-Brion (the only Graves added to the Médocs) and the promoted estate, Mouton-Rothschild. The general feeling among wine professionals is that this classification has always provided a good base for appreciating the wines of the Médoc (certainly at the high end of the classification) but that it is far from being infallible. On the one hand, while certain of these *crus* attempt to make the best wine possible others, either by incompetence or greed, produce wines that are below the level of their *terroir.* On the other hand, most of the châteaux, over a period of 140 years have made important extensions by the purchase of parcels of vines that were not originally classified.

The other classification in the Médoc, that of the *Crus Bourgeois*, dates from the 1930s and unites approximately 350 châteaux that do not figure in the 1855 classification. Among the Crus Bourgeois, certain offer very little interest while others today rival, in terms of quality, the Third and Fourth Growths.

Contrary to its rival in the Médoc, glued to the hierarchy of 1855, Saint-Emilion has, since 1955, possessed a classification that is revised every ten years. The classification not only takes into consideration the *terroir* of the properties but also their reputation and market price and also evaluates the wines by tasting. In September 1996 Saint-Emilion was, therefore, endowed with a new classification that includes 13 *Premiers Grands Crus Classés*, divided in to two categories A and B, and 55 Grands Crus Classés. One has to give credit to a system that incites the wine growers to improve and which attempts to regularly provide consumers with an order, references, and an evaluation of the best wines.

Finally, the Graves provides two classifications dating from 1959, one for the white wines and one for the reds.

BUYING IN BORDEAUX

The Bordeaux châteaux generally offer three or four vintages for sale. In 1997 and 1998 one could still find several '92s, a difficult year with little structure but one that if drunk now can provide a certain pleasure, particularly wines from the Médoc. The '93 vintage reveals a successful year for the Merlot and average for the Cabernet which didn't ripen well enough. The wines are fairly austere. The general level of the '94 vintage is good, providing wines to age (7 to 15 years), at the same time remaining on the limits of ripeness. As in '93 the best wines are found in the Libournais and in the north of the Médoc. The '95 vintage is a great year without being exceptional. The wines have fruit (the Cabernet was riper than in '94) but also, depending on the area, have a certain firmness (reminiscent of 1986). There are some particularly successful wines in the Médoc and the Libournais. As to '96, the wines appear to be for longer ageing than the '95s (10 to 20 years in the best *terroirs*), are remarkable in the Médoc, Graves (thanks to the late-harvested Cabernet Sauvignon), and Sauternes, a little less successful in the Libournais, and fairly mixed in the other appellations. The sweet wines, capricious by nature and sensitive to climatic variation, have in 1995 and 1996 resumed the excellence that has eluded them since 1990.

The prices at present have shown a huge increase, particularly in the great châteaux which are now virtually inaccessible. The market for the more moderate appellations is a little calmer but an increase in price of between 20 to 40% from the '94s to the '95s is a frequent occurrence.

ARBANATS

1 - RESTAURANT - **Le Luma**: *RN113, 33640 Arbanats. Tel. 05.56.67.53.55 Fax 05.56.67.26.37.* A large restaurant on the nationale route, much appreciated by Graves producers. Hearty cuisine and a Graves-only wine list with fifty entries at reasonable prices. Menu: 58 to 138 F. A la carte: around 120 F.

ARCINS

2 - RESTAURANT - **Le Lion d'Or**: *Place de la République, 33460 Arcins. Tel. 05.56. 58.96.79. Closed Sunday, Monday, in July and from 12/23 to 1/1.* A famous Médoc bistro with dishes smacking of tradition and seasonal rhythms. The freshness of their products is undeniable. Regulars (château staff, courtiers, etc.) often bring their own wine. Menu: 63,50 F. A la carte: around 190 F.

BARSAC

3 - HOTEL - **Le château de Valmont**: *33720 Barsac. Tel. 05.56.27.28.24 Fax 05.56.27.17.53.* Hotel and dining at a communal table, in an 18th-century castle. Very comfortable with a curteous welcome. Ideal for jaunts in the Sauternais and for living like a king without pauperizing oneself. 12 rooms: 395 to 700 F.

BLAIGNAN

4 - RESTAURANT - **Auberge des Vignobles**: *33340 Blaignan. Tel. 05.56.09.04.81.* Fresh regional products, informal atmosphere: a great stop for a simple meal. The client gets his money's worth. A la carte: around 120F.

BORDEAUX

5 - HOTEL - **Tulip inn Bayonne**: *15 cours de l'Intendance (entrance 4 rue Martignac and 11 rue Mautiec), 33000 Bordeaux. Tel. 05.56.48.00.88 Fax 05.56.48.41.60 or 05.56.48.41.61. Closed the last week in December and the first in January.* Near the Grand Théâtre, an elegant, completely refurbished hotel (rather small rooms). Warm welcome, good comfort, centrally located. 63 rooms: 450 to 695 F. 1 suite: 800 to 900 F.

6 - RESTAURANT - **Baud et Millet**: *19 rue Huguerie, 33000 Bordeaux. Tel. 05.56.79.05.77 Fax 05.56.81.75.48. Closed Sunday.* Few seats, reservations preferable. Serving only cheese and wine (with take-outs). Expansive and eclectic cellar welcoming the world's vineyards (1,000 different wines on the list). Heavenly prices. Menus: 105 to 165 F.

7 - RESTAURANT - **Bistro du Sommelier**: *163 rue Georges-Bonnac, 33000 Bordeaux. Tel. 05.56.96.71.78 Fax 05.56.24.52.36. Closed Saturday noon, Sunday and the week of August 15.* Honest bistro-style cuisine but above all a wine list that's well-chosen, lengthy (more than 100 Crus Classés from 20 appellations), and inexpensive. Menu: 121 F.

8 - RESTAURANT - **La Tupina**: *Jean-Pierre Xiradakis, 6 rue Porte-de-la-Monnaie, 33000 Bordeaux. Tel. 05.56.91. 56.37 Fax 05.56.31.92.11.* Southwestern products and folklore for a cosmopolitan clientele. 200 wines listed on a school notebook, but ser-

vice revolves around the selection of the moment (10 wines). Menus: 100 (lunch) to 250 F. A la carte: around 280 F.

9 - RESTAURANT - **Le Chapon fin**: *Francis Garcia, 5 rue Montesquieu, 33000 Bordeaux. Tel. 05.56.79.10.10. Fax 05.56.79.09.10. Closed Sunday and Monday.* Extravagant decor, classic fine cuisine, and a sumptuous list of great Bordeaux at appealing prices. Menus: 150 (lunch) and 260 to 400 F.

10 - RESTAURANT - **Claret's**: *46 rue du Pas-Saint-Georges, 33000 Bordeaux. Tel. 05.56.01.21.21. Closed Saturday noon.* Informal cuisine, lovely vaulted room and one of the most eclectic and expansive lists of accessible Bordeaux. Menus: 95 to 175 F.

11 - RESTAURANT - **Pavillon des boulevards**: *Denis and Nelly Franc, 120, rue Croix-de-Seguey, 33000 Bordeaux. Tel. 05.56.81.51.02 Fax 05.56.51. 14.58. Closed Sat. noon and Sun. and 2 weeks in August.* Dazzling dishes that harmoniously blend southwestern flavors, reasonable wine list. Menus: 220 (lunch) 270 and 420 F. A la carte: around 450 F.

BOULIAC

12 - HOTEL-RESTAURANT - **Hauterive Hôtel Saint-James**: *Jean-Marie Amat, 3 place Camille-Hostein, 33270 Bouliac. Tel. 05.57.97.06.00 Fax 05.56.20.92.58.* A brilliant chef, Jean-Marie Amat takes more liberties with his hotel's decoration than with his cuisine: excellent, but less dare-devil than what some critics have said it to be. Flavors are enhanced and precise (the pigeon grillé aux épices et sa pastilla is

divine). Bordeaux wines are everywhere (not necessarily the most expensive, especially by the glass): from the menu to the decor with its view of the cellar's racks. The selection from other regions is small, but right on the mark. The wine waiter is eloquent and discrete. Service is impeccable. This ultra-modern hôtellerie, with its decor signed by Jean Nouvel, is a diamond in the rough on the outside, high-tech on the inside. Unforgettable. Exceptional view of Bordeaux and the Gironde. Menus: 255 (lunch) to 380 F. Rotisserie: à la carte 160 F (closed Sun. and Mon.). 15 rooms: 700-950 F. 2 apartments: 1,200-1,550 F. Breakfast: 80 and 100 F.

13 - RESTAURANT - **Le Bistroy**: *3 place Camille-Hostein, 33270 Bouliac. Tel. 05.57.97.06.06.* Good bistro adjacent to the Saint-James (see above) with a large glass wall looking out on the garden and the hotel entrance. Brisk and pert southwestern cuisine. At night there's an informal night-goer ambiance. The small selection of wines (mostly young) changes frequently and

makes for a light bill. A la carte: around 200 F.

CAMBES

14 - RESTAURANT - **Auberge André**: *Le Grand-Port, 33880 Cambes. Tel. and Fax 05.56.78.75.23.* On the banks of the Garonne (terrace in summer), marine fish and shellfish cuisine, accompanied by a selection of Bordeaux at less than 100 F. Menus: 80 (weekdays) to 180 F.

CARBON-BLANC

15 - RESTAURANT - **Marc Demund**: *5 Avenue Gardette, 33560 Carbon-Blanc. Tel. 05.56.74.72.28. Closed Sunday evening and Monday.* Menus: 140 to 350 F. It's worth floundering out a little into this Bordeaux suburb, criss-crossed by the rocade and other thouroughfares: the products are good and flavorful, the wine list is well up to par.

CASTELNAU-DU-MEDOC

16 - BED & BREAKFAST - **Château du Foulon**: *33480 Castelnau-du-Médoc. Tel. 05.56.58.20.18 Fax*

05.56.58. 23.43. 5 guest rooms and 2 apartments (450 to 600 F, breakfast included) furnished with lovely antiques in a charming château set amidst an immense park. No meals.

17 - BED & BREAKFAST - **Domaine de Carrat**: *route de Saint-Hélène, 33480 Castelnau-de-Médoc. Tel. 05.56.58.*

24.80. Closed for the Christmas holidays. 3 rooms very tastefully appointed in the old stables, in a calm pastoral setting. Rooms: 260 to 300 F; suite (2 rooms): 450 F per night, breakfast included. No meals.

FRONSAC

18 - RESTAURANT - **Le Bord d'eau**: *Poinsonnet, route de Libourne, Fronsac. Tel. 05.57.51.99.91. Closed Sunday evening and Monday.* The best table in the Fronsac vineyard where fine products are displayed at their best and close attention is paid to vegetables. Good Bordeaux-only wine list, with 20 Fronsac and Canon-Fronsac. Excellent welcome. Menus from 100 F (except Saturday evening and Sunday lunch) to 260 F.

GAILLAN-EN-MEDOC

19 - HOTEL-RESTAURANT - **Château Layauga**:

33340 Gaillan-en-Médoc. Tel. 05.56. 41.26.83 Fax 05.56.41.19.52. Closed from January 15 to the end of February. The only gourmet table in northern Médoc, with a very classical and high-quality French bourgeois cuisine. Long wine list at fairly high prices. A la carte: around 350 F. Seven comfortable and cozy rooms (525 F) situated in the little castle. Breakfast: 65 F.

LANGON

20 - HOTEL-RESTAURANT - **Claude Darroze**: *95 cours du Général Leclerc, 33210 Langon. Tel. 05.56.63.00.48 Fax 05.56.63.41.15.* Menus: 210, 280 and 350 F. A la carte: around 450 F. Large comfortable rooms that play on the colors of the fabrics, at 320

and 420 F. A cuisine offering robust, concentrated flavors, but very refined and with remarkable products. Magnificent wine list (nearly 800 entries) with vintage Bordeaux reaching back to 1929 (château Latour) and even 1920 in magnum (Léoville-Barton). A hundred liqueurs from as early as 1936 (Yquem). Less prestigious appellations are not forgotten, with a large selection of old Sainte-Croix-du-Mont. Not to forget the 90 Armagnacs that span the century. Welcome and service to a tee.

LES ARTIGUES DE LUSSAC

21 - RESTAURANT - **Chez Servais**: *RN89, 33570 Les Artigues de Lussac Tel. 05.57.24.31.95. Closed Sunday evening and Monday.* Close to Lalande-de-Pomerol, bordering on the airfield's runways, an inviting table where food is simple and well prepared, with a good selection of Lalande-de-Pomerol.

LIBOURNE

22 - RESTAURANT - **Le Bistrot Chanzy**: *16 rue Chanzy, Libourne Tel. 05.57. 51.84.26. Closed Sunday and Monday. evening.* Menu: 85 F. A friendly bistro, clean (white table linens), simple and good, with a short, well-

prepared menu. Bordeaux-only wine list (80 entries) with some excellent vintages, moderate prices.

LISTRAC-MEDOC

23 - BED & BREAKFAST - **Château Cap-Léon-Veyrin**: *Maryse and Alain Meyre, Donissan, 33480 Listrac-Médoc. Tel. 05.56.58.07.28 Fax 05.56.58.07.50.* Kept by local growers. 5 doubles (with bathroom), simple, from 240 F per night (breakfast included) for 2 persons. Meals (October-May): 95 F.

MARGAUX

24 - HOTEL-RESTAURANT - **Le Pavillon Margaux**: *33460 Margaux. Tel. 05.57.88.77.54 Fax 05.57.88.77.73. As you enter Margaux.* This hotel-restaurant bordering on the Château Margaux vineyard, built in 1996 in the style of the 19th-century neoclassic châteaux, is the new Médoc address to discover. It offers 14 rooms (9 with

lounge). The most beautiful ones are in the main house: vast and cheerful, each has been tastefully decorated by the château that sponsored it. Rooms: 350 to 480 F. Breakfast: 45 F. Bright, colorful dining room looking out on the vineyard. Terrace in summer. Appetizing, creative cuisine built around regional products by a promising chef. Service is somewhat lacking. The outline of an enticing list of commendable vintages (priority given to Margaux) is beginning to take shape. Menus: 90 to 250 F. A la carte: around 300 F.

PAUILLAC

25 - HOTEL-RESTAURANT - **Château Cordeillan-Bages**: *Route des Châteaux, 33250 Pauillac. Tel. 05.56.59.24.24 Fax 05.56.59.01.89. Restaurant closed Saturday lunchtime, Monday. Hotel and restaurant closed in December and February.* Relais &

Châteaux, luxurious and tasteful, with a now well-established table. The elegant rooms, situated in the recent wings of this 17th-century Carthusian monastery, are equipped with the most modern comforts. Majestic wine list, mostly Médoc, with collector's bottles (therefore costly) presented by a knowledgeable wine waiter. Menus: 180 (lunch) to 380 F. 25 rooms: 900 to 1,200 F. Breakfast: 65 to 95 F.

26 - HOTEL-RESTAURANT - **Hôtel de France et d'Angleterre**: *3 quai Albert-Pichon, 33250 Pauillac. Tel. 05.56.59.01.20 Fax 05.56.59.02.31. Restaurant closed Sunday evening, Monday, and from October to April. Hotel closed from December 20 to*

January 10. Pleasing regional cuisine and wine list with around 400 entries from Médoc; rather recent vintages, with a preference for good-value Cru Bourgeois and Crus Classés. Menus: 85 to 220 F.

29 refurbished rooms, each bearing a different château name, that overlook the Gironde and Patiras island: 300 to 350 F.

PREIGNAC

27 - RESTAURANT - **Le Cap**: *Gilles and Maryse Lafarge, 33210 Preignac. Tel. and Fax 05.56.63.27.38. Closed Sunday evening and Monday.* A bucolic stop in a charming guinguette on the banks of the Garonne with a large arbor-shaded terrace in summer. Very informal. A summer bar was added in '97. Copious, straightforward regional cuisine at the right price. Short wine list with well-chosen local wines (12 Graves between 100 and 140 F, 5 Pessac-Léognan between 150 and 300 F). Menus: 100 and 140 F.

SAINT-ANDRE DE CUBZAC

28 - HOTEL - **Hostellerie du Vieux Raquine**: *Lugon 33340 Saint-André de Cubzac. Tel. 05.57.84.42.77 Fax 05.57.84.83.77. Closed mid-January to mid-February.* A lovely i7th-century mansion secluded in the tranquility of nature, with a view of the Fronsac vineyard and the Dordogne. 10 rooms: 440 to 700 F.

SAINT-CHRISTOLY

29 - RESTAURANT - **La Maison du Douanier**: *Port de Saint-Christoly de Médoc, 33340 Saint-Christoly. Tel. 05.56.41.35.25 Fax 05.56.41.56.60. Open from Pentecost to September 15. Closed Monday.* The cuisine is plain and conventional, but its water-level view with terrace on the Gironde is unique. Menus: from 100 F. A la carte: around 140 to 260 F.

SAINT-CHRISTOLY-DE-BLAYE

30 - BED & BREAKFAST - **La Bergerie**: *Les Trias, 33920 Saint-Christoly-de-*

Blaye. Tel. 05.57.42.50.80. In a park with pond, two houses for 2 or 6 persons that are nicely decorated in a rustic style with elegant fabrics and antiques. Each has its own kitchen and lounge with fireplace. 400 F (2 pers.) and 150 F (per extra pers.). Breakfast included. No meals.

SAINT-CIERS-DE-CANESSE

31 - HOTEL - **La Closerie des vignes**: *33710 Saint-Ciers-de-Canesse. Tel. 05.57.64.81.90 Fax 05.57. 64.94.44. Closed Sunday evenings (low-season) and from November 1 to March 31.* Rooms: 370 F. The only hotel in the Bourg area, modern and very pleasant with its

grey and blue tones. In the heart of the vineyards. Solicitous welcome, good, traditional family cooking. Short but well-chosen wine list with some old vintages.

SAINT-EMILION

32 - HOTEL - **Le Logis des Remparts**: *rue Guadet, 33330 Saint-Emilion. Tel. 05.57.24.70.43 Fax 05.57.74. 47.44. Closed mid-December to mid-January.* As its name suggests, the hotel adjoins the city's ramparts. Simple, partially refurbished rooms, some of which overlook the vineyard. A good value for this city. 17 rooms: 350 to 520 F. Breakfast: 50 F.

33 - HOTEL-RESTAURANT - **Château Grand Barrail**: *Route de Libourne, 33330 Saint-Emilion. Tel. 05.57.55.37.00*

Fax 05.57.55.37.49. This grand 19th-century castle, situated 2 km from Saint-Emilion in a park with vineyard and ornamental lake, got a royal make-over in 1995. Luxurious accommodations counting 20 vast, extremely comfortable rooms in the new wing (850 to 1,500 F) and 9 rooms and suites in the castle (1,200 to 2,900 F). Some are duplexes with jacuzzi. Pool. The restaurant, set up in the drawing room, possesses an

audacious chef, modern in contrasting textures and fastidious about the quality of his products, who makes up for some shortcomings (the menu is not always clear). An encyclopedic wine list in Saint-Emilion with 85 entries (mostly thanks to the château sales depot), one page devoted to old vintages (64, 66, 70 75, 78). Some notable omissions (Angelus, among others). Prices are high but not prohibitive. Menus: 170 (lunch weekdays) to 340 F.

34 - HOTEL-RESTAURANT - **Hostellerie de Plaisance**: *Place du clocher, 33330 Saint-Emillion. Tel. 05.57.74.41.11 Fax 05.57.74.41.11. Closed Sunday evening, Monday and in January.* Stilted decor, but with a lovely view of the village. A palatable table and a splendid wine list for Saint-Emilion and Pomerols. 10 smart rooms with lovely bathrooms: 580 to 1350 F, and 2 apartments: 950 to 1350 F.

35 - HOTEL-RESTAURANT - **Logis de la Cadène**: *Place du Marché-aux-Bois, 33330 Saint-Emilion. Tel. 05.57. 24.71.40 Fax 05.57.74.42.23. Open for lunch and dinner in summer, except Sunday evening and Monday. Low-season: open only for lunch, except on Monday.* Arbor of Virginia creeper, appetizing southwestern cuisine, wine list with 30 well-chosen entries from Saint-Emilion. Menus: 100 to 180 F. 3 simple guest rooms: 200 to 300 F.

36 - RESTAURANT - **Francis Goulée**: *27 rue Guadet, 33330 Saint-Emilion. Tel. 05.57.24.70.49 Fax 05.57. 74.47.96. Closed Sunday evening from November 15 to December 10.* In one of the city's steep streets, gourmet cuisine based on good products, combining modernity and classicism. A rich list of wines from the Libournais. Menus: 90 (lunch), 120 (except Sun.), 180, 190 and 230 F. A la carte: around 200 F.

37 - RESTAURANT - **L'envers du décor**: *11 rue du clocher, 33330 Saint-Emilion. Tel. 05.57.74.48.31 Fax 05.57. 24.68.90. Closed Sunday and evenings on holidays.* The only wine bar in the center of Saint-Emilion (two paces from the House of Wines). Terrace in summer. The château owners gladly meet up here in the good-natured atmosphere to enjoy hearty, regional bistro-style dishes and the worldly, varying wine list (wines of the day). A la carte: around 120 F.

SAINT-ESTEPHE

38 - RESTAURANT - **Restaurant Peyrat**: *Le port, 33180 Saint-Estèphe. Tel. 05.56.59.71.43.* Café-bistro set on the banks of the Gironde with summer terrace: easy-going meals and a small selection of Saint-Estèphes at smart prices. A la carte: around 110 F.

39 - HOTEL - **Château Pomys**: *Leyssac, 33180 Saint-Estèphe. Tel. information 05.56.59.32.26 Tel. reservation*

05.56.59.73.44 Fax 05.56.59.35.24. This lovely late 19th-century estate producing a Saint-Estèphe Cru Bour-

geois was converted into a hotel in 1991. 10 spacious, well-equipped rooms overlooking the park and vineyard. No restaurant.

SAINT-FERME

40 - BED & BREAKFAST - **Le château du Parc**: *33580 Saint-Ferme. Tel. 05.56.61.69.18 Fax 05.56.61.69.23.* Luxurious guest rooms and a very good table in an 18th-century castle. Remarkable welcome. Menu: 250 F, wine included. 7 rooms: 600 to 900 F. Breakfast: 50 F.

SAINT-GERMAIN-DE-LA-RIVIERE

41 - BED & BREAKFAST - **Château**

l'Escarderie: *Bénédicte Claverie, 33240 Saint-Germain-de-la-Rivière. Tel. and Fax 05.57.84.46.28.* A beautiful 1850 façade welcomes you to the La Rivière castle in the Fronsac vineyard, whose three spacious guest rooms overlook the park and vineyard. 260 F, breakfast included.

SAINT-JULIEN BEYCHEVELLE

42 - RESTAURANT - **Le Saint-Julien**: *2 rue des Acacias, place Saint-Julien, 33250 Saint-Julien Beychevelle. Tel. 05.56.59.63.87 Fax 05.56.59.63.89. Closed Tuesday evenings and Wednesday from October to May and in January.* Claude Broussard, who did his studies in Paris- notably under François Clerc-, came back home in 1996 to start up this restaurant in a village house across from the Léoville-Poyferré castle. Served amidst the stone and beam decor, his cuisine is downright tasty (delicious mild-garlic roasted Pauillac lamb), generous, and unpretentious. 3 menus: 95 (a great deal), 165 and 350 F (a medley of 6 dishes). The cellar, which is slowly but surely being stocked, favours Saint-Julien (30 references), from 135 to 3,600 F (Léoville-Barton '61) and Médoc in general. Few half bottles. To be discovered.

SAINT-LOUBES

43 - HOTEL-RESTAURANT - **Au vieux Logis**: *92, avenue de la République, 33450 Saint-Loubes. Tel. 05.56.78.92.99 Fax 05.56.78.91.18.* An establishment that recently moved into a large

family house while remaining in the village. 6 suitable rooms at a good value (225 to 285 F). Traditional regional cuisine. Good selection of Bordeaux and Entre-Deux-Mers. Menus: 125 and 250 F.

SAINT-MACAIRE

44 - RESTAURANT - **L'Abricotier**: *2 rue Bergoeing, 33490 Saint-Macaire. Tel. 05.56.76.83.63 Fax 05.56.76. 28.51. Closed Tuesday evening and from November 12 to December 5.* Savory and inventive local cuisine accompanied by a respectable wine list, all at reasonable prices. Menus: 105 to 210 F.

SAINT-MICHEL DE FRONSAC

45 - BED & BREAKFAST - **Clos Saint-Michel**: *1 rue Lariveau, 33126 Saint-Michel de Fronsac. Tel. 05.57. 24.95.81.* 250 F, breakfast included. A Girondin house with two guest rooms, kept by winegrowers.

SAINT-QUENTIN-DE-BARON

46 - BED & BREAKFAST - **Le Prieuré**: *33750 Saint-Quentin-de-Baron. Tel. 05.57. 24.16.75 Fax 05.57.24.13.80.* Two lovely ground-level rooms modernly

furnished in an ancient priory. No smokers. 175 (per pers.) to 480 F (2 pers.), breakfast included. Meals served in the evening, 140 F, wine included.

SAUTERNES

47 - BED & BREAKFAST - **Grand domaine du Ciron**: *Brouquet, 33210 Sauternes. Tel. 05.56.76.60.17 Fax 05.56.76. 61.74.* 4 simple, comfortable rooms (230 and 240 F, breakfast included)

in an attractive house set amidst the Sauternes vineyard. Pool.

48 - RESTAURANT - **Le Saprien**: *33210 Sauternes. Tel. 05.56.76.60.87 Fax 05.56.76.68.92. Closed Sunday evening and Monday.* Sober decor with exposed stonework; savory market-based cuisine, sophisticated but with a southwestern accent. Curteous and attentive female welcome. Large selection of Sauternes by the glass. Old vintages. View of the château Guiraud vineyard. Menus: 119 to 219 F.

49 - RESTAURANT - **Auberge les Vignes**: *23 rue Principale, 33210 Sauternes. Tel. 05.56.76.60.06 Fax 05.56.76. 69.97. Closed Monday evening and mid-January to mid-February.* A good provincial inn with modest, generous cooking and a lovely collection of Sauternes and Graves served by the glass. Menu: 60

(lunch) to 135 F. A la carte: around 180 F.

SOULAC-SUR-MER

50 - HOTEL - **Hôtel des pins**: *92 boulevard Amélie, 33780 Soulac-sur-Mer. Tel. 05.56.73.27.27 Fax 05.56.73.60.39. Closed from November 15 to March 15 (except from December 20 to January 10).* A house sitting between the sea and the pine forest. Comfortable and inviting. 31 rooms: 200 to 420 F. Breakfast: 40 F.

VILLENAVE D'ORNON

51 - RESTAURANT - **La Maison de Cuisine**: *33140 Villenave d'Ornon. Tel. 05.56.87.07.59. Closed Sunday. and Monday evening.* Alain Ponty's first restaurant (former student of Georges Blanc and Michel Guérard) opened on Christmas, '95. Modern but warm decor, chic regional cuisine attentive to ingredients. Good list of Graves (with presentation of the properties). Menu: 65 F (lunch weekdays). A la carte: around 145 F.

TO SEE

BLAIGNAN

VISIT - **Médoc " Noisettine "**: *33340 Blaignan. Tel. 05 56 09 03 09.* Free guided tour in costume all year - round by reservation (25 pers. min.). In July and August, Mon.-Sat. from 2:30 to 6:30 pm. A cottage industry confectionary (specialty: hazel nuts dipped in syrup until lightly candied, then dried and delicately coated in caramel).

BLASIMON

OUTING - Grandiose ruins of an ancient Benedictine abbey with its sculpted portal from the 12th century.

BLAYE

OUTING - An impressive military citadel (area: over 50 acres) on the banks of the Gironde that Vauban finished in 1689 to protect Bordeaux. From the opposite bank one can admire the Médoc region.

BORDEAUX

OUTING - **Chacun sa mer**: *Conservatoire de Plaisance, boulevard Alfred Daney, 33300 Bordeaux. Tel. 05.56.50.00.42 Fax 05.56.50.00.44.* A company that organizes group sailing-barge trips (22 persons) around the Gironde's islands. Departure from Bordeaux, Pauillac or Blaye with an organized picnic and wine tasting on Margaux island. Individuals can also sign up in Blaye's tourist office: tel. 05.57.42.12.09.

CIVRAC, BEGADAN, COUQUEQUES

VISIT - **Civrac, Bégadan, Couquèques**: Village churches that have conserved their beautiful 12th-century Romanesque apses.

LA BREDE

TOUR - **Château de la Brède**: *33650 La Brède. Tel. 05.56.20.20.49. Open*

April to June and October to November 11 on weekends and holidays from 2 to 6 pm. July to September every day except Tuesday from 2 to 6 pm. Admission: 30 F. The austere castle surrounded by a moat where Charles Louis de Secondat, baron of Montesquieu (1689-1755), president of the parliament of Bordeaux, philosopher, man of letters, and winegrower was born and lived. Tour of his chambers and library containing 7,000 volumes.

LA REOLE

VISIT - France's oldest city hall.

LA SAUVE-MAJEUR

VISIT - The most famous abbey in the Entre-deux-Mers. A ruin whose summit offers an impressive view.

LE VERDON-SUR-MER

OUTING - **Verdon-Royan ferry**: *Bacs-Gironde, 19 avenue du Phare de Cordovan, 33123 Le Verdon-sur-Mer. Tel. 05.56.09.60.84 (at the tip of Grave). Leaving Royan: tel. 05.46. 38.35.15. In summer, non-stop from 6:30am to 8:30pm, in winter: 7am, 9am, 11am, 2pm, 4:30pm, 6:30pm leaving Verdon.* 30 mn ferry ride across the Gironde (pedestrian: 16 F, car: 120 F)

MONTAGNE-SAINT-EMILION

MUSEUM - **Libournais Ecomuseum**: *Le Bourg, 33570 Montagne-Saint-Emilion. Tel. 05.57.74.56.89. Open mid-March to mid-November.* Admission: 25 F. Museum devoted to winegrowers (recreated workshops) and to the history of the vineyard and region.

MOULIS-EN-MEDOC

MUSEUM - **Château Maucaillou**: *Gare de Moulis-Listrac, 33480 Moulis-en-Médoc. Tel. 05.56.58.01.23. Open every day from 10 to 12:30 and 2 to 6.* Gironde's most interesting museum of the art and traditions of the wine and vineyard. Audiovisuel presentation on the making of a vintage wine.

PAUILLAC

MUSEUM - **Château Mouton Rothschild**: *33250 Pauillac. Tel. 05.56.73.21.29 Fax 05.56.73.21.28. Open every day by reservation from October to April and Monday to Friday in low-season.* Admission: 20 F, 70 F (with degustation of Mouton), 130 F (degustation of Mouton, Clerc-Millon, d'Armailhac). Complete and very professional tour of this prestigious winery's facilities and visit to the museum (completely restored in winter 96-97) displaying some rare works: paintings, tapestries, jewelry, porcelains. The personal collection of Baron Philippe de Rothschild and his daughter Philippine. Wine is sold in the boutique.

SAINT-EMILION

OUTING - The most touristy city in the Girondin vineyard is worth the pilgrimage. Avoid if possible in summer: the narrow streets often swarm with tourists like the Mont-Saint-Michel on August 15th. Of the city's fortified walls, the King's tower and the Guards' tower still remain. One can also still see two notable monastic sites: the monolithic church excavated in the chalky cliff that is unique

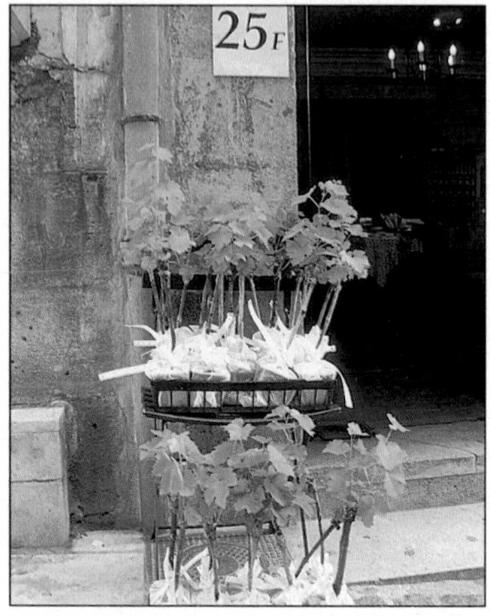

in Europe (tours every 45 mn, admission: 35 F) and the collegiate church with its cloisters. Too bad this lovely city is in the hands of the merchants of the temple who sell wine (at high prices) on every street corner.

SAINT-ESTEPHE

VISIT - **Château Cos-d'Estournel**: *33180 Saint-Estèphe. Tel. 05.56.73. 15.50. Monday-Friday from 10am to 12am and 2pm to 5pm.* For the traveller arriving from Pauillac on the D2, the first vision of the Saint-Estèphe is an oriental mirage: three angular towers crowned by copper Mandarin-style hats, a façade with sculpted arcades and honeylike reflections, and the dark wooden door of a Zanzibari palace appear high on the hill. You are not dreaming: this exotic construction, a Saint-Estèphe celebrity, is called Cos d'Estournel. So often described since Stendhal, this " pagoda " was erected in 1830 by Louis-Gaspard d'Estournel, a great traveller fascinated by India, who went broke building his estate and bringing it to perfection. Free access to the new exhibit room that recounts the history of Cos. Wine is sold in the boutique.

SAINT-FERME

VISIT - An abbey built by Clunisian monks that has stood the test of time. It now serves as town hall. Church with sculpted Romanesque capitals.

SAINT-GERMAIN D'ESTEUIL

OUTING - **The Brion Site**: *Saint-Germain d'Esteuil.* Brion's Gallo-Roman archeological site which will remind travellers that the history of the Médoc doesn't begin with the refined façades of the late 19th-century châteaux.

VEYRES

OUTING - The church, for the sculpted grapevines on the lintel and its view over the castle.

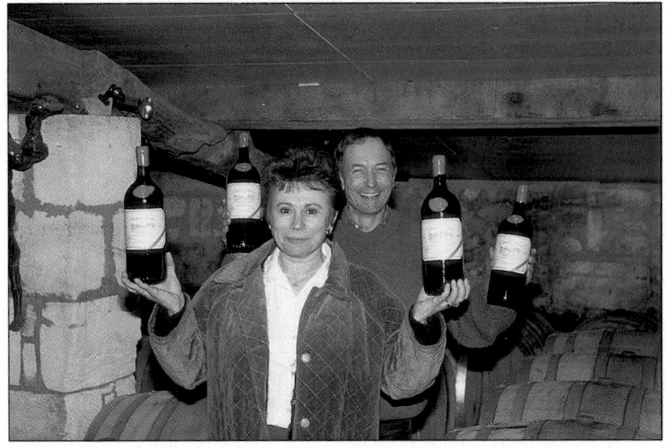

Guy and Maïthé Cenni.

Château de Blassan

Owners Maïthé and Guy Cenni. **Address** 33240 Lugon - Tel. 05.57.84.40.91 Fax 05.57.84.82.93. **Open** From Monday to Saturday, 8:00-12:00 and 14:00-18:00, by appointment.

Guy Cenni hasn't totally lost his accent despite abandoning his native eastern France 24 years ago to set up home with his wife, Maïthé, the daughter of a vine-grower in Lugon. His friends from the Peugeot car plant were among the first loyal clients, contributing to a winemaking adventure that continues today on 32 hectares dominated by Merlot (75%) and Cabernet Sauvignon. In the cellar he built himself, Guy Cenni, a passionate, hard working perfectionist, controls everything. Two *cuvées* of red Bordeaux dominate the range, the Tradition (aged in vat) and the Cuvée Spéciale (matured in barrel). The Bordeaux Supérieur Cuvée Spéciale '94 (31 F), aged in 50% new oak casks, will be good for drinking in four to five years. The nose is already beginning to open with fine toasted notes, and the palate is full with a firm but well balanced tannic structure which has been rounded out by the oak. The Bordeaux Supérieur '95 (25 F) is a generous, unoaked, fleshy wine, with spice and pepper flavors, and a satisfyingly tannic but unaggressive finish. It should be drinking well from 1998.

Our choice Bordeaux Supérieur Cuvée Spéciale '95 (31 F). The nose expresses a clear ripeness and the palate a sweet extract which the oak has softened without masking the fruit (redcurrant). The wine finishes with a firm, and present tannic structure indicating a potential for ageing. For the year 2000 or beyond.

Reception Warm and friendly, in a neatly arranged cellar.

How to get there *(Map 3): 14km west of Libourne via D670 to Saint-André de Cubzac. Turn right at Lugon then left passing behind the church in the direction of Vérac. The domaine is indicated.*

Cazalis.

Château Cazalis

Owner Claude Billot. **Address** 33350 Pujols-sur-Dordogne - Tel. 05.57.40.72.72 Fax 05.57.40.72.00. **Open** From Monday to Saturday, by appointment. **Spoken** Spanish, English.

Claude Billot hasn't forgotten that before becoming a vintner he was a lover of good wine. Located at Pujols, near the left bank of the Dordogne river, on 25 hectares of sand-clay-limestone soils (Merlot and Cabernet Sauvignon, average age 15 years), this former meat wholesaler firmly believes that a domaine should never disappoint its customers, regardless of the fickle form of nature. Consequently, having produced the superb Cuvée CL which gave him a certain notoriety and which was placed on the list of many a fine restaurant he decided that the '91, '92, and '93 vintages were not good enough to be bottled under this label and declassified them to a second label, Le Moulin de Cazalis. The Cuvée CL '94 (32 F) with its ripe fruit nose and black fruit palate with a hint of gaminess is still youthful and closed and should be cellared for another three or four years. The Cuvée CL '96 (available from June '98, 32 F) is ripe and silky with fine tannins, a slightly green finish but full fruit and plenty of finesse and needs to age to perfect maturity. The rosé, Les Tonnelles, is good.

Our choice Bordeaux Supérieur Cuvée CL '95 (32 F). Elegant but closed on the nose, the palate is soft and supple on the attack with a long, balanced finish and ripe, finely edged tannic structure. Drink from 1998 over a period of five to seven years.

Reception In a beautiful residence with a courtyard. Claude knows how to share his passion for wine.

***How to get there** (Map 3): 12km southeast of Saint-Emilion and 7km south of Castillon-la-Bataille via D17. The domaine is at the entrance to the village.*

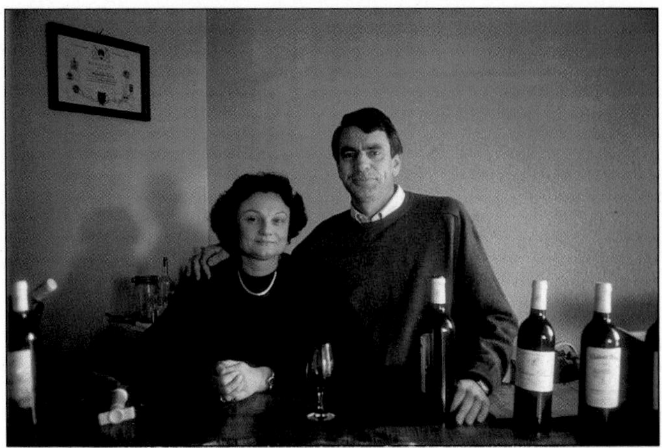

Patrick and Catherine Carteyron.

Château Penin

Owners Patrick and Catherine Carteyron. **Address** 33420 Génissac - Tel. 05.57.24.46.98 Fax 05.57. 24.41.99. **Open** From Mon. to Sat. afternoon, 9:00 -12:00 and 14:30-18:00. **Spoken** German.

The Entre-Deux-Mers may have given its name to a dry white Bordeaux but this region in the heart of the Gironde is also a nursery for good red wines. Enologist Patrick Carteyron returned to the family property (27 hectares) on the left bank of the Dordogne river in 1982 with an ambitious plan for restructuring the domaine within the economic constraints of the region. "I wanted, among other things, to increase the density of planting of my vines, reduce the number of grape bunches per vine and gain more concentration but these things are costly and in the appellations Bordeaux and Bordeaux Supérieur I cannot sell my wine for more than 35 francs." Indeed, but at this price and with Patrick's energy and professionalism the consumer is on to a good thing. The white Bordeaux '96 (29 F), tasted unfiltered before bottling, has a fruity, Sauvignon character, ample, fruit-driven palate and a ripe, flavorsome finish with the acidity slightly muted. It should be served chilled and consumed young. The red Bordeaux Supérieur '95 (27 F) offers a supple wine with fine, full tannins and a black currant note and can be drunk young. It will gain in complexity with some bottle age.

Our choice Bordeaux Supérieur Cuvée Sélection '95 (35 F). Tasted before bottling, this is a generous wine with ripe aromas and rich, full palate with notes of spice, black fruits, and tobacco and a long, fine, tannic finish. It can be appreciated young but will evolve well over five to six years.

Reception Between the office and barrel cellar with either Patrick or Catherine.

How to get there *(Map 3): 23km east of the Bordeaux Rocade and 7km south of Libourne. Take N89 from Bordeaux towards Libourne and exit at Génissac. Turn left at the stop sign towards the port of Génissac and follow the signs to the domaine.*

Stephane Asséo, one of Bordeaux's go-ahead young winemakers.

Domaine de Courteillac et Château Robin

Owners Béatrice and Stéphane Asséo. **Address** 33350 Ruch - Tel. 05.57.40.55.65 Fax 05.57.40.58.07. **Open** From Monday to Saturday, 10:00-12:00 and 14:00-18:00, bu appointment only. **Spoken** English.

Stephane Asséo's sailing trips in southern oceans have left him with the taste for a nomadic existence. Today, he navigates between four properties in the Entre-Deux-Mers and the Libournais. At his home port, the Domaine de Courteillac (27 hectares), acquired in 1982, he has forged the reputation of a rigorous winemaker. Here, he produces ripe, red Bordeaux with silky tannins and equally good white Bordeaux, particularly the *cuvée* Antholien, made from a predominance of Semillon vinified in new oak barrels. The excellent '95 (55 F) is particularly fresh, unctuous and distinguished. He has also applied his know-how with great zest at the new family property in the Côtes-de-Castillon, Château Robin (12.5 hectares), and in the space of four vintages has propelled the estate to the top of the appellation. One also finds Stéphane's mark at Château Fleur Cardinale (see Saint-Emilion) and in the management of Château Guillot-Clauzel, a little-known estate in Pomerol until "discovered in 1996.

Our choice Domaine de Courteillac Bordeaux red '95 (46 F). Neither filtered nor fined. Deep, bright hue with the aroma of ripe cherries and finely toasted oak. The palate is full and densely structured. To savor over six or seven years. Even richer with great suavity, full flavor, and powerful tannic structure, the Château Robin '95 (55 F) is also a must.

Reception In a cellar of antique charm among the barrels and vats. In a casual atmosphere this is a visit for wine lovers given by a wine lover.

How to get there *(Map 3): Between Blasimon and Castillon-la-Bataille via D17. Turn left opposite Ruch towards Courteillac.*

Stéphane Defraine.

Château de Fontenille

Owners Magdalena and Stéphane Defraine. **Address** 33670 La Sauve - Tel. 05.56.23.03.26 Fax 05.56.23.30.03. **Open** Every day 9:00-12:00 and 14:00-18:00, by appointment. **Spoken** English.

White Bordeaux is undergoing another economic crisis but there are still wine growers attached to this wine. Enologist Stéphane Defraine, installed at Château de Fontenille since 1988, believes in the appellation Entre-Deux-Mers, the dry, white wine produced in the region between the Dordogne and Garonne rivers. He is presently waiting impatiently to vinify a new parcel 60-year-old Semillon and Muscadelle. On his 36 hectare estate he also produces two red Bordeaux and a lightly macerated Bordeaux Clairet from 100% Cabernet Franc. The '96 (25 F) has plenty of character and is ripe with candied flavors. Two red Bordeaux were made in '95 from the same blend of 50% Merlot, 35% Cabernet Franc and 15% Cabernet Sauvignon. One matured in vat (27 F) is spicy with a soft tannic structure and the other aged in oak barrels (40 F) has a plummy flavor with roasted notes and is full and present on the palate. Since 1994 Stéphane Defraine has used the system of micro-oxygenation to round out the tannic structure in the red wines.

Our choice Entre-Deux-Mers '96 (27 F). Sauvignon, Semillon and Muscadelle vinified with skin contact and aged on lees for seven months in vat. Suave and aromatic without any "technical" nuance, the fruit is fresh, round, and present on the palate. A wine that provides simple but generous pleasure.

Reception One kilometer from the Abbey of La Sauve-Majeure (11th century) close to a sober 18th century house surrounded by woodland. The visit is conducted with attention and professionalism.

How to get there *(Map 3) From Créon towards Capian-Haux via D13. The domaine is indicated on the left.*

Thierry Bos, 34, has already produced a superb selection of wines which are regularly placed at the top in tastings of red Bordeaux.

Domaine de Bouillerot

Owners Véronique and Thierry Bos. **Address** Lacombe, 33190 Gironde-sur-Dropt - Tel. 05.56. 71.46.04 Fax 05.56.71.33.47. **Open** From Monday to Saturday, by appointment.

Thierry Bos took over the 7 hectare property from his father in 1989. The domaine, in family hands since 1874, is planted with 50% Merlot and a complement of Cabernet Franc, Cabernet Sauvignon and Malbec on clay and silt soils. His aromatic Bordeaux reds are regularly placed at the top in tastings. The Bordeaux '95 (20 F), produced from 80% Malbec and 20% Merlot, and aged for ten months in vat has a soft, fruity aroma, a palate accented towards the fruit, soft but present tannins and a crisp finish. The wine represents excellent value for money for everyday drinking and should be consumed over the next three to four years. The Bordeaux Supérieur Cuvée Passion '94 (33 F), produced from 80% Merlot and aged in barrel, has toasted aromas with a present but closed fruit content. Following the style of the domaine the palate is round but with a hard tannic structure typical of the 1994 vintage. A slightly austere nature should vanish in two to three years.

Our choice Bordeaux Supérieur Cuvée Passion '95 (35 F). Aged for one year in oak barrels and produced from 100% Merlot. Deep, black currant hue. The nose is much present with the elegant aroma of tobacco, toast, and black fruits. The palate has a velvety, round texture, rich, soft tannins, and slightly astringent finish, guaranteeing a good potential for ageing. Drink young from sheer *gourmandise* or cellar.

Reception The cellar offers nothing special, but Thierry is an enthusiastic host. His wife, Véronique, often receives visitors.

How to get there *(Map 3): 59km southeast of the Bordeaux Rocade. From A62 take Langon exit, towards La Réole, Marmande via N113. Turn left at Gironde-sur-Dropt towards Morizès. The house is 2-3km on the left near a brick-works.*

A vineyard between sky and water.

Domaine de l'Île-Margaux

Owners Families Nègre and Peugeot. **Supervisor** Lionel de Mecquenem. **Address** L'Île-Margaux 33460 Margaux - Tel. 05.56.88.30.46/05.57.88.35.19 Fax 05.57.88.35.87. **Open** From Monday to Friday, 9:00-12:00 and 14:00-17:30, by appointment only (little direct selling).

This is the most secret and exotic property in the Médoc. Perched on the smallest of the three islands in the Gironde estuary, facing Margaux, the 14 hectare domaine with its somber Girondin house was purchased and renovated in 1988 by three Parisians mad about Bordeaux wine. The isolated cellar master, Lionel de Mecquenem, lives year-round with his family on this stationary vessel in complete peace and solitude. His work is conditioned by the ebb and flow of the tide. When bottling, for instance, he transports the wine by vat on a barge to the other bank of the river. The deep but low-lying, silty soil of the vineyard, at one time part of Château Margaux, is classified in appellation Bordeaux Supérieur. Merlot (45%) is the principal grape variety. The '96, tasted before blending, looks to be excellent with rich, full Merlot, deep, generous Cabernet, and delicious Petit Verdot which has the aroma of violets. It's a great vintage. The only regrettable thing is that there weren't enough new oak barrels for the maturation.

Our choice Domaine de l'Ile-Margaux '95 (36 F). Typical Merlot dominated Bordeaux with black currant, ripe raspberry, and peppery aromas, generous palate, and firm structure which should mature well over six or seven years. A characterful wine.

Reception Lionel de Mecquenem transports visitors across the silty estuary by motor boat. Time has no importance in this unusual setting.

How to get there *(Map 3): Arriving from Bordeaux via D2 turn right at the entrance to Margaux towards Château Margaux. Straight on for 2km towards the Gironde. A sign indicates the landing-stage.*

Jean Duffau in his cellar.

Château Les Arromans

Owners Sylvette and Jean Duffau. **Address** 33420 Moulon - Tel. 05.57.84.50.87 Fax 05.57. 84.52.84. **Open** From Monday to Friday, 9:00 -12:00 and 14:00-18:00.

On the left bank of the Dordogne, opposite Saint-Emilion, the commune of Moulon with its south-facing slopes and limestone-clay and gravel soils is particularly adapted to the production of Merlot-based red Bordeaux. In great years (1990) the wines can rival without difficulty those of Saint-Emilion. Moulon is the fief of the Duffau family. Château Les Arromans (30 hectares) belongs to 72-year-old Jean, a personality in the Entre-Deux-Mers, who for 30 years has produced some of the wines of reference in the region. The wines of two neigboring domaines owned by his sons Joël (Château La Mothe du Barry), and Eric (Château Belle-Garde) are also worth discovering. They work in the same rigorous manner as their father and when he retires in three years they will divide his vineyard between themselves. The Entre-Deux-Mers '96 (19,50 F), produced from Semillon and Sauvignon, has crisp, expressive fruit and should be consumed young with a seafood dish. The simple red Bordeaux '95 (21 F) has a firmer tannic structure and should age longer than the round, fruity '96.

Our choice Château Les Arromans Prestige '95 (28 F). An excellent red Bordeaux which demonstrates the generosity and power of ripe Merlot that has been gently aged in barrel. It should drink well from 1999 to 2004.

Reception Visitors received with consideration by the Duffau family in the cellar.

How to get there *(Map 3): From Bordeaux towards Libourne via N89, then right towards Genissac and Moulon. Right in the village towards the cemetary then follow the signs.*

Nicole Noël.

Château Barrabaque

Supervisor Nicole Noël. **Address** 33126 Fronsac - Tel. 05.57.55.09.09 and 06.07.46.08.08 Fax 05.57.55.09.00. **Open** By appointment. **Spoken** English, German.

The Noêl family are a confident bunch. Nicole took over the domaine, 9 hectares planted with a predominance of old-vine Merlot (70%) on well-worked soils, from her father-in-law in 1984 and has vinified the wine in "her way" since 1988. Her ideas are now well established. She produces two very different styles of wine but with finesse as the common denominator. The *cuvée* Classique is all fruit and supple texture. The '94 (43 F) has good depth, structure and fruit. The '95 (approx. 47 F) has a lighter and fruitier style on the attack, opening out in the glass. The *cuvée* Prestige is a more ambitious wine produced from lower yielding vines, selected vats and with a maturation in oak varying according to the vintage. Older wines are available.

Our choice Château Barrabaque Prestige '94 (55 F). The nose has a toasted note with very ripe, black fruit (blackberry, black cherry) aromas and the palate is full and elegant. The wine has exceptional density and finesse, a long, fresh finish, and well integrated oak. A wine to drink or age a little. The '95 (approx. 60 F), tasted from barrel, will be very fruity (black currant), appetizing, fine, and well-balanced.

Reception Simple and attentive. At the beginning of the year the cuvée Prestige is offered *en primeur* with a reduction of approximately 20% on the eventual selling price.

How to get there *(Map 3): From Libourne to Fronsac via D670. Turn right in the center of Fronsac, towards Villegouge and Vérac, then first on the left. The tiny château is on the right.*

Jean-Jacques Dubois, a man of nuance rather than contrast.

Château Cassagne Haut-Canon

Owner Jean-Jacques Dubois. **Address** 33126 Saint-Michel de Fronsac - Tel. 05.57.51.63.98 and 05.57.51.18.24 Fax 05.57.51.62.20. **Open** By appointment. **Spoken** English.

Jean-Jacques Dubois prefers to emphasize the nuance in a wine rather than the contrast. He vinifies select parcels of grapes, practices a meticulous maturation in oak barrel to gain greater nuance, and blends stage by stage in the search for greater complexity. The importance of Cabernet in the prestige *cuvée* La Truffière produces a wine with a certain austerity and acidity which is well balanced by the ripeness and quality of the fruit. The regular wine has a greater percentage of Merlot and is rounder in style. The '92 (38 F) is ready for drinking but the splendid and still closed '94 (44 F) should be aged longer. It's not an obvious sort of wine but offers subtle aromatic notes of spice and coffee, finesse, and a long finish.

Our choice Two vintages of La Truffière. The '91 (60 F), which is ready for drinking, is dense, lively, elegant, crisp, and rounder than usual with a greater percentage of Merlot. The '94 (62 F) is a great wine and needs longer ageing. The palate is full, concentrated, and perfectly formed by the Cabernet with soft tannins, well-integrated oak, good length, and great persistence.

Reception The environment is wonderful with the château perched on a hill and completely surrounded by vines.

How to get there *(Map 3): From Libourne to Fronsac via D670. Turn right in the center of Fronsac, towards Villegouge and Vérac, then second on the left (sign to Moulin Pey-Labrie). Turn right after 700m and follow the sign.*

The *régisseur* Peter Kjellberg.

Château Grand Renouil & Château du Pavillon

Owner Michel Ponty. **Cellarmaster** Peter Kjellberg. **Address** Les chais du port, 33126 Fronsac - Tel. 05.57.51.29.57 Fax 05.57.74.08.47. **Open** From Monday to Friday, 8:00-12:00 and 14:00-17:00. **Spoken** English.

Michel Ponty cultivates two small domaines in Canon-Fronsac. Château Grand Renouil comprises 5.5 hectares of old vines, average age 40 years, exclusively planted to Merlot on well-worked soils. A severe system of selection has ushered in a second label, Le Petit Renouil, which is produced from grapes from the young vines (under 15 years) and those from lighter soils. Finesse in the wine is achieved by a moderate length of maceration and by the maturation in a percentage of new oak barrels (20%) for a period of around ten months in accordance with the vintage. The quality of the tannins provides a well constituted, deeply colored, and concentrated wine which is also very aromatic. This is a great Merlot-based wine with seductive aromas and firm structure. Château du Pavillon '95 (approx. 70 F) is a softer, more delicate wine with lovely extract, long, toasted finish, and remarkable persistence.

Our choice Château Grand Renouil '94 (76 F) for its fruit, concentration and finesse and definitely Château Grand Renouil '95 (approx. 80 F). This wine has greater depth and a more distinct character than the Château du Pavillon but will mature slowly. The palate is supple, fine, fruity (black currant), and spicy. The elegant oak complements without smothering the wine. The finish is long and persistent but the wine needs a little more bottle age.

Reception In the offices of the *negociant* house where a reception and tasting room are being completed.

How to get there *(Map 3): From Libourne to Fronsac via D670. Turn left at the entrance to the village towards the Dordogne river and the port. The cellars are on the right.*

Grégoire Hubau also knows how to repair toys.

Château Moulin Pey-Labrie & Château Haut-Lariveau

Owners Bénédicte and Grégoire Hubau. **Address** 33126 Fronsac - Tel. 05.57.51.14.37 Fax 05.57.51.53.45. **Open** By appointment. **Spoken** English.

Arriving from the north of France in 1988, Bénédicte and Grégoire Hubau chose to be ambitious in the way they managed the two domaines they had just acquired. They immediately set about working the soil, vinifying parcel by parcel in small vats, and making a strict selection of each vat. The soil and grape varieties, 70% Merlot and 20% Cabernet Sauvignon, were ideal for producing the powerful, well-extracted style of wine they wanted to make. "We like exaggerated things and certainly not those that are lifeless," they say in all honesty. For Château Haut-Lariveau (Fronsac) preference is given to the '95 (approx. 58 F) for its finesse, fruit, ripeness, and well-integrated oak. The '94 (55 F) also has elegance but the oak is still a little overstated. Château Moulin Pey-Labrie (Canon-Fronsac) provides a range of good vintages. The '93 (68 F) has the spicy aroma of cloves, a solid structure, power, and length. The '94 (70 F) is powerful with dense but fine extract, and a note of licorice. The oak still needs to mellow.

Our choice Château Moulin Pey-Labrie '95 (72 F). For its intense aroma, full and elegant palate, dense but silky tannins, and great length. A wine to age.

Reception A bed and breakfast will be opening shortly in the old windmill which is presently being restored.

How to get there *(Map 3): From Libourne to Fronsac via D670. Turn right in the center of Fronsac, towards Villegouge then second on the left. Shortly after turn right and follow the sign.*

Jacques Rodet in front of the stencils used for marking the barrels.

Château Brulesécaille

Owners Martine and Jacques Rodet. **Address** 33710 Tauriac - Tel. 05.57.68.40.31 Fax 05.57.68.21.27. **Open** From Monday to Saturday, 9:00 -12:00 and 15:00-19:00, Saturday afternoon and Sunday, by appointment. **Credit Cards** Visa, Eurocard, MasterCard.

Don't lose sight of the little Brouillon stream. It's the natural frontier, more eternal than any political barrier, which separates two linguistic cultures, the *oïl* and the *oc*. The name Brulesécaille means "the burning of the vine-shoots after pruning" and indicates that the vine wasn't planted here yesterday. The 13-hectare domaine is planted in one unit with a roughly equal percentage of Merlot and Cabernet. It is ideally situated on a clay-limestone hillslope which allows the grapes to ripen to full maturity and which provides naturally well-structured wines, even for the Merlot. The wines, which are not over-extracted, are velvety and well-matured, without being over-oaked. They have improved since 1993 when partial hand-picking and sorting of the grapes at the cellar were reintroduced. The white Côtes-de-Bourg '96 (27 F), tasted in barrel, is lemony, crisp, well-constituted, and harmonizes well with the oak.

Our choice Côtes-de-Bourg red '94 (36 F) for its open, fruity aroma, well-formed and elegant palate, lively and resolute character, and length and persistence. The '95 (approx. 40 F), tasted in barrel, has just about everything. It is loaded with fruit, has a velvety extract, good structure which balances out some fine but discreet oak. This is a wine to age for two or three years.

Reception Martine Rodet receives visitors in a large tasting-room installed in what was formerly the *vendangeurs* hall. It's possible to rent a *gîte* for the weekend (650 F) or the week (1,000 - 1,750 F according to the season).

How to get there *(Map 3): From Saint-André-de-Cubzac take D669 towards Bourg. Turn right at La Lustre (8km) and follow the signs.*

The beautiful 17th century château.

Château Falfas

Owners John and Véronique Cochran. **Address** 33710 Bayon - Tel. 05.57.64.80.41 Fax 05.57.64.93.24. **Open** By appointment. **Spoken** English, Spanish.

The present owners acquired this domaine in 1989 and now cultivate the land bio-dynamically, bringing a certain balance to the vineyard where Merlot, at the expense of Cabernet, is the dominant variety. In order to develop the aromatic aspect of the wines, often simply viewed in light of their structure, a long vatting-time, including a cold prefermentation maceration, has been introduced and the temperatures meticulouly controlled. Will Falfas become the iron fist in a velvet glove? Certainly, both *cuvées* for the vintages 1994 and 1995 should be "eye openers" as this domaine is making constant progress. The '94, theoretically an inferior vintage, could well surpass the '90, which we placed above last year, when the process of vinification and maturation has been assimilated. The *cuvée* Chevalier '94 (70 F) is in effect rich, reserved, with soft extract, and confirmed style and remains attractive with aromatic notes of spice and dried fruits on the palate following a spicy, floral nose. The oak is well-integrated and the finish long and crisp.

Our choice Côtes-de-Bourg '94 (43 F). For a sensible price here is a wine with ripe, open nose, full, dense palate, and plenty of extract that remains fine and present. The oak is well-integrated and the finish long, providing a wine that can age a little longer still. The quality of fruit in the '95 indicates an exceptional vintage.

Reception Excellent, in a small cellar.

How to get there *(Map 3): From Bourg towards Blaye via D669. Turn right after 4km towards Bayon. Go through the village. The château is on the right.*

The new cellar at the domaine, ultra-modern on the outside, traditional inside.

Château Haut-Macô

Owners Jean and Bernard Mallet. **Address** 33710 Tauriac - Tel. 05.57.68.81.26 Fax 05.57.68.91.97. **Open** From Monday to Saturday 8:00-12:00 and 14:00-19:00.

Historically, an important domaine in the appellation which constantly seeks to improve quality. The soils are now partially worked or seeded with grass, the vineyard managed in compliance with an hourly weather report and the vines trained in accordance with each parcel. Following a long vatting period the maturation in barrel is handled a stage at a time. "Like the pages of a novel, some are more interesting than others." Only the wines that have been rigorously selected are aged in oak. "'Into oak for you, you've merited it', we tell the wine," say the Mallet brothers with an amusing sense of imagery. The wood ageing produces wines that are rich, fine, and full with well-integrated oak. The Bordeaux Clairet '95 (23 F) aged on regularly stirred lees has a toasted aroma with plenty of volume, fruit, and a satisfyingly light tannic structure, making it a very agreeable rosé. The domaine also offers a simple Bordeaux, Domaine de Lilotte. The '95 (approx. 20 F) is all fruit, with marked "tears" and attractive character.

Our choice Cuvée Jean-Bernard '93 (43 F). This is a great success for a difficult vintage and is a wine with finesse. The '94 (approx. 41 F) will of course have more concentration and firmer tannins but the same elegance. It is on the other hand longer on the finish and more persistent and should be ready for drinking in a year.

Reception Don't miss the visit to the barrel cellar and the view of the barrels ranged in a semicircle.

How to get there *(Map 3): Saint-André-de-Cubzac to Pugnac via N137. Turn left at the cooperative in Pugnac and follow the signs.*

Philippe Estournet.

Château La Tuilière

Owners Philippe Estournet. **Address** 33710 Saint-Ciers de Canesse - Tel. 05.57.64.80.90 Fax 05.57.64.89.97. **Open** By appointment. **Spoken** English.

Philippe Estournet was previously an engineer (Boeing aircraft engines and pipelines in Borneo hold no secrets for him) and then a tour operator. When he acquired the domaine in 1991 he knew nothing about wine. Two years later this hard worker was top of his class at the Bordeaux Faculty of Enology, where he took all the courses. The 13.5-hectare vineyard, which surrounds the house, is mainly planted with Merlot (70%). The clay-limestone vineyard, formed in a south-facing circle, produces really ripe, well-built wines which are rounder and fruitier than in the early years when Philippe was trying to achieve recognition and impose a style. The barrel ageing will be better handled in the coming years with, in particular, a smaller percentage of new oak. It's a domaine which is still in a period of gestation and trying to find its mark but without doubt one to follow in order to have the pleasure of being one of the first to discover it.

Our choice Château La Tuilière '94 (33 F). Chosen for its teasingly fruity nose. The palate is defined, lively, and supple but structured with well-integrated wood. The '95, which is richer and more concentrated is also available. Tasted at the beginning of its stay in barrel, the '96 is better still and should be ready to drink within two to three years.

Reception Good. In a building that is still being restored.

How to get there *(Map 3): From Bourg to Blaye via D669. Turn right 4km after Bayon towards Saint-Ciers. Turn right at the post office and follow the signs.*

Gilbert Dubois, the *régisseur* and "memory" of the domaine.

Château de Belcier

Owner Assurances Macif. **Manageur** Gilbert Dubois. **Address** 33350 Les Salles de Castillon - Tel. 05.57.40.62.90 Fax 05.57.40.64.25. **Open** From Monday to Friday 8:00-12:00 and 14:00-16:00.

François de Belcier constructed the château around 1780 specially to receive a king who never came. It belonged to an old Bordeaux family who were linked to the Montaigne dynasty owing to the fact that one of the distant relations had married Madeleine Eyquem de Montaigne, niece of the author of *Essais*. Bought and sold a number of times, the domaine experienced mixed fortunes until acquired, as a status symbol, by an insurance company in 1986. The "memory" of the domaine is undoubtedly the *régisseur*, Gilbert Dubois, who has worked for three different owners. Remarkably restored, the château lies at the center of the 52-hectare vineyard which is planted with Merlot (60%), Cabernet (35%) and Malbec. The '93 (51 F), dominated by Merlot, has an intense, spicy aroma, and round, tannic, generous palate. The '92 (46 F), a surprise for the vintage, is light and supple and easy to drink now. The domaine also produces a second label, Château de Monrecueil, of which the '94 (39 F) is round and fruity with soft tannins.

Our choice Château de Belcier '94 (50 F). For its ripe nose, well-balanced and structured palate and well-integrated oak. It has good length and a persistent note of black fruits. The '95 will be a wine of great elegance.

Reception Pleasant. Visitors received in the cellar, often by the *régisseur.*

How to get there *(Map 3): 10km from Castillon-la-Bataille towards Villefranche via D21. Turn left just after Le Theolat and follow the signs.*

Tiny churches are spread throughout this little-known appellation.

Châteaux Puygueraud et Les Charmes-Godard

Owner Family Thienpont. **Address** Lauriol, 33570 Saint-Cibard - Tel. 05.57.40.61.04/ 05.57. 40.63.76 Fax 05.57.40.66.08. **Open** By appointment.

Have you heard of Oudenaarde? It's the fief of the Thienpont de Berlaere family. Have you heard of the Thienpont tribe? Perhaps not, unless you are a lover of Vieux Château Certan, a famous Pomerol estate, owned by this family who originated in Flanders. Georges, the patriarch, surrounded by his 13 children, settled at Puygueraud in 1946. It was a gamble as the Côtes-de-Francs vineyards had been virtually consigned to history. Thirty years later, entirely replanted, the domaine is the appellation leader. Nicolas Thienpont now vinifies the wines from the various domaines owned by the clan. Château La Claverie offers supple wines among which the '94 (40 F) is recommended. Château Les Charmes-Godard is the most Merlot-based wine with a round, fruity character. The '94 (40 F) is particularly successful. There is also a white wine, produced from Semillon (75%), Muscadelle (20%), and Sauvignon Gris, which has been barrel fermented and aged on regularly stirred lees. The '94 (40 F) and the '95 (45 F) are crisp, fruity, and rich.

Our choice Château Puygueraud '89 (60 F). Chosen for its intense, ripe aroma, ample and well-structured palate due to the higher than uaual percentage of Cabernet for the appellation. This generous, fruity wine is full of vitality and to be either drunk or aged a little.

Reception Welcoming, even if direct sales from the property are not the principal objective of the Thienpont family.

How to get there *(Map 3): Castillon-la-Bataille to Saint-Genès towards Villefranche via D17. Turn onto D123 to Saint-Philippe-d'Aiguille, Saint-Cibard and Saint-Cibard-Pimpine, then follow signs.*

Sunrise over the vineyard at Saillans.

Château Dalem

Owner Michel Rullier. **Address** 33141 Saillans - Tel. 05.57.84.34.18 Fax 05.57.74.39.85. **Open** By appointment. **Spoken** English, Spanish.

A well-situated vineyard, dominated by Merlot (85%), which after a long vatting period and ageing in a percentage of new oak, produces deeply colored wines which are dense, vigorous, tannic, and firmly structured. They need to age for a certain length of time in order to tame the acidic structure, mature the tannins and mellow the wine. Then they become supple but retain their natural character. As proof of this the domaine offers for sale an impressive collection of old vintages dating back 30 years. The '89 (84 F) is dominated by ripe Merlot, explodes with fruit and has a crisp, acidic freshness. The '88 (75.50 F) has begun to evolve but the palate which is powerful, balanced, and vigorous on the finish ensures that the wine is not past its best. The wine is austere without being disagreeable. The '85 (93.50 F), now at its peak, is balanced with soft, inviting tannins but is still garbed in a youthful structure.

Our choice The '90 (77.50 F). The nose is ripe but still reserved. The palate is Merlot dominated, fine with firm tannins. The attractive, chewy quality on the finish should diminish with age. A wine to age a little longer.

Reception A pretty château which overlooks the vineyard and the river Isle.

How to get there *(Map 3): From Libourne via D670 in the direction of Fronsac. Turn right before Fronsac towards Saillans via D128. The château is on the right just after Saillans.*

Château La Rivière, a patchwork of architectural styles.

Château La Rivière

Manager Jacques Santier. **Cellarmaster** Didier Gouyou. **Address** 33126 La Rivière - Tel. 05.57. 55.56.56 Fax 05.57.24.94.39. **Open** Juni - end September 9:00-11:00 and 14:00-17:00, the rest of the year by appointment. Admission price 25 F **Spoken** English, German. **Credit cards** Visa, Eurocard, MasterCard.

This is an astonishing and monumental château, renovated by Viollet-Le-Duc, which mixes the architectural styles of the Renaissance and 16th century. It possesses 5 hectares of undergroud cellars, hewn out of the limestone rock, where the wines are aged in barrel and bottle. This large domaine, consisting of 51 hectares planted mainly with old vines of 40 - 100 years of age, with Merlot the dominant variety (set to increase further with the new plantings), has just had a change of ownership. We will have to wait for the final presentation of the '95 vintage to judge the new style of vinification but the touch of Michel Rolland, the star enologist of the Libournais, is sure to be found. Based on tastings following the harvest the wine will have more weight and finesse. The '91 (70 F), which is still available, has started to evolve. The '93 (60 F) lacks concentration. It's the '94 (65 F) which marks the turning point in the evolution of the domaine with its well-constituted palate, concentration, and tannic structure.

Our choice The '95 (approx. 75 F). Tasted from a provisional blend, but the wine promises to be appetizing. The nose is ripe and present and the palate fine, linear, very elegant with cleverly worked oak. Wait to drink.

Reception Don't miss visiting the splendid and sumptuously arranged labyrinth of cellars.

How to get there *(Map 3): From Libourne towards Saint-André-de-Cubzac via D670 passing through Fronsac and Saint-Michel. The château is on the right on leaving La Rivière.*

Jean-Noël Hervé holds court in his cellar.

Château Moulin Haut-Laroque

Owner Jean-Noël Hervé. **Address** 33141 Saillans - Tel. 05.57.84.32.07 Fax 05.57.84.31.84. **Open** By appointment. **Spoken** English, German.

The 15-hectare domaine is scattered over a variety of soils including a limestone plateau and molasse hillsides. Merlot (65%) is the dominant grape variety and there are some old vines, one-third of which are over 65 years. All this allows Jean-Noël Hervé the possibility of gradually blending wines from the different parcels during the maturation period, for instance, each time the wine is racked or moved. From 42 different parcels he creates 20 batches of wine, all of which mature differently in the 250 barrels in the cellar. An '86 (price on request) is still available which has a bouquet evolving towards white truffles. The palate, with a note of cherry brandy, is particularly powerful. However, it doesn't have the glycerol "fat" which can only be perceived in the wines from 1988 onwards when the barrel ageing becomes more clearly defined. The '88 (price on request) has now opened out and has a dense extract which is well-balanced by the structure and acidity of the wine. It is rich with the attractive aroma of currants and raisins.

Our choice The '95 (70 F). This was tasted from barrel but with the final blend already made. The nose is clean and ripe and has the aroma of black fruits. The palate is full, rich, and impressive with well-formed tannins supplied by the old Cabernet Franc. The fruit is crisp and fleshy and the oak well-integrated. The finish is long and persistent with a spicy, smoky (Lapsang tea) note. This is a great wine and should be cellared.

Reception In the beautiful cellar which is Jean-Noël Hervé's "living-room".

How to get there *(Map 3): From Libourne via D670 in the direction of Fronsac. Turn right before Fronsac towards Saillans via D128. The château is on the left at the entrance to Saillans.*

François Dubrey, one of the leading lights in the southern Graves, in the *cuverie* of his property.

Château d'Ardennes

Owners Suzanne and François Dubrey. **Address** 33720 Illats - Tel. 05.56.62.53.80 Fax 05.56. 62.43.67. **Open** From Monday to Friday, 9:00 -12:00 and 14:00-18:00, preferably by appointment **Closed** Sept. 15 - Oct. 10. **Spoken** English.

This is a vast domaine of 60 hectares, a third white and two thirds red, and one of the leading lights of the southern Graves. It has patches of limestone soil which add a touch of power to the reds. This feature cannot be found in the neigboring properties, all of which have pure gravel soils. Fifty-year-old François Dubrey has been assisted since 1994 by his son Cyril, an enologist and agricultural engineer who also has a 5-hectare property, Château Mirebeau, in Pessac-Léognan. The first vintage, 1996, looks promising. François Dubrey has for a long time struggled alone to give recognition to the Graves appellation. He is tired of vintners who "only think about hunting game." This is his allusion to the lack of commercial dynamism there is in the region. To his credit Château d'Ardennes proves each year to be as good, if not better than certain wines in Pessac-Léognan. The powerful, oaky, white Graves '96 (56 F), produced from 70% Semillon and 30% Sauvignon, opens out on the palate with a little aeration and maintains a lively freshness.

Our choice The Château d'Ardennes '90 was one of the best in the appellation but there is none for sale. The '94 (60 F) is a transitional vintage while waiting for the '95 (61 F). As usual the wine has a dark-colored hue, resinous and chocolaty, and plenty of concentration with vegetal, smoky, black fruit notes and a complex finish. It should open out in two to five years.

Reception In the new vinification cellar, by an energetic family.

How to get there *(Map 3): 35km south of Bordeaux via A62, towards Toulouse. Exit at Podensac, towards Illats and Artigues. The domaine is on the left of D11.*

Jean-Noël Belloc studies the distinct gravel soils. "It's this that provides 80% of the quality of our wines."

Château Brondelle

Owner Jean-Noël Belloc. **Address** 33210 Langon - Tel. 05.56.62.38.14 Fax 05.56.62.23.14. **Open** From Monday to Friday, 8:00-12:00 and 14:00-19:00. **Spoken** English.

South of Langon, in the far southern corner of the Graves, the 41 hectares of Château Brondelle are located on deep stony-clay soils. "A hill similar to that of Haut-Brion," states Jean-Noël Belloc, until 1988 an accountant with IBM. The situation was different in 1925 when his grandfather bought the property. "In this region viticulture was only a complementary activity practiced alongside the cultivation of cereal and tobacco crops and the rearing of cattle. It was my grandfather who stopped this type of mixed farming." As a vestige of the era the cellar has been installed in a building that was formerly used for drying tobacco. If Brondelle is recognized for its well-built red wines, produced from 60% Cabernet Sauvignon and 40% Merlot, there is also an attractive selection of whites' made from Semillon and Sauvignon. The barrel aged Cuvée Anaïs '95 (60 F) has a toasted, ripe fruit nose with notes of vanilla and mandarin orange and a full, supple, powerful, and persistent palate. The sweet white Graves Supérieur '95 (45 F) has a deep golden hue, 14% alcohol, a toasted, crystallized fruit nose and slightly sugary palate with a lovely mellow attack. The wine is short on the finish but not cloying and is ideal with foie gras or as an aperitif.

Our choice The regular white Graves '96 (40 F). Tasted unfiltered. The nose expresses a ripe maturity without any dominant varietal characteristics. It is crisp, linear, refined with an attractive fruitiness and good weight without being heavy. It is already pleasant to drink.

Reception In the former barrel cellar, now traditionally restored.

How to get there *(Map 3): 42km southeast of the Bordeaux Rocade via A62. Exit at Langon, towards Bazas. Turn right after 4km towards Mazère. The château is on the left.*

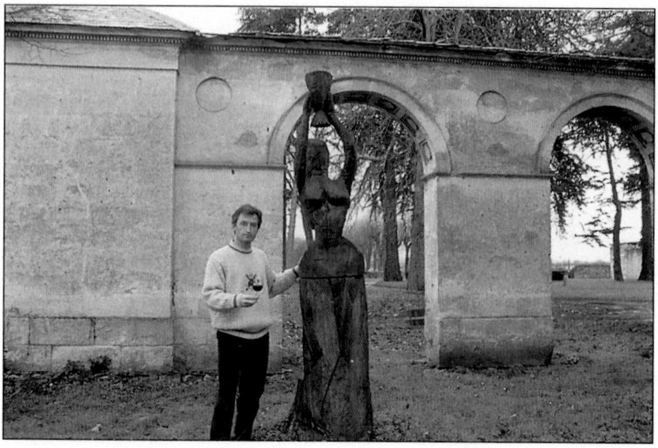

Dominique Haverlant in front of one of the archways of Vieux Château Gaubert which he started restoring in 1988.

Vieux Château Gaubert

Owner Dominique Haverlant. **Address** 33640 Portets - Tel. 05.56.67.04.32 Fax 05.56.67.52.76. **Open** From Mo. to Fri., 9:00 -12:00 and 14:00-17:30. Weekend by appointment **Spoken** English, German.

Dominique Haverlant is patiently restoring his château, a large *chartreuse* with archways surrounding the courtyard, which fell into ruin in the 18th century. "I reckon on finally installing my cellar here in two years. For the moment the priority has to be given to the vineyard." Dominique, the son and grandson of vintners, now has 35 hectares under production. A dynamic and ambitious man, he has also replanted the *clos* opposite the château with a high density of 8 500 vines per hectare. This is rare for the Graves appellation where the norm is usually 4 000 to 5 000 vines per hectare. Since the '93 vintage the Cabernet and Merlot in the red Graves appears more concentrated, the result of a long period of maceration. The wines have good fruit supported by barrel ageing in up to 40% new oak casks. This is a promising domaine with real quality-driven objectives. The white Graves '95 (57 F) has a steady golden color. The ripeness of the fruit is evident on the nose with a note of crystallized fruit and there is also a hint of toasted oak. The palate has fine extract, medium weight and an elegant finish.

Our choice The red Graves '94 (54 F). Vivid red hue, quite deep for the vintage with a spicy, resinous nose, and suave palate enriched by the toasted aroma and oak extract. The wine has the same generosity on the finish and a youthful vitality. A remarkable success for the vintage. Should be aged.

Reception In a tasting room at the entrance to the *chartreuse* managed by Dominique's assistant Sandrine.

How to get there *(Map 3): 21km southeast of the Bordeaux Rocade via A62. Exit La Brède, towards Langon. Follow N113 to Portets. The château is on the left at the entrance to the village.*

Marie-José Degas and her daughter Dany in the winter garden.

Château Haut-Gayat

Owners Marie-José and Dany Degas. **Address** La Souloire 33750 Saint-Germain du Puch - Tel. 05.57.24.52.32 Fax 05.57.24.03.72. **Open** By appointment. **Spoken** Spanish, some English .

Despite the slightly confusing name the appellation Graves-de-Vayres is not found in the Médoc but in the Libournais on the left bank of the Dordogne. This forgotten zone in the Entre-Deux-Mers has remained true to local viticultural tradition despite being broken up by the autoroutes, freeways and roundabouts which have dissected the countryside and vineyards. At the better producers there are some good wines at attractive prices to be discovered. Marie-José Degas, now assisited by her daughter Dany, tends her 15 hectare vineyard, with parcels scattered throughout the appellation, in the same way she cultivates her 3 hectare garden. Attention is given to every detail with each of the different parcels of vines occupying one of the 35 fermentation vats. The winemaking is clearly defined with the soils worked or seeded with grass, no white wines made and a fairly long vatting time for the reds. The barrel ageing is carefully reviewed with the wine placed in seasoned oak, one third of which is renewed yearly. As the wine evolves it resembles its environment, rigorous and formal in youth, more open when with age it comes to maturity. Only Marie-José Degas never changes, remaining optimistic and motivated.

Our choice Graves-de-Vayres '95 (31 F). For the clean, fruity, open nose and very ripe palate with fine tannins and a note of black fruits, then spices. There is also a fine but discreet oakiness. To drink now but can be aged a little.

Reception Attentive. In the tasting room.

How to get there *(Map 3): From Libourne towards Bordeaux via N89. Turn left after Arveyres towards Saint-Germain-du-Puch via D20. The cave is on the right in the centre of the village. Large sign.*

Over a period of 20 years Bernard Thomassin has elevated Château de France to a place alongside the best in Pessac-Léognan.

Château de France

Owner Bernard Thomassin. **Address** 33850 Léognan - Tel. 05.56.64.75.39 Fax 05.56.64.72.13. **Open** From Monday to Friday, 9:00-12:00 and 14:00-18:00. **Spoken** English, Portuguese.

The owner of Château de France evidently adores birds. This is proven by the names of exotic birds he has given to his second labels: Bec en Sabot (red) and Ganga Cata (white). "It's my father's passion," says Arnaud Thomassin, who manages on a daily basis the 32-hectare property (28 hectares of red and 4 white). The reds combine 60% Cabernet Sauvignon with 40% Merlot. Château de France '94 (70,40 F), powerful, firm, and direct is presently passing through an austere stage. It should taste better in 1998-1999. The Bec en Sabot '95 (39,80 F) with the aroma of red fruits and lightly oaked offers simple, easy drinking. Since 1992 the consequential percentage of Muscadelle used in the white Château de France has been transferred to the second wine, Ganga Cata. Consequently, the white Château de France, which is dominated by Sauvignon Blanc, has taken on depth and weight. The Ganga Cata '95 (36,25 F) with its discreet nose and crisp, fresh palate is ideal with seafood dishes.

Our choice Château de France white '95 (78 F). Aromatic and fresh with notes of citrus and tropical fruits that are also present on the palate. The oak dominates the attack but the finish is clean, crisp and long.

Reception Visitors are received by the domaine staff in a new shop which gives on to the terrace and vineyard. A tasting has to be requested. An appointment is needed for visits to the cellar.

How to get there *(Map 3): 9km south of the Bordeaux Rocade, exit Léognan (18B). Leave Léognan in the direction of Saucats and follow the signs.*

In 1989 and 1990 Francis Boutemy planted this vast hillock of 13 hectares which was formerly a pine forest.

Château Haut-Lagrange

Owner Francis Boutemy. **Address** 31, route de Loustalade, 33850 Léognan - Tel. 05.56.64.09.93 Fax 05.56.64.10.08. **Open** From Monday to Saturday, 9:00-12:00 and 14:00-18:00, by appointment.

Originally from a family in the north of France with long-standing ties in the Pessac-Léognan region, Francis Boutemy has built this domaine entirely. Neighbor to Château Larrivet Haut-Brion, there wasn't a single vine on this vast plateau until 1988. "But according to Cassini's famous map of 1764 this area was covered in vines," insists Francis Boutemy. The young vines were cultivated with care and attention. The soil was broken up a meter below the surface to install underground drainage. "This was done in order not to mix the surface soil and to keep the *terroir* homogenous and to make the development of the root system of the young vines easier." The vigor of these vines is held in check by green harvesting. The white wines, produced from 1.7 hectares of Semillon and Sauvignon, have rapidly expressed themselves. The '95 (55 F) has a full but discreet oaky nose, fine, long palate with medium intensity and should be ready to drink from 1998. Of the red wines, the '94 (55 F) displays the freshness typical of Haut-Lagrange, with a firmer extract than in '95. This wine is still a little austere on the finish and needs another three years bottle ageing.

Our choice Château Haut-Lagrange red '95 (58 F). Tasted from barrel this wine shows a firm, elegant extract with tannins that have the typical finesse and suppleness of a good Graves. It has an attractive, fresh finish. To drink within three to four years.

Reception In a recently restored cellar which is still undergoing change.

How to get there *(Map 3): 10km south of the Bordeaux Rocade, exit 18A. Take N113, towards Langon. Turn right at Bouscaut towards Léognan via D111. The domaine is signposted to the right after 5km.*

Jean de Laitre, the head of the most recently created domaine in Pessac-Léognan.

Château Le Thil - Comte Clary

Owner Family de Laitre. **Supervisor** Jean and Arnaud de Laitre. **Address** 33850 Léognan - Tel. 05.56.30.01.02 Fax 05.56.30.04.32. **Open** Every day by appointment. **Spoken** English.

In 1990, Jean de Laitre, a medical student resident in Paris, learned that his family had the opportunity to plant vines on agricultural wasteland. He abandoned his Hippocratic oath to construct this 10.6 hectare domaine in Pessac-Léognan with his brother Arnaud, a farmer in the Indre *département.* Located in the middle of a triangle of *Crus Classés* (Châteaux Bouscaut, Carbonnieux and Smith-Haut-Lafitte) the land, once cleared, revealed original soil of pure limestone-clay rock "with a number of characteristics similar to Saint-Emilion." The well-structured red wines show good ageing potential and already show a certain character. The '94 (62 F) has spicy, pomaded, Havana cigar flavors, a solid extract with toasted, crystallized fruit notes, but is still dominated by the oak which should mellow out in one to two years. The '95 (68 F), tasted in barrel, presents a solid, firmly knit, spicy extract with the flavor of black currant, blackberry and tobacco. Upright and very concentrated this looks like being a superb wine. Of the white wines, the excellent '95 (68 F) has a generously oaky nose, toasted notes and a crisp, elegant, fruity attack on the palate which continues with a delicate note of finesse.

Our choice Château Le Thil - Comte Clary white '96 (approx. 70 F). Tasted just before bottling. The nose is intense with smoky, toasted, ripe citrus fruit notes. The stylish palate shows real ripeness. In all a wine with great finesse, good balance and freshness on the finish. A very fine wine.

Reception The story of the domaine makes up for the rather uninteresting cellar.

How to get there *(Map 3): 10km south of the Bordeaux Rocade, exit 18A. Take N113, towards Langon. Turn right at Bouscaut towards Léognan, then left following the signs. The new cellar is on the left, before Smith-Haut-Lafitte.*

Charmail subjects the grapes to a cold prefermentation maceration in order to produce a maximum of elegance and suppleness in the wines.

Château Charmail

Owner Roger Sèze. **Address** 33180 Saint-Seurin de Cadourne - Tel. 05.56.59.70.63 Fax 05.56.59.39.20. **Open** From Mon. to Fri., 9:00 - 12:00 and 14:00-18:00. Weekend by appointment. **Spoken** English.

At the limits of Saint-Estèphe, Château Charmail extends over 22 hectares in one single unit. The property was acquired 15 years ago by Roger Sèze, the son of a vintner in Fronsac, following the completion of his studies in agronomy. In 1990, with the aid of enologist Michel Couasnon, he launched into a series of vinification experiments including cold prefermentation maceration. "The material can be extracted without any harshness, above all the tannins from the skins and not from the pips." Matured for a year in oak barrels and neither fined nor filtered the wines of Charmail possess a deep, violet color in their youth, the aroma of truffles, plums and then red fruits and an amazing softness. The '93 (44 F), intense in color, has well-integrated oak and has kept its fruit content. The wine is fluid but firm on the finish, expressing an attractive freshness in true Charmail style and should be ready to drink in two years. The '94 (46 F) has plenty of color, well-integrated toasted oak, subdued tannins which rest firm, a crisp, fluid extract, evident red fruit flavors, and a marked oakiness. This is a wine to age.

Our choice Château Charmail '95 (approx. 50 F). Extremely dark color. The intense nose has the aroma of pine resin, freshly ground coffee and black fruits. The attack on the palate is round with just a hint of vanilla. This is followed by the flavor of damp earth, evoking a nuance of Pauillac, and crushed black currant berries. The soft but present tannins impart a certain power. The wine has an attractive fresh finish.

Reception Visits to the cellar given by a passionate winemaker.

How to get there *(Map 3): 54km north of Bordeaux. Exit 7 on the Rocade, towards Blanquefort. Follow D2 to Saint-Estèphe, then signs to Saint-Seurin-de-Cadourne.*

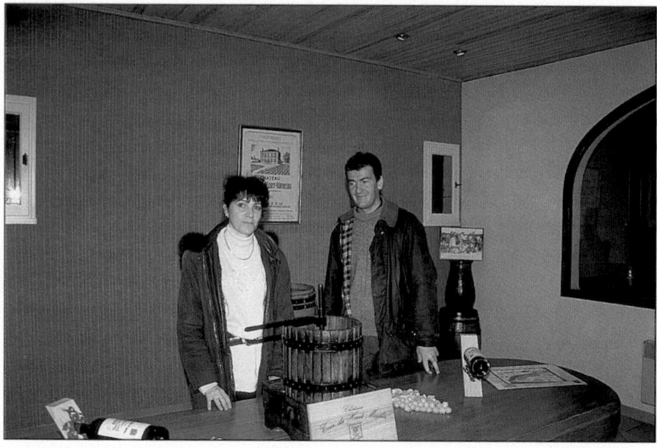

Béatrice Poitou and her brother Lionel whose red wines are perfect over six to eight years.

Château Tour du Haut-Moulin

Owners Béatrice and Lionel Poitou. **Address** Cussac-le-Vieux, 33460 Cussac-Fort-Médoc - Tel. 05.56.58.91.10 Fax 05.56.58.99.30. **Open** From Monday to Friday, 9:30 -12:00 and 14:00-17:00. **Spoken** English. **Credit cards** Visa, Eurocard, MasterCard.

Béatrice Poitou and her brother Lionel run this traditional *Cru Bourgeois* estate whose cellar is located at Lauga, 1km from the old castle, Fort-Médoc, in close proximity to the Gironde estuary. The domaine comprises 30 hectares divided into a number of parcels with 50% Cabernet Sauvignon, 45% Merlot and 5% Petit Verdot. Until 1990, the grape varieties were vinified together. "This became impossible with the difficult years of '91, '92, and '93 as the difference in ripeness was too great," explains Lionel, the winemaker. The wines are vinified in unlined, concrete vats, then aged carefully in oak barrels, one-third of which are renewed yearly. The château produces 200 000 bottles of the same wine and no second label. Château Tour du Haut-Moulin is a classic Médoc, lightly oaked, with substance and a good tannic structure which has become particularly refined over the last few years. The '94 (60 F) is mellowing out nicely and can be drunk today or in four years.

Our choice Château Tour du Haut-Moulin '95 (approx. 65 F). A fruity, linear, upright wine, with dense but fine, soft tannins, and a long spicy finish. The wine has plenty of charm.

Reception Welcoming visits given by Béatrice and Lionel.

How to get there *(Map 3): 31km north of Bordeaux. Exit 7 on the Rocade, towards Blanquefort. Follow D2 to Cussac Fort-Médoc. The château is indicated in the center of the village.*

Dep Ouadjet des Ors de Sothis (the dog) and Marianne Berry (the vintner).

Clos de l'Église

Owner Marianne Berry. **Address** 33500 Lalande-de-Pomerol - Tel. 05.57.51.40.25 Fax 05.57.74.17.13. **Open** By appointment.

Marianne Berry takes advantage of the fact that her 10 hectare vineyard is scattered over a variety of soils (gravel, clay-gravel, sandy-gravel) by planting different grape varieties and rootstocks in each parcel. This particularity continues in the cellar where each parcel of grapes is vinified separately. Her dislike of wood is remedied by a careful maturation of the wine enabling it to feed from the lees and breath a little during the process of racking. Despite the fact that the appellation Lalande-de-Pomerol is well suited to Merlot, Marianne Berry has a large percentage of Cabernet Franc and Sauvignon (40%) and also holds to her 2% Malbec. The wines have a particular style, accentuated when young, which is different from the rest of the appellation. “I like a wine which is harsh in the beginning and not at all attractive but which expresses its charm later on,” says Marianne Berry. You’d be convinced if she let you taste the older vintages which are often remarkably balanced and have plenty of finesse.

Our choice Clos de l’Eglise ’95 (approx. 70 F). Tasted during maturation. The nose is sound but still very closed. The palate is upright, with fine, delicate and present extract. A well-defined structure for a wine that is very long, persistent, and gourmand. A wine to age.

Reception Passionate.

How to get there *(Map 3): From Libourne towards Périgueux via N89. Turn left towards Lalande-de-Pomerol. The cellar is on the left at the entrance to the village, easily recognizable from the wooden panelling which gives it the appearance of a barn for drying tobacco. Small sign.*

Cellar master Vincent Duret.

Château Garraud

Owner Jean-Marc Nony. **Cellarmaster** Vincent Duret. **Address** 33500 Néac - Tel. 05.57.55.58.58 Fax 05.57.25.13.43. **Open** From Monday to Friday, 9:00-18:00, Saturday and Sunday morning by appointment. **Spoken** English. **Credit cards** Visa, Eurocard, MasterCard.

This is a large domaine of 32 hectares where plantings of Merlot are increasing but where the 80-year-old Cabernet Franc, which has resisted successive frosts, is still important for structure and finesse. The vines are meticulously cultivated with yields restricted and grapes sorted at the harvest. Each parcel is vinified separately and the wines partially aged in oak. This is a domaine that is making rapid progress and one of the rare estates in the appellation to offer older vintages. Of interest are the '94 (65 F), which is a little more tannic than the '95 (see our choice), the '93 (68 F) for its great structure in a difficult year and the smoky '89 (approx. 95 F) which is just beginning to open out. The '90 (196 F in magnums only) is of particular note for its richness, concentration, hint of red fruits and raw mushrooms, youth, and persistence of fruit. However, we prefer the more recent vintages which have clearly gained in finesse and texture.

Our choice Château Garraud '95 (67 F). Tasted during maturation from an early but not final blend. The nose is open and has ripe fruit aromas. The palate is fine and elegant with tightly knit, round tannins. The finish is long and persistent. A wine to keep.

Reception In a large reception room with bay-windows giving on to the vines.

How to get there *(Map 3): From Libourne towards Périgueux via N89. Turn right towards Néac then left following the signs. Pass in front of the pylons, cross the hamlet of Lavergne and the château is on the right.*

Bernard Levrault.

Château La Croix de la Chenevelle

Owners Madame and monsieur Levrault. **Address** La Grave, 33500 Lalande-de-Pomerol - Tel. 05.57.51.99.93 Fax 05.57.74.00.63. **Open** Every day 8:00-12:00 and 14:00-18:00. **Spoken** English. **Credit cards** Visa, Eurocard, MasterCard.

Following the tradition in appellation Lalande-de-Pomerol, Merlot dominates the blend here (90%) to produce round, fat, generally early drinking wines. This, however, is beginning to change. The latest vintages have benefited from grapes from recently acquired old vines and the cellar has been modernised to allow for the vinification of individual parcels. Since 1994 the wines have gained in concentration and finesse but without the loss of their fruit content. Bernard Levrault is particularly attentive to his vines and the *terroir* using only natural yeasts and working the soils. The maturation of the wines is also meticulously handled in 200 oak barrels of which one-third or one-quarter are renewed yearly according to the vintage. The length of ageing in barrel also varies according to the year so as not to dry out the wines. The extract is preserved by not filtering so if there is a deposit it's natural !

Our choice Château La Croix de la Chenevelle '95 (approx. 64 F). Tasted during maturation. The palate is dazzling, very ripe with black fruit, black currant, and wild cherry aromas, concentrated, and with fine tannins. The oak is well integrated and the wine has plenty of structure and good length. A wine to age. The '96 should be rich, fat and fruity.

Reception In a small tasting and sales room. The wines are also offered en *primeur* from Easter.

How to get there *(Map 3): From Libourne towards Périgueux via N89. Turn left towards Lalande-de-Pomerol. The cellar is in the center of the village, next to the beautiful Romanesque church.*

Patrice Pagès.

Château Fourcas-Dupré

Owner Patrice Pagès. **Address** 33480 Listrac-Médoc - Tel. 05.56.58.01.07 Fax 05.56.58.02.27. **Open** From Monday to Friday, 8:00-12:00 and 14:00-18:00. Weekend by appointment. **Spoken** English.

Acquired in 1843 by Jean-Baptiste Antoine Dupré, a barrister registered at the Bordeaux Court of Appeals, the estate was fully developed in 1844 with the addition of château, cellars and other agricultural buildings. Fourcas is the name of the gentle hillslope where the vines are planted. Assisted by his young enologist, Jean-Luc, Patrice Pagès has reorganized the vineyard to give an equal balance of Merlot and Cabernet Sauvignon (44% each) with a complement of 2% Petit Verdot. The vines are planted on Pyrenean gravel soils. The red wines of Fourcas-Dupré do not conform to the rustic image normally given to those of Listrac. Over the years the tannins have become refined and the wines have taken on weight and substance. As proof of this try the '94 (56 F) which is just beginning to open out. The '96 (available from summer 1998), tasted at an early stage, is soft and aromatic, and offers the character of an extremely ripe year. "The Cabernet came in at more than 12.3% and I've never seen that before," says Patrice. This will be a great wine.

Our choice Château Fourcas-Dupré '95 (60 F). The nose is ripe with notes of red fruits and licorice. The palate has been well-formed, with a passage through oak, and is round, velvety, powerful, with fine tannins. To drink from 1998.

Reception A welcome visit to the cellar is given by Patrice or one of the staff.

How to get there *(Map 3): 28,5km north of Bordeaux. Exit 7 on the Rocade, towards Castelnau-du-Médoc, then Listrac-Médoc. The château is on the right on the other side of Listrac.*

Lionel Bord.

Clos Jean

Owners Lionel and Nelly Bord. **Address** 33410 Haut-Loupiac - Tel. 05.56.62.99.83 Fax 05.56.62.93.55. **Open** By appointment.

The great sweet white wine appellations of Bordeaux, Sauternes and Barsac, tend to overshadow their little sisters. But Cérons, on the same bank of the river Garonne, Cadillac, Sainte-Croix-du-Mont and Loupiac, on the right bank, merit more than the condescension they are usually given. The situation, *terroir*, and climate of these appellations are also susceptible to producing great sweet wines providing the *vignerons* become completely involved. In addition, one of the principal advantages of these lesser known appellations is that the prices are far more attractive than those on the other side of the river. Lionel Bord makes wines "starting with the secateurs" by first nurturing the vines and the quality of the grapes. He regularly produces a delicious Loupiac which is balanced, floral, and has pure fruit flavors. The '95 (60 F) is particularly full and unctuous, spicy with notes of cinnamon and fruit kernel, with a long, dried apricot finish. Otherwise, have a fling and take the '55 (250 F) for its smoky, waxy nose and fullness on the palate with its waxy, sun-dried, curranty flavors.

Our choice Loupiac '95 (approx. 60 F). For the pure, clean nose and notes of apricot. The palate is fine and long on the attack, then settling to become dense without being syrupy thanks to a balancing freshness. Excellent length on the finish. A wine to cellar.

Reception In the cellar alongside the old hydraulic presses.

How to get there *(Map 3): From Bordeaux towards Langon via D10. Turn left 3km after Cadillac, at Loupiac, towards the village center then follow the signs up into the hills.*

The Siran *chartreuse*, formerly the property of the Comtes de Toulouse-Lautrec.

Château Siran

Owner William-Alain Miailhe. **Address** 33460 Labarde-Margaux - Tel. 05.57.88.34.04 Fax 05.57.88.70.05. **Open** Every day, 10:00-13:00 and 14:00-18:00. **Spoken** English, German. **Credit cards** Visa, Eurocard, MasterCard.

Under the supervision of Brigitte Miailhe, this historic 40-hectare estate, with 25 hectares in appellation Margaux, has over the last ten years made considerable efforts to put to good use its excellent sandy-gravel soil in the south of appellation Margaux. The soil has been drained, yields reduced, a new *cuverie* built, and the proportion of new oak barrels for maturing the wines increased. Before this Siran was already well-placed, producing wines for cellaring ('86, '89, '90) of the level of a *Cru Classé*. Since '95 a further impetus has been the arrival of consultant enologist Michel Rolland to oversee the vinification giving Siran additional power and velvety texture. The malolactic fermentation is now completed in new oak barrels, of which 70% are renewed yearly. Tasted during maturation the '96 looks like it will keep its promise of being a great year. Note: From the soil of the *palus* the Miailhes' produce an excellent Bordeau Supérieur, Le Saint-Jacques (35 F).

Our choice Château Siran '95 (130 F). Dark, intense on the nose and with an oaky exterieur. The texture of the palate is tight, mellow and long. A wine for long ageing. It defies the image of "lightweight" Margaux and in ten years will join the list of "greats" of the appellation with its complexity of bouquet.

Reception Well-organized and touristy. There is a tour through the long cellar, old fermenting room, cooperage and drawing-room. Visit and tasting: 20 F.

How to get there *(Map 3): 20km north of Bordeaux. Exit 7 on the Rocade, towards Blanquefort, Macau, Margaux via D2 route du Médoc. Turn right in Labarde and follow the signs.*

Château Paloumey, making a revival since 1990.

Châteaux La Bessane, Paloumey et La Garricq

Owner Martine Cazeneuve. **Address** Château Paloumey, 50, rue Pouge de Beau, 33290 Ludon-Médoc - Tel. 05.57.88.00.66 Fax 05.57.88.00.67. **Open** From Monday to Saturday, by appointment. **Spoken** English.

Leaving Blaye in 1990, the Cazeneuve family crossed the Gironde to install themselves at Paloumey, a *Cru Bourgeois* estate in the Haut-Médoc. The vines of this old property had been pulled up in 1954 and consequently no wines made since. Under the direction of Martine Cazeneuve, 18,5 ha were replanted with 55% Cabernet Sauvignon and 40% Merlot, including a good parcel on the plateau of La Lagune. The wines are marked by the ample fruitiness of the Merlot, accentuated by the youthful nature of the vines. This does not mean they lack concentration thanks to a severe selection of grapes at the harvest and to rigorous vinification. Under a rental agreement *(fermage)* the Cazeneuves' also took over in 1993 Château La Bessane in Margaux and Château La Garricq in Moulis. Both comprise 3 ha of vineyard. La Bessane is planted with 60-70% Petit Verdot, a variety that normally has a more minor rôle. Les Ailes de Paloumey, the second label of the Haut-Médoc, is an easy drinking, fruity, tender wine in '95 (52 F), to be consumed young.

Our choice Château Paloumey '95 (59 F). Very ripe, crystallized fruits, supple tannins, this is a vivid red to be appreciated young. Château La Garricq '95 (69 F) gains in substance and weight, with a finish marked by the barrel ageing. Age for another two years. Château La Bessane '95 (86 F) is a different style of wine. Still closed on the nose it is tight knit, airy, and long on the palate.

Reception Dynamic. Visitors are received by Martine Cazeneuve or her assistant Myriam.

How to get there *(Map 3): 18km north of Bordeaux. Exit 7 on the Rocade, towards Blanquefort, Macau via D2 route du Médoc Turn left towards the hamlet of Paloumey before Macau, at the level of Ludon, then right. The château is on the left after 1km.*

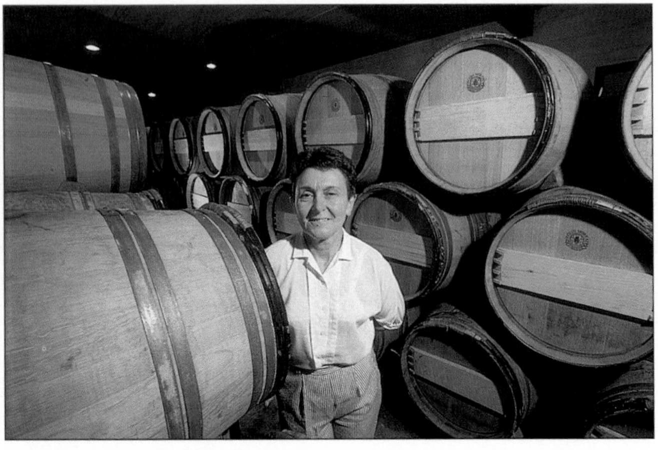

Jacqueline Gauzy-Darricade.

Château Les Grands Chênes

Owner Jacqueline Gauzy-Darricade. **Address** 33340 Saint-Christoly-de-Médoc - Tel. 05.56.41.53.12 Fax 05.56.41.35.69. **Open** Every day, preferably by appointment.

When Jacqueline Gauzy-Darricade worked in Paris she often told her father, a vinegrower attached to the local cooperative, to get rid of 7.5 hectares of vines. "As the only daughter, I never saw myself returning to the vines. The crunch came in the summer of 1982. The grapes were so wonderful in August that I decided to give up everything and throw myself into this new adventure." An irrepressible character, she improvised her first vintage and out of a mass of wines won a gold medal at the Concours Agricole de Paris. Since then, the dynamic Jacqueline has proved that she owes her success to her battling spirit and the quality of her land, including a very good plot behind the cellar. She produces two reds: Les Grands Chênes, matured in new and older oak barrels, and the *cuvée* Prestige, aged uniquely in new oak barrels. The '94s are brilliant. Les Grands Chênes (58 F) is balanced, fruity, with rustic tannins. The Prestige (69 F) has the aroma of coffee and toast on the nose and a rich, structured palate. These are wines to be appreciated over five to six years.

Our choice Château Les Grands Chênes Prestige '95 (approx. 72 F). The oak is present but discreet, well-supported by the fruit and tannin. Generous and long the wine explodes with a pronounced taste of black currant. A wine to keep.

Reception Visitors are received enthusiastically by Jacqueline in the cellar.

How to get there *(Map 3): 10km north of Saint-Estèphe via Saint-Seurin and Saint-Yzans. In the center of Saint-Christoly-de-Médoc. Signposted.*

Rémy Fauchey: "Mastering the evolution of the grape."

Château Lafon

Owners Isabelle and Rémy Fauchey. **Address** Prignac-en-Médoc 33340 Lesparre - Tel. 05.56. 09.02.17 Fax 05.56.09.04.96. **Open** Every day 9:30-19:30.

The path taken by Rémy Fauchey is similar to that followed by many wine growers in the northern Médoc. Initially attached to the wine growers cooperative like his father and grandfather before him, this 40-year-old made and bottled his first wine in 1985. It was then that he discovered the route to quality. "The most difficult thing is to master the evolution of the grape. After that, for the vinification, it's more a question of craft." The path to quality passes, in the Médoc as elsewhere, via reasonable yields in the vineyard. " I clearly saw the improvement in my wines when I started to seed grass in the vineyard and reduce the yields to around 45,50 hectoliters/hectare," he states. This 15 hectare domaine, with gravel hillock and clay-limestone plateau dominated by 55% Cabernet Sauvignon, has not ceased to surprise wine lovers for the last five years with its remarkably concentrated, textured, full, generous wines. In this vain the '94 (54 F), still impetuous and oaky, will settle down in a couple of years.

Our choice Château Lafon '95 (58 F). The wine has pronounced black currant notes, solid tannins, and a powerful, suave, full palate. A wine to age.

Reception Visitors cordially and professionally received in the barrel cellar where a space for tasting has been created.

How to get there *(Map 3): 60km north of Bordeaux. Exit 7 on the Rocade, towards Castelnau, Saint-Laurent. Turn right at the second set of traffic lights in Lesparre towards Prignac. Signposted.*

Jean Boivert, eighth generation *vigneron,* completed his 30th harvest at Ormes Sorbet in 1995.

Château Les Ormes Sorbet

Owners Hélène and Jean Boivert. **Address** 33340 Couquèques - Tel. 05.56.73.30.30 Fax 05.56.73.30.31. **Open** From Monday to Friday, 9:00-12:00 and 14:00-18:00. Saturday by appointment. **Spoken** English.

If the elm-trees (ormes), at one time owned by Monsieur Sorbet, have disappeared from this corner of the northern Médoc the vine appears to be in better health than ever. Jean Boivert is responsible for this 22-hectare domaine, one of the most regular and brilliant of the *Crus Bourgeois*. With a dominance of up to 75% Cabernet Sauvignon, which thrives on the limestone plateau, and a late harvest with severe selection, the wines, which are aged judiciously in barrel, speak the real language of the Médoc. "More Margaux than Saint-Estèphe, in fact, I never push the extraction too far," states Jean. Tasted from barrel, the '96, with two-thirds Cabernet Sauvignon, has ripe tannins and is deep and elegant and looks like it will be a classic. Note: Jean's son, Vincent, has just purchased a neighboring property, Château Fontis (AOC Médoc) and has produced an attractive '95 (65 F). The property was formerly known as Château Hontemieux and comprises 9 hectares opposite the windmill of Château Tour Haut-Caussan. In the process of installation at the time of our last visit, this is a domaine to discover.

Our choice Château Les Ormes Sorbet '95 (90). If the '96 (available winter 1998) offers a balanced ripeness, the '95 has greater power, pronounced spice and black currant aromas, a firm tannic structure and above all great length. This is for the year 2000 or beyond.

Reception Jovial and attentive. Conducted at the entrance to the cellar where there is a display of architectural objects found in the vineyard.

How to get there *(Map 3): 10km north of Saint-Estèphe, via Saint-Seurin and Saint-Yzans. In the center of Couquèques. Signposted.*

Parisian architect-decorator Jean Guyon has realized an old dream in successfully relaunching this tiny property in Bégadan.

Château Rollan de By

Owner Jean Guyon. **Address** By 33340 Bégadan - Tel. 05.56.41.58.59/01.40.67.19.17 Fax 05.56.41.37.82. **Open** From Monday to Friday, by appointment. **Spoken** English.

The vintages 1991 to 1993 and 1994 (less clearly) were Merlot years (the variety ripens earlier than the Cabernet) to the detriment of the Médoc and benefit of the Libournais. Except, that is, in the north of the peninsula where the Merlot is widely planted. In particular, it represents 75% of the plantings at Rollan de By. This young estate, at the time 2 hectares, was purchased by Jean Guyon in 1989 and now extends over 16 hectares of gravel and clay-limestone soils. It's a tiny jewel that has been completely renovated and is managed with the same attention to detail as a *Cru Classé*. The high proportion of Merlot gives Rollan de By a full, round charm which is honed into shape by the use of a high percentage of new oak (malolactic fermentation in barrel). Remember that the Merlot is firmer here than in the Libournais. The '91 (out of stock) launched the domaine with fanfare and since then Rollan de By has rarely disappointed. The '94 is maturing nicely, the oak well-integrated on the nose (suave with a discreet note of black fruits), the palate round and ample but structured on the finish with an austere note which is the hallmark of the vintage. The finish is long and honest. There is also a good second label, La Fleur de By, of which the '95 (65 F) can be appreciated young.

Our choice Château Rollan de By '95 (96 F) Sample. Deep, dark hue (black currant). The nose is suave with a note of pine resin, the palate "fat" with full, attractive fruit and marked oak. Good intensity but this sample was rather hard.

Reception Professional. Visits given by the young cellar master.

How to get there *(Map 3): 65km north of Bordeaux. Exit 7 on the Rocade, towards Castelnau, St-Laurent and Lesparre. At Lesparre towards Saint-Christoly, then Bégadan.*

Philippe Courrian's family have been resident in Blaignan since 1634.

Château Tour Haut-Caussan

Owner Philippe Courrian. **Address** 33340 Blaignan-Médoc - Tel. 05.56.09.00.77 Fax 05.56.09. 06.24. **Open** Every day by appointment.

In the beautifully undulating countryside of his northern Médoc Philippe Courrian dissects his land. This lover of country walks describes, with the enthusiasm of a gold prospector, the layers of blue and red clay "similar to Margaux" that are found on one parcel of 7 hectares on the Pontac plateau which, at 40 meters, is one of the highest spots in the Médoc. "People often forget that the soils of the Médoc have a longitudinal unity that follows the debris deposited by the Gironde and not a transversal." He respects the land of his fathers as well as the vine which he cultivates with due consideration. The Merlot appears at ease here even if it is obliged to share the soil of 17 hectare domaine with Cabernet Sauvignon. Fruit from the young vines of the latter goes into the second label La Landotte. Medocain but not chauvinistic, Philippe also possesses another "mistress" in the Corbières, Château Cascadais, where he produces some good rosés and reds.

Our choice Château Tour Haut-Caussan '95 (67 F). The ripe Merlot is the primary element in this generous, concentrated but not heavy wine. It has plenty of youthful charm but should age. In the '96 (available spring 1998) the Cabernet Sauvignon is the star over the Merlot, still with a balance between power and reserve.

Reception This is no aristocratic building, only a simple Girondin house. In the middle of the vines there is an 18th century windmill (depicted on the château label) which Philippe had restored.

How to get there *(Map 3): 62km north of Bordeaux. Exit 7 on the Rocade, towards Castelnau, Saint-Laurent and Lesparre. At Lesparre towards Couquèques, then right towards Caussan and Blaignan. The château is in the village.*

Serge Barbarin in the vines at Petit-Poujeaux.

Château Biston-Brillette

Owners Christiane and Michel Barbarin and son. **Address** Petit-Poujeaux, 33480 Moulis-en-Médoc - Tel. 05.56.58.22.86 Fax 05.56.58.13.16. **Open** From Mo. to Sat. morning, 9:00-12:00 and 14:00-19:00, Sat. afternoon and Sun. by appointment. **Credit cards** Visa, Eurocard, MasterCard.

Brillette is a place name and Biston the name of a mayor of Moulis in the 19th century. Destroyed by phylloxera, replanted, and resold on a number of occasions, the domaine fell into Michel Barbarin's hands in 1963. His sons Serge (sales and administration) and Jean-Paul (winemaker) now assist him in the management of this 22 hectare domaine which is located on gravel and clay-limestone soils. Over the last ten years, the aromatic, meaty wines of Biston-Brillette have acquired the rigorous nature of the best wines of Moulis: delicious when young but with good ageing potential. The vines have an average age of 18 years with the vineyard planted to 55% Cabernet Sauvignon, 40% Merlot and 5% Petit Verdot. The vinification is traditional and the percentage of new oak barrels never exceeds 35%. Faithful to the clients that buy direct from them, the Barbarins always have a number of older bottles at the cellar. Take advantage of the last of the '89s (67 F), ripe but firm, and '90s (69 F), still with a lively fruitiness, mature tannins, and notes of toast and spice. To drink or keep.

Our choice Château Biston-Brillette '95 (57 F). 55% Merlot. The nose is extremely ripe (crystallized cherries) predicting the weight on the palate. This is round, flavorsome and suave, and folded in soft tannins. The finish is spicy and not at all heavy. Real price-pleasure value.

Reception Family atmosphere with visitors received, in a capable manner, in a small reception room.

How to get there *(Map 3): 28km north of Bordeaux. Exit 7 on the Rocade, towards Castelnau-du-Médoc, Saint-Laurent. Turn right 3km after Listrac towards Moulis. The domaine is signposted on leaving the village, towards Poujeaux.*

The barrel cellar at Poujeaux - half the barrels are renewed yearly.

Château Poujeaux

Owner Jean Theil s.a. **Address** Grand-Poujeaux, 33480 Moulis - Tel. 05.56.58.02.96 Fax 05.56.58.01.25. **Open** Mon. to Sat., 9:00-12:00, 14:00-18:00. **Spoken** English **Credit cards** Visa, Eurocard, MasterCard.

"We have already won the *Coupe des Crus Bourgeois* (a competition that judges the estates over three vintages) but we were especially proud to win it again in 1995 for the vintages '90, '91, and '92, which are all so different," they announce enthusiastically at Poujeaux. Forgotten in the 1855 classification, the domaine is recognized as the best in Moulis and on a level with the Third Growths (1855). The single unit of 52 hectares of sand and fine gravel are planted with 50% Cabernet Sauvignon and 40% Merlot with a complement of Cabernet Franc and Petit Verdot which, unusually, often achieves good ripeness. "Hand of iron in a velvet glove," is the imagery for this wine which is fruity, structured, powerful, and round. Among the most recent successes, the '94 (approx. 100 F) has a dark hue, fine, oaky, acidulous nose without any heaviness, a ripe (black fruits), suave palate which is supple on attack with a nuance of humus. The tannins are firm but soft without any of the rusticity associated with the vintage. If there is still stock of the '90 in magnum (approx. 400 F) with its plum, coffee, licorice, and spice flavors, freshness, balance, and softness on the palate, do not hesitate. Old vintages are available.

Our choice Château Poujeaux '95 (approx. 120 F). Deep, dark hue. Polished, acidulous, oaky nose with notes of crystallized black fruits. The palate is full, round, and velvety, with a silky texture still endowed with a slight sweetness typical of the young wines of Poujeaux. Very good ageing potential.

Reception Visitors received in a small, well-appointed caveau with a view of the barrel cellar.

How to get there *(Map 3): 28km N of Bordeaux. Exit 7 on the Rocade, towards Castelnau-du-Médoc. Turn right 2km after Castelnau, towards Moulis. Traverse Moulis via D5, to Grand-Poujeaux.*

Fonbadet, hidden in the park.

Château Fonbadet

Owners Pierre and Pascale Peyronie. **Address** Saint-Lambert 33250 Pauillac - Tel. 05.56.59.02.11 Fax 05.56.59.22.61. **Open** From Monday to Saturday 9:00-12:00 and 14:00-18:00, by appointment.

If, 35 years ago, Pierre Peyronie hadn't decided to devote himself to the family property, developing sales and bottling his own wines, he would certainly have been the *régisseur* of a *Premier Cru Classé* in Pauillac, like his ancestors. After all these years he is happy with the choice he made. Fonbadet has created a reputation for regular quality and is one of the best non-classified growths in the appellation. This is recompense for the hard work undertaken at the 17 hectare vineyard (60% Cabernet Sauvignon) which has several large parcels of vines located near Lafite and Mouton-Rothschild. One of the specialities of Fonbadet is the continuing sales of a range of vintages, of which there is presently a good '94 (74 F) and an astonishing '86 (175 F) which is powerful but balanced and in the process of opening out. The prices are very reasonable.

Our choice Château Fonbadet '95 (80 F). A generous fruit is caressed by the nuance of tobacco and damp earth typical of the wines of Pauillac. The power on the palate is present but discreet without any aggressiveness. The finish is ripe and spicy. The wine provides at least ten years of guaranteed pleasure.

Reception Pierre Peyronie or his daughter, Pascale, welcome visitors in a somber tasting-room. Admire the variously scented trees and shrubs in the park, and in particular the two splendid old magnolias.

How to get there *(Map 3): 50km north of Bordeaux. Exit 7 on the Rocade, towards Blanquefort, Margaux, Saint-Julien, via D2 route du Médoc. The entrance to the château is on the left before Pauillac at Saint-Lambert. White gate and park.*

Roland Fonteneau's La Bécasse is much appreciated by lovers of wines of character.

Château La Bécasse

Owner Roland Fonteneau. **Address** 21 rue Édouard de Pontet, 33250 Pauillac - Tel. 05.56.59.07.14 Fax 05.56.59.18.44. **Open** By appointment only, (48 hours in advance).

Among the large and prestigious châteaux of Pauillac (some have over 100 hectares) Roland Fonteneau plays the rôle of Tom Thumb with his tiny 4,21 hectares estate comprising 22 parcels of vines dotted throughout the appellation. "Originally, the *cru,* La Bécasse, was located in Saint-Julien and belonged to my grandfather." His father Georges recreated the domaine in Pauillac in 1966. Thirty-nine-year-old Roland Fonteneau returned to the property ten years ago and continues, in a traditional manner, the small production based on grapes from old vines of more than 30 years. This consists of 100 barrels (never more than a third new oak) of red wine, "often austere when young," that need time to mature. Although, in '92 and '93, years where the Merlot unusually represents 50% of the blend, instead of 35%, the wines are that much easier. The '93 (75 F) is notable for its plum, blackberry, and earthy aromas (with a pronounced waxy note) and tannic palate which is gently softening.

Our choice Château La Bécasse '94 (80 F). This authentic and powerful Pauillac with its ripe flavors and tannins, firm structure, and rich taste is a great success. It needs to be carefully cellared for at least another three years.

Reception In a fairly spartan cellar, by appointment only as Roland is often in the vineyard.

How to get there *(Map 3): 50km north of Bordeaux. Exit 7 on the Rocade, towards Blanquefort, Margaux, Saint-Julien, via D2 route du Médoc. Turn left at the entrance to Pauillac, just after the Hotel Cordeillan-Bages. House with red shutters and doors in the village of Bages.*

Embroidered with cross stitch, grandmother's contribution to the reputation of the château.

Château Bertinerie

Owners Daniel, Éric and Frantz Bantegnies. **Address** 33620 Cubnezais - Tel. 05.57.68.70.74 Fax 05.57.68.01.03. **Open** From Monday to Friday 9:00-12:00 and 14:00-18:00, Saturday and Sunday by appointment. **Spoken** English, German. **Credit cards** Visa, Eurocard, MasterCard.

Daniel Bantegnies and his two sons know perfectly well that a great wine is made in the vineyard more so than in the cellar. This includes partially working the soil, severely pruning low-grown vines, training the vines in a particular fashion, known as "the lyre system," in order to acquire the necessary green canopy for ripening the grapes, following each parcel of vines, harvesting manually, and sorting the grapes at the cellar. The painstaking maturation adapted for each of the two *cuvées* represents the other side of this meticulous undertaking. The white wines of the second label, Château Bertinerie, are fruity and fleshy ('96: 31,90 F) while the reds are crisp and fine ('95: 35,90 F). Château Haut-Bertinerie '95 (approx. 48,50 F), the top label, has a high toast flavor, close to roasted coffee beans, although this is a characteristic of the *terroir* and not the ageing in oak barrel as the wines matured in vat have the same toasted note. It is rich, fine, and has a long finish. This is a remarkable wine to age for several years.

Our choice Château Haut-Bertinerie white '95 (48,90 F). Produced from the oldest Sauvignon vines and barrel fermented with the lees stirred, this wine has the ripe aroma of mango, white fruits, and licorice with a toasted note. The palate is full and rich with plenty of substance but remains fresh. The finish is long and persistent. This is one of the best whites in Bordeaux and can be cellared for a while.

Reception Excellent. Visitors received in a large tasting room.

How to get there *(Map 3): From Saint-André-de-Cubzac towards Angoulême via N10. After 8km exit at Cubnezais and follow the itinerary signposted.*

Pascal Montaut.

Château Les Jonqueyres

Owners Isabelle and Pascal Montaut. **Address** Courgeau n°7, 33390 Saint-Paul - Tel. 05.57.42.34.88 Fax 05.57.42.93.80. **Open** By appointment. **Spoken** English.

The domaine consists of 13 hectares of mainly Merlot vines in the Premières-Côtes-de Blaye with a small Cabernet Sauvignon dominated vineyard in the appellation Côtes-de-Bourg (Clos Alphonse Dubreuil). The vines are old, 40 to 60 years, and harvested manually. Pascal Montaut evidently prefers working in a traditional manner as the soils, limestone and clay, are worked and plowed. The wines are macerated for a lengthy period for maximum extraction and to produce long ageing wines. The fruit and extract is preserved by the absence of any filtration. The wine is matured in oak cask, with as much as 50% new oak according to the vintage. These are tannic, well-structured wines but with a dense, ripe, silky extract. The *cuvée* Domaine du Courgeau '95 (31 F), appellation Premières-Côtes-de Blaye, is produced from the youngest vines. The nose is more restrained than usual, the palate attractive with fine tannins, a note of oak, and good length. This is a wine for immediate pleasure.

Our choice Château Les Jonqueyres '95 (approx. 51 F). Tasted before the final blend but already astonishing. The nose is ripe and the palate dense with velvety tannins. This is a huge wine which is long and persisitent. It should be aged for another two years. The '96s will be in the same mold as the '95s with plenty of flesh and volume.

Reception Simple and passionate. Wines can be purchased *en primeur* at an interesting price.

How to get there *(Map 3): From Blaye towards Saintes via D937. Turn right at Saint-Martin (3km) and follow the signposted itinerary towards Saint-Paul.*

Angelus, admitted to the limited circle of *Premiers Grands Crus Classés* in 1996.

Château Angelus

Owners Hubert de Boüard de Laforest and Jean-Bernard Grenié. **Address** 33330 Saint-Émilion - Tel. 05.57.24.71.39 Fax 05.57.24.68.56. **Open** From Monday to Friday 9:00-12:00 and 14:00-18:00, by appointment. **Spoken** English.

The consecration of Angelus as *Premier Grand Cru Classé* in 1996, following the ten-yearly revision of the classification, was keenly anticipated. Since 1988, the estate has produced wines from one of the best *terroirs* on the southern slopes of Saint-Emilion. Of the 26 hectares of vineyard located on the clay-limestone soils of the upper slope and the clay-sand soils of the lower slope 23,4 hectares were classified. The vineyard is planted with 50% Merlot, 47% Cabernet Sauvignon and 3% Cabernet Franc, these proportions varying in the wine according to the vintage. The '96 will be marked by the Cabernet Franc (57%) and will be very upright with great freshness and length. "It will have less acclaim than the '95 but will be more revealing with time," states Jean-Bernard Grenié. Its attractiveness when tasted young, notably the suppleness and flesh produced by the malolactic fermentation in new oak barrels, should not hide the fact that Angélus is a wine that truly opens out with at least ten years ageing, providing a bouquet and texture of great complexity.

Our choice Château l'Angélus '95 (approx. 600 F). The wine displays enormous concentration further accentuated by the ripeness of the vintage. The palate is aromatic with complex notes of crystallized fruits and toast. The fruit is velvety and full with a densely grained, spicy, velvety extract. This is a vivid and erudite wine.

Reception Visits conducted by the château staff. A visit to the barrel cellar has to be requested.

How to get there *(Map 3): From Libourne via D17. Turn right at the roundabout at the entrance to Saint-Emilion, pass the church and continue down the hill for 1.5km.*

Beau-Séjour Bécot , once again among the ranks of the 13 *Premiers Grands Crus Classés* of Saint-Emilion.

Château Beau-Séjour Bécot

Owners Gérard and Dominique Bécot. **Address** 33330 Saint-Émilion - Tel. 05.57.74.46.87 Fax 05.57.24.66.88. **Open** From Monday to Saturday, by appointment. **Spoken** English.

Justice was handed to Beau-Séjour Bécot, stripped of the title of *Premier Grand Cru Classé* in 1986, at the ten-yearly classification in 1996. The verdict was already in the glass. Located a short distance from the old, walled town on the high part of the Saint-Emilion plateau on limestone soil, the domaine consists of 16 hectares planted with 70% Merlot and 30% Cabernet Sauvignon and Cabernet Franc. The characteristics of Beau-Séjour Bécot are elegance, a lively acidity and finesse with the depth provided by the *terroir* inherent. The hot years are usually the most successful for this estate. The wines are matured in 80% new oak barrels with the malolactic fermentation completed in cask. The Bécot family also manage Château Grand-Pontet (14 hectares), in close proximity to Beau-Séjour but on a more clay-based soil (attractive '95, firm and generous) and since '95, Château La Gomerie, a tiny estate of 2,5 hectares planted with 100% Merlot. During maturation the '96 was round, fluid with very soft tannins. A wine to follow.

Our choice Château Beau-Séjour-Bécot '95 (bottled in September '97, approx. 300 F). The attack is gentle (typical of this estate) and the wine well-knit, very fine, lively (a sensation rare in Saint-Emilion for this vintage), long, and spicy. This is an elegant wine for ageing.

Reception Visit and tasting: 30 F. Visitors received in a large hall with a video presentation of the domaine. Visit to the cellars, installed in 1 hectare of limestone tunnels originally quarried in the Middle Ages, where the bottles repose peacefully.

How to get there *(Map 3): From Libourne via D17. Turn right before the Great Wall of Saint-Emilion. Signposted.*

The hillock of Mondot is the highest point in Saint-Emilion.

Château Troplong-Mondot

Owner GFA Valette. **Directrice** Christine Valette. **Address** 33330 Saint-Émilion - Tel. 05.57.55.32.05 Fax 05.57.55.32.07. **Open** From Monday to Friday, by appointment. **Spoken** English, Spanish.

In 1850, Raymond Mondot, President of the Senate, having fallen in love with this site, purchased various parcels of land and constructed a domaine of 30 hectares which has not been modified since. At more than 100 metres above sea-level, the hillock of Mondot is the highest point in the commune of Saint-Emilion. The vineyard, planted with 90% Merlot of an average age of 45 years, is remarkably well exposed and covers the plateau dominating Saint-Emilion and the steep slope as far as Château Pavie. It is from this *terroir* that the wine acquires its rich constitution and vigorous tannins. Since 1981, Christine Valette has taken over the complete management of the domaine taking it to new levels of excellence. This has not been done without risk. The grapes are harvested late and severely selected and the wines matured in an important percentage of new oak. Consequently, the natural austerity in youth has been supplemented by a softness on the palate in the *en primeur* tastings, still with a firm structure, while the wines can mature over 20 years providing a complex range of tertiary aromas. The estate merits the classification *Premier Grand Cru Classé* which curiously escaped it in 1996.

Our choice Château Troplong-Mondot '95 (approx. 200 F). The oak is present (18 months maturation) with a dominance of spice. The palate is firm, powerful, tannic, and long. A great wine tailored for consumption in the 21st century.

Reception In an office of sober decor. There is the opportunity of visiting the cellars.

How to get there *(Map 3): From the Great Wall roundabout at Saint-Emilion take the exit Saint-Christophe. The château is signposted and lies at the base of a water tower.*

Former textile manufacturer Alain Asséo launched into the world of wine in 1983 with a 9-hectare property in Saint-Emilion.

Château Fleur Cardinale

Owners Claude and Alain Asséo. **Address** 333300 Saint-Étienne-de-Lisse - Tel. 05.57.40.14.05 Fax 05.57.40.28.62. **Open** From Monday to Saturday, 9:00-12:00 and 14:00-18:00, by appointment. **Spoken** English.

The Asséos are a good example of a family that has successfully changed direction. In 1983, Claude and Alain, former textile manufacturers, acquired Fleur Cardinale, a 10 hectare property (70% Merlot) located at Saint-Etienne-de-Lisse. Their son, Stéphane, established himself in the Entre-Deux-Mers in 1982 at the Domaine de Courteillac (see previous note). Partly abandoned, Fleur Cardinale, situated on the plateau above Saint-Etienne-de-Lisse at the eastern extremity of the appellation, near the Côtes-de-Castillon, is today one of the sure bets of the non-classified estates in Saint-Emilion. This is not an exceptional *cru* (owing to the *terroir*) but a regular, solid, aromatic wine given a certain polish by astute ageing in oak barrel (50% new oak with the malolactic fermentation in barrel). Stéphane Asséo's signature marks the wines. This is a Saint-Emilion that opens out with elegance over five to ten years.

Our choice Château Fleur Cardinale '95 (approx. 90 F). If a number of '95 in Saint-Emilion are dominated by rather heavy notes of over-ripeness this wine plays on ripe flavors, a defined oakiness (toast, tobacco) but also elegance and fresh fruit and floral notes. On the palate the wine is firm, well-knit, finely tannic and harmonious.

Reception Alain Asséo receives visitors at the cellar, a working environment rather than reception area.

How to get there *(Map 3): 7km east of Saint-Emilion via Saint-Christophe-des-Bardes towards Saint-Genès-en-Castillon. The property is signposted on the left.*

Danielle André: "I was born and grew up in the ambience of the property."

Château Haut-Segottes

Owner Danielle André. **Address** 33330 Saint-Émilion - Tel. 05.57.24.60.98 Fax 05.57.74.47.29. **Open** From Monday to Saturday 9:00-12:00 and 14:00-18:00, by appointment.

Haut-Segottes is one of those rare addresses which connoisseurs, in search of a good non-classified Saint-Emilion, have for many years passed on by word of mouth. Danielle André, the fourth generation at the domaine, has with exactitude and experience managed this tiny cru of 9 hectares since 1972. The main part of the vineyard, comprising 60% Merlot, 35% Cabernet Franc and 5% Cabernet Sauvignon, is not in fact located near the cellar (there are only 1,3 hectares here) but to the northwest of the appellation, near Pomerol. Here, the soils are very different from the limestone plateau of Saint-Emilion being composed of sand and clay with an iron content near Chauvin and Corbin. The yields are low for the appellation (48 hectoliters/hectare in '95) and the wines matured traditionally in oak barrels, of which one third are renewed yearly. The '94 (55 F) has a ripe Merlot style with slightly wild aromas of plum and leather and a round mouthfeel. Already a pleasure but still very young this is a wine to drink over five years.

Our choice Château Haut-Segottes '95 (approx. 60 F). The concentration in the fruit has produced an ample wine, powerful and rich in its youth with persistent flavors of black fruits, leather, and licorice. It finishes round with fine, soft tannins. Excellent value and pleasure.

Reception Charming. Madame André cordially receives visitors in her tiny but impeccably kept cellar.

How to get there *(Map 3): From Libourne towards Saint-Emilion via D243. On the right after the Hotel Grand Barrail. Signposted.*

Seven hectares in one single unit on the plateau of Saint-Emilion.

Château La Couspaude

Owner Family Aubert. **Supervisor** Jean-Claude Aubert. **Address** 33330 Saint-Émilion - Tel. 05.57.40.01.15 /05.57.40.15.76 Fax 05.57.40.10.14. **Open** Every day in Juli and Aug., 9:00-20:00. The rest of the year, Monday to Friday, 8:00-12:00 and 14:00-18:00, by appointment. **Spoken** English.

Winegrowers from father to son since 1750, the Auberts own 12 châteaux in the Libournais (225 hectares). La Couspaude is their flagship estate located some 500 meters from the Great Wall and Saint-Emilion's monolithic church. The domaine constitutes 7 hectares, in one single unit, of walled-in *clos* with the cellar in the middle. The soil consists of limestone rock and is planted with 70% Merlot, 20% Cabernet Franc and 10% Cabernet Sauvignon. Following the advice of enologist Michel Rolland, Jean-Claude Aubert has orientated La Couspaude towards a more modern expression of Saint-Emilion which is dominated by ripe Merlot from low-yielding vines and a maturation in new oak barrel. This is a marked style which leaves nobody indifferent. The '94 (165 F), more extrovert and generous in youth, is beginning to close up and should be cellared. La Couspaude was promoted to *Grand Cru Classé* in 1996.

Our choice Château La Couspaude '95 (approx. 300 F). Despite the heavy oak influence (resin, toast, roasted coffee beans) the extra-ripe Merlot shows through producing a round, suave wine with long, spicy finish and firm note typical of the *terroir*. Tasty when young this is also a wine that needs ageing.

Reception Well organized. In a large reception room. Visit the cellars hewn from the rock which are located underneath the vathouse.

How to get there *(Map 3): From Libourne via D17. Take the exit Saint-Christophe at the roundabout in front of the Great Wall in Saint-Emilion. The domaine is 400 meters on.*

This 55 hectare property at the border between Saint-Emilion and the Côtes-de-Castillon appeared on the scene in 1992.

Château Faugères

Owners Corinne and Péby Guisez. **Address** 33330 Saint-Étienne-de-Lisse - Tel. 05.57.40.34.99 Fax 05.57.40.36.14 – web : http://www.chateau-faugeres.com. **Open** From Monday to Friday 9:00-12:00 and 14:00-18:00, preferably by appointment. **Spoken** English.

Cinema producer, Péby Guisez, and his wife Corinne, a publisher, have entirely renovated the 18th century *chartreuse* that has been in family hands since 1823. They have also constructed a magnificent *cuvier*, one of the most original in Bordeaux, which has a rare functional beauty (a must to visit). Considerable sums have been spent but there is no ostentation at Faugères, only refinement. The domaine covers 55 hectares divided between Saint-Emilion (28 hectares, 70% Merlot) and the Côtes-de-Castillon (27 hectares, 50% Merlot). With the assistance of enologist Michel Rolland the red wines of Faugères are rapidly gaining respect in the Libournais. Château Cap de Faugères, Cotes-de-Castillon, '95 (49 F) is one of the stars of the vintage: full, rich, peppery, powerful, with ripe fruit, it is a generous wine that can be drunk young. The same can be said for the Bordeaux rosé, Les Roses de Château Faugères (39 F), produced from lightly macerated Merlot and Cabernet Sauvignon. The '96 is less fruity than the '95 but still round and full of charm.

Our choice Château Faugères, Saint Emilion Grand Cru, '95 (98 F). This has an exaggerated ripeness that is almost mediterranean in style with intense, viscous aromas of resin and cloves. The oak is well-integrated. The palate maintains this warmth and power and has toasted, spicy flavors. It will not appeal to everyone but will please connoisseurs.

Reception Polite, professional visits given in a sumptuous décor by the staff of the property

How to get there *(Map 3): From Saint-Emilion direction Saint-Etienne-de-Lisse, then Saint-Magne de Castillon via D130. The property is signposted on the left.*

Henri Duboscq: "In life, there is the sensual and the cerebral. I am a producer of the sensual."

Château Haut-Marbuzet

Owners Henri Duboscq and sons. **Address** 33180 Saint-Estèphe - Tel. 05.56.59.30.54 Fax 05.56.59.70.87. **Open** Every day 10:00-12:00 and 14:00-19:00. **Spoken** English. **Credit cards** Visa, Eurocard, MasterCard, Amex.

Starting with the 7 hectares that his father bought unplanted in 1952, Henri Duboscq has constructed a mini-empire of 70 hectares in Saint-Estèphe (Châteaux Haut-Marbuzet and Chambert-Marbuzet). As publicist for his own wines he likes sensation. "I am the provider of pleasure and my wines are sensual fiction." Consequently, Haut-Marbuzet doesn't have "customers" but "connoisseurs" who believe entirely in him. The style of his Saint-Estèphe is firmly marked by the Merlot and ageing in 100% new oak casks. Henri Duboscq plays the cabinet-maker by mixing oak from different regions (Nièvre, Tronçais, Sarthe and Vosges) according to the vintage. This artistic work endows the wines with amazing character in youth: bright, round, and full of charm. After six to eight years the *terroir* begins to show itself. Chambert-Marbuzet, aged in 50% new oak barrels, is less virile than Haut-Marbuzet and can be appreciated younger.

Our choice Château Haut-Marbuzet '94 (108 F). Deep, intense color. The nose provides a generosity and sweetness. The oak is marked but of great class. The palate is velvety, full, round, supple, with a clean, honest finish. A great wine.

Reception At the offices for a visit to the cellars with Cécile who is responsible for public relations. This is one of the rare great domaines of the Médoc where an appointment is not necessary.

How to get there *(Map 3): 51km north of Bordeaux. Exit 7 on the Rocade, toward Castelnau-du-Médoc, Saint-Laurent via D1, then Pauillac via D206 and Saint-Estèphe via D2. Turn right just after Cos d'Estournel for Marbuzet.*

René and Dany Rabiller, the outsiders of Saint-Estèphe.

Château La Peyre

Owners Dany and René Rabiller. **Address** Le Cendrayre, Leyssac 33180 Saint-Estèphe - Tel. 05.56.59.32.51 Fax 05.56.59.70.09. **Open** From Monday to Saturday, 9:00-12:00 and 14:00-18:00, preferably by appointment.

Landowners in Saint-Estèphe (11 hectares) for several centuries, the Rabiller family were members of the local wine cooperative like numerous other Stéphanois grape growers, as the inhabitants of Saint-Estèphe are called. In 1994, René Rabiller, an industrial engineer, succeeded his father, a respected grape grower, and disappointed with the quality initiative at the cooperative decided to bottle part of his own production. With his well-situated vineyard, constituting equal parts Merlot and Cabernet Sauvignon with an average age of 30 years, some classic methods of maturation, and the complicity of a few friends he produced his first *Cru Artisan* Saint-Estèphe in '94 (52 F). Generous, fruity, full on the palate, with present tannins, this is an honest, unsophisticated wine that can be appreciated young or which can age for four or five years. La Peyre is an outsider in Saint-Estèphe and needs to be discovered rapidly.

Our choice Château La Peyre '95 (58 F). Aromatic (black currant, blackberry), marked by the fruit and generosity of ripe Merlot in Saint-Estèphe and by robust tannins on the finish this is a wine of the future which should open out over ten years. Very good price-pleasure value.

Reception At the cellar, more often than not with Dany Rabiller who is attentive to her customers.

How to get there *(Map 3): 55km north of Bordeaux. Exit 7 on the Rocade, direction Blanquefort, then Pauillac, Saint-Estèphe via D2 route du Médoc. Turn right just after Cos d'Estournel, then left towards Leyssac. Le Cendrayre is next to the railway line.*

This beautiful *chartreuse* was practically abandoned until taken in hand in 1989. The rapid rise of this estate has not gone unremarked in Saint-Estèphe.

Château Tour de Pez

CEO Henry Duhayot. **Manager** Franck Duprat. **Marketing manager** F. Bellet. **Address** Lieu-dit L'Hereteyre, 33180 Saint-Estèphe - Tel. 05.56.59.31.60 Fax 05.56.59.71.12. **Open** From Monday to Friday, 9:00-12:00 and 14:00-17:00. **Spoken** English.

A family from Paris, owners of a number of pharmaceutical laboratories, acquired this 11-hectare vineyard in 1989. Until then the grapes had been transported to the local wine cooperative. Today, Tour de Pez 29 hectares planted with 45% Cabernet Sauvignon, 40% Merlot, 10% Cabernet Franc and 5% Petit Verdot. The new arrivals have worked hard to produce, since 1991, a Saint-Estèphe resulting from a severe selection of grapes which is aged in oak barrels, one-third of which are new. Château Tour de Pez represents 40% of the production, the rest being declassified down to the second label, Les Hauts de Pez. Château Tour de Pez is a supple, fruity (black currant) wine with plenty of charm which is marked by toasted oak and the inherent power of Saint-Estèphe. It is very much a contemporary style of wine which is flattering and easy to drink when young. The '94 (79 F) is representative of the style. The color is bright and the nose oaky with a toasted note. The palate is soft, without excessive weight, and with tannins that have already started to mellow out.

Our choice Château Tour de Pez '93 (76 F). Intense color. The nose has notes of coffee, chicory and toast. The palate is round, fat, without huge weight but very appetizing. The tannins are fairly discreet on the finish. It should be drinking well from the end of 1998.

Reception Visitors received by the *régisseur*, Franck Duprat, or his wife Valérie.

***How to get there** (Map 3): 51km north of Bordeaux. Exit 7 on the Rocade, direction Castelnau-du-Médoc, Saint-Laurent via D1, then Pauillac via D206 and Saint-Estèphe via D2. The château is signposted from the hamlet of Pez.*

Bruno Saintout, whose family have been resident in Saint-Julien for two centuries.

Château La Bridane

Owner Bruno Saintout. **Address** 33112 Saint-Julien - Tel. 05.56.59.91.70 Fax 05.56.59.46.13. **Open** In Juli and August, Monday to Saturday 9:00-12:00 and 14:00-18:00, the rest of the year by appointment. **Credit cards** Visa, Eurocard, MasterCard.

Planted by Bruno Saintout's father between 1960-1970, this property is one of the most recent in Saint-Julien (which has 11 *Crus Classés*), despite the fact that the family has been resident here for two centuries. The vineyard of La Bridane, which is located on fine gravel soils to the west on the Talbot plateau and to the north, towards Pauillac, near the vines of Léoville-Poyferré and Las Cases, comprises 15 hectares. It is planted with an atypical blend of grape varieties, namely 37% Cabernet Sauvignon, 33% Merlot and 30% Cabernet Franc, the last an important proportion for a variety more firmly linked with Saint-Emilion than the Médoc. These percentages, however, are not necessarily used in the final blend. The excellent '96 has 50% Cabernet Sauvignon. The wines of this *Cru Bourgeois* are lightly oaked with a firm, lively extract which is unusual for Saint-Julien.The Moulin de la Bridane, produced from a particular parcel of vines, is a much lighter wine.

Our choise Château La Bridane '95 (72 F). Resin, bell-pepper and peony flower aromas with a fresh, fruity palate (marked by the Cabernet Franc). The wine has fine tannins, perhaps a little angular, which will round out rapidly.

Reception In the barrel cellar in a corner arranged for tasting. Out of season it is possible to purchase the wine at Domaine du Cartujac, Bruno Saintout's other property located at Saint-Laurent du Médoc.

How to get there *(Map 3): 45km north of Bordeaux. Exit 7 on the Rocade, direction Blanquefort, Macau, Margaux and Saint-Julien-de-Beychevelle via D2. Turn left on the other side of the village, towards Pauillac. Signposted.*

Guy and Jean-François Delon, members of one of the Médoc's great winemaking families.

Châteaux Moulin de la Rose et Ségur de Cabanac

Owners Guy, Jean-François and Guylène Delon. **Address** Château Moulin de la Rose, 33250 Saint-Julien Beychevelle, Tel. 05.56.59.08.45 Château Ségur de Cabanac 33180 Saint-Estèphe, Tel.05.56.59.70.10. **Open** Monday to Saturday, 9:00-12:00 and 14:00-18:00, by appointment.

"Saint-Julien is feminine and Saint-Estèphe masculine," says 65-year-old Guy Delon. The former owner of Château Phélan-Ségur and member of one of the Médoc's great winemaking families is not particularly loquacious and prefers to let his wines speak for themselves. He is the owner of two *Crus Bourgeois*: the 6.25 hectare Château Ségur de Cabanac in Saint-Estèphe which was acquired in 1986 and 4.65 hectare Château Moulin de la Rose in Saint-Julien. The Saint-Estèphe is a wine of character, aromatic, fruity, and powerful with a solid structure. It is more at home with game dishes (the producer is an avid *chasseur*) than with nouvelle cuisine. This is one of the best *Crus Bourgeois* in the appellation Saint-Estèphe. The Saint-Julien also has a strong personality but is naturally more supple and elegant. The '95 and '96 are superb.

Our choice Château Ségur de Cabanac '94 (67 F). Powerful, tannic and warm with a typical note of moist earth. Château Moulin de la Rose '95 (approx. 87 F) has floral and ripe red fruit aromas. It is sweet and has a pronounced taste of black currant, ripe tannins and a long finish. Reserve the '96, it is a great wine made from 70% Cabernet Sauvignon.

Reception Guy Delon is a bear-like but sincere character. With his piercing look and a Médocain accent that can be cut with a knife, he is as direct as they come. Visitors are normally received at Saint-Julien where the two wines can be purchased.

How to get there *(Map 3): For Château Moulin de la Rose, arriving from Bordeaux via D2, pass by Château Beychevelle and continue straight on. In the village of Beychevelle 50m on the right. Ségur de Cabanac is located at the port of Saint-Estèphe on the corner of the road that climbs towards the village.*

The Louis XVI architecture of Saint-Georges, designed by Victor Louis.

Château Saint-Georges

Owner Family Desbois. **Address** Saint-Georges-de-Montagne 33570 Montagne - Tel. 05.57.74.62.11 Fax 05.57.74.58.62. **Open** From Monday to Friday 8:00-12:00 and 14:00-17:30. **Spoken** English, German. **Credit card** Visa.

In the jargon used in Bordeaux the four communes authorized to add their names to that of Saint-Emilion: Puisseguin, Lussac, Montagne and Saint-Georges, are known as the "satellites." Saint-Georges is the smallest of these with 170 hectares of which 50 hectares belong to the finest example, Château Saint-Georges. Owned by the Desbois family for more than a century the château displays a harmonious architecture between the four towers of the old medieval facade. The Merlot dominated wines are round, soft, and spicy with a good ageing potential of ten years in the good vintages and with a quality that is not far off that of the *Crus Classés* of Saint-Emilion. They are vinified in a traditional manner with, nevertheless, a high proportion of new oak barrels used for the ageing. There are always four vintages for sale. The second label, Château Puy-Saint-Georges, is soft and fruity and to drink young. Note: In France, Château Saint-Georges is sold directly to the public and essentially by correspondence.

Our choice Château Saint-Georges '95 (86 F). The oak is elegant with a hint of white pepper. The palate is tender with black fruit flavors and fine, ripe tannins. The finish is generous and has a note of chocolate. This is the most successful vintage since the excellent '90.

Reception The site is majestic, one of the most beautiful châteaux in the Libournais. Visits to the cellars by appointment only.

How to get there *(Map 3): From the roundabout at the Great Wall in Saint-Emilion take the direction Montagne. On the right after 2km is the entrance to the long alley that leads to the château.*

Yves Armand, always on the go.

Château La Rame

Owner Family Armand. **Address** 33410 Sainte-Croix-du-Mont - Tel. 05.56.62.01.50 Fax 05.56.62.01.94. **Open** From Monday to Friday 8:30-12:00 and 13:30-19:00, Saturday and Sunday by appointment. **Spoken** English, Spanish.

Yves Armand never stops. He could rest on the laurels he regularly obtains for his botrytized sweet wines. Instead, he continues to plant, modify the percentage of Sauvignon to the benefit of Semillon, and generally remodel his vineyard. The wines labeled Réserve correspond to a selection that has been matured in new or one-year-old barrels. They are powerful and need to be aged to allow the elegant oak to soften. There are still several old vintages for sale in limited quantities. The '90 (approx. 155 F) is pure on the nose with still a hint of oak. The palate is rich, long, and well balanced and structured by the acidity. The '88 (approx. 175 F) is clean and fresh with a rare purity on the nose. The palate is full, ample, powerful, soft, with a note of citrus fruits (orange). It is a very fine, structured wine, still with plenty of freshness, which is persistent and finishes with a hint of toast, leaving a lingering impression.

Our choice Château La Rame Réserve '89 (approx. 165 F). This wine is just beginning to open out. It has a fine nose and ample, botrytized, honeyed palate. It's long on the finish with notes of coffee and fig. A wine to age.

Reception Perfect. In a large, sober cellar. There are fixed allocations of wine for sale. The '88 and '89 are sold separately or in a presentation case (one bottle each of the '88,'89 and '90 vintages: 499 F). The '90 vintage is limited to six bottles.

How to get there *(Map 3): Follow signs from the center of Sainte-Croix.*

Roger Saint-Marc, who hates pressing his grapes.

Château L'Escaley

Owner Family Saint-Marc. **Address** Labat, 33410 Sainte-Croix-du-Mont - Tel. 05.56.62.06.12. **Open** By appointment.

Roger Saint-Marc is a young man, or at least he is younger than his vines. He is 66 and they are 71 years old. He makes the wine on his 8-hectare domaine which is planted with Semillon. He is used to late harvesting and picking over a long period of time (from 18 September to 27 October in 1990, 28 September to 25 October in 1989, 14 October to 19 November "under a small covering of snow" in 1985) to the extent that the pickers "often think that we have forgotten them and telephone to check that everything is alright." He likes to watch for the onset of botrytis and falls in love with the grapes. "In 1985 the grapes were the color of gold and I hated to have to press them." We could reproach him for doing successive bottlings of the same wine or for the variation in different lots of the same vintage. But with this quality the variations win the right to be called a nuance of expression. The '89 (approx. 48 F), which is actually on sale, is very botrytized and sweet but with a good balance between alcohol, acidity and sugar. It is long on the finish. There are also older vintages available at a very interesting price: '81, '85, and '86 (approx. 55 F).

Our choice Château L'Escaley '90 (approx. 47 F). The nose is intense and fruity (peach, pineapple). The palate is ample, rich, and very powerful with plenty of flesh. This is a wine with a soft texture and good balance between acidity, alcohol and sugar. It is very long with a lovely toasted finish.

Reception Simple. In the kitchen.

How to get there *(Map 3): Follow the signs for Château Louteau-Vieil from the center of Sainte-Croix. L'Escaley is just opposite.*

Hewn from a bed of fossilized oysters, the chapel where Louis XIII assisted at Mass in 1620.

Château Loubens

Owner Arnaud de Sèze. **Address** 33410 Sainte-Croix-du-Mont - Tel. 05.56.62.01.25 Fax 05.56. 76.71.65. **Open** By appointment.

Everything is peaceful here. The spirit of Monsieur Delancre, founder of the château and illustrious witch-hunter (he notched up five hundred witches) seems to have vanished, leaving the sweet wines to mature in peace. The domaine comprises 15 hectares in a single unit situated on the famous bed of fossilized oysters which makes the appellation unique (the fossiles can be seen under the terrace of Château Loubens or near Château de Sainte-Croix). The vineyard is planted with 95% Semillon. Arnaud de Sèze systematically seeks out noble rot and concentration by often harvesting very late (21 October to 22 November in 1985). Several older vintages are still available. The '90 (110 F) has exceptional botrytized concentration, the '89 (106 F) is finer, and the '88 (106 F), and '86 (104 F) are also available. The '85 (120 F) is astonishing for its truffle nose, delicate rather than powerful palate with biscuit and vervain notes and its length and persistence.

Our choice Château Loubens '83 (130 F). This was a year where "the vintage was like a holiday, a real dawdle. It lasted two months, with seven or eight successive passages through the vines and plenty of botrytis." The palate is ample, fat and unctuous with fruit on the attack and a powerful toasted finish. The wine has plenty of persistence and the balance and structure will allow it to age further.

Reception Don't forget to ask to see the bank of fossilized oysters under the terrace, the chapel that was hewn from the rock and the old cellars lit by candles.

How to get there *(Map 3): 300m from the church of Sainte-Croix.*

The reserve of old vintages.

Château Haut-Bergeron

Owners Robert, Hervé and Patrick Lamothe. **Address** 33210 Preignac - Tel. 05.56.63.24.76 Fax 05.56.63.23.31. **Open** From Monday to Saturday 9:00-12:00 and 15:00-19:00, Sunday by appointment. **Spoken** English, Spanish, Italian.

The Lamothe family have two treasures. Their old Semillon vines (26 hectares with an average age of 60 years) which are worked in a traditional manner: severe pruning, organic manure, precise and selective harvesting, and a collection of old vintages that date back to 1978. Wine lovers can, therefore, discover great sweet wines in full maturity. Sold in small quantities, one can find collectors vintages like '89 and '90 (150 F), '86 (165 F) and '82 (185 F). The prices are very reasonable with regard to the quality. As throughout the region, Robert Lamothe and his two sons, Hervé and Patrick, are delighted with the '95 and, in particular, the '96 vintages. Tasted during barrel ageing the latter seems better than the '90. For those in search of a rarity, a micro-*cuvée* of two barrels made from grapes picked one by one from 100-year-old vines is looking exceptional. We'll come back to it again in the year 2000.

Our choice Château Haut-Bergeron '95 (108 F). Matured in oak barrels for 18 months. Deep, golden hue. Plenty of power and sweetness with the flavor of crystallized fruits. Full and fat on the palate. Without the point of acidity evident in the '96 this is a very imposing wine. To drink now or forget for ten years. The second label, Château Fontebride '95 (70 F) is a simpler wine without great complexity. It makes an excellent aperitif.

Reception In the Lamothe house. Easy-going, family atmosphere.

How to get there *(Map 3): From Bordeaux towards Toulouse via A62 autoroute, exit Cadillac. At péage towards Cérons, Barsac and Preignac via N113. Turn right at Preignac and follow the signs.*

An acclaimed figure and celebrated wines.

Châteaux Gilette, Les Justices et Respide-Médeville

Owners Andrée and Christian Médeville. **Address** 33210 Preignac - Tel. 05.56.76.28.44 Fax 05.56.76.28.43. **Open** From Monday to Friday, 9:00-12:00 and 14:00-18:00, by appointment. **Spoken** English, Spanish. **Credit cards** Visa, Eurocard, MarsterCard.

Christian and Andrée Médeville manage three excellent properties in Sauternes and Graves. The legendary Château Gilette and its very old vintages of Sauternes provide an opportunity, unique in Bordeaux, to delve back in to the past. After a long period of ageing in vat the wines are offered for sale no sooner than 20 years after the harvest. The Crème de Tête '78 (approx. 741 F) became available in June 1997. It offers the elegant aromas of crystallized grapefruit and white fruits (peach, apricot). Creamy on the palate, it has a fresh finish with notes of lemon and Mocha coffee. It is finer than the '76. Don't forget, however, the other Sauternes, Château Les Justices, which is fermented in barrel and sold two years after the harvest, or Château Respide-Médeville, a young vineyard of 30 acres (12 hectares) in the Graves at Toulenne which is improving regularly. The white Graves '95 (67 F) is finely aromatic (menthol, white fruits), crisp, and linear. It should be ready for drinking in 1998.

Our choice Château Réspide-Médeville, red Graves, '95 (77 F). Aromatic (plum, blackberry, violet), round on the palate with soft tannins, this is a delicious wine which is attractive young. Château Les Justices, Sauternes, '95 (149 F) is the fruit of finely selected grapes which offers depth, weight, and toasted flavors. It is rich without being massive. A very classy wine.

Reception They talk passionately about their wines in a tasting room next to the office.

How to get there *(Map 3): From Bordeaux towards Toulouse via A62 autoroute, exit Cadillac. At péage towards Cérons, Barsac and Preignac via N113. The office is behind the church in Preignac.*

Uprooted in 1976 then replanted in 1988, Myrat is unique in the recent history of Sauternes.

Château de Myrat

Owners Xavier and Jacques de Pontac. **Address** 33720 Barsac - Tel. 05.56.27.15.06 Fax 05.56.27.11.75. **Open** From Monday to Friday 9:00-12:00 and 14:00-18:00. Weekend by appointment.

From 1976 until 1990, not a drop of Sauternes appeared from the cellars of Château de Myrat. There was good reason, for this *Deuxième Grand Cru Classé* no longer possessed any vines. The economy in Sauternes could not have been worse between 1960 and 1970 and Myrat, who no longer bottled at the estate, had difficulty selling the wine to the *négociants*. In 1976, the Comte de Pontac, persuaded that the deathknell for sweet wines had been rung, decided to pull up the entire 22 hectares of vines. The story of Myrat, eradicated from viticultural maps, could have finished there. However, following the death of the Comte in 1988, his sons, Xavier and Jacques, learned that the entitlement to replant still existed but that it was nearly null and void. A mad race against time ensued and in six weeks the 22 hectares were totally replanted. Unfortunately, a series of disappointing vintages followed (frost, rain) and it wasn't until 1994 that Myrat made its mark. In 1995 and 1996 nature was more clement. Despite the youth of the vines one can sense the finesse of Myrat's *terroir* in these early vintages.

Our choice Château de Myrat '95 (125 F). The style of the wine is one of finesse, typical of Barsac, with menthol and lemon peel aromas and soft, sweet, refined extract. The '96, presently being matured in barrel, looks superb.

Reception By Xavier de Pontac who receives visitors in one of the outbuildings of the château.

How to get there *(Map 3): From Bordeaux towards Toulouse via A62 autoroute, exit Cadillac. At péage towards Cérons, Barsac via N113. Turn right by Château Nairac at the entrance to Barsac and continue 2km. Signpost.*

Nairac, designed by Mollié, a student of Victor Louis, prolific architect of the 18th century, and the garden which was restored in 1992.

Château Nairac

Owner Nicole Heeter-Tari. **Supervisor** Nicolas Heeter-Tari. **Address** 33720 Barsac - Tel. 05.56.27.16.16 Fax 05.56.27.26.50. **Open** From Monday to Friday, 9:00-12:00 and 14:00-17:00, by appointment. **Spoken** English.

Situated on the right bank of the Ciron (the tiny river which is instrumental in the development of noble rot, *botrytis cinerea*), Barsac can claim its own appellation for sweet wines (a Barsac can also take the appellation Sauternes but not the reverse). The characteristics of Barsac are a persistent aroma and more finesse on the palate. However, Nairac, *Cru Classé* in 1855, has a more powerful style. “The Sauternes of Barsac,” as described by one of the neighbors in an admiring way. The wines provide the proof, the product of an careful selection dictated by Nicole Heeter-Tari and her son Nicolas who have managed the 16-hectare vineyard (90% Sémillon) and vinified the wines since 1993. Consequently, in 1991 and 1992 Nairac only produced 12 barrels! In 1993 and 1994 the same rigorous selection was imposed and the production was tiny but the wines were among the best in the appellation. The ’95 (available from spring 1998) is very concentrated, fleshy, with a strong apricot sensation and dried fruit flavors, the product of raisining on the vine.

Our choice Château Nairac ’94 (price on demand). Fine citrus, lime-tree, elderberry, and honey nose. The palate, without exceptional length, is one of the richest in Sauternes-Barsac for this vintage. This is a very full, silky, and agreeable wine.

Reception Professional. Visits conducted by Nicolas. Admire the château and garden.

How to get there *(Map 3): From Bordeaux towards Toulouse via A62 autoroute, exit Cadillac. At péage towards Cérons, Barsac via N113. The château is clearly visible on the right at the entrance to Barsac.*

BOURGOGNE

4
Charny
D16
D3
A6
Senan
18
38
Pontigny
Seignelay
Ligny-le-C.
Tonnerre
Arthonnay
Cruzy-le-Châte
Aillant-s.-Th.
Sommecaise
Appoigny
30
238
Tanlay
St-Maurice-s.-Aveyron
D955
10
N7
241
Châblis
44
D965
D950
Auxerre
Yonne
D965
14
D944
18
Lézinnes
Les Forges
D41
Champignelles
Villiers-St-Benoît
Pourrain
D965
21
240
21
Ste-Vertu
Ancy-le-Franc
Ravières
Toucy
St-Cyr-les-Colons
236
237
11
12
Nuits
Bléneau
D950
2
3
D956
Pasilly
20
Ouanne
A6
Mézilles
N6
D956
Étivey
D90
N151
21
22
239
Nitry
D49
Ouanne
Vermenton
Aisy-s.-Armançon
St-Fargeau
St-Sauveur-en-Puisaye
234
Cure
89
19
D85
26
Courson-les-Carrières
Mailly-le-C.
L'Isle-s.-Serein
D965
Lavau
D2
D32
D944
D957
Vassy
St-Amand-en-P.
D955
Druyes-les-Belles-Fontaines
21
235
D957
Voûtenay-s.-Cure
Montréal
Neuvy-s.-L.
N6
Époisses
Coulanges-s.-Yonne
Guillon
Cousin
D955
Alligny-Cosne
D957
D957
Clamecy
Avallon
45
Cussy-les-Forges
D954
A67
Entrains-s.-Nohain
24
14
D5
15
D36
23
N6
Chamont
Cosne-Cours-s.-L.
La Chapelle-St-André
D34
Dornecy
D958
D944
D70
D19
D5
N151
Nuars
N7
Donzy
Varzy
D23
Canal du Nivernais
D985
Quarré-les-Tombes
18
27
15
48
St-M.-du-Puy
Asnan
D5
Châteauneuf-Val-de-Bargis
Lormes
Dun-les-Places
Cousin
Saulieu
Pouilly-s.-Loire
Garchy
Champlemy
Corbigny
D6
D977B
N151
D977
Brinon-s.-B.
D34
D945
N7
23
Ardan
D977B
Vauclaix
D920
St-Révérien
D985
Montsauche
Herry
Les Bertins
D38
D977B
D977B
Yonne
Ternin
18
Premery
Nièvre
L'Huis-Picard
26
La Charité-s.-Loire
15
D34
D37
Poiseux
D977
D38
D958
Planchez
Aunay-en-Bazois
D945
D944
D37
Guérigny
St-Saulge
58
25
D45
D9
Châtillon-en-B.
Anost
Lucenay-l'Évêque
Pouques-les-Eaux
Varennes-Vauzelles
16
D978
Bona
Château-Chinon
36
D26
Tammay-en-Bazois
Rouy
D37
La Petite-Verrière
Fourchambault
14
35
16
D18
Nevers
D978
St-Bénin-d'Azy
Moulins-Engilbert
D10
D18
D985
St-Léger-s/s-Beuvray
La Guerche-s.-l'Aubois
Challuy
Imphy
D9
D34
D26
Vandenesse
N81
D13
St-Honoré-les-Bains
Étang-s.-Arroux
D920
19
D37
La Machine
Cercy-la-Tour
24
Mesvres
17
La Chèvre
Maison-de-Bourgogne
Sancoins
N7
Decize
D979
Luzy
N81
D994
N76
Fours
N81
29
Arroux
St-Pierre-le-Moûtier
D978A
D116
St-Hilaire-Fontaine
D985
Canal latéral
D979A
Neuville-lès-Decize
Acolin
Le Veurdre
27
Saône-et-Loire
D13
Lurcy-Lévis
31
Dornes
Lucenay-lès-Aix
Cronat
D973
Issy-l'Évêque
Toulon-s.-Arroux
Limoise
Villeneuve-s.-Allier
D979A
Maltat
Couleuvre
Allier
11
71
Franchesse
35
à la Loire
Bourbon-Lancy
Perrecy-les-Forges
N7
D1
Bourbon-l'Archambault
D13
Chevagnes
D60
Gueugnon
N79
D15
Loire
D953
D973
St-Aubin-s.-Loire
Yzeure
Ygrande
St-Menoux
Moulins
26
17
Génelard
D945
Bourbince
D979
19
D73
12
D985
D11
Souvigny
N9
11
N1079
Dompierre-s.-Besbre
St-Agnan
D994
D945
5
D55
26
D1
N145
Neuilly-le-Réal
Saligny-s.-Roudon
N79
Digoin
Chavenon
Le Montet
20
Châtel-de-Neuvre
Bessay-s.-Allier
D989
Vaumas
9
Paray-le-Monial
17
D1
17
N7
17
D480
Liernolles
St-Yan
26
D21
Jaligny-s.-B.
D994
D15
D989
Arconce
D982
Allier
Chazeuil
Le Donjon
Neuilly-en-Donjon
D46
Bransat
Besbre
9
Varennes-s.-Allier
03
Trézelles
Anzy-le-Duc
Montmarault
D989
St-Pourçain-s.-Sioule
21
St-Gérand-
Chambilly
Marcigny

5
Châtillon-s.-Seine
Gurgy-la-Ville
St-Loup-s.-A.
Haute-Marne
Bannes
Langres
Terre-Natale
Laignes
Maisey-le-Duc
Voulaines-les-T.
Perrogney
Auberive
Chaudenay
Chalindrey
Fayl-la-F.
Chamesson
Recey-s.-Ource
52
Longeau
Pierrefaite
Genevrières
Coulmier-le-Sec
Chassigny-Aisey
Grenant
St-Marc-s.-Seine
St-Broing-les-Moines
Étais
Prauthoy
Montvaudon
Villaines-en-Duesnois
Aignay-le-Duc
Grancey-le-Ch.-Neuvelle
Pierrecourt
Montbard
Baigneux-les-Juifs
Côte-d'Or
21
Selongey
Champlitte
Alise-Ste-Reine
Moloy
Chazeuil
Fontaine-Française
Lamargelle
Chanceaux
Is-s.-Tille
Venarey-les-L.
Vernot
Autrey-lès-Gray
Gray
Semur-en-Auxois
Bèze
Savigny-le-Sec
St-Seine-l'Abbaye
Mirebeau
Vitteaux
Fontaine
Précy-s/s-Thil
Talant
Arc-s.-Tille
Grosbois-en-M.
Pont-de-Pany
Dijon
Pontailler-s.-S.
Chenôve
Sombernon
Lamarche-s.-S.
Marsannay
Gevrey-Chambertin
Genlis
Auxonne
Liernais
Pont-d'O.
Villers-Rotin
Pasquier
Meuilley
Trouhans
Arnay-le-Duc
Nuits-St-G.
Brazey-en-P.
Rochefort-s.-Nenon
St-Jean-de-L.
Dole
Bligny-s.-O.
Corgoloin
Broin
Aloxe-Corton
Tavaux
St-Aubin
Beaune
Seurre
Chemin
Épinac
La Rochepot
Trugny
Chaussin
Autun
Nolay
Navilly
Doubs
Les Essards-Taignevaux
St-Loup-de-la-Salle
Verdun-s.-le-D.
St-Émiland
Chagny
Gergy
Pierre-de-Bresse
Chaumergy
Mercurey
Bellevesvre
Marmagne
Saône-et-Loire
Sellières
St-Martin-en-Bresse
Mervans
Montcenis
Le Creusot
Givry
St-Germain-du-Bois
Chalon-s.-Saône
Thurey
Bletterans
Montchanin
Frangy-en-B.
Lons-le-Saunier
Blanzy
Buxy
St-Germain-du-Plain
Montret
Beaurepaire-en-Bresse
Montceau-les-Mines
Sennecey-le-Grand
Louhans
Conliège
St-Vallier
Mont-St-V.
Genouilly
St-Gengoux-le-National
Tournus
Chantemerle
Montpont-en-Bresse
Beaufort
La Guiche
Cormatin
Brancion
Cuisery
Orgelet
Salornay
Lugny
Varennes-St-Sauveur
Cuiseaux
St-Trivier-de-Courtes
St-Bonnet-de-Joux
Fleurville
St-Amour
Pont-de-Vaux
Cormoz
Cluny
Charolles
Ste-Cécile
Azé
Coligny
St-Julien
Arinthod
St-Julien-s.-Reyssouze
Manziat
Trambly
Charnay-lès-Mâcon
Montrevel-en-Bresse
Marboz
St-Étienne-du-Bois
Matour
Tramayes
Mâcon
Thoiretté

B O U R G O G N E

INTRODUCTION

Many a wine lover has quickly succumbed to Burgundy's delicate, sensual wines, the aromatic, fruity progeny of a single grape variety: Pinot Noir or Chardonnay. Delightful, too, is the experience of savoring the complexity of the region's innumerable *terroirs*. But how to make our way through the labyrinth of Burgundian appellations and domains? There are eight hundred Appellations d'Origines Contrôlées in Burgundy, twice as many as in the Bordelais and yet Burgundy has a fifth as many vines (23,000 hectares, excluding the Beaujolais). It is a patchwork of *terroirs* parcelled out by medieval monks after herculean labor. Sometimes enclosed by walls called *clos*, chopped up into a myriad of parcels as big as a curate's garden, the *terroirs* reflect the infinitely diverse geological and climatic combinations which affect these hillside vineyards that fan out over three *départements*: the Yonne, the Côte-d'Or, and the Saône-et-Loire.

Burgundy has thus remained on a human scale in which small properties reign supreme. Behind each label are usually a couple of *vignerons* who cultivate a necklace of small plantings scattered over several communes and produce a tiny quantity of wine. Often crafty, they need to be coaxed into parting with a few bottles of their best wine.

In Chablis, the region's most northerly outpost, a somewhat harsh countryside of fossilized white limestone, you will find the largest properties. In the Côte d'Or on the other hand, a narrow strip of vineyards just thirty miles long, micro-domains abound. Their old cellars piled high with large wooden barrels nestling beneath the houses are like small craftsmen's ateliers, a far cry from the Bordelais' vast cellars with modern stainless-steel vats. In the Côte Chalonnaise and the Mâconnais, estate-bottling is a more recent tradition, with most cellars having been built over the last thirty years.

A vineyard tour of Burgundy is a marvelous pretext to stop off and see the various villages: the medieval cellars of Saint-Bris, the Gallo-Roman site of Prémeaux-Prissey, Saint-Romain and its spectacular cliff, the Mâconnais and its Romanesque churches. Along the way the region's superb restaurants beckon, offering deliciously hearty dishes prepared with a delightful neglect for fashion and calories that cry out to be washed down with the local *crus.* The vineyards selected for this Guide are not intended to be a *Who's Who* of Burgundy. Great winemakers rub shoulders in these pages with those of modest reputation. But these men and women share the common goal of fighting for their idea of good Burgundy. And while their methods of winemaking are sometimes divergent, their wines in the long run--in the glass--offer a genuine character and that extra modicum of soul which will never leave you indifferent.

BURGUNDY APPELLATIONS

Appellations in Burgundy are quite simply organized in a vertical hierarchy of ascending quality, like a pyramid. The *terroirs* classifications are quite complex. At the base of the pyramid, the regional appellations are produced in all or part of a given region. This large family accounts for 65% of all Burgundy produced. It includes the simple Bourgogne appellation (red, white, rosé); the grape variety (Bourgogne Aligoté, white only); a vinification method (Crémant de Bourgogne); the name of a sub-region (Bourgogne Côte-d'Auxerre, Bourgogne Haute-Côte de Nuits, Bourgogne Haute-Côte de Beaune, Bourgogne Côte Chalonnaise); or a commune (Bourgogne Irancy). Appellations soon to disappear include Bourgogne Passe-Tous-Grains, a blend of Pinot Noir and Gamay; and Bourgogne Grand Ordinaire, from the least desirable *terroirs.*

Next up the scale are the communal or Villages appellations (23% of production). These are the appellations with the famous names: Chablis, Gevrey-Chambertin, or Meursault for example. There are fifty-three in all. In each village, the vineyards are divided into a myriad of parcels or *lieux-dits*, called *climats* in Burgundy. The Villages appellations can thus be followed by the name of these *climats*, with a view to greater precision. Be careful: *climats* with the same name can be found in different villages.

The best *climats* are promoted to the rank of Premier Cru. Five hundred and sixty-one *climats* are classed Premier Cru and represent 11% of Burgundy wines. Their labels bear the name of the commune followed by that of the *climat*. For example: Meursault-Perrières Premier Cru; or Mercurey Clos du Roi Premier Cru. There are also blends from several Premier Cru *climats*. In this case, the name of the commune is followed by the term Premier Cru: Puligny-Montrachat Premier Cru.

Finally, the élite Grands Crus stand proudly at the top of the pyramid, accounting for only one per cent of Burgundy wines. These prime vineyard areas are of very variable size (Clos de Vougeot: 50.6 hectares; Montrachet: 8 hectares; La Romanée: 0.85 hectares); they are appellations in themselves, relegating the name of the village to second position on the label: Chambertin in the commune of Gevrey-Chambeurtin, or Chevalier-Montrachet in that of Puligny-Montrachet. It is of course essential to avoid confusing the name of the Grands Crus with that of their villages. There are thirty-two Grands Crus in the Côte-d'Or. In Chablis, the Grand Cru appellation covers 97 hectares and seven *lieux-dits.*

This patchwork of appellations is extremely meticulous, the result of centuries of work on the part of Burgundy's winegrowers who have astutely pinpointed differences in soils and locations--the region's *terroirs*--in a totally empirical way. They have demonstrated the peasant's innate sense of observation which recent scientific studies, notably geological, have shown to be justified. But the subtlety of Burgundy's *terroirs* doesn't stop there. There is also an informal hierarchy among the Premiers and Grands Crus. For example, of the many white Grands Crus planted in Puligny-Montrachet and Chassagne-Montrachet, Chevalier-Montrachet at the top of the slope expresses extraordinary finesse and elegance; at the bottom of the slope, Bâtard-Montrachet yields a very fat, rich Burgundy. In the middle of the hillside you will find the holy of holies, Montrachet, combining finesse with opulence. Thus, the best vines here are located half-way up, in the heart of the hillside. This gift of nature and these expressions of an infinitely nuanced vineyard region must be complemented, of course, by the winemakers' skill in vinifying and ageing their wines. All the great Burgundies are aged in oak barrels called *pièces*, containing 228 liters. This volume corresponds to the grapes that a winegrower in the past could harvest from a parcel called an *ouvrée.* (Still used, the measurement represents about one twenty-fourth of a hectare). The symbiosis between wine and oak is one of the main characteristics of Burgundy wines. Depending on the variable proportion of of new oak barrels ("new" can apply to barrels having contained the wine of several harvests) and the length of bottle ageing, the winemaker puts his own style on his wines. Finally, it is essential to carefully follow the vintage of these great wines, for Burgundy is subject to wide variations in climate from one year to the next.

BUYING IN BURGUNDY

There are two main grape varieties in Burgundy: Pinot Noir for red wines, and Chardonnay for whites. The grapes are never blended here, but are vinified and aged separately.

The northernmost vineyards are those of the Yonne *département* and its star, Chablis, with 2720 hectares in Chablis and neighboring communes. The grapes here, yielding only white wines, are grown in four appellations, Petit Chablis, Chablis, Chablis Premier Cru, and Chablis Grand Cru, and yield a mineral character, straightforward, a wine of great breeding from the Chardonnay. Exported in great quantities, Chablis today is renowned internationally as *the* dry white wine, making the best Chablis quite rare and expensive. The Yonne also produces excellent Burgundies at very reasonable prices: Irancy, a tannic, solid red wine which ages very well; Epineuil, Chitry, Coulange-la-Vineuse, Tonnerre, and Côtes-d'Auxerre, lighter, more gulpable wines produced in red, white, and rosé versions. They are superior in quality to the simple generic Bourgogne appellation.

More than 78 vineyard-free miles separate Chablis from Dijon, the gateway to the Côte de Nuits, ending at Corgoloin. Grown in a 12-mile necklace of vineyards nestling side by side are the most famous red wines of Burgundy: the greatest concentration of Grands Crus and certainly the most powerful and complex red wines, including Nuits-Saint-Georges, Gevrey-Chambertin, Vosne-Romanée and Clos Vougeot. It is quite rare to discover little-known gems in the necklace, although they might be found in two or three villages somewhat overshadowed by their great neighbors, such as Marsannay or Fixin, pronounced "Fis-*sin*" in Burgundy.

Continuing south, with no natural boundary, the Côte de Beaune begins several kilometers north of Beaune in the commune of Ladoix-Serigny. In the cradle of great white wines like Corton-Charlemagne, Meursault, Puligny-Montrachet, and of several voluptuous red pearls such as Pommard and Volnay, the wine lover can also find the largest palette of little-known intermediary *crus* here, in both red and white wines: Ladoix, Pernand-Vergelesse, Savigny-lès-Beaune, Chorey-lès-Beaune, Auxey-Duresse, Saint-Romain, Saint-Aubin, Maranges...

The Côte Chalonnaise marks the transition between the Côte d'Or and the Mâconnais. Here, Mercurey, Givry, and Rully offer less complex whites and reds than in the Côte d'Or, but at reasonable prices. Finally, the Mâconnais is essentially a breeding ground for white wines, still very little-known except for its famous *cru*, Pouilly-Fuissé.

Both at the bottom of the pyramid with simple regional appellations or on top with Grands Crus, Burgundies are expensive wines. Burgundy is a small vineyard region, terribly fragmented in its wines and its properties, and the world demand for Burgundies continues to grow. For this reason, no matter what the appellation, the wine buyer must in effect pay a surcharge, a kind of entrance fee imposed by the market, before paying the real price of the wine. In these conditions the wine connoisseur has every reason to find the price too high and thus to forego buying wine in Burgundy. Unless, unless...the buyer is an aficionado of Pinot Noir and Chardonnay. From 1960 to the early 1980s, this "surcharge" could seem exaggerated given the quality of the wine: at the height of its fashion, Burgundy was drowning in mediocrity. But over the last fifteen years, Burgundies have not only improved but have attained a general level of quality never before approached. Finally, while the thirty-two Grands Crus have attained such summits that they are practically unaffordable to most connoisseurs, there are still many Burgundies for 50 to 80 francs, offering remarkable quality for the price. More than any other region, Burgundy belongs to wine lovers who have the curiosity to travel off the beaten path and shatter myths.

Among the vintages available, you can still find some '93s, an excellent year for wines that age well, and for whites of slightly inferior quality, quite severe, vigorous, and crisp. The '94 reds and whites are not charming, big Burgundies and are therefore very pleasant to drink young. 1995 was a small-yielding harvest, a rich, mature vintage for red wines, at once well structured and delicate; it also yielded well-balanced white wines. 1996, with heavy yields in volume and despite worrisome rains before the harvest, turned out to produce wines of a very high but heterogenous quality. From those *vignerons* who harvested late, the results were wonderful, especially in the Côte de Nuits. The grapes picked too early, on the other hand, produced diluted, somewhat acid wines, especially the Pinot Noirs, which are more likely to become diluted with heavy yields. Depending on the wine, the '96s will be good to drink with three to ten years' bottle age for whites and four to fifteen years for reds.

Wines are rare in Burgundy and the good domains quickly run out of bottles to sell. But that doesn't mean that they cannot be found, especially if you meet the winemakers on their property: they love knowing their customers, and this is also the best way of winning their confidence and obtaining their best wines regularly, since the great vintages are often reserved for their faithful clientele. In 1998, therefore, you should reserve the very good 1996s, which will be bottled in the spring or autumn of 1998. And above all, don't hesitate to say that you found them in our Guide.

INTRODUCTION

A TABLE WITH BURGUNDIES

As opposed to Bordeaux wines (which generally should be kept for five to ten years), red Burgundies open up more quickly and offer enormous pleasure when they are young: Fleshy, thick, and still fruity, they go well with pork, lamb stew, farm-bred chicken, and giblets like sweetbreads. With longer bottle aging (six to eight years), they are good accompaniments for *boeuf bourguignon* and slowly simmered meat dishes in general. After ten years the great Côte-de-Nuits are marvelous with game. White Burgundies make a beautiful complement to seafood: Chablis with oysters, shellfish, marinated salmon; Meursault or Puligny-Montrachet (after five to six years in bottle) with fresh-water fish in a cream sauce; Corton-Charlemagne or another Grand Cru with lobster. White Burgundies are also good company for parsleyed ham, snails and frogs' legs, as well as cheeses like Comté or Pont-l'Evêque, with which they are much finer escorts than red wines.

ALOXE-CORTON

1 - HOTEL - **Villa Louise**: *21420 Aloxe-Corton. Tel. 03.80.26.46.70 Fax 03.80.26.47.16 web: www.villa louise.com.* Formerly the Hôtel Clarion, this 17th-century family mansion (sans restaurant) facing the Aloxe vineyard still offers 10 modern, refined, and perfectly quiet

rooms. A truly charming stop. From 500 to 800 F. Breakfast: 75 F.

AUXERRE

2 - RESTAURANT - **Le bistrot du Palais**: *69 rue de Paris, 89000 Auxerre. Tel. 03.86.51.47.02. Closed Sunday and Monday.* Friendly atmosphere and cuisine (bouchon lyonnais: excellent traditional French cuisine). Good finds in wines at reasonable prices. A la carte: around 80 F.

3 - RESTAURANT - **Le Jardin Gourmand**: *56 bd Vauban, 89000 Auxerre. Tel. 03.86.51.53.52 Fax 03.86.52.33.82. Closed Tuesday and Wednesday.* Market products, straightforward fine cuisine. Good selection of Burgundies with a truly lyric list of Chablis. Service by the glass. Menus: 140 to 270 F.

BEAUNE

4 - HOTEL - **Château de Challanges**: *Challanges, 21200 Beaune. Tel. 03.80.26.32.62 Fax 03.80.26.32.52. Closed December to March.* Traditional mansion set in a park. Rooms redone in a classic style. No restaurant. 9 rooms and 5 suites: 530 to 800 F. Breakfast 60 F.

5 - HOTEL - **Hôtel Le Home**: *138 route de Dijon, 21200 Beaune. Tel. 03.80. 22.16.43 Fax 03.80.24.90.74.* On the way into Beaune (the road is well travelled, but the house well insulated from noise): a charming hotel with park, tastefully furnished with antiques. 23 rooms: 325 to 450 F. Breakfast: 35 F.

6 - RESTAURANT - **Bernard Morillon**: *31 rue Maufoux, 21200 Beaune. Tel. 03.80.24.12.06 Fax 03.80. 22.66.22. Closed Monday, lunch Tuesday, and in February.* High-class bourgeois cuisine in the Burgundian tradition, served in an old private residence in the town center. Friendly welcome. An almost Bur-

gundy-only wine list with some very expensive old vintages (49, 59, 64); average prices per bottle: 280-300 F. Menus: 180 to 480 F. A la carte: around 400 F.

7 - RESTAURANT - **Le Benaton**: *25 rue du Faubourg-Bretonnière, 21200 Beaune. Tel. 03.80.22.00.26 Fax 03.80.22.51.95. Closed Wednesday and lunch Thursday.* Spartan decor. Sober, personalized cuisine and wise pricing of the Burgundy wine list. Terrace in summer. Currently the best value in Beaune. Menus: 108 to 230 F.

8 - RESTAURANT - **Le Jardin des Remparts**: *10 rue de l'Hôtel-Dieu, 21200 Beaune. Tel. 03.80.24.79.41 Fax 03.80.24.92.79. Closed Sunday, Monday (except holidays), and mid-February to mid-March.* Along Beaune's circular boulevard: a modernly furnished family house from the 30's. Fine cuisine (traditional and original), wise prices for the first menus and a wine list that gives a boost to little-known appellations. For around 150 F you can find a bottle that will put a smile on your face. Menus: 135 to 305 F.

BOUILLAND

9 - HOTEL-RESTAURANT - **Le Vieux Moulin**: *21420 Bouilland. Tel. 03.80.21.51.16 Fax 03.80.21.59.90. Closed Wednesday (except evenings in high-season), Thursday noon (except holidays) and from January 5 to 21.* Somewhat isolated from the Côte, 10 km northwest of Savigny-lès-Beaune, near the ruins of Sainte-Marguerite's. Contemporary cuisine combining seafood and " landfood ". Wine list with 450 good-looking but expensive entries. Menus: 195 to 350 F. 24 rooms and 2 suites with modern comfort and decor from 380 to 1,200 F. Perfectly calm.

BUSSIERES

10 - HOTEL-RESTAURANT - **Relais Lamartine**: *71960 Bussières. Tel. 03.85.36.64.71.* An honest and loyal regional cuisine (product origins are proudly displayed) accompanied by an enticing list of Mâconnais wines. Menus: 110 to 220 F. 8 rooms: 345 to 395 F.

CHABLIS

11 - HOTEL-RESTAURANT - **Hostellerie des Clos**: *18 rue Jules-Rathier, 89800 Chablis. Tel. 03.86.42.10.63 Fax 03.86.42.17.11. Closed Wednesday and Thursday (low-season) and from mid-December to mid-January.* Quiet rooms and fine dining. Numerous references in Chablis which gains somewhat by the service. Menus: 175 to 420 F. 26 rooms: 288 to 530 F.

12 - RESTAURANT - **Au Vrai Chablis**: *Place du Général-de-Gaulle, 89800 Chablis. Tel. 03.86.42.11.43 Fax 03.86.42.14.57. Closed Tuesday evening and Wednesday.* Unpretentious local cuisine accompanied by a relatively full list of Chablis. Menus: 78 (weekdays) to 135 F. A la carte: around 135 F.

CHAGNY

13 - HOTEL-RESTAURANT - **Château de Bellecroix**: *71150 Chagny. Tel. 03.85.*

87.13.86 Fax 05.85.91.28.62. Closed mid-December to mid-February. A medieval castle modified in the 18th century with beautiful slate-roofed turrets. Twenty-one rooms, some overlooking the park. Some are quite small, while others, with mullioned windows, are much larger. Swimming pool. From 580 to 1,000 F. Breakfast: 65 F.

14 - HOTEL-RESTAURANT - **Jacques Lameloise**: *36 place d'Armes, 71150 Chagny. Tel. 03.85.87.08.85 Fax 03.85.87.03.57. Closed Wednesday, Thursday noon, and mid-December to late January.* Relais & Châteaux. Excellent preparation of Burgundian specialties. Remarkable list of estate bottled wines. Menus: 390 and 600 F. 17 rooms: 700 to 1,500 F.

CHALON-SUR-SAONE

15 - RESTAURANT - **Le Moulin de Martorey**: *Jean-Pierre Gillot, Saint-Rémy, 71100 Chalon-sur-Saône. Tel. 03.85.48.12.98. Closed Sunday evening and Monday.* In a former grain mill: a cuisine that's powerful (wine sauces) and innovative (variations in seasoning). The premier menus are faultless. Well-chosen Burgundy wine list, especially for Côte Chalonnaise. Suitable prices. Menus: 180 to 410 F.

CHAMBOLLE-MUSIGNY

16 - HOTEL - **Château-Hôtel André Ziltener**: *Rue de la Fontaine, 21220 Chambolle-Musigny. Tel. 03.80.62.41.62 Fax 03.80.62.83.75.* In the heart of the village, a vast bourgeois house (fomerly the Cistertian monks' cellar) completely renovated in great luxury and pomp. For well-to-do amateurs. Three rooms: 900 to 1,000 F. Seven apartments: 1,100 to 1,800 F. Breakfast: 80 F. Visit and wine sales in the cellar of the establishment that also acts as négociant.

CHARRECEY

17 - RESTAURANT - **Le Petit Blanc**: *Pont Pilley, 71510 Charrecey. Tel. 03.85.45.15.43. Closed Monday.* Towards Autun, 5 min from Mercurey. A welcoming inn with friendly bistro-style cuisine and a selection of Chalonnais vintages that's just as nice. Menus: 68 to 158 F.

CHOREY-LES-BEAUNE

18 - BED & BREAKFAST - **Château de Chorey-lès-Beaune**: *21200 Chorey-*

lès-Beaune. Tel. 03.80.22.06.05 Fax 03.80.24.03.93. Open from March 1 to November 30. 5 rooms and a suite in this castle of the 13th and 17th centuries belonging to a wine-growing family. From 710 to 810 F, breakfast included.

19 - HOTEL-RESTAURANT - **L'Ermitage Corton**: *RN74, 21200 Chorey-lès-Beaune. Tel. 03.80.22.05.28 Fax 03.80.22.86.01. Closed Sunday evening, Monday, and mid-January to mid-February.* Generous regional cuisine (excellent for traditional sauces and reductions) and an equally lavish Burgundy wine list. High prices. Menus: 170 to 650 F. 10 very comfortable rooms (850 to 1,800 F).

CURTIL-VERGY

20 - HOTEL - **Le Manassès**: *21220 Curtil-Vergy. Tel. 03.80.61.43.81 Fax 03.80.61.42.79. Closed December through February.* A small hotel (7 rooms: 400 F. Breakfast: 50 F) kept by winegrowers in an entirely

renovated house. Modern comforts and a first-rate welcome.

FLAGEY-ÉCHEZEAUX

21 - RESTAURANT - **Robert Losset**: *Place de l'Église, 21640 Flagey-Échezeaux. Tel. 03.80.62.88.10. Closed Wednesday, and Sunday evening.* A bar-tobacconist with surprisingly good Burgundian cooking, hearty and generous. Low prices. Honest Burgundy wine list. Menus: 140 to 250 F.

FUISSE

22 - RESTAURANT - **Au Pouilly-Fuissé**: *71960 Fuissé. Tel. and Fax 03.85.35.60.68. Closed Sunday evening and Wednesday, and the first week of August and first 3 weeks of January.* Good quality Bressan cuisine for the price. 25 Pouillys, Mâcons and Saint-Vérans, mostly from village producers. Menus: 85 to 222 F. A la carte: around 150 F.

GEVREY-CHAMBERTIN

23 - BED & BREAKFAST - **Le Relais de**

Chasse: *Chambœuf, 21220 Gevrey-Chambertin. Tel. 03.80.51.81.60 Fax 03.80.34.15.96.* 4 rooms (400 F) in a lovely Burgundian manor offering a warm welcome. No meals. No smoking.

24 - HOTEL - **Hôtel des arts et Terroirs**: *28 route de Dijon, 21220 Gevrey-Chambertin. Tel. 03.80.34.30.76 Fax 03.80.34.11.79.* 20 comfortable, well-arranged rooms (250 to 580 F).

Breakfast: 45 F. Bicycles available for rides around the vineyard.

25 - RESTAURANT - **Bonbistrot**: *Rue du Chambertin, 21220 Gevrey-Chambertin. Tel. 03.80.34.33.20. Closed Sunday evening, Monday (except in February), three weeks in February and two in August.* Countryside setting, good cuisine, convivial atmosphere. Short wine list at reasonable prices. A la carte: around 125 F.

26 - RESTAURANT - **Rôtisserie du Chambertin**: *Rue du Chambertin, 21220 Gevrey-Chambertin. Tel. 03.80.34.33.20 Fax 03.80.34.12.30. Closed Sunday evening and Monday (except in February), three weeks in February and two in August.* Traditional cuisine and tongue-in-cheek Burgundian folklore. Relatively complete wine list, with very costly collector's bottles. Menus: 210 to 330 F.

27 - RESTAURANT - **Les Millésimes**: *25 rue de l'Église, 21200 Gevrey-Chambertin. Tel. 03.80.51.84.24. Closed Tuesday, noon Wednesday, and December 20 to January 29.* Generous cuisine with a regional accent at an elegant table. Boggling selection of Burgundies at the usual prices. Menus: 315 to 595 F.

GILLY-LES-CITEAUX

28 - HOTEL-RESTAURANT - **Château de Gilly Clos Prieur**: *21640 Gilly-les-Citeaux. Tel. 03.80.62.89.98 Fax 03.80.62.82.34. Closed Wednesday.* Relais & Châteaux. A dining hall with Gothic columns and ogives, rooms wonderfully furnished. Long wine list. Palatial welcome. Menus: 195 to 410 F. 39 rooms: 680 F to 1,000 F and 8 apartments from 1,590 to 2,500 F.

IGE

29 - HOTEL-RESTAURANT - **Château d'Igé**: *71960 Igé. Tel. 03.85.33.33.99 Fax 03.85.33.41.41. Closed in February.* A 12th-century feudal castle at 12 km from Cluny. Well-seasoned cuisine, cooked just right, and an honest wine list that could do better in the region. Menus: 155 (lunch weekdays) to 365 F. 7 charming rooms: 495 to 750 F. 6 apartments: 905 to 1,125 F.

LADOIX-SERRIGNY

30 - RESTAURANT - **Les Coquines**: *N74, 21550 Ladoix-Serrigny (4 km from the Beaune-Nord exit on the A6 towards Dijon). Tel. 03.80.26.43.58 Fax 03.80.26.40.49. Closed Wednesday evening and Thursday, and for February vacation.* In a former fermenting room, Burgundian cuisine with a modern twist. Short list of Burgundies at moderate prices. Menus: 155 to 225 F.

MARSANNAY-LA-COTE

31 - RESTAURANT - **Les Gourmets**: *8 rue du Puits-de-Têt, 21160 Marsannay-la-Côte. Tel. 03.80.52.16.32 Fax 03.80.62.03.01. Closed Sunday evening, Monday, one week in August and two in February.* One of Burgundy's great refined tables. Most of the good Marsannays are on the wine list at smart prices. Menus: 145 to 410 F.

MERCUREY

32 - RESTAURANT - **Hôtellerie du Val-d'Or**: *Grand' Rue, 71640 Mercurey. Tel. 03.85.45.13.70 Fax 03.85.45. 18.45. Closed Monday and noon Tuesday, and 4 weeks between December and January.* Classic regional cuisine with a large selection of Côte-Chalonnaise. Menus: 165 to 345 F. A la carte: around 350 F.

MEURSAULT

33 - HOTEL - **Hôtel des Magnolias**: *8 rue Pierre-Joigneaux, 21190 Meursault. Tel. 03.80.21.23.23 Fax 03.80.21. 29.10. Closed early December to mid-March.* A bourgeois house in the village, renovated and well-equipped (no restaurant). Charm and character. 12 rooms: 400 to 750 F.

MONTHELIE

34 - BED & BREAKFAST - **Domaine de Suremain**: *21190 Monthelie. Tel. 03.80.21.23.32 Fax 03.80.21.66.37.* Refurbished old vacation house (independant, with courtyard) that can house 5 persons. Run by renowned winegrowers. Rental by the week from Easter to Halloween.

NUITS-SAINT-GEORGES

35 - BED & BREAKFAST - **Domaine de Loisy**: *28 rue Général-de-Gaulle, 21700 Nuits-Saint-Georges. Tel. 03.80.61. 02.72 Fax 03.80.61.36.14.* Four rooms (500 to 850 F, breakfast included). A little noisy due to the proximity of the road. The owner organizes cellar visits.

36 - HOTEL-RESTAURANT - **La Gentilhommière**: *13 vallée de la Serrée, 21700 Nuits-Saint-Georges. Tel. 03.80.61. 12.06 Fax 03.80.61.30.33. Closed Tuesday, noon Wedday (restaurant) and mid-December to mid-January.* In a pastoral setting, away from the Côte de Nuits, a large one-story hotel with txenty average-sized rooms (390 F) that are simple, comfortable and very quiet. We didn't try the restaurant. Menus: 195 to 275 F. Breakfast: 50 F.

PULIGNY-MONTRACHET

37 - RESTAURANT - **Le Montrachet**: *Place des Marronniers, 21190 Puligny-Montrachet. Tel. 03.80.21.30.06 Fax 03.80.21.39.06. Closed noon Wednesday and in December.* Elegant decor, cuisine with a regional inspiration. Lovely list of great white wines at high prices. Menus: 190 to 415 F. thirty-two rooms: 450 to 1,000 F.

38 - RESTAURANT - **La Table d'Olivier Leflaive**: *Place du Monument, 21190 Puligny-Montrachet. Tel. 03.80.21.37.65/ 03.80.21.95.27 Fax 03.80.21.33.94. Lunch only (12 to 2pm) every day (except Sun.) from mid-March to mid-November.* Simple specialty cooking (plate of cold cuts, cheese board) and degustation of the wines of this very good

Puligny property. Menus at 180 F (with eleven appellations villages)

or 230 F (seventeen appellations villages Premier Cru). Take-outs.

REPLONGES

39 - HOTEL-RESTAURANT - **La Huchette**: *01750 Replonges. Tel. 03.85.31.03.55 Fax 03.85.31.10.24. Closed mid-November to mid-December and Monday.* 4 km east of Mâcon: a vast Bressan house offering 12 very comfortable rooms with view of the park. Pool. From 400 to 1,200 F.

SAINT-GERVAIS-EN-VALLIERE

40 - HOTEL-RESTAURANT - **Moulin de Hauterive**: *Chaublanc, 71350 Saint-Gervais-en-Vallière. Tel. 03.85.91.55.56 Fax 03.85.91.89.65. Closed Monday, noon Tuesday and in January.* Leaving the vineyard (12 km east of Beaune), one discovers this very beautiful, Virginia-creeper-covered mill surrounded by a park. 10 rooms and 12 suites, very comfortable, from 530 to 850 F. Breakfast: 70 F. Menus: 105 to 400 F.

SAINT-LAURENT-SUR-SAONE

41 - RESTAURANT - **Le Saint-Laurent**: *1 quai Bouchacourt, 01750 Saint-Laurent-sur-Saône. Tel. 04.85.39.29.19 Fax 04.85.38.29.77. Closed from November 15 to December 15.* On the left bank of the Saône (of which one takes full advantage from the terrace), another of Georges Blanc's addresses (see following). His bistro, offering good regional cuisine at moderate prices, is worth the detour for the first menus. Wine list in keeping with the cuisine. Menus: 98 to 210 F. A la carte: around 200 F.

SANTENAY

42 - RESTAURANT - **Le Terroir**: *Place du jet d'eau, 21590 Santenay. Tel. 03.80.20.63.47. Closed Thursday and Sunday evening except in July and August.* A simple and savory regional cuisine, professional service, smart prices and a serious wine list. Menus: 83 F (lunch weekdays), 98 to 220 F.

SAVIGNY-LES-BEAUNE

43 - BED & BREAKFAST - **Le Hameau de Barboron**: *Odile Nominé, 21420 Savigny-les-Beaune. Tel. 03.80.21.58.35 Fax 03.80.26.10.59.* Meals by reservation. 15 mn from Beaune, a

vast hunting lodge secluded in the forest. Magnificently restored, it offers guest rooms in great comfort and country-style refinement. Worthy of a Relais & Châteaux, with

conviviality to boot. Hunting weekends organized from October to March. Single rooms: 450 to 500 F, doubles: 550 to 900 F, duplex: 1,000 to 1,200 F. Breakfast: 65 F.

TONNERRE

44 - HOTEL-RESTAURANT - **L'Abbaye Saint-Michel**: *Montée Saint-Michel, 89700 Tonnerre. Tel. 03.86.55.05.99 Fax 03.86.55.00.10. Closed in January.* This very luxurious renovated abbey affords a view over the two churches in Tonnerre and Épineuil's reviving vineyard. Beautiful garden. Creative and elegant cuisine by one of Joël Robuchon's disciples. Preference given to Tonnerrois wines, especially Chablis. High prices. A la carte: around 550 F. Eleven rooms, two suites and one apartment: 590 to 1,500 F, breakfast included.

TOURNUS

45 - RESTAURANT - **Restaurant de Greuze**: *Jean Ducloux, 1 rue A. Thibaudet, 71700 Tournus, Tel. 03.85.51.13.52 Fax 03.85.51.75.42.* A colorful character in French gastronomy, Jean Ducloux and his table, with a pre-war bourgeois flavor, are a must along the road toward the Mâconnais. Elegant decor, hearty and generous cuisine, genuine conviviality- in short, destined to entertain both the eyes and the palate. Classic and serious selection of great wines from the region and elsewhere. Menus: 260 F (weekdays) and 490 F. A la carte: count on 400 F.

46 - HOTEL - **Hôtel de Greuze**: *Jean Ducloux, 5/6 place de l'abbaye, 71700 Tournus, Tel. 03.85.51.77.77 Fax 03.85.51.77.23.* Same proprietor as the restaurant de Greuze. Beautiful hotel looking out on the abbey. Twenty-one rooms and two apartments: 620 to 1,900 F.

47 - HOTEL-RESTAURANT - **La Montagne de Brancion**: *Brancion, 71700 Tournus. Tel. 03.85.51.12.40 Fax 03.85.51.18.64.* A new hotel advantaged by

its view over the vineyard and the village of Martailly. Modern comforts and a smiling welcome. Pool. Rooms: 460 to 760 F. Breakfast: 70 F. Menus: 250 to 330 F.

VEZELAY

48 - HOTEL-RESTAURANT - **L'Espérance**: *Marc Meneau, Saint-Père-sous-Vézelay, 89450 Vézelay. Tel. 03.86. 33.20.45 Fax 03.86.33.26.15. Closed Tuesday, noon Wednesday and in February (restaurant only).* Magnificent hostelry and exceptional cuisine. Authoritative wine list leaning toward the Yonne, particularly Vézelay. Menus: 360 to 860 F. 34 rooms: 420 to 2,000 F.

VOUGEOT

49 - HOTEL - **Hôtel de la Perrière**: *18 rue du vieux Château, 21640 Vougeot. Tel. 03.80.62.80.49 Fax 03.80.62. 83.65.* At the foot of the Vougeot hill, a few hundred yards from the castle, a hotel with 12 simple (no TV), but comfortable rooms shared between three houses (new or restored), most of which look out on the vineyard. Ask for those in the little one-story house bordering on the vineyard. From 320 to 440 F.

TO SEE

BEAUNE

MUSEUM - **Hospices de Beaune, Musée de l'Hôtel-Dieu**: *2 rue de l'Hôtel-*

Dieu, 21200 Beaune. Tel. 03.80.24. 45.00 Fax 03.80.24.45.99. Open every day mid-November to mid-March from 9 to 11:30 and 2 to 5:30. The rest of the year from 9am to 6:30pm. Admission: 32 F.

MUSEUM - **Burgundy Wine Museum**: *Rue d'Enfer, 21200 Beaune. Tel. 03.80.22.08.19. Open every day*

(except Tuesday from December 1 to March 31) from 9:30 to 6. Admission: 25 F. In the residence of the dukes of Burgundy. Collection of rare works evoking wine and vineyards, tapestries from Lurçat and Tourlière. Tours every day.

CANAL DE BOURGOGNE

OUTING - **Boat rental**: Almost 1200 km of rivers and canals, near deserted by commercial transporters, are open for boating. Well-equipped houseboats (for four to twelve persons) can be rented for the weekend, a week or longer. No license required. Prices vary on rental period. *Information:* **Bateaux de Bourgogne**: *1/2 quai de la République, 89000 Auxerre. Tel. 03.86.51.12.05.* From

3,000 to 8,000 F per week for a 5-person boat, depending on rental period. **Locaboat Plaisance**: *Quai du Port-au-Bois, 89300 Joigny. Tel. 03.86.91.72.72.* From 5,000 to 8,600 F per week for a 5-person boat, depending on rental period.

CHENOVE

OUTING - **The wine presses of the dukes of Burgundy**: *8 rue Roger-Salengro, 21300 Chenôve, Tel. 03.80.52. 82.83. Every day between 6/15 and 9/30 from 2 to 7pm.* Free admission. Two counter-balance wine presses dating from the reign of Jean Sans-Peur (1404). September 20 and 21: 10th anniversary of the grape-crushing fête.

COTES-DE-BEAUNE

FETE - **Les Trois glorieuses de Bourgogne**: The third weekend in November of each year. The region's most popular festival, including the general exhibition of wines from all of Burgundy (impressive tasting of 3,000 wines, open to all, on Saturday and Sunday in Beaune's Palais des Congrès), the Hospices de Beaune's auction (hall de Beaune, Sunday afternoon), the degustation of the Hospices' most recent vintage (Saturday and Sunday), and the Paulée de Meursault (Monday). Prestigious private lunches at the Meursault castle.

COULANGES-LA-VINEUSE

OUTING - **Coulanges-la-Vineuse**: An 18th-century press-down wine press.

MACON

OUTING - **Domaine Saint-Philibert**: *Loché 71000 Mâcon. Tel. 03.85.35. 61.76. Open all year.* Tours daily by reservation. It's only after lengthy searching all throughout France that Philippe Bérard, chosen in our guide for his Pouilly-Loché white wines, was able to set up this vast museum devoted to vineyard and winery tools. Our man has a real passion, and a stop here can leave nothing but good memories.

POUILLY-EN-AUXOIS

OUTING - **Hot-air balloon rides**: **Air Adventures**: *Rue du Chat Fou, 21320 Pouilly-en-Auxois. Tel. 03.80. 90.74.23 Fax 03.80.90.72.86.* Hot-air balloon rides above the vineyards (approximately one hour), every day year-round, weather per-

mitting. Lift-off in the morning or late afternoon. By reservation. Group rates beginning at five persons.

Air Escargot: *71150 Rémigny. Tel. 03.85.87.12.30 Fax 03.85.87.08.84.* Hot-air balloon ride over the vineyards, year-round. Take-off in Beaune. Count on a 3-hour adventure (including inflating and return trip). Early morning or late afternoon lift-offs. By reservation. Discount group rates with six or more persons.

POUILLY FUISSE

OUTING - **The church's porch sculp-**

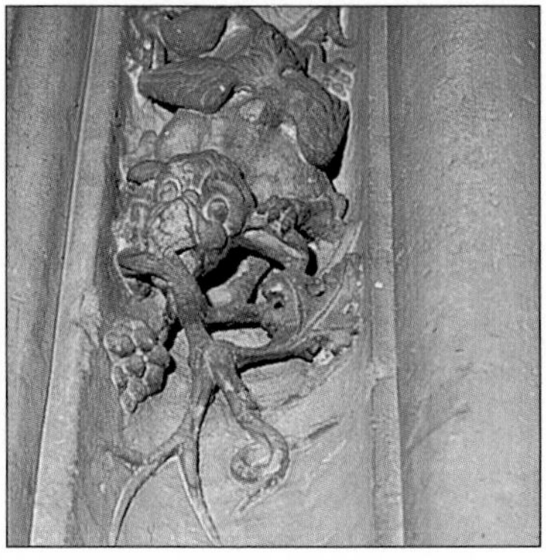

tures: blights devour the grapevine.

RULLY

FETE - **Saint-Vincent tournante de Bourgogne 1998 in Rully**: last weekend in January. Two days of celebrations in the villages of the appellation, tasting of the appellation's collegial wine.

SOLUTRE

OUTING - **Roche de Solutré**: made famous by the press-covered presidential outings, this majestic rocky spur- an important prehistoric site- can be climbed easily in an hour and a half. View over the Pouilly vineyard and the plain of the Saône.

VERGISSON

OUTING - **Ânes et sentiers**: *Roger Lassarat, Le Martelet, 71960 Vergisson. Tel. 03.85.35.84.28. Every day in July and August, weekends in low-season.* Reservations suggested. Visit the Pouilly-Fuissé vineyard by donkey (for one or more days): such is the odd and exciting adventure offered by an excellent winegrower settled in at the foot of the roche de Solutré, in Vergisson. Fifteen donkeys available. Plan on 250 to 300F per donkey per day.

VOUGEOT

VISIT - **Château du Clos-Vougeot**: *21640 Vougeot. Tel. 03.80.62.86.09 Fax 03.80.62.82.75. Open April to September from 9 am to 6:30pm (5pm Sat.), October to March from 9 to 11:30 and 2 to 5:30 (5pm Sat.). Closed December 24, 25, 31 and January 1.* Admission: 17 F; children (less than 13): 13 F; less than 8: free. A one-hour tour: the historic 12th-century castle, followed by a

film on the guild's activities.

In each vintage, Jean-Hugues Goisot's simple Burgundies are exceptionally pure and straightforward.

Domaine Ghislaine et Jean-Hugues Goisot

Owners Ghislaine and Jean-Hugues Goisot. **Adresse** 30, rue Bienvenu-Martin, 89530 Saint-Bris-le-Vineux - Tel. 03.86.53.35.15 Fax 03.86.53.62.03. **Open** Monday to Saturday, 8:00-12:00 and 13:30-19:00, by appointment. **Credit cards** Visa, Eurocard, MasterCard.

The Goisots have been dominating the white-wine scene in the Yonne *département* (Chablis aside) for years. A hard-working perfectionist, Jean-Hugues Goisot is a disciple of the school that makes straightforward wines, deliciously fruity, without cosmetic effects: hymns to their *terroir,* the picture of freshness and elegance that could serve as a model for many a *grand cru* winemaker. Of the nine wines available (the estate covers 24 hectares), his '96 Bourgogne Aligoté (29 F) serves as a benchmark: fruity, full-bodied taste of ripe grapes, finishing with a vivacious touch. The '96 Bourgogne Côtes d'Auxerre (33 F), from 15-year-old Chardonnay vines, is distinguished by beautiful concentration, an ample, generous taste. Superb. The Corps de Garde *cuvées,* vinified and aged in barrels, needs some bottle age: 'the '95 Chardonnay (41 F), mellow, buttery, mouth-filling; and the '95 Pinot Noir (37 F): bouquet of red berries, well structured, is delicious.

Our Choice Saint-Bris is the home territory of the Burgundian Sauvignon and the Goisots are its prime growers: their '96 Sauvignon de Saint-Bris (29 F) has a mentholated, pink-grapefruit aroma; very smooth and mellow in taste; and the latest '96, the Sauvignon Corps de Garde Gourmand (36 F), from Fié Gris grapes, the ancestor of Sauvignon, yields a very aromatic white wine (mango, aniseed), soft, with an extraordinary taste of exotic candied fruits. Delicious.

Reception By Jean-Hugues Goisot, discreet and reserved, but most often by his wife and alter ego, Ghislaine. Old cellar with 11th-century guardroom.

How to get there *(Map 4): On A6, take Auxerre Sud exit (15km). From the toll gate, direction Auxerre, then Avallon (N6). 4 kms south of Auxerre, direction Saint-Bris.*

Irancy is famous for its cherries, for Germain Soufflot (1713-1780), the architect of the Panthéon in Paris, and for its native son, Jean-Pierre Colinot.

Domaine Colinot

Owners Anita and Jean-Pierre Colinot. **Adresse** 1, rue des Chariats, 89290 Irancy - Tel. and Fax 03.86.42.33.25. **Open** From Monday to Saturday, 8:00-20:00, Sunday until 16:00, by appointment. **Spoken** English, German.

He's often described as *volubile* in French, which the French dictionary defines as "a person who talks a lot, quickly. Antonym: silent." Thank you, *Petit Robert*, for having devoted several lines to Jean-Pierre Colinot during his lifetime! You won't soon forget turning in to this small lane in Irancy. For Colinot is a magnificent raconteur who tells you all about his village--colorful, "red, in fact, it was Communist for a long time"; explains his *terroirs,* which are about to crowned with the communal appellation in 1998--"'Irancy', and no longer 'Bourgogne Irancy', with the *lieux-dits* mentioned on the label"; and champions the César, "the archaeological grape variety of Irancy", tannic and deeply colored. Like the man, the red wines here have character and they talk back. Using traditional, old techniques, Colinot owns eight hectares of Irancy, giving wines that are deep red in color, well structured, never lacking in body or fruit. All the grapes are vinified by individual parcels of vines. The '96s are remarkable, on a par with the '90s, especially Les Mazelots, Palotte, Côte du Moutier (43 to 48 F). Don't hesitate.

Our choice The '96 Bourgogne Irancy Vieilles Vignes (48 F). Pinot Noir filled out with 15% César, from 70-year-old vines. Very deep color, full, mellow aroma of black fruit, remarkably mouth-filling, velvety, robust, textured, densely tannic finish. An original wine, like its maker.

Reception Generous and picturesque, with Anita and Jean-Pierre, in their 13th-century cellar.

How to get there *(Map 4): On A 6, exit Auxerre Sud (24.5km). From the toll gate, direction Auxerre, then Avallon (N6). 10 kms south of Avallon, direction Irancy. In the center of the village.*

Founded in 1815, this estate has undergone complete modernization over the past ten years, resulting in finer Chablis.

Domaine J. Billaud-Simon

Owners Bernard and André Billaud, Jeanine Pimpaneau. **Adresse** 1 quai de Reugny, 89800 Chablis - Tel. 03.86.42.10.33 Fax 03.86.42.48.77. **Open** From Monday to Saturday, by appointment. **Spoken** English.

"The grapes and the *terroir*" are the essential preoccupations of Bernard and André Billaud, and the latter's son, Samuel, who is in charge of winemaking on the twenty-hectare estate lying on the best *terroirs* of Chablis. Excessive barrel-ageing, which sometimes conceals the typical mineral edge of Chablis, is not their style. Vinification in barrels is used sparingly. The crystalline Chardonnay speaks here with a crystal-clear, graceful voice. The winemakers aim for a forthright picture of the *terroir,* combined with the maturity of the vintage: the Chablis raised eyebrows in 1995. Of the four Premiers Crus, their Mont de Milieu (about 70 F), concentrates its fruit and mineral edge, opening up long on the palate with traces of honey and chalk. In the Vieilles Vignes version (about 85 F), 30% of which is barrel aged, the *terroir* is less evident in the aroma, accenting the full and remarkably lingering taste. The 1994 Grands Crus are Chablis of great generosity: Vaudésir is long, complex, of great breeding; Les Clos is demonstrative, powerful.

Our choice The '95 Chablis Premier Cru Les Vaillons (about 70 F). A wine of perfect maturity but still ethereal, elegant, all lace and length. An excellent résumé of the spirit of the estate's Chablis.

Reception On the banks of the River Serein, in a 19th-century estate; you will see the modern architecture of the cellars and the tasting cellar. Professional and attentive.

How to get there *(Map 4): On A6, take exit Auxerre Sud, direction Chablis (12km). In Chablis, direction Tonnerre,before crossing the Serein (in front of the public wash house), turn right and follow the river bank for 500 meters.*

Daniel Defaix, a champion of Chablis wines at their peak.

Domaine Daniel-Étienne Defaix au Vieux Château

Owners Daniel and Fabienne Defaix. **Address** Vieux château de Milly, Le Monde du Vin, 14 rue Auxerroise, 89800 Chablis - Tel. 03.86.42.42.05 Fax 03.86.42.48.56. **Open** Every day, 9:00-12:00 and 14:00-18:00. Jan 1 - Feb 15 by appointment. **Spoken** English. **Credit cards** Visa, Eurocard, MasterCard.

As opposed to the usual practice in Chablis, Daniel Defaix built the entire organization of his estate (26 hectares, with 2/3 in Premier Cru vineyards) on selling his wines only once they are fully mature. This strapping gastronome likes to take his time. Which begins with the harvest, when the grapes are very ripe, and continues with vinification and ageing uniquely in vats, including a complex and delicate lees manipulation and yeast autolysis. As a result, Defaix' Chablis is very delicate, soft, "well fed". The exception to this long-haul work is his simple Chablis, a lovely wine in 1995 (55 F). Of the Premiers Crus, the '92s came out only in 1997 and this great year for white Burgundy kept its promise. The '92 Vaillons (85 F) is a Chablis of great maturity, the richest, most powerful, and spiciest of the vintage: a gastronomic wine that is marvelous with red mullet. The 1992 Lys (85 F) is more discreet, while mouth-filling, liquid, with a firm, mineral finish and fine length.

Our choice The '92 Chablis Premier Cru Côte de Léchet (85 F). Defaix's Chablis that invariably opens up the most quickly, with aromas and tastes of candied fruits (citrus fruit, pineapple); buttery on the palate, soft, not heavy, finishing with a mineral edge. To drink or to keep.

Reception *Caves Defaix - Le Monde du Vin* in the center of Chablis. Most often by a secretary or by Fabienne, Daniel's wife. Tasting cellar recently renovated.

How to get there *(Map 4): On A6, exit Auxerre Sud, direction Chablis (12km). In the center, tasting room on the corner of the Rue Auxerroise and the Rue Paul-Bert.*

Jean-Paul Grossot has acquired an excellent reputation with his Chablis and Premier Cru Chablis from the best hillsides of Fleys.

Domaine Grossot

Owners Corinne and Jean-Pierre Grossot. **Address** 4 route de Mont-de-Milieu 89800 Fleys - Tel. 03.86.42.44.64 Fax 03.86.42.13.31. **Open** From Monday to Saturday by appointment. **Spoken** English.

A young couple who have had a vineyard in Fleys for eighteen years, Corinne and Jean-Pierre Grossot have risen in the ranks of Chablis fame over the years. Their vines are plated on sixteen hectares, including eleven in Fleys, a well-exposed *terroir* where Chardonnay ripens well; and five hectares in the Chablis Premier Cru appellation. Several *cuvées* are only briefly aged in oak, the great majority of the Grossots' wines vinifying in stainless steel vats. The wines are lovely, notably the excellent '95 Chablis (46 F for second bottling), with a fine, fresh citrus-fruit bouquet, and a mellow taste that doesn't overpower that finesse. Of the Premiers Crus, the two "easiest" wines are the Côte-de-Troëmes, more fruity and round than mineral (63 F for the '95); and Les Fourneaux, from a hillside located just in front of the cellar: silky, delicate, promising fullness and length. If the '95 is no longer available, ask for the '96. For Chablis to cellar, we will rely on those from the villages of Fourchaume, Vaucoupin, (for concentration and finesse; 67 F); and Mont-de-Milieu.

Our choice The '95 Chablis Premier Cru (67 F). Fluid, very mellow extract but typically Chablis in its elegance, its hints of chalk and mineral tastes, delicate and long. To drink or to cellar for five years.

Reception Simple and discreet, in the barrel-vaulted cellar of the Grossots' recently built home.

How to get there *(Map 4): A6, exit Auxerre Sud, direction Chablis (12km) via D965. Leave Chablis in direction Tonnerre. Fleys is in 5km. The cellar is at the entrance to the village on right.*

A vast estate with modern equipment reflects the expansion and dynamism of Chablis winegrowers over the past twenty years.

Domaine de Sainte-Claire

Owner Jean-Marc Brocard. **Address** Rue de Chablis, 89800 Préhy - Tel. 03.86.41.49.00/03.86.42.45.76 (tasting room) Fax 03.86.41.45.09. **Open** From Monday to Saturday, 8:00-12:00 and 13:30-18:00. Sunday and national holidays by appointment **Spoken** English. **Credit cards** Visa, Eurocard, MasterCard.

Beginning in late 1960 with several hectares of vines on the estate of his parents-in-law in Saint-Bris-le-Vineux, Jean-Marc Broccart, a former industrial draftsman, is today the director of a vast winery in Préhy, with eighty hectares of vineyards, mainly in the Chablis appellation at Préhy. He also is a *négociant.* A recently built winery with modern equipment reflects the expansion and dynamism of Chablis' winegrowers over the past twenty years. The wines are in the hands of a young oenologist, Clotilde Davenne. "We must sell our difference, our soil, we have only that," she explains. Thus she uses no oak at all, favoring contemporary vinifications, close to the grape and the *terroir.* Of a large range of wines, we enjoyed the '96 Sauvignon de Saint-Bris (25 F), aromatic, elegant, very crisp; the Bourgogne Chardonnay (35 F), close to a Chablis with a pronounced mineral accent. Among the Chablis, the Vieilles Vignes (50 F) is beautifully mouth-filling, with a dense texture; while the Premier Cru Montée de Tonnerre (60 F) has a typical Chablis mineral edge and lingering taste. Very reasonable prices.

Our choice The '96 Bourgogne Aligoté (30 F). A wine from the lower priced range that still is fruity and mellow, charmingly balanced, clean. To be drunk now.

Reception In a modern, bright boutique/tasting room with view over the vines.

How to get there *(Map 4): On A6, exit Auxerre Sud, direction Chablis (D 965). In 1km, right towards Montallery, Courgy, then Préhy. From Chablis (8km), direction Nitry, then Préhy. Large new building, at the entrance to village.*

Frédéric Prain in one of his Chaprons.

Domaine d'Élise

Owner Frédéric Prain. **Address** 89800 Milly-Chablis - Tel. 03.86.42.40.82 Fax 03.86.42.44.76. **Open** From Monday to Saturday, by appointment. **Spoken** English, German, Italian.

An aficianado of antique DS cars with a body by Chapron (of which he has a magnificent collection), travel, and cinema (Kurosawa), Frédéric Prain is "also" a winemaker in Chablis. An unusual figure in the world of Chablis, where he arrived at Milly in 1982, this former civil engineer discovered wine in later life, while retaining his adolescent passions. Uninterested in the commercial side of winemaking, Prain devotes himself mainly to his vines--13 hectares on a white-chalk *terroir* typical of Kimmeridgian limestone--and to making wine. Close to the Defaix school of Chablis (see preceding vineyard), Frédéric harvests late, selects his crop severely by picking small lots of individual parcels; leaves his wines on the lees and autolyses the yeasts; and he bottles late. The point is to make "fatter", firmer Chablis. The wine is aged only in vats. The excellent '95 is still available, a vintage with overripe layers (quince, honey, candied citrus fruits), which can be drunk in three years.

Our choice The '96 Chablis (45 F). A reflection of the crispness and maturity of the vintage: bouquet of white peaches and grape blossom; fat, rich, velvety, with a clean, delightful finish. Mouth-filling.

Reception Informal, in the kitchen or basement of a large, recently built house with a panoramic view over Chablis. With Frédéric, we talk of wine and everything else.

How to get there *(Map 4): On A6, exit Auxerre Sud, direction Chablis (11km). 1km before Chablis, on the right, just before the road to Milly. Small sign.*

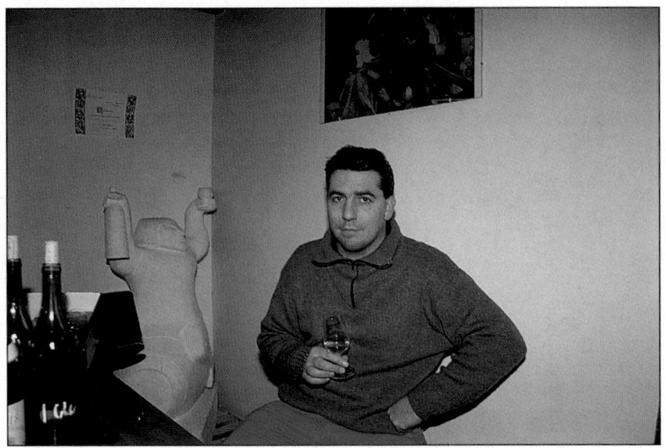

Olivier Savary: little by little, the bird made his nest.

Domaine Savary

Owners Francine and Olivier Savary. **Address** 4 chemin des Hâtes, 89800 Maligny - Tel. 03.86.47.42.09 Fax 03.86.47.55.80. **Open** From Monday to Sunday morning, 9:00-12:00 and 13:30-18:30. **Credit card** Visa. **Spoken** English.

Considering the affluence of this Chablis winemaker today, it is difficult to imagine that Olivier Savary's parents were obliged to leave their vineyard--in the not so distant past--in order to find more profitable work and to feed their family. As a child, Olivier returned regularly during school vacations to play with his cousins in the lovely rolling hills of Maligny. "I always loved the land here and I knew that I would return," he recollects. Following studies at the School of Oenology in Dijon, the young man decided to set up as a winemaker in 1984, beginning almost from scratch: one and a half hectares from his grandfather. Little by little, the bird made his nest. At thirty-five, Olivier today owns a vineyard of twelve hectares, mainly in the Chablis and Petit Chablis appellations. "I had to fight, but I acquired a hectare each year." It is a success story for this winemaker who has sold all his production in bottles since 1989. His '96 Petit Chablis (38 F) is lemony, straightforward, very crisp, light, lively. A good '96 red Bourgogne Epineuil (35 F): more intense than in '95, very fruity and peppery.

Our Choice The '96 Chablis Vieilles Vignes (52 F). A barrel-aged Chardonnay, bouquet of ripe citrus fruit, flavor opens up fully on palate, slightly oaky, youthful and lively; lemony, mineral finish. A fresh, lively Chablis.

Reception By Olivier, open and good-natured, in a small modern cellar with a charming tasting corner adjacent to the vat room. His wife also participates.

How to get there *(Map 4): A6, exit Auxerre Sud, direction Chablis (12km) via D965. On leaving Chablis, direction Tonnerre, towards Maligny (7.5km). Arrow to cellar.*

Vincent Prunier, the latest in a prestigious line of winemakers in Auxey.

Domaine Vincent Prunier

Owner Vincent Prunier. **Address** 21190 Auxey-Duresses - Tel. 03.80.21.27.77 - 03.80.21.21.90 Fax 03.80.21.68.87. **Open** Every day, 8:00-12:00 and, 14:00-19:00, preferably by appointment. **Credit cards** Visa, Eurocard, MasterCard.

Vincent Prunier (32 year-old) is the youngest in a long line of prestigious winemakers who virtually monopolize the village of Auxey-Duresse. Vincent is the son of Pierre, the only member of the family to have preferred machines to winemaking. After an apprenticeship with his uncle and godfather, Michel, a leading winemaker in Auxey, Vincent went into business for himself in 1988, with some parcels of his own vines and many which he sharecropped. Today, his vineyard covers 11 hectares producing both red and white wines. The competition between the Pruniers is strong but Vincent succeeds in imposing his style. His reds are intense, full-bodied, balanced wines; the whites, very mellow but always elegant. The '96s are outstanding, particularly the white Meursault Vireuil, and the red Saint-Aubin Premier Cru Les Combes, a wine of very beautiful structure. Of the '95s, taste the white Saint-Aubin Premier Cru (55 F), charming, fruity, light, best drunk young; and the red Auxey-Duresses Premier Cru Grands Champs (58 F), big and tannic, long, lingering taste. It will be perfect in three years. For a thirst-quenching white: the '96 Aligoté(27 F).

Our choice The '95 white Auxey-Duresses (57 F). Very aromatic bouquet of mint and mango; fat, generous, buttery and mouth-filling, it finishes elegantly for the vintage.

Reception By Vincent or his parents, charming people, in an improvised tasting room in what was intended to be a garage for his father.

How to get there *(Map 5): On A6, exit Beaune. From Beaune: N74, towards Châlon, then D973 via Pommard, then Auxey-Duresse. On leaving village, towards Nolay, last house on left.*

Pierre Heilly has always worked in organic agriculture.

Domaine d'Heilly et Huberdeau

Owners Pierre d'Heilly and Martine Huberdeau. **Address** Cercot 71390 Moroges - Tel. 03.85.47.95.27 Fax 03.85.47.98.97. **Open** From Monday to Saturday, preferably by appointment.

Pierre d'Heilly and Martine Huberdeau met at university. They had a passion in common, organic agriculture, which they put into practice when they moved to this beautiful rolling countryside near Givry in 1978. They restored the family house and cellars, planting a small, 5 1/2 hectare vineyard on the slopes of Mont Avril, in front of the cellar: a hiking area known for its botanical path. Martine is in charge of the business side of the vineyard, while Pierre cultivates the soil and vines. There is no *grand cru* here, just good Pinot Noir, Chardonnay, and Aligoté. The latter, in the '96 vintage (31 F), is crisp, fruity, a wine of lovely finesse. It's good on its own, or in a traditional Kir with blackcurrant liqueur. The '95 red Passe-Tout-Grains (28 F): aroma of peonies and red berries, high in alcohol, somewhat gamey, lightly tannic. We prefer to drink the reds young before they develop pronounced animal notes.

Our choice The '95 red Bourgogne Côte Chalonnaise (35 F). Combines red berries and rustic traces, forthcoming on the palate, spicy, firm tannins. Very pleasant *crémant* (40 F), from Pinot Noir, Chardonnay, and Aligoté: delicate rim of bubbles, fresh and flowery aroma, not aggressive on palate, creamy finish with a hint of sweetness.

Reception Friendly. Honey for sale (Pierre's brother is a beekeeper.

How to get there *(Map 5): On A 6, exit Châlon-Sud. Turn left onto RN80, direction Le Creusot-Montceau-les-Mines. Exit at Moroges, turn right and follow direction Cercot. Sign in village.*

Vines in the Bourgogne Hautes-Côtes-de-Beaune appellation, pruned on the lyre system of trellising.

Domaine Christine et Didier Montchovet

Owners Christine and Didier Montchovet. **Address** Nantoux 21190 Meursault - Tel. 03.80.26.03.13 Fax 03.80.26.05.19. **Open** From Monday to Saturday, by appointment.

Breaking with his family's traditional winemaking techniques, Didier Montchovet, 35, planted his own vineyard of 8 hectares in the Bourgogne and Bourgogne Hautes-Côtes-de-Beaune appellations, with some vines in those of Beaune Premier Cru and Pommard. That was 12 years ago, when this graduate of the Dijon and Bordeaux Schools of Oenology was one of the first to employ biodynamic viticulture. With his wife, Christine, he champions this "natural" method even though it requires herculean work: The vineyard must be plowed and manually spaded, forsaking the use of chemical weedkillers beneath the vines. During fermentation, stems are left on the red grapes, which are vinified in vat for 20 to 25 days; the wine is *pigé* manually, keeping the skin caps in contact with the juice for deeper color; and it is aged in seasoned barrels. The '96 Bourgogne Passe-Tout-Grains (30 F) is a lovely, grapey thirst-quenching wine, with a rustic, crisp texture. The '95 Hautes Côtes (45 F) is full-bodied, well balanced, with excess tannins which will soften with bottle age. Try to find a few bottles of red Beaune Premier Cru Vignes Franches, of fleshy, round, beautiful complexity. Note also a delicious white '96 Aligoté (30 F) and a charming Gamay sold by the bulk (15 F a liter).

Our choice The '95 red Beaune Premier Cru Au Coucherias (85 F). A mellow Pinot Noir with a bouquet of figs, pepper, red berries, but crisp and long on the palate, with a graceful finish. To be drunk or cellared.

Reception In a bucolic village away from the vineyard, in the basement of the house under completion; enthusiastic, sincere owners.

How to get there *(Map 5): From Beaune, direction Châlon (N74), then Pommard (D973). On the Pommard village square, right towards Nantoux (3km).*

Claire Naudin and Folie Douce, "Sweet Folly".

Domaine Henri Naudin-Ferrand

Owners Henri Naudin-Ferrand and daughters. **Address** Magny-les-Villers 21700 Nuits-Saint-Georges - Tel. 03.80.62.91.50 Fax 03.80.62.91.77. **Open** From Monday to Saturday, 8:00-12:00 and 13:30-19:30. Sunday and national holidays by appointment. **Spoken** English. **Credit card** Visa.

After brilliant studies in agronomy and oenology, Claire Naudin, 28, returned to the family vineyard of 22 hectares in the Hautes-Côtes in 1993. With her sister Anne, also an oenologist, Claire maintains the standards of quality set by their father, Henri. In this area, Chardonnay arrived quite late, in the mid-1960s. Grandfather Naudin made only Bourgogne Aligoté, which he sold in barrels to cafés in Dijon. Still a good wine from the estate (there are vines planted in 1902), this Aligoté yields an excellent, small fruity wine. The '96 (26 F) is aromatic, flowery, fruity, rich, with a vigorous finish. Of the reds, Claire aims at intensity but "without trying for great power", producing balanced, sincere wines, like their maker. Her '95 Bourgogne Hautes-Côtes-de-Nuits, peppery, spicy, somewhat rustic, tastes deliciously of red berries. The '95 Côte-de-Nuits Villages Vieilles Vignes (53 F): intense aroma mingling plums and rustic notes, generous and full-flavored, with dense but discreet tannins. A beautiful bottle in three years.

Our choice The '95 Bourgogne Hautes Côtes-de-Beaune Cuvée d'Automne (37 F). Light red color, peppery bouquet develops notes of blackcurrants and black berries, mellow taste with soft tannins, delicate and dense.

Reception the whole family, excellent, very helpful; at the entrance to the cellar.

How to get there *(Map 5): 10km north of Beaune. On A 31, exit Nuits-Saint-Georges (10km). On N74 towards Beaune, turn right at Corgoloin, direction Magny-lès-Villers. In the village, sign.*

With her father, Ghislaine Barthod owns six and a half hectares of Pinot Noir vines in Chambolle-Musigny.

Domaine Ghislaine Barthod

Owner Family Barthod-Noëllat. **Address** Ruelle du Lavoir, 21220 Chambolle-Musigny - Tel. 03.80.62.80.16 Fax 03.80.62.82.42. **Open** From Monday to Saturday, by appointment. **Spoken** English, German.

It isn't easy to find Chambolle wines in Chambolle: 70% of the vines are grown by "foreign" winegrowers, meaning those from neighboring villages! Its Premiers Crus have entrancing names like Les Amoureuses, "The Lovers", Aux Beaux Bruns, "Men Dark and Handsome", and Charmes, which translates itself. Winemaking here is extremely classic: grapes are destemmed, fermented in wooden vats, and frequently *pigés*. Ghislaine's Chambolles are remarkably silky and elegant. Following a '94 vintage of average concentration, to be drunk young, the 1995s are Burgundies to be cellared and coveted. The vineyard offers a beautiful series of Premiers Crus, all perfectly typical Chambolles. We especially enjoyed the '96 Les Cras (about 125 F), very firm and dense now, and a magnificent bottle in ten years; and Les Charmes (about 130 F, available in small quantities): the synthesis of them all, fruity and complex, finishing with silky structure. Don't forget the excellent '95 Chambolle-Musigny (about 90 F). Few wines are available but Ghislaine does her best to satisfy faithful customers.

Our choice The '95 Chambolle-Musigny Premier Cru Aux Beaux Bruns about 125 F). Located at the bottom of the slope on quite deep soil. In its youth, the wine has a profoundly smooth, velvety, fruity style not shared by its alter egos. A "dark and handsome" Burgundy, long on charm.

Reception In the cellar, by friendly Ghislaine.

How to get there *(Map 5): On A31, exit Nuits-Saints-Georges. 7.5km north of Nuits-Saint-Georges via N74, direction Dijon. In Chambolle-Musigny, the estate is sign-posted.*

Jean-Marc Pillot keeps the balance between white and red Chassagne.

Domaine Jean Pillot et Fils

Owners Béatrice, Jean-Marc and Jean Pillot. **Address** Le Haut des Champs or 1 rue Combard, 21190 Chassagne-Montrachet - Tel. 03.80.21.33.35 Fax 03.80.21.92.57. **Open** Every day by appointment, 9:00-12:00 and 14:00-18:00.

"The estate saw the light of day in 1910, planted by my great-grandfather, who was a barrel maker. Today, the 10 hectares of vines are tended by my father, Jean, my sister, Béatrice, and me," says Jean-Marc Pillot, a young winemaker of dependably good humor. The Pillots produce as much red wine as white, resisting the mad fashion that is inspiring winemakers here to uproot their Pinot vines and replant them with Chardonnay, which is more profitable. Chassagne whites are often more aromatic, with notes of grilled almonds and honey, and more lush than those of Puligny, its twin village, and they open up easily as they age. The five white Premiers Crus from the '96 vintage are distinct, good pictures of the *terroir,* well defined. The Chenevottes (about 140 F) is flowery and fresh; the Champs Gain (140 F) more powerful and generous; the Morgeot (about 150 F) even more massive; Les Caillerets (about 150 F) goes back to a Chassagne of finesse and a long mineral finish. The red Chassagnes, a specialty of Jean-Marc's father, show remarkable finesse and fruit in the '96 vintage.

Our choice Of the whites, the '96 Chassagne-Montrachet Premier Cru Les Macherelles (about 140 F), the most open of them all, is delicious when young. Rich, deep, toasty, buttery, slightly chalky finish. The red Chassagne-Montrachet Premier Cru Morgeot (about 140 F): prunes, wild strawberries, cherries; very smooth and full taste, on a par with the great Côtes-de-Nuits.

Reception Family-style, helpful; in the vinification cellar.

How to get there *(Map 5): 14km south of Beaune via N74. At the Châlon-sur-Saône/Chagny interchange, go under the bridge and turn towards Chagny.*

The Château de la Tour and its neo-medieval architecture from the late 19th century.

Château de La Tour

Owners Jacqueline Labet and Nicole Déchelette. **Supervisor** François Labet. **Address** Clos Vougeot, 21640 Vougeot - Tel. 03.80.62.86.13 Fax 03.80.62.82.72. **Open** Every day, 9:00-12:00 and 14:00-19:00, Jun - Oct; the rest of the year by appointment. **Spoken** English, German. **Credit cards** Visa, Eurocard, MasterCard.

Several meters down the slope from the Château du Clos-de-Vougeot, in the heart of the eponymous enclosure, the Château de la Tour has the largest estate (5.5 hectares) in the Grand Cru Clos-Vougeot appellation. François Labet is the winemaker here as well as at the Domaine Pierre Labet. Since the late 1980s, his Clos-Vougeot has been once again at the top of the appellation, typically yielding wines of powerful structure and tannic backbone. The Clos de la Tour is often distinguished by its pure fruit, its fine extraction and balance: a wine made to age well. Several vintages are available (from 200 to 300 f). From the Domaine Pierre Labet, were were enchanted by the Beaune wines: the white '96 Clos des Mosnières (85 F), charming, soft Burgundy with lovely oakiness; the same Clos in the red '95 vintage (83 F): pure fruit, licorice and resins, soft tannins; and the red Coucherias Premier Cru (110 F), with great breed, firm and long.

Our choice The '95 Clos-Vougeot (250 F). This concentrated vintage offers the entire spectrum of this great vineyard: intensely aromatic bouquet (black berries, licorice, cocoa, violets), solid, dense tannic structure which explodes on the palate, with a powerful finish and exceptional length. Cellar it, and forget it.

Reception Upstairs in the château, by competent staff. Vast tasting room with visible beams and large oak table.

How to get there *(Map 5): On A31, exit Nuits-Saint-Georges. 5km north of Nuits-Saint-Georges via N74 (direction Dijon). Arrows.*

The Clos-Vougeot gates.

Domaine Bertagna

Owners Mark and Eva Reh-Siddle. **Address** Rue du Vieux Château, 21640 Vougeot - Tel. 03.80.62.86.04 Fax 03.80.62.82.58. **Open** Every day, 9:00-19:00, closed in Jan. **Spoken** English, German. **Credit cards** Visa, Eurocard, MasterCard.

Acquired in 1982 by a German family specializing in sparkling wines in their country, this estate today comprises more than thirty hectares, including five Grands Crus and seven Premiers Crus, as well as sixteen hectares of red grapes in Hautes-Côtes-de-Nuits, the Dames Huguettes parcel. This makes a large sweep of vineyards from Gevrey-Chambertin to Aloxe-Corton, with a large part of them in Vougeot, notably the Vougeot Premier Cru Clos de la Perrière, a Bertagna monopoly; the Les Cras Premier Cru, Les Petits Vougeots Premier Cru, and the Clos-Vougeot Grand Cru. Bertagna's wines from these vines are the most distinguished. In the most recent vintages, viticultural methods have become more strict (grapes are very rigorously sorted during the harvest), resulting in much finer wines than in the past. The '95 Clos-Vougeot (270 F) is very firm, austere, concentrating on its length of flavor, spicy and powerful. To be cellared.

Our choice Two rare wines. The '95 white Vougeot Premier Cru (170 F), a wine grown on only two estates and one of the rare whites of the Côte de Nuits. The Chardonnay vines are young (10 years), but they are already expressing their red-grape soil: big, massive wines with little acidity, very full-bodied, imposing taste. Original. Of the reds, the '95 Vougeot Premier Cru Clos de la Perrière (170 F) is rich, soft, with marked oak, between the firmness of a Clos-Vougeot and the elegance of a Musigny.

Reception Touristic and aimed at selling, in a large boutique.

How to get there *(Map 5): Exit Nuits-Saint-Georges. 5km north of Nuits-Saint-Georges via N74, direction Dijon. Arrows in Vougeot.*

Philippe Senard, who is constantly analyzing his techniques, offering a beautiful range of Corton Grands Crus.

Domaine du Comte Senard

Owners Daniel and Philippe Senard. **Address** 21420 Aloxe-Corton - Tel. 03.80.26.41.65 Fax 03.80.26.45.99. **Open** From Monday to Saturday evening, by appointment. **Spoken** English. **Credit cards** Visa, Eurocard, MasterCard.

"In 1996, we began harvesting at the beginning of October, when everybody else had almost finished. I think we were right." Smiling, holding his pipette, Philippe Senard invited us to taste his latest red wines with a gourmet's satisfaction. We shared his satisfaction and his enthusiasm as we savored Senard's Aloxe-Corton, its intense bouquet of blackcurrants, its tannins rare for this *terroir;* the Corton Clos des Meix, graceful, velvety, and full-bodied; the Corton-Charlemagne, spicy, lingering in taste; the Corton Bressandes, dense in texture, a perfect picture of its *terroir* with its notes of moist earth; and finally, the Corton Clos du Roi, which we have rarely tasted in such a smooth, velvety expression, yet one with monumental backbone. All will be available in the spring-summer of 1998. Of the '95s, only a few bottles are left: try to find the Clos des Meix and the Clos du Roi (about 180 F), which should be cellared. A wine to drink young is the charming white Chorey-lès-Beaune (about 50 F), all fruity softness.

Our choice The '95 Corton Clos des Meix Grand Cru (about 165 F). It reflects the style sought for the '96s: an emphasis on velvet and full-body, often lacking in Cortons. Less powerful than the Cloy du Roy, it can also be enjoyed younger, as of 1999.

Reception By Philippe Senard, a picture of good humor, in his beautiful 14th-century barrel-vaulted cellar.

How to get there *(Map 5): On A 31, exit Beaune. 5km north of Beaune via N74, then left towards Aloxe-Corton. At the fork in the road before the village, turn left. On the small square, entrance to Domaine on immediate left. No signs.*

Maurice Chapuis.

Domaine Maurice Chapuis

Owners Anne-Marie and Maurice Chapuis. **Address** 21420 Aloxe-Corton - Tel. 03.80.26.40.99 Fax 03.80.26.40.89. **Open** From Monday to Saturday, by appointment. **Spoken** English, German. **Credit cards** Visa, Eurocard, MasterCard.

Maurice Chapuis took over the familial vineyard in 1985, growing ten hectares of red grapes in Aloxe-Corton, Aloxe-Corton Premier Cru, and Corton Grand Cru, and one hectare of white grapes in the Corton-Charlemagne appellation. Prudent by nature, he doesn't try to revolutionize Burgundy's time-honored winemaking techniques. Accordingly, he can be expected each year to offer wines that are balanced, straightforward, respectful of their *terroir,* and of good quality for their appellation. His '95 Aloxe-Corton Premier Cru (90 F) delivers a mellow fruity bouquet, with a full spicy taste and firm tannins. The red Corton Grand Cru comes from two different vineyards: the Languette parcel, planted on the Corton-Charlemagne appellation, thus white-grape country, is a quite elegant wine, with finesse ('95: 130 F); while the Perrières (our choice) is a real macho, typically Corton, tannic, powerful, a wine that keeps. "As for white wines, I don't like them to impose themselves. The more precise and finer the wine, the greater the intellectual pleasure in tasting them." The '93 (170 F) is still closed, a wine to be cellared.

Our choice The '95 Corton Grand Cru Perrières (130 F). Powerful bouquet of cocoa, leather, smoky notes. On the palate, we found the masculinity of Corton, mouth-filling, fat, tannic backbone, lingering taste. Beautiful balance. For the 21st century.

Reception In a traditional old Burgundian cellar, with a helpful, conscientious winemaker.

How to get there *(Map 5): On A 31, exit Beaune. 5km north of Beaune via N74, direction Dijon, then left towards Aloxe-Corton. At the fork in the road before the village, turn right. The house is 200 meters on the right.*

Pierre Marey and his son, Eric: the tasting ritual.

Domaine Pierre Marey & Fils

Owners Pierre and Éric Marey. **Address** 21420 Pernand-Vergelesses - Tel. 03.80.21.51.71 Fax 03.80.26.10.48. **Open** Every day, 9:00-12:00 and 14:00-19:00, preferably by appointment.

Good humor is the order of the day at this ten-hectare family domaine presided over by Pierre Marey and his son, Eric. "I was born in this house and everything is handled by the family here, from the vines to the customers," exclaimed Pierre. The style of wines made by the Mareys is concentrated more on power with balance; as they have only a hint of oak, they are pleasant to drink young, even the *grands crus*. As is often the case in Pernand-Vergelesses, you can find a good Aligoté here, from 50-year-old vines (30 F). Grown on a hectare in the commune of Pernand-Vergelesses, the '95 Corton-Charlemagne (185 F), flowery and honeyed with a toasty trace is intense and lacy for the *cru*, with a crisp, mouth-watering finish. It is already good to drink. We found the '96, before its bottling, a fruity, vigorous Burgundy. Of the reds, the '95 Corton (130 F), spicy and well structured, with firm, long tannins, needs bottle age.

Our choice The '95 white Pernand-Vergelesses (60 F): bouquet of ripe white fruit, crisp, elegant, fluid, thirst-quenching, good length. Delicious drunk young.

Reception In a small, typically Burgundian tasting cellar--watch your head going down. Cheerful, bon vivant atmosphere.

How to get there *(Map 5): On A 31, exit Beaune. 5km north of Beaune via N74, direction Dijon. 800 meters after the Boulevard Circulaire, turn left towards Savigny, then Pernand. At the fork in the road before the village, turn right. The cellar is 30 meters before the church, on the right.*

Corton-Charlemagne is a vast, (48 hectares) Grand Cru appellation. The Bonneau du Martray vineyard is a good reflection of its excellence.

Domaine Bonneau du Martray

Owner Family Le Bault de la Morinière. **Supervisor** Jean-Charles de la Morinière. **Address** 21420 Pernand-Vergelesses - Tel. 03.80.21.50.64 Fax 03.80.21.57.19. **Open** From Monday to Friday, by appointment. **Spoken** English.

The south-facing slopes of Corton's "mountain", about 1200 feet high, are home to the prestigious Corton-Charlemagne white Grand Cru, planted in the 3 communes of Ladoix-Serigny, Aloxe-Corton--pronounced "Alosse"--and Pernand-Vergelesses. It is the least sophisticated great white wine of the Côte de Beaune, giving expression to its *terroir* in a direct, clear, and even abrupt manner. Many tasters find it has a masculine side, even a certain austerity in its youth. With 9.5 ha of vines, Bonneau du Martray is the largest property in the Corton-Charlemagne appellation. Above all, it is the benchmark of the *cru.* As with no other domain here, we found the straightforward style of the *terroir* in these long-lived white wines, opening up only after 8 to 20 years (depending on the vintage) to reveal the depth and the monumental structure of the *cru.* This domaine also has 1.5 ha of Pinot Noir in the Corton Grand Cru. Currently sold out, it is a powerful, intense wine which has gained enormously in depth in the recent vintages. Reserve the '96s.

Our choice The '94 Corton Charlemagne (299 F). Bouquet of average intensity, more mineral than ripe Chardonnay--as with the '93--without heaviness (you can sense that the grapes were severely sorted at the harvest in order to produce this clean style), straightforward, still closed. An intermediary vintage which should be drunk in 2000.

Reception No tasting cellar but we were courteously received by Monsieur de la Morinière.

How to get there *(Map 5): 5 kms north of Beaune via N74, direction Dijon. 800m after the Boulevard Circulaire, turn left towards Savigny, then Pernand. At the foot of the village, turn right. The cellar is 50m before the church, on the right.*

Denis Berthaut pays homage to Fixin, one of "the common little Burgundies".

Domaine Berthaut

Owners Vincent and Denis Berthaut. **Address** 9, rue Noisot, 21220 Fixin - Tel. 03.80.52.45.48 Fax 03.80.51.31.05. **Open** Every day (except weekends in Dec and Jan), 8:00-12:00 and 14:00-18:00. **Credit cards** Visa, Eurocard, MasterCard.

In the shadow of its famous neighbor Gevrey-Chambertin, Fixin is a discreet village in the northern Côte de Nuits which lives with the memory of Napoléon Bonaparte: a museum is dedicated to the Emperor, filled with the souvenirs of Claude Noisot, a Bonaparte fan retired in Fixin, and the famous statue by François Rude: *Napoléon Awakes*. In fact some red wines here are said to have had an imperial reputation, with a *pièce* of Clos Perrière having once sold for the same price (expensive) as Chambertin. The Berthaut brothers own thirteen hectares, mainly in Fixin, of which they are ardent champions. Their vinifications are traditional, leaving the *terroirs* to express themselves. The appellations are Fixin Village, with mention of the *lieu-dit* on the label (Les Clos and Les Crais); and Fixin Premier Cru Les Arvelets. These red wines are "wild" and fruity in taste, powerful and chewy, with none of the rusticity often found in Fixin wines. The '95 Les Crais (about 85 F) is an elegant Burgundy, suggesting mellow red berries and dense tannins; Les Clos (about 85 F) reveals the concentration and complexity worthy of a Premier Cru.

Our choice The '95 Fixin Premier Cru Les Arvelets (about 100 F). Bouquet of blackcurrants, raspberries, ripe figs; soft, rich, mouth-watering and delicate on the palate, following through with fine tannic structure. A well-built and well-aged wine.

Reception Friendly, in a small, pleasantly decorated tasting cellar, and an evocation of Napoléon.

***How to get there** (Map 5): On A 31, exit Dijon. 10km south of Dijon via N74, direction Beaune. In the center of Fixin, in front of "La Poste", near the restaurant Chez Janette.*

A magnificent cellar for displaying magnificent wines.

Domaine Bernard Dugat-Py

Owner Bernard Dugat-Py. **Address** Rue de Planteligone, 21220 Gevrey-Chambertin - Tel. 03.80. 51.82.46 Fax 03.80.34.16.45. **Open** From Monday to Saturday, by appointment.

A traditional winemaker in good Burgundian style, Bernard Dugat-Py passionately devotes himself to his 5.1 hectares of vines, many of them old, planted in the best *terroirs* of Gevrey-Chambertin: three Village sites (Vieilles Vignes, Coeur de Roi, and Evaucelles); three Premiers Crus (Petite-Chapelle, Lavaux-Saint-Jacques, and Fonteny); and two Grands Crus (Charmes-Chambertin, Mazis-Chambertin). We were enthusiastic about all the '95s. Unfortunately, the demand exceeding the supply, there isn't a bottle left. However, the '96s are coming out in the spring of 1998. Reserve them right away because we found this vintage a benchmark. Bernard Dugat-Py's '96 Burgundies have extraordinary velvety smoothness. The Gevrey Vieilles Vignes (90 F), with violets in the bouquet, offers a texture of delicacy and breed; with Les Evocelles, a parcel recently taken over, there are blueberries and wild blackberries, with more silkiness and length; while the Premiers Crus are sensational, the Mazis Grand Cru (250 F) is intensely voluptuous.

Our choice The '96 Gevrey-Chambertin Coeur de Roy (110 F). From selected vines more than 50 years old (yield 33 hectoliters per hectare). Concentrated fruit, generous oakiness, fleshy, full, spicy. The top of the Villages wines.

Reception Very hospitable, in a magnificent cellar from the 11th and 13th centuries.

How to get there *(Map 5): On A 31, exit Dijon Sud. 10km south of Dijon via N74, direction Beaune. In Gevrey, after the "Mairie", first street on left. At the stop sign, in front of the church, on left. The Rue de Planteligone is 150 meters on left.*

Pierre Damoy, at the controls of one of the largest domaines of Gevrey-Chambertin.

Domaine Pierre Damoy

Owner Family Damoy. **Supervisor** Pierre Damoy. **Address** 11 rue du Maréchal de-Lattre-de-Tassigny, 21220 Gevrey-Chambertin - Tel. 03.80.34.30.47 Fax 03.80.58.54.79. **Open** From Monday to Saturday, by appointment. **Credit cards** Visa, Eurocard, MasterCard.

The great-great-grandson of Julien Damoy, who made a fortune in the early 20th century and bought wines in the Médoc and Gevrey-Chambertin, Pierre Damoy, 31, arrived on the family domaine in 1992. He had no experience, just the desire the do an excellent job, opting for lower yields, very ripe grapes, and careful ageing in new oak barrels. The domain's reputation grew, and today it is difficult to buy wine on the property. However, astute wine lovers can always find some Gevrey Villages (about 90 F), with a very aromatic bouquet of crushed blackcurrants in '96, with fine, elegant tannins. Try also to find a Vieilles Vignes Clos Tamisot (about 120 F): soft, sweet bouquet, velvety, generous on the palate. With patience, you can approach the holy of holies, a trilogy of Grands Crus of which the domain is one of the largest owners: Chapelle-Chambertin, Chambertin, and Chambertin-Clos de Bèze. There are '92s left, a denigrated vintage but a good one here, ready to drink and reasonably priced.

Our Choice The '96 Chapelle-Chambertin Grand Cru (175 F from the latest harvest; then about 250 F). A majestic wine, with powerful tastes of damp earth and black berries, very lingering on the palate, with delicate, dense tannic structure. To be cellared.

Reception By the dogs (well-behaved) of the domaine, who act as doorbells. Impassioned tastings with Pierre in the large cellar.

How to get there *(Map 5): On A 31, exit Dijon Sud. 10km south of Dijon via N74, direction Beaune. Go into Gevrey-Chambertin, direction Centre Ville. After the Place des Marronniers, 200 meters on right.*

Philippe Charlopin, a champion of mature grapes.

Domaine Philippe Charlopin

Owner Philippe Charlopin. **Address** 18, route de Dijon, 21220 Gevrey-Chambertin - Tel. 03.80.51. 81.18 Fax 03.80.51.81.27. **Open** From Monday to Saturday.

Eleven hectares in Marsannay, Gevrey-Chambertin, Morey-Saint-Denis, Vosne-Romanée, Chambolle-Musigny, and Gevrey Grand Cru: all are benchmarks in their category. Because Philippe Charlopin makes draconian selections of his grapes, he works the lees (which is rare for red wines), he does not run off the wine, and he uses carefully selected new barrels. Above all, Charlopin harvests his Pinot Noir at peak maturity. Taking advantage of a beautiful Indian summer in 1996, his late harvests made their mark. The wines have a perfectly mellow tannic structure, "jovial" and round like the winemaker himself. As the '95s are sold out, reserve the '96s, which came out in late 1997. The red Marsannay En Montchenevoy (80 F), a lovely, pleasant wine when young, is sure to have many delighted takers. The Morey-Saint-Denis (120 F), a full bouquet of cherries, is firm, more austere than the Chambolle (145 F), a very silky Burgundy with remarkable finesse. Explosive bouquets and tastes are delivered by the Grands Crus Clos-Saint-Denis (255 F, of magisterial fullness); and Charmes-Chambertin (225 F), is very lingering on the palate, elegant and vigorous.

Our choice The '96 Gevrey-Chambertin Vieilles-Vignes (145 F). Oakiness with great class, a bouquet of freshly roasted coffee layered with ripe cherries; fat, full-flavored, becoming quite firm on the palate, with vigorous tannins.

Reception On the edge of the Route Nationale, by a winemaker who loves his work.

How to get there *(Map 5): On A 31, exit Dijon Sud. 10km south of Dijon via N74, direction Beaune. On N74, at entrance to Gevrey, on left.*

René Bourgeon, in charge of vinifications, and his wife, Danielle.

Domaine René Bourgeon

Owners Danielle, Jean-François and René Bourgeon. **Address** 71640 Jambles - Tel. 03.85.44. 35.85 Fax 03.85.44.57.80. **Open** All the week, 9:00-12:00 and 14:00-19:00. Preferable to call ahead.

René Bourgeon suffered a back injury during the 1992 harvest and since then has concentrated his tremendous energy on vinifications. He is helped by his wife, Danielle, and their son, Jean-François, who manages the 10 hectares estate in the Bourgogne and Givry appellations. A master of winemaking techniques, René keeps a close eye on the latest research in oenology. He makes wines of straightforward, very pure fruitiness (the rewards of cold maceration), which are delicious drunk young and can age 10 years with charm. His '95 white Givry Clos de la Brûlée (40 F) yields a bouquet of intense toastiness, delicate and easy to drink, and a lingering, elegant taste of great distinction. The '95 red Côte Chalonnaise Les Pourrières (30 F) suggests blackcurrants, very ripe cherries, a soft, charming wine which will open up fully in 1998. Another red, the '95 Givry (40 F) yields a touch of red-berries acidity, a lively, crisp palate, its soft tannins developing at the finish. Each sip is a mouthful of grapes! All the domain's wines offer excellent value for the price.

Our choice The '95 Givry La Barraude (110 F, only in 1.5 liter magnums). From 80-year-old Pinot Noir vines. Complex bouquet (black berries, leather, truffles), intense grapiness on the palate, with soft, mellow extract, delicate, dense tannins, but not excessive. Remarkable. Like all wines from Bourgeon, it should be served and aired in a carafe.

Reception (Map 5): A6 exit Châlon-Sud, then direction Montceau-les-Mines (express highway). Exit Saint-Désert. In 3km, directin Jambles. The cellar is on the square at top of village.

How to get there: *(Map 5): A6 Chalon-Sud exit, then towards Montceau-les-Mines (voie express). Saint-Désert exit. 3km, towards Jambles. The cellar is on the village Square.*

Chantal and Yvon Contat-Grangé in front of a work by David Wicress.

Domaine Contat-Grangé

Owners Chantal and Yvon Contat-Grangé. **Address** 71150 Dezize-les-Maranges - Tel. 03.85. 91.15.87 Fax 03.85.91.12.54. **Open** Every day, by appointment. **Credit cards** Visa, Eurocard, MasterCard.

In January 1997, the rollicking, itinerant Festival of Saint-Vincent, the patron saint of wine, made its traditional stopover in Les Maranges. It was the occasion for many wine lovers to discover this young, spirited *cru* (with 230 hectares of vines, declared AOC in 1989), planted in three communes--Cheilly, Sampigny, and Dezize--on the southern gateway to the Côte de Beaune. You'll find a handful of good cellars there, including that of Chantal and Yvon Contat-Grangé, who have been in their old village house for fifteen years. They own six and a half hectares of vines, planted in the "bio" spirit: manual harvests, no yeast, quite long maceration. Yvon's well-structured reds gradually mature their tannins, especially in 1996. The '95s, somewhat firm when we tasted, will open up in late 1998. Of the whites, the '96 Hautes Côtes-de-Beaune (35 F) is mouthwateringly fruity, to be enjoyed young; while the Maranges (42 F), of remarkable maturity (13° natural alcohol), its bouquet of ripe peaches, soft and full-bodied, needs two years' bottle age.

Our choice The '95 Maranges Premier Cru (50 F). The most generous wine, with well-structured tannins not overpowering the black berries and truffles typical of the *terroir.* The '96 is gaining in finesse.

Reception Excellent, informal, in a small, traditional cellar.

How to get there *(Map 5): A 6 exit Beaune. 18km southwest of Beaune via N74, directon Châlon. Before Chagny, direction Santenay (D974), then Dezize-lès-Maranges. The cellar is on the left in the main street.*

In the Audoins' cellar, husband and wife both have their say in making the wine.

Domaine Charles Audoin

Owners Françoise and Charles Audoin. **Address** 7, rue de la Boulotte, 21160 Marsannay-la-Côte - Tel. 03.80.52.34.24 Fax 03.80.58.74.34. **Open** From Monday to Sunday morning by appointment. **Credit card** Visa. **Spoken** English.

In many vineyards, the husband makes the wine and his wife handles the business side. But with the Audoins, the couple obviously work hand in hand. They have their preferences, which are quite complementary: Françoise likes delicate bouquets, the impressions on the nose more than on the palate; Charles, forty-eight years old, with thirty-three years in the vineyard, has a penchant for well-structured, tannic wines. "When we vinify, we also try to keep a balance." You notice the balance in their range of Marsannays (without Premier Cru status), which were very regular and especially well made in 1995, an excellent vintage to be cellared and which will mature in three years. Of the red wines, taste above all the Marsannay (45 F), very mouth-filling, soft, with delicate tannins. The Marsannay Les Favières (50 F) is a touch more mature and concentrated, firm without being aggressive. There is a small quantity of excellent white '96 Marsannay, flowery and lemony on the nose, generous, full-bodied, with hints of ripe citrus fruit, and a crisp finish.

Our choice The '95 Marsannay Clos du Roy (53 F), the most textured wine, soft and mouth-filling, with dense, silky tannins (to bottle age); and the '96 Marsannay Rosé (34 F): youthful, fruity aroma, red berries, supple but crisp at the finish. Delicious.

Reception Family-style, friendly, in the cellar finished in 1995.

How to get there *(Map 5): A 31, exit Dijon Sud. 5.5km south of Dijon via N74, direction Beaune. In Marsannay, go in front of the "Mairie", first street on left. Cellar on right.*

Laurent Juillot: "Since the 1993 vintage, I've been 99% responsible for vinification, my father 1%. But it's the 1% that counts the most."

Domaine Michel Juillot

Owners Michel and Laurent Juillot. **Address** Grande-Rue, 71640 Mercurey - Tel. 03.85.45.27.27 Fax 03.85.45.25.52. **Open** From Monday to Saturday, 8:00-19:00. Sunday by appointment. **Spoken** English. **Credit cards** Visa, Eurocard, MasterCard, Amex.

If you want to tease Michel Juillot, tell him that you find his Pinot Noir quite good but that it lacks a bit of color. You'll see a look of total disbelief on the face of this jovial, rotund winemaker who loves his job with a passion. Actually, this great figure of the Côte Chalonnaise leaves most of the winemaking job to his son, Laurent, who presides over twenty-six hectares of vines, half of which are in Mercurey Premier Cru: Les Combins, Clos Barrault, Les Champs-Martins, and the Clos Tonnerre parcel, a Juillot monopoly. The Juillots have mastered the art of barrel-ageing (serious studies were carried out here on this subject); and they constantly test and compare various winemaking techniques, notably various means of handling the harvested grapes. Many wines and vintages are available. Among others, we took special note of the '94 white Mercurey Premier Cru Les Champs Martins (105 F): powerful, minerally, still somewhat vegetal, very lingering taste; and of the reds, the '94 Mercurey Les Champs Martins (73 F), solid but still firm; while it's ageing, we will enjoy the '94 Clos Tonnerre (68 F), soft, youthful, a charming wine to drink now.

Our choice The '94 red Mercurey Clos des Barraults (95 F), still an aroma of red berries and its youthful softness, with a well-structured finish and good length for the vintage. Drink as of 1998.

Reception In a large cellar-boutique with many bottles on display.

How to get there *(Map 5): A 6, exit Chalon-Nord. 16.5km northwest of Chalon-sur-Saône via the road to Autun (D978). In the main street of Mercurey. Cellar on left coming from Chalon.*

Henri Darnat, three daughters and four hectares in Meursault.

Domaine Darnat

Owner Family Darnat. **Supervisor** Henri Darnat. **Address** 20, rue des Forges, 21190 Meursault - Tel. 03.80.21.23.30 Fax 03.80.21.64.62. **Open** From Monday to Saturday, by appointment. **Spoken** English, Italian.

In Meursault, the many *lieux-dits* mean that the *terroir* has more marked variations than in Puligny or in Chassagne. Thus there is no typical Meursault but rather a diversified range of Meursaults on which the winemaker of course puts his stamp. With his four hectares of vines which are cultivated and harvested manually, Henri Darnat makes Meursault Villages and Premier Cru which are clear-cut and rather lacy in style. He likes his wines to be delicate, fruity, and crisp. "Somewhat more Puligny than Meursault". If you like this style, you'll be delighted with his simple '96 Meursault (90 F), mouth-filling but also fruity, graceful, very clean. The '96 Saint-Aubin Premier Cru En Remilly (75 F), from young vines, has a flowery bouquet of white peaches; all finesse and subtlety. Delicious. Still ageing, the '96 Meursault Premier Cru Goutte d'Or (140 F) was reticent when we tasted it, while showing power and mineral notes. Don't overlook the two simple '96 Burgundies (40 F): a very fruity white and an aromatic red wine, silky and savory.

Our choice The '96 Meursault Premier Cru Clos Richemond (150 F). Very crisp, vine-flower bouquet, full-bodied and generous attack, straightforward, long, complex. Beautiful when bottle aged.

Reception Enthusiastic, by a winemaker who loves to discuss his work. In the basement of a 19th-century building.

How to get there *(Map 5): A 6, Beaune exit. 8.5km south of Beaune via N74 (direction Chalon). From the center of Meursault, direction Auxey-Duresse, then Rue des Forges.*

Patrick Javillier, Meursault Villages champion.

Domaine Patrick Javillier

Owner Patrick Javillier. **Address** 7 impasse des Acacias, 21190 Meursault Caveau - 19 place de l'Europe - Tel. 03.80.21.27.87 (office) - Tel. 03.80.21.65.50 (cellar) Fax 03.80.21.29.39. **Open** Tasting room, Mar - Nov from Fri. afternoon to Monday, 10:00-12:30 and 14:30-19:00. The rest of the year, in the cellar by appointment. **Spoken** English. **Credit cards** Visa, Eurocard, MasterCard.

A sensitive winemaker with great curiosity, and a demanding taster, Patrick Javillier has refined his style over the years. Starting with quite simple, fruity wines, this oenologist "gives them extensive rest on their lees, and matures them in order to highlight their *terroir*". His whites have gained in relief and in definition. In 1995, a low-yielding vintage dominated by its rich extract, you can sense this evolution beginning with his white Burgundies: the Oligocène (69 F), discreet and mineral in aroma, straightforward, amazingly lingering on the palate, is a first cousin of the Meursaults. The white Savigny-lès-Beaune Montchenevoy (85 F): flowery, honeyed in bouquet, very mellow, soft, sweet on the palate, it is the charming expression of young wines. Of his six *cuvées* of Meursault Village, Les Tillets (115 F) is exceptionally powerful; the late-bottled Clos du Cromin (125 F), its nose of ripe grapes, is supple and mouth-filling, "well fed", without the length of Les Clous (130 F).

Our choice The '95 Meursault Les Murgers (140 F). From old vines, a wine reticent in its youth, less immediate, but with an elegant texture, straightforward and firm, which matures with time. For the year 2000 and beyond.

Reception In the tasting cellar (in summer) or in the Javilliers' house.

How to get there *(Map 5): A 6 exit Beaune. 8.5km south of Beaune via N74. Cellar at entrance to Meursault, on left, in 500 meters. The house is at the exit from the village, direction Volnay, before the stop sign on D973, on left (sign).*

Michel Dupont-Fahn, a member of the Harmonie de Meursault, and his wife, Leslie, a native of Los Angeles.

Domaine Dupont-Fahn

Owners Leslie and Michel Dupont-Fahn. **Address** Clos des Toisières, Monthelie, 21190 Meursault - Tel. 03.80.21.26.78 Fax 03.80.21.21.22. **Open** From Monday to Saturday, by appointment. **Spoken** English.

The sound of a baritone voice coming up from the cellar of the Dupont-Fahns' modern house reminds the visitor that, like many of his Meursault winemaker friends, Michel Dupont is a member of the local band. "Groups of friends get together and it's always the occasion for great tastings." Michel Dupont, a fifth-generation winemaker, married Leslie Fahn, a young American who had come to France to learn about wine nineteen years ago. In 1989, they set up on their estate, with 4 1/2 hectares in three Meursault-Villages lieux-dits, several ares in Puligny-Montrachet and a few red vines in Auxey-Duresses and Monthelie. They harvest late ("we play with fire"), use new oak moderately (25%), yielding "Meursaults you can drink quite young, between two and seven years." Making the point was the '95 Puligny-Montrachet Les Grands Champs (95 F): rich, buttery, balanced, with a firm finish which has not yet had its last word. Of the reds, the '95 Auxey-Duresses (45 F) has a lovely bouquet of very ripe black berries and equally appealing softness.

Our choice The '95 Meursault Les Vireuils (85 F), from vines more than 60 years old. A concentrated white wine with an intense, open bouquet, round on the palate, which opens up generously while retaining mineral overtones.

Reception Courteous and helpful, in the basement of a modern house.

How to get there *(Map 5): A 6 exit Beaune. 9.5km south of Beaune via N74, direction Chalon. Leave Meursault direction Monthelie. At the stop sign on D973, turn right towards Volnay. Cellar 50 meters on left.*

Romain Lignier brought out majestic Burgundies in 1995.

Domaine Hubert Lignier

Owners Hubert and Romain Lignier. **Address** 45 Grande-Rue, 21220 Morey-Saint-Denis - Tel. 03.80.34.31.79 Fax 03.80.51.80.97. **Open** From Monday to Friday, 9:00-12:00 and 14:00-18:00, by appointment. **Spoken** English, German.

Morey-Saint-Denis has 35 winemakers, one 100 hectares of vineyards, several very good Premiers Crus and five Grands Crus. Wines from this domaine are made by young Romain, 26, who depends on his father's experience: his Burgundies have "the finesse and the elegance of Chambolles along with the power and backbone of Gevreys." The Lignier style can be resumed by his keeping strict control of production (30 hectoliters per hectare in 1995) and classic, careful vinification. Grown on 8 hectares, his range of red wines is extensive. We concentrated on the Moreys. Rarely have we found Pinots so deeply colored, ripe, and full-bodied in the '95 vintage: the Morey-Saint-Denis Village (about 100 F) has a beautifully deep-red color, an intense bouquet of licorice, black berries; a soft, mouth-filling Burgundy; and the Morey-Saint-Denis Premier Cru Les Chaffots (about 140 F) is still deeper in color, dense; with abouquet of very ripe blackcurrants, licorice, tar; a very youthful, grapy wine, well structured, thickly textured, gloriously velvety.

Our choice: The Morey-Saint-Denis Premier Cru Vieilles Vignes (about 160 F). We weren't dreaming: it was truly a Pinot Noir with this color of crushed blackberries, this extraordinary maturity, concentration and mouth-filling volume. An incomparable wine, very rich, with powerful blackberries lying over massive rôtis tannins. Majestic.

Reception By Romain or Hubert, generous, open-minded, who must be credited for the fame of the domaine.

How to get there *(Map 5): A 31, exit Nuits-Saint-Georges. 6.5km north of Nuits-Saint-Georges via N74 (to Dijon). The Grande-Rue is the main street that goes down to N74.*

Overlooking Prémeaux-Prissey, the Domaine de l'Arlot is located on the narrowest stretch of vines in the Côte de Nuits.

Domaine de l'Arlot

Owner Axa Millésime. **Responsable** Jean-Pierre de Smet. **Address** 21700 Prémeaux-Prissey - Tel. 03.80.61.01.92 Fax 03.80.61.04.22. **Open** From Monday to Saturday, by appointment. **Spoken** English.

Owned by Axa Millésime since 1987, this domaine is planted on 15 hectares, with a parcel in the Beaune Premier Cru Les Grèves appellation since 1996. It is headed by Jean-Pierre de Smet, a formidably demanding winemaker with a conviction in his work that might well inspire many a born *vigneron.* A native of Nice, a crack skier and sailor who has crossed the Atlantic several times, de Smet has succeeded in boosting Arlot up to its rightful rank so that today it includes three Premiers Crus which are Arlot monopolies: red grapes in the Clos de l'Arlot and the Clos des Forêts Saint-Georges; and white grapes in the Clos de l'Arlot, a great rarity and quickly sold, remarkable in the '95 vintage (225 F). The '95 reds are mature and elegant in style and can be enjoyed young. The '95 Nuits-Saint-Georges (98 F) is already open, with animal and blackberry notes, elegant and pleasant to drink, with soft tannins. Perfect in late 1998. The '95 Clos de l'Arlot Premier Cru (145 F), its bouquet of spices and cloves, is both rustic and delicate, finishing with soft tannins.

Our choice The '95 Nuits Saint-Georges Premier Cru Clos des Forêts Saint-Georges (170 F). Bouquet of leather and glazed black berries; complex, firm, full-bodied, with a lingering taste of licorice and tobacco. A very beautiful Burgundy.

Reception By appointment. Wine lovers are welcome and on request can visit the deep cellars of the domaine.

How to get there *(Map 5): A 31, exit Nuits-Saint-Georges. 3.5km south of Nuits-Saint-Georges via N74 (direction Beaune. On N74, in the village, on right, large, light-blue door.*

The Dubois' home and cellar.

Domaine R. Dubois et Fils

Owner Family Dubois. **Address** 21700 Prémeaux-Prissey - Tel. 03.80.62.30.61 Fax 03.80.61.24.07. **Open** From Monday to Saturday, 8:00 30-11:30 and 13:30-19:00, Sunday and national holidays by appointment. **Spoken** English.

Until recently, the majority of the vines in Prémeaux-Prissey, the heart of the Côte de Nuits, belonged to *négociants* who hired the inhabitants of the village to work in the vineyards. Louis Dubois (1874-1947) was one of them, devoting his life to working for a *négociant* while acquiring his own two hectares of vines. Three generations later, the Dubois family today presides over an estate of twenty-two hectares. The expansion of the domain owes much to Régis, 54, who began bottling his own production in 1968, seconded by his son, Raphaël, the business manager, and his daughter, Béatrice, a young, globe-trotting oenologist who returns regularly to follow vinifications. With this new generation, wine-making has taken a youthful turn. The Dubois' range of wines is vast, with nineteen AOCs, mostly red wines, with regional and village appellations. Of the '96s, don't miss the Nuits-Saint-Georges (about 75 F), a perfect portrait of the appellation; or the Chambolle-Musigny, beautifully silky. In '95, the Nuits-Saint-Georges (about 75 F), with glazed red berries, leather, is powerful and imposing; the Porêt-Saint-Georges Premier Cru (about 95 F) is dense, long, and tannic.

Our choice The '95 Nuits-Saint-Georges Premier Cru Clos des Argillières (about 100 F). Deep, rich, fat, mouth-filling, finishing firmly without being hard. An excellent Premier Cru. The '96s are promising the same, if not superior, style.

Reception Friendly, family-style, in the basement of a modern building.

How to get there *(Map 5): 3.5km south of Nuits-Saint-Georges via N74 (direction Beaune). On N74, in the village, on left; go down into the village and follow arrows.*

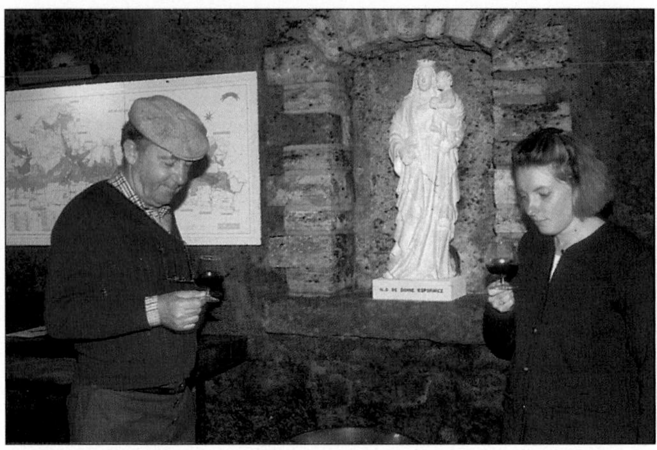

Bernard Dubreuil and his daughter, Christine.

Domaine Dubreuil-Fontaine

Owners Bernard and Christine Dubreuil-Fontaine. **Address** Rue Rameau-Lamarosse, 21420 Pernand-Vergelesses - Tel. 03.80.21.55.43 Fax 03.80.21.51.69. **Open** From Monday to Saturday afternoon, 9:00-12:00 and 14:00-18:00. **Spoken** English. **Credit card** Visa.

In Pernand-Vergelesses, perched on an escarpment and keeping watch over the "mountain" of Corton, the Dubreuil-Fontaine family owns a wide range of parcels planted on twenty hectares of vines (75% red), all in the Côte de Beaune. The largest is the Pernand-Vergelesses site on six hectares, whose wines are representative of the cellar's quality even though we prefer the Ile des Vergelesses Premier Cru (our choice). We ascended into the spheres of Corton with the trio Perrières, Bressandes, and Clos du Roi. The '94s currently on offer are definitely inferior to the '93s. But the Clos du Roi (142 F), richly textured, already beautifully balanced, can be enjoyed while we wait for the '95s. Of the whites, top billing goes to the Corton-Charlemagne, always long to open up. Take note also of the '95 Pernand-Vergelesses, its bouquet of licorice and ripe fruit, soft and full-bodied on the palate. Good Bourgogne Aligoté with mentholated, flowery aroma.

Our choice The '94 Pernand-Vergelesses Premier Cru Ile des Vergelesses (90 F). From a good terroir for red grapes, facing the Corton hillside, invariably yielding wines that are easy and charming to drink. This '94, a modest vintage, displays soft grapiness though somewhat aggressive, well-balanced extract, rather tannic. To be drunk in 1998.

Reception With simplicity and sincerity.

How to get there *(Map 5): A 31, Beaune exit. 6km north of Beaune, direction Dijon (N74). 800 meters after the Boulevard Circulaire, left towards Savigny, then Pernand. At the foot of the village, at the fork in road, turn left. Go into village. Also: A6, Beaune exit.*

Jean-Luc Joillot.

Domaine Jean-Luc Joillot

Owner Jean-Luc Joillot. **Address** Rue de la Métairie, 21630 Pommard - Tel. 03.80.22.47.60 Fax 03.80.24.67.54. **Open** From Monday to Saturday, 9:00-12:00 and 14:00-19:00, by appointment. **Credit cards** Visa, Eurocard, MasterCard.

At age thirty-six, Jean-Luc Joillot already has sixteen years of winemaking experience, having returned home as a young man to help his mother on the family domaine. It covers thirteen hectares of vines, mostly red, planted in the Bourgogne, Hautes Côtes-de-Beaune, Beaune, and Pommard appellations. Jean-Luc has progressively enlarged the domaine and oriented it towards estate-bottling and direct sales. He also presides over the Winemakers' Syndicate of Pommard, a 320-hectare appellation confronted with the problem of scattered vineyards: more than half of them today belong to domaines outside of Pommard. We enjoyed delicious tastings of a beautiful series of Pommards Villages and Premier Cru, all with lovely concentration. The '93 Villages (90 F) is young and delightful, still fruity on the palate, to be drunk now or cellared. The '95 Noizons (about 102 F) is deeply colored, full-bodied, well-balanced, powerfully tannic: perfect with long bottle age. The same can be said for the even more promising Premier Cru Epenots (about 143 F), complex, very long. Jean-Luc, who doesn't push his wines, is still selling vintages from 1991 through 1994.

Our choice The '95 Pommard Rugiens (about 123 F). A powerful bouquet of damp earth, truffles, leather; full-bodied taste of chocolate, black berries, dense, deep texture. A Pommard Villages easily on a par with some Premiers Crus.

Reception Friendly, instructive, in the small tasting cellar beneath the family home.

How to get there *(Map 5): 4km south of Beaune via N74, direction Chalon, then D973. On the Pommard village square, on right, then left behind the church.*

This domain has been in Jérôme Sordet's family since 1790.

Domaine Coste-Caumartin

Owner Jérôme Sordet. **Address** Rue du Parc, 21630 Pommard - Tel. 03.80.22.45.04 Fax 03.80.22.65.22. **Open** Every day 9:00-12:00 and 14:00-19:00. **Credit card** Visa.

Pommard varies in structure depending on its vineyard site. At Jérôme Sordet's domain, the comparative tasting of his two Premiers Crus is thus a good lesson in *terroirs.* Located on the Volnay side, the Les Fremiers, a beautiful '95 (118 F), soft and elegant, displays "the delicate overall quality of the Volnays and the powerful finish of the Pommards." The Clos des Boucherottes (our choice), a Caumartin monopoly, faces in the Beaune direction, surrounded by Les Petits Epenots. Its chewy texture and powerful tannins are more Pommard in style. The newcomer on this 13-hectare family domain, producing wines of regular character, is a '95 Beaune Premier Cru Les Chouacheux (82 F). A round, delicious wine, it can be drunk while the Pommards are ageing. The '95 Pommard (93 F) is an excellent *Villages* wine with gamey, black-fruit hints, structured with dense tannins, well balanced. Also good red and white Burgundies (45 F) and two white Saint-Romains: flowery, straightforward, and very crisp in its '96 Classique version (53 F); the '96 Sous-Roche (56 F) is more complex and more powerful.

Our choice The '95 Pommard Premier Cru Clos des Boucherottes (125 F). Soft, mouth-watering attack, developing into a long finish with delicate, spicy tannins; we could sense the maturity of the wine, but also the reticence of one which will become beautiful with age.

Reception Outstanding, especially in the often closed doors of Burgundian winemaking. The Sordets don't look at their watches during an extensive tasting, in a beautiful barrel-vaulted cellar from the early 17th century.

How to get there *(Map 5): A 6 Beaune exit. 4km south of Beaune via N74, direction Chalon, then D973. Before entering Pommard, on right (sign).*

Jean-René Chartron and his son, Jean-Michel, owners of the 2 1/2 hectares of the Puligny-Montrachet Premier Cru Clos de Cailleret, a family monopoly.

Maison Chartron et Trébuchet

Owners Jean-René Chartron and Louis Trébuchet. **Address** 13, Grande-Rue, 21190 Puligny-Montrachet - Tel. 03.80.21.32.85 Fax 03.80.21.36.35. **Open** From Monday to Friday, 9:00-12:00 and 14:00-18:00, by appointment. **Spoken** English, German. **Credit cards** Visa, Eurocard, MasterCard.

Jean-René Chartron and his son, Jean-Michel, own 9 ha of vines in Puligny-Montrachet; since 1984, they have been associated with Louis Trébuchet, a *négociant,* and the current President of the *Interprofession Bourguignonne.* Their dynamic wine brokerage makes a clear distinction between the wines of the Domaine Chartron and those of the *négoce.* The latter are made from grapes bought in the form of must--unfermented grape juice--which is subsequently vinified and aged with extreme care. These are essentially white wines from the Côte de Beaune, which often call more attention to the finesse of their *terroirs* than to their intensity. There are very few '95s left, but you won't be disappointed with the '96 Burgundies, which open up more readily, with grace and delicacy. Apart from Puligny, we tasted some 20 white wines, including an unforgettably delicious Rully (about 69 F), hazelnutty and soft; the Saint-Romain, a white Burgundy of distinct character; the powerful Auxey-Duresse, the elegant Saint-Aubin Premier Cru Les Chatenières, and the Chassagnes Village and Premier Cru Morgeot (about 150 F), which are simply outstanding. Of the Pulignys, the Villages (about 130 F) is reliably good. Le Clos de la Pucelle and Les Folatières are distinguished Premiers Crus.

Our choice The '94 Puligny-Montrachet Domaine Chartron Clos des Caillerets Premier Cru (about 210 F). Flowery, concentrated, mouth-filling, firm, full-bodied and lingering on the palate: a great gastronomic wine in five years.

Reception By Sharon in a small tasting room at the entrance to the cellar.

How to get there *(Map 5): 11km south of Beaune via N74, direction Chalon.*

A meal at the Maison Oliver Leflaive.

Maison Olivier Leflaive

Owner Olivier Leflaive. **Head winemaker** Franck Grux. **Address** Place du Monument, 21190 Puligny-Montrachet - Tel. 03.80.21.37.65 Fax 03.80.21.33.94. **Open** From Monday to Saturday afternoon, by appointment. **Spoken** English.

Founded in 1984 by the heir of a prestigious family of winemakers in Puligny, this wine brokerage has built an international reputation for its wines from the Côte de Beaune and the Côte Chalonnaise. With 11 ha of its own vines, it also buys small *lots* of grapes or must (75% of its needs in 1996), which it vinifies and ages. Since 1995, the Maison Olivier Leflaive has had a large cellar at its disposal in which Franck Grux, the winemaker, oversees vinifications on an increasingly large scale, while maturing wines by separate parcel. A skilled professional, Frank describes the '96 whites as "delicate, well-balanced wines, typical of their *terroir*, less powerful and immediately appealing than the '95, but they will be delicious with meals." Of the wines we tasted, the most outstanding were the Auxey-Duresses, the Saint-Romain, the Puligny Village (a mineral taste in '96), and all the Meursaults from the hillside vineyards, including a superb Narvaux. Of the '95s available, the Puligny (114 F), full-bodied, buttery, mouth-watering, will be marvelous in 1998, like the Saint-Romain (61 F), reflecting the opulence of its vintage; and the Saint-Aubin Premier Cru En Rémilly (79 F), a more elegant wine, with great finesse for the vintage.

Our choice The '95 Meursault Premier Cru Charmes (159 F). Powerful, fat, spicy, imposing. Truly a big wine. Uncork it as of the year 2000.

Reception By the sales staff of the cellar, in a convivial tasting room near the offices. Lunch with wines every day except Sun. (230 F all included).

How to get there *(Map 5): A 6 Beaune exit. 11km south of Beaune via N74, direction Chalon. Offices next to tasting room.*

Vincent Dureuil-Janthial treading the grapes with his feet, in good Burgundian tradition.

Domaines Dureuil-Janthial

Owners Raymond and Vincent Dureuil-Janthial. **Address** 7, rue de la Buisserolle, 71150 Rully - Tel. 03.85.87.02.37 Fax 03.85.87.00.24. **Open** From Monday to Saturday, 9:00-12:00 and 14:00-19:00; Sunday by appointment. **Spoken** English.

The Dureuil-Janthials are true artisans of wine who perpetuate traditional techniques, from growing the grapes to vinifying them with monastic strictness. Raymond, the father, owns six hectares of red and white grapes, mainly in the Bourgogne, Mercurey, and Puligny-Montrachet appellations. Son Vincent, 25, began working on the domain in 1994, helping his father with winemaking and also producing his own Rully from three hectares. The white wines are fermented in oak, then aged and stirred on the lees for a year and a half. The red grapes are crushed, stems and all, and undergo cold maceration in wooden vats, where they are *pigés* by foot, keeping the caps in contact with the juice for deeper color. They are aged over a long period in new oak barrels, *pièces*: about two years for Raymond's wine, only a year for Vincent's. The father's wines are very concentrated and tannic, wines that will keep well. Vincent's wines can be enjoyed young, for their grapiness. Several vintages are on offer. Don't hesitate.

Our choice The '95 white Rully (55 F). Flavor of very ripe citrus fruit, smooth with toasty hints. A powerful wine but not heavy. The '93 red Rully (60 F): complex, full bouquet; structured and meaty, with overlying tannic structure and spices.

Reception Excellent, in the office or the cellar. Welcoming customers (soon to be friends) is a point of honor with the Dureuil-Janthials.

How to get there *(Map 5): A6 Beaune exit. 20km south of Beaune via N74, direction Chalon. Then, in Chagny, D981, direction Rully. Domaine indicated beginning in center of Rully.*

Gilles Buisson.

Domaine Henri et Gilles Buisson

Owners Monica and Gilles Buisson. **Address** Impasse du Clou, 21190 Saint-Romain - Tel. 03.80.21.27.91 Fax 03.80.21.64.87. **Open** From Monday to Saturday, 8:00-12:00 and 14:00-19:00, Sunday by appointment. **Credit cards** Visa, Eurocard, MasterCard.

Between the Hautes-Côtes and the Côte de Beaune, Saint-Romain is a delightful village nestling in the hills above Meursault. Its wines, mostly white, are attracting a growing number of connoisseurs for their good quality/price ratio. The appellation Saint-Romain covers 135 hectares of vineyards. Without the breeding of a Puligny or the vitality of a Meursault, white Saint-Romains, when young, deliver a quite powerful bouquet, flowery, toasty, and somewhat honeyed; fine vivacity, average intensity on the palate, and a texture which softens with two to four years of bottle age. There is no Premier Cru here, but the *lieux-dits* are well known: Sous la Velle, Sous-Roche, Sous le Château, Jarrons. Gilles Buisson took over the domaine from his father, adding parcels of Corton, Pommard, and Volnay to the Saint-Romain vineyard. The small production of red '96 Saint-Romain Sous la Roche (about 50 F) has a gloriously fruity bouquet of cherries; a lively, solidly tannic taste, somewhat vegetal. The good Corton Le Rognet is about 140 Francs.

Our choice The '96 white Saint-Romain Sous La Velle (about 52 F). Very fruity (white peaches) on the nose and palate, with extract sustained by ripe acidity, providing a long finish. To be drunk as of 1999.

Reception Very open, in a recently opened tasting room. The domaine has two houses to rent in the village, for seven to eight people.

How to get there *(Map 5): On A6, exit Beaune. Take N74 in Chalon direction, turn right onto D973 towards Pommard, Volnay, Monthelie. At Meursault, right towards Saint-Romain. Going into the village, cellar on left.*

Santenay, dominated by the Trois-Crois hillsides: famous for its salt-water springs, its casino, and its wines.

Domaine Lucien Muzard & fils

Owners Lucien, Claude and Hervé Muzard. **Address** 11 bis, rue de la Cour Verreuil, 21590 Santenay - Tel. 03.80.20.61.85 Fax 03.80.20.66.02. **Open** From Monday to Sunday morning, by appointment. **Spoken** English. **Credit cards** Visa, Eurocard, MasterCard.

Lucien Muzard and his two sons, Claude and Hervé, the ninth generation of *vignerons* in this family, work hard on their twenty-hectares of vines, including seven hectares which they sharecrop on the Domaine de l'Abbaye de Santenay. Ninety-five percent of the wines are red, from the Bourgogne, Santenay, Santenay Premier Cru, Pommard, and Chassagne-Montrachet appellations; and five percent are white Santenays. The reds are not destemmed at this writing. We tasted a series of '96 red wines, solid and firm (to be drunk in 1999 or 2000), less mellow than the '95s (sold out), but there are some lovely bottles. For example, the Santenay Clos des Hâtes, combining fruity acidity and projecting tannins; the Maladière Premier Cru (68 F), the most open when young, a grapy taste finishing with good tannins for ageing; and the Gravières Premier Cru (68 F), full-bodied, with a well-structured texture. The Clos de Tavannes (70 F) was very closed during our tasting. Of the whites, the Santenay Champs Claude (72 F), from young vines on the Chassagne-Montrachet border, yielded a pronounced citrus-fruit bouquet, softness on the palate, and a firm finish. It will mature nicely with barrel ageing.

Our choice The '96 red Santenay Champs Claude Vieilles Vignes (56 F). Bouquet of black currants with a touch of acidity; structured on the palate but with soft tannins; crisp, fruity finish. It is not the most concentrated red, but it is beautifully balanced.

Reception In the tasting room of the family home, with good humor and attentiveness.

How to get there *(Map 5): On A 6 exit Beaune, then 17km southwest of Beaune via N74. Before Chagny, towards Santenay (D974). In Santenay, signs.*

Maurice Ecard: forty-eight years of winemaking and enthusiastic as ever.

Domaine Maurice Écard & fils

Owner Maurice Ecard. **Address** 11, rue Chanson-Maldant, 21420 Savigny-lès-Beaune - Tel. 03.80.21.50.61 Fax 03.80.26.11.05. **Open** From Monday to Sunday afternoon, by appointment.

Maurice Ecard's "recipe" for winemaking could be summed up as follows: mass selection of vines; grapes harvested in baskets, sometimes sorted and dried; yields kept low by debudding; in the cellar, the fermenting grapes are *pigés* and wine is aged in oak barrels, 20% of which are new. So much for the technical side. While the wines from Maurice Ecard and his sons are invariably among the best in Savigny, it is also because they come from the finest *terroirs* of the village, of which 85% are Premiers Crus. The result is solid red Savignys with backbone, aromatic intensity and the soft tannins that are typical of the appellation, making them lovely to drink young or capable of ageing gracefully. The domaine's '94s are good now, while the '95s should be cellared. Few bottles are available in this vintage, but the '96s are good (70 to 85 F). Of the Premiers Crus, Peuillets highlights the firmness characteristic of the eastern slopes of Savigny; Narbenton, the most austere Savigny in its youth, yields its habitual power; while Jarron is a spicy and vigorous red Burgundy.

Our choice The '96 red Savigny-lès-Beaune Premier Cru Serpentières (about 85 F). From the southern hillside of Savigny, it is always the silkiest, softest, and most mouth-watering of the domaine's Premiers Crus. This vintage is no exception to the rule.

Reception Generous, very helpful towards customers. In the cellar.

How to get there *(Map 5): On A 6, Beaune exit. 5.5km northwest of Beaune, towards Dijon (N74). 800 meters after getting off the Boulevard Circulaire, on left towards Savigny. Signs beginning at Place du Château.*

Claude Maréchal: in favor of "the vine's self-sufficiency".

Domaine Claude Maréchal

Owner Claude Maréchal. **Address** 6, route de Chalon 21200 Bligny-les-beaune - Tel. 03.80.21.44.37 Fax 03.80.26.58.01. **Open** Every day, by appointment.

Claude Maréchal tends nine hectares of vines in five communes--Bligny, Ladoix, Savigny, Auxey-Duresses, Pommard--essentially as a sharecropper or tenant farmer. Since the 1980s, this sincere young man, as natural as his wines, has veered into biodynamic viticulture as a means of "feeling the *terroir*" and allowing the vine to find its "self-sufficiency". "Man puts nourishment into his mouth, not intravenously. Why should it be different with vines?" During fermentation, sulfur, while not entirely banished, is used to a minimum, yielding extremely digestible wines. We were delighted with the Bourgogne Rosé (28 F), its aroma of raspberries and strawberries, full-bodied and lively. The '95 red Savigny (66 F) is solid but its tannins are velvety, very charming. The Les Lavières Premier Cru is more concentrated, with a bouquet of licorice and ripe raspberries. Maréchal's '95 white Auxey-Duresses (67 F) is totally original. The Chardonnay and Pinot Blanc are harvested very late, yielding a very rich wine (14.1% alcohol by volume), complex, with notes of humus and toast.

Our choice The '95 Pommard Les Vignots (105 F). From vines planted in 1932: Pinot Noir, Chardonnay, Aligoté, and Pinot Beurot. Its color is quite pale but it is a very powerful Pommard: wet earth, truffles, while very crisp on the palate, rich, long, silky, complex. Unforgettable.

Reception Very enthusiastic, in the barrel-ageing cellar of a recently built farmhouse.

How to get there *(Map 5): On A 6, exit Beaune, towards Bligny. The cellar is at the exit in Chalon direction, on right. Large courtyard.*

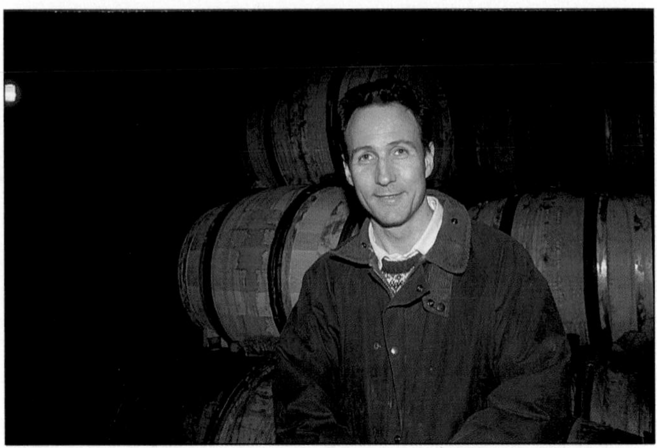

Etienne Grivot made magnificent 1994 vintages of Chambolle-Musigny, Vosne-Romanée, Vougeot, and Nuits-Saint-Georges.

Domaine Jean Grivot

Owners Jean and Étienne Grivot. **Address** 6, rue de la Croix-Rameau, 21700 Vosne-Romanée - Tel. 03.80.61.05.95 Fax 03.80.61.32.99. **Open** From Monday to Saturday, by appointment. **Spoken** English.

You can judge great winemakers by their so-called "small" or "average" vintages. Such was the case with Jean Grivot, whose red 1994s were the best we tasted from the Côte de Nuits. On his family domaine covering fifteen hectares of vines in the Vosne-Romanée, Nuits-Saint-Georges Village and Premier Cru, Chambolle-Musigny and Grands Crus (Echezeaux, Clos-Vougeot, Richebourg) appellations, he succeeded in the difficult task of balancing concentration and fruit in a year when the Pinots Noirs were on the diluted side. His Vosne-Romanée Les Boissières (98 F) delivers direct fruit, sensual and charming. The Vosne-Romanée Premier Cru Les Rouges (124 F) expresses seduction and power, without aggressivity. Of the Grands Crus, Grivot's success is spectacular. There are bottles of Clos Vougeot left (190 F): it does not have the hard extract we encountered elsewhere, retaining the characteristics of the *terroir* with the softness and youth of the vintage. The '96 bottlings, very rich Burgundies but marked with Etienne's velvet imprint, are available in small quantities.

Our choice The '96 Clos Vougeot (about 240 F, on reservation). "This is a big strong wine that has to be taught manners," says Etienne. It is deep red in color, with a remarkably concentrated bouquet (violets, glazed blackberries, licorice), a very lingering taste. Needs seven to eight years' bottle age.

Reception Etienne's enthusiasm for his work is contagious.

How to get there *(Map 5): On A 31, exit Nuits-Saint-Georges. 2.5km north of Nuits-Saint-Georges via N74, towards Dijon. 100 meters from church. On the Place de l'Eglise, a map shows all the domainees in the village.*

Jean Thévenet in front of his cellar, which won a First Prize for architecture.

Domaine de Bongran

Owner Jean Thévenet. **Address** Quintaine 71260 Clessé - Tel. 03.85.36.94.03 Fax 03.85.36.99.25. **Open** From Monday to Saturday, by appointment. **Credit cards** Visa, Eurocard, MasterCard.

On his fifteen hectares of Chardonnay grapes planted on the Quintaine hillsides and entirely cultivated with machines, Jean Thévenet perpetuates the tradition of late harvests which made the reputation of the Mâcons from Clessé and Viré in the 19th century. This is an exception in a Mâconnais whose wines are inevitably linked with cooperative cellars and the nondescript "dry little white wine". This meticulous *vigneron* likes to quote Pierre Ramonet, a legendary winemaker in Chassagne-Montrachet: "To make a great white wine, a third of the harvest must have *pourriture noble"*, overripe grapes locally called *levroutés*. Two outstanding wines are made in this spirit: the *Levrouté,* with an '87 (150 F) yielding a bouquet of Riesling (gasoline and truffles) with notes of wet earth and honey, a powerful wine, half-way between dry and sweet; and the '89 Botrytis (400 F): honeyed color, glazed oranges, linden bouquet, very rich in sugar but a wine of finesse, of rare persistence.

Our choice The '94 Mâcon Clessé Tradition (90 F): very ripe bouquet, slightly exotic; soft on the palate, with sugary attack developing into a very long, mineral finish. To be drunk.

Reception In the modern cellar, which won a First Prize in architecture, illuminated by two "portholes"; by a great but modest winemaker.

How to get there *(Map 5): On A 6, exit Mâcon-Nord. 15km north of Mâcon via N6, towards Tournus; before Fleurville, towards Quintaine (5km). Cellar at top of village, sign.*

Renée Michel and sons.

Domaine René Michel & Fils

Owners René Michel and Sons. **Address** Cray, 71260 Clessé - Tel. 03.85.36.94.27 Fax 03.85.36.99.63. **Open** Every day, by appointment. **Spoken** English, German.

The majority of Mâcons are to white wines what Beaujolais is to reds: simple wines, intended to be drunk rapidly. However, you can find certain Chardonnays which are good expressions of their *terroir* (from yields below the 72 hectoliters per hectare authorized!), as only Burgundy can make them. The Michel family belongs to that small number of stubborn *vignerons*. Organized, frank, honest, the father and his three sons sacrifice nothing to quality, carefully tending their 60-year-old vines planted on one of the best *terroirs* of the Mâconnais. Two white Mâcons Clessés stand out: one, aged traditionally in vats (35 F for the '96), with a sweet, slightly exotic bouquet; straightforward, firm, and powerful on the palate; and the other vinified and aged in oak barrels for eight to twelve months. The grapes are harvested manually (very rare in the Mâconnais) and late. In 1996, the Chardonnays were harvested with about 13.2% potential alcohol. The wines are sold following three years of bottle age, but we will be patient as we drink the excellents 1994s, powerful Mâcons with rich extract and marked alcoholic strength.

Our choice The '94 Mâcon Clessé aged in oak barrels (45 F). Beautiful golden color, bouquet of toast, tobacco, spice cake. Very mellow taste, still somewhat closed, opulent and persistent. Rare quality for the price.

Reception Very informally by a charming family of genuine *vignerons.*

How to get there *(Map 5): On A 6, exit Mâcon-Nord. 15km north of Mâcon via N6, towards Tournus; drive towards Clessé (5km). The hamlet of Cray is at the exit from Clessé on the road to Viré.*

Jean-Gérard Guillot-Broux with Saint Vincent, the patron saint of wine-makers.

Domaine Guillot-Broux

Owners Jean-Gérard and Jaqueline Guillot-Broux and children. **Address** 71260 Cruzille-en-Mâconnais - Tel. 03.85.33.21.89 / 03.85.33.29.74 (cellar) Fax 03.85.33.01.94. **Open** From Monday to Saturday, 8:00-12:00 and 14:00-19:00. Sunday by appointment. **Credit cards** Visa, Eurocard, MasterCard. **Spoken** English.

Hit by phylloxera in the early 19th century, vineyards in the northern Mâconnais virtually disappeared. A winegrower in Cruzille since 1978, Jean-Gérard Guillot-Broux is striving to bring them back. From his apprenticeship with Bernard Michelot in Meursault, he has retained a preference for wines with an oaky edge, good expressions of the *lieux-dits* on which his fifteen hectares of grapes are planted. "On the surveyor's map, some parcels had the same names as in Meursault; they were abandoned hillsides too difficult to cultivate which I plowed up entirely." He could be criticized for an ambiguous use of famous names elsewhere: Perrières, Genevrières, Combettes...But his work is certainly remarkable, as we discovered in tasting his remarkable Mâcons Blancs Villages, including a powerful, minerally '96 Mâcon-Cruzille Les Perrières (about 45 F; limited stock); and a '95 Mâcon-Cruzille (about 45 F): a wine of breeding, with long, mellow acidity on the palate.

Our choice The '96 Mâcon Chardonnay Les Combettes (about 55 F): ripe, typical Chardonnay bouquet, delicate oakiness, graceful and mouth-watering. Five years' bottle age.

Reception In the barrel cellar with Jean-Gérard, as Burgundian as they come.

How to get there *(Map 5): On A 6, exit Tournus; 15km southwest of Tournus, towards Ozenay (road to Cormatin), Martailly, then Cruzille. In the village, on right, white door, big house.*

The 1996 harvest at the Domaine du Vieux Saint-Sorlin.

Domaine du Vieux Saint-Sorlin

Owners Corinne and Olivier Merlin. **Address** 71960 La Roche-Vineuse - Tel. 03.85.36.62.09 Fax 03.85.36.66.45. **Open** From Monday to Saturday, by appointment. **Spoken** English.

Between the famous wines of the Côte d'Or and the much-publicized Beaujolais, the Mâconnais, the comet's tail of the Burgundian vineyards, has some marvelous discoveries in store for the adventurous wine lover, such as those to be made here at La Roche-Vineuse, "Vinous Rock", in the south of the appellation. Corinne and Olivier Merlin have six hectares of old vines planted on an excellent *terroir* in Mâcon La Roche Vineuse (Chardonnay and Gamay) and Bourgogne Pinot Noir. Their philosophy: small yields, manual harvests in baskets, vinifications by parcel, (very careful) ageing on the lees in barrels, and very little filtration. But the Merlins are in the Mâconnais and promoting their wines is far from being as easy as in the Côte d'Or. Of the whites, the domaine's strong selling point is the '96 Mâcon Vieilles Vignes (48 F): flowery aroma, very mellow taste for the vintage, graceful and straightforward, a very beautiful wine. Their '96 red Bourgogne Vieilles Vignes (41 F) is a soft, balanced wine with a trace of acidity, quite lively, finishing with a round, red-berry taste. To be drunk in 1999.

Our choice The '95 Mâcon Blanc La Roche-Vineuse Les Cras (70 F). Powerful, delicately oaky bouquet on a par with the best Pulignys, a mellow yet lacy texture, mouth-watering, elegant finish. Great character. Don't be put off by its price: the wine is worth every centime.

Reception In the cellar, by a couple of impassioned winemakers.

How to get there *(Map 5): On A 6, exit Mâcon-Nord. 10km west of Mâcon via N79, towards Cluny. At the top of the village. Signs.*

Fuissé and its vineyards.

Domaine Robert-Denogent

Owner Jean-Jacques Robert-Denogent. **Address** 71960 Fuissé - Tel. 03.85.35.65.39 Fax 03.85.35.66.69. **Open** From Monday to Saturday, by appointment. **Spoken** English.

Very old Chardonnay vines, varied *terroirs* in the best *climats* of Fuissé, an expert hand at fermentation and barrel ageing: decidedly, Jean-Jacques Robert-Denogent has a lot of good things going for him. This is where we had our most beautiful tastings of Pouilly-Fuissé. Five hectares of white grapes yield wines on a par with the best Premiers Crus of the Côte de Beaune, while delivering their Fuissé identity as regards finesse and precise tastes, with overlying mineral structure. The 1995s confirmed our majestic tasting last year. The Mâcon Solutré Clos des Bertillonnes (47 F), its bouquet of ripe fruit with exotic hints, supple, soft, very full glazed citrus on the palate, is a Mâcon unlike the others. The Pouillly Fuissé La Croix (72 F), harvested even later when the grapes were super-ripe, delivers a delicate, intense bouquet of quince and honey; round, fat, very rich extract with a pronounced mineral (schist) finish. The Pouilly Fuissé Les Carrons (120 F), from Chardonnay vines almost a century old, is still very closed but we already could sense its enormous fullness on the palate, with appetizing mineral edges, and its very great potential. In ten years, it will be explosive.

Our choice The '95 Pouilly-Fuissé Cuvée Claude Denogent (87 F), from limestone-clay soils. Very big bouquet: slightly sugary hints, glazed citrus, exotic fruit preserves. Magnificent, fat taste, almost ethereal, mineral backbone. An extraordinary wine.

Reception By Jean-Jacques, very enthusistic and pleasant, in his small cellar full of barrels.

How to get there *(Map 5): On A 6, exit Mâcon-Sud. 8km west of Mâcon via Loché. In the center of Fuissé (lieu-dit Le Plan).*

Françoise, Nicolas and Adeline Melin.

Domaine de la Soufrandise

Owners Françoise and Nicolas Melin. **Address** 71960 Fuissé - Tel. 03.85.35.64.04 Fax 03.85. 35.65.57. **Open** Every day, by appointment. **Spoken** English.

In 1986, Nicolas Melin, 35, an engineer with the French Forestry Service, and his wife, Françoise, took over the property that had been in the family since 1853. Their vines--four hectares are more than 35 years old--are planted entirely in Fuissé, including a large parcel next to "La Soufrandise", their old house surrounded by high walls. Very promising winemakers who should be closely followed, the Melins favor slow vinifications without yeast. They use a touch of oak for the Pouilly (about 20%), which is always blended with vat wine "for people who enjoy an oaky edge without its opulence". They quietly impose their style, aiming at "wines that are not too lively, which open up rapidly and can be drunk in five years." Their '95 Mâcon-Fuissé Le Ronté (39 F) yields a lovely glazed taste, without heaviness, straightforward, soft, typical of the *cru.* The '95 Pouilly Fuissé Vieilles Vignes (60 F) has an appealing bouquet of glazed citrus, fluid, elegant, flowery (fern, lilies) and slightly mineral. It can be enjoyed young.

Our choice The '95 Pouilly-Fuissé Levrouté Vieilles Vignes (70 F). *Levrouté* means late-harvested in the Mâconnais. From a *terroir* of crumbly schist, delivers aromas of very ripe raisins with toasty hints, a powerful, rich taste marked by alcohol, long, a wine of great character. To be cellared.

Reception Family-style, informal.

How to get there *(Map 5): On A6, exit Mâcon-Sud, towards Fuissé. At the entrance to Fuissé on the road to Mâcon, on right.*

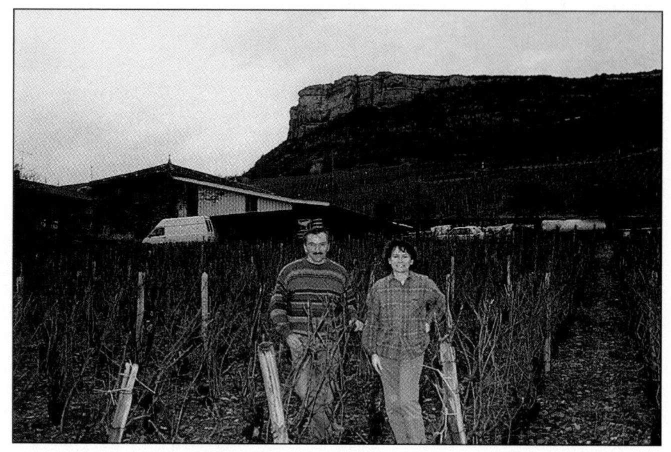

Domaine Barraud

Owners Martine and Daniel Barraud. **Address** Les Nembrets, 71960 Vergisson - Tel. 03.85.35.84.25 Fax 03.85.35.86.98. **Open** Every day, 9:00-12:00 and 14:00-19:00, by appointment.

Vergisson is one of the four communes in the Pouilly-Fuissé appellation, with Fuissé, Solutré-Pouilly, and Chaintré. "Here, as opposed to Fuissé, estate bottling is quite recent. We are discovering the potential of our *terroirs,"* explains Daniel Barraud, who is far ahead in this area. He favors traditional mass vine selections and champions the slopes facing Vergisson beneath the rock of that name. "We must wait for the wines, which mature slowly." Careful-barrel ageing complements his search for quality. On their 6 1/2 hectare-vineyard, the Barrauds' Chardonnay is a straightforward wine, without artifice and with the minerality of Vergisson. There is an excellent '96 Mâcon Vergisson La Roche, from a superb parcel which touches the vines of Fuissé: beautifully intense fruit, mellow, mineral taste, lingering. More mature (slightly soft, round, very charming taste), 25 % of the '96 Saint-Véran En Crèche (45 F) is aged in oak. The '96 Pouilly-Fuissé La Verchères (about 75 F) yields a sweet bouquet of white fruit, with mouth-watering softness and fine mineral edges. To be cellared.

Our choice The '96 Pouilly-Fuissé Vieilles Vignes (about 90 F). Gold straw color, toasty, sweet bouquet, marvelously intense on the palate, remarkable balance, without heaviness. A great wine which calls attention to the crispness of its vineyard origin.

Reception Most often by charming Martine, in their modern home. A beautiful location.

How to get there *(Map 5): On A 6, exit Mâcon-Sud. 10km west of Mâcon via Davayé. At entrance to Vergisson, on a small square with a map of the domaines, take small road towards the hillside.*

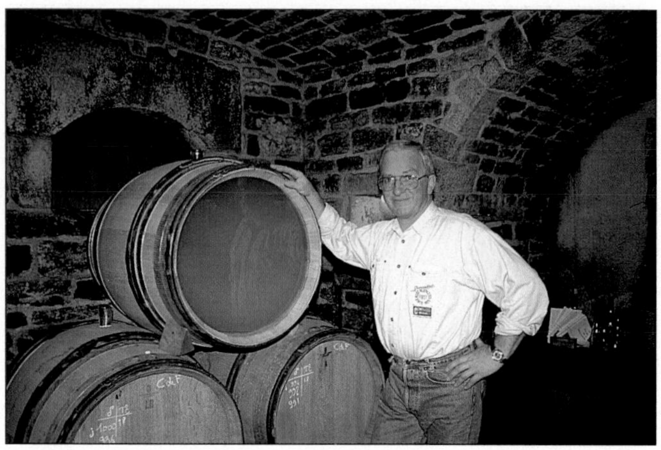

Roger Lassarat, the Mayor of Vergisson, and his demonstration barrel for watching the wine "at work".

Domaine Roger Lassarat

Owner Roger Lassarat. **Address** Le Martelet 71960 Vergisson - Tel. 03.85.35.84.28 Fax 03.85. 35.86.73. **Open** From Monday to Saturday, 9:00-12:00 and 14:00-18:00, by appointment.

Mayor Lassarat has twenty-four donkeys, all members of the association *Anes et Sentiers*, Donkeys and Footpaths, organized to take tourists through the vineyards of his village and the surrounding countryside. An active man in Pouilly-Fuissé, Roger Lassarat is also a winemaker with nine hectares of vines primarily in Saint-Véran and Pouilly-Fuissé. Many wines are aged in oak, which makes its presence quite evident in them, and there are beautiful bottles from old vines or individual parcels, depending on the vintage. We took special pleasure in the '96 Pouilly-Fuissé Clos de France (74 F): vine blossoms, chalk, fern, long, graceful, a good reflection of the minerally character of Vergisson wines. The '96 Pouilly Prestiges, "from old vine stumps", furnished a fruity, candied bouquet, a dense, tight taste: a wine to cellar (and to be reserved). Note that prices were reduced in 1995 and didn't budge in 1996. A marvelous policy, *Monsieur le Maire!*

Our choice The '94 Saint-Véran Le Cras (79 F). From late-harvested, overripe grapes. Intense roasted-coffee bouquet, very fat, with notes of quince and glazed citrus rind, mellow yet crisp.

Reception By friendly Roger Lassarat, in a beautiful barrel-vaulted cellar giving onto the tasting room.

How to get there *(Map 5): On A 6, exit Mâcon-Sud. 10km west of Mâcon via Davayé (D177). Access indicated in upper part of Vergisson, at Le Martelet.*

Gilles Guerrin.

Domaine Gilles Guerrin

Owners Sylvie and Gilles Guerrin. **Address** 71960 Vergisson - Tel. 03.85.35.80.38 Fax 03.85.35.87.07. **Open** Every day, by appointment.

In the southern Mâconnais, we are in a country of high cliffs, a great geological upheaval from which rise the famous Rocks of Solutré and of Vergisson, the impressive rocky spurs that tower over the plain of the Saône to the east and, to the west, the famous vines of Pouilly-Fuissé. In a small village house in Vergisson, Gilles Guerrin began estate-bottling his Mâcons, Saint-Vérans, and Pouillys in 1987. Today, he sells scarcely half of his production directly from the vineyard, with quite modest means but energy to spare. His wines are clean on the palate, with a hint of oak, and sold at angelic prices. His '96 Mâcon Vergisson reveals a flowery, acidulated peach aroma, mouth-wateringly soft extract, a supple, distinct taste with a mineral touch. Of the Saint-Vérans, the '96 Prestige (37 F) is softer and slips down more easily, with less minerality than the Mâcon.

Our choice The '96 Pouilly-Fuissé Vieilles Vignes (59 F). A very ripe, exotic bouquet (mango, pineapple), full-bodied and mature on the palate, with a typical Pouilly mineral finish. Excellent quality for the price.

Reception Informal and friendly, in a small tasting cellar stacked with bottles, beneath a traditional Mâconnais house.

How to get there *(Map 5): On A 6, exit Mâcon-Sud. 10km west of Mâcon via Davayé (D177). Access indicated in Vergisson.*

Philippe Bérard with part of his collection of viti-vinicultural tools.

Domaine Saint-Philibert

Owner Philippe Bérard. **Address** Loché 71000 Mâcon - Tel. 03.85.35.61.76 / 04.78.43.24.96 Fax 04.78.35.90.87. **Open** Every day, 9:00-12:00 and 14:00-19:00, by appointment. **Spoken** English.

A great collector of objects related to wine, Philippe Bérard has arranged a 2700 square-foot museum beneath his vat room, displaying one thousand of his most beautiful pieces. It has taken him ten years to make an allegorical display retracing the history of the viticulture of France in general and of the Mâconnais in particular. Exhibited in this manner, such objects as old barrel spigots take on a new dimension reminiscent of contemporary art. It is extremely interesting, as is the spectacle that takes place here in the glass. On his old family property of 6.3 hectares, including 4.7 in Pouilly-Loché and Mâcon-Villages, Philippe Bérard makes only Blanc de Chardonnay and outstanding Pouilly-Loché--a small appellation, the first cousin of Pouilly-Fuissé. His '95 Mâcon-Loché is soft, very fruity, full-bodied, with little acidity. There are two *cuvées* of Pouilly-Loché: the classic Pouilly (our choice), which is fermented in vats; and Le Clos des Rocs (46 F), a parcel vinified in large barrels and casks. It is a lively, straightforward wine in the 1993 vintage.

Our choice The '95 Pouilly-Loché (39 F). A fresh, citrus aroma balanced by softness on the palate (the result of partial malolactic fermentation), with fine mineral character. It can be drunk now.

Reception Good humored, instructive, by a winemaker who loves his work; in a typical Mâconnais house.

How to get there *(Map 5): On A 6, exit Mâcon-Sud. In 3.5km, towards Gare TGV (train station), then Loché. Domaine in front of church, at top of village.*

CHAMPAGNE

Laon
Athies
Sissonne
Château-Porcien
Rethel
Tourteron
Le Chesne
Attigny
Aniz
Festieux
Chavignon
Cerny-en-L.
Craonne
Vailly-s.-Aisne
Pontavert
Berry-au-Bac
Roizy
Neufchâtel-s.-Aisne
Juniville
Vouziers
Leffincourt
Machault
Bourg-et-Comin
Braine
Ventelay
Bourgogne
Isles-s.-S.
Fismes
Witry-les-R.
Pontfaverger-Moronvilliers
Sommepy-Tahure
Beine-Nauroy
Reims
Tramery
Cormontreuil
Fère
Prosnes
L'Espérance
Ville-s.-Tourbe
Coincy
Ville-en-Tardenois
Mourmelon-le-Grd
Suippes
Verzy
Châtillon-s.-Marne
St-Hilaire
La Cheppe
Valmy
Dormans
Aÿ
Dizy
Condé-s.-M.
Auve
Crézancy
Igny-C.
Épernay
Chouilly
Juvigny
La Grande-Romane
Dommartin
Condé-en-B.
Avize
Courtisols
Mareuil-en-B.
Châlons-en-Champagne
Compertrix
Moivre
Montmort-Lucy
Vertus
Chaintrix-Bierges
Marson
Posses
Montmirail
Maclaunay
Champaubert
Étoges
Villeseneux
Écury
Nuisement
Pogny
Vanault-les-D.
Marne 51
Vitry-la-V.
Morsains
Bannes
Vatry
Fontaine-s.-Coole
Songy
Chapton
Normée
Esternay
Fère-Ch.
Coole
Vitry-le-François
Sézanne
Sommesous
Sompuis
Châtelraould-St-Louvent
Montceaux
Pleurs
Mailly-le-Camp
Humbauville
Thiéblemont-F.
Larzicourt
St-Ouen-Domprot
Barbonne-Fayel
La Chapelle-Lasson
Anglure
Aube
Dampierre
Margerie-Hancourt
Conflans
Pouan
Arcis-s.-A.
Giffaumont
Nogent-s.-S.
Romilly
Méry-s.-Seine
Chavanges
St-Martin-de-Bossenay
La Belle-Étoile
Montier-en-Der
Coclois
Montmorency-Beaufort
Trainel
Voué
Marigny-le-Châtel
Aube 10
Lesmont
Louze
Soulaines-Dhuys
Brienne
Piney
Sognes
Marcilly-le-Hayer
Le Pavillon-Ste-Julie
Troyes
Luyères
Dierrey
Ste-Savine
Pont-Ste-M.
Géraudot
Jessains
Thorigny-s.-Oreuse
Villemaur
Lusigny
Vendeuvre
Estissac
Bucey
Aix-en-Othe
Bar-s.-A.
Villeneuve-l'Arch.
Bouilly
Fournaudin
Jeugny
Eguilly
Cerisiers
Arces
Auxon
Bar-s.-S.
Lantages
Polisy
Silvarouvres
Neuvy-Sautour
Ervy
Chaource
Pargues
Essoyes
Cunfin
Joigny
St-Florentin
Vanlay
Mussy-s.-S.
Migennes
Bagneux-la-Fosse
Les Riceys
Montigny-s.-A.
Flogny-la-C.
Hauterive
Coussegrey
Arthonnay
Villedieu
Brion-s.-O.
Canal
Suippe
Vesle
Marne
Aube
Seine
Vanne
6
9 10 11 12
301 314
324
6
322 2
317
3 4
311
310
316
305
325
307 309
313
7
323
302
318
303 319 8
312
306
5
308 315
13 14
326
1
321
304
320

CHAMPAGNE

INTRODUCTION

The Champagne vineyards are divided into two sometimes querulous families. On one side are the great *maisons de négoce* with the prestigious names, who usually own extremely well-located vineyards but buy most of their grapes to satisfy their large needs. On the other side are the *vignerons* themselves, who vinify only the grapes from their own vineyards. Their wine is usually made from a single grape variety and is thus more sensitive to variations in vintage. Champagnes from a single grape also give greater expression to their *terroir*, their vineyard origin. From one cellar to the next, we thus have a clear picture of a minerally Chardonnay from Le Mesnil, followed by the full-bodied style of a Pinot Noir grown in Mailly. So that you can discover these *terroirs* of the Champangne, we have deliberately presented only individual winemakers in this Guide, called Récoltants-Manipulants: growers who vinify and sell only the Champagne from their own grapes. They are designated by "RM" on their label, as opposed to the Négociants-Manipulateurs, the *maisons de négoce* with "NM" on the label.
From a strictly tourist point of view, however, the *négociants'* cellars are often more impressive and more attractively designed than those of the small *vignerons*: Thus, we have suggested a choice of the most beautiful Champagne houses which can be visited in Epernay and in Reims, the two Champagne capitals. Seriously damaged during World War II, the Champagne villages themselves, with the exception of Hautvillers, are not of great interest. However, those in the Aube vineyards on the edge of the Champagne near Burgundy are truly charming.

FROM STILL WINE TO CHAMPAGNE

These are the most northerly vineyards in which grapes can ripen, which means that they often have little sugar and great acidity. During the Champagne-making process these weaknesses become strong points: The bubbles modify our perception of the wine's acidity and confer body on wines which are sometimes weak.
Up until this essential operation, vinification resembles that in all the other winegrowing regions of France. Picked by hand, the grapes from each different vineyard or parcel of vines are pressed separately, with careful distintion made of

each vineyard origin. The juice undergoes alcoholic fermentation during which yeasts are released which transform it into wine. A second, malolactic, fermentation takes place in the bottle, transforming strong malic acid into softer lactic acid. The different wines are then blended: the *assemblage*. This is the first fundmental operation in making Champagne. The object is to achieve a harmonious combination of the different wines from different vineyards, the different grape varieties, and possibly from different vintages, in order to perpetuate the "house style" which sets each Champagne producer apart. Actually making the Champagne, *champagnisation*, can then begin.

First, the bottling, *tirage,* and the second fermentation in bottle, called *prise de mousse*: once the blend has been created, it is enriched with new yeasts and 24 grams of sugar per litre and bottled. Yeasts now bring about a second fermentation in the bottle, the *prise de mousse*, slowly transforming the sugar in the cool temperature of the cellar and creating the bubbles that make sparkling Champagne.

During bottle-ageing, the bottles are kept lying horizontally, *sur les lattes*, for a long period, enhancing the exchange of the wine and the dead yeasts, nourishing the wine and developing its aromas. The ageing period depends on the Champagne: two to three years for ordinary Champagnes, three to five years for vintage Champagnes, and much longer for the *cuvées de prestige*.

During the secondary fermentation, the bottles are turned daily (*le remuage*) in order to concentrate the deposit formed by the dead yeast cells and causing it to slide down onto the cork. *Remuage* may be done by hand, with the bottles placed on wooden racks and slowly turned until they are almost vertical. It can also be done mechanically, using *gyropalettes.*

The final steps are *dégorgement*, expelling the dead-yeast deposit, and *dosage.* Once the yeast deposit is firmly concentrated on the cork, the bottle is plunged into a freezing liquid. A small block of ice is formed, imprisoning the deposit which is then expelled by the natural pressure of the gas in the bottle. The final step is the *dosage*, in which the *liqueur d'expédition* is added, a syrup of wine and sugar whose quantity varies depending on the Champagne desired: Brut, the driest Champagne; Sec; or Demi-Sec.

GRAPE VARIETIES

Three *cépages* (grape varieties) are planted in the Champagne: two black-skinned grapes, the Pinot Noir and Pinot Meunier; and one white, the Chardonnay. Pinot Meunier makes fruity, balanced Champagnes which develop and age quite quickly, and is therefore most often found in ordinary Champagnes which have had less bottle age *sur lattes*. The vines are planted mostly in the Valley of the Marne between Château-Thierry and Epernay. Pinot Noir produces more vigorous, full-bodied wines, low in acidity. Champagne made from either Pinot or from a blend of them is called Blanc de Noir, "white wine from black-skinned grapes." Chardonnay is distinctly more acid, conferring crispness and structure to the blends. It is grown essentially in the Côte des Blancs but also in some parts of the Montagne de Reims, where it produces a very different wine with greater backbone. A Champagne made from Chardonnay exclusively is called Blanc de Blanc.

INTRODUCTION

MAIN VINEYARD REGIONS

The large Vallée de la Marne from Cumières to Mareuil is the kingdom of the powerful, solidly built Pinot Noir, which is grown in the famous vineyard regions of Aÿ, Ambonnay, and Bouzy. Chardonnay is a minor grape there, producing very different wines with much more structure, especially from the Aÿ vineyards, than those grown on the Côte des Blancs. The Montagne de Reims is another home to the Pinot Noir, yielding lively, vigorous wines, the best known being those from Mailly-Champagne, Verzy, and Verzenay. Several Chardonnay vineyards there are of fine quality, notably those in Villers-Marmery. As the name Côte des Blancs indicates, it is the home territory of Chardonnay, with a necklace of prestigious *crus* planted south of Epernay in Avize, Cramant, and Le Mesnil. The vines around Troyes in the Aube *département supply* the Champagne houses with a large amount of Pinot Noir grapes which, unjustifiably, do not carry the prestige of the other regions.

TYPES OF CHAMPAGNE

The most common Champagne is the Brut Sans Année (BSA), a blend of various vintages, generally including some wines from previous years, called reserve wines. Despite the variations in each harvest, the Brut Sans Année must regularly reflect the "house style", year in and year out.

Vintage Brut Champagne may be a blend of various wines and grape varieties but they must be from the same harvest. Made only in years of exceptional harvests, vintage Champagnes should translate the climatic realities of the harvest, as should all the other wines of France.

The Cuvées Spéciales, vintage or not, are considered the *crème de la crème* of the Champagne house. They are usually distinguished by a prestigious name and a special bottle. The Cuvée Spéciale is above all the creation of the large Champagne *négociants.*

Pink Champagnes, both vintage and non-vintage, are usually obtained by blending white and red wines from the Coteaux Champenois, and more rarely by maceration and vinification of black grapes.

The Champagne region still produces non-sparkling red and white wines under the appellation Coteaux Champenois. Sold for the same price as Champagne, they are rarely of interest, except for the wines mentioned in this Guide.

Finally, in the Aube *département*, the lovely village of Riceys produces the very special Rosé des Riceys, a still wine made from Pinot Noir, with good color and a fleshy, fruity taste that becomes spicy with age.

BUYING CHAMPAGNE

Once the *dosage* has been added to Champagne, it generally is good for drinking. If you have an excellent cellar, you can keep Champagne and discover an unusual aspect of it as it ages: What Champagne loses in bubbles, it gains in body and smoothness. But your cellar must truly be perfect; otherwise, deprived of the nourishment of its lees, Champagne will rapidly deteriorate and dry out. As the great 1989 and 1990 vintages are currently available, you should make these your first choice. In addition, try our selections of the several old vintages still available and recently disgorged; and taste the Extra Brut and other un-dosed Champagnes for their inherently beautiful balance.

INTRODUCTION

A TABLE WITH CHAMPAGNE

Varying as Champagnes do with the grape varieties used, their proportion in the blend, their vineyard origins, the amount of *vins de réserve*, and the *dosage*, it is difficult to give advice on matching Champagne with food. Nevertheless, here are several tips on serving an all-Champagne meal.

Non-vintage Blanc de Blancs: As an apéritif, as long as it is not too sweet. Full-bodied Champagnes go well with grilled fish and, more rarely, chicken, veal, and pork.

Vintage Blanc de Blancs: Often bigger wines than those above, these accompany a wider choice of dishes, including fish in a sauce. If you have old Champagnes from Avize or Le Mesnil, they are marvelous with firm, succulent fish like turbot; or shellfish in an aromatic sauce, like a civet of lobster. Vintage Blanc de Blancs is also good with cooked, mature cheeses like old Comté or old Beaufort.

BRUT SANS ANNEE, Non-vintage dry Champagne: From the winemakers we have selected here, we have often greatly enjoyed non-vintage Champagnes with white meats or small game birds, provided the Champagnes were predominantly Pinot Noir and sufficiently aged. Vintage Bruts, generally fuller and more vigorous Champagnes, can even accompany large game like venison.

Rosés: If they have begun to mature and if they are made with a high proportion of Pinot Noir (from the Montagne de Reims or Les Riceys Grands Crus), try them with lamb or goat cooked pink.

BAR-SUR-SEINE

1 - RESTAURANT - **Le Parc de Villeneuve**: *N71 (toward Châtillon), hameau de Villeneuve, 10110 Bar-sur-Seine. Tel. 03.25.29.16.80. Closed Sunday and Monday evening and Wednesday.* Menus: 175 and 240 F (weekdays); 260 and 320 F. A la carte: around 400 F. A beautiful manor house nestled in its park offering real southern cuisine (one of the Caironi brothers worked under Ducasse). Attractive wine list, well-stocked with Champagnes.

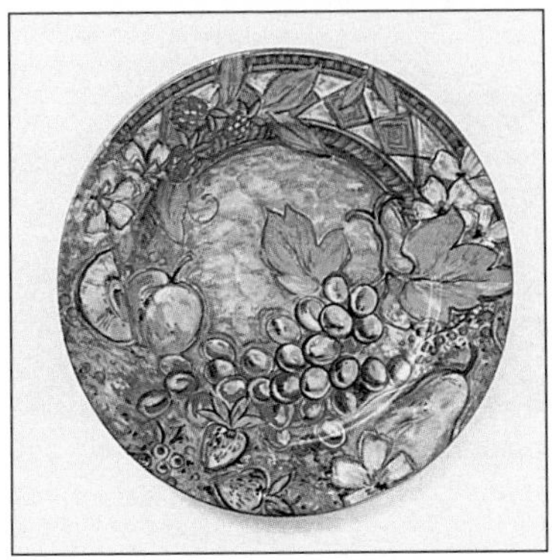

BEAUMONT-SUR-VESLE

2 - HOTEL-RESTAURANT - **La Maison du champagne**: *51360 Beaumont-sur-Vesle. Tel. 03.26.03.92.45. Closed Sunday evening and Monday.* Tasty home-style cooking, but it's the wine list that attracts the most attention. Fifty entries from Champagne, classed by village, that show a stronger preference for winegrowers than for négociants. Perfect selection with minute and precise information on each vintage. The rest of the list (around 400 entries) holds some lovely surprises: judicious selection in the great appellations (particularly in Alsace and Rhône), several finds in regions not generally on wine lists (Savoie, Jura, Corse), and a generous welcome for wines from abroad. Menus: 77 to 200 F. Rooms, however (200 to 350 F), could do with refurbishing.

ÉPERNAY

3 - RESTAURANT - **Chez Pierrot**: *16 rue de la Fauvette, 51200 Epernay. Tel. 03.26.55.16.93. Fax 03.26.54.51.30. Closed Sunday.* Creative cuisine. Very attractive list with Champagnes at reasonable prices, served by the flute. Menu: 120 F. A la carte: around 250 F.

4 - RESTAURANT - **La Table Kobus**: *3 rue du Docteur-Rousseau, 51200 Epernay. Tel. 03.26.51.53.53 Fax 03.26. 58.42.68. Closed Sunday evening and Monday.* Bistro ambiance and reinterpreted home-style dishes. Good choice of wines and Champagnes. Menu: 130 F. A la carte: around 250 F.

ÉTOGES

5 - HOTEL - **Château d'Étoges**: *51270 Etoges. Tel. 03.26.59.30.08 Fax 03.26.59.35.57.* A 17th-century

castle surrounded by a moat that now welcomes guests. Vast, magnificently-decorated rooms from 600 to 800 F and suites at 1,200 F. Breakfast is at 70 F. The restaurant is less inspiring.

FERE EN TARDENOIS

6 - HOTEL-RESTAURANT - **Château de Fère**: *02130 Fère en Tardenois. Tel. 03.23.82.21.13 Fax 03.23.82.37.81.* Rooms and suites: 850 to 1950 F depending on dates. Menus: 180 (except weekdays) to 480 F. A little way out of the vineyard, this address is nevertheless one of our favorites in Champagne: a beautiful site with nearby ruins (visible from the rooms) that bring together the Middle Ages and the Renaissance; a dining room decorated with paintings of animals; a full-flavored cuisine, spicy but not impertinent, moderately exotic (but the menu's style is a bit too precious). Above all a pleasure for wine-amateurs: the former waiter, now enthusiastic young wine waiter, Frédéric Pagneux; an attractive list of Champagnes with old vintages, a good selection of well-chosen Bordeaux vintages, and good choices in other viticultural regions.

IGNY-COMBLIZY

7 - BED & BREAKFAST - **Château du Ru Jacquier**: *51700 Igny-Comblizy. Tel. 03.26.57.10.84 Fax 03.26.57.11.85.* A beautiful 18th-century edifice, transformed into a castle by its turrets, in the middle of a park . Warm welcome. 6 guest rooms at 400 and 450 F, breakfast included. Meals (by

reservation): 150 F, wine not included.

LE-MESNIL-SUR-OGER

8 - RESTAURANT - **Le Mesnil**: *2 rue Pasteur, 51190 Le-Mesnil-sur-Oger. Tel. 03.26.57.95.57 Fax 03.26.57.78.57. Closed Monday evening and Wednesday, from 1/23 and 2/5 and from 8/16 to 9/3.* Impressive list of Champagnes offering old vintages,

and a good selection of Mesnil wines at tame prices. Menus: 100 to 350 F. A la carte: around 280 F.

REIMS

9 - HOTEL-RESTAURANT - **Les Crayères**: *64 boulevard Henri Vasnier, 51100 Reims. Tel. 03.26.82.80.80 Fax 03.26.82. 65.52. Restaurant closed Mon. and noon Tues. Hotel and restaurant from 12/22 to 1/12.* A large bourgeois dwelling in the middle of a park that once belonged to Louise Pommery. Rooms are spacious, the bar very pleasant. Cuisine with a fondness for spices, but which is not dominated by them. Good choice of coffees. Sumptuous wine list (650 entries, of which 200 in Champagnes, from only very important négociants, with some old vintages for amateurs of mature Cham-

pagnes; wines from the rest of France are perfectly chosen in sufficiently aged vintage years). Menus: 850 to 950 F (wine included). Rooms and suites: 990 to 2,400 F. Breakfast: 110 F.

10 - RESTAURANT - **Au petit Comptoir**: *17 rue de Mars, 51100 Reims. Tel. 03.26.40.58.58 Fax 03.26.47.26.19. Closed noon Sat. and Sun.* Home-style cooking and a short but well-chosen wine list. A la carte: around 250 F.

11 - RESTAURANT - **Le Vigneron**: *Place Paul-Jamot, 51100 Reims. Tel. 03.26.47.00.71 Fax 03.26.47.87.66. Closed noon Sat. and Sun., the first 2 weeks in August and from Christmas*

to 1/1. Lovely collection of objects, especially Champagne posters. Solid, square meals. Attractive list of Champagnes (nearly 300 entries representing one hundred vineyards). Menu: 160 F. A la carte: around 250 F.

12 - BED & BREAKFAST - **La Maison du potier**: *5 rue des Tournelles, 51100 Reims. Tel. 03.26.77.67.77 Fax 03.26.77.67.78.* Guest rooms in a very old half-timbered house whose windows look out on the cathedral. Good welcome. Rooms: 295 F (2 pers.), 260 F (1 pers.) breakfast included.

TROYES

13 - RESTAURANT - **Le Clos Juillet**: *22 boulevard du 14-Juillet, 10000 Troyes. Tel. 03.25.73.31.32 Fax 03.25.73.98.59. Closed Sat. noon and Sun.* Menus: 160 to 290 F. A la carte: around 400 F. Philippe Colin knows only one law: the product and

nothing but the product. Therefore, simple flavors, lovely products, and precise cooking. Good list of Champagne combining négociants and winegrowers. The Aube, of course, is not forgotten. Good choices from other wine-producing regions. Large selection of half bottles.

14 - HOTEL - **Le champ des oiseaux**: *20 rue Linard-Gonthier, 10000 Troyes. Tel. 03.25.80.58.50.* A group

of half-timbered houses huddled around a paved courtyard. Rooms are large and quiet. Choose among the suites under the roof. Rooms: 490 to 790 F. Breakfast: 60 F.

TO SEE

AŸ

MUSEUM - **The Aÿ Wine Museum**: *Champagne Pierre Laurain, 2 rue Roger Sondag, 51160 Aÿ. Tel. 03.26.55. 18.90 Fax 03.26.55.19.34. From 9 to 12 and 2 to 5.* Collections of viticultural tools and old Cham-

pagne labels. An exhibit on the history of Aÿ wines.

BAYEL

MUSEUM - **The royal glassworks of Champagne**: *10310 Bayel. Tel. 03.25. 92.42.68 (Office of tourism). Factory tours every morning, Mon. to Fri., at 9:30 and 11am, Sat. at 9:30am. Visit to the eco-museum, Mon. to Sat., from 9 to 12am and 2 to 6pm, Sun. from 2 to 6pm.*

CHAVOT

VISIT - The church hemmed in by the vineyard.

COLOMBE-LE-SEC

OUTING - The magnificent 12th-century cellar in an annex to the Clairvaux abbey, now a farm. *Visits each Sat. from May to October, 3 to 7 pm.*

CUIS

VISIT - The Romanesque church surrounded by vines.

EPERNAY

VISIT - **The cellars**: the main tourist attraction is, of course, touring the cellars of the great Champagne estates. The easiest to visit is that of **Champagne Mercier** with its famous little train *(70 avenue de Champagne, 51200 Epernay. Tel. 03.26.51.22.22 Fax 03.26.51.22.23. Open every day from 9:30 to 11:30 and 2 to 4:30, to 5:30 on weekends and holidays; closed Tues. and Wed. from December to late February).* The tour most adapted to connoisseurs, but from which amateurs will greatly benefit, is that of the **Moët et Chandon cellars** *(20 avenue de Champagne, 51200 Epernay. Tel. 03.26.51.20.20 Fax 03.26.51.20.21. Open Mon. to Fri. and weekends from April to late October, from 9:30 to 11:30 and 2 to 4:45).* Among the numerous activities offered by the Castellane house (live butterfly gardens; visit of the giant

tower dominating the city; label, printing-press and Champenois wildlife museums), one should especially keep in mind the collection of posters by Capiello, the graphic artist for whom Champagne was a favorite subject. In the beautiful cellars, a wine museum with a fascinating retrospective of all the different processes invented for the remuage (riddling) of Champagnes. *(57 rue de Verdun, 51200 Epernay. Tel. 03.26.51.19.19 Fax 03.26.54. 24.81. Visits from 5/1 to late October, from 10 to 12 and 2 to 6).*

VISIT - Slightly out of the city center, **la maison Leclerc-Briant** displays a collection of tools and objects promoting Champagne. *(67 rue Chaude Ruelle, BP 108, 51204 Epernay cedex. Tel. 03.26.54.45.33 Fax 03.26.54. 49.59. Mon. to Fri. from 9 to 12 and 1:30 to 5:30 (weekends by reservation).*

OUTING - Avenue de Champagne, where Champagne's great estates own some magnificent private residences.

ESSOYES

MUSEUM - **The House of the Vineyard**: *10360 Essoyes. Tel. 03.25.29.64.64. Open from Easter to Halloween, from 2:30 to 6:30 pm; the rest of the year by reservation.* Lovely ethnographic museum next to Renoir's studio.

GRAUVES

OUTING - In the church, a Madonna carved in a wine press screw. Some say mischevously that " elle a fait plus de tours que de miracles... " (she has performed more tricks (/rotations) than miracles).

HAUTVILLERS

OUTING - This village, surrounded by vineyards, is also famous for its hundreds of polychromatic wrought iron signs evoking the inhabitants' different professions: from the thatcher to the winegrower, almost each profession has one.

LE-MESNIL-SUR-OGER

OUTING - Climbing through the vineyards behind the village affords a view over the legendary Clos du Mesnil, one of the region's few hedged-in vineyards.

LES RICEYS

OUTING - A very beautiful wine-producing village in the Aube whose streets are lined with low stone walls.

NESLE-LE-REPONS

OUTING - The 16th-century church shelters a 15th-century Madonna with grapes.

ŒUILLY

MUSEUM - **House of Champagne**: *51480 Oeuilly. Tel. 03.26.57.10.30. Open every day from 5/1 to 11/15 (except Tues.) from 2 to 6 pm. Admission: 25 F (adults), 10 F (children 10-18).* A collection of viticultural tools in an 18th-century building.

REIMS

OUTING - *5 place du Général-Gouraud, 51100 Reims. Tel. 03.26.61.62.55 Fax 03.26.61.63.98. April to late October, every day from 9 to 5:30. The rest of the year by reservation.* The cellars of the great Champagne négociants. Pommery is famous for its impressive staircase and the lightning sculpted by Emile Gallé.

OUTING - *9 place Saint-Nicaise, 51100 Reims. Tel. 03.26.85.45.35 Fax 03.26.85.44.39. From 9:30 to 11 and 2 to 4:30. Closed weekends December to late February.* The Taittinger cellars bring together crayères (the quarries from which limestone was taken in the Gallo-Roman period), the remains of a 13th-century chapel, and its 15th-century crypt.

OUTING - *51 Boulevard Henri-Vasnier, 51100 Reims. Tel. 03.25.84. 43.44 Fax 03.26.84.43.49. Every day (except Tues. and Wed. from December to late February) from 9 to 11 and 2 to 5:15.* Piper-Heidsieck has opted for the " scenic railways " visit with its automated tubs that glide in an astonishing way through decor illustrating wine-growing and wine-making.

RILLY LA MONTAGNE

OUTING - A church whose sculpted stalls evoke viticulture.

TROYES

OUTING - In the basilica of Saint-Urbain, the lovely " Madonna with grapes ".

VERZENAY

OUTING - The mill dominating the vineyard.

Patrick Arnould and his father, Michel.

Champagne Michel Arnould et Fils

Owner Family Arnould. **Address** 28 rue de Mailly, 51360 Verzenay - Tel. 03.26.49.40.06 Fax 03.26.49.44.61. **Open** From Monday to saturday, 9:00-18:00, Sunday by appointment. **Spoken** English. **Credit cards** Visa, Eurocard, MasterCard.

The Verzenay vineyards are special in that their slopes face north, giving greater finesse and more acidity to the Pinot Noir which is predominant in the commune. With the exception of the Brut Réserve and Carte d'Or produced by the Arnoulds, their wines are made from pure Pinot Noir, light, elegant, and aromatic. A fine illustration is the family's Brut (about 71 F): intense, buttery on the nose, vigorous on the palate, with hints of white fruit and hot plum tart; a "muscular" Champagne, perfect *à table*. The Brut Réserve (about 76 F) concentrates on its lingering Chardonnay taste, with traces of ripe pears and agelica. Those who turn up their nose at pink Champagne should taste this one for its vinosity, hinting of fruit kernels and plums, its élan characteristic of all the wines from this cellar (about 76 F).

Our Choice The Carte d'Or (about 100 F). In fact, a 1990 vintage but not indicated as such on the label. Full, mellow, powerful, concentrated taste, will become a great wine with bottle age. Bottling was planned for Christmas 1997 "to give it that much extra sap, firmness and bouquet," according to Michel Arnould. While it's in the cellar, drink the Brut.

Reception Michel is occasionally rather gruff, but not for long; Patrick is more convivial. Don't miss Verzenay's two curious sights: its windmill and its incongruous lighthouse.

How to get there *(Map 6): From Reims to Epernay via N51. At Montchenot (11km), turn left. The cellar is at the entrance to Verzenay, on the left.*

Philippe Secondé, a descendent of Edmond Barnaut, the founder of the house in 1874.

Champagne Edmond Barnaut

Owner Philippe Secondé. **Address** 2 rue Gambetta, 51150 Bouzy - Tel. 03.26.57.01.54 Fax 03.26.57.09.97. **Open** Everyday by appointment. **Spoken** English. **Credit cards** Visa, Eurocard, MasterCard.

The Bouzy vineyards have a way of producing very ripe Pinot Noirs, "sometimes excessively so", to quote Philippe Secondé's aimiable euphemism. Translation: they can be heavy. Except when the winemaker knows how to play with his *terroirs.* The parcels at Sur Les Brousses, Feuchère, and the Côte aux Lièvres contribute density and vinosity to the wine; Les Houardes, Les Monts de Tauxières, Les Moulins, and Les Monts-Rouges, whose soils are thinner, offer their light touch to the *assemblage.* Philippe Secondé thus chose to vinify by parcel, depending on the age of the vines, in order to have a broad palette of Pinots Noirs for his *assemblages.*

The '90 Grand Cru (120 F) reveals a round, fruity bouquet, opening out with spices and honey on the palate.

Our Choice The Extra Brut (91 F). Very Pinot Noir (90%), softened with a touch of Chardonnay. The blend highlights the great 1990 vintage. The reserve wines from '88 lend maturity, while those of '92 contribute vivacity. Golden color, fruity, generous, powerful bouquet; vinous and mouth-filling: "very Bouzy, but without wooden clogs," commented Philippe Secondé. Persistent toasty, apricot finish.

Reception By an impassioned Champagne maker.

How to get there *(Map 6): From Epernay to Chalon via D1 to Tours/sur/Marne. Turn left toward Bouzy (D19). In the village, follow the arrows. The cellar is on the right.*

Philippe Charlemagne.

Champagne Guy Charlemagne

Supervisor Philippe Charlemagne. **Address** 4 rue de la Brèche d'Oger, 51190 Le Mesnil/Oger - Tel. 03.26.57.52.98 Fax 03.26.57.97.81. **Open** From Monday to Saturday midday 8:00-12:00 and 14:00-18:00. **Spoken** English. **Credit cards** Visa, Eurocard, MasterCard.

Guy Charlemagne's ordinary Champagnes are made largely from grapes grown in the region of Sezanne or from *vins de taille*, wines from the second and third grape pressings, yielding balanced, pleasant Champagnes. His Brut Extra and particularly the Réserve Brut are lovely apéritif wines, delicate and graceful, happily with little *dosage* (about 80 F). You should take special note of the vintage Champagnes, from grapes grown in the Le Mesnil Grand Cru vineyards. This is a *terroir* which yields difficult, demanding wines, slow to open up, strongly marked by their acid structure, often developing aromatic, mineral notes (gunflint).

The '90 Grand Cru is now available only in large bottles: magnum (220 F), jeroboam (520 F), and mathusalem (1430 F). Its bouquet is intense, of hot butter; delicate, spicy, fat, rich on the palate, with lingering, fine acidity which is not masked by the *dosage.* The Mesnillésimes bottlings are available only in small quantities. The '88 (125 F) is very soft, pure on the palate, with hints of grilled almonds, while you should take special note of the '89 (called Cuvée du Centenaire, 125 F) is it is still available: a mellow, toasty Champagne, softened by partial malolactic fermentation, highly structured and ample.

Our choice The '90 Mesnillésime (125 F). As the name suggests, this is a pure Chardonnay from the oldest vines in the Le Mesnil Grand Cru vineyards. Its color is flecked with gold, the bouquet open and mellow. Full flavor, firmly supported by acidity, its amplitude beginning to open out.

Reception Pleasant, in a large tasting room.

How to get there *(Map 6): From Epernay to Le Mesnil via D10. (signposted).*

Pascal and Eric Cheurlin.

Champagne Cheurlin et Fils

Owner Family Cheurlin. **Address** 13 rue de la Gare, 10250 Gyé-sur-Seine - Tel. 03.25.38.20.27 Fax 03.25.38.24.01. **Open** From Monday to Saturday, 8:00-12:00 and 13:30-18:00, Sunday and national holidays from Apr. 26 - Dec. 31. **Spoken** English. **Credit cards** Visa, Eurocard, MasterCard.

Pascal largely mans the cellar while Eric presides over the vines at this Champagne house which is quite typical of the Aube, with the lion's share of the domaine devoted to Pinot Noir. In certain Champagnes, however, Chardonnay is predominant, as with the '91 Brut Originel, which came out in September 1997 (145 F). Before their *champagnisation,* the still wines in this *cuvée* are partially vinified in oak, giving them a pleasant smoky edge and enhancing a vigorous, powerful taste which might surprise those accustomed to more neutral Champagnes. Of the more traditional Champagnes, we tasted a beautiful Grande Cuvée (87 F): a mix of finesse and crispness. This return to the source of oak vinification will be continued for some other *cuvées.*

Our choice The Cuvée Prestige (98 F). Very Pinot Noir, a powerful, big Champagne, mouth-filling, giving a physical sensation of the extract. The bouquet is complex (toast, plums). The finish is long, with traces of mint.

Reception Friendly, in a large tasting cellar.

How to get there *(Map 6): Southeast of Troyes towards Châtillon (N71). 11kms after Bar-sur-Seine, turn left toward Gyé, following the signs "Maisons de Champagne". The cellar is on the right, indicated by a large inscription on the wall.*

Old machines in the cellar.

Champagne Gaston Chiquet

Supervisors Antoine and Nicolas Chiquet. **Address** 890-912 Avenue du Général Leclerc, 51530 Dizy - Tel. 03.26.55.22.02 Fax 03.26.51.83.81. **Open** From Monday to Friday, 8:00-12:00 and 14:00-18:00, Saturday and Sunday by appointment. **Spoken** English. **Credit cards** Visa, Eurocard, MasterCard.

Gaston Chiquet has some thirty parcels of vines scattered over twenty-two hectares, mainly in Hautvilliers, Dizy, and Aÿ, thus in the fiefs of the Montagne de Reims generally devoted to Pinot Noir. But this *maison* stands out with its large proportion of Chardonnay in the *assemblages* (35% in the Bruts) and with its exclusive use of the grape in its Cuvée de Prestige. The result is Champagnes of power and backbone, very different from their cousins from the Côte des Blancs. It's only a shame that the base wines have a little too much *dosage.*

Taste the 1990 predominantly Chardonnay vintage (about 120 F) for its maturity, fullness, and explosive fruit; the predominantly Pinot Noir '89 (about 110 F), a powerful, honeyed Champagne; and above all the Blanc de Blancs d'Aÿ, especially the '91 unlabelled as a vintage (about 92 F): open and mellow bouquet, full and vigorous on the palate. It is typically Chardonnay in bouquet (toasty, nutty, *brioché*), but with the fullness and vinosity of the Pinot.

Our choice The '88 Blanc de Blancs d'Aÿ (only in magnums and in limited quantities, about 250 F). Wheat flour on the nose, very intense, toasted on the palate, well balanced by acidity, with a delicate smoky finish.

Reception In the living room of the house. Beautiful cellar.

How to get there *(Map 6): Dizy borders Epernay, in the north. In the village, take the road to Hautvillers. The cellar is on the right.*

Erick de Sousa.

Champagne De Sousa

Owner Érick de Sousa. **Address** 12 Place Léon Bourgeois 51190 Avize - Tel. 03.26.57.53.29 Fax 03.26.52.30.64. **Open** By appointment.

The family name stands out from the traditional names of the Champagne: Erick de Sousa's grandfather was Portuguese and came to France as a soldier during World War I, finally settling in the Champenois. His descendents remained and shortly were producing one of the best Champagnes of Avize, made from old Chardonnay vines. Their low yield gives concentrated wines, often non-chaptalized; they are naturally well-balanced and crisp because of low *dosage.*

Apart from our choice below, we enjoyed the Brut Réserve (98 F) for its balance, fruit, and crispness, its taste evoking *brioche* and wheat, and its bouquet of moist bread. These are the characteristic aromas of the Chardonnays from Avize and Oger, two Grands Crus on the Côte des Blancs which are classified 100% on the scale of grape prices from a particular Champagne vineyard, and thus an indication of high quality.

Our choice The '92 (127 F), from old Chardonnay vines. Mellow bouquet, ample, well structured on the palate, naturally ripe (no chaptalization); crisp because of low *dosage.* Beautiful notes of dried fruit, long, persistent finish, aromatic and toasty.

Reception With an affable winemaker in a large tasting cellar. Don't miss a stroll through the village, which Erick de Sousa and other young *vignerons* have decorated with giant enlargements of old postcards describing the work in the vines and the cellars.

How to get there *(Map 6): From Epernay to Avize via D10. The cellar is in the center of the village, indicated by arrows.*

Paul et Pierre Déthune.

Champagne Paul Déthune

Owner Paul Déthune. **Address** 2 rue du Moulin, 51150 Ambonnay - Tel. 03.26.57.01.88 Fax 03.26.57.09.31. **Open** By appointment. **Spoken** English. **Credit card** Visa, Eurocard, MasterCard.

Made from a single vineyard in the Ambonnay Grand Cru appellation, wines from Paul Déthune are very fruity and round due to a large proportion of old wines in the blends (as much as 50%). Partial oak vinification of the wines (30%) is well integrated so as not to mark the final Champagne. The Brut, however, (78 F) has a little too much *dosage.* The 1990 vintage (135 F) reveals a lovely bouquet of wheat, an elegant, fruity taste evoking plums and grilled almonds, and a lingering lemon tart finish. This cellar also offers two good still wines from the Côteaux Champenois: a red (78 F), a 1990 but labelled non-vintage: fruity, good extract, mixing traces of cherry pits and peat; and a white wine (48 F), golden and mellow. This is an old vintage which had been forgotten in a corner of the cellar, whose "birthdate" Paul Déthune has forgotten, "between 1970 and 1980", but which is still rich, crisp, and has beautifully softened.

Our choice The Prestige Grand Cru (120 F). Equally balanced between Pinot and Chardonnay, a blend of wines from the great '89 vintage and 50% of older wines. Very mellow and open, with dried-fruit bouquet. Creamy, very fruity, apricot-sauce taste, lingering and fresh.

Reception By friendly father and son in a large tasting room.

How to get there *(Map 6): From Epernay to Châlons via D1. In Tours-sur-Marne, turn left to Bouzy (D19). In center of village, turn right to Ambonnay. The Déthune cellar is at entrance to Ambonnay, on right, next to the Coopérative.*

Jacques Diebolt.

Champagne Diebolt-Vallois

Supervisor Jacques Diebolt-Vallois. **Address** 84 rue Neuve, 51530 Cramant - Tel. 03.26.57.54.92 Fax 03.26.57.53.74. **Open** By appointment. **Spoken** English, Spanish.

All the Champagne *négociants* aim at vinification and blending so as to create their special house style, especially in their non-vintage Champagnes: their identity card year in and year out. Not so with Jacques Diebolt, who is "always insatiable, never satisfied", and forever in pursuit of new experiences. Either you go along with him, or you look for another Champagne!

Today, Diebolt wants to "redo what I learned in my youth": vinifying still wines in oak, bottling without *collage* to clarify the wines, and without filtration "in order to make Champagne the way my grandfather did."

His non-vintage Tradition, fruity and vinous, is a blend of Chardonnay and one-third Pinots (73 F). The Blanc de Blancs, partly aged in oak before *champagnisation*, is smooth, fruity, with firm extract, and just a hint of oak on the long, persistent finish (79.50 F).

Our Choice The Prestige (101 F). Purely from the Cramant vineyards, blended with the 1992 base wine, rounded out with almost equal proportions of '90 and '91. It comes from old vines in the Les Pimonts *lieu-dit*. The Champagne is powerful, concentrated, full-bodied, long, with marked aromatic overtones of peaches and almonds. Very persistent.

Reception Extremely enthusiastic.

How to get there *(Map 6): From Epernay toward Avize via D10. At the entrance to the village, after the giant bottle, take second street on left, then first on right (route marked). The Diebolt-Vallois' house is at the end of the "impasse", on right, facing the cellar.*

Jacqueline Egly-Ouriet has begun a collection of old winemaking tools.

Champagne Egly-Ouriet

Owners Michel and Francis Egly-Ouriet. **Address** 9-15 rue de Trépail, 51150 Ambonnay - Tel. 03.26.57.00.70 Fax 03.26.57.06.52. **Open** By appointment. **Credit cards** Visa, Eurocard, MasterCard.

This house owns seven hectares in Bouzy, Verzenay, and most importantly, in the heart of the Ambonnay vineyards and their beautiful south-facing slopes: Les Crayères, Les Secs, Les Feuchères, and Les Beurys. Along with the traditional Pinot Noir grown on the Montagne de Reims, the house owns a good amount of Chardonnay, which is more delicate here than on the rest of the Montagne de Reims. Michel and Francis Egly-Ouriet's vines are old, thirty-five years on the average, and each parcel is vinified in small vats separately. Only the grapes intended for the vintage Champagnes are vinified together in order to obtain a more harmonious blend and to spotlight the character of the vintage.

The Brut Tradition (79 F) is open and fruity, quite powerful, solid, and softened by the large proportion of reserve wine from the great '90 and '91 vintages. The Rosé (85 F) is very vinous, with smoky, dry-apricot, nutty overtones. The Blanc de Noir Vieilles Vignes (95 F), from the Pinot Noir vines on the Les Crayères parcel planted in 1947, is a Champagne of character and finesse.

Our choice The '90 (125 F) for its intense bouquet, its graceful, fruity taste, and slightly toasty finish.

Reception Around the winemaking tools that Jacqueline Egly-Ouriet is beginning to collect.

How to get there *(Map 6): From Epernay toward Châlon via D1. In Condé-sur-Marne, turn left to Ambonnay on D37. The cellar is at the exit from village, on the road to Trépail, on left.*

From the courtyard of the Cheval-Gatinois' house, the view over the angular rooftops.

Champagne Gatinois

Owners Pierre and Marie-Paule Cheval-Gatinois. **Address** 7 rue Marcel Mailly, 51160 Aÿ - Tel. 03.26.55.14.26 Fax 03.26.52.75.99. **Open** By appointment. **Spoken** English, German. **Credit cards** Visa, Eurocard, MasterCard.

Pierre Cheval-Gatinois used to work in the Budget Ministry, while his wife, Marie-Paule, was a dietician. Winemaking beckoned to them in 1980, and took the couple to the Champenois, or more precisely, to the élite vineyards in Aÿ, whose nuances Pierre knows by heart. Talking wine with him, we feel as if he transports us right into his vines, explaining exactly how they should be pruned, and asking us to "listen to the grapes, which should knock against each other when the bunches are shaken and not remain stuck together." All the wines from this small house (7 hectares, mainly Pinot Noir) deserve high praise but they are also in demand, the still wines as well as the Champagnes. The Brut Réserve Grand Cru (91 F) is deep copper, with a full bouquet of honey and brioche; it is lacy, smooth, and fruity on the palate. If you can still find one of the 2681 bottles of '93 Coteaux Champenois still red wine (120 F), you should jump at the chance. This is one of the finest wines from this appellation, much superior to the usually overrated red Bouzy. A delicious wine of great character, it is made from a variety of Pinot Noir, the Petit Pinot d'Aÿ; the grapes are sorted a number of times during the harvest, accounting for the wine's smoothness, finesse, and purity.

Our choice The 1990 (105 F). "The Sunday pot of honey", says Pierre Cheval. Mature, spicy bouquet, taste of honey, quince, dried apricots. A rich, lively Champagne. The subsequent '91 is fine.

Reception Attentive and very enthusiastic.

How to get there *(Map 6): From Epernay to Aÿ via D201 3km). The cellar is in the center of the village, behind the church.*

Barrel-cum-sign at the entrance to the cellar.

Champagne René Geoffroy

Owner Family Geoffroy. **Address** 150 rue du Bois des Jots, 51480 Cumiéres - Tel. 03.26.55.32.31 Fax 03.26.54.66.50. **Open** By appointment. **Spoken** English. **Credit card** Visa, Eurocard, MasterCard.

This house is notable for its extensive vinification in oak casks, the renunciation of malolactic fermentation, and moderate *dosage.* As a result, René Geoffroy Champagnes have many aromatic qualities while remaining fresh and crisp.

The Réserve (75 F) is made with Pinot Noir and Pinot Meunier, yielding fruitiness on the nose and a soft, persistent taste: an immediately delightful Champagne. The Cuvée Sélectionnée (86 F) has a more closed bouquet, but the taste is already round and powerful, with well integrated oakiness. A large proportion of Chardonnay confers vivacity and length of flavor.

We tasted these same qualities in the Prestige (108 F), a Champagne of great finesse. René Geoffroy also produces good Coteaux Champenois still reds, which bear the vintage label in great years. The non-vintage wine currently available is grapy and pleasant, with a slightly smoky taste (71 F).

Our choice The Rosé (84 F). As opposed to most pink Champagnes which are colored by means of blending red and white still wines, the color in this Rosé is obtained by the *saignée* method: skins are left in contact with the juice during fermentation, which is "bled" off the vat when it is the desired pink. Powerful and vinous, with marked extract and lovely smoky overtones, this is a real Champagne, and delicious with meals.

Reception By hospitable René Geoffroy or his son, Jean-Baptiste, in the cellar. Take time to listen to them explain their work with passion.

How to get there *(Map 6): From Epernay to Reims via N51. On the other side of the Marne, at the traffic circle, turn left toward Cumières (D1). The cellar is at the bottom of the village, indicated with arrows.*

Didier and Pierre Gimonnet.

Champagne Pierre Gimonnet

Owner Family Gimonnet. **Address** 1 rue de la République, 51530 Cuis - Tel. 03.26.59.78.70 Fax 03.26.59.79.84. **Open** From Monday to Friday, 8:00-12:00 and 14:00-18:00, Saturday by appointment. **Spoken** English. **Credit cards** Visa, Eurocard, MasterCard.

With Premier Cru vines in Cuis and Grands Crus parcels in Chouilly and Cramant, the Gimonnet house has reached for the stars to create its various Champagnes with little or no *dosage*, and often no chaptalization. The '92 Crémant Gastronome (93 F) is bright and sparkling, with small bubbles as light and scented as a brioche; the '92 Club (107 F) is a firmer Champagne of great backbone, reflecting its origins in Cramant's old vines; the Fleuron '90 (107 F) well deserves its name, "The Finest Jewel", for its ample bouquet and full flavor. Those who like old Champagnes will find the Fleuron in the '85 vintage as well (112 F, very limited quantity), which is distinguished by overtones of dried fruits and nuts. Apart from the Gimonnets' Gastronome, which is intended to be drunk young, all their Champagnes develop marvelously in power and Burgundy-like richness with a little bottle age.

Our choice Two variations on the 1989 vintage. The large proportion of Cramant Chardonnay in the Club gives a Champagne whose bouquet blossoms fully, with a persisent finish of beeswax (118 F). The Oenophile is an '89 Champagne, not labelled as such. From a high proportion of Cuis Chardonnay, it is graceful, lively, supremely elegant. With no chaptalization and no *dosage,* it has a floral bouquet of great finesse, with mint and lichen on the palate, and a smoky finish evoking Lapsang Souchong tea (112 F).

Reception Hospitable. Don't miss seeing the vine-covered church.

How to get there *(Map 6): From Epernay toward Avize via D10. At the entrance to Cuis, immediate right turn (signposted).*

Pierre Lallement.

Champagne Juillet-Lallement

Owner Pierre Lallement. **Address** 21 rue Irénée Gass oder 30 rue Carnot, 51380 Verzy - Tel. 03.26.97.91.09 Fax 03.26.97.93.29. **Open** By appointment. **Credit cards** Visa, Eurocard, MasterCard.

Les Champs Saint-Rémi, Les Montants, La Croix de l'Aumonier, Les Vins Mousseux, Les Vignes de l'Evêque: These are the finest vineyards in Verzy and Sillery, two Grand Cru sites of the Montagne de Reims where Pierre Lallement's family has owned vines for four generations. Two-thirds of the small, four-hectare vineyard are planted in Pinot Noir, but some Lallement Champagnes are made with a high proportion of Chardonnay, and others, the Blanc de Blancs, are entirely Chardonnay.

Champagnes from this house receive very little *dosage*: 5 grams for the Brut, less still for the vintage Champagnes; they should therefore have some bottle age because wines from Verzy are quite vigorous. That quality, on the other hand, ensures ageing potential. Such is the case with the Brut (70 F), the '94 Blanc de Blancs (74 F), vigorous and powerful; and above all with the '91 Grande Tradition: very round with apricot overtones, lacy, delicate, and lively.

Our choice The '89 (110 F). Intense toasty bouquet, ample taste mixing roses, new-mown hay, tobacco, and rum. With very little *dosage*, crisp and firm.

Reception Rotund and friendly, like the wines.

How to get there *(Map 6): From Reims to Epernay via D51. In Montchenot, turn left to Verzy. In the village, the Rue Irénée Gass joins N44. The cellar is on the left. Near Verzy, you might want to see the unusual twisted beech trees that look like giant bonzais. (Signs in Verzy for "Les Faux de Verzy").*

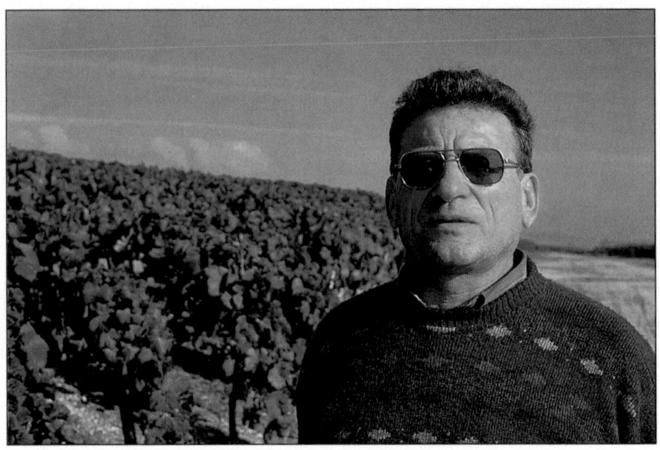

Jean Lallement.

Champagne Jean Lallement

Owners Jean, Louisette and Jean-Luc Lallement. **Address** 1 rue Moët and Chandon 51360 Verzenay - Tel. 03.26.49.43.52 Fax 03.26.49.44.98. **Open** By appointment.

Jean, Louisette, his wife, and now Jean-Luc, their son, own 4 1/2 hectares of vines, 80% Pinot Noir, in Verzy, Ludes, and mainly Verzenay, where they also have Chardonnay vines; their parcels are planted on the best *lieux-dits* of the commune there: Les Livrys, Le Champ du Clerc, Les Pertois, and La Voie de Reims, on either side of the Côte de la Barbarie. There is nothing barbaric, however, about these wines.

The Lallemonts aim for a vinous Champagne, meaty and big, in which the *terroir* is well reflected: the wines are not filtered and no yeast is added. The house limits itself to two Champagnes: a non-vintage Brut rounded out by wines from the previous year; and a Réserve whose vintage is not labelled. Both wines take their time to develop and they mature well.

The Brut (69 F) is fine, delicate, and flowery on the nose, opening up with hints of wheat. The taste is full, elegant, vigorous but not hard, lingering on the palate with overtones of toast, orange, and plums.

Our choice The Brut Réserve (78 F). From the '90 harvest, with a non-vintage label. Lacy, delicate bouquet, mellow, hints of fresh butter, citrus, smoke. Very full, soft taste, vigorous, big backbone, lean. Great finesse, finishing with dry citrus fruit. With very little *dosage*, a remarkable Champagne.

Reception Informal and attentive.

How to get there *(Map 6): From Reims to Epernay via D51. In montchenot, turn left to Verzenay. The cellar is indicated in the center of the village going down toward Beaumont on right.*

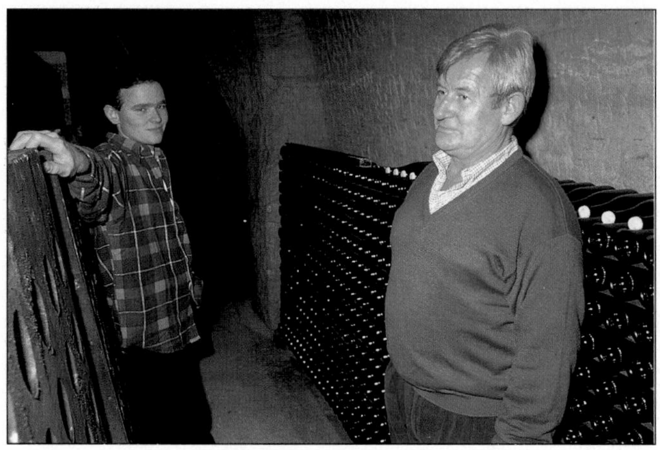

Georges and Bertrand Lilbert, father and son.

Champagne Lilbert Fils

Owner Georges Lilbert. **Address** 223 rue du Moutier, 51530 Cramant - Tel. 03.26.57.50.16 Fax 03.26.58.93.86. **Open** By appointment. **Spoken** German.

This domaine has holdings in the Grand Cru sites of Chouilly and Cramant, where the wines are less solid than in Avize, less round than in Oger; they are are noted for their elegance and finesse. The Lilberts have no Pinot Noir, and thus no pink Champagne. *Père et fils*--after Jules and André, now there are Georges and Bertrand--swear by Chardonnay, and long bottle age. With little *dosage*, their Champagnes typically have a persistent flow of bubbles and overall finesse of style.

A good apéritif Champagne is the simple Brut (80 F), very fruity and soft, with a honeyed finish. For serving with meals, try the '85 vintage at 150 Francs: intense bouquet of tobacco, linden, slightly smoky; rich, powerful yet delicate taste, with notes of tangerines and spices (cinnamon); very fresh, verbena finish. With bottle age, it will develop power on a par with the great Burgundies.

The cellar also produces a good white Coteau Champenois still wine (68 F), with pear bouquet, delicate, elegant on the palate with blackberries and fruit.

Our choice The '90 (112 F, if still available. Otherwise, it will be cellared until the year 2000). Beautiful golden yellow color. Fresh, flowery bouquet. Small, pleasant bubbles and bread taste, finishing with exotic hints of papaya.

Reception In a corner of the shipping room decorated with enlargements of old postcards.

How to get there *(Map 6): From Epernay to Cramant via D10. In the center of the village, follow marked itinerary on left. Cellar indicated by a plaque beside a large porch.*

Gérard Frémaux and the *maître de chai*, Hervé Datan

Champagne Mailly grand cru

Honorary director Gérard Frémaux. **Managing director** Jean-François Preau. **Cellarmaster** Hervé Dantan. **Address** 28 rue de la Libération, 51500 Mailly-Champagne - Tel. 03.26.49.41.10 Fax 03.26.49.42.27. **Open** (20F) and tasting (10 F) by appointment from Monday to Saturday midday, 8:00-12:00 and 14:00-18:00. Fom May to Sept. 15, Saturday and Sunday afternoon, 15:00-17:00. In Juli and Aug. everyday, 8:00-18:00. **Spoken** English, German, Spanish. **Credit cards** Visa, Eurocard, MasterCard.

This is an exemplary *coopérative* for whom seventy winegrowers tend a third of the Mailly Grand Cru vineyards. Only Mailly's own grapes, white and black, go into its Champagnes. They are thus picture-perfect expressions of the *terroirs*: earthy wines with body but not heavy. Mailly's ability to stock large quantities means that the wines on offer are well aged and include several old vintages. The '91 (labelled non-vintage) Blanc de Noirs (124 F) has an intense, honeyed bouquet with a powerful yet delicate taste, opening up with traces of yellow plum. The cellar also offers the '83s (226 F): a nice balance between rhubarbe on the nose and spices on the palate, ample but delicate. Finally, those who are against overly sweet Champagne will enjoy the Extra Brut (117) without *dosage,* whose mature blend yields a round, harmonious wine.

Our choice The '90: round, balanced, fruity with much less acid than the '89. (132 F).

Reception A very competent explanation of the *terroir* and its wines.

How to get there *(Map 6): From Reims to Epernay via D51. In Montchenot, turn left to Mailly Champagne. The cellar is at the entrance to the village, on the left.*

Bernard Margaine and his son, Arnaud.

Champagne A. Margaine

Owner Family Margaine. **Address** 3 Avenue de Champagne, 51380 Villers-Marmery - Tel. 03.26.97.92.13 Fax 03.26.97.97.45. **Open** From Monday to Saturday, 8:00-12:00 and 14:00-18:00. **Spoken** English. **Credit cards** Visa, Eurocard, MasterCard.

This house was founded in 1920 by Gaston Margaine, a taxi driver in the Marne *département.* He eventually bought a café in the region, finally inheriting a vineyard belonging to a customer who died without heirs.

Wines from Villers-Marmery have built up a solid reputation in Chardonnays, as opposed to the rest of the Montagne de Reims where Pinot is preponderant. Bernard and Arnaud Margaine's seven hectares of vines are 90% Chardonnay. They juggle the diversity of their soils and emphasize the blending job, using several years of reserve wine (for the non-vintage Brut) to add complexity to their Champagnes. Their aim is wines of character and full flavor, vinosity and softness, qualities which can already be perceived in the still wines before *champagnisation.* The Brut Tradition (71 F) is attractively round and balanced, unusual for a 90% Chardonnay. This is due to the large proportion (40%) of old wines in the blend. The Rosé (80 F), a perfect apéritif Champagne, is amazingly exotic: litchis, yellow plums and even rose water, an aroma so typical of Alsatian Gewürztraminers.

Our choice The '89 Blanc de Blancs (113 F). Fine bouquet mixing flowers and red berries. Full, long, on the palate, aromatic bouquet of peaches and honey. A mellow Champagne, sustained by beautiful acidity and little dosage.

Reception By hospitable father and son in their new tasting-room/museum.

How to get there *(Map 6): From Reims to Epernay via D51. In Montchenot, turn left to Villers-Marmery. The cellar is at the entrance to the village, on the left.*

The sign at José Michel.

Champagne José Michel

Owners José and Bruno Michel. **Address** 14 rue Prélot, 51530 Moussy - Tel. 03.26.54.04.69 Fax 03.26.55.37.12. **Open** By appointment.

The Champagne villages often seem at odds with their churches. Instead of clustering around them, the villages relegate churches to the edge of town. Could it be to keep watch over the vines? If so, Chavot, just outside of Epernay, is a perfect example of such town planning. Chavot's church turns it back to the village and looks out over the vines--and the cellar of José Michel.

Along with their Chardonnay vines, José Michel and his son, Bruno, own Pinot Noir as well as Pinot Meunier, a grape variety often denigrated in the Champagne vineyards. But the vine comes into its own at this house, where it is extensively used in all the wines, including the vintage Champagnes. Contrary to the pejorative reputation it has with many people, the Pinot Meunier in these wines shows a real ability to age well, developing lovely notes of wax and honey, as in the 1982 vintage (110 F). You can still find bottles of the great vintages from 1989 (96 F) and particularly 1990 (120 F, for the Club Champagne). These wines have now attained their maturity, while remaining fresh and elegant. And with little dosage, they are good with meals.

Our choice The Extra Brut (85 F), a blend of 40% Chardonnay and Pinot Meunier. Very little dosage (2 grams); the Meunier and reserve wines contribute softness and balance. It is fine, mellow, very long, a gastronomic Champagne.

Reception With kindness and great enthusiasm.

How to get there *(Map 6): Leave Epernay by the south, toward Moussy. On the right after the Auberge Champenoise, then on left at the Monument aux Morts. The cellar is at the end of the street on the right.*

An angelic welcome.

Champagne Pierre Moncuit

Supervisor Nicole Moncuit. **Address** 11 rue Persault-Maheu, 51190 Le Mesnil/Oger - Tel. 03.26.57.52.65 Fax 03.26.57.97.89. **Open** From Monday to Friday, 9:00-12:00 and 14:00-18:00, Saturday and Sunday by appointment. **Spoken** English. **Credit cards** Visa, Eurocard, MasterCard.

Nicole Moncuit is a *vigneronne* in heart and soul. Her Champagnes are fine expressions of both vineyard and vintage (the non-vintage Champagnes are not rounded out by reserve wines). As opposed to the traditional blend, the Cuvée Nicole Moncuit is made from old vines planted in the single village of Chétillons.

The non-vintage Cuvée Réserve (82 F) is in fact from the '93 harvest, with a bouquet of grapefruit and tree bark. The '89 (104 F) is flowery with a touch of mint; and a soft, rich taste. A crisp, fresh Champagne, thus an excellent apéritif. The '89 Vieille Vigne Nicole Moncuit (127 F) is ample and rich on the palate, delivering an almost sweet taste (dried and glazed fruit, dried orange, tea), very long and persistent. You will find excellent magnums of '86 (218 F) and '85 (221 F).

Our choice The two '88s. The 110 F Champagne: minerals and licorice on the nose, opening up with fruit and then truffles, and licorice again on the finish. The Vieille Vigne Cuvée Nicole Moncuit (137 F) is still more impressive with its bouquet of hot butter and verbena, an ample, balanced taste, with caramel and licorice. Spicy, long finish.

Reception Pretty tasting room under the watchful eye of two plump cherubs. The beautiful, skillfully illuminated cellars are worth a visit.

How to get there *(Map 6): From Epernay to Mesnil-sur-Oger via D10. In the village, take direction Montmort. The house is on the left.*

Pascal Morel.

Champagne Morel Père et Fils

Owner Pascal Morel. **Address** 93 rue du Général de Gaulle, 10340 Les Riceys - Tel. 03.25.29.10.88 Fax 03.25.29.66.72. **Open** By appointment. **Credit cards** Visa, Eurocard, MasterCard.

The Champagne region is known mainly for its sparkling Champagne and somewhat less for its still wines, red and white, from the Coteaux Champenois appellation. The Rosé des Riceys is still less known. In essence it is made from a quite long maceration of Pinot Noir which is then *saigné*, bled out of the vat before the juice becomes too tannic or too deeply colored. It is more than a rosé and not yet a red wine, just an enticing pink compromise between the two.

The Rosé des Riceys is a passion with Pascal Morel and yet, in 1997, he launched into sparkling Champagnes and has already demonstrated masterly skill. The old wines in his blends, very Pinot Noir in character, yield a Champagne of maturity and balance with a beautiful aromatic bouquet (apricots, yellow plums) and length on the palate. The Champagne now available will be more lively and, fortunately, shorter on dosage.

Our choice The '93 Rosé des Riceys (about 76 F). Fruit and a touch of cinnamon on the nose. Mouth filling, a wine of backbone whose tannins are hardly perceptible. Very persistent. Like all the Rosés des Riceys from this cellar, the wine will become more powerful with several years' bottle age.

Reception Pascal Morel and his wife do not look at their watches when they explain the vinification idiosyncracies of this singular rosé.

How to get there *(Map 6): From Troyes to Châtillon-sur-Seine via N71. After Bar-sur-Seine, turn right at Celles-sur-Ource to Les Riceys. The cellar is in the center of the village, next to the church.*

François Moutard.

Champagne Moutard Père et Fils

Owner Family Moutard. **Address** 6 rue du Pont, 10110 Buxeuil - Tel. 03.25.38.50.73 Fax 03.25.38.57.72. **Open** From Monday to Saturday, 8:00-12:00 and 14:00-19:00. **Credit cards** Visa, Eurocard, MasterCard, Amex.

Does wine from the Aube have a special taste? Yes, replies François Moutard without hesitating: "It is a wine of dimension, above all in the vintage years, a very old wine. You can see that mainly in the Chardonnays from the clay soils that are close cousins to Chablis." The two regions are on the extreme edge of the Champagne and Burgundy, respectively.

Champagnes from Moutard will please connoisseurs of wines with body and little acid. Those who enjoy old vintage Champagnes will be especially well served with the '83 (96 F), its honeyed bouquet and flavor evocative of rum. For a more youthful Champagne, try the Réserve (68 F), a 100% Chardonnay Champagne, fresh, crisp, and lemony.

Our choice The Extra Brut (91 F). Very little dosage, long bottle age (from the '90 vintage), fine backbone lent by Chardonnay and Pinot in equal proportions; beautiful gold color, mellow bouquet, dense, toasty taste--almost like roast coffee; balance contributed by "fat" extract and not by dosage sugar. Lovely, ethereal finish.

Reception Friendly and competent. The house also has a small distillery and sells good *marcs.*

How to get there *(Map 6): Southeast of Troyes (N71), towards Châtillon. 6kms after Bar-sur-Seine, turn left to Buxeuil. The cellar is in the center of the village, on the right. (Signposted).*

Jean-Louis Portier, tuba player in the local brass band.

Champagne Virgile Portier

Supervisor Jean-Louis Portier. **Address** 21 route nationale, 51360 Beaumont/Vesle - Tel. 03.26.03.90.15 Fax 03.26.03.99.31. **Open** From Monday to Saturday, 8:00-20:00. **Credit cards** Visa, Eurocard, MasterCard.

Grandfather Virgile Portier founded this family domaine with the purchase of vines in the Verzy and Beaumont Grand Cru villages, and particularly in the Ecrevisse, "crayfish", vineyard, thus providing the motif depicted on the capsules. Grandson Jean-Louis perpetuates the family's winegrowing tradition, while taking time out to play the tuba in the Beaumont Brass Band.

The large proportion of Pinot Noir in his blends accounts for wines of character and power. Jean-Louis Poirier does not currently sell vintage Champagne. The difference between the two Champagnes on offer lies in different proportions of Pinot and Chardonnay in the blends.

The Brut Extra (71.15 F), made with 70% Pinot Noir, is fine, fruity, and mellow, sustained by the Chardonnay's clean acidity (no malolactic fermentation). The result is a delicious Montagne-de-Reims for an apéritif, a Champagne with body and a beautiful gold color.

Our choice The Brut Spécial (82 F). Solid, well structured (Chardonnay and Pinot in equal parts), very Chardonnay bouquet: toasty, hot bread crust, veering to Pinot Noir on the finish, powerful and ample. Ample taste and extract, with aromatic notes (spices, cinnamon, dried fruit), diminishing with fresh finish.

Reception Bucolic.

How to get there *(Map 6): Reims toward Châlons via N44. The cellar is at the entrance to Beaumont, on the right.*

Henri Quenardel, a lover of old Champagnes.

Champagne J.H. Quenardel

Owner Henri Quenardel. **Address** 5 rue de Reims 51500 Ludes - Tel. 03.26.61.10.52 Fax 03.26.61.14.28. **Open** By appointment. **Spoken** English, German. **Credit cards** Visa, Eurocard, MasterCard.

Henri Quenardel stands out in Ludes. In a part of the Champagne dominated by Pinot Meunier to produce balanced, quickly drinkable wines, he decided to conserve the family's old Pinot Noir and Chardonnay vines and its tradition of making Champagnes with long bottle age. You will thus find vintages of great character in this cellar: '89, '85, '82, and even the 1975 vintage in more traditional Champagnes.

His '89 (120 F), with little dosage, is very expressive on the nose, with a fine, white-fruit taste. The '85 yields the same explosive bouquet, an even more beautiful taste: smoky, lichens, smooth, with acidity. The '82 offers an exceptional bouquet of rice powder and flowers. The taste is ample, round, with notes of black and yellow plums. The three Champagnes are very fresh and crisp.

Our choice The '75 vintage (180 F), a delightful old Champagne. Subdued color, intense bouquet, notes of *café au lait* and caramel. Extraordinary taste of roasted arabica coffee. Very dense extract, with great power, but the wine still has fine acid structure. Very long and persistent.

Reception Most often by attentive Madame Quenardel.

How to get there *(Map 6): From Epernay to Reims via N51. At Monchenot, turn right to villers-Allerand, then Rilly, Chigny and Ludesd. In the center of the village, sign on left. The cellar is at the exit from village, on the right.*

François Secondé.

Champagne François Secondé

Owner François Secondé. **Address** 6 rue des Galipes, 51500 Sillery - Tel. 03.26.49.16.67 Fax 03.26.49.11.55. **Open** By appointment.

For a long time, Sillery was Champagne's most *recherché* still white wine, sought after for its fruitiness and balance. Eugène Sue regularly served it, unfortunately iced, in his novels. Neighboring the vineyards of Mailly and Verzenay, Sillery has a chalky spur with very thin topsoil which is highly favorable for growing Chardonnay. The grape acquires a finesse here that is unequalled except in the Côte des Blancs.

But we preferred François Secondé's sparkling Champagne Brut Intégral, with very little dosage. The bouquet is flowery, the taste full-bodied, ample, balanced (77 F). His Rosé is excellent also (81 F), a pink champagne made by the *saignée* coloring process and thus vinous and good with food, yielding an apricot and dried-fruit finish.

Our choice The '94 Blanc de Blancs (98 F), from Chardonnay from Sillery, normally the homeland of Pinot Noir. There is brioche in the bouquet, continuing and opening up on the palate with nutty, yellow-plum notes. Great finesse, much more delicate than the Chardonnays from Aÿ. The aromatic palette and delicious acidity reminded us of Chenin, and François Secondé was delighted with the comparison.

Reception Informally by Madame Secondé, enthusiastically by François Secondé, who knows every inch of his vineyard by heart.

How to get there *(Map 6): From Reims to Châlons via N44. In 10km, turn right toward Sillery. The cellar is in the center of the village, indicated by arrows.*

Jean-Mary Tarlant.

Champagne Tarlant

Owner Family Tarlant. **Address** 51480 Oeuilly - Tel. 03.26.58.30.60 Fax 03.26.58.37.31. **Open** From Monday to Saturday, 8:00-12:00 and 14:00-18:00, Sunday by appointment. **Spoken** English, German. **Credit cards** Visa, Eurocard, MasterCard.

Champagne's viticultural kingdoms might be said to lie on the Côte des Blancs in the Epernay region, reigned over by Chardonnay, and on the Montagne de Reims, where Pinot Noir flourishes. Two other less prominent regions however, the Vallée de la Marne and the Aube *département* in the region of Troyes, deserve the wine lover's attention; strolling through the lovely vineyards is also not to be missed. Certain producers here make excellent Champagnes. Those from the Tarlant family, for example, where we tasted a delicious Extra Brut (84 F), without dosage, crisp but mellow; the Blanc de Blancs (95 F), with a smoky bouquet and depth of flavor; the '89 Prestige (104 F), light and elegant; as well as the powerful Cuvée Louis, vinified in oak (136 F). This is a blend of the great '89 and '90 vintages, yielding a Champagne of great richness. The same blend exists in a Champagne which has not been vinified in oak, developing a lovely smoky, nutty style (125 F).

Our choice The '88, if it is still available (112 F). The wine is beginning to develop its full potential but remains fresh. Enticing smoky bouquet, somewhat minty taste. If unavailable, ask for the '89.

Reception By a member of the charming family. Simple, comfortable guest rooms with breakfast (250 F). Be sure to visit the Maison Vigneronne, an ecomuseum evoking the life of a family of winemakers in the 19th century (open from May to October, every day except Tues. from 2 to 6 PM.)

How to get there *(Map 6): From Epernay toward Château-Thierry via N3 for 10km. In Oeillly, go to top of village. The cellar is on the right, on leaving the village (signposted).*

Denis Velut.

Champagne Jean Velut

Owner Denis Velut. **Address** 9 rue du Moulin, 10300 Montgueux - Tel. 03.25.74.83.31 Fax 03.25.74.17.25. **Open** By appointment. **Spoken** German.

The little-known Aube vineyards near Burgundy, while bravely holding their own in making Champagne, also invite the visitor to explore their beautiful old villages with timber-fronted houses and a host of excellent restaurants.

Denis Velut has suddenly found his farmhouse to be part of the urban spread of Troyes but his vineyard in Montgueux is still in the bucolic countryside. We especially liked his Champagne Rosé (75 F), with little dosage and bursting with fruit. His white Champagnes are 100% Chardonnay: the limestone soil of Montgueux is especially favorable to the grape here, yielding wines of finesse and verve.

Our choice The Blanc de Blancs (75 F). Bouquet of flour, delicate, fresh taste, with notes of apricot and almonds, persistent on palate. The base wine is 1990, with 20% from 1989. The subsequent *cuvée* is based on the 1991 vintage, with reserve wines from 1990. Dense, fine, lemony finish.

Reception Simple but open, in the shipping room. The church has an interesting rustic sculpture of Saint Vincent, a work of the curate, and an unusual belfry without a bell. In Troyes, there is a beautiful *Virgin With Grapes* in the Saint-Urbain Church.

How to get there *(Map 6): In Troyes, take direction Paris via Sens (N60) for 7km, then turn right toward Montgueux. At entrance to village, turn left.*

CORSICA

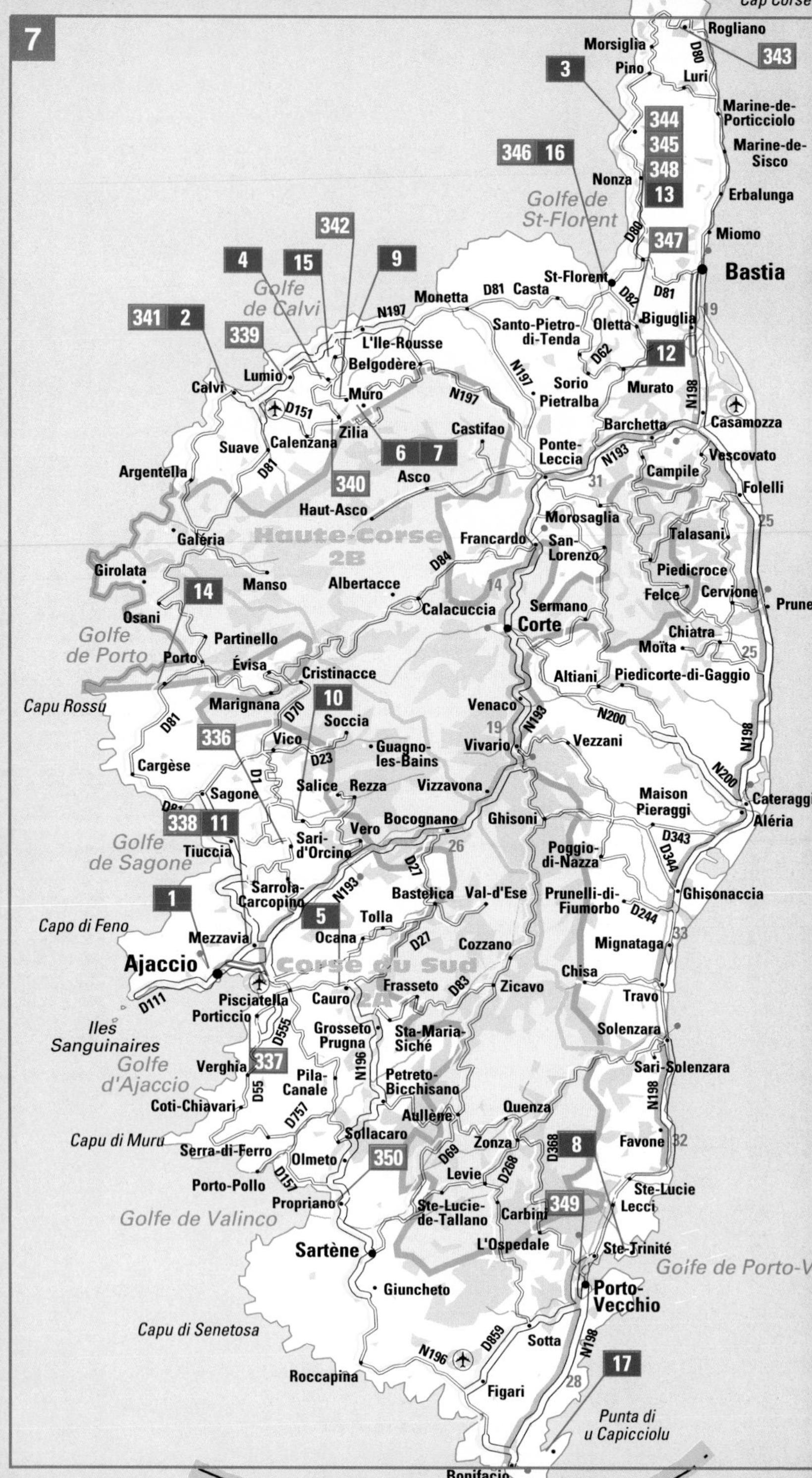

7
Cap Corse
Rogliano
343
Morsiglia
D80
Pino
Luri
3
344
345
348
13
Marine-de-Porticciolo
Marine-de-Sisco
Nonza
Erbalunga
346
16
Golfe de St-Florent
D80
347
Miomo
Bastia
342
4
15
9
St-Florent
Golfe de Calvi
Monetta
D81
Casta
D82
D81
341
2
N197
Santo-Pietro-di-Tenda
Oletta
Biguglia
19
339
L'Ile-Rousse
D62
12
Belgodère
N197
Sorio
Murato
Lumio
N197
N198
Calvi
Muro
Pietralba
D151
Barchetta
Casamozza
Zilia
Castifao
Suave
Calenzana
6
7
Ponte-Leccia
N193
Vescovato
Argentella
D81
Asco
Campile
340
31
Folelli
Haut-Asco
Morosaglia
25
Galéria
Haute-Corse 2B
Francardo
San-Lorenzo
Talasani
D84
Girolata
Manso
Albertacce
14
Piedicroce
14
Felce
Cervione
Prunete
Osani
Calacuccia
Sermano
Golfe de Porto
Corte
Chiatra
Partinello
Moïta
25
Porto
Évisa
Altiani
Piedicorte-di-Gaggio
Cristinacce
Capu Rossu
Marignana
10
Venaco
N200
D70
Soccia
D81
336
19
N193
Vico
Vivario
Vezzani
N198
Guagno-les-Bains
D23
Cargèse
D1
Salice
Rezza
Vizzavona
N200
Sagone
Maison Pieraggi
Cateraggio
D81
Aléria
338
11
Bocognano
Ghisoni
Vero
D343
Golfe de Sagone
Tiuccia
Sari-d'Orcino
26
Poggio-di-Nazza
D344
D27
Sarrola-Carcopino
N193
Bastelica
Val-d'Ese
Prunelli-di-Fiumorbo
Ghisonaccia
1
D244
Capo di Feno
5
Tolla
Ocana
33
Mezzavia
D27
Cozzano
Mignataga
Ajaccio
Corse du Sud 2A
Chisa
D111
Fasseto
D83
Zicavo
Pisciatella
Cauro
Travo
Iles Sanguinaires
Porticcio
D555
Grosseto Prugna
Sta-Maria-Siché
Solenzara
N196
Golfe d'Ajaccio
Verghia
337
Pila-Canale
Petreto-Bicchisano
Sari-Solenzara
D55
N198
Coti-Chiavari
D757
Aullène
Quenza
Capu di Muru
Sollacaro
Zonza
D368
8
Favone
32
Serra-di-Ferro
Olmeto
350
D69
D268
Levie
D157
Porto-Pollo
Ste-Lucie
Propriano
Ste-Lucie-de-Tallano
Carbini
349
Lecci
Golfe de Valinco
Sartène
L'Ospedale
Ste-Trinité
Golfe de Porto-V
Porto-Vecchio
Giuncheto
Capu di Senetosa
D859
Sotta
N196
N198
17
Roccapina
Figari
28
Punta di u Capicciolu
Bonifacio
Capo Pertusato

C O R S E

INTRODUCTION

You might say that there are two Corsicas, at least in summer: That of the seashore, a paradise for lovers of sunshine and waterskiing; and Corsica of the interior, a land of forests, mountains, breathtaking views of the sea from its towering red cliffs, Baroque and Romanesque churches scattered here and there, and finally the imprint of Italy with its Pisan bridges and Genoese watchtowers. The latter is the Corsica we love. And it is the latter, interior, Corsica that its winemakers are bringing back to life, tirelessly plowing up the steep hillsides and planting new vines on these old terraces that have been long overrun by the maquis.

Crisscrossing the island to visit its fifteen outstanding vineyards also allows you to see Corsica's most beautiful sites: the Baroque and Romanesque churches of Balagne in the Calvi vineyards; the Romanesque church of San-Michele decorated with sculpted vines in the Patrimonio appellation; Genoese towers and the omnipresent windswept sea in the Cap Corse vineyards; chalk cliffs buffeted by the wind and sea at Bonifacio in the Figari appellation; the great megalithic sites in the Sartène vineyard region; and the island's remarkable museums: that of Aleria, in particular, has a beautiful collection of old objects related to wine. The mountain roads of the interior and their chestnut forests are also worth the detour.

CORSICAN APPELLATIONS

The regional Appellation d'Origine Contrôlée (AOC) may be followed by the name of one of five sub-regions: Calvi, Côteaux du Cap Corse, Figari, Porto-Vecchio, and Sartène. Two appellations are named after their commune: Patrimonio and Ajaccio. The latter appellation, declared in 1993, applies to Muscat from Cap Corse, a *vin doux naturel*, a sweet, fortified wine made in the manner of port. Corsica's AOC vineyards currently cover almost two thousand hectares, planted mostly with red grapes and with only 20% in white vines.

MAIN GRAPE VARIETIES

Barbarossa, Aleatico, Carcaiolo, Codiverta, Elegante, and Bella Donna are no longer allowed in the Corsican vineyards. These vines are being extensively replanted with such varieties as Syrah, Grenache, and Mourvèdre.

C O R S E

INTRODUCTION

The Vermentino, a white grape, is in fact the Malvoisie vine which is found under various names throughout the Mediterranean basin. It produces very different wines depending on how they are made, from the flowery light wines of modern vinification to big, well-structured wines with a firm backbone.
The Nielluciu, a red grape, is the Sangiovese which has made the reputation of Chianti wines. It is essentially cultivated in the region of Patromonio in the north of the island and is vinified alone, as a varietal wine. Planted in the only chalky soil of the appellation, this "Jupiter's blood" is a marvelous wine for its deep color, its tannins, and its solid structure. In the region of Calvi, a buffer vineyard between Patrimonio and Ajaccio, it is often blended with Sciaccarellu.
The red Sciaccarellu is typically grown on the granite soil around Ajaccio, but it also found in other vineyard regions: Calvi, Figari, Sartène, and Porto-Vecchio. Often pale in color, it is enjoyed for its aromatic palette with peppery overtones and its finesse. Like the Nielluciu grape, Sciaccarellu yields wines that can improve with age, but they are invariably drunk too young in Corsica.
"Cracking in the mouth", as the local sciaccarellu translates,
it is the most typically Corsican grape as it has never been found elsewhere.

SPECIAL VINIFICATIONS

Muscat, which has recently been promoted to AOC standing, is a specialty of Cap Corse. The grapes are poured into baskets or onto flat *lauze* stones and left to dry, causing their water to evaporate and their natural sugar to concentrate. (The same method is used for *vins de paille* in the Jura and in the Rhône Valley). After vinification, the wine is *muté*, its fermentation stopped by the addition of alcohol before all its sugar has been converted into alcohol, thus leaving a *vin doux naturel*: a wine with its own natural sweetness, like its homologues in the Languedoc-Roussillon.
Rappu, also a specialty of Cap Corse, is a wine reminiscent of Banyuls. Vinified like Muscat, it is made with the Grenache grape, and occasionally some Aléatico, a less prominent grape on the island.
Impassitu is the third specialty of Cap Corse: a dry white *passerillé* wine usually made with Vermentino grapes; harvested late when they are overripe, they vinify dry as their sugar totally ferments. The wine is then aged some ten years in barrels, thus becoming a deliberately oxidized wine.

BUYING WINE IN CORSICA

As almost all Corsican wines are sold during the year following the harvest, vintage really isn't a consideration when buying Corsican wines. 1996 red wines will have less ageing potential than usual because the end of the harvest was often rainy; thus it isn't the best vintage if you want to experiment with cellaring. Try wines from another, more balanced vintage: you could have pleasant surprises, especially with those from the vineyards around Patrimonio.

A TABLE WITH CORSICAN WINES

The white Vermentino makes an excellent apéritif and it is also a good accompaniment for delicate fish provided the wine is not too aromatic. A full-bodied Vermentino should accompany dry or smoked sausages and cold cuts; rich, fleshy fish either baked or cooked in butter or cream; and fatty cheeses like Camembert or Brie.

INTRODUCTION

Sciaccarellu Rosé is good with golden fried chicken and cheeses like Tomme, Saint-Paulin, and Gruyère. Nielluciu Rosé, often more robust, goes well with hearty dishes and cheese.

Sciaccarellu, whose grapiness takes precedence over its structure, enhances grilled meat and small game. Often more tannic and robust, Nielluciu makes a good choice with sauced game and meat.

Muscat is of course marvelous with desserts like Corsican pastries with *brocciu* or those made with chestnut flour.

AJACCIO

1 - RESTAURANT - **Le Floride**: *Port de l'Amirauté, Niveau 1, 20000 Ajaccio. Tel. 04.95.22.67.48.* Very large offering of baked fish dishes (denti, sar, chapon, corbe, pageot). Good selection of Corsican wines. Menus at 61 (lunch weekdays), 135 (all fish) and 325 F (all spiny lobster).

CALVI

2 - RESTAURANT - **Émile's**: *Quai Landry, 20260 Calvi. Tel. 04.95.65.09.60/ 04.95.65.00.37 Fax 04.95.65.27.34. Closed October to April and lunchtime in July and August.* Remarkable fish cuisine and good wine list (mostly Corsican, but the Continent is well-represented). Menus: 120 a 450 F.

CANARI

3 - RESTAURANT - **U Scogliu (The Rock)**: *Marine de Canelle, 20217 Canari. Tel. 04.95.37.80.06. Open every day, lunch and dinner from April to late September. On the west coast of Cap corse.* The day's catch. Attractive wine list (41 entries) based on Patrimonio and le Cap. A la carte: around 150-250 F.

CATERI

4 - RESTAURANT - **Auberge Chez Léon**: *20225 Cateri. Tel. 04.95.61.73.95.* 17 km northwest of Calvi. Family cuisine both excellent and Pantagruelian. Menus: 90 (lunch) to 120 F.

CAURO

5 - RESTAURANT - **U Barracone**: *20117 Cauro. Tel. 04.95.28.40.55. Open every day from Easter to 9/15 (low-season, closed Sun. evening and Mon.).* On the Sartène route. Excellent Corsican cuisine. Remarkable wine list from Corsica and the Continent. Menu: 135 F.

FELICETO

6 - BED & BREAKFAST - **Mare Monti**: *20225 Feliceto. Tel. 04.95.63.02.00.* 20 km east of Calvi. An old house with an antiquated charm (ask to see the surprising Napoléon III salon) offering guest rooms from 270 to

280 F (1 pers.), 630 F (4 pers.), apartment: 490 F. Half and full board available.

7 - BED & BREAKFAST - **U Mulinu**: *20225 Feliceto. Tel. 04.95.61.73.23.* Informal dining set up in an oil-mill that's still running. The cabaret atmosphere is ensured by the owner, Joseph Ambrosini. 160 F wine included, reservations necessary.

LECCI-DE-PORTO-VECCHIO

8 - HOTEL-RESTAURANT - **Grand Hôtel de Cala-Rossa**: *20137 Lecci-de-Porto-Vecchio. Tel. 04.95.71.61.51 Fax 04.95.71.60.11.* 10 km from Porto-Vecchio. Terrace dining room looking out on the pines and the sea.

Full-flavored cuisine and attractive insular wine list. Menus: 180 (lunch except Sunday) to 350 F (dinner).

Buffet: 200 F (Wednesday and Sunday high-season) The new rooooms (some with terrace) are very pleasant and bright. Prices can double depending on the season: 500 to 3,800 F. Half board obligatory in July and August.

L'ÎLE-ROUSSE

9 - HOTEL-RESTAURANT - **La Bergerie**: *Route de Monticello, 20220 Île Rousse. Tel. 04.95.60.01.28 Fax 04.95.60.06.36. Closed November 20 to late March.* An inviting restaurant, mainly seafood menu (very fresh) by an enthusiastic fisherman.

A la carte: around 250 F. Rooms: 240 to 380 F.

LOPIGNA

10 - RESTAURANT - **Le Relais**: *20139 Lopigna. Tel. 04.95.28.94.38.* Around 8 km from the clos d'Alzeto. A table whose secret is kept by Pascal Albertini. On the suspended terrace that rubs up against the mountain (the cherry tree reaches up to the railing), Nenette Angelotti serves copious dishes that can be had for a song. A memorable meal that's handmade and homemade, Corsican from top to toe. As for dessert, you serve yourself...

MEZZAVIA

11 - RESTAURANT - **Restaurant A Casetta**: *Plaine de Cuttoli, 20167 Mezzavia. Tel. 04.95.25.66.59 Fax 04.95.25.87.67. Closed Sunday evening and Monday.* Forget the stock tourist-area pizza menus (although they are good) and treat yourself to the Corsican menu at 180 F. Solid cooking, both tasteful and colorful. Wines of the appellation are well represented.

MURATO

12 - BED & BREAKFAST - **Campo di Monte**: *20239 Murato. Tel. 04.95.37.64.39. Open every evening in high-season (low-season, open Friday and Saturday evenings and noon Sunday).* 20 km south of Saint-Florent, going towards Rutali on the Murato route. An informal table devoted to traditional cuisine, served in a series of

small dining rooms. Menu: 220 F.

PATRIMONIO

13 - BED & BREAKFAST - **Château Calvello**: *Monsieur Ficaja, 20253 Patrimonio. Tel. 04.95.37.01.15.* A splendid fortified edifice from the late 16th century, facing the vineyard. Three vacation houses by the week (2,500 and 2,800 F) and three rooms by the night (380 F, breakfast included).

PIANA

14 - HOTEL-RESTAURANT - **Les Roches Rouges**: *20115 Piana. Tel. 04.95.27.81.81 Fax 04.95.27.81.76.* South of Porto. The impressive building, a former luxury hotel, has taken on a patina that gives it a weathered-palace charm. Rooms are simple and clean. Choose those in the angles: their windows look

out on both the rocky Calanches and the gulf of Porto. Lovely historic dining room. Rooms: 320 F (2 pers.), 400 F (3 pers.) and 550 F (4 pers.). Breakfast: 45 F. Menus: 110 to 380 F.

PIGNA

15 - HOTEL-RESTAURANT - **Casa Musicale**: *20220 Pigna. Tel. 04.95.61.77.31. Closed in January and February, and Monday in low-season.* 8 km

southwest of Île-Rousse. A wonderful and inviting old house. Meals are served on the terrace overlooking the village. Excellent local cuisine: to be discovered. A la carte: around 150 F. Some delightful rooms: 260 to 400 F in high-season (195 to 280 F in winter).

SAINT-FLORENT

16 - HOTEL-RESTAURANT - **Hôtel Bellevue**: *20217 Saint-Florent. Tel. 04.95.37.00.06 Fax 04.95.30.14.83.* The Bellevue offers very handsome rooms from 350 to 450 F (low-season). In high-season and with obligatory half board, from 750 to 1,100 F and from 1,100 F to 1,700 F depending on dates. Breakfast: 60 F.

SANTA MANZA

17 - RESTAURANT - **L'Epave (Chez Louis)**: *Santa Manza, 20169 Bonifacio. Tel.*

04.95.73.05.81. Open every day. Northwest of Bonifacio. For dining alongside the fishing boats. The owner catches the rarest of fish in the morning, that are then impeccably cooked. Menus: 80 to 120 F.

TO SEE

ALERIA

MUSEUM - **The Jérôme-Carcopino Museum**: *Fort de Matra, 20270 Aleria. Tel. 04.95.57.00.92 Fax 04.95. 57.05.50. Open 5/16 to 9/30 from 8 to 12am and 2 to 7pm. Until 5pm*

from 10/1 to 5/15. Closed 1/1, 5/1, 11/1 and 11 and 12/25. The museum is in the Matra fortress. Several rooms contain sumptuous Etruscan and Roman objects found during the excavations: amphorae, magnificently decorated craters, dog- and mule-headed rhytons (drinking vessels), sculpted wine ladels.

BASTIA

MUSEUM - **The ethnographic museum** in the former palace of the Genoese governors. *Place du Donjon, la Citadelle. Tel. 04.95.31.09.12. Open 9 to 12 and 2 to 6. Closed weekends during the current remodeling.*

CORTE

MUSEUM - **The Corsican museum**: *20250 Corte. Tel. 04.95.61.00.61.* Two thousand objects relating to the island's pastoral and agricultural life from the 18th to the 20th century.

MURATO

OUTING - The lovely multi-colored church of San Michele and its sculpted bands devoted to the grapevine.

SAINT-FLORENT

OUTING - Two paces from the magnificent Pisan cathedral of the Nebbio, along the road leading to the Leccia cellar, one can see a row of pillars christened the " Bishop's trellis " on the left side.

On the Aguida slopes, the highest vineyard in Corsica.

Clos d'Alzeto

Owner Pascal Albertini. **Address** 20151 Sari-d'Orcino. Tel. 04.95.52.24.67 Fax 04.95.52.27.27. **Open** From Monday to Saturday, 8:00-12:00 and 14:00-19:30 (13:30-17:30 in winter). **Spoken** Italien, English, German. **Credit Cards** Visa, Eurocard, MasterCard.

This mountainous vineyard spreads out over the Aguida hillsides like a summer frock, its red leaves at harvest time adding a crimson trim.

Pascal Albertini rarely leaves his eagle's nest, occupied as he is with bringing the vineyard back to life, replanting olive trees on the terraced slopes, and restoring the old houses. He was not offended that his oak-aged Rosés were not truly to our liking, offering the marked taste that the locals enjoy (31 F for the '94). We much preferred the structured, fresh 1996 (about 31 F) and the white wine, which can be laid down: the '94 (33 F) is smooth, powerful, evoking "the maquis" with its notes of myrtle and fennil. Our favorites were his red wines (32 F), like the '91: figs, macerated raisins, lively on the palate; and the '93, which is full-bodied and dense.

Our choice The '90 red Prestige (70% Sciacarellu, 20% Grenache, some Syrah). The closed bouquet and the soft attack are deceptive: the wine opens up to deliver dense extract, power and length on the palate. Drinkable now, but can be cellared (48 F).

Reception By an attentive winemaker with contagious enthusiasm, in one of the most beautiful vineyards on the island.

How to get there *(Map 7): Leave north of Ajaccio via N194. In Mezzavia (7km), turn left onto D81 to the Golfe de la Liscia. In the center of Masorghja, turn right (large sign) and follow the itinerary indicated.*

A bull's head for a headstrong winemaker.

Clos Capitoro

Owner Jacques Bianchetti. **Address** Pisciatella, 20166 Porticcio - Tel 04.95.25.19.61 Fax 04.95.25.19.33. **Open** From Monday to Saturday, 8:00-12:00 and 14:00-19:00 (18:00 in winter), Sunday by appointment. **Spoken** Italian. **Credit Cards** Visa, Eurocard, MasterCard.

The name means "Bull's Head Vineyard" and the *torrero* is headstrong indeed when it comes to championing Corsican wines, preserving "the memory of the vineyard" by bringing back old tools, and reflecting his grandfather's passionate determination to replant the vineyard from seed after it was devastated by phylloxera. Today, Jacques Bianchetti has planted thirty hectares of Sciacarellu, the predominant grape variety in the Ajaccio region, along with Grenache and, for white wines, Vermentino. His '96 Rosé (38 F), full-bodied and fresh, is better with food than as an apéritif. The '96 white wine (42 F), flowery and delicate, is a good escort for grilled fish; while the delicious Malvoisie, a *vin doux naturel*, has little sugar and softened alcohol, with traces of spice, rum, and honey (80 F). The Clos Capitoro also makes two red wines. The first is a blend of Sciacarellu, contributing a highly aromatic palette, and of Grenache for "chewiness" in its youth: explosive bouquet, intense and ample on the palate, with overtones of hay, tobacco, and spices (38 F). A few years' bottle age will allow the tannins to soften.

Our choice The '94 red wine, from pure Sciacarellu (50 F). A somewhat finer bouquet than the above red, more delicate on the palate, with round tannins and spicy notes. To be drunk now.

Reception Charming, in a new tasting room which overlooking the cellar.

How to get there *(Map 7): Leave Ajaccio going toward Sartène via N196. Turn left toward Pisciatella in 12km. The cellar is on the immediate right, indicated by a large sign.*

The walls of the cellar are covered with frescos celebrating the vine and the cellar.

Domaine Peraldi

Owner Guy de Poix. **Winemaker** Christophe Georges. **Address** Chemin du Stiletto, 20167 Mezzavia - Tel 04.95.22.37.30 Fax 04.95.20.92.91. **Open** From Monday to Saturday, 8:00-12:00 and 14:00 - 19:00 (18:00 in winter). **Spoken** English. **Credit Cards** Visa, Eurocard, MasterCard.

The visitor feels certain that the owners of this domaine would like to move elsewhere, surrounded as they are by the encroaching suburbs of Ajaccio and their accompanying eyesores. As if in reaction against this disorder, the vineyard is a model of propriety. The wines also evoke order and precision. Domaine Peraldi's white wines have fine acid structure (they need a little bottle age), and a soft, fine taste coupled with verve and length on the palate (39 F for the '96).

The first red wine made by the domaine is a "melting pot" combining grapes from the island with those from the continent. Along with Sciacarellu, it is a blend of Cinsault, Grenache, and Carignan. The '96 (39 F), which we tasted from the barrel, is fruity, balanced, with silky tannins; the product of a difficult harvest during which half the grapes had to be thrown away, the 1995 (39 F) has an attractive aromatic aroma but lacks the characteristic structure of wines from this cellar. The most beautiful wine from the domaine is invariably the Clos du Cardinal, a pure Sciacarellu aged in oak.

Our choice The '96 Clos du Cardinal, tasted at the beginning of its barrel age, has a beautiful "cardinal red" color. Its bouquet has the marked smoky and fruity overtones typical of the Sciacarellu. On the palate, the extract is fine and dense, with a lovely, soft oakiness. (58 F).

Reception Good, but mainly aimed at sales.

How to get there *(Map 7): Leave Ajaccio from north via the road to Corte (N194). Before Mezzavia, turn right before the shopping center (signposted).*

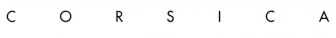

The famous *culombu*, a seashell transformed into a horn.

Clos Culombu

Owner Étienne Suzzoni. **Address** Chemin de la chapelle San-Petru, 20260 Lumio - Tel 04.95.60.70.68 and 04.95.60.60.56 Fax 04.95.60.63.46. **Open** Every day, 8:00-20:00. **Spoken** English, Italian. **Credit Cards** Visa, Eurocard, MasterCard.

Culombu? This is a large triton seashell whose tip has been cut off in order to make it into a horn. Corsican shepherds once used the horn to communicate from one valley to the next, as Etienne Suzzoni can demonstrate with some sonority.

The wines from his Clos are typically Corsican: the reds are a blend of Sciacarellu, the traditional grape of the Ajaccio region, and Nielluciu, which has made the reputation of Patrimonio wines. Depending on the year, they can be very supple or more tannic. The '95 Prestige (35 F) belongs to the latter type: its extract is tannic but not hard; it is chewy, with fruitiness and pleasant smoky overtones.

Our choice The '96 Rosé Prestige (32 F), made from a beautiful blend of grapes: Nieluciu for body and volume, making it good with meals; Sciacarellu, contributing generous fruit, and a touch of Vermentino for crispness. To be enjoyed now.

Reception By a member of the family, in the cellar.

How to get there *(Map 7): Leave Calvi heading for Lumio (N197). At the entrance to village, sign on right. The small Romanesque Chapel of San-Petru is decorated with two lions on the porch.*

At the foot of the villages of La Balagne, the vineyards of Alzipratu.

Couvent d'Alzipratu

Owners Maurice and Pierre Acquaviva. **Address** 20214 Zilia - Tel 04.95.62.75.47 Fax 04.95.60.42.41. **Open** Everyday, 8:00-19:00. **Spoken** Italian.

Saint Restitute, the patron saint of La Balagne, is an obstinate saint. Her chapel, a stone's throw from the Couvent d'Alzipratu vineyards, is said to have been built on the very spot where she was tortured. But the inhabitants of Calenzara had originally chosen another site for the chapel. It is said that every night, the building materials intended for the chapel were miraculously transported on a cart and pulled by two white oxen to the site of the present chapel.

Pierre Acquaviva is almost as obstinate. This former student of medieval history recently decided to resurrect the family vineyard, beginning by uprooting the vines and slowly replacing them with continental grape varieties, principally Cinsault and Nielluciu. The old cellar is soon to have a serious facelift. A determined winemaker, Acquaviva deserves to be followed attentively: the Couvent d'Alzipratu is surely to become the outstanding new vineyard of the region. His 1996 white wine (24 F) is fine and delicate, the red (23 F) is fruity in the '95 vintage, more concentrated and tannic in the 1996.

Our choice The '96 Prestige Rosé (30 F). Beautiful grey-pink color, clean bouquet, soft on the palate, delicately smoky, lovely finish. Delicious. Ready to be drink.

Reception In the old vinification cellar.

How to get there *(Map 7): From Calvi to Calenzana (D151), then drive towards Zilia. After the Chapelle Sainte-Restitute, domaine is on the left, facing the former convent.*

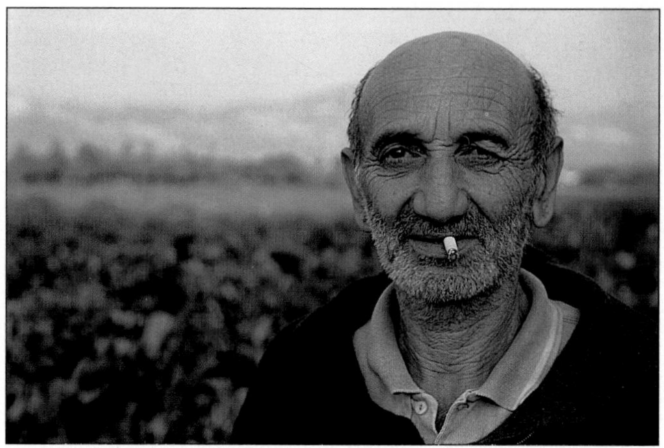

Fabien Paolini: the "cactus" beard in imitation of the real thing in his garden.

Clos Landry

Owner Fabien Paolini. **Address** Carrefour de l'aéroport, 20260 Calvi - Tel 04.95.65.04.25 Fax 04.95.65.37.56. **Open** In Summer, at the refreshment bar at the entrance of the property, de 8:00-20:00; in winter, in the cellar, 8:00-12:00 and 13:30-18:00. **Spoken** Italian. **Credit Cards** Visa, Eurocard, MasterCard.

"Here we have cactus...". What was once the field where wheat was threshed is today Fabien Paolini's cactus garden, possibly the inspiration for his prickly beard. But there is nothing prickly about the man, who has a heart of gold. He is a tireless story teller--recounting the pine trees planted by his father, the winds that blow over his vines, changing name as they change direction. He regularly makes one of the loveliest Rosés imaginable, the pink color obtained by direct pressing. It is fruity, full-bodied, but invariably fresh. The same might be said of his white wine: Fabien and his daughter, Cathy, made a 1996 white from very old vines, yielding a smooth but light wine, flowery and persistent on the palate (32 F). The red wine is improving greatly (29 F): fleshy, fruity, fine tannic structure.

Our choice The '96 Rosé (29 F): beautiful "gray" color obtained by direct pressing of Sciacarellu, Nielluciu, and Grenache. Firm, fine, fresh bouquet. The taste is meaty, solid, well balanced, with overtones of red berries, nuts, and spices. Lingering on palate. Good to drink now.

Reception Excellent. The small bar at the entrance to the domaine is a good, inexpensive spot for a glass of wine and a snack in the shade.

How to get there *(Map 7): Leave Calvi and turn right towards Aéroport Sainte-Catherine. The domaine is at the intersection of N197 and D81, immediately on the right.*

The Clos Reginu in the early morning.

Clos Reginu

Supervisor Michel Raoust. **Address** Felicetto, 20225 Muro - Tel 04.95.61.72.11 Fax 04.95.61.80.16. **Open** From Monday to Saturday, 8:00-12:00 and 16:00-19 h in summer, 8:00-12:00 and 14:00-17:00 in winter. **Spoken** Italian **Credit Cards** Visa, Eurocard, MasterCard.

The Clos Reginu is an atypical vineyard in Corsica, with seven hectares of continental Grenache and five hectares each of Nielluciu and Sciacarellu. And yet it's not a practical joke played by Michel Raoust, locally called a *pinzuti,* meaning foreigners but mainly French people from the mainland. Some Corsicans think the word comes from Parisians' "pointed" accent.

Pinzuti by birth but Corsican by devotion to his wines, Michel Raoust is skillful at blending Grenache with traditional local grapes to create tannic wines, with backbone and fine structure, particularly his E Prove red wines. The white wines need a certain bottle age to open up on the nose, but their structure and delicate acidity on ageing make the wait worth it. The '96 E Prove (36 F) is flowery and long, very elegant. The '96 Rosés are beautiful: the regular *cuvée* (25 F) with its notes of tangerine, as well as the E Prove (36 F), which is more earthy.

Our choice The '96 Red (25 F). Mellow, appetizing bouquet, full-bodied, fleshy taste, powerful and solid. Drinkable now.

Reception Informally, in the vinification cellar.

How to get there *(Map 7): From Calvi to Lumio, then Lavatoggio (D 71), Cateri and Muro. Go back in the direction of Ile Rousse on the left for 3km. The domaine is on the left (signposted).*

The panorama from the terrace of "the Americans' house".

Clos Nicrosi

Owner Jean-Noël Luigi. **Address** 20247 Rogliano - Tel 04.95.35.41.17 Fax 04.95.35.47.94. **Open** From Monday to Saturday 9:30-11:30 and 15:00-19:00. **Spoken** Italian.

There are a thousand reasons for coping with the narrow, winding roads that take you to the tip of Cap Corse. First, the beauty of the countryside with fewer and fewer houses as you drive, leaving you alone with just the land and the sea. Then, at the very top of Rogliano, looms the sumptuous "Americans' house" towering far above the village. Such is the local name for the houses built by natives of Cap Corse who emigrated to America and, once their fortune was made, gave them a home on their return. Thirdly, you will find Jean-Noël Luigi's Muscat wines here, the envy of the island and continental wine lovers in the know.

His Muscat is partially *passerillé*: the grapes are put into crates and left to dry in the sun in order to increase their sugar concentration as the water in the grapes evaporates. Other producers on the island achieve the same result by spreading the grapes on stones called *lauzes.*

Our choice The '96 Muscatellu (58 F). Fine, flowery bouquet with aromatic overtones of raisins, citrus rind, and dried roses on the palate and good sugar-alcohol balance. But it must be bought between May and the end of July. Otherwise, the sign *"Plus de vin"*, "No more wine", is hung on the gate.

Reception an aunt or Jean-Noël Luigi, in the old family home.

How to get there *(Map 7): Rogliano is the most northerly commune on Cap Corse. In the center of the village, head for the former convent "(couvent)", then left in 2km (signposted). Be careful of the many hairpin curves.*

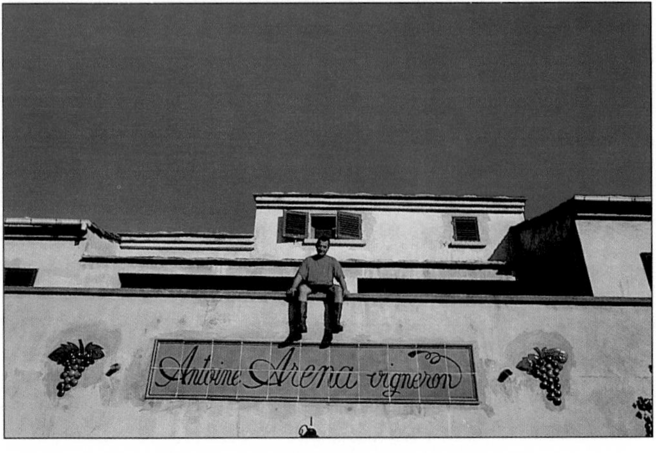

Antoine Arena, *Winemaker*, says the sign.

Domaine Antoine Arena

Owner Antoine Arena. **Address** 20253 Patrimonio - Tel 04.95.37.08.27 Fax 04.95.37.01.14. **Open** Everyday, 7:00-21:00, except Aug. 15. **Spoken** English, Italian.

A former law student, Antoine Arena plows up his vineyard the way he must have plowed through his law books: with determination and attention to detail. His vineyard is divided equally between red and white grapes. Depending on the harvest, one or the other produces the most wine. But Antoine Arena knows how to keep an even balance so that his average wines are never far behind those from the outstanding vintages.

The domaine's white wines are currently in the spotlight. A first '96 *cuvée* (40 F) is a flowery wine; a second, La Grotte di Sole (40 F) is more toast and almonds; and the Carco is our choice. There are still several bottles of '95 Vieilles Vignes, non filtered: intense, mineral bouquet, structured taste with fine acid backbone; it needs more bottle age. The Muscat (50 F) is ample and powerful; and the *vin de table*, from over-ripe Vermentino, is marvelously glazed (100 F for 50 cl).

Our choice The '96 Carco (40 F). Long fermentation, not finished when we tasted it, already ensures smoothness and body. Beautiful structure, length on the palate, persistence, overtones of yellow plums: the most beautiful white wine on the island. Needs some bottle age.

Reception In the cellar, perfect: Antoine knows every grape in the vineyard; Marie, his wife, all the good shops for authentic regional products.

How to get there *(Map 7): Leave Saint-Florent via D81. The cellar is at the entrance to Patrimonio, just after the traffic circle, on the left (signposted).*

Roger Le Stunff and his son, Laurent.

Domaine de Catarelli

Owner Roger Le Stunff. **Address** Marine de Farinole, 20253 Patrimonio - Tel 04.95.37.02.84 Fax 04.95.37.18.72. **Open** Every day 9:00-12:00 and 14:00-19:00. **Spoken** English, Italian.

A former flyer and a native of Brittany, Roger Le Stunff settled in Corsica after his marriage, planting his vineyard on the water's edge. His wines seem the reflection of the elements surrounding them: ethereal as the air, dense as the water, tannic as the clay-chalky soil they come from, yet tender as the clay itself.

Le Stunff used to vinify his wines instinctively, like a flyer following the stars, "my nose over the vat sniffing the aromas". With the construction of a new cellar and the arrival on the domaine of his son, Laurent, winemaking here took a more serious turn but did not alter the straightforward style of his wines. While the '96 red (32 F) does not have the fruit, the maturity or the extract of the previous vintages, the '96 white (32 F) is round and flowery; and the '96 rosé (30 F) is round, with little acidity but no heaviness, and lovely smoky, tangerine notes.

Our choice The '96 Muscat du Cap Corse (48 F). Intense, fine bouquet, overtones of linden and raisins on the palate, balanced, lingering, spicy finish. Can be drunk now.

Reception Hospitable

How to get there *(Map 7): From Saint-Florent to Patrimonio. At the traffic circle, turn left onto D80 to Les Marines de Farinole (marinas) (8km). The domaine is on the left (signposted).*

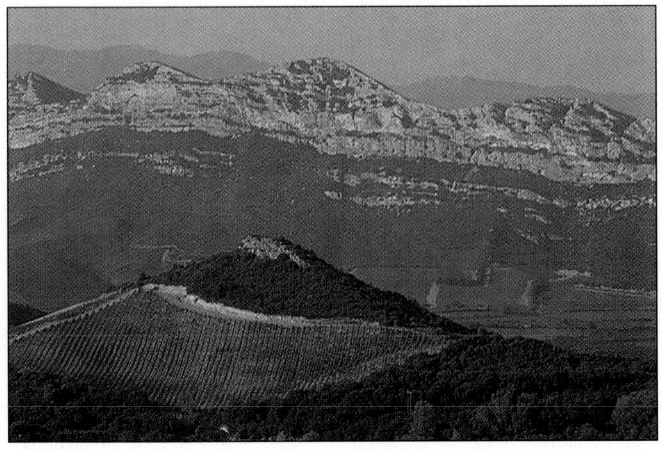

The domaine is climbing high.

Domaine Gentile

Owner Dominique Gentile. **Address** 20217 Saint-Florent - Tel 04.95.37.01.54 Fax 04.95.37.16.69. **Open** From Monday to Saturday, 8:00-12:00 and 14:00-18:00 in high season; by appointment in low season. **Spoken** Italien, english.

Dominique Gentile knows what he wants. He fought long and hard, successfully, to gain recognition of the Muscat du Cap Corse as an AOC. But he often prefers not to use the appellation on his labels because the criteria established do not correspond to his idea of a balanced wine. His best Muscats therefore have very little sugar and are elegant and light, mingling musky notes with exotic rose water overtones (62 F for the '96). Championing traditional grapes, he has systematically replanted his Grenache vines with Nielluciu. A perfectionist, Gentile bottle-ages his wines before making them available, despite heavy demands from tourists. While the '96 is pleasant, fruity, and round (39 F), we preferred the older vintages which are still available in the Sélection Noble *cuvée*. The '94 ('52 F) is beginning to open up with gamey, earthy notes, while the '92 (52 F), which is once again avaialble, offers flavors that open up gradually on the palate, becoming more tannic but softly so.

Our choice The '96 Muscat VDN (62 F), lacy and delicate, with very little sugar (75 F), mixing musky notes with exotic rose water. In the Muscat du Cap Corse appellation (53 F), it is more powerful and sweeter (95 grams of sugar), and more classic. We prefer the lightness of the first, which with bottle age often blossoms out with linden and toast. To drink or to cellar.

Reception In a simple sales room decorated with beautiful black-and-white photos of vines.

How to get there *(Map 7): On the edge of Saint-Florent, head for Patrimonio (D 81). Sign on left.*

Yves Leccia at the controls of the tasting room.

Domaine Leccia

Owner Yves Leccia. **Address** 20232 Poggio-d'Oletta - Tel 04.95.39.03.22 and 04.95.37.11.35 Fax 04.95.37.17.03. **Open** Every day 9:00-18:00. **Spoken** English.

"I like," says Yves Leccia, "the rough power of the Nielluciu, its tough character, its powerful aromas of tar and game." But his wine will undergo careful bottle ageing before it pleases him: a soft wine, yet mirroring the clout of the vineyard.

His '95 white Nielluciu (35 F) is fresh, slightly mentholated, with a mineral finish. The '96 will be distinctly softer and more ample. In an especially difficult vintage in Corsica, the red '95 Classique (35 F) is supple, fruity with a smoky overtone, round, and immediately enticing. The '96 Muscat (55 F), very sweet, needs bottle age to mature.

Our choice The '95 red Pietra Bianca (45 F). Concentrated, fine tannins, soft, fruity, elegant. Some bottle age.

Reception Next to the vinification cellar, in a large tasting room, simply and tastefully decorated.

How to get there *(Map 7): The easiest itinerary is via the Place de Saint-Florent and D238. 3km after the Cathedral of Le Nebbio (open in summer; beautiful sculpted capitals and the prayer book of the "unknown saint"), the cellar is on the left (signposted). We prefer the scenic Route de la Corniche, from Patrimonio toward Bastia on D81. At the Col de Teghime peak (6km), turn right towards Oletta, then go back down toward Saint-Florent. The road is difficult but offers a magnificent view over the vineyards of Patrimonio. By this road, the cellar is on the right.*

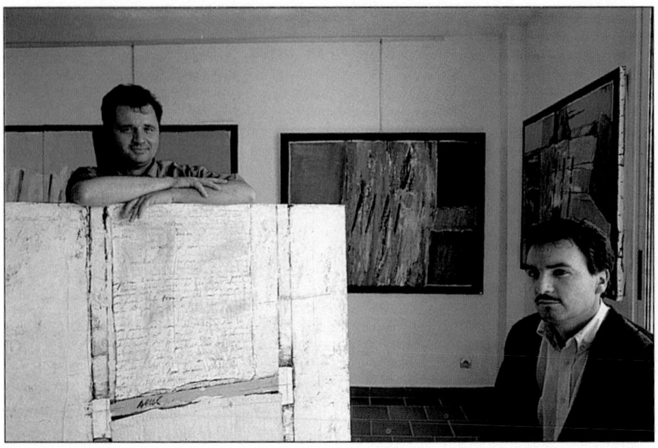

Henri Orenga (left), while paintings by Jean-Paul Pancrazi are being hung for exhibit.

Domaine Orenga de Gaffory

Owners Pierre and Henri Orenga de Gaffory. **Winemaker** Xavier Enu. **Address** 20253 Patrimonio - Tel 04.95.37.11.38 Fax 04.95.37.14.25. **Open** Every day, 8:00-12:00 and 14:00-18:00, except weekend in low season. **Spoken** English, Italian. **Credit Cards** Visa, Eurocard, MasterCard.

Although this winery regularly holds interesting exhibits of contemporary art, the large patches of color on the surrounding hillsides unfortunately have nothing to do with art: They are the sad remains of the latest fires in the maquis and the trails left by the fire-fighting airplanes.

Henri Orenga's domaine for several years now has had an ambitious policy of using oak barrels to vinify white wines and Muscat and to age red wines (the Gouverneurs *cuvées*), with variable results depending on the vintage. In addition to their principal vineyard, Pierre and Henri Orenga have just taken over another domaine, San Quilico, which is being replanted. The vines are still too young but promising. Among the wines currently available, we enjoyed the '96 Rosé San Quilico for its power; the '96 Orenga (34 F), a dense, fruity wine; and the red '95 Orenga Cuvée des Gouverneurs (48 F) for its overtones of bay.

Our choice The '95 Blanc Orenga de Garrory (40 F): delicate bouquet; soft taste with little acid, minerally and minty. The '96, tasted from the vat, will be soft and long on the palate.

Reception The entrance to the cellar has regular exhibits of modern art in the summer: Maddalena Rodriguez-Antoniotti, Claude Viallat, François Retali.

How to get there *(Map 7): Coming from Saint-Florent via D81, the cellar is 1km before Patrimonio, on the right (signposted).*

The vineyard was cleared and planted in 1964.

Domaine de Torraccia

Owner Christian Imbert. **Address** Lecci, 20137 Porto-Vecchio - Tel 04.95.71.43.50 Fax 04.95.71.50.03. **Open** From Monday to Saturday, 8:00-12:00 and 14:00-18:00. **Spoken** English, Italian, German, Spanish, Potuguese, Arab.

Like his cat, Christian Imbert has led several lives. After a spell in Chad, he came to Porto-Vecchio to undertake a new adventure, clearing and planting a beautiful vineyard of forty hectares. This "Corsified" native of Burgundy displays his motto in his cellar: "Love, believe, and dare." Not taking the easy route, he began as a winemaker in 1964, defying the industrial-scale viticulture which was then overtaking the island, plowing the soil completely and planting traditional Corsican grapes.

His rosé is generally vinous and spicy, but fine and creamy, very fresh and good with meals (about 30 F); the white (about 35 F) is smooth, aromatic, with overtones of fruit kernels and verbena. Imbert's '94 red (about 30 F) is fine and long on the palate, opening out with notes of the garrigue.

Our choice The '94 Oriu Réserve (52 F). (*Oriu* means "to hide"in Corsican). Made from Nielluciu (80%) and Sciacarellu. Deep red in color, smoky bouquet, long and powerful on the palate, sustained by delicate, structured extract; velvety tannins, very mellow, with aromatic olive notes (*tapenade*). Drink now or bottle age.

Reception Hospitable, in the cellar where you will also find the olives, oil, and vinegar produced on the domaine. The nearby vineyard is a sight to see, like a formal garden planted on a breathtaking site.

How to get there *(Map 7): Coming from Porto-Vecchio (N198), in 13km, turn right in the center of Leccif and follow the marked itinerary to the domaine (on the left).*

The Genoese bridge shown on the domaine's labels.

Domaine Fiumicicoli

Owner Family Andréani. **Address** Route de Levie, 20100 Sartène adresse postale Simon and Felix Andréani, Marina II, 20110 Propriano - Tel 04.95.76.14.08 and 04.95.77.10.20 Fax 04.95. 76.24.24. **Open** From Monday to Saturday, 8:00-12:00 and 14:00-18:00 in high season, by appointment in low season. counter sales, every day, 8:00-20:00 on the Propriano road in Olmeto. **Spoken** English.

Up until 1992, the 12th-century Genoese bridge shown on the Domaine Fiumicicoli's labels was overrun by trees and shrubs, and almost invisible. Today, it rises out of a stark landscape, cruelly razed by the floods of the River Rizzanese. A part of this vineyard is very old, mixing all the Corsican grape varieties over seven hectares of land. The other parcels, planted with white Vermentino and red Grenache, Nielluciu and Sciacarellu, are planted in equal shares.

Fiumicicoli's white wine (38.50 F) is typically soft and fruity, with a trace of almonds in the '96, opening out with a beautiful and unusual touch of acidity for wines of the south. The '94 red (33.50 F), a blend of Grenache, Nielluciu, and Sciacarellu in equal proportions, is not up to the previous vintages, which are generally supple but more concentrated. Ask if there are remaining bottles of the '90 pure Sciacarellu (about 45 F), with lingering aromas of coffee.

Our choice With the ups and downs of the various vintages, the domin has earned a justified reputation for rosés made by direct pressing. The '96 (33.50 F) is soft, vinous, a fine wine with body, verve, and lingering taste. Can be drunk now.

Reception Simple, in the vat room.

How to get there *(Map 7): Sartène via N196. After 7km from Propriano, turn right on D268. After the bridge (on left), the domaine is on the right (signposted).*

JURA

8
Chassigny-Aisey
Genevrières
Grenant
Combeaufontaine
Port-s.-S.
Flagy
Saulx
Prauthoy
Montvaudon
Vauconcourt-Nervezain
Scey-s.-S.
Chamoille
Mollans
Pierrecourt
Vesoul
Quincey
Selongey
Champlitte
Vaite
Haute-Saône
Seveux
Fresne-St-Mames
Vellefaux
Chazeuil
Fontaine-Française
Dampierre-s.-Salon
70
Frétigney-et-Velloreille
Rougemont
Montbozon
Autrey-lès-Gray
Gray
La Chapelle-St-Quillain
Bèze
Rioz
Oiselay-et-G.
Mirebeau
Rigney
Choye
Gy
Baume-les-Dames
Étuz
Arc-s.-Tille
Bonboillon
Pontailler-s.-S.
Roulans
Dijon
Marnay
Aïssey
Lamarche-s.-S.
Longvic
Audeux
Besançon
Genlis
Gendrey
Auxonne
Villers-Rotin
St-Vit
Tarcenay
Étalans
Trouhans
Dampierre
Épeugney
Brazey-en-P.
Ornans
St-Jean-de-L.
Rochefort-s.-Nenon
Quingey
Nods
Dole
Samson
Broin
Arc-et-Senans
Amancey
Doubs
25
Tavaux
St-Aubin
Seurre
Chemin
Vaudrey
Mouchard
St-Gorgon-Main
La Vrine
Trugny
Chaussin
Salins-les-B.
Levier
Navilly
Les Essards-Taignevaux
Chaffois
Verdun-s.-le-D.
Aumont
Arbois
Pierre-de-Bresse
Chaumergy
Poligny
Pont-d'Héry
Frasne
St-Point-Lac
Bellevesvre
Censeau
Jura
Sellières
Martin-Mervans
-Bresse
St-Germain-du-Bois
Picarreau
Nozeroy
Voiteur
Champagnole
Thurey
Bletterans
Mouthe
Frangy-en-B.
Lons-le-Saunier
Beaurepaire-en-Bresse
Doucier
Pont-de-la-Chaux
Montret
Conliège
Foncine-le-Bas
Louhans
Nogna
Bonlieu
Le Chenit
Chantemerle
St-Laurent-en-Grandvaux
Montpont-en-Bresse
Beaufort
Clairvaux-les-lacs
Bois-d'Amont
La Tour-du-Meix
Morbier
Orgelet
Morez
Étival
Varennes-St-Sauveur
La Rixouse
Les Rousses
St-Cergue
Trivier-Courtes
Cuiseaux
St-Amour
Cormoz
Moirans-en-Montagne
St-Claude
Mijoux
St-Julien
Nyon
Coligny
Arinthod
Divonne
St-Julien-s.-Reyssouze
Lavans
Gex
Dortan
Les Bouchoux
Versoix
Montrevel-en-Bresse
Marboz
St-Étienne-du-Bois
Thoirette
Ferney-Voltaire
Oyonnax
Chézery-Forens
Genève
Izernore
Vonnas
Bourg-en-Bresse
St-Germain-de-Joux
Collonges
Annemasse
St-Julien-en-G.
Péronnas
Ceyzériat
Nantua
Neuville-les-Dames
Reignier
Bellegarde-s.-Valserine
Lent
Châtillon-s.-

INTRODUCTION

The Jura loves its vineyards. You have only to see its house fronts decorated with vineyard motifs, its statues invariably laden with grapes, and omnipresent Saint Vincent, the patron saint of winemakers, paid homage throughout the region. Museums are richly evocative of wine and the popular wine festivals--in Arbois Montigny, Pupillin--are dependably joyous events in the wine calendar. If you add the beauty of the countryside, the cellars warmly open to the public, notably in Arbois, and the fine restaurants of this *département*, the Jura can be a high point in your tour of French vineyards.

JURA APPELLATIONS

The Côtes-du-Jura appellation covers the entire vineyard region and applies to all kinds of Jura wines, from Chardonnay to yellow wine, still and sparkling wines, and the full range of blends. There are also more restricted geographical areas, whose appellations also apply to all kinds of wines : Arbois and Arbois-Pupillin, from the name of the two villages. The Côtes-du-Jura AOC also produces Crémants and *macvin*, a *vin de liqueur* made by adding *marc eau-de-vie* to the fresh must before fermentation.

The other appellations, from a small geographial area, apply only to certain kinds of wine. Thus, the L'Etoile appellation, named after the small star-shaped fossils abundant in the soil around the village of that name, applies only to white, yellow, and sparkling wines from L'Etoile; the village of Château-Chalon also has its own appellation, which applies only to yellow wines produced there.

SPECIAL VINIFICATIONS: YELLOW WINE AND STRAW WINE

The legend has it that *vin jaune*, yellow wine, was developed by the abbesses of Château-Chalon. As the pleasures of the flesh were forbidden to them, they are said to have poured their love into the creation of this wine.

What is known is that *vin jaune* is made from the Savagnin grape alone. It is harvested late, when it has a potential alcoholic content of at least 12°. Vinification is

similar to that of all white wines: the grapes are pressed and undergo alcoholic fermentation followed by malolactic fermentation.
But it is the ageing of yellow wine that is special. It is aged for more than six years in barrels of 228 liters, which are not filled completely in order to keep the wine in contact with the air: the barrels are said to be en *vidange*. The practice is thus totally opposite to that of Bordeaux vinification, during which the barrels are constantly topped up, a procedure called *ouillage*, in order to keep the wine from oxidizing. The yeasts present in the cellar, notably the *bayanus* saccharomines, cause a veil to form on the surface of the wine, protecting it from maderization while promoting slow oxidation. This gives the wine its famous "yellow", nutty taste. So that visitors can visualize the veil phenomenon, many wineries explain the process by means of small, illuminated glass-bottom barrels.
With a view to making a whole range of different wines for subsquent blends, the winemaker places his ageing barrels in very different places, from the cellar to the loft (a dry cellar will give more flowery wines), deliberately exposing them to changes in temperature.

If the veil does not develop properly to make a barrel of Savagnin "go yellow" (especially if the volatile alcohol increases too quickly), it is removed from the ageing vat and usually blended with Chardonnay to produce what is called here a "*blanc typé*", a white wine of marked character.
Yellow wines are sold in a bottle with a special shape, the *clavelin*. It contains 62 centiliters, which is intended to represent what remains of a liter of wine after evaporating over a long ageing period.

The *vin de paille*, straw wine, is a liquorous wine whose sugar is concentrated by leaving the grapes to dry for at least two months. Harvested early to preserve their acidity, bunches of grapes are placed on straw mats, thus the name, or hung suspended from the ceiling. Water in the grapes evaporates during this time and after long and difficult pressing, because they are so dry, they yield only several hectoliters of juice. As the cost of producing *vin de paille* is high, this rare wine is sold only in half-bottles of 37.5 centiliters, and is often sold in limited quantities.

GRAPE VARIETIES
At the end of the last century, some fifty different grape varieties were grown in the Jura, most planted for their heavy yields. The Appellation Contrôlée criteria ruled out all but five: Chardonnay, Pinot Noir, Savagnin, Trousseau, and Poulsard. The first two are planted principally in Burgundy; the latter three are typical of the Jura. Half of the vineyards are planted in Chardonnay, while Poulsard and Savagnin each represent somewhat less than 20% of the vines here. A little more than 10% of the vines are Pinot Noir, while about 5% are Trousseau. The grapes are used to make either varietal wines or blends, making the range of Jura wines very large indeed.
A native of Burgundy, Chardonnay was introduced into the Jura as early as the 14th century. Some winemakers plant a Chardonnay clone, locally called the "red-stemmed melon" because of the deep pink color of its stalk. Certain vignerons consider this a variety on its own. For others, it is a simple reversible mutation depending on the soil: the Chardonnay may become red-stemmed in one vineyard and in another

the red-stemmed grape becomes Chardonnay again. Modern ampelography does not yet know why. It is found throughout the Jura vineyard, growing on all kinds of soil, light or heavy.

Pinot Noir was also brought from Burgundy at the same time. Compared with the grape of its homeland, it yields wines of similar fruit but rarely structure, except on several fine *terroirs*; but it is found in almost all the Jura vineyards. Pinot Noir is most often found in blends with the other two more typical Jura red grapes, the Trousseau and the Poulsard.

The first mentions of Trousseau date from 1731. It perhaps came from Savoie or the Valais. Its name is said to come from the old word *toursel*, meaning "package", because of the bundled look of its grape bunches. The book *Vins*, *Vignes*, et *Vignoles du Jura* by one of the greatest winemakers of the region, Lucien Aviet (see page), explains the name amusingly: "*Vignerons* of the past kept Trousseau wine for a very long time, until their daughter married; then they sold it to pay for...her trousseau". Planted in deep soil, on red Keuper marl or gravel, the grape yields wines of deep color, tannic, rich, solid, long-lived. The Poulsard grape is often called "Ploussard" in Pupillin, the small village near Arbois which proclaimed itself the world capital of the grape. Some of the *vignerons* presented in this Guide, notably Pierre Overnoy, stubbornly hold to the local name. Certainly of local origin, the grape is mentioned in texts dating back to the early 14th century. It prospers on heavy, rich soils like marls and clays. Planted mainly in the Arbois region, especially in Pupillin, Poulsard is sometimes vinified as a white wine--in the L'Etoile appellation--but it most often goes into red wines. It is often very pale (sometimes offered as a rosé), delicately scented, fine, a wine of longevity when it is vinified to this end.

The leading grape variety of the Jura, the Savagnin, still called *naturé* in the Arbois region, is thought to have come from Germany and introduced into the Franche-Comté when the region was still part of Germany. Late-maturing, the grape favors hot soils with a limestone or siliceous topsoil on a base of Liassic marl. It is most often vinified to make powerful yellow wines, but some winemakers use it like the other grape varieties to produce fresh, fruity wines.

BUYING WINE IN THE JURA

Yellow wines and *vins de paille* can keep a very long time. The latter attain peak maturity at about five years of bottle age. The yellow wines currently available are mostly 1988 and 1989 vintages. Some wineries still offer older vintages of great interest: they are indicated in the vineyard descriptions which follow.

The taste in Jura winemaking is for ageing wines in bottle before they are offered for sale. The various vintages in either white or red wines currently available are thus good to drink now, but they can also be cellared: Jura's Chardonnay often reveals amazing qualities after ageing, thus reflecting its kinship with its Burgundian cousin.

A note of caution however if you wish to stray from the vineyards we have selected here: The 1994 vintage was difficult for red wines, but you can still find bottles of the famous 1990.

A TABLE WITH THE WINES OF JURA

Yellow wine is good with richly flavored dishes, like foie gras, lobster, Comté cheese, and of course, the traditional *coq au vin jaune et aux morilles*. The *blanc typés*, white wines like no others, are often lovely accompaniments for mushrooms. Poulsard is best with charcuteries, sausages and cold cuts, while Trousseau and blended red wines traditionally accompany grilled meats.

ARBOIS

1 - HOTEL-RESTAURANT - **Jean-Paul Jeunet**: *9 rue de l'Hôtel de Ville, 39600 Arbois. Tel. 03.84.66.05.67 Fax 03.84.66.64.20. Closed Tuesday and Wednesday noon (except during school vacation and summer), and in December and January.* Rooms are modern and comfortable. Rooms: 450 to 520 F. Those in the annex, a former presbytery, overlook the rose bushes in the parish priest's garden, cared for by father Jeunet. Very good breakfast: 62 F. Menus: 190 (lunch) to 500 F. Jean-Paul Jeunet enhances textures and flavors with near forgotten wild plants (amaranth, melilot), roots and bark. 600 entries on the wine list, with 200 from the Jura upheld by an excellent wine waiter.

2 - RESTAURANT - **Le Caveau**: *3 route de Besançon, 39600 Arbois. Tel. 03.84. 66.10.70 Fax 03.84.37.49.62.* Overhanging the river, a respectable traditional table. The wine list invites you to leave the path well taken. Menus: 88 to 295 F.

BAUME-LES-MESSIEURS

3 - RESTAURANT - **Restaurant des Grottes**: *39210 Baume-les-Messieurs. Tel. 03.84.44.61.59. Closed evenings and late September to Easter.* Northeast of Lons, snuggled in a blind valley, a modest restaurant (menus: 82 to 145 F) with a simple but decent wine list. Lovely site, at the foot of the falls.

4 - BED & BREAKFAST - **Abbaye de Baume-les-Messieurs**: *Ghislain Broulard, 39210 Baume-les-Messieurs. Tel. 03.84.44.64.47.* Within the abbey's walls, vast guest rooms at 320 F with breakfast. Possibility of light dining, regional products.

COURLANS

5 - RESTAURANT - **Auberge de Chavannes**: *39570 Courlans. 6 km from Lons, on the N78. Tel. 03.84.47.05.52 Fax 03.84.43.26.53. Closed Sunday evening, Monday and in January.* Menus: 130 to 265 F. One of the best tables in the Jura where regional cuisine always has its place. Exemplary welcome. As for wine, 13 exceptional Juras and 6 great vins jaunes from old vintages. Good choices from other regions.

DOLE

6 - RESTAURANT - **Les Templiers**: *35 Grande-Rue, 39100 Dôle. Tel. 03.84. 82.78.78 Fax 03.84.72.12.52. Monday and Sunday evenings on reservation only.* Menus (200 to 250 F) and dishes oscillating between tradition and creation.

Attractive wine list for Jura wines, particularly from Arbois.

MOUCHARD

7 - HOTEL-RESTAURANT - **Chalet Bel'Air**: *Tel. 03.84.37.80.34 Fax 03.84.73. 81.18. Closed Wednesday, except during school vacations.* For a quick meal, choose the rotisserie room; for a more leasurely repast, the gastronomic room, subtly anchored in regional cuisine. The wine list is equally faithful to the region, with 80 entries mostly from Arbois. Menus: 185 to 380F. Nine simple, well-kept rooms: 245 to 400F.

PASSENANS

8 - HOTEL-RESTAURANT - **Auberge du Rostaing**: *39230 Passenans. Tel. 03.84. 85.23.70 Fax 03.84.44.66.87. Closed Monday evening (low-season) and noon Tuesday.* Rustic and straightforward cuisine at the right price. Menus: 63 to 177 F. Decent rooms: 135 to 250 F.

9 - RESTAURANT - **Le Bon Pays**: *Tel. 03.84.85.28.90. Closed Wednesday.* Regional and not costly. Menus: 80 to 130 F.

POLIGNY

10 - HOTEL-RESTAURANT - **Hostellerie des Monts-de-Vaux**: *39800 Poligny. Tel. 03.84.37.12.50 Fax 03.84.37.09.07.* An elegant and cheery inn, full of nooks and recesses, with treasures lovingly collected (glasses, silverware). Rooms: 550 to 850 F. Menus: 180 F (lunch). A la carte: around 350-400 F.

11 - HOTEL-RESTAURANT - **Domaine de la Vallée Heureuse**: *Route de Genève, 39800 Poligny. Tel. 03.84.37.12.13 Fax 03.84.37.08.75. Restaurant closed Wednesday in low season and noon Thursday.* Rooms from

400 to 550 F, apartments from 700 to 900 F. Pool and sauna. Try for the room in the old bread oven; one drifts asleep there lulled by the babbling brook. Menus: 95 (lunch) to 220 F. Simple but well-prepared cuisine. Attractive wine list with fifty well-chosen entries from the Jura.

SALINS-LES-BAINS

12 - HOTEL - **Hôtel des Deux Forts**: *Place du Vigneron, 39110 Salins-les-Bains. Tel. 03.84.37.93.75.* A modest hotel for vineyard travellers, at the north end of the region, facing the magnificent old Salines buildings. Rooms: 160 to 250 F.

TO SEE

ARBOIS

MUSEUM - **Franche-Comté's Wine and Vineyard Museum**: *Château Pécauld, rue des Fossés, 39600 Arbois. Tel. 03.84.66.26.14 Fax 03.84.66.10.29 e-mail: Pécauld@ Jura.vins.com. Open February to November from 10 to 12 and 2 to 6, except Tuesday. In July-August from 10 to 6.* The beautiful 18th-centruy

castle houses a collection of wine-related tools and objects, and explains viticulture and vinification, including particularities of the Jura (vin jaune, vin de paille), in a lecturing but lively way. Admission: 20 F.

OUTING - The archivolts of the porch of the **church of Saint-Just** are decorated with bunches of grapes and vine leaves.

CHAMPLITTE

MUSEUM - **Museum of popular arts and traditions and Museum of arts and techniques**: *Château de Champlitte 70600 Champlitte. Tel. 03.84.67. 82.00. Open from 9 to 12 and 2 to 5 (6pm in summer) except Sunday morning. Closed Tuesday from September to May.* The viticulture section displays a collection of 12 wine presses,

including that of the bishops of Langres dating from 1680, as well as a cooper's workshop and a distillery.

CHÂTEAU-CHALON

OUTING - This lovely village perched on its peak lends its name to the vins jaunes and shelters beautiful winegrowers' houses that are particularly well upkept.

LODS

MUSEUM - **Wine and Vineyard Museum**: *25930 Lods. Tel. 03.81.60. 93.54. Visits 7/1 to 8/31 from 10 to 12 and 2 to 6, except Tues.* In a 16th-century winegrower's house. An interesting collection of viticultural tools.

LONS-LE-SAUNIER

OUTING - Several ancient houses on the place de la Comédie display lérods (vinedresser's pruning knives) sculpted on the doorway lintels.

MIEGES

OUTING - The church's bell-tower porch (15th/16th centuries) is decorated with viticultural motifs (vine-branches, harvesters).

MONTAIGU

OUTING - The Carthusian cellars, occupied by the Pignier estate.

NANS-SOUS-SAINTE-ANNE

MUSEUM - **Edge-tool Industry Museum**: *25330 Nans-sous-Sainte-Anne. Tel. 03.81.86.64.18 Fax 03.81.86.54.70. Open every day 4/1 to 11/1 from 10 to 12:30 and 2 to 6:30. In March and November open Sun., holidays and during school vacation from 2 to 6pm.* In beautiful vaulted cellars. All of the machinery, tools and products of an edge-tool workshop, with a collection of vine-dresser's hoes.

POLIGNY

OUTING - In the Saint-Hippolyte collegial, a magnificent sculpted " Madonna with grapes " (18th century). In the church of Mouthier-Vieillard, a 17th-century vintner's tomb decorated with viticultural tools.

VADANS

OUTING - The church's stoop is decorated with grapes.

VITICULTURAL FESTIVITIES

JANUARY
Arlay: Saint Vincent's day, the last Sunday in January.

APRIL
Château-Chalon and Poligny: Saint Vernier's day, patron saint to Jura winegrowers, the third Sunday in April.

JULY
Arbois: wine festival, the third Sunday in July.

AUGUST
Montigny-les-Arsures: Trousseau vine festival, the last Sunday in August.

SEPTEMBER
Arbois: the first Sunday in September is the Biou, the big Jura wine festival. The procession of winegrowers carries a giant bunch of grapes made with hundreds of branches from their vines that can weigh up to 100 kilos. It's then displayed in the church nave.

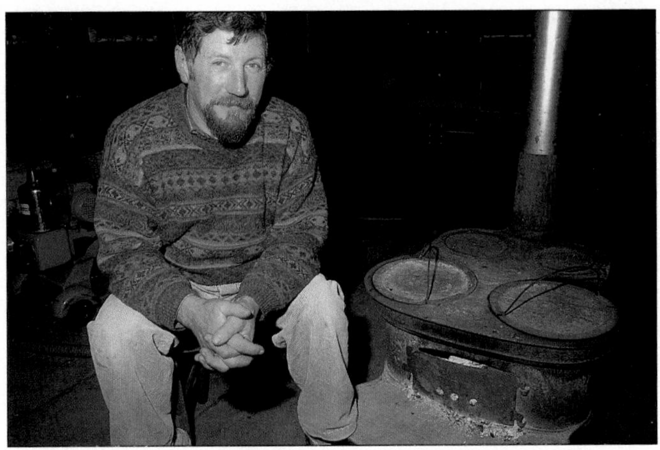

Lucien Aviet, alias Bacchus.

Lucien Aviet

Owner Lucien Aviet. **Address** Montigny-lès-Arsures, 39600 Arbois - Tel. 03.84.66.11.02. **Open** By appointment.

"All men are born free and equal in their right to drink Melon, Trousseau, Poulsard, and Savagnin." Lucien Aviet's cellar is full of such wise old sayings. But those who are expecting rustic wines will be surprised. Here, they are all lightness and finesse: "Bacchus" is a sophisticated winemaker.

Each grape variety is dedicated to the buyers who were the first to express their interest in wines from Lucien Aviet: the Cuvée des Docteurs designates the Poulsard, while the Cuvée des Géologues is made from Trousseau.

Aviet's '95s are already available. We tasted them from the ageing barrel. The '95 Chardonnay Cuvée des Docteurs (45 F) comes from 80-year-old Poulsard vines with a touch of Savagnin: impressive, almost massive on the palate, with a very lingering taste. In a lighter, fruitier style, we liked the '95 Trousseau Cuvée des Géologues. The "young" vines (everything is relative here, because they are some twenty years old) yield a pale wine, with fruit on the nose and promising smoothness and body.

Our choice The '95 Arbois Trousseau Vieilles Vignes, Cuvée des Géologues (about 50 F). No more color than the above Trousseau, but much more concentrated extract, bursting with fruit, with a mysterious smoky touch. Some bottle age.

Reception Entertaining winemaker, interesting cellar.

How to get there *(Map 8): Leave north Arbois toward Besançon. After 2km, right toward Montigny. Follow itinerary indicated.*

An old cask in Frédéric Lornet's cellar: a work of art.

Frédéric Lornet

Owner Frédéric Lornet. **Address** l'Abbaye 39600 Montigny-lès-Arsures - Tel. 03.84.37.44.95 Fax 03.84.37.40.17. **Open** Every day, 9:00-12:00 and 14:00-19:00. **Credit cards** Visa, Eurocard, MaterCard.

Frédéric Lornet currently works as a carpenter, restoring the old buildings of the former Montigny Abbey. He is also restoring his vineyard in the northern Arbois appellation.

Color seems to matter to his vines. Planted on red marl soils, his Chardonnay is minerally and powerful in the '94 vintage, but smoother and fattier from the '95 harvest, grown on blue marl. His red wines also have a strong "identity", with a fruity '95 Poulsard (40 F) and a mouth-filling '94 Trousseau Les Dames (50 F): soft tannins, fleshy taste with notes of plum.

The '89 yellow wine (150 F) is flowery on the nose, its powerful attack softening at the finish; even more dramatic is the '94 *vin de paille* (130 F for half-bottle): intense, very delicate bouquet of quince, dried flowers, minerals; straightforward on the palate, clean, bread-crust hints, well balanced.

Our choice The '94 Savagnin Réserve Evelyne (50 F). A Savagnin vinified to express its own character, without seeking a "taste of yellow". Bouquet blossoms sumptuously, very honeyed. The palate confirms the bouquet in volume, density, smoothness; very long on the palate, with notes of citrus. Some bottle age.

Reception Among the casks in the cellar, until the new tasting room is opened in the renovated buildings.

How to get there *(Map 8): Leave north Arbois heading for Besançon. After 2km, turn right to Montigny; follow posted itinerary.*

Pruning at the Domaine de la Pinte.

Domaine de la Pinte

Owner Family Martin. **Supervisor** Philippe Chatillon. **Address** BP16, 39601 Arbois Cedex - Tel. 03.84.66.06.47 Fax 03.84.66.24.58. **Open** On the week, in tasting room from 9:00-12:00 and 14:00-19:00 (tel. 03.84.37.42.62), by appointment. **Spoken** English. **Credit cards** Visa, Eurocard, MasterCard.

"Plante beau, cueille bon, pinte bien." Plant precisely, harvest properly, drink well. The Domaine de la Pinte adheres scrupulously to the two first parts of its motto. The third must be judged by its visitors. For our part, we give them flying colors.

The Domaine's '94 red Poulsard (41 F) is fruity and slightly peppery, while the '95 (about 35 F) will have somewhat more body. Of the whites, we tasted a lovely '95 Chardonnay (45 F): aniseed and moist chalk bouquet; delicate, buttery taste, hints of fruit kernels; long and persistent, it was reminiscent of Alsatian Pinot Gris. A '93 Savagnin (85 F) opened up with an aromatic finish evocative of fresh dates. Several yellow wines are available: the 1990 (150 F), very candied and long; the '83 (198 F): mushroom bouquet, caramel taste opening up with incense; and the spicy, persistent 1986 for 168 Francs.

Our choice The '92 *vin de paille* (190 F for half bottle). Very liquorous bouquet evoking toast, spice cake, dried apricots, and glazed angelica. The taste is very expressive and sweet, with notes of raisins and coffee. Sugar and acidity are well balanced; very lingering taste. Can be drunk now.

Reception If you wish simply to buy these wines, they are available in the tasting room in the center of town on the Rue de l'Hôtel de Ville, just off the Grand-Place. If you have more time, you can go to the Domaine itself and visit the three beautiful cellars, 210 feet long.

How to get there *(Map 8): Leave south of Arbois heading for Poligny. After 2km, turn left onto the small road with itinerary posted.*

Kimi the cat, (with Jacques Puffeney.)

Jacques Puffeney

Owner Jacques Puffeney. **Address** Montigny-lès-Arsures 39600 Arbois - Tel. 03.84.66.10.89 Fax 03.84.66.08.36. **Open** By appointment.

Six hectares of vines on fifteen parcels, the oldest vines dating from 1939: Jacques Puffeney is not exactly a modernist. His labels are printed with old-fashioned but elegant typeface and his bottles are, one by one, sealed with wax. Every bottle awakens a memory in him. The touch of rose and peony in the bouquet of his '94 Arbois Poulsard, a fresh red wine, light but concentrated, (about 32 F) takes him back to the schoolboy processions of his youth.

Other wines deserve remembrance of things past. His '94 Trousseau Les Bérangères (55 F), for its dense, voluptuous extract; the '93 Savagnin (60 F), for its elegance; and the '88 yellow wine (160 F) for its spicy, graceful taste.

Our choice The '94 Arbois Chardonnay (40 F). Chardonnay is a mutant grape variety which varies depending on the soil and the graft. On poor soils, it becomes a cousin of the Chardonnet in the Jura, the *melon à queue rouge* as it is called here, yielding soft wines with little acidity and beautiful overtones of angelica. Mellow and buttery, very lingering on the palate, this Chardonnay is a mouth-watering delicacy. Ready to drink.

Reception By a reserved but helpful winemaker, in his cellar surrounded by barrels. If you're a hunter, you might enjoy the sight of woodcocks hanging from the ceiling, "as subtle as a Savagnin."

How to get there *(Map 8): Leave northern Arbois heading for Besançon. After 2km, turn right to Montigny; follow itinerary posted. The cellar is at the top of the village, on the left (signposted).*

The tasting room, an Arbois tradition.

Domaine Rolet

Winemaker Guy Rolet. **Address** Rue de l'hôtel de ville, 39600 Arbois - Tel. 03.84.66.08.89 Fax 03.84.37.47.41. **Open** Every day, 9:00-12:00 and 14:00-19:00. **Spoken** English. **Credit cards** Visa, Eurocard, MasterCard.

With an impressive new vinfication and ageing cellar, this large domaine of over sixty hectares nevertheless adheres to traditional winemaking: grapes are harvested manually (by eighty workers in 1995), and its yellow wines are made in the old-fashioned way, without producing the veil on the fermenting wine which is the normal procedure in making this rare wine. Guy Rolet goes so far as to age each barrel of yellow wine in different places in order to create a large palette of wines--they become more flowery in a dry cellar--which will then yield blends of greater complexity. As the 1994 harvest was difficult for Jura's red wines, try instead the '90 Mémorial (60 F), a blend of two-thirds Trousseau with Pinot Noir. The bouquet is smoky, gamey; it is full-bodied in taste, with fine tannic structure and overtones of hay, tea, roses. Of the whites, try the '95 Chardonnays, vinified in oak barrels and and aged on their delicate lees: the Arbois (46 F) is buttery and full-bodied, with notes of ripe pears and a long finish; the Côtes-du-Jura (47 F) is somewhat more structured.

Our choice The '88 Arbois Jaune (170 F), "a wine that is still proud", says Guy Rollet, referring to its reticence as a young wine. It is a good representative of the un-veiled yellow wines, with young aromas of citrus and dry fruit. The characteristic traces of nuts and curry will develop with bottle age. The delicate taste is beginning to develop its potential power. To be cellared.

Reception Helpful and attentive, in the traditional Arbois tasting room.

How to get there *(Map 8): In the center of Arbois, in front of the "Mairie", next to the Hôtel de Paris.*

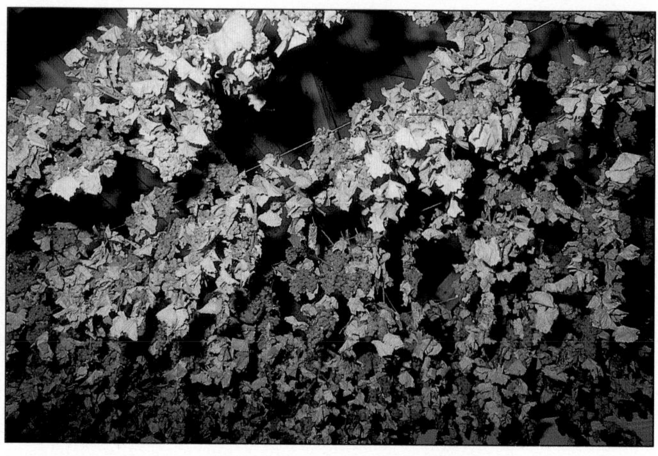

Hung from the rafters to dry, the grapes that will make the *vin de paille*.

André et Mireille Tissot

Owner Family Tissot. **Address** Montigny-lès-Arsures, 39600 Arbois - Tel. 03.84.66.08.27 Fax 03.84.66.25.08. **Open** Every day, 8:00-12:00 and 14:00-19:00. **Spoken** English. **Credit cards** Visa, Eurocard, MasterCard.

The Tissot family has a large 23-hectare expanse of vines in many beautiful vineyards favorable to growing two typical grapes of the Jura, Poulsard and Savagnin, red and white respectively, and in such reputable sites as Les Bruyères. If you visit the domaine during the harvest, you can see the cellar where the Tissots' *vin de paille* is aged. Hung from the rafters or spread out on straw mats, whence the name of the wine, the bunches of grapes are left to dry slowly: the water in them evaporates, thus concentrating their sugar and aromatic elements to yield an unparalleled liquorous wine.

The '93 straw wine (115 F for half-bottle), naturally vinified without artificial yeast, underwent fermentation of a year and a half. It has an intense bouquet of quince, its taste very concentrated, caramelly sweet, long and persistent. Of the traditional wines, taste the '94 white Arbois Sélection (44 F), a blend of 75% Chardonnay and 25% Savagnin: buttery, powerful backbone, lingering taste.

Our choice The '89 yellow Arbois (165 F). Bouquet already open and spicy; deep, full flavor opening up with curry, very long on the palate. The beautiful result of a blend of grapes from different parcels: the Les Bruyères slopes contribute maturity and power; the La Vasée marls, finesse and acidity. To be cellared.

Reception Marvelous, by a member of the family, all in love with their work.

How to get there *(Map 8): From Arbois head toward Besançon. After 2km, turn right direction Montigny. Just before the village church, turn left. Signposted.*

Jacques Tissot and his son, Philippe.

Jacques Tissot

Owner Jacques Tissot. **Address** 39 rue de Courcelles, 39600 Arbois - Tel. 03.84.66.14.27 Fax 03.84.66.24.88. **Open** Every day, 9:00-12:00 and 14:00-19:00. **Spoken** English, German. **Credit cards** Visa, Eurocard, MasterCard.

Rotund, garrulous, his cap ever present, Jacques Tissot is a colorful figure in Arbois. He has two "secrets", which he willingly reveals: his beautiful cellars full of ageing casks in the center of town where Louis Pasteur carried out his pioneering experiments in wine fermentation, and his old *cuvées* of Trousseau and yellow wines which he meticulously ages before making them available.

Jacques Tissot likes wines of character, such as his blend of Chardonnay and Savagnin used to make a regional specialty, the *blanc typé* with the "yellow" taste (65 F), beautifully round and balanced; the '94 Poulsard Arbois (40 F), a good example of the appellation; a smoky, licorice wine in the Pupillin appellation (45 F); and a powerful yellow wine (155 F for the 1988). Tissot's liquorous, very spicy '93 *vin de paille* (120 F for half-bottle), evokes spice cake, licorice, and white fruit.

This *vigneron* ages simpler wines with similar exactitude. The 1994 Chardonnay, for example, (44 F), whose minerally bouquet is softened by a more flowery taste.

Our choice The '93 Savagnin (70 F). Vinified without the oxidation induced in yellow wines. Powerful, waxy bouquet; full-bodied, well structured on the palate, with a hint of curry. Beautifully fresh. Can be drunk now.

Reception In the tasting room, usually presided over by charming Madame Tissot.

How to get there *(Map 8): From the center of Arbois, 500 meters on left going toward Louis Pasteur's house. Tasting room on left, clearly indicated.*

Pierre Overnoy, the soul of Poulsard.

Pierre Overnoy

Owner Pierre Overnoy. **Address** Rue du Ploussard, 39600 Pupillin - Tel. 03.84.66.14.60. **Open** By appointment.

The Jura's traditional Poulsard is pronounced "Ploussard" in Pupillin, which you should know because the sign at the entrance to the village proclaims that it is the world's capital of the grape variety.

Pierre Overnoy makes his wines in the traditional manner, plowing the soil completely, refusing to use chemical fertilizers, adding no yeasts during fermentation or sulphur during the harvest or bottling; he neither fines nor clarifies his wines. They are thus "living" wines, constantly developing; they mature badly in improper cellars but in good bottle-ageing conditions they age beautifully. They must be decanted before serving.

We especially liked the 1990 Ploussard Arbois Pupillin (48 F) for its smoky bouquet, fruity, deep flavor, delicate tannins, and its elegant, persistent structure: it should not be drunk too cool. Overnoy's '87 yellow wine (160 F) is full-bodied but delicate.

Our choice The '89 Arbois Pupillin Savagnin (148 F, sale limited to 4 bottles): very sweet bouquet, toasty, spicy; graceful, delicate, vigorous on palate. Very fat and soft, beautiful aromatic notes of curry and roasted coffee. The most outstanding wine in the Jura today.

Reception Charming, attentive; Pierre Overnoy enthusiastically explains the concept of his wine.

How to get there *(Map 8): In front of the Arbois church, take D246 to Pupillin. The cellar is in the center of the village, marked by a sign.*

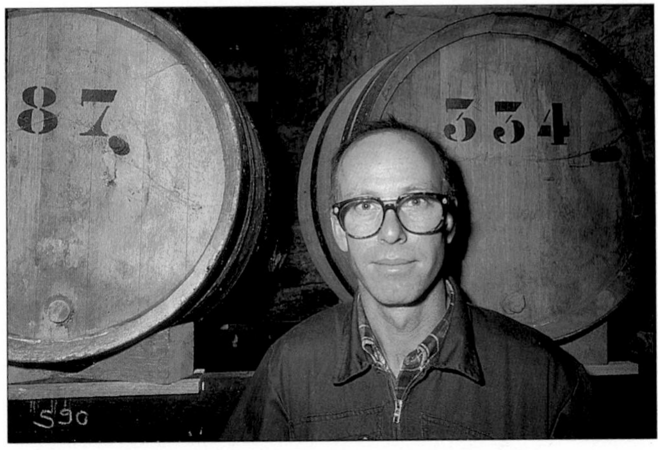

Jean Berthet-Bondet.

Domaine Berthet-Bondet

Owner Jean Berthet-Bondet. **Address** 39210 Château-Chalon - Tel. 03.84.44.60.48 Fax 03.84.44.61.13. **Open** By appointment. **Spoken** English. **Credit cards** Visa, Eurocard, MasterCard.

An agricultural engineer specializing in ageing wines, Jean Berthet-Bondet planted his vineyard here following his training with Jean Macle (see next page). Far from copying the wines of his former boss, Berthet-Bondet turns out wines of decidedly different styles although the two winemakers share a common passion for the importance of vineyard sites. Jean Berthet chose his on the compact, marly soils of Les Dames.

He systematically seeks wines with a yellow taste, even his Côtes-du-Jura, which are aged in casks without *ouillage,* or replacement of evaporated wine. He likes explosive bouquets, as with his '92 Savagnin (77 F), which is aged in casks without *ouillage* for three years. His '93 Côtes-du-Jura (47 F) is certainly a *blanc typé* but without a false yellow taste; its pear overtones are predominant, while its crispness keeps it fresh. This winery also makes a good *macvin*, an apéritif specialty of the Jura blending grape juice with *marc* grape brandy. It is very fat, almost liquorous, but well balanced.

Our choice The '89 yellow Château-Chalon (165 F). Intense bouquet of glazed citrus, spices; enticing attack, lovely extract, full-bodied, rich, hints of spice, great length and finesse. Some bottle age.

Reception In the Savagnin ageing cellar.

How to get there *(Map 8): From Arbois via N83 towards Lons. 18km after Poligny, turn left toward Voiteur, then Château-Chalon. The winery is at the top of the village, clearly indicated.*

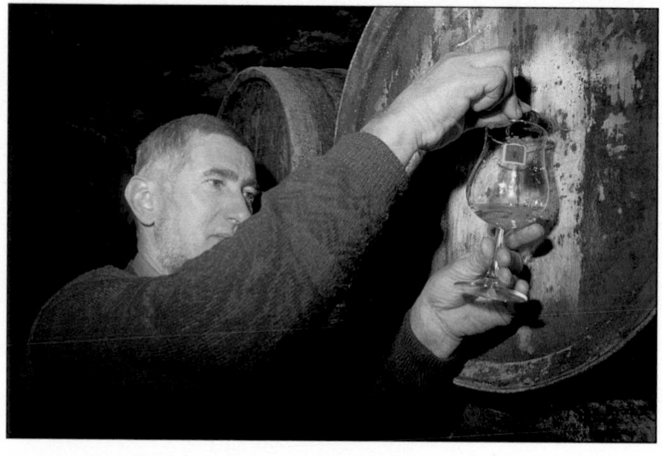

Jean Macle at the *guillette.*

Jean Macle

Owner Jean Macle. **Address** Rue de la Roche, 39210 Château-Chalon - Tel. 03.84.85.21.85 Fax 03.84.85.27.38. **Open** Every day by appointment.

Called the *dzi* in Arbois and *guillette* in Château-Chalon, it is the small horn taster with which the winemaker tastes the wine from the barrel and follows the ageing of yellow wine. We accompanied Jean Macle at various *guillette* tastings of wines soon to be made available. His '94 Côtes-du-Jura (about 45 F), from Chardonnay with 10% Savagnin, has a delicate bouquet, a powerful taste, rich and full of extract, almost tannic, with beautiful overtones of mint, aniseed, and citrus. It has great length on the palate. The wine is made according to the techniques special to the Jura: the two varietals age separately, without *ouillage* (wine evaporated through the oak is not replaced) but they are protected from oxidation by the veil of yeast which forms on the surface during fermentation.

Our choice The '90 Château-Chalon yellow wine (about 170 F): pure, fine bouquet (spice and Oriental *kamoun*), still closed. Concentrated, delicate flavor, very long, big structure. Low acidity will make it mature more rapidly than the '89 (170 F). For Jean Macle's faithful customers, note that you can begin to drink the '88s and '85s; the '87 needs some bottle age, but the '86s and '83s should still be cellared. All should be opened 24 hours before serving.

Reception Excellent and competent, usually by Jean Macle or his wife, in a room reserved for tasting.

How to get there *(Map 8): From Arbois via N83 towards Lons. 18km after Poligny, turn left towards Voiteur, then Château-Chalon. The winery is at the center of the village, indicated by arrows and a sign.*

Luc Boilley.

Luc et Sylvie Boilley

Owners Luc and Sylvie Boilley. **Address** 39380 Chissey-sur-Loue - Tel. 03.84.37.64.43 Fax 03.84.37.71.21. **Open** Every day, 9:00-12:00, on the afternoon by appointment. **Spoken** English, German, Spanish. **Credit cards** Visa, Eurocard, MasterCard.

Luc and Sylvie Boilley's necklace of vines sparkles up and down the Côte du Jura appellation. But they pay special attention to their vineyard in the north, which they are attempting to revitalize. The vines there are unusual in that they are planted *en foule*, with white and red grapes mixed together.

Of the Boilleys' many wines, take note of the '95 Chardonnay (38 F): smooth and full-bodied; the '89 yellow wine (145 F), with concentration and finesse, but it needs bottle age; and the '92 Côtes-du-Jura Flor (62 F). From their vines at Champagne-sur-Loue, the latter is a blend of white Savagnin and Chardonnay with red Poulsard and Trousseau; a white wine, it is pressed immediately after the harvest so as not to take on the color of the red-grape skins. The wine is, however, lightly tinged with pink. It is flowery, delicate, and pure on the nose, with an ample, rich taste and toastiness.

Our choice Two Savagnins from overripe grapes. The '94 (54 F) is ample and powerful, very full-bodied and fine, with pleasant, lingering overtones of very ripe grapes. The '92 Cuvée Sainte-Catherine, picked on November 25, reflects the late harvest in its beautiful overtones of fresh mushrooms due to *botrytis*. The taste is lively and appealing, with a touch of white pepper lingering on the palate. Can be drunk now.

Reception Helpful and attentive.

How to get there *(Map 8): From Dôle to Arc-et-Senans via D7. In Chissey, take the road to Mouchard. The cellar is on the left (signposted).*

The curious sculpted faces in the cellar.

Cellier des Chartreux

Owner Family Pignier. **Address** 39570 Montaigu - Tel. 03.84.24.24.30 Fax 03.84.47.46.00. **Open** From Monday to Sunday morning, 8:00-12:00 and 13:30-19:00 **Spoken** English, German. **Credit cards** Visa, Eurocard, MasterCard.

The principal vineyards of the Jura lie north of Lons-le-Saunier, yet the growers in the south should not be overlooked, even if their labels bear the generic Côtes-du-Jura appellation. The wines here, very different from those in the north, come from vines grown on soils with more limestone or blue marls, favoring white grapes. Chardonnay is the predominant grape variety in the Pignier family's vineyard.

The Pigniers are the seventh generation of Montaigu's oldest winegrowing family, who have been in the village since 1794. They occupy the childhood home of Rouget de l'Isle, who was a *vigneron* here before he became famous as the composer of *La Marseillaise*.

Their wines are typically marked by strong, but beautiful, acidity and are aged at length in casks in the cellar, which was built by Carthusian monks in the 13th century, thus the name of the vineyard.

Our choice The '93 Cellier des Chartreux Côtes-du-Jura (42 F). Aged in oak casks and barrels for three years: fresh and lively, with bouquet of yellow flowers and gun flint; lingering on the palate, with notes of hazelnuts and irises. Long, persistent, clean finish. Can be drunk now.

Reception See the beautiful cellar, built in 1225 by Carthusian monks.

How to get there *(Map 8): Leave Lons heading for Oyonnax. Montaigu is on the right, just after the large slope. The cellar is on the village square, on the right.*

The old sign of the Clavelin vineyard.

Hubert Clavelin et Fils

Owners Hubert Clavelin and sons. **Address** Rue du Serin, Le Vernois, 39210 Voiteur - Tel. 03.84.25.31.58 Fax 03.84.25.35.27. **Open** From Monday to Sunday midday 8:00-12:00 and 14:00-19:00.

The so-called "English" bottle holding 62 centiliters and made by the Vieille-Loye glassworks in the 19th century became famous after Abbot Paul Clavelin insisted on this unusual size for his wines. As was the case for the words *godillot* and *poubelle*, *clavelin* became the accepted word for the bottle used exclusively for Jura's yellow wine. Representing the present generation of the long family line, Patrick Clavelin describes the bottle as having "more stomach than backside."

Apart from our choice, we enjoyed his yellow wines. The '89 (128 F) is delicate on the nose, opening out with a robust, powerful taste, full-bodied and concentrated. Decanted several hours before serving, it blossoms with an orange-like bouquet.

The '90 Château-Chalon yellow wine (145 F) is more powerful on the nose, with a powerful taste. Bottle age is indispensable.

Our choice The '93 white Côte-du-Jura (36 F). A vin typé, very marked by the special vinification of Jura wines in contact with air, protected by a veil of yeasts which keeps the wines from oxidizing completely. From Chardonnay and Savagnin vines which are planted together, *en foule*, the wine is delicate and minerally. Can be drunk now.

Reception See the beautiful ageing cellars.

How to get there *(Map 8): From Poligny to Lons via the Route des Vins (D57, then D70). The cellar is in the center of Le Vernois, on the left, marked by a sign.*

Michel Geneletti.

Michel Geneletti

Owner Michel Geneletti. **Address** Rue de l'Église 39570 L'Étoile - Tel. 03.84.47.46.25 Fax 03.84.47.38.18. **Open** From Monday to Saturday, 9:00-12:00 and 14:00-18:00. **Spoken** German.

It is generally said that the appellation L'Etoile owes its name to the tiny star-like fossils which are often found in the soil here. But perhaps it might also refer to the five hills which surround the village that look like a large star. The name might also be a form of gratitude, for these hills endow the small appellation with a microclimate which protects the vines from the cold morning air blowing off the Jura plains.

Michel Geneletti pursues his lucky star in wines "of great finesse, lacy, not too *typés*, more like hazelnuts than nuts. L'Etoile is light rather than powerful." The two vintages available meet that description. There is a mineral trace in the '93 (42 F); while the '95 (about 40 F) has a a clean bouquet, and full-bodied but fresh taste. Geneletti also has a good *vin de paille* (99 F for half-bottle): liquorous but well balanced taste, evoking coffee, toast, mint.

Our choice The '88 and '89 yellow wines (148 F and 146 F respectively). The '88 has an intense bouquet, a delicate, rich flavor with minerally, spicy notes, and length on the palate. It is more mature than the '89: powerful bouquet; structured, strong, spicy taste, following through to the finish. The '89 needs more bottle age.

How to get there *(Map 8): From Arbois towards Lons via N83. 24kms after Poligny, turn right towards L'Etoile (careful, it's a sharp bend). The cellar is at the entrance to the village, on the right, indicated by a large sign.*

Calligraphy exercise in the Montbourgeau cellar.

Domaine de Montbourgeau

Owner Jean Gros. **Address** 39570 L'Étoile - Tel. 03.84.47.32.96 Fax 03.84.24.41.44. **Open** Every day, 9:00-12:00 and 14:00-19:00. **Credit cards** Visa, Eurocard, MasterCard.

Jean Gros is a legend in L'Etoile and today his daughter, Nicole, is carrying on his work.

Wines from the Domaine de Montbourgeau are blended according to the winery's needs, drawn off barrel by barrel while respecting the ageing of each.

When they are available, look for the special white wines, which are made from Chardonnay, Savagnin, and Poulsard jointly, and then aged on their lees to confer full body and smoothness. Montbourgeau's '94 white L'Etoile (40 F) reveals a delicate bouquet and a fleshy, silky flavor, lingering on the palate. The '93 Cuvée Spéciale (49 F), aged on the lees, is more open, enticing, ample, and smooth in taste, with dense, fine extract and length on the palate. Nicole Gros' '90 yellow wine (150 F) offers an attractive, fine bouquet with a delicate taste of glazed fruit and oranges, and a long, spicy finish.

Our choice The '92 straw wine (105 F for half-bottle). From 20% Poulsard, 20% Savagnin, and 60% Chardonnay: powerful bouquet, some sweetness and spice cake. Ample on the palate, still closed but will soon open up with toast, nutmeg, a trace of mint, very fresh. Persistent finish. Bottle age but it can be drunk now.

Reception By a competent and kind winemaker in a pleasant tasting room.

How to get there *(Map 8): From Arbois towards Lons via N83. 24km after Poligny, turn right towards L'Etoile (careful, it is in a sharp curve). Go through the village. The cellar is at the exit from the village, on the right, with arrows.*

LANGUEDOC

9
Villefranche-de-Rouergue
Colombies
Rodez
Palmas
Laissac
Séverac-le-Château
La Primaude
Ségur
Vézins-de-Lévézou
Le Massegros
Rieupeyroux
Sauvensa
Baraqueville
Pont-de-Salars
Bois-du-Four
La Fouillade
La Salvetat-Peyralès
Naucelle
Salles-Curan
St-Beauzély
Aguessac
Cassagnes-Bégonhès
Laguépie
Mirandol-Bourgnounac
Pampelonne
Bouloc
Millau
Monestiés
Tanus
Villefranche-de-Panat
Aveyron
St-Georges-de-Luzençon
Carmaux
St-Jean-Delnous
Réquista
La Cavalerie
Blaye-les-M.
Noailles
St-Rome-de-Tarn
St-Rome-de-Cernon
L'Hospitalet-du-Larzac
Valderiès
Valence-d'Albigeois
Vabres-l'Abbaye
Roquefort-s.-Soulzon
Marssac-s.-Tarn
Albi
St-Juery
St-Affrique
Plaisance
Ambialet
St-Félix-de-Sorgues
Cornus
Villefranche-d'Albigeois
St-Sernin-s.-Rance
Alban
Cadalen
Petit-St-Jean
Fondamente
Teillet
Montfranc
Camarès
Ceilhes-et-Rocozels
Lombers
Montdragon
Le Masnau-Massuguiès
Belmont-s.-Rance
Fayet
Réalmont
Montredon-Labessonnié
Viane
Brusque
Avène
Lacaze
Murat-s.-Vèbre
Tarn
St-Paul-Cap-de-Joux
Roquecourbe
Vabre
Lacaune
Lunas
Lacrouzette
Cambon-et-Salvergues
Brassac
St-Gervais-s.-Mare
Bédarieux
Puylaurens
Castres
Le Bez
Valdurenque
Anglès
Hérépian
Soual
Labruguière
Mazamet
Laurens
Roquebrun
Labastide-Rouairoux
St-Pons-de-Thomières
Murviel-lès-B.
Revel
Dourgne
Aussillon
Courniou
Cessenon
St-Amans-Soult
Rieussec
Cazouls-lès-Béziers
Les Martys
St-Chinian
Cébazan
Cuxac-Cabardès
Mas-Cabardès
Lespinassière
Aigues-Vives
Saissac
Caunes-Minervois
Cruzy
Maureilhan
Castelnaudary
Brousses-et-Villaret
Peyriac-Minervois
Capestang
Villepinte
Olonzac
Nissan-lez-E.
Conques-s.-O.
Ginestas
Alzonne
Aigues-Vives
Coursan
Bram
Carcassonne
Trèbes
Canal du Midi
Narbonne
Montréal
Lavalette
Lézignan-Corbières
Narbonne-Plage
Fanjeaux
Leuc
Capendu
Rouffiac-d'Aude
Ferrals-les-Corb.
Alaigne
Gruissan
Gruissan-Plage
Moulin-Neuf
St-Hilaire
St-Laurent-de-la-C.
Portel
Limoux
Lairière
Sigean
St-Benoît
Ajac
Aude
Durban-Corbières
Port-la-Nouvelle
Félines-Termenès
Lanet
Ste-Colombe-s.-l'Hers
Couiza
Arques
Villeneuve-les-Corbières
Cap Leucate
Mouthoumet
Espéraza
Puivert
Leucate
Tuchan
Quillan
Soulatgé
Port-Leucate
Bugarach
Cubières-s.-Cinoble
Vingrau
Salses
St-Paul-de-Fenouillet
Port-Barcarès
Belcaire
Axat
Maury
St-Hippolyte
Rivesaltes
Caudiès-de-F.
Ste-Colombe-
Ansignan
Le Barcarès
Estagel
Agly
A61-E80
A9
N88
N112
N113
N126
N9
D911
D999
D902
D622
D613
D611
D118
D620
D623
D629
D600
D81
D25
D10
D903
D91
D86
D83
D89
D63
D907
D74
D607
D5
D11
D610
D14
D16
D36
D12
D922
D908
D7
D8
D709
D627
D168
D332
D1118
D83
D117
414 415
426
32
19 20
12 13
419 424 34
17
425
4
421
393
7
28
402
403
5 6
420
422
423
399
23 24 25
26
394
29
418
9
406
11
396
38
33
398
400
37
36
401
27
417
397
416
395
35

10
La Capelle
Ispagnac
Le Pont-de-Montvert
St-Maurice-de-Ventalon
Génolhac
St-Paul-le-Jeune
La Maison-Neuve
Vallon-Pont-d'Arc
La Malène
St-Chély-du-Tarn
Florac
St-Julien-d'Arpaon
Sauvas
Les Vignes
Le Mazel
Ste-Cécile-d'Andorge
Bessèges
Barjac
Laval-S
La Parade
Barre-des-Cévennes
St-Ambroix
St-Germain-de-Calberte
La Grand-Combe
Le Rozier
Meyrueis
St-Étienne-Vallée-Française
St-Martin-de-Val.
Navacelles
La Roque-Ste-Marguerite
St-André-de-Valborgne
Salindres
Lussan
St-Jean-du-Gard
Alès
Seynes
Trèves
L'Estréchure
L'Espérou
Valleraugue
Anduze
Vézénobres
Foissac
St-Jean-du-Bruel
Lasalle
Nant
Uzès
Sauclières
St-Hippolyte-du-Fort
Lédignan
Alzon
Le Vigan
Montdardier
Ganges
Sauve
St-Chaptes
Pompignan
Quissac
Montmirat
La Calmette
Le Caylar
St-Maurice-Navacelles
St-Bauzille-de-Putois
St-Mamert-du-Gard
Marguerittes
Nîmes
Causse-de-la-Selle
Roqueredonde
St-Pierre-de-la-Fage
Tréviers
Calvisson
St-Martin-de-Londres
Sommières
Galargues
Boisseron
Viols-le-Fort
Lodève
Vergèze
Les Matelles
Vauvert
Aniane
Castries
Lunel
Aimargues
Montarnaud
St-Gille
Clermont-l'Hérault
Gignac
Montpellier
Marsillargues
Vendargues
Juvignac
Mauguio
Aigues-Mortes
Albaro
St-Jean-de-Védas
Faugères
Paulhan
Fabrègues
Pérols
La Grande-Motte
Le Grau-du-Roi
Sylvéréal
Villeveyrac
Gigean
Palavas-les-Flots
Roujan
Montagnac
Pointe de l'Espiguette
Pézenas
Frontignan
Stes-Maries-de-la-M
Mèze
Golfe d'Aigues-Mortes
Montblanc
St-Thibéry
Sète
Florensac
Béziers
Bessan
Marseillan
Vias
Sérignan
Agde
Le Cap-d'Agde
Vendres
Cap d'Agde
Valras-Plage
St-Pierre-s.-Mer
Gard 30
Hérault 34
GOLFE DU LION

L A N G U E D O C

INTRODUCTION

Fanning out from seashore to mountains, richly dotted with abbeys and citadels, few regions can boast such a great diversity of landscapes, country paths, colors, and scenery as Languedoc. And its wines? The common notion that the Appellation d'Origine Contrôlée Languedoc is accorded to vineyards of similar quality should be forgotten. The traveller who comes here in the spring and winds through the small roads leading from the Roussillon border to the western portals of Nîmes, from the foothills of the Cévennes to the Mediterranean, has the impression of an ever unfolding panorama. In the Corbières and the Minervois, when the vines begin lazily to awaken from winter, it is an unforgettable spectacle to see them suddenly burst in an explosion of celadon green. In fewer than sixty miles the vine can be seen in all its elements, in an infinity of different climates in which a vineyard, its soil and exposition, can be helped or hindered by winds off the sea and the rocky hills. To this diversity of climates must be added a greater diversity still: that of the continual progress being made in the leading vineyards of Languedoc, contributing a further reason for visiting them attentively, listening to the men and women who make the wines, and observing their environment: In the Minervois, from chapel to lock on the Canal du Midi; along the ancient Aquitaine Road that snakes through the Lézignan region and leads to the historic sites of the Cistercian Fontfroide Abbey and the medieval village of Lagrasse; high up in the hills of Corbières, its fortresses perched atop rocky spurs--Queribus, Aguilar, Duilhac, which were major sites in the Albigensian crusades; in the tranquillity of the seashore, its salt flats like a patchwork of vines, lagoons, and indigo lakes. Languedoc, too, means discovering the rare villages of protected architecture--Gruissan, Bages, Peyriac-sur-Mer: breaths of oxygen on a seafront asphyxiated by high-rise residences. Envisioning the Roman patricians opening up the Via Domitia, towering over the Narbonne flatland vineyards from the summit of the Massif de la Clape. Humming a Brassens song on the banks of Lake Thau, facing Sète and a platter of oysters from Bouzigues. Yet Languedoc is much more still. And if wine were only a pretext to explore this charming region? Its winemakers would understand: They are the first to love their region as much as their wine, to tell you of a marvelous place to see, a favorite restaurant, or an inn where they like to send their friends.

LANGUEDOC APPELLATIONS

The search for improved quality which has revolutionized Languedoc viticulture began some twenty years ago, a time when the golden age of the region's *gros rouge*, mass-produced, cheap "plonk", was dying a slow death. Under pressure from the European Union, winegrowers have uprooted thousands of hectares of inferior vines, a practice which continues today and subsidized by the EU. New AOC areas have been designated, favoring the superior hillside vineyards instead of the vast plains of the past. Grape varieties have been chosen with a view to greater quality, and yields allowed per hectare have been reduced. In 1996, Languedoc had 308,000 hectares of vines, 35,600 of which were Appellation Contrôlée. The race for quality had taken on the speed of a marathon. Thus wine lovers setting out to explore the vineyards of Languedoc will doubtless find their judgments varying between admiration and vexation. Admire the vineyards in the midst of modernization, with the arrival of new domains eliciting formidable competition among the winegrowers: whether natives of the region or new arrivals from the cities (often with limited means, these *vignerons* are building the future of Languedoc around Mediterranean wines of genuine quality. Admiration is in order, too, for the resurrected vineyard regions which had been abandoned and whose excellence today is incontested. Vexation sets in, however, when we see that today there is still much too much Coteaux-du-Languedoc, Corbières, and Minervois being produced, the best of them drowned in a sea of wines sold for less than some *vins de pays*. It is also unfortunate that this region is in the hands of enormous groups of *coopératives*, who are only too happy to supply wine in volume to large supermarkets. The coming twenty-five years, which will usher in the new generation of pioneers, will be decisive. In the meantime, let's not deprive ourselves of the good wines, of which 89% are red, made by *vignerons* who have set their sights on quality.

The second largest appellation of the Languedoc with 8255 hectares, the Coteaux-du-Languedoc vineyards occupy a long stretch from Nîmes to Narbonne, along the ancient Via Domitia between the Mediterranean and the Cévennes foothills. Twelve vineyard regions are entitled to mention their name on the label, in addition to the Coteaux-du-Languedoc appellation. This is the result of a decisive policy aimed at delineating the various *terroirs*, and even individual wines. Of them, the most sought after is incontestably Pic-Saint-Loup, north of Montpellier, whose specialty is beautifully structured Syrahs, with no dryness. Red wines represent 75% of the production, from Carignan, Cinsault, Grenache, Mourvèdre, and principally Syrah, a Rhône Valley grape variety which is being extensively planted here. Quite solid wines marked by their Mediterranean identity, they can vary from pleasant wines for everyday enjoyment, somewhat rustic and best in their youth, to ambitious wines, often carefully aged in barrels, which can be cellared for four to seven years. There is a small amount of white wine made, dry, half-dry, or *moelleux*, in the Clairette-du-Languedoc appellation.

Faugères and Saint-Chinian are two wines from the vineyards north of Béziers, west of the Coteaux-du-Languedoc, planted in soils of schist and limestone. In the foothills of Mount Le Caroux (3273 feet in altitude), Saint-Chinian is planted with

2890 hectares of vines, largely dominated by Carignan. The *coopératives* often vinify the wine by means of carbonic maceration in order to offer a fruity wine, easy to drink. On the other end of the spectrum, several private wineries make wines which can age well in bottle; they have great extract, backbone, and a rustic style, all of which is more in keeping with the vineyards. In Faugères with its 1695 hectares, Syrah is a beautiful wine, with distinctive aromatic finesse and velvety extract. In the past, Faugères was known for its brandy, which is making a comeback today.

On the slopes of the Montagne Noire in the foothills of the Cévennes, the Minervois appellation occupies a vast amphitheater facing due south, high over the Vallée de l'Aude and the Canal du Midi. Its 5130 hectares of vines are planted on terraces between the *causse*, limestone plateaux, and the *garrigue* scrubland, which is dotted with almond trees, century-old olive trees and majestic cypresses.

96% of the wines from these arid terraces of pebbles, sandstone, schist, and limestone are red: generous, softly tannic, long, and quite dry. There is also a small promising production of a late-harvest white wine, the Minervois Noble.

Corbières, Languedoc's largest appellation with 14,160 hectares and 94% red grapes, lies at the center of a rectangle formed by Carcassonne, Narbonne, Perpignan, and Quillan, in a succession of very varied vineyards of complex geology, including soils of schist, limestone, sandstone, and marl. Reflecting this diversity, the appellation includes eleven distinct vineyard regions (the vineyard origin is not always easy to pinpoint in the wine) lying between Hautes Corbières, Corbières Centrales, and Corbières Maritimes. Today inferior in quality to Coteaux-du-Languedoc wines, Corbières remains very heterogenous: the best, long-lived red wines come from near Lézignan in the Boutenac vineyards; around the village of Moux, they offer greater acidity and natural fruitiness; in the hillside vineyards, the wines gain in freshness and finesse; wines from the ocean vineyards are charmingly delicate and soft, with the reds characterized by solid alcoholic structure.

With a name like that of a Belgian comic-strip character, Fitou's 2500 hectares hold the oldest red AOC rating in the Languedoc, awarded in 1948. Fitou is a Janus-like appellation composed of vineyards on the coast facing Lakes La Palme and Leucate, and others in the Corbières toward Tuchan and Paziols, on the boundary of the Aude *département* and the Catalan region. Resting on its old laurels, Fitou no longer has the status it once did. Many producers, led by the *coopératives*, make it into a fruity wine for summer, although it should be the quintessence of a Mediterranean wine: powerful, concentrated, solid, with long ageing potential.

West of Carcassonne, Malpère and Cabardès are the most westerly appellations of the Languedoc, still labelled Vins Délimités de Qualité Supérieure, VDQS, the stepping stone to AOC status. Planted on the last foothills of the Montagne Noire, 330 hectares of vines in Cabardès and 550 hectares in Malpère ripen in the sunshine of the Midi but are also affected by the rainfall of the Southwest: 28 inches per year compared with 19 inches in Narbonne. This double influence is reflected in a large panoply of Southwestern grape varieties--Merlot, Cabernet, Cot--along with Mediterranean grapes: Syrah and Grenache. These vineyards produce several good simple reds and rosés that are reasonably priced.

Four appellations apply to the Limoux vineyards of 1230 hectares south of Carcassonne. The oldest appellation (1938) and the most famous is Blanquette-de-

Limoux, a sparkling white wine from the Mauzac grape, which is made by classic vinification with a second fermentation in bottle; and by the ancestral method involving spontaneous fermentation in bottle, the addition of sugar, and an alcoholic content of less than 7%. Crémant-du-Limoux, promoted to AOC in 1990, is made with less Mauzac and more Chardonnay and Chenin (40% for each), yielding a more vigorous "creaming" wine. The Limoux appellation was created in 1993, designating a non-sparkling white wine made from a large proportion of Chardonnay, vinified and aged in oak barrels. It is one of the rare southern Chardonnays of elegance.

A vast number of wines are labelled *vins de pays* in the Languedoc. This is either because the authorities have neglected or refused AOC status for a *vin de pays* vineyard or because the winemaker wishes the freedom to plant certain grape varieties which are forbidden by AOC in the Languedoc. Most *vins de pays* come from the Hérault *département*. Winemakers are free to produce a varietal *vin de pays* from Chardonnay, Sauvignon, Cabernet, or Merlot. These are of limited interest, but sometimes they are wines equal or superior to those bearing the AOC label.

BUYING WINE IN THE LANGUEDOC

While the red wines of the Languedoc today have won the wine lover's recognition, the rosés, and to a lesser degree, the white wines are still far from noteworthy: Be careful. In the 1996 vintage the region was hard hit by bad weather and torrential rains. The best wines are reds, which are round, mouth-filling, grapey. Their extract lends them little concentration. The majority of the Coteaux-du-Languedoc, Minervois, and Corbières should thus be drunk within two years of the harvest. The '95s that are still available are more appealing, with good structure and maturity. You can find good classic wines for 20 F to 30 F. The prices for special, barrel-aged wines quickly attain greater heights, usually around 50 F, while some, with a Syrah base, may attain 100 F, although this is not always justified.

***A TABLE* WITH LANGUEDOC WINES**

The white wines from the coastal vineyards--Picpoul de Pinet, Coteaux-du-Languedoc, Corbières--are ideal companions for the strongly iodized oysters from Bouzigues and rock fish. The red wines, evoking the piney scrubland, red and black berries, and somewhat rustic in taste, are excellent with the new Mediterranean recipes based on herbs and spices. Barrel-aged wines with two to three years' bottle age make good accompaniments for hearty autumn and winter dishes: preserved duck and goose, meat stews, red meat, and game.

AGDE

1 - HOTEL-RESTAURANT - **La Tamarissière**: *Lieu-dit " La Tamarisière ", 34300 Agde. Tel. 04.67.94.20.87 Fax 04.67. 21.38.40. Restaurant closed Sun. evening and Mon. (except lunch in summer), from 3/15 to 6/15 and from 9/15 to 1/2.* 4 km south of Agde, facing the Hérault canal: a lovely, renovated hotel with bucolic garden. We haven't tried the restaurant recently, though it's quite renowned. Attractive wine list, local wines at reasonable prices given the hotel's excellent standards. Menus: 155 to 350 F. A la carte: around 400 F. 27 rooms: 380 to 550 F.

BEZIERS

2 - RESTAURANT - **Le Framboisier**: *12 rue Boïeldieu, 34500 Béziers. Tel. 04.67. 49.90.00 Fax 04.67.28.06.73. Closed Sun. and Mon.* Masterly classical cuisine and an attractive list of regional wines. Reasonable prices. Menus: 180 to 380 F. A la carte: around 300 F.

3 - RESTAURANT - **Le Jardin**: *37 avenue Jean-Moulin, 34500 Béziers. Tel. 04.67.36.41.31 Fax 04.67.28.72.55. Closed Sun. evening, Mon. and 2 weeks for Mardi-Gras and the first 2 weeks in July.* Precise, fresh and seductive market-based cuisine and above all a wonderful offering of regional wines, some served by the glass. Menus: 115 to 295 F (children's menu: 65 F). A la carte: around 200 F.

CAPESTANG

4 - BED & BREAKFAST - **Domaine de la Redonde**: *Montels, 34310 Capestang. Tel. 04.67.93.31.82 Fax 04.67. 93.40.34.* A suite and a flat (for 2 or 4 persons) in a small castle that's typical of the plain of Béziers. Classic and elegant decor. Pool. From 400 to 500 F.

CARCASSONNE

5 - HOTEL-RESTAURANT - **Hôtel de la Cité, la Barbacane**: *Place Saint-Nazaire, 11000 Carcassonne. Tel. 04.68.25. 03.34 Fax 04.68.71.50.15. Closed November to April, Sunday evening and noon Monday (except July and August).* In the city, a palace with a Hollywood-Gothic character, in the manner of Viollet-le-Duc. Excellent welcome, first-rate comfort. The best table in the region. More than 300 wines from Languedoc and Roussillon (80 to 1,050 F) on a wine list that boasts 1,200 entries. Menus: 180 to 420 F. 26 rooms: 750 to 1,900 F.

6 - HOTEL-RESTAURANT - **Domaine d'Auriac**: *Route de Saint Hilaire BP 554, 11009 Carcassonne. Tel. 04.68.25. 72.22 Fax 04.68.47.35.54 e-mail: auriac@relaischateaux.fr. Closed 2/15 to 3/2 and 11/15 to 12/7. Hotel closed Sunday from 10/1 to 10/31 and Sunday and Monday from 11/1 to Easter. Restaurant closed Sunday from 10/1 to 10/31, Sunday evening and Monday from 11/1 to Easter.*

4 km from the walled city, a large and impressive house (Relais & Châteaux) in a park, bordering on a golf course. Elegant accommodations, flavorful cuisine served in the garden in summer. Menus: 190 to 390 F. 28 rooms: 400 to 1,500 F.

CAUNES-MINERVOIS

7 - HOTEL-RESTAURANT - **Hôtel d'Alibert**: *Place de la Mairie, 11600 Caunes-Minervois. Tel. 04.68.78.00.54. Closed Sun. evening and Mon.* From the outside, one doesn't expect to find the lovely Renaissance courtyard in this simple but comfortable house. Warm and informal welcome followed by fine regional and seasonal cooking (generous portions of cèpe-mushrooms and game). Fine selection of Minervois and Corbières: ask for the young proprietor's advice, he knows them like the back of his hand. Perfect menu at 120 F. Rooms: 220 to 320 F. Breakfast: 35 F.

ESPONDEILHAN

8 - HOTEL - **Château de Cabrerolles**: *34270 Espondeilhan. Tel. 04.67.39.21.79 Fax 04.67.39.21.05.* 10 km north of Béziers. A lovely bourgeois edifice set amidst the woods and vineyard, kept by a couple whose welcome is more than warm. A place to stay while navigating through the plain of Béziers and Faugères. Wise prices. 5 rooms: 320 to 480 F. 5 suites: 450 to 590 F. 5 apartments: 320 to 380 F.

FABREZAN

9 - HOTEL - **Le Clos des Souquets**: *Avenue de Lagrasse, 11200 Fabrezan. Tel. 04.68.43.52.61. Fax 04.68. 43.56.76. Closed 11/1 to 3/1.* For excursions in the Corbières, a little one-story hotel, soberly decorated, where prices are as low as the welcome is warm. Private pool for

some rooms. Daily menus, simple and informal. Short list of local wines. 5 rooms: 280 to 380 F.

FLORENSAC

10 - RESTAURANT - **Léonce**: *8 place de la République, 34510 Florensac. Tel. 04.67.77.03.05 Fax 04.67.77.88.89. Closed Sunday evening (except in July and August), Monday and from mid-February to mid-March, the last week in September and the first in October.* Excellent and innovative bourgeois cuisine, perfectly done. Charming welcome. Service and decor are burdensome. Interesting wine list, but disappointing for regional wines. Menus: 150 to 350 F. A la carte: around 350 F.

FONTJONCOUSE

11 - RESTAURANT - **L'Auberge du Vieux Puits**: *11360 Fontjoncouse. Tel. 04.68.44.07.37 Fax 04.68.44.08.31. Closed Sunday evening year-round, Monday except in July and August and from mid-January to mid-February.* Generous cuisine with a strong

southern accent. Generally attractive wine list, welcoming many Languedoc wines. Excellent welcome. Menus: 155 to 320 F.

HOMPS

12 - HOTEL-RESTAURANT - **Auberge de l'Arbousier**: *Route de Carcassonne, 11200 Homps. Tel. 04.68.91.11.24. Closed Wednesday, Sunday evening (low-season), from February 15 to March 15 and from November 10 to 27.* A former cellar along the canal du Midi, bright, with a tree-shaded terrace facing the canal. Simple regional cuisine and an attractive wine list counting 30 Languedoc wines, with a preference for Minervois. Menus: 80 to 205 F. Very quiet rooms from 210 to 250 F.

13 - HOTEL - **Le Clos des Muscats**: *Grand' Rue, 11200 Homps. Tel. 04.68.91.38.50 Fax 04.68.91.36.94. Closed in December and January.* Lovely village house with small yard and pool. Woodwork decor, very comfortable. 10 rooms: 300 to 680 F.

LATTÈS

14 - RESTAURANT - **Maison des vins du Languedoc**: *Mas Saporta, 34970 Lattès. Tel. 04.67.06.88.66. Closed noon Saturday and Sunday.* Good bistro with a vast selection of regional wines at heavenly prices. Wines sold in the cellar of the mas, open all week round. Menus: 79 to 140 F.

15 - HOTEL - **Mas de Couran**: *Route de Fréjorgues, 34972 Lattès. Tel. 04.67. 65.57.57 Fax 04.67.65.37.56.* 5 km from Montpellier. A large and impressive house built in the last century in a sumptuous park. Pool. 18 well-equipped rooms: 300 to 465 F.

LAURET

16 - HOTEL-RESTAURANT - **L'Auberge du Cèdre, domaine de Cazeneuve**: *34270 Lauret. Tel. 04.67.59.02.02 Fax 04.67.59.03.44. Closed January to March inclusive. Restaurant open weekends, by reservation for visitors.* Vast, beautiful family mansion in a mountain setting, that the name hardly suggests. 18 " friends' rooms ", simple and arranged to please visitors with 2, 3, or 4 beds. Informal group atmosphere. Good, colorful market-based cuisine served in a sunny old orangery. Good Pic-Saint-Loup wines at around 100 F. Menu: 130 F. Rooms: 100 F per person, 165 F for half board.

LIGNAN-SUR-ORB

17 - HOTEL-RESTAURANT - **Château de Lignan**: *34490 Lignan-sur-Orb. Tel. 04.67.37.91.47 Fax 04.67.37.99.25.* 7 km north of Béziers, a vast, beautiful edifice transformed into a hotel-restaurant with a seminary atmosphere. Wonderful seasonal cuisine, wine list coming into its own served by a competent wine waiter. A la carte: around 400 F. Fourty-six rooms: 400 to 650 F, three suites: 600 to 750 F.

MAGALAS

18 - RESTAURANT - **La Boucherie**: *Place*

de l'Eglise, 34480 Magalas. Tel. 04.67.36.20.82. Closed Sunday (except evenings in July and August) and Monday. A guenine butchery that welcomes " meat-lovers and their friends ". Copious and original, good-humored atmosphere. Nice list of local wines at reasonable prices. Menus: 52 (lunch weekdays) to 130 F.

MINERVE

19 - BED & BREAKFAST - **Les Aliberts**: *Monique and Pascal Bourgogne, 34210 Minerve. Tel. 04.68.91.81.72 Fax 04.68.91.22.95. By reservation.* A heart-warming stop in the Minervois. Lovely, restored 12th-century farm house surrounded by the garigue and vineyard that dominates the Minervois hills. Five bright, charming houses with garden or large private terrace. Household amenities of a luxurious vacation house. Large pool carved in the rock. Four-room unit: 2,000 F per weekend to 10,000 F per week in summer. Three rooms: 1,500 F per weekend to 6,500 F. Two rooms: 1,200 to

6,000 F. Low-season and according to availability, a room-suite: 400 F, breakfast included.

20 - HOTEL-RESTAURANT - **Le Relais Chantovent**: *34210 Minerve. Tel. 04.68. 91.14.18 Fax 04.68.91.81.99. Closed Monday and January to*

March. In a lovely village clinging to the rock, friendly regional cuisine with a view over Cesse canyon. Short list of Minervois. Menus: 95 to 200 F. Seven charming rooms scattered throughout the village, from 220 to 300 F.

MONTPELLIER

21 - RESTAURANT - **Le Jardin des Sens**: *11 avenue Saint-Lazare, 34000 Montpellier. Tel. 04.67.79.63.38. Closed Sunday.* A distinguished table offering a fine preparation of products, especially the sauces and jus, with a fondness for contrasting textures. Regional wines are well represented. Menus: 210 (lunch except Saturday) to 580 F.

22 - HOTEL - **Le Guilhem**: *18 rue Jean-Jacques Rousseau, 34000 Montpellier. Tel. 04.67.52.90.90 Fax 04.67. 60.67.67.* Centrally located hotel, in one of the old city's pedestrian areas (parking at the prefecture). Garden and view of the cathedral. Thirty-three rooms: 330 to 650 F. Breakfast on the terrace: 49 F.

NARBONNE

23 - RESTAURANT - **La Table Saint-Crés-**

cent: *Domaine de Saint-Créscent-le-Viel, 11100 Narbonne. Tel. 04.68.41.37.37 Fax 04.68.41.01.22. Closed Sunday evening and Monday.* In a beautiful 8th-century stone vaulted room, an excellent regional cuisine prepared by a very talented chef. Great quality for the price. The wine list was not complete for our visit, but seems off to a good start. Menus: 100 to 248 F. A la carte: around 200 F.

24 - HOTEL-RESTAURANT - **Hôtel du Languedoc, La Petite Cour**: *22 boulevard Gambetta, 11100 Narbonne. Tel. 04.68.65.14.74 Fax 04.68.65.81.48. Restaurant Tel 04.68.90.48.03 Fax 04.68.32.76.27. Restaurant closed Sunday from October to April.* Good regional gourmet cuisine, grand list of Corbières. Menus: 63 (lunch) to 105 F. Fourty rooms: 200 to 480 F.

25 - BED & BREAKFAST - **Domaine de l'Hospitalet**: *Route de Narbonne-Plage, 11100 Narbonne. Tel. 04.68.45.34.47. Reservations and rooms: l'Auberge des vignes Tel. 04.68.45.28.50.* A 60 ha seaside estate " created " by Jacques Ribourel, where wine plays the lead role in a vast tourist and cultural site composed of museums devoted to harnesses, collector's cars, telephones, fauna and flora, fossils, honey, cooperage,... Dining and guest rooms.

ORNAISONS

26 - HOTEL - **Le Relais du Val-d'Orbieu**: *D24, 11200 Ornaisons. Tel. 04.68.27.10.27 Fax 04.68.27.52.44.* In a vineyard between Narbonne and Lézignan: a perfectly quiet one-story hotel with a very professional welcome. High prices. Twenty rooms: 440 to 720 F. Swimming pool and tennis.

PALAJA

27 - BED & BREAKFAST - **La Ferme de la Sauzette**: *Route de Villefloure, Cazil-*

hac, 11570 Palaja. Tel. 04.68.79.81.32 Fax 04.68.79.65.99. A few kilometers from Carcassonne. An old farm surrounded by vines and fields offering five comfortable mansarded rooms. From 270 to 355 F. Possibility of dining in the evening (125 F, wine included).

PEYRIAC-MINERVOIS

28 - HOTEL-RESTAURANT - **Château de Violet**: *Route de Pépieux, 11160 Peyriac-Minervois. Tel. 04.68.78.11.44/04.68.78.10.42 Fax 04.68.78.30.01.* A 19th-century residence converted into a hotel. Vast rooms with old-fashioned charm, some with beautiful furniture (prefer the " chambre de l'archevêque "). The castle of Violet, run by Emilie Faussié, is also a good viticultural estate (especially for whites) that can be visited on

request. Menus: 150 to 250 F. Twenty rooms: 300 to 850 F.

PORTELS-LES-CORBIERES

29 - RESTAURANT - **Château de Lastours**: *11490 Portels-les-Corbières. Tel. 04.68.48.29.17.* A vast 700-ha estate that produces good Corbières, organizes 4 x 4 racing on the property, and offers a good vintner's table. Menu: 95 and 190 F.

SAINT-GUIRAUD

30 - RESTAURANT - **Le Mimosa**: *34725 Saint-Guiraud. Tel. 04.67.96.67.96 Fax 04.67.96.61.15. Closed in November, December, January and February, as well as Sunday evening (except July and August) and Monday (except holidays). By reservation.* Ten kilometers north of Clermont-l'Hérault. Shaded patio, refined decor, competent service, excellent and harmonious Mediteranean cuisine: a simple and pleasant location. The local wine list is superb, the best in the region. A must. Menus: 170 to 290 F.

SAINT-MARTIN-DE-LONDRES

31 - RESTAURANT - **Les Muscardins**: *19 route des Cévennes, 34380 Saint-Martin-de-Londres. Tel. 04.67.55. 75.90 Fax 04.67.55.70.28. Closed Monday, Tuesday, and in February.* Serious and imaginative kitchen-work, fine selection of local wines. Menus: 170 to 390 F A la carte: around 300 F.

SAINT-NAZAIRE DE LADAREZ

32 - RESTAURANT - **Domaine Borie La Vitarèle**: *34490 Saint-Nazaire-de-Ladarez. Tel. 04.67.89.50.43. By reservation. Open June to September, every day except Monday.* The rest of the year, weekends and holidays. Closed in September. In a little village house, a farm-inn kept by nice Saint-Chinianais winegrowers. Kind and informal, they receive in the kitchen and serve generous regional cuisine accompanied by wine from the property from 31 to 64 F. Menus: 95 to 150 F, children: 45 F.

SIGEAN

33 - HOTEL - **Château de Villefalse**: *Route de Narbonne, Le Lac, 11130 Sigean. Tel. 04.68.48.54.29 Fax 04.68.48. 34.37.* South of Narbonne, a luxurious hotel surrounded by a 100-hectare vineyard. Very professional welcome, great comfort, tranquility. Ten duplexes and fiveteen suites: 350 to 1,000 F. Pool.

SIRAN

34 - HOTEL-RESTAURANT - **La Villa d'Eléis**: *Avenue du Château, 34210 Siran.*

Tel. 04.68.91.55.98 Fax 04.68.91. 48.34. The new hotel-restaurant of the Minervois House of wines. A vast and lovely village farm house, extremely well-restored. The twelve rooms are vast, well-furnished, very comfortable, and look out on either the vineyard or the interior courtyard. Rooms from 350 to 800 F. The high-quality gourmet restaurant was, however, still trying to find its bearings during our visit in winter 96-97.

Exhaustive list of Minervois, at smart prices. Menus: 125 (weekdays) to 360 F (wine included). A la carte: around 300 F.

SOULATGE

35 - BED & BREAKFAST - **La Giraudasse**: *11350 Soulatgé. Tel. 04.68.45. 00.16.* Guest rooms in an 18th-century house situated near the Galamus gorges and the Cathar castles. Rooms: 260 F, breakfast included. Meals: 110 F, by reservation.

VILLENEUVE-LES-CORBIERES

36 - BED & BREAKFAST - **Domaine Lerys**: *Maguy and Alain Izard, avenue des Hautes Corbières, 11360 Villeneuve-les-Corbières. Tel. 04.68.45.95.47 Fax 04.68.45.86.11.* Two rooms in the village kept by good Fitou producers, recently arranged above the cellar, with small terrace. For two to four persons. 240 F per night for two, breakfast included.

37 - RESTAURANT - **Le Corbiérou**: *11360 Villeneuve-les-Corbières. Tel. 04.68. 45.83.05.* A rustic and informal village café-inn where vintners come for a simple meal. Game in season. A dozen Corbières and Fitou, mostly from the area. Menus: 67 to 170 F.

VILLESÈQUE-DES-CORBIÈRES

38 - BED & BREAKFAST - **Château Haut-Gléon**: *Villesèque-des-Corbières CD611, 11360 Durban. Tel. 04.68. 48.85.95 Fax 04.68.48.46.20. By reservation.* West of Sigean, a splendid estate restored in '93 with great taste and at great expense. Offering

six lovely guest rooms: bright, sober Mediteranean decor, seperate from the castle and worthy of the best accommodations in the region. Prices on request.

TO SEE

CANAL DU LUNCH

BOAT RIDE - **Boating on the canal du Lunch**: Boat rentals (no license required) by the week, weekend or day. One-way trips possible with divers destinations, depending on the company. **Minervois Cruisers**: *38 chemin des Patiasses, Le Somail, 11120 Ginestas. Tel. 04.68.46.28.52 Fax 04.68.46. 23.09.* **Locaboat-Plaisance**: *Port Occitanie, 11200 Argens-Minervois. Tel. 04.68.27. 03.33 Fax 04.68.27. 71.96.* **Luc Lines**: *BP2, 11220 Homps. Tel. 04.68.91.24.00 Fax 04.68.91.24.11.* **Connoisseurs**: *Port de Plaisance, 11800 Trèbes. Tel. 04.68.78.73.75 Fax 04.68.78.92.79.* 23 boats, rental by the week. **Crown Blue Line**: *Le Grand Bassin, BP21, 11401 Castelnaudary. Tel. 04.68.94.52.72 Fax 04.68.94.52.73 web: www.crownblueline.com - e-mail: boathols@crown-blueline.com.*

CAUNES MINERVOIS

VISIT - **Romanesque abbey**: *Tel. 04.68.78.09.44. Open every day from 10am to 12am and 2pm to 7pm.* Guided tour only. Admission: 20 F. The chevet can be seen for free.

CESSERAS

OUTING - **Les Capitelles du Minervois**: *Place de la Gare, 34210 Cesseras. Tel. 04.68.91.17.17 Fax 04.68. 91.23.85. June to September.* Minervois women's association that organizes picturesque outings in the Haut Minervois: enchanting walks, vineyard and wine outings, etc. Full day: 45 F per person, 1/2 day: 25 F.

CUCUGNAN

VISIT - **Château de Queribus (13th and 14th centuries)**: *11350 Cucugnan. Tel. 04.68.45.03.69. In February, March, November and December open weekends and school vacations from 10am to 5pm. In April and October, every day from 10am to 6pm. In May, June and September, every day from 10am to 7pm. In July and August every day from 9am to 8pm.* Admission: 25 F, children: 10 F. The tour also includes a show: " Le Sermon du curé de Cucugnan ".

DUILHAC

OUTING - **Château de Peyrepertuse**: *Open every day from 9am to 7pm.* Admission: adults 15 F, children 10 F.

FONTFROIDE

VISIT - **Romanesque abbey**: *Tel. 04.68. 45.11.08. Open September to June from 10 to 12 and 2 to 5, in July and August from 9:30 to 6.* One-hour guided tour. Admission: 35 F, children: 13 F.

LAGRASSE

OUTING - **Abbey of Sainte Marie**

d'Orbieu: *Origo SARL, 11220 Lagrasse. Tel. 04.68.58.11.58 Fax 04.68.58.11.52. Open every day (except Sunday morning) from 10:30am to 12:30pm and 2pm to 6:30pm. March 29 to April 30 and October 1st to November 3, from 2pm to 5pm.* Southern France's largest Benedictine abbey. Admission: 20 F, children: 13 F.

LEZIGAN-CORBIERES

MUSEUM - **Wine and vineyard museum**: *3, rue Turgot, 11200 Lézignan-Corbières. Tel. 04.68.27.07.57. Open every day from 9am to 7pm.* Across from the station. Admission: 25 F. Presentation of the region's viticultural environment and dwellings. The facilities are somewhat antiquated.

MINERVE

OUTING - Natural bridges of the Cesse, dolmens of the Lacs.

MUSEUM - **Hurepel Museum**: *Rue des Martyrs, 34210 Minerve. Tel. 04.68.46.10.28. Open April to June 14 and in September and October from 2 to 6pm. June 15 to September 1 from 11am to 7pm.* Admission: 15 F (free for children). Small museum with figurines and miniature scenes recreating the Cathar epic (1209-1210). Excellent introduction to this great historic event in the region.

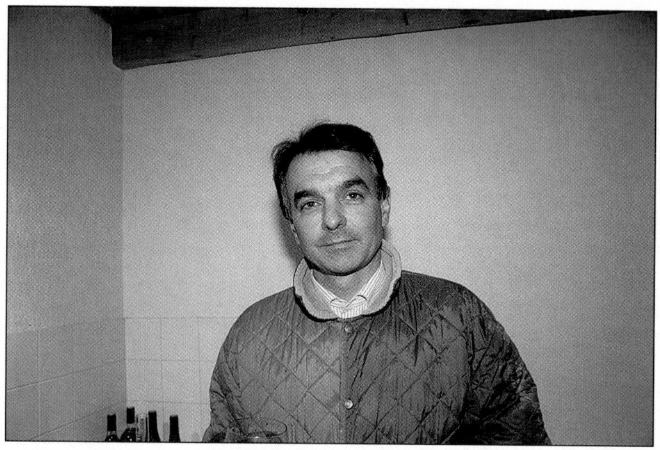

Alain Maurel on his vineyard in Cabardès, the most westerly appellation in the Languedoc.

Château Ventenac

Owner Alain Maure. **Address** 1 place du Château, 11610 Ventenac-Cabardès - Tel. 04.68.24.93.42 Fax 04.68.24.81.16. **Open** From Mon. to Sat. 8:00-12:00 and 14:00-19:00, by appointment.

Planted on the last foothills of the Montagne Noire, vines in the small Cabardès appellation ripen in the sunshine of the Mediterranean, while often affected by the rainfalls of the Southwest. This double influence is translated into a diversity of grape varieties in the vineyard. Growing on the Château Ventenac's seventy hectares are thus Southwestern vines: Merlot, Cabernet, Gros Manseng; the Mediterrean Grenache and Muscat; Burgundy's Chardonnay; and even the Loire Valley's Chenin. Of his red Cabardès wines, Alain Maurel makes no secret of his preferences for Bordeaux grapes: "The Cabernets and Merlots create much more interesting wines than the Grenache." His white wines come from an amazing "confrontation" between Chardonnay, Chenin, Gros Manseng, and Muscat à Petit Grain: the '96 (22 F) opens up with white flowers and citrus on the nose, a lively taste, and a somewhat soft, exotic finish. We will be interested in the new '96 Stéphanie *cuvée* (27 F), in which some of the Chardonnay is aged in oak. For a thirst-quenching bottle, try the lovely '96 Cabardès Rosé (20 F): crushed-raspberry aroma, charming and light on the palate.

Our choice The '95 red Château Ventenac Cabardès (22 F), from Merlot, Cabernet, and a touch of Grenache, vinified in vats. Aroma of slightly cooked blueberries and blackcurrants; solid extract on the palate balanced with softness, making it pleasant to drink young. Fruity, mouth-filling finish. Excellent quality for the price.

Reception In the office, in the heart of a lovely village in the western Aude *département*.

How to get there *(Map 9): 10km west of Carcassonne via N113 (exit Castelnaudary-Toulouse). After Pezens, right towards Ventenac (arrows).*

Souvenirs of the Ivory Coast decorate Marthe and François Lemarié's cellar.

Château Aiguilloux

Owners Marthe and François Lemarié. **Adresse** 11200 Thézan-des-Corbières - Tel. 04.68.43.32.71 Fax 04.68.43.30.66. **Open** From Monday to Saturday, 9:00-12:00 and 14:00-19:00, preferably by appointment. **Spoken** English.

Normandy, the Antilles, Paris, the Ivory Coast (where they met): the Lemariés had been around before they put down their suitcases here in the Corbières in the mid-1980s. Their vines spread over 125 hectares, 35 of which are planted on the clay-limestone slopes of a small rocky mountain chain. This is a good region for red wines (made with carbonic maceration) and rosés, vinified by direct pressing. The Lemariés, who are convivial people, offer visitors a barrel of wine (7500 F for 300 bottles) and the chance to bottle it with the winemakers: "bottles, corks, capsules, labels, and our help all included", followed by a magnificent feast at the Château. Such generosity is found in their wines: the '95 red Tradition (25 F) is deeply colored, round, with notes of cherries and a somewhat rustic finish. It needs three years' bottle age. The '96 Rosé (25 F), fruity but discreet, is vinous but not heavy, its finish dry and straightforward; it does not betray the winery's reputation for good rosés.

Our choice The red '94 Château Aiguilloux Corbières, Cuvée des Trois Seigneurs (32 F): somber color, still youthful aroma, rustic and fruity, a fleshy taste, spicy and savory. To drink now for its fruitiness, or keep while its tannins soften. For private customers, three or four vintages of this *cuvée* are still available.

Reception By Marthe, friendly and a good teacher, in a charming tasting room.

How to get there *(Map 9): 28km from Narbone via D613 then D123 towards Montséret. Go through the village and continue towards Donos. The domaine is on the left.*

Montgaillard, a village of some fifty people in the Hautes-Corbières, is coming back to life thanks to this small vineyard.

Cellier Avalon

Managing Director Michel Larregola. **Manager** Franck Galangau. **Address** 11330 Montgaillard - Tel. 04.68.45.41.98 Fax 04.68.45.01.37. **Open** From Monday to Saturday, 9:00-18:00.

The setting here is majestic, rocky, rugged, and wild, lost in the confines of the Corbières just a few kilometers as the crow flies from the Cathar chateaux of Queribus and Peyrepertuse. The destiny of Montgaillard, a tiny, sleepy mountain village, was to take another direction in 1990, when four young *vignerons* decided to revitalize viticulture there and to open a small cooperative cellar. Today, they have 140 hectares of vines, with 100 in Corbières, planted on unusual schistous soil at an altitude of 1200 feet. The red wines, predominantly from Syrah, display the vivacity of their youth, maturing well for two to four years, while conserving their freshness and spicy notes. The '96 Rosé d'Octobre (22 F), from young late-harvested Syrah vines, is deeply colored, aromatic with a touch of acidity; very fruity and lively finish. This *terroir* is also good for white grapes (Grenache, Roussanne, Maccabeu): the '96 Domaine de Mitounes is light, flowery, with a touch of acidity, a popular style today. Drink now.

Our choice The '95 red Château Avalon Corbières (29 F). 80% Syrah (carbonic maceration vinification) and Grenache. A purple color typical of young Syrah; powerful aroma of very ripe grapes, fleshy taste, very fruity; the tannic finish will round out by the end of 1988.

Reception You won't be disappointed for having made the trip, given the beauty of the site, facing Mount Tauch, and the friendly reception in a recently built tasting room.

How to get there *(Map 9): 54km south of Narbonne. From Tuchan, drive towards Padern then Montgaillard. At the entrance to the village.*

Christian Baillat: "Wines have a story to tell."

Domaine Baillat

Owner Christian Baillat. **Address** 2 rue Montlaurier, 11220 Montlaur - Tel. 04.68.24.08.05 Fax 04.68.24.00.37. **Open** From Monday to Friday, by appointment, Saturday, 11:00-18:00. **Spoken** German, English.

While we realize how excellent Languedoc vineyards can be, we can also be irritated to see that certain winemakers are not doing justice to their vines. As an antidote to this disappointment, we went to taste Christian Baillet's wines. In ten years, this young, dogged, impassioned Franco-Austrian, with the help of Benoît Huchin from the Dubernet Laboratory, has made a line of red Corbières "all of which, individually, have a story to tell" and bear the imprint of low-yield Syrah vines. His '95s, tasted before bottling, are remarkable. The Domaine Baillat (28 F), made with carbonic maceration, is immediately appealing, with overtones of ripe cherries, tar, and spices. It will be perfect with three years' bottle age. We next tasted two more complex barrel-aged wines: the Clos de la Miro (40 F), from 70% Syrah, quite full-bodied but also austere; and the Cuvée Emilion (our choice), more ample and concentrated. Baillat makes a very good Rosé (28 F), with fresh, young fruitiness.

Our choice The '95 red Cuvée Emilien Baillat (54 F). Although the vines are young, this destemmed Syrah, *pigé* in Burgundian style and aged in 70% oak barrels, is already a wine of real character: straightforward extract, fresh, "muscular", with dense, long tannins and oakiness. To be cellared. The '94 (54 F), somewhat less structured, is slowly beginning to open out.

Reception By Christian, a sensitive winemaker and great champion of Corbières. In a small boutique.

How to get there *(Map 9): 24km southeast of Carcassonne: N113 towards Narbonne. In Trèbes, turn right onto D3 towards Fontiès, Monze, Pradelles, then Montlaur. Winery next to church.*

Patrick de Marien, President; and Bernard Pueyo, Director.

Cave d'Embres-et-Castellemaure

Managing Director Patrick de Marien. **Manager** Bernard Pueyo. **Address** 4 route des Canelles, 11360 Embres-et-Castelmaure - Tel. 04.68.45.91.83 Fax 04.68.45.83.56. **Open** Sep. 16 - June 14, visit from Monday to Friday 8:00-12:00 and 14:00-18:00. June 15 - Sep. 15, open every day. **Credit Cards** Visa, Eurocard, MarsterCard, Amex.

This small cooperative winery with 300 hectares of vines and 125 members, has put Embres-et-Castelmaure on the wine map: two villages which are now one, they nestle in the Hautes-Corbières massif, half-way between the Cathar citadels and the Mediterranean. Managed by a dynamic team, the winery fiercely defends its independence vis-à-vis the large cooperative groups of the region. Offering its private customers specially selected wines, with three red, rosé, and white Corbières wines (we prefer the reds): Castelmaure, an excellent '95 red Grains Entiers (20.50 F), a wine of sunny fruitiness, round, without heaviness, to be drunk young; the '94 red Col des Vents (26 F), with rustic, resinous overtones, to be drunk now. And finally, Pompadour, from old Carignans (50%) grown on schistous hills, Grenache, and Syrah: the wine ages extremely well.

Our choice The '93 red Pompadour Corbières (32.50 F). Delicate tannins, subdued power; this wine is currently the winery's best, even if it can be criticized for a slightly dry finish. This sensation disappears when the wine is drunk with a simmered dish in a sauce. Three old vintages are still available, offering excellent value for the money.

Reception Very friendly, in a tasting room hung with contemporary art in the summer.

How to get there *(Map 9): 40km south of Narbonne. On A9, exit Sigean, towards Portel and Durban. One kilometer after Villeneuve, on left (D205) to Embres.*

A magnificent estate reconstructed in 1991 by the founder of the K-Way brand of clothing.

Château Haut-Gléon

Owners Léon-Claude and Léon-Nicolas Duhame. **Address** Villesèque-des-Corbières, 11360 Durban - Tel. 04.68.48.85.95 Fax 04.68.48.46.20. **Open** From Monday to Saturday, 9:00-12:00 and 14:00-19:00. **Spoken** English. **Credit cards** Visa, Eurocard, MarsterCard, Amex.

In 1990, at the age of fifty-five, Léon-Claude Duhamel sold his large textile company and realized his life's dream: he bought a 250-hectare estate, including 30 hectares of vines, in the heart of the garrigue and the appropriately named Paradise Valley (he didn't make it up!), east of Corbières. Investments worthy of a great Bordeaux château went into reviving the vineyard, uprooting and replanting half of the vines, and restoring the vast mansion as well as the vinificaton equipment: the barrel cellar is magnificent. Duhamel's wines are outstanding, and are beginning to show their excellence with the 1994 vintage. The Haut-Gléon style, far from yielding wines of thick concentration, is one of elegance and balance as the result of skillful ageing in oak which never produces heavy wines. There are good vins de pays from the Vallée du Paradis-Domaine de la Passière: the red is very round and the white bears the marked imprint of ripe Sauvignon, with exotic tastes. The wines come in a squat bottle, a reproduction of an old flacon found on the estate.

Our choice The '95 red Corbières Château de Haut-Gléon (50 F): 60% Syrah, with Grenache and Carignan, aged in oak eight months. Delicate bouquet of ripe grapes layered with spicy, vanilla hints; delicate extract, fresh, fruity, soft tannins.

Reception In a verdant, magnificent setting where hospitality takes priority.

How to get there *(Map 9): 30km south of Narbonne. On A 9, exit Sigean, towards Portel-des-Corbières. After going through Portel, the domaine is 6km on the left.*

Guido Jansegers, from Flanders to Corbières.

Château Mansenoble

Owners Guido Jansegers and Marie-Annick De Witte. **Address** 11700 Moux - Tel. 04.68.43.93.39 Fax 04.68.43.97.21. **Open** From Monday to Saturday, 9:00-12:00 and 14:00-19:00, preferably by appointment. **Spoken** English, German, Flemish.

We always knew that the Belgians were great connoisseurs of French wines. We've now learned that they can also be formidable winemakers, like Guido Jansegers, who bought twenty hectares of vines in Moux in 1993. In four years, this former insurance man and sprightly fifty-year-old has made a spectacular success here, ranking among the Top Ten Winemakers in the Languedoc. From vines on the Montagne Alaric, a 20-kilometer rocky barrier stretching from east to west between Carcassonne and Lézignan, his red wines are quite fresh and above all very "*masculine*", as is demonstrated by the '95 Vin de Pays des Coteaux de Miramont (25 F): fruity (raspberries), corpulent, and dense; and the '95 Cabernet-Sauvignon (25 F) with a distinctive peppery style, less rustic than the Miramont, but also less original. Jansegers' Corbières are showing increasing finesse, such as the '95 Château (34 F): aromatic, round, with blackberries and acidulated cherries on the palate; lively finish. Can be drunk now.

Our choice The '95 red Corbières Réserve du Château (54 F). Comes in a tall bottle. Selected Syrah (60%), Grenache, and Mourvèdre, destemmed, half aged in oak for 14 months. Beautiful black-plum color, sweet overtones, disceetly oaky bouquet. Silky, round attack develops out with mouth-filling volume, not heavy; tannic, balanced finish. A generous, delicious wine, to be enjoyed as of 1988, for three to four years.

Reception Charming, informative, in an immaculately kept tasting room.

How to get there *(Map 9): 27km east of Carcassonne. On N113, between Carcassonne and Lézignan. In Moux, the cellar is in the main street that crosses the village.*

The tasting room is in a 12th-century chapel.

Château Les Palais

Owners Anne and Xavier de Volontat. **Address** 11220 Saint-Laurent-de-la-Cabrerisse - Tel. 04.68.44.01.63 Fax 04.68.44.07.42. **Open** Every day, 9:00-12:00 and 14:00-19:00. **Spoken** English. **Credit cards** Visa, Eurocard, MarsterCard.

Anne and Xavier de Volontat own a large 120-hectare estate in the Corbières appellation, planted on one of the best vineyards of the Aude, La Pinède, around the village of Boutenac. The Château Les Palais has a long reputation for red wines from predominantly Carignan grapes vinified by carbonic maceration. "I defend Carignon not out of snobbism as some people do, but because it is our distinctive style," says Xavier de Volontat. It's true that here, as at La Voulte-Gasparets (see page), the often denigrated grape yields smooth, full-bodied wines of real depth, spicy and peppery. Such quality demands meticulous winemaking, notably during the harvest when each parcel is picked only when the grapes are perfectly ripe. A *crescendo* tasting here began with the simple, aromatic '96 white wine (28 F); the very good '96 rosé (28 F), fruity and generous; and the five red wines which reflect the age of the vines and their exposition. Several vintages are available, enabling you to follow the development of each wine.

Our choice The two extremities of the red palette: The '94 Les Palais-Merveille (25 F), from young wines: fruity, "thick" and supple, to be drunk young; and the '93 Les Palais-Randolin (56 F), from Carignan vines more than 80 years old, Grenache, and Syrah, offering superb concentration with full-body; firm, dense, long, peppery tannins. A Languedoc *grand cru*, not to be opened before 1999.

Reception Professional and attentive. The courtyard of the domaine lies at the end of a long lane of olive trees, where visitors taste "religiously" in the restored chapel.

How to get there *(Map 9): 12km south of Lézignan. Between Fabrezan and Saint-Laurent-de-la-Cabrerisse, on D611; on left (signposted).*

Claude Vialade and Jean-Paul Salvagnac.

Château Saint-Auriol

Owners Claude Vialade and Jean-Paul Salvagnac. **Address** 11220 Lagrasse - Tel. 04.68.58.15.15 Fax 04.68.58.15.16. **Open** From Monday to Friday, 9:00-12:00 and 14:00-19:00. Saturday by appointment. **Spoken** English, Spanish, German.

In Cathar country, working for a wine syndicate is no bed of roses, as Claude Vialade can tell you. A hard-working soldier at the head of the Corbières Wine Syndicate until 1994, she participated in the battle to improve the quality of this vast appellation. To lead by way of example, her domaine has made regular, irreproachable wines for the last fifteen years. They are the result of intensive work undertaken by her husband, Jean-Paul Salvagnac, an architect by training, who patiently uprooted and replanted their 37 hectares of vines. Their holdings have expanded with the addition of a new vineyard, the 10-hectare Château Salvagnac in Saint-Laurent. The '96 Saint-Auriol Rosé (28 F), with acidulated fruit, power and verve, is a wine of character. Of the whites, try the '94 vintage (35 F): fennil and glazed citrus, discreet oakiness, a hint of softness at the finish. It can be drunk now, as can the '95 red Salvagnac: wet fur and black berries, very round, charming on the palate.

Our choice We couldn't resist the '95 red Corbières Château Saint-Auriol (35 F), vinified in oak barrels: fruity, gamey taste, delicate oakiness, still very youthful extract, firm, good ageing potential. Can be drunk now.

Reception Hospitable. Exhibit of archeological objects (signet vases) found on the property.

How to get there *(Map 9): 20km southwest of Lézignan. Leave Lagrasse in the Saint-Laurent direction. After 3km, turn right onto D42. Right again after a small bridge (arrows).*

The Fauna Museum at the Espace Octaviana.

Les Vignerons du Mont-Ténarel d'Octaviana

Managing Director Henri Barbe. **Manager** Alain Cros. **Address** caveau Gasparets 11200 Boutenac - Tel. 04.68.27.09.76 Fax 04.68.27.58.15. **Open** Every day, 9:30-12:00 and 14:00-18:00. **Credit cards** Visa, Eurocard, MarsterCard.

Famous for their Fauna Museum where many visitors come to admire a vast collection of stuffed birds, wild boars, foxes, and deer, the Vignerons du Mont-Ténarel d'Octaviana sell wine from three communes and the vineyards around Lézignan, Boutenac, and Fontfroide: 1400 hectares with seven hundred in the Corbières appellation. Most of the wines from from old Carignan vines and Grenache for structure; and, for the past fifteen years, from newly planted Syrah vines. We took special note of two wines, the Château Hauterive Le Haut and the Cuvée Sextant, which reflect the winemakers' experience in selecting vineyard sites and in oak vinification. The '95 white Château Hauterive Le Haut (41 F), from old Grenache vines and Macabeu, is very full-bodied while remaining crisp and fruity. The old Carignan vines grown around Boutenac, fermented by carbonic maceration, make marvelous red wines. Their free-run juices have an aromatic power of cherries and blackcurrants and a velvety quality which is found in the '95 Hauterive Le Haut at 39 Francs.

Our choice The '95 red Corbières Prestige Sextant (48 F). 80% Syrah with Carignan, carbonic maceration for twenty days. Toasty aroma with powerful vanilla overtones; soft, oaky, dense tannins on the palate: a "New World" style, very fashionable in France.

Reception 365 days a year in a vast tasting room in an ageing cellar, beneath the Fauna Museum (entrance to Museum: 25 F).

How to get there *(Map 9): A 61 exit Lézignan (12km). From Lézignan drive towards Ornaison and Gasparet. In the center of the village. Signposted.*

Patrick Reverdy has managed this domaine since 1982.

Château La Voulte-Gasparets

Owners Messieurs Bergès and Reverdy. **Responsabe** Patrick Reverdy. **Address** Gasparets, 11200 Boutenac - Tel. 04.68.27.07.86 Fax 04.68.27.41.33. **Open** Everyday 8:00- 12:00 and 14:00-19:00. **Credit cards** Visa, Eurocard, MasterCard.

The Carignan grape variety is the object of great debate in the Languedoc. Planted in massive quantities on the flat plains following devastation of the hill vineyards by the phylloxera louse, it has actively contributed to the detestable image of the region's red wines. Many winemakers are fighting for its elimination. But there are those who hold that Carignan gives great wines if they are made from old low-yielding vines and planted on hill vineyards. Tasting La Voulte's red wines from 60% Carignan with Grenache and Syrah only proves how right those winemakers are. Apart from the grapes themselves, they are above all planted on a sumptuous 45 ha vineyard of round stones, like Châteauneuf-du-Pape, which is owned by Patrick Reverdy. His La Voulte Gasparets is also one of the rare domaines where carbonic maceration yields wines that can be laid down, and where ageing in oak is handled smoothly. The '95 Cuvée Réserve (35 F) is mouth-watering, soft, rather gamey, still marked by oak, but a wine of undeniable breed. Cellar it for three years. Note the good '96 Rosé (28 F), very pale, acidulated fruit, slightly tannic; and a '96 white (28 F): powerful, predominantly exotic notes lent by the Rolle grape.

Our choice The '95 red Romain Pauc (63 F). Deep purple, inky color, aroma still closed (unguent, blueberry preserves), but already magnificently velvety taste, fleshy, mouth-filling; firm, very dense tannic finish, promising a beautiful wine with bottle age. Patience.

Reception In a sober stone tasting room, by Patrick Reverdy, the "orchestral conductor" of the winery.

How to get there *(Map 9): On A 61 exit Lézignan (12km). From Lézignan towards Ornaison and Gasparet. In the center of the village.*

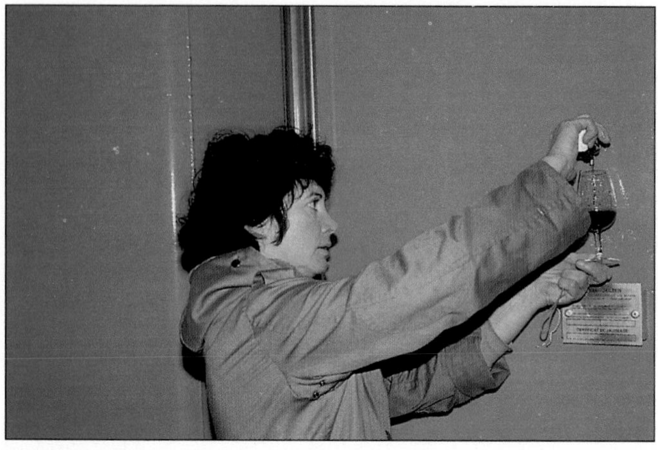

Marlène Soria.

Domaine Peyre-Rose

Owners Marlène and Philippe Soria. **Address** 34230 Saint-Pargoire - Tel. 04.67.98.71.88. **Open** Every day, by appointment only. **Spoken** English.

In 1983, Marlène Soria left Montpellier and her job in real estate to set up on the Saint-Pargoire plateau, a *garrigue* of large limestone rocks isolated behind the Valmagne Abbey. She planted a small 25-hectare vineyard with ridiculously low-yielding vines (20 hectoliters per hectare) imposed by this arid country on the borderline of profitability. Marlène Soria takes risks permanently: highly alcoholic wines in '95, with an average of 14.8%; and very long fermentations. The result is that the red wines from Peyre-Rose, two Syrah *cuvées*, the Clos des Cistes and the Clos Syrah Léone, are unlike any others. Without wishing to flatter the winemaker, we find that they have formidable concentration and volume. The '92s are beginning to open out, while the '93s and '94s should be cellared. The '94 Clos des Cistes (140 F) is a diamond in the rough: opaque, with a myriad of velvety tannins and a long, chalky finish. The '94 Syrah Léone (140 F) has greater finesse and freshness. The Novembre 1995, Marlène Soria's very dry, powerful white wine (90 F) is amber in color, its bouquet of honey and raisins. An autumn wine.

Our choice The '93 Clos des Cistes (120 F): anthracite, leather, tar, garrigue, black olives, very mouth-filling and dense, mellow, soft, complete. To our knowledge, one of the greatest red wines from this vintage in the Languedoc.

Reception The cellar has been slightly enlarged with a small tasting area. Marlène always greets visitors warmly.

How to get there *(Map 10): Take N113 (Montpellier-Mèze). At entrance to Saint-Pargoire coming from Villeveyrac, take a small road on left located behind a sawmill.*

Wine has been made at Bébian since the 11th century.

Prieuré de Saint-Jean-de-Bébian

Owners Chantal Lecouty and Jean-Claude Le Brun. **Address** Route de Nizas, 34120 Pézenas - Tel. 04.67.98.13.60 Fax 04.67.98.22.24. **Open** From Monday to Saturday, in July/August, 9:00-12:00 and 15:00-19:00 or by appointment. **Spoken** English, Spanish.

In 1994, the former owner of the magazine *La Revue du Vin de France*, Jean-Claude Le Brun and his companion, Chantal Lecouty, a wine writer, bought this beautiful priory and 26 hectares of outstanding vines. The vineyard's reputation had been well established by its former owner, Alain Roux, who had planted Grenach, Syrah, and Mourvèdre here in the 1960s. The way was thus prepared for Chantal Lecouty, who took over the winemaking, aided by François Serre, an enologist from Béziers. We can only pay homage to her first two vintages. While retaining the Bébian style, Chantal has added a personal touch by softening the red wines, which had often had a rough edge previously. She has also created a second red wine ('94 La Chapelle, fluid and rustic) and a small amount of oak-vinified white wine, powerful and fleshy (110 F). The '93 Prieuré (80 F) should be bottle aged: the tannins are becoming soft but remain solid and firm. The '94 Le Prieuré (82.50 F) is softer and more "feminine".

Our choice The '95 red Prieuré Saint-Jean-de-Bébian (90 F). Tasted before bottling, it is fresh (pine resin, ripe red berries), ample, generous, without rustic edges; finishes with beautiful, dense, long tannins and tastes of coffee and spice. A great Mediterranean wine of breeding. Ready to drink in late 1998.

Reception By Chantal and Jean-Claude Le Brun, happy to welcome wine lovers to their beautifully restored priory.

***How to get there** (Map 10): 3km from Pézenas, towards Nizas.*

Facing the Mediterranean, the earliest ripening grapes in the Côteaux-du-Languedoc.

Château Mire-l'Étang

Owners Jacqueline, Pierre and Philippe Chamayrac. **Address** 11560 Fleury-d'Aude - Tel. 04.68.33.62.84 Fax 04.68.33.99.30. **Open** From Monday to Saturday 8:00-12:00 and 15:00-19:00. **Credit cards** Visa, Eurocard, MasterCard.

La Clape is one of the twelve vineyard regions in the Coteaux-du-Languedoc appellation, named after a 660-foot massif on the coast east of Narbonne. The vineyards are planted around this mountain, which was an island in Roman times. Its surrounding swamps were drained during the reign of Napoleon III in the late 19th century. The Château Mire-l'Etang covers forty-eight hectares of vines southeast of La Clape, where the maritime influence is strong. In a generation, Pierre and Jacqueline Chamayac have done everything on the domaine, from planting the vines to equipping the cellar. Their dogged determination is being ensured by their son, Philippe. Quite lively and iodized, the Chamayracs' '96 white wine (28 F)--whites are much sought-after in La Clape--is not quite up to par with the '95. These wines are good with the local oysters from Bouzigue. The winery's '96 Corail Rosé (28 F) is a model of powerful, fleshy style, more that of a light red wine than a neutral rosé. Of the Mire-l'Etang's red wines, they are distinguished by fine, mature tannins sustained by a solid alcoholic structure.

Our choice The '95 red Coteaux-du-Langudoc La Clape Cuvée des Ducs (45 F), from Syrah (70%) and Grenache, with nine months in barrels, 1/3 of which are new. The Syrah in this wine is reminiscent of Bandol's Mourvèdre in its powerful extract and silky tannins, with overtones of glazed black berries and spices. Bottle age for five years.

Reception Informal, by Pierre or Philippe in a tasting room much frequented by tourists in summer.

How to get there *(Map 9): On A9, exit Narbonne-Est. Follow coastal road: Narbonne-Plage, St-Pierre, Fleury and Les Cabanes. The vineyard is indicated with arrows.*

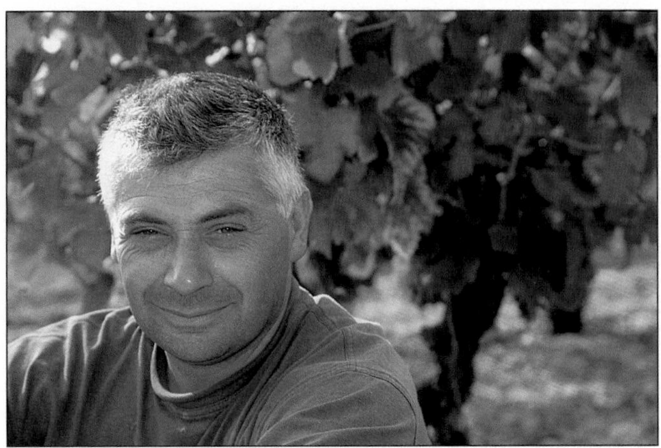

Pierre Clavel.

Domaine Clavel

Owner Pierre Clavel. **Address** Rue du Languedoc, 34160 Saint-Bauzille-de-Montmel - Tel. 04.67.86.97.36 Fax 04.67.86.97.37. **Open** From Monday to Saturday, by appointment. **Spoken** English.

Pierre Clavel is a travelling *vigneron.* His forty hectares of vines are planted on the eastern periphery of Montpellier on the excellent vineyard site of La Méjanelle, with early-ripening grapes and red sandstone-pebbly soil; but his winery, since the summer of 1996, is located in Saint-Bauzille, near his home 15 kilometers farther north at the foot of the mountains. There are more comfortable ways of life, but Pierre is now "at home". An engaging person with a sly smile, full of energy, Pierre Clavel has become one of the leading winemakers of the Languedoc. But few of his countrymen can enjoy his wines: 95% are exported. Clavel's red wines are basically made from Syrah, Mourvèdre, and Grenache. If the quality of a winery can be judged by its least expensive wine, Clavel's is remarkable. His '95 Cuvée Gourmande (25 F), from Syrah and Grenache, is a generous wine, evoking spices and licorice, and offering excellent value for the price. You will also find one of the best rosés in the appellation (21 F for the '96) and a rare white wine made predominantly from the Rolle grape.

Our choice The '95 red Coteaux-du-Languedoc La Copa Santa (50 F), from 80% Syrah, 20% Mourvèdre, aged in seasoned barrels. Aromas of black berries, roasted coffee; fruity, velvety and full, with spicy tannins, long on the palate. A marvelous wine, to be cellared five to six years.

Reception Generous, very enthusiastic, by Pierre or Jannick, the young enologist who oversees vinification.

How to get there *(Map 10): From Montpellier to Sommières (N110). In 10km, left to Sussargues, Saint-Drézéry and Saint-Bauzille. Cellar in center of village.*

Sylvain Fadat, champion of blended wines.

Domaine d'Aupilhac

Owner Sylvain Fadat. **Address** 28 rue du Plô, 34150 Montpeyroux - Tel. 04.67.96.61.19 Fax 04.67.96.67.24. **Open** From Monday to Saturday, 14:00-19:00, preferably by appointment.

With fifteen hectares of terraced vines on rocky, quite deep soil on the Montpeyroux vineyards at the Larzac border, Sylvain Fadat has in eight years forged a unique style in the Coteaux-du-Languedoc world of contemporary wines. While he makes an array of varietal wines often from Syrah (the Carignan of the 21st century?), Fadat says that "our future lies in blended wines." Of course he owns Syrah and Mourvèdre parcels but he continues to pamper his old Cinsault and Carignan grapes. His red Coteaux-du-Languedoc Montpeyroux (our choice) is a unique reflection of those vines. Among the domaine's rare wines, be sure to taste the Le Carignan vin de pays. The '95 (42 F), evoking moist leather and ripe fruit, is a velvety, round red wine with a firm, long finish, unlike any other. We found Fadat's '96 rosé (26 F) absolutely mouth-watering: fruity, generous, remarkable.

Our choice The '96 white *vin de pays* (42 F), from Ugni, Grenache, and Chardonnay, aged in wood. A dry wine with very mellow extract, soft and honeyed, but with rare crispness on the finish. And the delicious '95 red Coteaux-du-Languedoc Montpeyroux (40 F), with overtones of fresh cigar, *garrigue,* full, supple, magnificently balanced. Ready to drink now; can be kept.

Reception Informal, in a small tasting room on the ground floor of a village house.

How to get there *(Map 10): 36kms northwest of Montpellier. On N109 (Montpellier-Clermont-l'Hérault) in Gignac, go into village: then follow Laganas, Montpeyroux. In center of village.*

André Leenhardt with Saint-Loup Peak in the background.

Château de Cazeneuve

Owners Anne and André Leenhardt. **Address** 34270 Lauret - Tel. 04.67.59.07.49 Fax 04.67.59.06.91. **Open** Every day, 17:00-21:00 and Saturday, by appointment. **Credit cards** Visa, Eurocard, MasterCard.

Lying between the cool Cévennes mountains and the Mediterranean with its maritime influence, the vineyards at the foot of Saint-Loup Peak (2550 feet) are planted predominantly with red Syrah grapes. Young André Leenhardt, formerly on the technical staff at the Chamber of Agriculture, bought sixteen hectares of vines here and made his first wines at the Château de Caseneuve in 1991. Since then, he has totally reorganized and enlarged his vineyard to twenty-five hectares, planting 60% Syrah red grapes, along with Mourvèdre and old Grenache vines. 40% of the latter grapes are used for his '96 Terres Rouges (28 F), reminiscent of red berries and *garrigue*, a soft, fresh wine, delicious young. The barrel-aged Syrah made its début with the '95 Classique (38 F): toasty, a touch of acidity, supple, long, and more concentrated in the Grande Cuvée. Of Casenave's whites, the 1996 vintage saw the arrival of Grenache and Viognier grapes, lending structure to the Roussanne in the wine. Along with the excellent Classique ('96: 45 F), 1996 also ushered in a *barrique*-aged Grande Cuvée for 60 Francs.

Our choice The '95 red Pic Saint-Loup Grande Cuvée (60 F), from 90% Syrah, aged in oak barrels, half of which were new. Deep color, with typical soft bouquet and overtones of roasted coffee, long on the palate, velvety, powerful, with tannins softened by the fattiness of the oak. Good to drink beginning late 1998.

Reception Charming, in a magnificent location surrounded by chalk cliffs, which alone deserve a long visit. Good inn in front of winery (See Good Addresses in Languedoc).

How to get there *(Map 10): 35km north of Montpellier towards Anduze via D17. 3km after Valfaunès, turn left towards Lauret. Arrows.*

Jean-Benoît Cavalier's tasting cellar.

Château de Lascaux

Owners Isabelle and Jean-Benoît Cavalier. **Address** Place de l'Église, 34270 Vacquières - Tel. 04.67.59.00.08 Fax 04.67.59.06.06. **Open** Every day 10:00-12:30 and 15:00-19:00, except Sunday (by appointment). **Spoken** English, Spanish.

The Lascaux vines are planted on soils of crumbly red clay and limestone pebbles *(lascaux* means "limestone rock" in the *langue d'oc*, the dialect spoken in Languedoc). An agricultural engineer, Jean-Benoît Cavalier has owned the family vineyard since 1984. 80% of his vines are Syrah, the Rhône Valley grape that enjoys favorable rainfall here, thus yielding less aggressive tannins than elsewhere in Languedoc. Logically, these conditions should make it possible for the Pic Saint-Loup appellation to be promoted in coming years to the status of a *cru*. Before tasting the reds which have made the reputation of the Château de Lascaux, try the revelation of 1996: the vineyard's two white wines made from young Rolle, Marsanne, and Viognier grapes. The Classique (34 F) is soft, delightfully drinkable, fresh, and exotic on the palate. The Pierres d'Argent (52 F) is vinified in oak, with some new barrels: tasted before bottling, it is more mature, a soft and forthcoming wine evoking dried apricots and pinepples

Our choice The '95 red Coteaux-du-Languedoc Les Nobles Pierres (52 F), from 90% Syrah with Grenache, aged in oak barrels, 1/3 new. Its fruitiness and aromatic distinction are remarkable. It is round and supple, already very pleasant, without aggressive tannins, following through with a lingering taste of ripe cherries. A mouth-watering, distinguished wine.

Reception Hospitable, in a barrel-vaulted, 11th-century tasting cellar in the upper part of Vacquières.

How to get there *(Map 10): 35km north of Montpellier towards Anduze via D17. In Sauteyrargues, go through the village in Vacquières direction. On the "Place de l'Eglise".*

Christophe Peyrus dropped anchor in Lauret in 1992.

Clos Marie

Owner Françoise and Christophe Peyrus. **Address** Route de Cazeneuve, 34270 Lauret - Tel. 04.67.59.06.96 Fax 04.67.59.08.56. **Open** Every day, preferably by appointment.

Christophe Peyrus, 29, spent part of his youth at sea in the French Navy before dropping anchor in 1992 at the foot of Saint-Loup Peak. The call of the sea was replaced by the call of *l'amour*: his companion, Françoise, owns twenty hectares of vines, enabling the young couple to go into business. The grandson of a winemaker in Cahors, Christophe first learned by doing: tending the vines and then, in 1995, making his first wines--with improvised equipment. "To cool my fermenting rosés, I used twenty cubitainers of ice water which I had cooled in a freezer." Christophe emerged from the experience with flying colors. His '95 rosé was delicious and the red Tradition (34 F), from 60% Syrah and 40% Grenache, is very fruity (blackcurrants and black berries), soft on the palate, while revealing the power that comes from this soil. Since then, thanks to the efficient enologist Claude Serra, Christophe has launched into barrel-ageing, with a red wine ('95: 52 F) and a white ('96: 42 F), from traditional old grape varieties: Maccabeu, Grenache, and Clairette. His adventure has only begun.

Our choice The '96 Coteaux-du-Languedoc Rosé (28 F). Made by "bleeding" Syrah and Grenache juice after skin contact: soft, full-bodied, mouth-watering, very fruity. Delicious.

Reception Hospitable and simple.

How to get there *(Map 10): 35km north of Montpellier towards Anduze via D17. 3km after Vaulfaunès, turn left towards Lauret. In the center of the village, Cazeneuve direction.*

Serge Martin-Pierrat, between vineyard and orchard.

Château des Hospitaliers

Owner Family Martin-Pierrat. **Address** 34400 Saint-Christol - Tel. 04.67.86.01.15 Fax 04.67.86.00.19. **Open** Every day 8:00-12:00 and 14:00-20:00. **Credit cards** Visa, Eurocard, MasterCard.

In 1978, following his studies in plant physiology, Serge Martin-Pierret bought an estate in Saint-Christol which today comprises twenty-four hectares of vines and ten hectares of orchards. His credo is respect for fruit, whether from the vine or the tree. West of Montpellier, Saint-Christol is a land of deep red-clay and pebbly soils with beneficial rainfall. The vine roots thus rarely suffer from drought. Traditional Languedoc grape varieties predominate in the Hospitaliers vineyards: Grenache, Cinsault, and Carignan, which are vinified by carbonic maceration. The red wines, lively and aromatic, are never massive, but soft and elegant: restful, digestive wines. Of the dozen wines available, we took special note of two *vins de pays*. A '96 Chardonnay (40 F), from 60-year-old vines, among the oldest vines of this variety in the Languedoc: vinified in oak, ample and mellow; and a '94 Merlot (30 F), a wine of character. From the hill vines, the '95 Spéciale (18 F) is a good, thirst-quenching wine, while the '94 Prestige (25 F) is softer, more full-bodied, evoking black berries.

Our choice The '93 red Coteaux-du-Languedoc Saint-Christol Réserve (40 F). Pepper, gooseberries, *garrigue*, solid extract, while remaining fluid and graceful; beautiful spicy finish. Good with red meat.

Reception Given priority. In their small tasting room, the Martin-Pierrats sell a large part of their production: wines, apples, cherries, peaches, apricots, almonds.

How to get there *(Map 10): From Montpellier towards Sommières (N110). After 25km, turn right towards Saint-Christol. Tasting room in center of village. Signposted.*

Salagou is reminiscent of a Central American volcanic-crater lake.

Mas des Chimères

Owner Guilhem Dardé. **Address** 34800 Octon - Tel. 04.67.96.22.70 Fax 04.67.88.07.00. **Open** Evry day, 11:30-12:30 and next 18:00, Saturday, 14:00-19:00 and Sunday 10:00-12:30, preferably by appointment.

Guilhem Dardé's vineyard lies on the northwest boundary of the Coteaux-du-Languedoc appellation. Lying at the foot of Mount Larzac and on the edge of Lake Salagou, the vines are planted on an exotic terrain of red soil composed of crumbly schist colored by iron salts called *ruffe*. Poor and difficult to tend, they nevertheless yield genuine, foursquare wines at the hands of Dardé. A member of the wine syndicate, he is a proponent of "meeting other winemakers and keeping the doors open". Dardé opened his own winery after twenty years of belonging to a *coopérative*. An unusual wine is his white *vin de pays* from the Chassan grape--a cross between Chardonnay and Listan--giving a charming, somewhat tannic wine (27 F); and the rare red Oeillade varietal, made from the Cinsault table grape: with peonies, fruit, pepper (24 F), it is best after a year of bottle age.

Our choice The '94 red Coteaux-du-Languedoc (35 F), from 70% Syrah with Grenache and Carignan, aged in 400-liter oak barrels. Very forthcoming fruitiness (blueberries, cherries, unguent), powerful, solid taste, textured with dense tannins. The same can be said for the '95, which promises to be even better.

Reception By an enthusiastic, dedicated "winemaker peasant", as Guilhem Dardé describes himself. Ask to see the small barrel cellar in one room of the house where roquefort used to be aged.

How to get there *(Map 10): From Pezenas towards Clermont-l'Hérault, then in Bédarieux direction. On this road (D908), after 15km, turn right to Octon.*

Michel Louison, the mover and shaker of Faugères, with the sketch of his future cellar.

Château des Estanilles

Owners Monique and Michel Louison. **Address** Lenthéric, 34480 Cabrerolles - Tel. 04.67.90.29.25 Fax 04.67.90.10.99 **Open** From Monday to Saturday, 8:00- 12:00 and 14:00-19:00, preferably by appointment.

Michel Louison, a native of Tours who came to Faugères without a centime in 1975, is today one of the leading winemakers of the Midi: a just reward for over twenty years of hard work. Famous for his temper and his no-nonsense way of speaking, this self-taught man is a perfectionist in everything. In his 25-hectare vineyard, which he planted predominantly with low-yielding Syrah vines; in the cellar, where he has perfected oak-ageing as it is rarely seen in the Languedoc. In fact, Louison revealed Lenthéric to be a good vineyard site, whose schistic soils are excellent for aromatic white wines and mouth-watering red Syrah varietals. In 1996, with the harvest disrupted by rain, his Mourvèdre yields a barrel-aged rosé (75 F) which is very unusual, soft, and peppery. The white Coteaux-du-Languedoc (40 F), from barrel-aged Marsanne, Roussanne, and Viognier, is a beautifully exotic, fruity wine, with a vivacious length on the palate. Of the reds, the '96 Faugères Tradition (27.50 F) is youthful, delicate, with Mediterranean tastes: aromatic herbs and black berries. Good young, excellent value for the price.

Our choice The '95 red Faugères Syrah (80 F). More like a Saint-Joseph than a Côte Rôtie in freshness, it has a distinctive aroma of cocoa, black plums, raspberries, pepper; full-bodied taste and remarkable texture. Good now or can be cellared.

Reception With enthusiasm and élan, in the vinification cellar beneath the family's house.

How to get there *(Map 9): 24km north of Béziers. On D909 (Béziers-Bédarieux), at Laurens, turn left onto D136 to Lenthéric.*

Frédéric Albaret, in his "Bronx" stables.

Domaine Saint-Antonin

Owner Frédéric Albaret. **Address** La Liquière, 34480 Cabrerolles - Tel. and Fax 04.67.90.13.24. **Open** Every day by appointment (answering machine).

Among the new estate-bottling vineyards, which have been regularly created over the last fifteen years in the Languedoc, you will meet more young winemakers than elsewhere because the price of land is still affordable. Often from non-winemaking backgrounds and with limited means, many chose the job out of a love for wine. At the age of thirty, Frédéric Albaret fell for the mountain charm of Faugères. After harvesting grapes at the Domaine Léon Barral in Lenthéric in 1994, the fledgling winemaker bought thirteen hectares of land which he partially replanted with Syrah and Mourvèdre vines, making his first wine in 1995. This talented young *vigneron*, bursting with energy, already has an idea for the "signature wines" that he wants to create. "I don't want to make wines with exaggerated extraction, a taste of *marc*; I would like to channel the power of the vineyard." His first Syrah, with a third Mourvèdre, was aged in barrels. Tasted from the barrel, this wine has promise, even though Frédéric has the feeling that it "escaped me somewhat." We can highly recommend a visit with this winemaker who searches, doubts, and discovers.

Our choice The '95 red Faugères Tradition (30 F). A blend of traditional Languedoc grape varieties: Grenache, Carignan, Cinsault, all destemmed, vinified in vat. The vineyard is left to deliver its traces of schist wrapped in charming, delicious fruit. Good now.

Reception In the vinification cellar or the small ageing cellar improvised in a stable ("the Bronx" as Frédéric calls it.)

How to get there *(Map 9): 24km north of Béziers. On D909 (Béziers-Bédarieux); at Laurens, turn left on D136 to La Liquière. Cellar in center of village.*

Bernadette and Jean-Pierre Faixo.

Domaine de Roudène

Owners Bernadette and Jean-Pierre Faixo. **Address** 11350 Paziols - Tel. and Fax 04.68.45.43.47. **Open** From Monday to Saturday, 9:00-12:00 and 14:00-19:00.

Neighboring the Pyrénées-Orientales *département*, Fitou is an unusual Janus-like appellation composed of two vineyard regions several kilometers apart, one on the coast facing Lakes La Palme and Leucate, and the other in the mountains of Corbières, towards Tuchan and Paziols. In this village of six hundred inhabitants, Jean-Pierre Faixo, the Deputy Maire, opened his own winery eleven years ago, after leaving a coopérative. He favors low-yielding vines, vinifying his red wines to yield extraction and power: "That is a real Fitou, a powerful, Mediterranean wine which ought to have rustic, gamey aromas," as he explains his philosophy. He doesn't like carbonic maceration because "those wines don't keep their promise over time." In 1995, Faixo harvested magnificent Carignans but he turned up his nose at the Grenache, which was "too diluted". In 1996, the opposite happened, with his Carignans suffering from large yields while the Grenaches were remarkable at the end of the harvest. Jean-Pierre offers two Fitous: the Sélection, vinified in vat, and the Fût de Chêne, for 35 Francs.

Our choice The '95 Fitou Sélection (25 F). A very aromatic Fitou evoking cherries, plums, wet fur; full-bodied, smooth, mellow and powerful. Can be drunk or kept, to be served with game.

Reception Family-style, cordial, in a well-appointed tasting room, cooled with a fan in summer.

***How to get there**: (Map 9): A 9, Sigean exit, towards Portel-des-Corbières, Durban, Turchan. In Paziols, the Cellar is on left, after the school, at the end of thecourtyard.*

The upper valley of the Aude, favorable to Chardonnay and Pinot Noir.

Domaine de l'Aigle

Owner Jean-Louis Denois. **Address** Roquetaillade, 11300 Limoux - Tel. 04.68.31.39.12 Fax 04.68.31.39.14. **Open** From Monday to Friday, by appointment. **Spoken** English.

In 1989, Jean-Louis Denois, an enologist from Champagne, bought his 20-hectare Domaine de l'Aigle here. Located 7 kilometers from Limoux, his choice was not made by chance. An adventurous explorer of the region, Dubois had noticed the excellent dry white wines made from these beautiful hillside vineyards in the Aude Valley, cool despite their latitude, and especially favorable for growing Chardonnay (a Limoux Blanc AOC has recently crowned the vineyards). The wines from l'Aigle are of very high quality for the region: 2 red *vins de pays* in 1995, the Pinot Noir (40 F), spicy, lovely fruit, quite lively; and the Terres Rouges (50 F), from selected old Pinots, more mellow, soft, and tannic. Good to drink as of 1999. Of the barrel-aged white Limoux, the '95 Classique (40 F), from Chardonnay and Mauzac (15%), is fleshy, round, mouth-watering and can be drunk while you bottle-age the '95 Les Aigles (50 F): 100% Chardonnay, slightly oakier but also more mellow, ample, and long on the palate. It's a wine for Burgundy lovers.

Our choice The sparkling Tradition Brut (45 F). Pinot Noir (70%) and Chardonnay, first fermentation in barrels. You will be surprised by the fruitiness and body of this sparkling white wine. It is entitled to no appellation (Pinot Noir is not accorded AOC status in Limoux), which doesn't keep it from being better than many small Champagnes that abound on supermarket shelves.

Reception By Madame and Monsieur Denois, in their home on the side of the Pic de Brau overlooking the village of Roquetaillade. Look up at the sky: the name "Eagle's Nest" was not chosen out of the blue.

How to get there *(Map 9): 7km south of Limoux via D121, via Magrie. In Roquetaillade, the road to the domaine is indicated.*

Ageing Blanquette.

Domaine de Fourn

Owner Famille Robert. **Address** 11300 Pieusse - Tel. 04.68.31.15.03 Fax 04.68.31.77.65. **Open** From Monday to Saturday 8:00-12:00 and 14:00-19:00. Sunday by appointment. **Credit cards** Visa, Eurocard, MasterCard.

With its 120 hectares of vines, including 80 with AOC status, the Robert family pioneered the Crémant-de-Limoux appellation and has upheld it for fifty years. Vinified in deep underground cellars, their sparkling Blanquette and Crémant-de-Limoux are made with a large proportion of the local Mauzac grape variety (some vines are a century old); the Roberts also make a large range of varietal vins de pays de l'Aude, from Chardonnay and Cabernet. Of the thirteen sparkling wines we tasted, we especially enjoyed the dry wines: the Blanquette Brut Domaine de Fourn Médaille d'Or (33 F), evoking glazed fruit, toast--a soft, quite delicate wine; the Crémant (43 F), from Mauzac, Chardonnay, and Chenin, with fine, tiny bubbles and a creamy, chalky, very distinct taste. Among the dessert wines, we noted the Blanquette Au Temps de Pépé, demi-sec (34 F): licorice, mint, glazed fruit, delicate and light, with ripe-apricot sweetness; and the sweet Blanquette Ancestrale (32 F): aromatic bouquet, sweet taste of preserved citrus and ginger, reminiscent of Asti Moscato.

Our choice The '93 Blanquette-de-Limoux Brut Cuvée du Cinquantenaire (36 F), from 100% Mauzac. Aromas of ripe apple, hawthorn, orange rind; generous, ample, slightly sweet taste, yet retaining a distinct, straightforward finish. An apéritif and dessert wine.

Reception By members of the Robert family, in a bucolic setting of the Limoux countryside.

How to get there *(Map 9): On A 61, exit Carcassonne-Ouest. 29km from Carcassonne and 6km from Limoux. From Limoux towards Saint-Hilaire via Pieusse. Road to the domaine is indicated.*

12th-century Notre Dame de Centeilles, with thyme and lavender wafting on the air, stands high above this eponymous vineyard.

Clos Centeilles

Owners Patricia and Daniel Boyer-Domergue. **Address** Campagne de Centeilles, 34210 Siran - Tel. 04.68.91.52.18 Fax 04.68.91.65.92. **Open** From Monday to Saturday, 10:00-12:00 and 16:00-18:30, preferably by appointment. **Spoken** English.

A teacher and winemaker, Daniel Domergue and his wife, Patricia, grow thirteen hectares of vines as naturally as possible, thorougly plowing the soil, using no weedkillers and highlighting regional grape varieties which are denigrated elsewhere: Cinsault, “the only grape left from the glorious period of Languedoc wines in the 18th century”; Carignan: “We take pity on its disgrace”; and the little-known Pinot Noir Fin, a clone of Burgundy's famous grape. The Domergues' Mourvèdre is pruned in lyre shapes, “a prototype of subversion,” thus willingly disregarding local conventional wisdom. Their wines are the antithesis of banal. The '95 Carignanissime (28 F), reminiscent of glazed black berries, is soft, elegantly balanced, a charmingly youthful wine to drink. The '94 Campagne (37 F), from 90% Cinsault, is very fresh, with light fruitiness, spicy, and peppery. The '94 Clos (57 F), from Mourvèdre, Syrah, Grenache reveals deep color, black berries; a complete, complex wine that needs bottle age. The '93 Guiniers (57 F), from Pinot Noir, is round and powerful, opening out on the finish with figs and cocoa.

Our choice The '94 Capitelle de Centeilles (57 F), from 100% Cinsault, late harvested, *pigeage* in open vats, with grape caps kept in contact with fermenting juice. Bouquet of black plums and cooked cherries, hinting at the mouth-filling volume and balanced taste with some acidity and very young, firm tannins, lingering on the palate.

Reception In the Domergues' house; they love to share their passion for Mediterranean viticulture.

How to get there *(Map 9): From Olonzac, take direction Pépieux and Siran. Go around the village and take the road to the Eglise de Centeilles, going up the hillside.*

The Orosquettes in their cellar hewn out of the rock, unusual in the Minervois.

Château La Grave

Owners Josiane, Jean-Pierre and Jean-François Orosquette. **Address** 11800 Badens - Tel. 04.68.79.16.00 and 04.68.79.01.69 Fax 04.68.79.22.91. **Open** June 15 - Sep. 15, every day 9:00-12:00 and 14:00-19:00. In low season, open from Monday to Friday, weekend by appointment. **Credit cards** Visa, Eurocard, MasterCard.

Since 1978, the Orosquette family has invariably made the most of their 90 hectares of vines in Badens, producing varietal *vins de pays* and Minervois appellation wines. They have a predilection for white wines, to which they lend an elegant, modern style, emphasizing the grape by skin maceration and aiming at wines to be drunk young. Of the *vins de pays*, the Chardonnay (25 F) is invariably soft, delicate, light, and quite balanced. Of the Minervois appellations, the '96 Expression (29 F), evoking peaches and fresh grapes, is clean, distinctive, and fresh; the Privilège (50 F) has greater body, with a honeyed, lingering taste: good accompaniments for Mediterranean fish cooked in foil. But La Grave's modern-style red wines should not be overlooked. The '93 Minervois Privilège (39 F), from Syrah, Carignan, and Grenache, barrel-aged, conveys black berries with gamey notes and soft tannins. It can be drunk or cellared.

Our choice The '94 red Minervois Expression (28 F), 60% Syrah. Can be enjoyed now for its generous fruitiness, its round, soft, delicious extract.

Reception By a charming family who divide their time between sailing their boat on the Mediterranean, and their vineyard.

How to get there *(Map 9): 12km east of Carcassonne. From Carcassonne towards Olonzac via D610. 3km after Trèbes, turn left to Badens.*

André Iché.

Château d'Oupia

Owner Famille Iché. **Address** Oupia, 34210 Oupia - Tel. 04.68.91.20.86 Fax 04.68.91.18.23. **Open** Every day by appointment. **Credit cards** Visa, Eurocard.

The Château d'Oupia is a large village house dating from the 12th century and comprising 53 hectares of vines, including 30 in the Minervois appellation. It was made famous several years ago by the Swiss rock star Stephan Eicher, who loves the wines from Oupia and designed the illustration for the Nobilis bottle. And yet Château d'Oupia's owner, André Iché, is hardly a media-seeking person. A serious traditional winemaker, one of the best in Languedoc, he turns out a range of red Minervois which we put at the very top. They are based on old Carignans, Grenaches, and Syrahs, which undergo long vinification in vats. The '95 Tradition (23 F) is a powerful, charming wine, fleshy, without hard edges, offering excellent value for the money. The '95 Les Barons (35 F), is fruity, with somewhat more vanilla, leather and structure. Iché's '94 Nobilis (60 F): leather, cigars, still closed and oaky, long, dense, will be a beautiful wine of breeding in five to six years. For those who like rare wines: the '94 Emerantine (50 cl., 100 F) is a sweet white wine with a bouquet of glazed citrus, concentration, and magnificent smoky overtones. The best "Vin Noble" of the Minervois.

Our choice The '95 red Minervois Al 26 (about 38 F). The strange name comes from the name of a parcel of Grenache on the town cadastral map. The grapes were picked overripe and vinified separately in 1995, as an exception. Strawberries, gooseberry jelly, very mouth-filling, structured, velvety, amazingly fresh. A collector's item.

Reception By André Iché, in a simple cellar.

How to get there *(Map 9): From Narbonne, drive towards Lézignan on N113, then right towards Olonzac on D611, and Oupia. Tasting room in center of village.*

In the heart of the Petit-Causse, La Livinière should be promoted to the Appellation Village status in the near future.

Domaine Piccinini

Owners Jean-Christophe and Maurice Piccinini. **Address** Route des Meulières, 34210 La Livinière - Tel. 04.68.91.44.32 Fax 04.68.91.58.65. **Open** Every day, by appointment. **Spoken** English.

The town of La Livinière and its surrounding communes should over the coming years accede to the rank of *cru*, with the first Villages appellation in the Minervois. It will be the reward for a good *terroir* in the heart of the Petit-Causse, made up of terraced vineyards on limestone and sandstone soil; but most importantly, the reward goes to a small group of dogged winemakers spearheaded by Maurice Piccinini. The former president of a cooperative, he and his son, Jean-Christophe, created their own winery in 1990, with twenty hectares of vines, and vinification equipment purpose-built for controlled barrel ageing, including proper cellar hygrometry. The red wines deliver fruit, fluid extract, a fleshy texture and can be enjoyed quite young. The whites, deliberately aromatic and lively, need even less bottle age. Picinini made a lovely '96 Vin de Pays d'Oc Merlot (22 F) for thirst-quenching everyday drinking. Of his red Minervois, the '95 Clos de l'Angély (30 F), from selected, barrel-aged Syrah, Grenache, and Mourvèdre, is not quite up to the '94: it is reticent, very fluid, and somewhat dry. The '96 white barrel-aged Minervois (35 F), exotic, minty, vine-flowery, with a firm finish, is a better wine.

Our choice The '96 red Minervois Tradition (25 F). Beautiful, generous fruit, round, harmonious taste, delicate, dense tannins, somewhat chalky (the Minervois mark), open, good to drink now.

Reception In a small, cool cellar, contiguous with the medieval town wall of La Livinière.

How to get there *40 km northwest of Narbonne. In Olonzac, towards Pépieux, Siran and La Livinière.*

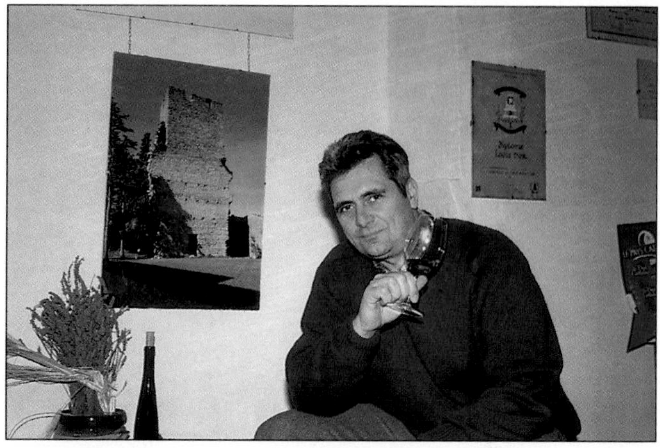

Jean-Poudou and his wooden tower, at the top of the small fortified village of Laure-Minervois.

Domaine de la Tour-Boisée

Owners Marie-Claude and Jean-Louis Poudou. **Address** 11800 Laure-Minervois - Tel. 04.68.78. 10.04 Fax 04.68.78.10.98. **Open** From Monday to Saturday, by appointment only. **Spoken** English.

A strapping man, loquacious in good Mediterranean style, Jean-Louis Poudou is not one to rest on his laurels. His business a success--Poudou's Minervois wines are frequently on offer in the great restaurants of France--the hard-working winemaker uses his success to promote the ideas he holds dear. "Making good wine is one thing, but now we've got to let the vineyards speak. For a long time, people were preoccupied with grape varieties in our region. But it's the *terroir* that will make our living tomorrow." Vintage after vintage, wines from the "Wooden Tower" are becoming more natural. In its youth, the '96 red Marielle et Frédéric (26 F), from Grenache and Syrah, is an aromatic, fruity delight. The '96 Rosé (26 F) also holds its own, yet with a somewhat harder edge than in '95. The '95 Marie-Claude (55 F) is a beautiful white wine, aged in oak, which repeats the success of the '90s and '93s: fennil, vanilla, honey, round, full. Bottle age for two years. Collectors should note the '95 Chardonnay Vendange Tardive (50 cl., 160 F), a mix of honey and preserved tangerines.

Our choice The '94 red Minervois Cuvée Marie-Claude (40 F): Macerated Carignan and Syrah, aged 12 months in oak barrels. Cloves and plum jelly, generous taste, still with pronounced oakiness during our tasting. Somewhat less body than the '93, needs 3 years' bottle age.

Reception Jovial and impassioned, in an inviting tasting room.

How to get there *(Map 9): 20km northeast of Carcassonne. From Trèbes, towards Laure-Minervois. In upper village, signs.*

With his companion, Irène, Paul Durand has created a wine of original style in the Minervois.

Domaine Paul Louis Eugène

Owners Paul Durand and Irène Prioton. **Address** 34210 Siran-Minervois - Tel. 04.68.91.52.87 Fax 04.68.91.59.20. **Open** Every day by appointment. **Spoken** English, German.

Although he is entitled to the Minervois appellation on his labels, Paul Durand chose to deliberately class his wines as *vins de table*, "a wine for a *very good* table," he emphasized with a smile. He did so because he is demanding, wants to make wine his own way, refuses to compromise, and is not concerned with wine "fashion". He is an artisan's winemaker who puts the individual first and does not fear to make "marginal" wines. With the enologist Eugène Sanchez, Durand blends wines from various grape varieties grown in the vineyards "being reconquered"- L'Alzabe, La Perrière, Cassagnoles- pursuing wines with his personal touch. His barrel-aged wines do not shout "wood"; instead, they cause the extract to gracefully mature and purify. We have been greatly enthusiastic about Durand's small five-hectare vineyard for several years because we have found that each vintage brings an extra style often non-existent elsewhere. The Habilis (43 F) is a hymn to Carignan, forthcoming, and very fresh; the Rouge Feuille (47 F) is Cabernet with a Languedoc accent, fruity and softly tannic; while the Dernière Cueillette (47 F) is, by virtue of its maturity and complexity, a sculpture of the Mourvèdre grape.

Our choice The '95 white Cassagnoles (50 F), from Marsanne and Sauvignon. Delicate, generous fruitiness laced with candy and honey; dry, full-bodied, very mellow taste, suggesting quince and glazed fruit. The '93, which can still be found on restaurant wine lists, is at its peak.

Reception Paul and Irène talk of their job with verve and modesty, leaving no one indifferent. Ask to taste the olive oil (their other passion.) Delicious.

How to get there *(Map 9): 35km northwest of Narbonne. From Olonzac, drive towards Pépieux and Siran. In the village, signs.*

Marc Valette.

Domaine Canet-Valette

Owner Marc Valette. **Address** 22, rue Waldeck-Rousseau, 34370 Cazouls-lès-Béziers - Tel. and Fax 04.67.93.60.84. **Open** From Monday to Saturday, by appointment.

Cooperative cellars are the treasure of the Languedoc. Not, unfortunately, because of the irreprochable quality of their wines, but thanks to the fantastic human potential behind them: Men who know how to tend the vines and understand the vineyards better than anyone. Marc Vallette is an excellent example of them. A member of a cooperative for years, like his father, this hard worker owns eighteen hectares of vines between Cessenon and Causse-et-Vayran (including seven hectares which he plowed up on the hillside), planted on clay-limestone soil. Since 1992, Valette has been bottling part of his Saint-Chinian. And we're glad he did, because we have never tasted a cooperative wine of this quality. His friend Jean-François Izarn (see following page) passed on to Vallette his tastes in wine and vinification, with pigeage and ageing in wood barrels. They share the same views on Saint-Chinian, which they feel should be wines with body and power, made from low yields, with ageing potential. Vallette's '93 Fût de Chêne (55 F) was magnificent, but the vintages to come are even better.

Our choice The '95 Saint-Chinian. A classic wine (45 F) from Syrah, Grenache, Cinsault, Carignan. Smooth, full, with solid tannins, very peppery. And the Cuvée Maghani, barrel aged (75 F), from Grenache and Syrah; tasted before bottling, it is more dense and velvety, very rich, tremendous backbone. To be cellared.

Reception In the vinification cellar or in Marc's neighbor's house.

How to get there *(Map 9): 12km northwest of Béziers, go towards Saint-Chinian on N112, then right towards Cazouls-lès-Béziers. Go through the village towards Cessenon; the cellar is on the right.*

In 1995, Jean-François and Cathy opened a farmhouse inn.

Domaine Borie La Vitarèle

Owners Cathy Planès and Jean-François Izarn. **Address** Chemin de la Vernède, 34490 Saint-Nazaire-de-Ladarez - Tel. 04.67.89.50.43 Fax 04.67.89.50.43. **Open** Every day 9:00-19:00, preferably by appointment. Closed in Septembre. **Spoken** English.

You will be doubly rewarded for this excursion into the land of schist: you will discover Cathy and Jean-François' excellent Saint-Chinians and vins de pays, as well as their modest but good farmhouse restaurant which they opened in their house in 1995. "We began with two and a half hectares of plum trees which eventually made it possible for us to buy vines." Six hectares of grapes yielded their first wines in 1990. They are good reflections of low-yielding grapes and precisely chosen vineyard sites, with predominantly Syrah planted on clay and limestone soils. There is a delicious '96 Vin de Pays d'Oc Merlot (29 F), made with little filtration: explosive raspberry aroma, animal overtones, balanced, soft. It can be drunk young. But the '95 Vin de Pays d'Oc La Combe (46 F) needs bottle age: black color, muscular extract, very tannic, "tastes straight out of the barrel", but very promising. Sincere wines of character.

Our choice The '95 Saint-Chinian (58 F), 100% Syrah, 27 hl/ha, destemmed, 21 days' vatting, barrel aged one year, unfiltered. Somber as a moonless night, aroma still very closed, powerful on the palate, with black berries, spices, extracted tannins. Long peppery, chalky finish. Two to three years' bottle age will yield a lovely wine.

Reception Generous, by Cathy and Jean-François. Best to reserve a table for lunch in the inn and taste the wines with food. (See Hotels and Restaurants in Languedoc).

How to get there *(Map 9): 26km north of Béziers. From Béziers, direction Murviel-les-Béziers, Causses-et-Veyran, and Saint-Nazaire-de-Ladarez.*

Isabelle and Rémi Ducellier and Régis Abbal, three adventurers who set out for Les Chemins-de-Bassac.

Domaine Les Chemins-de-Bassac

Owners Isabelle and Rémi Ducellier. **Address** Place de la Mairie, 34480 Puimisson - Tel. 04.67.36.09.67 Fax 04.67.36.14.05. **Open** Every day, 9:00-12:00 and 14:00-19:00, preferably by appointment. **Spoken** English.

Rémi and Isabelle Ducellier are among the young Languedoc winemakers who offer vins de pays much superior in quality than many an ordinary AOC. History professors suddenly out of work, they took over the family vineyard with the help of their friend Régis Abbal in 1987, and made their first wines in 1991. Reducing the size of their vineyard to twenty hectares, the trio planted Syrah, Cabernet, Pinot Noir, Roussane, and Viognier, thoroughly plowing the soil, aiming at low-yielding grapes, manually harvested. An ambitious project, it is already paying off despite the youth of the vines, as we could already observe in tasting a series of three reds, a rosé, and a white. The latter first came out in 1996 (45 F), made from Roussane and Viognier: aromatic, peachy, not heavy, to be drunk young. Of the reds, the '95 Chemin-de-Bassac (30 F), 80% Syrah, is also good young, with notes of black fruit and damp earth, with soft tannins. A wine to lay down is the '95 Cap de l'Homme (50 F), from barrel-aged Grenache. Beautiful labels are illustrated with Rémi's watercolors.

Our choice The '94 vin de Pays d'Oc Pierre Elie (about 35 F), Syrah and Grenache. Aroma of toast, black fruit, unguent; powerful, round, lingering taste of licorice, damp leather; spicy finish. Excellent quality for the price.

Reception In a tasting area arranged above the vats in the large cellar, by courteous Isabelle, Rémi or Régis.

How to get there *(Map 10): 10km north of Béziers. From Béziers, direction Bédarieux on D909. Turn left towards Puimisson. The house is in the center of the village.*

Pugibet and sons.

Domaine de la Colombette

Owners François, Lionel, Gilles and Vincent Pugibet. **Address** Ancienne route de Bédarieux, 34500 Béziers - Tel. 04.67.31.05.53 Fax 04.67.30.46.65. **Open** From Monday to Saturday, 9:00-12:00 and 14:00-19:00. **Spoken** English.

In 1967, François Pugibet bought a vineyard on the northern edge of Béziers. Since then, his nineteen hectares of vines planted around the isolated house have been replanted, mainly with Chardonnay, Sauvignon, Muscat, Cabernet-Sauvignon, and Syrah. The density of plantings has progressively been increased to 8000 Chardonnay vines per hectare, with total plowing of the soil and vines pruned low and short. With unusual mastery for the region, the Pugibets vinify wines using gentle pneumatic presses, ageing in small vats and oak barrels and *demi-muids*, large, 600-liter barrels. The Chardonnay Vins de Pays d'Oc made this winery's reputation, and today they are benchmarks. One is vinified partially in barrels (35 F), yielding the grapiness of white kernel-fruit; the other is vinified and aged in *demi-muids* (60 F): smooth, full-bodied, voluptuous, long, almost suave. The '96s tasted from the barrel are perfect. There is no room to describe all the reds, although our favorites are the Puech d'Hortes, an aromatic red Syrah-Grenache (17 F), an amazing price for the quality; and the explosive '94 or '95 barrel-aged Grenache (30 F).

Our choice the '96 dry Vin de Pays des Coteaux-de-Libron Muscat (30 F). Aromatic but not excessively so, a lively white on the palate, a delicious apéritif. Of the reds, the '94 Lladoner Pelut (60 F), from a Catalonian grape variety akin to the Grenache, aged 18 months in barrels: concentrated, solid, spicy. A discovery.

Reception By a hospitable family who love their work.

How to get there *(Map 9): 5km from Béziers. Leave in the Bédarieux direction on D909. After 4km, in front of the junction towards Boujan, sign on left.*

PROVENCE

11
Bourg-Andéol
Pierrelatte
Valréas
Nyons
Verclause
Eyguians
Montjay
St-Paul-Trois-Ch.
Drôme
Suze-la-Rousse
Mirabel-aux-Baronnies
D546
Châteauneuf-de-Chabre
Pont-St-Esprit
Bollène
Tulette
Buis-les-Baronnies
Montauban-s.-l'O.
Ste-Cécile-les-V.
Vaison-la-Romaine
Mollans
St-Léger-du-V.
Séderon
Curel
Mondragon
Sérignan
Malaucène
Les Omergues
Orange
Vacqueyras
Bédoin
Vaucluse 84
Sault
Revest-du-Bion
Jonquières
Mormoiron
St-Étienne-les-Orgues
Courthézon
Châteauneuf-du-P.
Roquemaure
Monteux
Carpentras
Monieux
St-Christol
La Bastie
Bédarrides
Sorgues
Entraigues
Pernes-les-Font.
Simiane-la-Rotonde
Villeneuve-lès-A.
Avignon
Le Pontet
Fontaine-de-V.
L'Isle-s.-la-Sorgue
St-Saturnin-d'Apt
Rustrel
Forcalquie
St-Michel-l'Observatoire
Reillanne
Aramon
Le Thor
Caumont
Apt
La Bégude
Châteaurenard
Le Coustellet
Maillane
Cavaillon
Robion
Bonnieux
Céreste
St-Rémy-de-Prov.
Plan-d'Orgon
Tarascon
St-Étienne-du-Grès
Lauris
Ansouis
Mirabeau
Fontvieille
Maussane-les-A.
Eyguières
Sénas
Mallemort
Cadenet
Arles
Mouriès
Salon-de-P.
Lambesc
Rognes
Pertuis
Durance
Jouques
Rians
Pélissanne
St-Cannat
Peyrolles-en-P.
Le Merle
St-Martin-de-Crau
Miramas
La Fare-les-Oliviers
Éguilles
Vauvenargues
Mas-Thibert
Canal d'Arles à Port-de-Bouc
Istres
St-Chamas
Aix-en-Provence
Pourrières
Rognac
Berre-l'Ét.
Vitrolles
Gardanne
Trets
Bouches-du-Rhône 13
Fos-s.-M.
Marignane
St-Zachari
Salin-de-Giraud
Port-de-Bouc
Martigues
Septèmes-les-Vallons
Port-St-Louis-du-Rhône
Lavéra
Golfe de Fos
Allauch
Auriol
Roquevaire
Pointe de Beauduc ou du Sablon
Carro
Carry-le-Rouet
Marseille
Gémenos
Cap Couronne
Aubagne
Le Camp-du-C.
Ile Pomègues
La Penne-s.-H.
Cassis
Ceyreste
Cap Croisette
Cap Canaille
Ile de Riou
La Ciotat
St-Cyr-s.-M.
Bandol
MER MÉDITERRANÉE
24 25 26
3
461
454
36
459
484
16
475 480 34
462
460 37
31
463
455 456 39
1 2
5
6
469
43
485 32
7
35
8
483
29 30
15
457 11 12
458
38
446 447 448
449 452 453
19
4

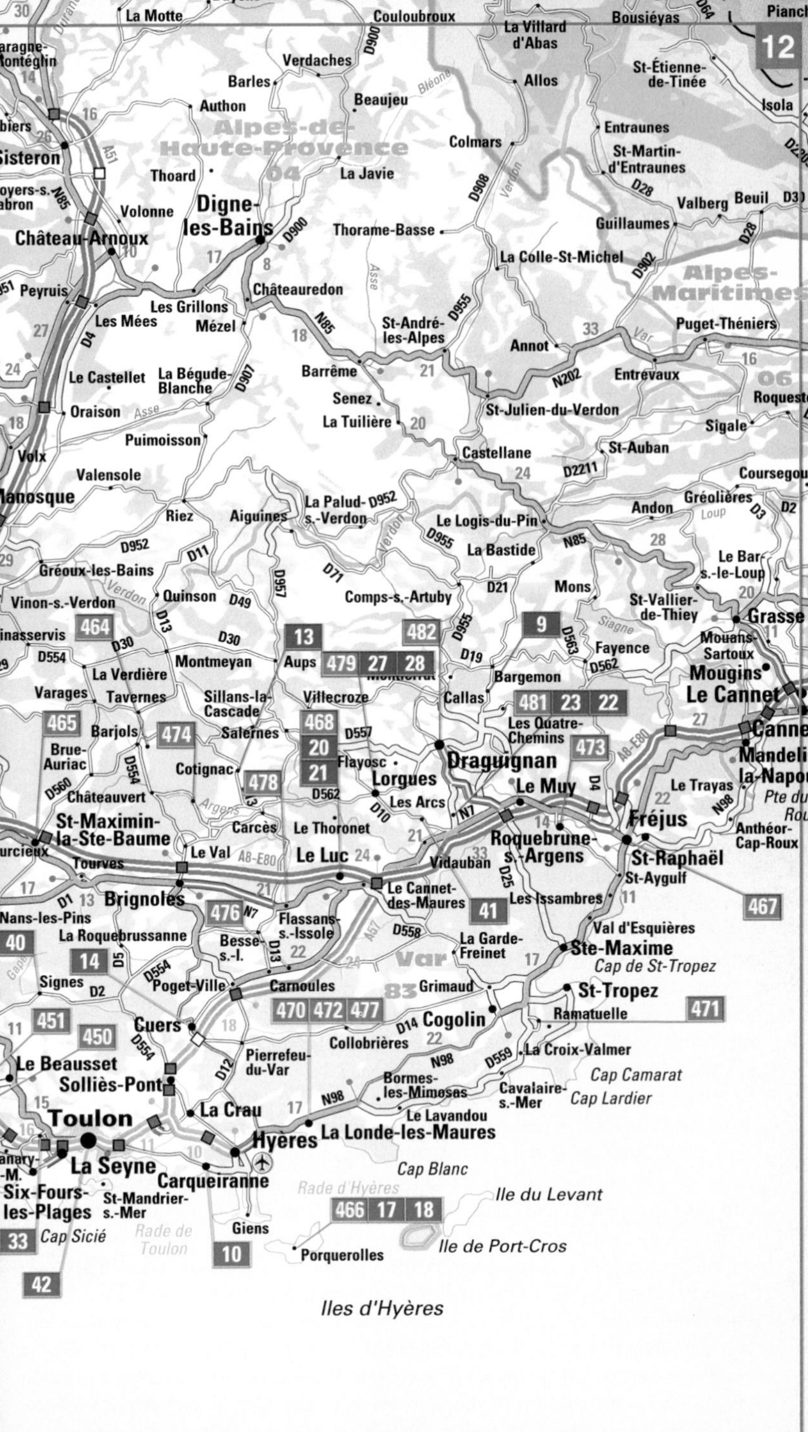
12
Alpes-de-Haute-Provence
04
Alpes-Maritimes
06
Var
83
Sisteron
Château-Arnoux
Digne-les-Bains
Manosque
Castellane
Grasse
Mougins
Le Cannet
Cannes
Mandelieu la-Napoule
Fréjus
St-Raphaël
Draguignan
Le Muy
Roquebrune-s.-Argens
Ste-Maxime
St-Tropez
Cogolin
Le Luc
Brignoles
St-Maximin-la-Ste-Baume
Toulon
La Seyne
Hyères
La Londe-les-Maures
Six-Fours-les-Plages
Le Beausset
Solliès-Pont
La Crau
Cuers
Carqueiranne
Lorgues
Les Arcs
Vidauban
Bayons
Seyne-les-Alpes
Pra-Loup
La Motte
Couloubroux
Bousiéyas
Pianche
La Villard d'Abas
Allos
St-Étienne-de-Tinée
Isola
Verdaches
Barles
Beaujeu
Authon
Colmars
Entraunes
St-Martin-d'Entraunes
Thoard
La Javie
Valberg
Beuil
Volonne
Guillaumes
Thorame-Basse
La Colle-St-Michel
Peyruis
Les Grillons
Châteauredon
Les Mées
Mézel
St-André-les-Alpes
Annot
Puget-Théniers
Le Castellet
La Bégude-Blanche
Barrême
Entrevaux
Roquestero
Oraison
Senez
La Tuilière
St-Julien-du-Verdon
Sigale
Puimoisson
St-Auban
Volx
Valensole
Coursegoules
Gréolières
Andon
Riez
Aiguines
La Palud-s.-Verdon
Le Logis-du-Pin
La Bastide
Le Bar-s.-le-Loup
Gréoux-les-Bains
Quinson
Comps-s.-Artuby
Mons
St-Vallier-de-Thiey
Vinon-s.-Verdon
Mouans-Sartoux
Fayence
Montmeyan
Aups
Bargemon
La Verdière
Varages
Tavernes
Sillans-la-Cascade
Villecroze
Callas
Barjols
Salernes
Les Quatre-Chemins
Brue-Auriac
Cotignac
Flayosc
Le Trayas
Pte du Cap Roux
Anthéor-Cap-Roux
Châteauvert
Carcès
Le Thoronet
Le Val
Tourves
Le Cannet-des-Maures
Les Issambres
St-Aygulf
Nans-les-Pins
La Roquebrussanne
Flassans-s.-Issole
Val d'Esquières
Besse-s.-I.
La Garde-Freinet
Cap de St-Tropez
Signes
Poget-Ville
Carnoules
Grimaud
Ramatuelle
Collobrières
La Croix-Valmer
Pierrefeu-du-Var
Cap Camarat
Bormes-les-Mimosas
Cavalaire-s.-Mer
Cap Lardier
Le Lavandou
Cap Blanc
Rade d'Hyères
St-Mandrier-s.-Mer
Ile du Levant
Giens
Cap Sicié
Rade de Toulon
Ile de Port-Cros
Porquerolles
Iles d'Hyères
A8-E80
A51
A57
N85
N202
N7
N98
D900
D908
D902
D955
D952
D907
D957
D2211
D28
D30
D4
D11
D13
D49
D71
D554
D560
D557
D562
D563
D19
D21
D10
D25
D558
D14
D559
D12
D1
D2
D3
D17
D64
D2205
D5
D951
D22
Durance
Bléone
Verdon
Asse
Var
Loup
Siagne
Argens
Gapeau
464
465
474
478
13
479
27
28
482
9
481
23
22
468
20
21
473
41
467
476
40
14
451
450
470
472
477
471
466
17
18
33
10
42

P R O V E N C E

INTRODUCTION

Nature has endowed Provence with two facades, that of the beaches, of *dolce farniente*, and traffic jams along the coast; and that of the mountains and forests, of hidden retreats and tiny winding roads snaking up to remote villages. There are two styles of Provençal viticulture, also: that which aims at making gulpable wines for the region's tourists without too much further ado, and the winemaking designed to emerge from the beaten path and to create wines of true distinction, capable of attracting the connoisseur's recognition. Obviously, the traveller will be the most surprised by the latter family of wines and delighted by the charming hospitality of the people who make them.

The vast Provençal vineyards span three *départements*, the Bouches-du-Rhône, the Var, and the Alpes-Maritimes, strung out from the Baux-de-Provence to the outskirts of Nice in a necklace of nine appellations. Most produce red, white, and rosé, the latter evoking the very heart and soul of Provence. Planted on the plains with Provençal abandon or laboriously pruned on *restanques* (terraced vineyards) vines here are everywhere and nowhere, reflecting a countryside and climate of enormous diversity. Some vineyards even double as the last rampart against forest fires and urban spread, common blights in Provence.

An enviable, carefree vacationland, the Provencal vineyards over the last twenty years have attracted more neophyte winemakers than any other region. Among them flourishing companies or wealthy French businesspeople, and foreigners above all, are providing the means to make the great wines of tomorrow, breaking with old-fashioned winemaking techniques and mentalities. Compared to the reputation of their wines, their investments are colossal. These investors are creating imposing reception centers, such as the Château de Berne and the Château de Sainte-Rosaline in the Côtes-de-Provence appellation, and in Romanin in the Baux-de-Provence vineyards. This "Californian" approach is revitalizing wine tourism here, which is widely developed elsewhere in France. But the Provençal wine world also includes the many *pieds-noirs* families--French nationals born in North Africa--who in the mid-1960s shook up French viticulture, along with several rare aristocratic families from Marseilles, Bandol, and Aix-en-Provence who remained faithful to the land of their ancestors. This melting pot of strongly individual winemakers is reflected in a production of extremely singular wines, individual in the choice of grape varieties (the Provençal range of grapes is one of the widest in France), in winemaking techniques, and even in the bottles and labels, with producers vying for the most original designs. But who is complaining? Certainly not the wine lover, for whom Provence is a veritable haven of delightful wine and food.

PROVENÇAL ROSÉ

Provence is an unusual piece in the French viticultural puzzle. Its heart beats mainly to the the rythm of one season and one color: the summertime rosé intended for the vast numbers of tourists here and today representing three-fourths of its wine production. For the masses of tourists who began flocking to Provence in the post-war years, undemanding in their wine tastes, Provençal *vignerons* turned out equally unambitious wines. But over the last fifteen years, the Provençal wine picture has been changing--apace with the number of tourists.

The region's rosés today are of much greater quality because of investments made in vinification equipment (rosé requires perfect temperature control and precise pressing techniques). Well-made rosé, like any good wine, is a real wine with its own identity, reflecting its vineyard origin and its grape varieties. Provençal *vignerons*, who often make red, white, as well as rosé, will tell you that rosé is technically the most difficult wine to vinify if they want to find the correct balance between its color (crimson yellow, Indian pink, onion skin, or pale pink), its freshness and its body. Rosés are made from a large array of grape varieties, Cinsault, Grenache, Syrah, Mourvèdre, and Tibouren; and with two vinification methods: direct, rapid pressing of red grapes; or by skin contact with red grapes followed by "bleeding" the juice from the fermentation vat once the proper pink is attained: the *saignée* method. The various vineyard sites are thus given subtle expression, yielding wines of finesse from the vineyards near the Montagne Sainte-Victoire; body for those of the Haut-Var; round, balanced qualities for those from the coastal vineyards, and so on: There is not one Provençal rosé, but many.

PROVENCAL APPELLATIONS

Today, there are nine Appellations d'Origine Contrôlée in Provence.

Bandol, with 1250 hectares; Cassis, 20 hectares; Palette, 20 hectares; and Bellet, with 38 hectares, are the appellations from the "old school", having been promoted to AOC status between 1936 and 1948. They are the most reputable appellations today. Its vineyards planted around eight communes northwest of Toulon, Bandol is the outstanding region for Mediterranean red wines, even though rosé today represents more than 60% of its production. Tannic, rough wines in their youth, vinified to keep at least ten years, it contains at least 50% of a very capricious grape variety, Mourvèdre, filled out with Grenache and Cinsault. The vineyards are strongly influenced by their maritime climate and location. Bandol wines are usually aged eighteen months in oak casks. Lying several *calanques* (inlets) east of Marseilles, Cassis is the stronghold *par excellence* of marvelous white wines, at once smooth and lively, made from the Ugni Blanc, Sauvignon, Doucillon (Bourboulenc), Clairette, and Marsanne grape varieties and planted on the hillsides along the sea. West of Aix-en-Provence, Palette is the least known appellation, producing

70% red wines and 15% rosé and 15% white. The predominant vines are Mourvèdre, Grenache, Cinsault, Carignan, Syrah, and Clairette. There are only two producers of Palette, including the famous Château Simone, with 80% of total production. In the Alpes-Maritimes *département* near Nice, Bellet is also a small vineyard region producing distinctive wines in all three colors, dominated by its white wines made from the Rolle grape. Bellet reds and rosés come from Cinsault and Grenache as well as from two local *cépages* which are becoming extinct, the Braquet and the Folle Noire grapes.

The Cotes-de-Provence (17,000 hectares), Coteaux-d'Aix-en-Provence (2900 hectares), Côtes-du-Luberon (2730 hectares), Coteaux-Varois (1600 hectares), and Coteaux-des-Baux (300 hectares) are much newer appellations, covering about 90% of Provençal vineyards They are owned by many cooperatives and by individual domains almost everywhere in Provence, to whom we owe the region's improved wine quality. Within these very heterognous recent appellations, you will find the best red wines in the young Coteaux-des-Baux vineyards, which were promoted to AOC with the 1995 vintage; and a few beautiful wines in the Coteaux-d'Aix-en-Provence, Coteaux-Varois, and Côtes-du-Luberon appellations. Finally, Côtes-de-Provence is the most sweeping appellation of them all. Rosé accounts for 80% of its production, but you should not overlook its red and white wines, some of which are beginning to be wines of great distinction, notably from the vineyards around Montagne Sainte-Victoire near Aix and in the Haut-Var.

BUYING WINE IN PROVENCE

The first rosés are available in late February. Most are intended to be drunk during the year following the harvest. The most full-bodied rosés, similar to those of Bandol, can attain their peak in one to two years: the longer you keep a rosé (within a limit of two to three years), the less fruity and more vinous it becomes. The 1996 harvest was marked by cool, damp weather conditions. Whatever the appellation, the rosés are quite pale, with unusual acidity. The whites are often diluted, with some exceptions: the best are from Cassis and Palette, and they all should be drunk young. The same can be said for a great majority of the red wines, which will not be wines to keep, even from vineyards like Bandol or the Baux-de-Provence, which are known for their long-lived wines. On the other hand, 1995 was a beautiful year for red wines, which are quite concentrated and Mediterranean in style despite troublesome rainfall in September. In 1998, you can begin to enjoy the Côtes-de-Provence red Syrah varietals; the Coteaux-Varois, Coteaux-d'Aix-en-Provence, and the Coteaux-de-Baux. The Bandols will just be coming out and should be patiently bottle aged for five to eight years. In this appellation, you can find older vintages: look for the '93s, '90s, '89s, or the 1988s.

A TABLE WITH PROVENCAL WINES

Rosé cries out for Provençal and more generally Mediterranean cuisine: cold or hot first courses like salads with aromatic herbs, vegetable pâtés, and stuffed vegetables with a tomato *coulis*. Whites and rosés both go well with grilled fish like red mullet, sea bass, sardines, and codfish; *bourride* fish stew and shellfish with a high iodine content like sea urchins and violets.

Certain Côtes-de-Provence rosés from coastal vineyards, particularly Bandol, stand up to more pungent tastes: *pistou* vegetable and basil soup; *anchoïade* anchovy crusts, and *aïolli* garlic mayonnaise. Provençal red wines intended to be drunk young often fill the same bill as rosés. Concentrated wines from old Grenache or Syrah vines call for grilled red meats with herbs, as well as sweet and sour Oriental cuisines--curry, lacquered duck--and Mexican dishes like tacos and enchilladas.

In their "adolescence" (about 18 months' bottle age), red Bandols can match their tannins with meat roasts. More mature Bandols are good in the autumn and winter, entering the exclusive circle of wines that go well with game.

Generally speaking, rosés should be drunk cool, between 46°F and 50°F. For certain vinous, full-bodied rosés such as Bandol and Cassis, and for Palette and Cassis white wines, it is preferable to increase the temperature slightly to 54°F, thus allowing their aromas to open out in the glass. Red wines should be served between 59°F and 64°F.

AIX-EN-PROVENCE

1 - HOTEL - **Villa Gallici**: *Avenue de la Violette (impasse des Grand Pins), 13100 Aix-en-Provence. Tel 04.42. 23.29.23 Fax 04.42.96.30.45.* Nestled in the greenery on the heights of Aix, a superb Provençal mas with original, luxurious, and refined rooms offering great comfort while avoiding stock uniformity. nineteen air-conditioned rooms: 950 to 2,950 F. Breakfast: 100 F. Swimming pool. The Clos de la Violette restaurant is 5 min on foot.

2 - RESTAURANT - **Le Clos de la Violette**: *10 avenue de la Violette, 13100 Aix-en-Provence. Tel 04.42.23.30.71 Fax 04.42.21.93.03. Closed Sunday and Monday lunch.* The best table in Aix, in a lovely family house with garden. Inventive, savory cuisine full of the southern sun. All the major Provençal and Corsican estates are on the wine list. Too bad the wine waiters change so often. Menus: 230 (lunch except holidays) to 500 F. A la carte: around 450 F.

AURONS

3 - BED & BREAKFAST - **Château Petit Sonnaillier**: *Dominique Brulat, 13121 Aurons. Tel 04.90.59.34.47.* A lovely little castle in the Coteaux-d'Aix that offers, since late 1995, a very beautiful independant room (for a couple with two children), tastefully restored in Provençal country style. Rooms: 330 F, breakfast included.

BANDOL

4 - HOTEL-RESTAURANT - **Hôtel Île Rousse**: *17 boulevard Lumière, 83150 Bandol. Tel 04.94.29.33.00 Fax 04.94. 29.49.49.* Vast 4-star hotel on the seaside, elegant, very comfortable, well kept. Ask for rooms looking out on the bay. fifty-three rooms and two suites: 350 to 1240 F. Swimming pool, beach.

BEAURECUEIL

5 - HOTEL-RESTAURANT - **Le Relais Sainte-Victoire**: *René Bergès, 53 avenue Sylvain-Gauthier, 13100 Beaurecueil. Tel 04.42.66.94.98 Fax 04.42.66.85.96. Closed Sunday evening, Monday, Friday noon and the first week in January.* An excellent inn set in a Cézanne landscape, sophisticated cuisine accompanied by the best Provençal wines and some old vintages. Menus: 175 to 420 F. Ten spacious, comfortable rooms: 400 to 700 F. There are a terrace and swimming pool.

6 - HOTEL-RESTAURANT - **Mas de la Bertrande**: *Madame Six, 13100 Beaurecueil. Tel 04.42.66.75.75 Fax 04.42.66.82.01. Closed February 15 to March 15.* 10 km east of Aix on the N7, a perfectly serene stop-off at the foot of Sainte-Victoire mountain. A perfectly commendable table (regional menu: 90 F). A personal touch in the choice of wines from Aix and the environs. Ten rooms: 380 and 550 F. Terrace and salt-water pool.

BONNIEUX-EN-PROVENCE

7 - HOTEL-RESTAURANT - **La Bastide de Capelongue**: *84480 Bonnieux-en-Provence. Tel 04.90.75.89.78 Fax 04.90.75.93.03.* A new luxury hotel built by the family who owns the

Moulin de Lourmarin. Provençal cuisine based on homegrown produce. Menus: 180 F (lunch) and 250 F (3 dishes and desserts). 17 majestic, perfectly comfortable rooms. From 900 to 1,500 F (duplex). Superb heated pool overlooking Bonnieux.

CABRIERE D'AIGUES

8 - RESTAURANT - **Restaurant de La Roque**: *Campagne La Roque, 84240 Cabrière d'Aigues. Tel 04.90.77. 63.74. Closed Sunday and Monday, the last week in September and the first three in October. By reservation.* In the Luberon, a farm restaurant isolated in the countryside. Excellent regional cuisine (scrambled eggs with truffles, game, stews, etc.). Small selection of local wines. Menus: 145 to 230 F.

CALLAS

9 - HOTEL-RESTAURANT - **Les Gorges de Pennafort**: *83830 Callas. Tel 04.94.76.66.51 Fax 04.94.76.67.23. Closed January 15 to March 15.* A

farm house isolated in the bucolic setting of a rocky cirque. Menus: 205 to 275 F. Thirty-five Côtes-de-Provence and seven Bandols, all sure to please (between 150 and 200 F). Attentive and efficient headwaiter. Somewhat gaudy 80's decor. Twelve rooms and four suites, extremely comfortable: 480 to 950 F. Breakfast: 65 F.

CARQUEIRANNE

10 - RESTAURANT - **Les Pins Penchés**: *Avenue du Général de Gaulle, port des Salettes, 83320 Carqueiranne. Tel 04.94.58.60.25 Fax 04.94.58.69.04. Closed Sunday evening and Monday except in July and August.* Two paces from the Mediteranean, a regional cuisine prepared with brio by a young chef. Marvellous wine list (100 Provençal wines) but at prices typical of the coast (rosé around 125 F). Menus: 165 to 215 F. A la carte: around 250 F.

CASSIS

11 - HOTEL-RESTAURANT - **Le Clos des Arômes**: *10 rue Paul-Mouton, rue Agostini, 13260 Cassis. Tel 04.42.01.71.84 Fax 04.42.01.31.76. Closed October to April.* A cozy village house with small rooms draped in Provençal fabrics. Breakfast (45 F) in the garden. 8 rooms: 295 to 570 F.

12 - HOTEL-RESTAURANT - **Le Jardin d'Emile**: *Plage du Bestouan, 13260 Cassis. Tel 04.42.01.80.55 Fax 04.42.01.80.70.* Across the road from the Bestouan beach, a beautiful house completely redone in fashionable Mediteranean tones. 6 handsome, fairly good sized, air-conditioned rooms (400 to 600 F). Breakfast: 50 F. The cuisine wagers on southern classics. Chic. A still modest wine list, but which offers some pleasures. Menus: 98 (lunch) to 195 F.

COTIGNAC

13 - BED & BREAKFAST - **Domaine Nestuby**: *83570 Cotignac. Tel 04.94. 04.60.02 Fax 04.94.04.79.22. Closed November to February.* Four spacious guest rooms, nicely decorated, in a Côtes-de-Provence estate. 320 F per night per couple, breakfast included. Meals: 100 F, wine from the property at will.

CUERS

14 - RESTAURANT - **Le Lingousto**: *Route de Pierrefeu, 83390 Cuers. Tel 04.94.28.69.10 Fax 04.94.48.63.79. Closed Sunday evening and Monday.* Good Provençal cuisine prepared with talent by Alain Ryon,

served in a stylish decor with large covered terrace in summer. Exemplary wine list with eighteen Côtes-de-Provence and twelve Bandols. Satisfaction at around 100 F. Strongly recommended. Menus: 180 to 380 F, with a menu at 290 F wine included.

GEMENOS

15 - RESTAURANT - **Baron Brisse**: *48 chemin de Jouques, 13420 Gemenos. Tel 04.42.32.00.60 Fax 04.42.32.09.60. Closed Sunday evening and Monday.* Flavorfully seasoned cuisine (excellent market fish). The menu at 145 F is one of the best deals we've found. Excellent selection of Provençal wines that won't run up the bill. Menus: 145 to 225 F.

GRAMBOIS

16 - HOTEL-RESTAURANT - **Le Clos des Sources**: *Quartier Le Brusquet, 84240 Grambois. Tel 04.90.77. 93.55 Fax 04.90.77.92.96.* A modern hotel with Provençal architecture situated in the heart of the

Luberon, open since summer 95. Panoramic view. Twelve rooms: 390 to 520 F (1 pers.), 440 to 680 F (2 pers.).

ÎLE DE PORQUEROLLES

17 - HOTEL-RESTAURANT - **L'Oustaou**: *Île de Porquerolles, 83400 Hyères. Tel 04.94.58.30.13 Fax 04.94.58.34.93.*

Closed in January and February. In the port, five simple, comfortable, air-conditioned rooms from 450 to 550 F. Restaurant on the premises.

18 - HOTEL-RESTAURANT - **Le Mas du Langoustier**: *Baie du Langoustier, Île de Porquerolles, 83400 Hyères. Tel 04.94.58.30.09 Fax 04.94.58.36.02. Closed mid-October to late April.* A luxurious little paradise. The hotel has been completely renovated. Based on excellent local products, the fine cuisine is subtle and savory. Not to be missed while on the island. Menus: 320 to 550 F. A la carte: around 500 F. 47 rooms and 3 apartments: 900 to 1,650 F.

LA CADIERE-D'AZUR

19 - HOTEL-RESTAURANT - **Hostellerie Bérard**: *Rue Gabriel-Péri, 83740 La Cadière-d'Azur. Tel 04.94.90. 11.43 Fax 04.94.90.01.94. Closed Sunday evening, Monday (low-season) and mid-January to late February.* Sunny cuisine featuring piquant seasonings and savors. Game in season. Large and interesting selection of Bandols by the lady of the house who also

knows how to spot good wines in other regions. Let her guide you. New wine list of old Bandol vintages (notably a 1966 Tempier). Menus:

160 to 450 F. 40 very comfortable rooms situated in the old houses around the restaurant, from 455 to 1,200 F. Swimming pool, sauna, exercice room.

LE LUC

20 - BED & BREAKFAST - **Château de Roux**: *Le Cannet des Maures, 83340 Le Luc. Tel 04.94.60.73.10 Fax 04.94. 60.89.79.* 5 mn from the Luc toll booth, this good Côtes-de-Provence estate offers a comfortable room for 2 and a suite for 4 (300 and 600 F, breakfast included) in its old, ocher rough-cast family manor. Very good communal table by reservation (150 F).

21 - RESTAURANT - **Le Gourmandin**: *8 place Brunet, 83340 Le Luc. Tel 04.94.60.85.92 Fax 04.94.47.91.10. Closed Sun. evening and Mon. and from 8/20 to 9/10.* In a village house, copious and tasty seasonal cuisine (excellent first menus, truffles in winter). 15 Côtes-de-Provence between 80 and 120 F. Service on the veranda. Menus: 106 (lunch weekdays) to 235 F. A la carte: around 250 F.

LES ARCS-SUR-ARGENS

22 - HOTEL-RESTAURANT - **Le Logis du Guetteur**: *Place du Château, 83460 Les Arcs-sur-Argens. Tel 04.94. 73.30.82 Fax 04.94.73.39.95. Closed mid-January to March 1.* Cool, vaulted rooms and poolside terrace. Traditional Provençal cuisine. Good selection of Côtes-de-Provence. Menus: 135 to 290 F. Ten comfortable rooms (470 to 520 F) in an old

castle. Breakfast: 50 F.

23 - RESTAURANT - **Le Bacchus Gourmand**: *Maison des Vins, N7, 83460 Les Arcs-sur-Argens. Tel 04.94.47. 48.47. Closed Sunday evening and Monday.* Bright dining rooms and terrace. Fine cuisine with a Provençal accent. An exhaustive wine list for Côtes-de-Provence and, for once, at reasonable prices (70 to 160 F). Menus: 150 to 270 F.

LES-BAUX-DE-PROVENCE

24 - HOTEL-RESTAURANT - **L'Oustau de Baumanière**: *Val-d'Enfer, 13520 Les-Baux-de-Provence. Tel 04.90.54. 33.07 Fax 04.90.54.40.46. Closed Wednesday and noon Thursday from October 15 to April 1 and in February.* Relais & Châteaux. Distinguished table, one of the most renowned in Provence. The wine list

is the best in Provence but prices are in keeping with the establishment. Menus: 450 to 690 F. Twelve rooms and eight suites: 1,250 to 2,200 F. Breakfast: 120 F.

25 - HOTEL-RESTAURANT - **La Benvengudo**: *Vallon de l'Arcoule, 13520 Les-Baux-de-Provence. Tel 04.90.54.32.54 Fax 04.90.54.42.58. Closed from November to early February.* At the foot of Baux, a comfortable

hotel in a charming old farm house. seventeen air-conditioned rooms: 530 to 930 F. Breakfast: 62 F.

26 - HOTEL-RESTAURANT - **Le Mas d'Aigret**: *D27, 13520 Les Baux-de-Provence. Tel 04.90.54.33.54 Fax 04.90.54.41.37.* Reopening early 1998. A surprising troglodytic (carved into the rock) restaurant with good regional cuisine. Unoriginal wine list, but which welcomes regional wines. sixteen comfortable rooms (some with garden, others troglodytic) looking out on the Crau.

LORGUES

27 - BED & BREAKFAST - **Domaine Saint-Jean-Baptiste**: *1525 Route de des Arcs, 83510 Lorgues. Tel 04.94.73.71.11 Fax 04.94.73.26.91.* In her viticultural estate surrounded by vineyards, Brigitte Grivet offers three simple, very quiet guest rooms. Warm welcome, good breakfast. 260 F (1 night, 2 pers.).

28 - HOTEL-RESTAURANT - **Chez Bruno**: *Bruno Clément, 83510 Lorgues. Tel 04.94.73.92.19 Fax 04.94.73.78.11. Closed Sunday evening and Monday.* Charming mas with shaded terrace run by a real character: earthy, imposing, and outspoken. Lots of truffles (estivum in summer). Trust him for wine; the best of Provence are on his wine list. Menu: 280 F. Three extremely comfortable rooms: 480 to 750 F.

LOURMARIN

29 - HOTEL-RESTAURANT - **Auberge La Fenière**: *Reine and Guy Sammut, Route de Cadenet BP 18, 84160 Lourmarin. Tel 04.90.68.11.79 Fax 04.90.68.18.60. Closed noon Monday and in January.* In the spring of 1997, Reine Sammut moved into this beautiful, bright house looking out on the Durance valley. Her cooking is always savory, based on the region's best products. Guy, her talkative and considerate husband, is in the dining room, assisted by Eric Sertour, a brilliant Parisian wine waiter. Marvellous wine list for southern wines, including the Languedoc. Menus: 190 to 490 F. Seven rooms with refined country-

style decor from 550 to 950 F. Breakfast: 80 F. Swimming pool.

30 - HOTEL-RESTAURANT - **Le Moulin de Lourmarin**: *84160 Lourmarin. Tel 04.90.68.06.69 Fax 04.90.68.31.76. Closed early January to February 15.* Modern, somewhat gaudy accommodations set up in a former

mill with view of the castle. Flavorful, pert and innovative cooking by Edourad Loubet. Attractive wine list. Menu: 195 to 400 F. A la carte: around 500 F. Eighteen rooms and two suites: 500 to 2,100 F. Breakfast: 85 F.

MAUSSANE-LES-ALPILLES

31 - RESTAURANT - **La Petite France**: *15 avenue Vallée des Baux, 13520 Maussane-les-Alpilles. Tel 04.90.54.41.91 Fax 04.90.54.52.50. Closed noon Thursday and Wednesday, in January and one week in November.* Cozy decor with bacchic posters, warm welcome, and generous Provençal cuisine based on excellent local products. All Baux wines are on the list. Menus: 175 to 350 F. A la carte: around 300 F.

MEYREUIL

32 - RESTAURANT - **L'Auberge Provençale**: *RN7, Quartier Le Canet, 13590 Meyreuil. Tel 04.42.58.68.54 Fax 04.42.58.68.05. Closed Tuesday evening and Wednesday.* A renovated dining room with a Provençal twist and a generous cuisine using regional products. Attractive list for Provençal as well as Rhône valley wines at reasonable prices. Menus: 100 to 240 F.

OLLIOULES

33 - RESTAURANT - **La Table du Vigneron**: *Domaine de Terrebrune, Chemin de la Tourelle, 83190 Ollioules. Tel 04.94.74.01.30 Fax 04.94.74.60.54. By reservation. Closed Monday and Sunday evening from September to June.* The Delille brothers, renowned Bandol vintners, run the inn. On the menu: anchovy sauce, grilled meats, brandade, good Provençal cuisine accompanied by their own wine. Tour and degustation in the cellar. Menus: 200 to 260 F.

PUYLOUBIER

34 - RESTAURANT - **Les Sarments**: *4 rue Qui-Monte, 13114 Puyloubier. Tel 04.42.66.31.58. Closed Monday and noon Tuesday.* In one of Puyloubier's narrow streets, a rustic, family-style Provençal cuisine served in a small, cool dining room. Ten good Côtes-de-Provence at smart prices. Informal service. A la carte: around 150 F.

PUYVERT

35 - BED & BREAKFAST - **Château Saint-Pierre de Mejans**: *Laurence Doan*

de Champassak, 84160 Puyvert. Tel 04.90.08.40.51 Fax 04.90.08.41.96. An apartment and a double with

salon (750 F) in a majestic priory that produces Côtes du Luberon. Stylishly personalized decor in an idyllic location.

SAINT-ANDIOL

36 - HOTEL-RESTAURANT - **Le Berger des Abeilles**: *Nicole Grenier, 13670 Saint-Andiol Tel 04.90.95.01.91 Fax 04.90.95.48.26. Closed Sunday*

evening and Monday (low-season), in January and February. A friendly little house offering fresh, locally-inspired, motherly cooking served under a lush plane tree in summer. Short list of Rhône and Provençal wines. Menus: 140 to 250 F. 6 well-equipped rooms: 300 to 370 F.

SAINT-CANNAT

37 - BED & BREAKFAST - **Château de Beaupré**: *Marie-Jeanne and Christian Double, Les Plantades, RN7, 13760 Saint-Cannat. Tel (cellar) 04.42.57. 23.83 Tel (reservations) 04.90.59. 49.40 Fax 04.42.57.27.90.* In the charming viticultural buildings of this lovely 18th-century farm house (see the Coteaux d'Aix estates), two calm and comfortable vacation houses for 2: 1450 to 1780 F, or 5 persons: 1860 to 2630 F, by the week.

SAINT-CYR-SUR-MER

38 - RESTAURANT - **La Calanque de Port-d'Alon**: *83270 Saint-Cyr-sur-Mer. Tel 04.94.26.20.08. Closed evenings and Tuesday from October to April. Closed in November.* On a private beach (admission: 50 F, reimbursed in the restaurant). A protected site surrounded by pine groves and facing the Big Blue, where one feasts on fresh grilled fish or bouillabaisse in a summery, good-natured atmosphere. Attractive wine list with ten very good white, red and rosé Bandols. Menus: 149 to 198 F. A la carte: around 275 F.

SAINT-REMY-DE-PROVENCE

39 - HOTEL - **Château des Alpilles**: *D31, 13210 Saint-Rémy-de-Provence. Tel 04.90.92.03.33 Fax 04.90.92.45.17. Closed mid-November to mid-December and 1/9 to mid-February.* High quality and refinement for VIP

voyagers in an entirely restored 19th-century manor. 15 air-conditioned rooms, 4 suites and 1 small seperate house: 900 to 2,000 F. Pool.

SIGNES

40 - RESTAURANT - **Espace Thélème**: *Sainte-Fleur, 83870 Signes. Tel 04.94.32.80.69 Fax 04.94.32.80.70. By reservation only.* A renowned oenologist in the region, M. Aubanel conceived this location, with its contemporary Greco-roman decor, for organizing initiations to wine tasting. Competent service and a variety of excellent wines, particularly those from Bandol.

TARADEAU

41 - BED & BREAKFAST - **Château de Saint-Martin**: *83460 Taradeau. Tel 04.94.73. 02.01.* Of the 70 rooms in this 18th-century manor, three welcome guests for princely stays. 500 F, breakfast included.

TOULON

42 - RESTAURANT - **Le Jardin du Sommelier**: *20, allée de l'Amiral-Courbet, 83000 Toulon Tel 04.94.62.03.27 Fax 04.94.09.01.49.* The Provençal bistro of a young wine waiter, Christian Scalisi, who previously worked in fine restaurants. Pert cuisine, informal welcome, a good value and a fond tribute paid to wines of the south (selection of Bandols and Côtes-de-Provence) and from elsewhere that won't run the bill sky-high. Very strongly recommended. Menus: 160 to 220 F. A la carte: around 220F.

TRETS

43 - RESTAURANT - **Le Clos Gourmand**: *13 bd de la République, 13530 Trets. Tel 04.42.61.33.72.* Traditional Provençal cuisine in a discreet, contemporary ambiance. Good menu for Provençal flavors at 170 F. On the wine list, 15 Côtes-de-Provence from Sainte-Victoire mountain from 85 to 150 F.

TO SEE

CASSIS

OUTING - Creek tours. Year-round boat

tours. Departure from the port on request. See 5 or 8 creeks.

LES ARCS-SUR-ARGENS

OUTING - **The House of " Côtes de Provence " wines**: *RN7, 83460 Les Arcs-sur-Argens. Tel. 04.94.99. 50.20 Fax 04.94.99.50.29. Monday-Friday from 8:30 to 12am and 2 to 6pm (closing at 7pm in June and September, at 8pm in July and August).* Brochures on the Côtes-de-Provence wines and vineyard, in a vast, modernly decorated cellar where one can choose among 650 Côte-de-

Provence, 12 of which are continuously offered for a free tasting.

MENERBES

MUSEUM - **Corkscrew museum, Domaine de la Citadelle**: *84560 Ménerbes.Tel 04.90.72.41.58. Open 4/1 to 9/30 from 9 to 12am and 2 to 7pm (weekends and holidays from 10 to 12am and 3 to 7pm). 10/30 to 3/31 from 9 to 12am and 2 to 6pm, Saturday from 9 to 12am. Museum closed Sunday and holidays.* West of Bonnieux, in the Luberon mountains, the property of Yves Rousset-Rouard (theatre and cinema producer) displays more than one thousand well-presented corkscrews (some one of a kind) from the 17th century to the present. The location also has a bookstore specializing in works on vineyards and wines, as well as a vine garden.

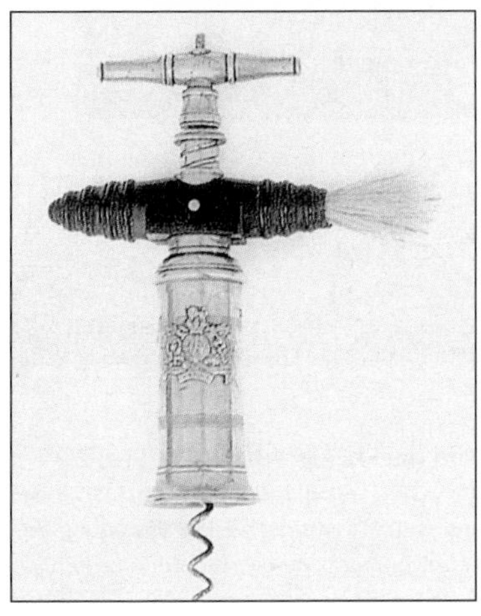

TARADEAU

OUTING - **Château de Saint-Martin**: *83460 Taradeau. Tel 04.94.73.02.01 Fax 04.94.73.12.36. 9am-8pm, in summer. Cellar open from 9am to 5pm Monday-Saturday from November to April. From 9am-8pm from May to October.* Show: 30 F. A 25-minute light and sound show (10 shows per day) in the magnificent 15th-century cellars of this great Côtes-de-Provence viticultural estate (no showings in harvesting season).

VITICULTURAL FESTIVITIES

JULY
The Coteaux d'Aix fair on the cours Mirabeau in Aix-en-Provence, the last weekend in July.

DECEMBER
The Vintage fête in Bandol: first Sunday in December. In the port, huge tasting of the last red Bandol vintage, served from the cask. Attractions and an excellent popular atmosphere.

Claude Jouve-Férec and Madame Castell, his winemaker, perpetuate the tradition of great red wines from Bandol.

Domaine Lafran-Veyrolles

Owner Claude Jouve-Férec. **Address** Route de l'Argile, 83740 La Cadière-d'Azur Tel. 04.94.90.13.37 (office) or 04.94.98.72.59 Fax 04.94.90.11.18. **Open** From Monday to Friday, 8:30-12:00 and 13:30-17:00. Week-end by appointment.

A far cry from the media's spotlight on certain Provençal vineyards, the discretion of Lafran-Veyrolles (like that of its owner) is equalled only by the regular quality of its wines. Owned by the Férec family since the 19th century, the domaine comprises ten hectares of vines which are meticulously tended--no chemical weedkillers are used--and planted on one of the best clay-limestone *terroirs* of La Cadière. Somewhat restrained in their youth, Férec's red Bandols blossom with ten years' bottle age. Since 1993, when destemming was initiated, there have been two cuvées. The Classique, from 60-70% destemmed Mourvèdre with Grenache, Cinsault, and Carignan; and the Spéciale, from 90-100% Mourvèdre, a wine of great longevity in the finest Bandol tradition. The '94 Classique (61 F), its bouquet of leather and black berries, and soft, delicate tannins on the palate, is a graceful Bandol which can be drunk now. Jouve-Férec's white wine (55 F, '96), from Clairette and Ugni, and his rosé (54 F, '96) are wines of great character, combining fruitiness and body.

Our choice The '94 red Bandols Cuvée Spéciale (65 F). Lacking the concentration of the '93s and '91s (if they are still available, snap them up!), this 90% Mourvèdre Bandol is one of the most beautiful wines from the vintage. Balanced and fruity bouquet, discreet, velvety, fresh taste, tannins perceptible but not austere. Five to six years' bottle age.

Reception By Claude Jouve-Férec, an erudite native of Provençe and an attentive host.

How to get there *(Map 11): On A50, exit La Cadière-d'Azur. In the first turn going up to La Cadière, turn left (sign) in 2km. Domain on the left, on edge of autoroute.*

Jean-Pierre Gausen speaks out for Mourvèdre.

Domaine de la Noblesse

Owners Julia and Jean-Pierre Gaussen. **Address** 1585 route de l'Argile, 83740 La Cadière-d'Azur - Tel. 04.94.98.75.54 Fax 04.94.98.65.34. **Open** Every day, 8:00-12:00 and 13:30-20:00. **Spoken** Espagnol, some English.

To get an idea of the strong personality of Bandol's Mourvèdre, its virile tannins and powerful extract, a tasting with Jean-Pierre Gaussen is de *rigueur*. He planted his first vines here twenty-five years ago, today totalling twenty hectares, most of which are on an excellent hillside, Les Costes, facing east-southeast. Gaussen vinifies the old-fashioned way, using large wooden vats shaped like a flattened cone which are installed in his cool cellar hewn out of the rock.
Gaussen also has a permanent stock of five vintages on offer. The '89 (79 F), with a bouquet of leather and glazed figs, still very young, dense, tight extract, needs two years' bottle age. We can begin to drink the '91 (79 F), delivering fruit and tannin but without hard edges. Gaussen's '93 (79 F) impressed us with its brilliant, inky color, its bouquet of *garrigue*, blackberry preserves, and its extremely structured, explosive taste: to be laid down until the year 2000. On the other hand, the domaine's whites and rosés (48 F), aromatic, soft, and mouth-watering, can be enjoyed young.

Our choice In 1994, a vintage of little concentration in Bandol, Gaussen made an outstanding wine, the Longue Garde (79 F): somber, deep-purple color, bouquet of black fruit, vanilla, roasted coffee, opening up with an immediate softness on the palate, and smooth, firm, powerful extract. Can be drunk now.

Reception Informal, family-style, at the cellar entrance.

How to get there *(Map 11): On A 50, exit La Cadière-d'Azur. In the first turn going up to La Cadière, turn left (signposted) after 1.5kms.*

Henri de Saint-Victor, who discovered the Pibarnon terroir, and his son, Eric.

Château de Pibarnon

Owners Catherine, Henri and Éric de Saint-Victor. **Address** 83740 La Cadière-d'Azur Tel. 04.94.90.12.73 Fax 04.94.90.12.98. **Open** From Monday to Saturday, 8:00-12:00 and 14:00-18:30. **Spoken** English, Spanish. **Credit cards** Visa, Eurocard, MasterCard.

The Château de Pibarnon is magic. Its sheer location is magic: towering above the sea at an altitude of 900 feet, the Château stands on an escarpment scattered with Alep pines and 45 hectares of terraced vines, some planted in a rocky amphitheater, others on a balcony facing Saint-Cyr. Its *terroir* is magic: the Pibarnon hillside and its active limestone-clay soils are "150 million years older than the other local formations." Its men are magic: Henri de Saint-Victor discovered the potential of this site, planting his grapes here and vinifying them with his considerable winemaking talent. Finally, the Château de Pibarnon's wines are magic: they have the stupendous ability of Pibarnon reds to enthrall the taster as young wines, while developing into great wines in their maturity. No longer available at the domaine, the excellent '89s, '91s and '92s can still be found in good wine shops and restaurants. There is a fine rosé (63 F), a *saignée* wine from 50% Mourvèdre, with body and balance: a good escort for spicy dishes.

Our choice We found the '94 red Bandol (74 F), somewhat thinner and dryer than usual, preferring the '93 (76 F), with the full, unctuous bouquet and taste typical of young Pibarnons (cocoa, pine sap, cherries, leather); silky, balanced, mouth-filling, persistent but delicate tannins.

Reception In the château's beautiful cellars lined with casks; Henri has transmitted his contagious enthusiasm to his son.

How to get there *(Map 11): On A 50, exit La Cadière-d'Azur. In the first turn going up to La Cadière, second road on left (sign). Go 5km over a winding road up the hillside.*

At the foot of the hillside in La Cadière-d'Azur, Geneviève and Henri Tournier brought out their first Bandol in 1989.

Domaine de la Roche-Redonne

Owners Geneviève and Henri Tournier. **Address** 83740 La Cadière-d'Azur - Tel. 04.94.90.11.83 Fax 04.94.90.00.96. **Open** Thursday, Friday and Saturday 10:00-12:00 and 16:00-20:00 from Easter to Nov. 1, and by appointment. **Spoken** English.

A newcomer to the exclusive Bandol wine scene, Roche-Redonne was established in 1989 from a regrouping of family vineyards whose production until then had been vinified by the local cooperative cellar. The young domaine shows outstanding promise, making its way quietly through the Bandol wine world of historic properties. It has already become known for its contemporary red wines, whose intense fruit and elegant extract make them drinkable when they are young (what are restaurateurs waiting for before discovering this wine?). Roche-Redonne's vines are planted on twelve hectares divided into three vineyards located around the cellar on the north hillside of La Cadière; on the south hillside; and in Sainte-Anne, where the famous Redonne Rock is located. Although it isn't (yet) mentioned on the label, there are two red Bandols from domaine: one from predominantly Grenache, supple and charming; the other from pure Mourvèdre, more dense and tannic, of greater longevity but rarely austere. You will find a very good white Bandol (55 F), from 95% Clairette with Ugni, vinified in vats and barrels, a fine balance between ample licorice tastes and vibrant fruit.

Our choice The '93 Bandol, predominantly Mourvèdre. Bouquet of black currants, cocoa, leading on to musky notes; silky on the palate, with fine, dense, long tannins. It's best to begin with the '94 (60 F), with more balance but similar style.

Reception Informally, in the vinification cellar or a small, rustic tasting room.

How to get there *(Map 11): On A 50, exit La Cadière-d'Azur. Go into La Cadière then back down towards Saint-Cyr. 1km on right, on edge of autoroute.*

Managed by Jean-Marie (above) and François Peyraud, the Domaine Tempier is benchmark for aficianados of red Bandol.

Domaine Tempier

Owners Jean-Marie and François Peyraud. **Address** 83330 Le Plan-du-Castelet - Tel. 04.94.98.70.21 Fax 04.94.90.21.65. **Open** From Monday to Saturday morning, 9:00-12:00 and 14:00-18:00, except national holiday. **Spoken** English. **Credit cards** Visa, Eurocard, MasterCard.

Owned by the Peyraud family since 1834, Tempier is an exception with its thirty hectares of vines in the communes of Le Beausset, La Cadière, and Le Castellet meticulously planted in tiny parcels. Certain parcels are vinified separately, offering red Bandols which differ depending on the vines' expositions and the more or less marked presence of Mourvèdre. No red wine is either filtered or fined. At the base of the quality pyramid is the '94 Bandol Classique (80% Mourvèdre): *garrigue*, pepper, extract more present but still balanced in '94 (74 F): a small vintage, it must be remembered. Then come the Bandols from the major vineyards: La Migoua, 50% Mourvèdre from hillside vines, with Grenache and Cinsault: concentrated bouquet, dense but delicate tannins, especially in '94 (82 F), which is already opened up; La Tourtine (60% Mourvèdre, 82 F), suave and smooth, with more volume; and Cabassou, 100% Mourvèdre from 40-year-old vines: the darkest color, tannic, depth of flavor (our choice). The Peyraud family, the guarantor of Bandol quality, has older vintages available, including several excellent '93s and the '89 Turtine in magnum for 233 Francs.

Our choice The '94 red Cabassaou Bandol (98 F): brilliant cardinal red; spicy, eucalyptus bouquet, beautifully round attack, with a powerful but fluid middle taste; fine, fruity finish. Good to drink as of late 1998.

Reception Charming, in an old tasting cellar.

How to get there *(Map 12): On A 50, exit Number 11 at La Cadière-d'Azur, towards Le Plan du Castellet. After 2km on left, small road behind the new school.*

The Tour du Bon vineyards, the great discovery in Bandol in 1990.

Domaine de La Tour du Bon

Owner Family Hocquard. **Supervisor** Agnès Henry-Hocquard. **Address** 83330 Le Brûlat-du-Castellet - Tel. 04.94.32.61.62 Fax 04.94.32.71.69. **Open** From Monday to Friday, 9:00-12:00 and 14:00-18:00, weekend preferably by appointment. **Spoken** English.

In the course of our last blind tasting (label concealed) of the 1994 vintage in Bandol, we wrote about one wine: "elegant oaky edge, straightforward style, direct; great, classic Mourvèdre." And we put in the margin of our tasting notes, "Tempier?". No, this lovely wine came from the "recent" domaine of the young people behind it, Agnès Henry and her *maître de chai* from Saumur, Antoine Pouponneau. The domaine comprises twelve hectares in the north of the Bandol appellation, with low-yielding vines planted on a mixture of white (Saint-Ferréol) and red soils; grapes are carefully selected by parcel; during vinification, they are partially destemmed and a minimum of sulphur is used. The Tour du Bon makes a very good white wine (57 F) from Rolle and Clairette grapes, which are partially vinified in barrels; the '96 is especially vibrant and delicate. The two red Bandols get better by the vintage: the Classique (60-70% Mourvèdre, with Cinsault and Grenache) and the Saint-Ferréol, from selected parcels of destemmed Mourvèdre, aged in oak, excellent in '95 (80 F) but produced in limited quantity.

Our choice The '94 red Bandol (60 F). Soft bouquet of mocha and grilled tomatoes, supple taste with good tannin extraction and no hard edges; lingering on palate. Ready to drink. The '95 (60 F), dense and vigorous, should be kept longer.

Reception In a small, intimate tasting room, by an enthusiastic young team.

***How to get there** (Map 12): On A 50, exit Number 11 at La Cadière-d'Azur. Between Le Castellet and Sainte-Anne-du-Castellet. The road to the domaine is indicated.*

At the Château Vannières, you can still find old vintages of Bandol.

Château Vannières

Owners Colette and Éric Boisseaux. **Address** 83740 La Cadière-d'Azur - Tel. 04.94.90.08.08 Fax 04.94.90.15.98. **Open** From Monday to Saturday, 8:00-12:00 and 14:00-18:00. Sunday by appointment. **Spoken** English. **Credit cards** Visa, Eurocard, MasterCard.

In 1957 by the Boisseaux family from Burgundy, the 34-hectare Château Vannières is unusual in two ways. First, its sole red Bandol is less marked by the imposing Mourvèdre (50% filled out by Grenache and Cinsault grapes) than those from the other great historic vineyards in the Bandol appellation. As a young wine, it is by nature silkier and more balanced, while retaining beautiful qualities with age: complex notes of humus, leather, truffles, wet fur. Secondly, Vannières is one of the rare Bandol properties where old bottles are regularly stocked and brought out. Eight vintages are available, from 1975 (175 F) to 1993 (75 F). Thus offered is a great array of splendid sensations, such as those of the '89 (95 F), a powerful Bandol laced with roasted coffee and cocoa, marked by the grapes' advanced maturity and soaring, delicate tannins. Don't miss the '96 white Bandol (75 F) with its tastes of aniseed, honey, and apricot.

Our choice The '93 red Bandol (75 F): ripe fruitiness (prunes, blackberry preserves), silky, dense tannins. Very pleasant today, it can also age beautifully. The '85 (120 F), suave and earthy (truffles), with perfectly soft tannins, is at its peak now.

Reception Very professional, in a medieval-style barrel-vaulted tasting cellar. Summer art exhibits.

How to get there *(Map 12): On A 50, exit Number 11 at La Cadière-d'Azur direction Le Castellet; then stay on D82, going along the autoroute to your left, towards Saint-Cyr for 4km. Signposted.*

The tasting room is always amusingly decorated.

Domaines Bunan

Owners Paul, Pierre and Laurent Bunan. **Manager** Paul Bunan. **Address** Moulin des Costes, 83740 La Cadière-d'Azur - Tel. 04.94.98.58.98 Fax 04.94.98.60.05 **Open** From Mon. to Sat., 9:00-12:30 and 14:30-19:00 (18:00 in winter). Sunday and national holidays only from Apr. to Oct., 10:00-12:00 and 16:00-19:00. **Spoken** English, Spanish **Credit cards** Visa, Eurocard, MasterCard.

In perpetual movement, the Bunan clan is constantly perfecting their vineyard and winery since they set up on the Bandol *restanques* in 1962. The vat room could serve as a model, with impeccably maintained casks and a beautiful cellar, which was restored in 1996; and their vast, magnificent 85 ha of vines bearing the Côtes-de-Provence and Bandol labels for reds, whites, and rosés. The two outstanding vineyard sites are Moulin des Costes, with 18 ha producing red Bandol (70% Mourvèdre and 30% Grenache), supple and round; and the 6 ha Château La Rouvière: the 100% Mourvèdre is a Bandol of great longevity, a collector's item, and is made only in the great vintages. From the 1994 vintage, we will not be sad to console ourselves with the Moulin des Costes (about 50 F), very well made for the vintage, with a powerful bouquet of ripe fruit and resin, soft tannins: a charming wine which can be enjoyed now. The white and rosé Moulin des Costes (50 F), delicate and light, are lovely with the first warm days of summer. Those from the Château de la Rouvière (55 F; '96), more structured, will improve with a year in bottle.

Our choice The '93 red Château de la Rouvière (74 F). Still dominated by powerful fruit; generous, full-bodied taste, spicy, tannic finish; it is maturing beautifully. Pour it into a carafe two hours before serving.

Reception A priority, exemplary professionalism, in a vast tasting room, always amusingly decorated.

How to get there *(Map 11): On A 50 exit Bandol (6km). From Bandol towards Beausset (D 559) for 4km. 300 yards after the autoroute bridge, on left.*

The warm atmosphere in Luc and Frédéric Cartier's tasting room.

Mas de Gourgonnier

Owners Luc and Frédéric Cartier. **Address** Le Destet, 13890 Mouriès - Tel. 04.90.47.50.45 Fax 04.90.47.51.36. **Open** Week: 9:00-12:00 and 14:00-18:00. Sunday (closed in Jan. and Feb.) 9:00-12:00 and 15:00-17:30. **Spoken** English. **Credit cards** Visa, Eurocard, MasterCard.

As we crossed their valley dotted with vines, olive trees, rosemary, and green oaks, we could see why the Cartier brothers don't need an arsenal of chemicals to cultivate their land. Biodynamic viticulture is very widespread here and enjoys a microclimate favorable for it. Luc and Frédéric grow 42 hectares of vines and 20 hectares of olive trees in the valley, selling their wine and olive oil with the label *Nature et Progrès*. The Cartiers' olive oil (55 F for 50 cl.), delicate and aromatic, is as regular and straightforward as their white AOC Coteaux-d'Aix-en-Provence and their rosé and red wines, 60% of their production, made predominantly from Grenache grapes and bearing the Baux-de-Provence label. The rosé is vinous while remaining a wine of fruit and verve, as is highlighted by the '96 (31 F). Of the red wines, four vintages are available, including a good Tradition (31 F): aroma of *garrigue* and fur; red berries come out strongly on the palate, with less evident tannins. For a wine of greater complexity, try the Réserve du Mas: the delicious '89 (60 F) invites an analogy with venison and glazed prunes.

Our choice The '95 red Réserve du Mas Baux de Provence (42 F), from Grenache, Syrah, Cabernet: very aromatic bouquet (a characteristic of the appellation) suggesting unguent, crushed black olives, licorice. Silky, smooth taste. Good to drink now or to cellar for two years.

Reception Affable, in a charming tasting room. For children, homemade apricot and grape juice is for sale.

How to get there *(Map 11): On A 7, exit Cavaillon (34km), towards Saint-Rémy-de-Provence, then Maussanne-les-Alpilles and Le Destet. The domaine is on the left.*

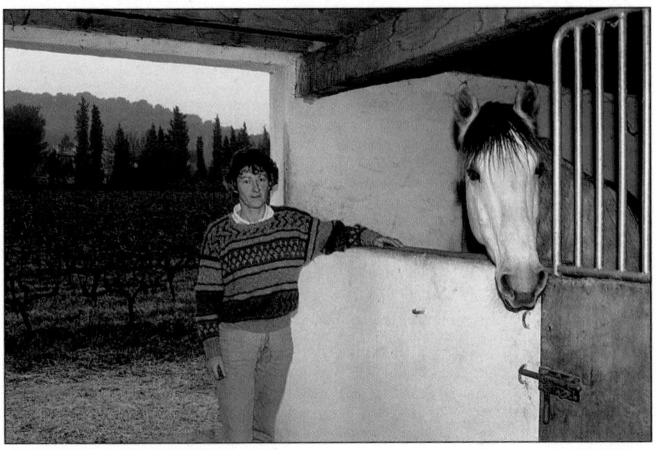

Dominique Hauvette and her faithful travelling companion in the Alpilles Mountains.

Domaine Hauvette

Owners GFA du Domaine Hauvette. **Address** Chemin du Trou-des-Bœufs, La Haute Galine 13210 Saint-Rémy-de-Provence - Tel. 04.90.92.03.90 Fax 04.90.92.08.91. **Open** Only by appointment.

Formerly a ski instructor on the slopes of her native Val-d'Isère, Dominique Hauvette studied agricultural law in Paris and, in the early 1980s, settled on a six-hectare vineyard in Les Baux, in the northern piedmont of the Alpilles Mountains. Her vines include five hectares of red grapes in the Baux-de-Provence appellation, and one hectare of white grapes in the Coteaux-d'Aix-en-Provence. An independent spirit, Dominique does everything herself, from tending the vines using biodynamic viticulture techniques (wines are labelled Nature et Progrès) to actually selling the wine. 1994 and 1995 were excellent vintages at the vineyard, especially in red wines, which are made from low-yielding vines (30 hectoliters per hectare) which give the domaine's wines an original taste with a glazed, resinous edge. Good in its youth, the '95 Jeunes Vignes (60 F) is deliciously fruity, suggesting crushed raspberries, and delicately tannic. Dominique Hauvette makes a small amount of a splendid white wine (85 F; '96) from pure Clairette vinified in oak; and an exquisite rosé: the 1996 vintage costs 48 Francs.

Our choice The '94 red Baux-de-Provence (66 F), predominantly Grenache, with Syrah and Cabernet-Sauvignon; for the first time 100% destemmed and vatted at length. Aromatic finesse (resin, red berries), dense, fresh, lingering on the palate: a great Provençal wine of admirable breed. Ready to drink.

Reception Countrified, surrounded by the dogs and horses Dominique adores. We tasted in the quiet dining room of her *mas.*

How to get there *(Map 11): On A 7, exit Cavaillon (34km), direction Saint-Rémy-de-Provence. Before Saint-Rémy, on D99, turn left to La Galine. Signs.*

Hollowed out of a rocky flank in the Alpilles, the cellar is one of the most spectacular French vinicultural achievements of recent years.

Château Romanin

Partner Colette and Jean-Pierre Peyraud and Jean-André Charial. **Address** 13220 Saint-Rémy-de-Provence - Tel. 04.90.92.45.87 Fax 04.90.92.24.36. **Open** From Monday to Friday, 9:00-13:00 and 14:00-18:30. Weekend and national holidays 11:00-19:00. **Spoken** English. **Credit cards** Visa, Eurocard, MasterCard, Amex.

Château Romanin opened its doors in 1993 following colossal investments and construction: 16,200 square feet of subterranean cellars hewn out of the Alpilles Mountains, including a sensational cathedral-like cellar with neo-Egyptian columns and cement neo-Gothic flying buttresses supported by the bare rock: a grandiloquent, esoteric setting. For the owner, a financier, and the manager, the famous two-star chef of *L'Oustau-de-Baumanière* in Les Baux, talking about the wine seems as important as tasting it. In the chateau's initial years, imparting information seemed more important than making good wine. But the young 50-hectare vineyard, under biodynamic cultivation, is finding its style, producing shimmering, straightforward red wines and undeniably gaining in depth today. The '96 Rosé (46 F) is crimson-yellow in color, with a red-currant aroma; a full, vibrant taste; and good length on the palate.

Our choice The '95 red Château Romanin Baux-de-Provence (69 F), from Cabernet-Sauvignon, Grenache, Syrah, aged in oak casks. Brilliant ruby-red color, suave bouquet mixing red berries, *garrigue* and black olives. On the palate, the attack offers soft extract, opens up and concentrates on freshness and breed at the finish. The best red wine made so far at Romanin. Good to drink now.

Reception California-style dramatic presentation, with video projection. The site is worth the visit.

***How to get there** (Map 11): On A 7, exit Cavaillon (34km), towards Saint-Rémy-de-Provence. Before Saint-Rémy, on D99, turn left and follow the signs towards the mountain.*

Overlooking the Bay of Cassis at the foot of Cape Canaille, a vineyard out of a dream.

Clos Sainte-Magdeleine

Owners Georgina and François Sack-Zafiropulo. **Address** Avenue du Revestel, 13260 Cassis - Tel. 04.42.01.70.28 Fax 04.42.01.15.51. **Open** From Monday to Friday, 10:00-12:00 and 15:00-19:00. Sunday and national holidays by appointment. **Spoken** English.

On the edge of the Mediterranean with the lofty cliff of Cape Canaille towering above it, the Clos Sainte-Magdeleine is a vineyard out of a dream, unforgettable. Mirrored in the turquoise sea are the ochres of the cliff and the Clos' twelve-and-a-half hectares of vines clinging to the terraced *restanques*. Planted at the end of the 19th century, the domaine has been in the Zafiropulo family for more than seventy years, principally producing its great specialty, white Cassis, and some rosé. The predominant Marsanne grape, contributing full body and complexity, is complemented by Ugni and Clairette, yielding white wines which age very well. Malolactic fermentations are systematically carried out. "Our wines have little acidity; we aim for rich, soft Cassis, which is our hallmark," says François Sack, the ship's captain. In the 1995 2-1/2 hectares of white vines were uprooted and replanted, yielding a wine that is already much in demand. The Clos produces a beautiful, powerful rosé of the Bandol style for 55 F.

Our choice The '95 white Cassis (55 F). More aromatic than the '94, its bouquet is layered with honey, vanilla, a touch of menthol and iodine. The generosity continues on the palate: full-bodied, long, mouth-watering tastes of peach and glazed citrus. Sensational with Mediterranean seafood and shellfish.

Reception In the vinification cellar, informally. Ask if you can tour the property: a dream, as we said.

How to get there *(Map 11): 35km east of Marseille. On Autoroute 50 exit Cassis. Drive towards "Centre Ville", then Casino. At the Casino traffic circle, head towards the seashore. 450 feet on right.*

Sophie, Loustic and Gribouille.

Clos Val Bruyère - Château Barbanau

Owner Family Cerciello. **Supervisor** Sophie Cerciello. **Address** Hameau de Roquefort, 13830 Roquefort-La-Bédoule - Tel. 04.42.73.14.60 Fax 04.42.73.17.85. **Open** Every day, 10:00-12:00 and 15:00-19:00. **Spoken** English. **Credit card** Visa, Eurocard, MasterCard.

Natives of Serre-Chevalier in the Southern Alps, the Cerciello family moved to this beautiful valley ten years ago after Madame Cerciello inherited the 7-1/2 hectares of white grapes in Clos Val-Bruyère in the Cassis appellation. In 1988, the Cerciellos bought the Château Barbanu property where the cellar is located, with 16 hectares in Côtes-de-Provence producing red, white, and rosé wines. The daughter of the house, Sophie, manages the entire vineyard with enthusiasm and energy. Only eight kilometers apart, the vines in the Cassis and the Côtes-de-Provence appellations produce very different white wines, our favorites from this domaine: the '96 is excellent. The white '96 Côtes Barbanu (34 F), made mainly from the Rolle grape, is distinct, straightforward, quite short. The '96 Grande Cuvée version (41 F), with 20% aged in new oak with malolactic fermentation, is rich and smooth: the finest Grande Cuvée made so far. The domaine's '96 rosé is more balanced than the '95 but it is a wine of finesse.

Our choice The '95 white Val Bruyère Cassis (49 F). Vibrant style (malolactic fermentation stopped) if compared with the other Cassis wines but more intense in taste than the Côtes-de-Provence. Discreet floral aroma, lengthy lime and grapefruit tastes leading to a beautiful, vigorous finish; delicious with lunch in the heat of summer.

Reception In a lovely isolated estate at the foot of the cliff, in a tasting room decorated in pale blue and apricot. Careful: nice dogs.

How to get there *(Map 11): On A 50 exit La Bédoule (15km from Cassis), towards Roquefort-La-Bédoule, then Roquefort, domaine on right.*

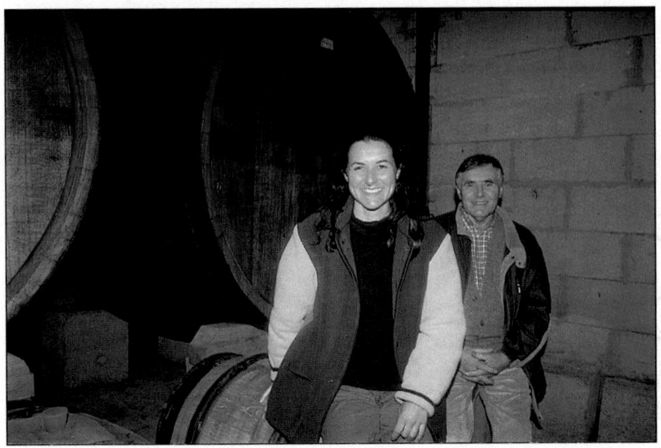

Jean Salen and his daughter Carole, masters of red Coteaux-d'Aix wines and guardians of the Provençal cooked wine tradition.

Domaine Les Bastides

Owners Carole and Jean Salen. **Address** 13610 Le Puy-Sainte-Réparade - Tel. 04.42.61.97.66 Fax 04.42.61.84.45. **Open** Every day, 9:00-12:00 and 14:00-19:00. **Spoken** English. **Credit cards** Visa, Eurocard, MasterCard.

It is difficult to imagine that Provençal weather can be devastating. Jean Salen and his daughter, from an old Provençal country family wth thirty hectares of vines north of Aix, know better. In 1994, a merciless hailstorm ruined their vineyard, and their vines took two years to recover. And then, as if to excuse herself, nature was kind in 1996, offering the Salens a sumptuous late harvest, with magnificent Grenaches yielding wines of more than 13° alcohol and Cabernets that would put the Médoc vineyards to shame. The '96 red wines will not come out before 1999, but the '93s are still available (our choice). Of the rosés and whites, the '96 white wine (38 F) is very mellow, full, mouth-filling, and the '96 rosé (34 F) is in the same style, hinting of strawberry and raspberry preserves. Don't miss the rare mulled wine (78 F): caramel, apricot preserves, orange peel, made from an old Provençal recipe. Delicious.

Our choice The '93 red Coteaux-d'Aix-en-Provence Cuvée Valéria (46 F), Cabernet-Sauvignon and Grenache, aged in oak casks. Spicy bouquet, fur, *garrigue*. Mouth-filling, mellow, powerful pepper, leather taste, with dense tannins on aftertaste. Cellar for three years.

Reception Sincere, in a newly renovated tasting room.

How to get there *(Map 11): 12km north of Aix-en-Provence. Drive towards Le Puy-Sainte-Réparade, via D13. After Saint-Canadet, the domaine is on right.*

Marie-Jeanne and Christian Double aim for elegance and fruit in their Coteaux-d'Aix.

Château de Beaupré

Owners Marie-Jeanne and Christian Double. **Address** Les Plantades 13760 Saint-Cannat - Tel. 04.42.57.33.59 (cellar) or 23.83 Fax 04.42.57.27.90. **Open** Every day, 9:00-12:00 and 14:00-18:00 (19:00 in summer). **Spoken** English. **Credit cards** Visa, Eurocard, MasterCard.

The Château de Beaupré is one of the lovely 17th-century bastides that were once aristocratic country houses dotting the landscape around Aix. The vineyard, today comprising 40 ha, and the cellar were created in 1890. The domaine currently produces a regular range of good Coteaux-d'Aix red, rosé, and white wines marked by their elegance and fruit. "To increase concentration in the reds, I orient my efforts towards the vineyard," Christian Double emphasizes. We were delighted with the '96 Rouge Soleil, from Grenache and Syrah grapes and carbonic maceration: fruity, balanced, soft, a small, charmingly thirst-quenching wine. We next tasted the '95 Château (30 F), a blend of Cabernet, Grenache, and Syrah, offering a touch of acidity and resin, its tannins still obvious; it will be good in 1998; and the red Collection (our choice). Beaupré's white wines are interesting, one with the Château label made from 80% Rolle young vines and vinified in vat, suggesting aniseed and ripe citrus, very full-bodied in '96 (35 F); the other Collection (56 F; '96), is from barrel-vinified Sémillion and Sauvignon, evoking quince paste; strong oakiness is still evident.

Our choice The '92 red Coteaux-d'Aix-en-Provence Collection du Château (55 F). More dense than the '93, this Cabernet (90%) and Syrah blend vinified in vat can be enjoyed now for its fine tannic structure, lovely softness, suave, gamey tastes, and good length on the palate.

Reception Courteous and distinguished, in a lovely, rustic tasting room. Accommodations for 2 or 5 people available in two quiet, comfortable guest houses.

How to get there *(Map 11): From Aix-en-Provence (13km), on N7 towards Lambesc. In 6kms on right, take in Rognes direction. Follow the arrows.*

The haven of Sylvette Jauffret, an impassioned winemaker, was a royal postal relay station from 1740 to 1890.

Château Pont-Royal

Owners Jacques-Alfred and Sylvette Jauffret. **Address** Route nationale 7, Pont-Royal, 13370 Mallemort - Tel. 04.90.57.40.15 Fax 04.90.59.12.28. **Open** Tuesday, Thursday, Friday, Saturday, 9:00-12:00 and 15:00-19:00. Monday and Wednesday, 15:00-19:00. Sunday and national holiday, 9:30-12:00. **Spoken** English, Italian. **Credit cards** Visa, Eurocard, MasterCard.

"I'm a nervous wreck for three weeks while I vinify my rosés, but I have such fun," Sylvette Jauffret admits with gourmet satisfaction. This enthusiastic winemaker, totally wrapped up in her beautiful sixteen-hectare property, never stops, even finding time to visit the wine fairs and salons around the country. Her "pets" are of course the rosés, which she masters to perfection and which she can talk about for hours. A good wine for everyday drinking is the '96 Tradition (25 F): elegant, balanced, straightforward fruitiness; for special meals, the Grande Cuvée (our choice) is one of the most beautiful wines of Provence. For her red wines, Sylvette goes back to her "first love": Grenache. Out of ten vintages tasted, the Grenache red is a finer expression than the Cabernet, which is too dry here. The '95 Tradition (25 F) is a good, "all-purpose" wine for informal meals with friends, while the '94 Grande Cuvée (37 F) is more serious, tannic, and should be laid down one year.

Our choice The '96 rosé Coteaux-d'Aix Grande Cuvée (37 F): 80% Grenache, 20% Mourvèdre. A smooth wine full of fruity, wild-strawberry tastes, slightly smoky, mouth-filling, with a generous finish from ripe Mourvèdre, but not heavy. Great art.

Reception Excellent, attentive, professionaml, in the former stable of the chateau. Depending on the season, Sylvette presents her "other passions" along with her wines: from beautiful china to Provençal fabrics and recurring art and sculpture exhibits.

How to get there *(Map 11): On A 7, exit Senas (11.5km) take in Aix-en-Provence direction via N7. On N7, 9km before Lambesc (30km from Aix).*

Peter Fischer and his Bacchic fresco, one of the many works left each year by his artist friends.

Château Revelette

Owner Sandra and Peter Fischer. **Address** Chemin Palunette, 13490 Jouques - Tel. 04.42.63.75.43 Fax 04.42.67.62.04. **Open** From Monday to Friday, 14:00-18:00. Saturday 9:00-12:00 and 14:00-18:00 (except national holidays). **Spoken** German, English.

Provençal wines are on the road to quality thanks to winemakers like Peter Fischer, who are curious, cultivated, and demanding vis à vis their *terroir*. Trained in California, this young German bought twenty-five hectares of vines here in the northern Coteaux-d'Aix only twelve years ago. "We have a cool climate here for white grapes, and a *terroir* for reds. I don't like to extract the grapes too much, which would impair the wine's rustic qualities, and yet I still seek depth of flavor and smoothness." Peter achieved this subtle balance perfectly in 1995. There are two labels: the Château Revelette red, white, and rosé wines: fruity, straightforward, charmingly drinkable (good red '95, 35 F, spicy, supple, ready to drink); and take special note of the red and white Grands Vins, vinified and aged in oak. The '95 Grand Blanc (52.50 F) from Chardonnay: suave bouquet of cinnamon, glazed citrus, very mellow and pleasant to drink; will be an explosive Chardonnay in three years. One of the most interesting new white wines of Provence.

Our choice The '95 Grand Rouge de Revelette (63 F). Deep color, bouquet of ripe blackcurrant, toasty, suave edges. On the palate, the Cabernet and the Syrah express a balance never before attained by this wine; deliciously velvety, Mediterranean tastes, dense, soft tannins, still marked by oak but it is distinguished. To cellar for six to seven years. Remarkable.

Reception First by the peacocks, the symbol of the chateau, who roam freely over this beautiful property, and then by Peter or his wife, both convivial and professional.

How to get there *(Map 11): From Aix (31km), take in the direction of Venelles, Meyrargues, Peyrolles, Jouques, and Rians. 5km from Jouques on D561, on the right.*

The chateau dating from the 13th and 14th centuries: certain scenes were shot for the film *Le Hussard Sur le Toit*, adapted from the novel by Jean Giono.

Château du Seuil

Owners Jeanine and Philippe Carreau-Gaschereau and children. **Address** 13540 Puyricard - Tel. 04.42.92.15.99 Fax 04.42.92.18.77. **Open** Every day, 9:00-12:00 and 14:00-19:00. **Spoken** English **Credit card** Visa.

As you go to the tasting room, you will see the Château du Seuil in the distance, hidden behind vegetation tumbling down from the Trévarèse hillside. Philippe and Jeanine Carreau Gaschereau, former lawyers, thus preserve their privacy from the hordes of tourists in the summer. Their vast estate includes almost 380 ha of vines, 45 ha of which are planted on hillsides at an altitude of 1050 feet and are an average of twenty years old. The white Coteaux-d'Aix wines have made the reputation of the Château du Seuil, offering finesse and crispness previously unknown in the region. While competition is now more stiff, the domaine still remains a benchmark. Its classic white wine, from Sauvignon, Grenache, and Ugni, is invariably aromatic (linden, peaches), both imposing and vibrant (30 F; '96), gaining in texture in the Grand Seuil version (our choice). Of the reds, which need two to seven years' bottle age, the wines have typical aromas of blackcurrants, spice, and thyme, and are marked by the vegetal aspect of Cabernet, which comes through strongly in the '94 Grand Seuil Prestige (50 F). The good '96 rosé (30 F) is balanced and fruity.

Our choice The small amount of '95 white Coteaux-d'Aix-en-Provence Grand Seuil Prestige (50 F), from Sauvignon and Grenache, vinified partially (70%) in barrels. The bouquet is discreetly oaky with a hint of apricot; creamy, elegant, ripe tangerines, good length on the palate. Cellar for two years. The '96 is also promising.

Reception Professional, in a recently opened tasting room adjacent to the vinification cellar.

How to get there *(Map 11): From Aix-en-Provence (13km), N7 towards Lambesc. After 6km, turn right towards Rognes, then 3kms on right (signposted).*

Jean-Marc Etienne, *vigneron*, his wife, Brigitte, a teacher of dance, and Bouchon ("cork"), the dog.

Domaine des Alysses

Owners Jean-Marc and Brigitte Étienne. **Address** Le Bas Deffend, 83670 Pontevès - Tel. 04.94.77. 10.36 Fax 04.94.77.11.64. **Open** From Monday to Saturday, 9:00-12:00 and 14:00-18:00, preferably by appointment. **Spoken** English, Italian.

The Coteaux Varois, (AOC since 1993), is located around Brignoles, in the center of the Haut Var. These vineyards produce red, white, and rosé wines, the majority unpretentious, thirst-quenching wines and a few more ambitious ones. Those from Jean-Marc and Brigitte Etienne, for example. Their 20 ha of vines, planted in biodynamic viticulture, are located in the northern part of the appellation at an altitude of 1200 feet: a region where Provençal grape varieties grow in difficult conditions, as opposed to Cabernets and Merlots. Priority is given to red wines of strong constitution, products of lengthy maceration, which must be aged in bottle three to 7 years. They are straightforward, very fresh, in a word, genuine. In 1996, a first white Chardonnay *vins de pays* was made (30 F), and aged in 400-liter barrels. Tasted from the barrel, it is a wine of interesting finesse. Of the reds, by way of introduction, we tasted an original *vin de pays*, the '96 Angélique (25 F), a blend of Carignan and Pinot Noir: black berries and bay, supple, to be drunk young.

Our choice The '94 red Coteaux Varois Domaine des Alysses Prestige (60 F), aged eighteen months in barrels. Typical inky purple color, fine bouquet of prune preserves, *garrigue*, vanilla. The taste is fruitier than the '93, accompanied by marked, dense, clear-cut tannins and a fresh finish. 5 years' bottle age. Decant two hours before serving.

Reception Sincere, convivial, attentive, in unspoiled countryside.

How to get there *(Map 12): On A8, exit Saint-Maximin, direction Barjols and Pontevès. Go into Pontevès and through the village; on leaving, go around a curve, keep straight ahead: take road to Les Valettes, follow the arrows to domaine.*

Jacques de Lanversin: "the terroir comes first".

Domaine du Deffends

Owners Suzel and Jacques de Lanversin. **Address** 83470 Saint-Maximin - Tel. 04.94.78.03.91 Fax 04.94.59.42.69. **Open** Every day, 9:00-12:00 and 14:00-18:00 (15:00-19:00 in summer). **Spoken** English. **Credit cards** Visa, Eurocard, MasterCard.

This Domaine is a mover and shaker in the young Coteaux Varois appellation, which was promoted to AOC in 1993. Jacques de Lanversin and his wife, Suzel, who manages the domaine, have made their 14.5 ha property on the Saint-Maximin hillsides into a leading vineyard of Provence. Well before the vineyards were recognized as AOC quality, the de Lanversins had always worked to make wines that gave full expression to the vineyard, the *terroir*. Their star red wine, named the Clos de la Truffière, the "Truffle Oak Vineyard" in homage to Brillat-Savarin's "culinary diamond", can be found in many starred restaurants. 1996 throughout Provence was a "combat" vintage with difficult climatic conditions. Grapes had to be severely sorted during the harvest, with yields dropping to 35 hl/ha for red wines and 20 hl/ha for whites. But the reward is in the bottle: the Rosé d'Une Nuit (30 F), a *saignée* rosé from Grenace and Cinsault is typically subtle and aromatic; and the second vintage of the *vin de pays* Var Champ du Sesterce 1996 (45 F), a blend from young Rolle and Viognier vines, barrel aged: aromatic bouquet of apricots and yellow plums, delicate on the palate, more lively than in 1995. Good to drink now.

Our choice The '95 red Coteaux Varois Clos de la Truffière (40 F). We found the power of the good vintages (we were reminded of the '85s) in this Cabernet-Syrah blend, aged in *demi-muid* and casks: generous tastes of leather, truffles, well-structured extract, good ageing potential.

Reception Courteous and helpful, in a small tasting room at the entrance to the cellar.

How to get there *(Map 12): On A 8, exit Saint-Maximin (40km east of Aix). The road to the domaine is marked with arrows. Indicated also on N7.*

Surrounded by trees and greenery on the Island of Porquerolles across from Hyères, the domaine was created in 1983.

Domaine de la Courtade

Owner Henri Vidal. **Directeur** Richard Auther. **Address** Île de Porquerolles, 83400 Hyères - Tel. 04.94.58.31.44 Fax 04.94.58.34.12. **Open** From Monday to Saturday (except national holidays), by appointment. **Spoken** English, German.

If the Island of Porquerolles one day receives the honors of a "Villages" appellation, it will be the consecration of a unique *terroir* created by the combination of a maritime climate and soil composed of primary metamorphic schist. And it will be due to Henri Vidal, the "inventor" of a great thirty-hectare vineyard here, mainly planted in white Rolle and red Mourvèdre vines. From the beginning, the Courtade adventure has been associated with the young manager, Richard Auther, an Alsatian by birth who knows his vines by heart. His two wines get better with every vintage: the Alycastre, from the youngest vines, and the domaine's great wine, La Courtade. The '96 white Alycastre (47 F) is a blend of Rolle and Sémillon: elegant aroma of grapefruit; round, balanced on the palate, fruity citrus taste, a wine of character. But La Courtade also means great oaky red wines, including a 1993 (86 F) with smoky, mocha traces, rich, dense, and long on the palate. It is just now beginning to soften.

Our choice The white '95 Cotes-de-Provence La Courtade (86 F). Golden color, unusual aroma of aniseed and peppermint, quite intense; in the glass, it opens up with citrus and glazed pineapple. Fluid, mouth-filling extract, with the palate confirming the exotic aroma; a quite firm finish, with a trace of iodine. Good to drink now.

Reception By Richard Auter or Françoise, both enthusiastic and instructive. A visit to the island can include the National Botanic Conservatory and its collection of varietal grapes.

How to get there *(Map 12): Take the ferry (20 mins.) from La Tour Fondue on the Giens peninsula (10km from Hyères). It's a 25 mins. walk from the port of Porquerolles.*

Jean Paquette and his son, Jérôme, an enologist.

Domaine de Curebéasse

Owners Jean Paquette and fils. **Address** Route de Bagnols, 83600 Fréjus - Tel. 04.94.40.87.90 Fax 04.94.80.75.18. **Open** From Monday to Saturday, 9:00-12:00 and 15:00-19:00, except national holidays.**Spoken** English, Italian.

Travelling the world from Ethiopia to Chile, studying marketing, geology, and enology at the University of Bordeaux, the Paquette family has been at the Domaine de Curebéasse for five generations. They own twenty hectares of vines near Fréjus five kilometers from the sea, where the climate is gentle and humid and the soils are those of the Esterel volcanic massif. Planted in a coastal area where grapes are the latest to ripen, the vines are a palette of Provençal varieties: Mourvèdre, Grenache, Syrah, and Rolle. In a small, well-planned cellar, red, white, and rosé wines are meticulously vinified. The rosés, colored by skin maceration, as well as the white wines are full-bodied, with a strong presence on the palate, but without heaviness. The '96 Blanc de Blancs (41 F), from 80% Rolle, reveals a pleasant aroma of ripe exotic fruit and rice pudding, a fruity, fleshy taste, and a refreshing finish. The '93 red Les Roches Noires (41 F), 50% Mourvèdre, barrel-aged, has a spicy aroma of pepper and cloves; its structure is still solid. The '92 (44 F) is a softer wine, with greater length on the palate and breed.

Our choice The '96 rosé Côtes-de-Provence Angélico (41 F), dominated by Mourvèdre and Tibouren: round, somewhat suave, ripe, delicious fruitiness. An excellent rosé with food, its taste more prominent than its aroma.

Reception In a small tasting room. Behind his professorial air, Jean Paquette is a hospitable man who loves his Provençal vineyard.

How to get there *(Map 12): On A 8, exit Fréjus, Saint-Raphaël: follow direction Bagnols. In less than 2km, the entrance to the domaine is at the third traffic circle.*

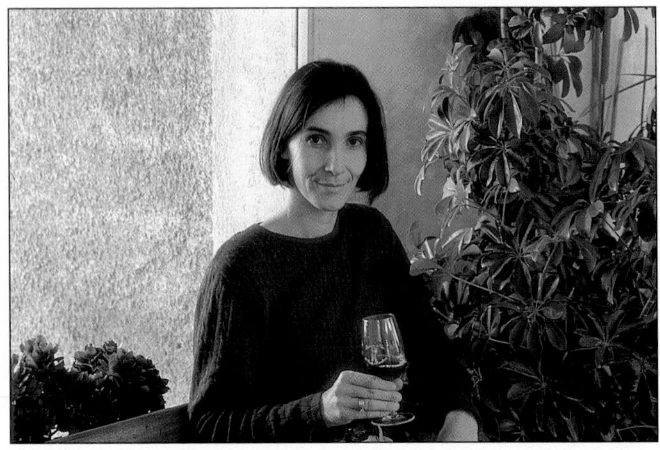

With talent and determination, Roselyne Gavoty has raised the family vineyard to the top of the Côtes-de-Provence appellation.

Domaine Gavoty

Owners Pierre and Roselyne Gavoty. **Address** Cabasse, 83340 Le Luc - Tel. 04.94.69.72.39 Fax 04.94.59.64.04. **Open** From Monday to Saturday, 8:00-12:00 and 14:00-18:00. Sunday by appointment. **Spoken** English, German. **Credit cards** Visa, Eurocard, MasterCard.

The Gavoty brothers entrusted their daughter and niece, Roselyne, with their 110-hectare estate composed of two family vineyards. An energetic winemaker, she has raised Gavoty to the summit of Côtes-de-Provence wines. Unusual for Provence, she has enjoyed equal success with reds, whites, and rosés, offering also a collection of old vintages. Her great wines are labelled "Clarendon", the pseudonym of the most famous member of the family, Bernard Gavoty, the music critic of the daily *Le Figaro* in the 1970s. Harvested very late, grapes suffered from hail and rain in 1996 and Roselyne did not make red Clarendon in the vintage, doing her best to maintain quality in her whites and rosés. The '96 white Clarendon (45 F), evoking vanilla and cinnamon, is well structured and quite vibrant. It will be at its peak in three years. There are several good '93s and '90s left (60 F), which are available by the bottle. The '96 rosé Clarendon (44 F) is fruity but more vinous than in previous years.

Our choice The '88 red Côtes-de-Provence Clarendon (52 F): black olives, bay, dried tomatoes on the nose; round, mouth-filling taste, with traces of leather, crushed black olives, leading on to soft, somewhat dry tannins. A beautiful expression of a red Provençal wine at its peak. One of the best vintages from the domaine.

Reception Charming, by Roselyne or an associate, in the tasting room. Farm products for sale.

How to get there *(Map 12): A 8, exit Brignoles or Le Luc. On N7, between Brignoles and Le Luc, tke D13 direction Cabasse. After 4km, go under the autoroute; entrance to domaine on left.*

Nicolas Gruey at the tasting-room door.

Château Grand'Boise

Owner Nicolas Gruey. **Address** 13530 Trets - Tel. 04.42.29.22.95 Fax 04.42.61.38.71. **Open** Every day, 9:00-12:30 and 15:00-19:00, preferably by appointment (closed in national holidays). **Spoken** English, Italian, Spanish. **Credit cards** Visa, Eurocard, MasterCard.

The beautiful old farmhouse named *La Grenobloise* offers a marvelous view out over the Montagne Sainte-Victoire. All around, the Château Grand'Boise spreads out over 390 hectares of forest and 45 hectares of vines (including 73 different parcels!), clinging to Mount Aurélien and overlooking the village of Trets: the vines are covered by the Côtes-de-Provence Villages appellation. A winemaker of tremendous energy, Nicolas Gruey manages the vast estate, continuing the job begun by his mother and devoting the same passion to it. Of his Classique wines, which should be drunk within the year, we especially enjoyed the '96 Blanc de Blancs (38 F), a blend of Rolle, Sémillon, and Ugni: very mellow aroma of quince paste, but quite vibrant and crisp on the palate; and the '96 rosé (34 F), with traces of cherry candy, very fruity and delicate: a lovely thirst-quenching wine. The Mazarine wines can be kept somewhat longer. The '95 white Mazarine (50 F) is deep gold in color, its aroma of pine resin, licorice, cooked peaches, and its ample taste leading to a firm finish; the wine is still marked by its ageing in oak and needs two years to soften.

Our choice The '90 red Côtes-de-Provence Mazarine (52 F). Still pale in color; powerful, subtle bouquet: resin, black olives, truffles, cherry preserves. Perceptible, supple extract with soft tannins. Good to drink now, with sauced meat dishes.

Reception Friendly, by Nicolas or an associate, in the cellar.

How to get there *(Map 11): From Aix, take Brignoles direction on N7; after 19km, turn right to Trets. The domaine is indicated with arrows beginning in village center.*

Benjamin Defresne, a former restaurateur in Neuilly, near Paris.

Château de Jasson

Owners Marie-Andrée and Benjamin Defresne. **Address** Route de Collobrières, 83250 La Londe-Les-Maures - Tel. 04.94.66.81.52 Fax 04.94.05.24.84. **Open** From Monday to Sunday morning, 9:00-12:30 and 14:00-20:00. **Spoken** English, Spanish. **Credit cards** Visa, Eurocard, MasterCard.

Benjamin Defresne comes from an old family of winemakers from...the Oise Valley near Paris! To be precise, from Argenteuil where, as you can see from the geneological tree displayed in his tasting room, his ancestors were making wine as far back as the 14th century. In 1991, Defresne left his restaurant, the *Jarasse* in Neuilly, and bought this 16-hectare domaine between the sea and the Maures Massif. He knew exactly what kind of wines he wanted to make: modern, soft, fruity, immediately appealing, wines which he is henceforth making for his restaurateur friends. Six months after the harvest, his rosés and whites are as delicious as ripe fruit as a result of skin maceration and low-temperature fermentation at 61 F. His '91 Eléanore Rosé (42 F), pale salmon in color, evocative of red berries, is round, soft, charmingly drinkable. Even the red '95 Victoria (45 F), from Cabernet in carbonic maceration with Syrah and Grenache, is good to enjoy now for its soft, somewhat gamey overtones.

Our choice The '96 white Côtes-de-Provence Cuvée Jeanne (42 F), from young Rolle and old Ugni vines. Pale, brilliant color, very aromatic and delicate on the nose, with white flowers and grapefruit; vibrant, elegant, lacey, lingering on the palate. An excellent white summer wine. Good now.

Reception Affable, in a small, neat tasting room.

How to get there *(Map 12): Coming from Hyères, in the center of La Londe-Les-Maures, turn right onto D88 in the Les Jassons direction. Domain 1km on left.*

The new boutique-tasting room, "to give the sun and the sea some competition".

Les Maîtres Vignerons de la presqu'île de Saint-Tropez

Manager Robert Zimmer. **Address** La Foux, 83580 Gassin - Tel. 04.94.56.32.04 Fax 04.94. 43.42.57. **Open** From Monday to Friday, 8:30-12:00 and 14:30-19:00. Saturday, 10:00-12:00 and 16:00-19:00. Sunday only in Juli, August, September. **Spoken** English, German, Italian. **Credit cards** Visa, Eurocard, MasterCard, Amex.

Who hasn't been to Saint Tropez at one time or another? The peninsula today is perhaps not so glamorous as it was in the '60s, but it still draws the crowds. And so if you're coming to "Saint Trop"', forget the mediocre wines there and visit this association of eight domaines located around the village, with a cooperative cellar in Cuers, which has taken a turn in the right direction in recent years. Out of the multitude of wines available, look for two labels: the Carte Noire wines in a flute-shaped bottle, and the Château de Pampelonne. The '96 rosé Château de Pampelonne (41.50 F) concentrates on acidulted fruit and beautiful, refreshing vitality. The '95 red Carte Noire (35 F) suggests crushed black currants and its tannins will soften in 1998.

Our choice The '96 rosé Côtes-de-Provence Carte Noire (35 F): brilliant salmon color, suave aroma of ripe grapes leading to a round, vinous, generous taste. Good now. The '95 red Château de Pampelonne (41.50 F): deep, cardinal-red color, oaky, suave, cherry-preserve aromas, fruity extract, solid finish. Good now or can be cellared.

Reception By hostesses in a vast, new boutique-tasting room called *Petit Village*, which also sells regional products. "Saint Tropez is known for tourists rather than wines," explains the cooperative's Director, Robert Zimmer. "Our two competitors are the sun and the sea; so we do everything to attract customers."

How to get there *(Map 12): Before entering Saint-Tropez, at the large intersection with RN98 (Toulon-Nice), take in the Cogolin direction. The tasting room with a large parking lot is on the immediate left.*

Nathalie and Jean-Louis Gourjon in their tasting room just a stone's throw from the beaches of La Londe-les-Maures.

Château Maravenne

Owners Nathalie and Jean-Louis Gourjon. **Address** Route de Valcros, 83250 La Londe-Les-Maures - Tel. 04.94.66.80.20 Fax 04.94.66.97.79. **Open** From Monday to Sunday morningk, 9:00-12:00 and 15:00-19:00. **Spoken** English.

Natives of the Rhône Valley, the Gourjon family came here in 1980 to take over this vast 71-hectare domaine, its vines planted on terraces facing the sea and Porquerolles Island. Until 1985, "I played it by ear," confessed Jean-Louis Gourjon, speaking of his vinification techniques. Since then, the Château Maravenne has been showered with medals and first prizes. The large cellar is equipped with a system for cooling the grapes as soon as they arrive. Goujon then subjects the grapes to cold maceration before fermentation, a technique which makes it possible to obtain balanced extract and the expression of intense fruitiness in young wines. In short, these are "fashionable" wines. "The '96 is the most difficult vintage I've encountered in sixteen years," he said. Habitually charming, his wines from the 1996 vintage are somewhat more austere because they lack maturity. Of the Grande Réserve wines, there is a good rosé from Grenache and Tibouren: red berries with a touch of acidity, delicate, crisp; and the white wine (36 F), a Rolle varietal, evokes citrus and white peaches in a quite vibrant wine.

Our choice The '96 rosé Côtes-de-Provence Collection Privée (36 F), Grenache and Tibouren. From the same grape varieties as the Grande Réserve but a blend of different cuvées: it has greater aromatic finesse, fuller-body, and more fruitiness on the palate.

Reception In a convivial atmosphere; many people in summer come to the tasting room, set up in a 19th-century Provençal residence.

How to get there *(Map 12): 2km from the center of La Londe-Les-Maures, towards Golf de Valcros. Signposted.*

Pierre Chauvier (with his brother, Robert) makes one of the best, and above all the most regular, rosés of Provence.

Domaine de Marchandise

Owners Pierre and Robert Chauvier. **Address** 83520 Roquebrune-sur-Argens - Tel. 04.94.45.42.91 Fax 04.94.81.62.82. **Open** Every day, 9:00-12:00 and 14:00-19:00.

Pierre Chauvier is not given to discussing his Côtes-de-Provence rosé for hours. If you ask him about his winemaking techniques, he reveals just the bare minimum: temperature is important, as is vinification on the lees in order to obtain the smooth, velvety wines that bear his personal touch. But the vineyard (30 hectares) also makes a difference, with a predominant role played by Tibouren, the grape variety that combines finesse and power and is expressed marvelously in rosés from the coastal vineyards; it is blended with Grenache, Cinsault, and grapes from young Mourvèdre vines. They are all planted on deep soil over clay, "which always waters the vine." That being said, it isn't necessary to determine the secret of this nectar in order to find it absolutely delicious. And there is no special wine, but just one rosé. "We sell 100,000 bottles directly to private individuals and we want everyone to have the same wine." Caution: the winery is often out of wine from October to March.

Our choice The '96 rosé Côtes-de-Provence. Pale pink, aroma of ripe red berries; rich, full, ample flavor, good persistence. Ideal with white meats and fish seasoned with spices and herbs.

Reception For a clientele of wine lovers rather than tourists, in the new, immaculate cellar.

How to get there *(Map 12): 13km from Fréjus, 22km from Draguignan. On A 8, exit Le Muy or Puget-sur-Argens. On N7, between Le Muy and Puget, direction Bagnols-en-Forêt. Go 2km to the hamlet of La Marchandise.*

A former outbuilding of the Château de Miraval, Réal-Martin is named after a Provençal river.

Château Réal-Martin

Owner Jacques Clotilde. **Supervisor** Gilles Meimoun. **Address** Le Val, 83143 Correns - Tel. 04.94.86.40.90 Fax 04.94.86.32.23. **Open** Every day, 9:00-12:00 and 14:00-18:00. **Spoken** English. **Credit cards** Visa, Eurocard, MasterCard.

A businessman by training and the son-in-law of Jacques Clothilde, the owner of Château Réal-Martin, Gilles Meimoun began here by waging a successful campaign to promote the domaine's wines vis à vis the leading restaurants of France. He is now in charge of winemaking on this 35 hectare vineyard. In 1996, his second vintage, nature was cruel, as it was throughout Provence. But Réal-Martin's vines, planted 36 miles from the sea at an altitude of 900 to 1200 feet, stood up quite well in this year of late-ripening grapes, which were healthy at harvest time. The '96 rosé (55 F), a blend of Grenache, Cinsault, and Syrah, is more vigorous and less vinous than in '95: a perfect rosé for a summer lunch. The reds reflect the elegance of the old Grenache vines, yielding fine, soft tannins with spicy overtones and extra crispness due to the altitude of the vineyard. They blossom beautifully after three to four years' bottle age. The '95 (55 F), the progeny of an average vintage, can be enjoyed now.

Our choice The '96 white Côtes-de-Provence. One of the whites from old Ugni vines, vinified in vat, the most interesting white wines in Provence. In 1996, the wine was the "success of the vintage" at Réal-Martin. Its beautiful acidity sustains its clean, fresh aromas; the attack is balanced, becoming straightforward, graceful, very dry. To drink now or to cellar.

Reception Réal-Martin is off the tourists' beaten track and is all the more charming for it. The Clotilde-Meimoum family has the gift of hospitality.

How to get there *(Map 12): On A 8, exit Brignoles (10kms). From Brignoles, drive towards Le Val and Barjols on D554.*

The wheat field, the *mas*, and the Montagne Sainte-Victoire.

Domaine Richeaume

Owner Henning Hoesch. **Address** D57b, 13114 Puyloubier - Tel. 04.42.66.31.27 Fax 04.42.66.30.59. **Open** From Monday to Friday 8:00-17:00 (preferable to call ahead), weekend by appointment. **Spoken** German, English, Italian.

A Doctor of Canon Law and former university professor of German origin, Henning Hoesch restored this *mas* in the early 1970s and built a contemporary underground cellar. The overall effect is plain, in keeping with the poetry of the red, rocky *garrigue* and the magic Montagne Sainte-Victoire: it is one of the most moving natural settings of Provence. The Domaine Richeaume comprises twenty-five acres of vines planted in biodynamic viticulture. The red wines from Richeaume are among the best Mediterranean wines today, especially the Syrah and Columelle *cuvées*, from Syrah, Cabernet, and Grenache grapes (65 F; '95): soft, clear-cut wines with a subtle oaky edge. Also excellent is the rosé, revealing an unusual aroma of peonies and red berries, quite a vigorous wine in '96 (50 F); as well as the '96 Blanc de Blancs (50 F), just as fruity (peaches, apricots), with a lemony finish.

Our choice The '95 red Côtes-de-Provence Syrah (about 80 F). Very deep color; crushed red currants, quite powerful oak on the nose with resinous notes, leading to ripe black fruit. Soft, spicy, fruity attack with a charming oaky hint, neither hard nor dry. Straightforward finish. Simply delicious. Good as of now.

Reception Professional, in the cellar, usually by Sylvain Hoesch.

***How to get there** (Map 11): From Aix, take N7 towards Saint-Maximin-Brignoles. After 15km, at the Château de la Bégude, turn left towards Saint-Antonin (D56c), then right towards Puyloubier (D57b). 3km before Puyloubier, on left; entrance indicated by two cypresses and a stone marker. No sign.*

Marc Jacquet, Manager of the Domaine de Rimauresq, designed the new cellar, a model of sobriety and efficiency.

Domaine de Rimauresq

Owner Family Wemyss. **Directeur** Marc Jacquet. **Address** Route de Notre-Dame-des-Anges, 83790 Pignans - Tel. 04.94.48.80.45 Fax. 04.94.33.22.31. **Open** From Monday to Friday, 9:00-12:00 and 14:00-18:00. **Spoken** English.

The Domaine de Rimauresq has been revitalized since it was bought by a Scottish family in 1988. In 1994, a vinification cellar was built, an architectural reflection of the original old Provençal building. Designed by Marc Jacquet, the enologist who manages the domaine, the cellar has proven its efficiency at the vineyard, which covers thirty-two hectares of vines on excellent *terroir*, facing northwest in the shadow of the Notre-Dame-des-Anges hillside, where several magnificent vines more than 70 years old are planted. Harvests at Rimauresq are always quite late, yielding reasonable alcohol levels. This is especially advantageous for the white wines, the domaine's specialty, which are very Mediterranean in taste while remaining delicate and graceful. The rosé, marked by the Cinsault grape, is vibrant in the '96 (39.50 F), with overtones of acidulated fruit and boxwood, lacier than in '95. Of the reds, we tasted only the '93 (4450 F): prunes, mocha, delicate tannins, mouth-filling, good to drink now; and the '96, generous, promising fruit, enjoyable as a young wine.

Our choice The '96 white Côtes-de-Provence, predominantly from Rolle grapes. Aroma of white fruit and custard, still closed when we tasted it. Ample, mellow taste with little acidity and a delicately aromatic finish. A wine of character.

Reception Very professional, in a recently built, plain tasting room.

How to get there *(Map 12): On A 8, exit Le Cannet-Le Luc (18km). From Le Luc, towards Toulon (N97). In Pignans, on N97, turn left towards Notre-Dame-des-Anges. Signposted.*

Alain Combard and Agnès, who supervises the tasting room.

Domaine Saint-André-de-Figuière

Owner Alain Combard. **Address** 83250 La Londe-Les-Maures - Tel. 04.94.66.92.10 Fax 04.94.35.04.46. **Open** Mon. to Sat., 9:00-12:00 and 14:00-19:00. **Spoken** English. **Credit cards** All major.

Associated with the Domaine Laroche in Chablis for 22 years, Alain Combard rapidly made a place for himself in the Provençal sun. A native of Salon-de-Provence, he bought the Domaine Saint-André-de-Figuière in La Londe in 1992, 2 minutes as the seagull flies from the sea. His made a wise choice with this domaine, with 20 ha of vines planted in healthy biodynamic viticulture, several parcels of old vines, and a cellar already equipped. Combard set out to make further progress and above all, to put his personal stamp on his wines. In 5 years, he has succeeded brilliantly and it was here that we tasted some of the most beautiful wines during our last visit to Provence. The rosé Vieilles Vignes will reconcile wine connoisseurs to this color: the '96 (49.50 F), dominated by Mourvèdre and Syrah, is a charming rosé, fruity but with substance: a gourmet's wine that will be good for 2 years. The '96 Blanc de Blancs (41.50 F), a blend of Rolle, Sémillon, Ugni, with delicate citrus overtones, is vibrant and elegant. Tasted from the ageing barrel, the new '96 Blanc Barrique Grande Cuvée Delphine (62 F) was also beautifully promising. Adding the red wine to this list (our choice), Saint-André-de-Figuière has successfully achieved the difficult task of making excellent wines in all three colors.

Our choice The '95 red Côtes-de-Provence Cuvée Spéciale (51 F), mainly from Mourvèdre. Brilliant carmine-red color; fresh, appetizing bouquet of strawberries and pine, very meaty, fruity taste with perceptible but soft tannins; delicious to drink for three years.

Reception By Agnès, the secretary, who is a charming hostess.

How to get there *(Map 12): 3km from the center of La Londe-Les-Maures, towards Bormes-les-Mimosas. Follow the signs for "Jardins d'Oiseaux".*

Hervé Goudard and Ordizan, a 30-year-old thoroughbred who roams freely over the Oppidum parcel of vines.

Château Saint-Baillon

Owner Hervé Goudard. **Address** RN7 83340 Flassans-sur-Issole - Tel. 04.94.69.74.60 Fax 04.94.69.80.29. **Open** From Monday to Saturday, 9:00-12:00 and 14:00-18:00. **Spoken** English, German. **Credit cards** Visa, Amex.

If Provençal vineyards were to be classified today, the Château Saint-Baillon would deserve the rank of Premier Cru. Hervé Goudard, a judge by training with the gentlemanly air of a character out of F. Scott Fitzgerald, is one of the rare Provençal winemakers to use oak barrels in moderation, without a heavy hand; to pick his Cabernet-Sauvignons at peak maturity; and to have placed his bets on the Syrah grape 20 years ago. Located in the northen part of the Côtes-de-Provence appellation, the domaine covers 200 hectares, including 25 hectares of vines on terraced slopes in the midst of the *garrigue*; they are planted on very rocky clay-limestone soil at an average altitude of 900 feet. Despite five delicate vintages, the Saint-Baillon reds--the Roudaï *cuvée*, from Cabernet-Sauvignon and Syrah; and Oppidum, more strongly Syrah (80%, and the oldest vines)--invariably come out first in our tastings. "We don't make any rosé here which would collapse after 6 months in the bottle," explains Hervé. His '96 rosé Opale (66.50 F) is somewhat biting, with delicate fruit and length on the palate. In the same style, the '96 white Opale is marked by the Rolle grape (lime), a wine of distinction and finesse.

Our choice The '92 red Côtes-de-Provence Oppidum (79 F). Lovely wine, mainly from Syrah, in a small vintage: brilliant, youthful color; gamey bouquet; soft, oaky-vanilla taste, still fleshy and velvety. To drink now.

Reception In a small tasting room in front of the 15th-century bastide.

How to get there *(Map 12): On A8, exit Brignoles. On N7, between Brignoles (9km) and Flassans-sur-Isole. Road to domaine marked with arrows.*

Brigitte Grivet's vines are planted around a chapel dedicated to Saint John the Baptist, the symbol of rebirth and purifying waters.

Domaine Saint-Jean-Baptiste

Owner Brigitte Grivet. **Address** Route des Arcs, 83510 Lorgues - Tel. 04.94.73.71.11 Fax 04.94.73.26.91. **Open** Everyday 9:00-18:00 in winter and 9:00-19:00 in summer. **Spoken** English, German.

Before buying her own ten-acre vineyard in Lorgues in 1994, Brigitte Grivet had gained broad winemaking experience from Châteauneuf-du-Pape to the Coteaux-d'Aix-en-Provence appellation. Returning to a vineyard on a more human scale, she supervises everything at the Domaine Saint-Jean-Baptiste, even finding the time to extend warm hospitality to guests in her three bed-and-breakfast rooms. Brigitte makes red, white, and rosé wines, seeking to express fruit rather than concentration. Offered at reasonable prices, her wines are intended to be drunk young: hers is the kind of address that wine lovers exchange by word of mouth. The '96 white wine (31 F), mainly from Sémillon, has a fragrant aroma of fennil, white flowers, green apple; fruity with a touch of acidity on the palate, very balanced, delicious. Of the reds, the '95 Classique (31 F) is straightforward, fruity, with a somewhat rustic finish; while the '95 Harmonie (41 F), from selected Cabernet and Syrah in a tall Italian bottle, is more delicate, more precise, with a taste of blackcurrants and spice.

Our choice The '96 rosé Cotes-de-Provence (31 F). An excellent rosé from Cinsault and Grenache; simple, round, enticing, thirst-quenching, very fruity, perfect for informal meals with friends. Good to drink now.

Reception By Brigitte, in the cellar, simple and attentive. Homemade vinegars for sale. Bed-and-breakfast rooms.

How to get there *(Map 12): 15km southwest of Draguignan. On A 8, exit Le Luc-Vidauban. On N7, exit Vidauban (or Les Arcs), towards Lorgues. 2km before Lorgues, domaine on the right, in front of the restaurant "Chez Bruno".*

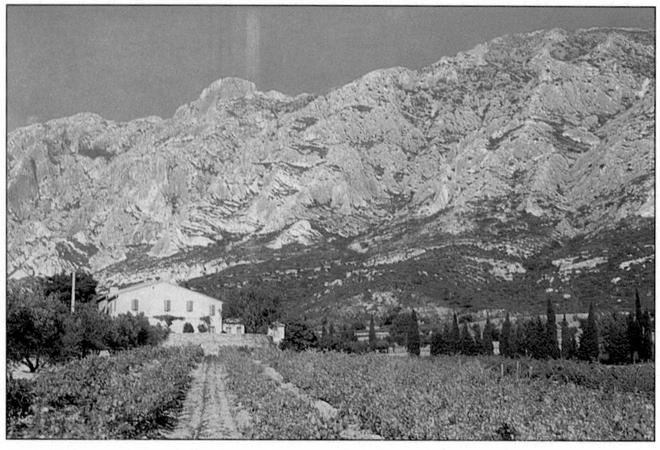

The only vineyard planted on the southern flank of the Montagne Sainte-Victoire: a privileged, breathtaking sight.

Domaine de Saint-Ser

Owners Bernard and Renaud Pierlot. **Address** Mas de Bramefan, Route de Saint-Antonin, D17, 13114 Puyloubier - Tel. 04.42.66.30.81 Fax. 04.42.66.37.51. **Open** Every day 10:00-17:00 (18:00 in summer). **Spoken** English. **Credit card** Visa.

Lovers of Cézanne will be jealous of Renaud Pierlot. A young native of the Champagne, he moved to the family domaine in the late 1980s, living in this magic countryside "possessed" by the Montagne Sainte-Victoire. The towering mountain of changing luminosity and colors provides the background for Pierlot's twenty-six hectares of young vines planted on terraces at an altitude of 1350 feet and facing due south. The *mas* houses the efficiently equipped cellar where Renaud, a young father, carefully blends *saignés* rosés from Grenache, Cinsault, and Cabernet; and other Syrah rosés colored by direct pressing. We also enjoyed the '96 white wine (41 F), made from Rolle, planted in 1991 and vinified by skin maceration and by direct pressing. Pale, limpid yellow, with aromas and tastes of citrus peel and glazed lemons, it is vibrant with a touch of acidity, and beautifully crisp.

Our choice The '96 rosé Côtes-de-Provence Prestige (41 F); diaphanous Indian pink, more aromatic than the '95 (its acid support is important), still delicate on the palate--the hallmark of Saint-Cer--fruity, and flowery. A classic.

Reception Very open, by workers on the property or Renaud, in a recently built tasting room. Hiking paths laid out for touring the vineyard and the Montagne Sainte-Victoire (count on three hours to get to the top).

How to get there *(Map 11): 26km east of Aix-en-Provence. From Aix, take direction Saint-Maximin-Brignoles on N7. In 15km, at the Château de la Bégude, turn left towards Puyloubier (D57b). Just before Puyloubier, turn left towards Saint-Antonin (D17). 2km on the right.*

The cloister and the chapel of the abbey containing the relics of Saint Rosaline, as well as a remarkable mosaic by Marc Chagall.

Château Sainte-Roseline

Owner Bernard Teillaud. **Address** 83460 Les Arcs-sur-Argens - Tel. 04.94.99.50.30 Fax 04.94.47.53.06. **Open** Every day, 9:00-12:00 and 14:00-18:00. **Spoken** English. **Credit cards** Visa, Eurocard, MasterCard.

Originally the Celle Roubaud Monastery founded in the 11th century and later an abbey which attained its apogee under Prioress Roseline de Villeneuve, who died in 1329, the Saint Roseline Abbey is a highlight of Provençal religious history. Classed as an Historic Monument, the abbey and its vineyard changed hands in 1993. The ambitious new owner, Bernard Teillaud, undertook colossal restoration work to renovate the old cloister, the vines, and the cellars. The vineyards, with 50 hectares of vines, was partly replanted and the cellars considerably enlarged (to 45,000 square feet!). For the 1996 vintage, the young winemaker, Christophe Bernard, was well in command of the vineyard's new potential. There are three families of red, white, and rosé wines: the Cloître de Sainte-Roseline, the Château Sainte-Roseline, and the barrel-aged Tête de Cuvée. The '96 rosé and white Cloître wines (32 F) are very thirst-quenching, grapey, simple, and balanced. The red '93 Château (64 F) offers a lovely, soft oaky bouquet of cocoa and mocha, a vigorous wine with firm tannins.

Our choice The '96 white Côtes-de-Provence Château Sainte-Roseline (52 F), from a high proportion of Rolle. Tall, flute-shaped bottle. Beautiful aromatic intensity, charmingly smooth, delicate, lingering extract. In the same range, the '96 rosé (52 F) is delectably fruity.

Reception Recently renovated tasting room and impressive barrel-vaulted reception room. Chapel open to the public every afternoon except Monday.

How to get there *(Map 12): 8km south of Draguignan. On A8, exit Draguignan-Le Muy, towards Draguignan on N557; 4kms on left towards Les Arcs, on D91. Signposted.*

The Domaine Rabiega, a center of active viticultural experimentation, belongs to a Swedish company.

Domaine Rabiega

Owner Vin & Sprit. **Directeur** Lars Torstenson. **Address** 83300 Draguignan - Tel. 04.94.68.44.22 Fax 04.94.47.17.72. **Open** From Monday to Friday, 9:00-12:00 and 14:00-17:00 (9:00-12:00 in winter). **Spoken** Swedish, English. **Credit cards** Visa, Eurocard, MasterCard, Amex.

Innumerable foreigners have bought vineyards in Provence over the last twenty years. Some of them are dilettantes, and have a hard job ahead of them. Highly organized and ambitious, others aim at improving the wines, especially the reds, and make a brilliant success of their domaine. A perfect example of the latter breed is *Vin & Sprit*, formerly a distributor of Swedish spirits, which bought the ten-hectare Domaine Rabiega in 1986. Supervised by an outstanding winemaker, Lars Torstenson, the domaine has become a benchmark, notably for its Clos d'Ière wines. The classic line, Christine Rabiega, is less spectacular, although there is a pleasant '96 rosé, thirst-quenching, with a touch of acidity. Since 1995, Lars has also made wines from the Château d'Esclans in La Motte, which has ultra-modern vinification equipment, offering promising wines, notably the '96 white wine.

Our choice The red '94 Côtes-de-Provence Clos d'Ière I (about 100 F). The last bottles of this sumptuous Syrah varietal. A wine of deep, mellow flavor (blackcurrants, black berries), full, complete, with silky tannins magnified by oak ageing. The '94 Clos d'Ière II (60 F), Grenache and Carignan, is less complex, more developed and soft; can be enjoyed now for its fluid tannins and chocolate finish.

Reception In a recently built tasting room, guided tour of the vineyard (30 minutes) available.

How to get there *(Map 12): On A 8, exit Le Muy-Draguignan (14km), towards Draguignan. From Draguignan towards Lorgues. At the Lorgues-Flayosc intersection, continue towards Logues on D562. Domain indicated by arrows on right.*

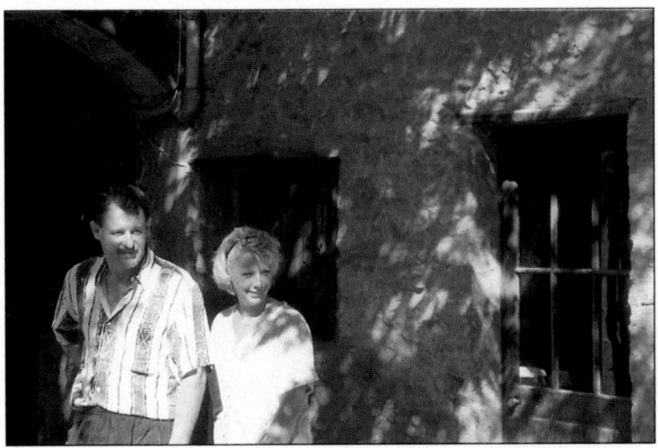

Jean and Catherine Levêque in the courtyard of the Château Fontenille, whose name refers to the many springs on the estate.

Domaine de Fontenille

Owners Pierre and Jean Lévêque. **Address** 84360 Lauris - Tel. 04.90.08.23.36 Fax 04.90.08.45.05. **Open** From Monday to Saturday, 9:00-12:00 and 14:00-19:00. **Spoken** English.

In 1949, Jules Levêque, the grandfather of the present owners of Domaine de Fontenille, Pierre and Jean, bought this estate, which had long been devoted to mixed farming. Pierre and Jean's father, Michel, progressively replanted the 18-hectare vineyard and brought out his first bottles of Côtes-du-Luberon in 1978. "But wine was certainly made here before that, because the vaults in our cellar are inscribed '1535'", Jean explained. Strongly marked by Grenache Noir planted on clay-limestone soil and blended with Syrah and 90-year-old Carignan, the red Fontenilles are deeply colored, powerful, spicy, heady, and keep well, from four to eight years. They are aged in cement and stone vats, thus no oak, and are not moved. In some years, fifty hectoliters are isolated and bottled after five to six years of vat age. This was the case with the '88 (62 F), spicy and "animal", velvety, peppery on the palate, a good accompaniment for game dishes. There is a simple, flowery '96 white wine (30 F), based on Ugni and Clairette.

Our choice The '95 red Côtes-du-Luberon (34 F). Purple color, very aromatic (blackberries, pepper, resin), combining solid structure with vibrant taste, dense tannins. It will develop beautifully in five years.

Reception Simple and cordial, in an old cellar of this historic Luberon estate.

How to get there *(Map 11): On A 7, exit Cavaillon (27km), towards Pertuis. In Lauris, drive towards Roquefraîche (2km). On A8, exit Aix-en-Provence (32km), to Pertuis then Lauris.*

Val-Joanis, a vast 400-hectare property, has a luxuriant park and vegetable garden which you can visit.

Château Val-Joanis

Owner Family Chancel. **Address** 84120 Pertuis - Tel. 04.90.79.20.77 Fax 04.90.09.69.52. **Open** From Monday to Friday, 9:00-12:00 and 14:00-19:00. Weekend 10:00-13:00 and 15:00-18:00 (19:00 in summer). **Spoken** English, German. **Credit cards** Visa, Eurocard, MasterCard.

Jean-Louis Chancel, a former Marseilles manufacturer and now a banker in London, built this magnificent property in the late 1970s. Located in the south of the Luberon, the Château Val-Joanin covers 180 hectares, 80% in the Côtes-du-Luberon appellation and the rest with the *vin de pays* label. The young vines are planted on the edge of a pine forest and bathed by its heady fragrances, yielding resinous aromas which are amazingly perceptible in Val-Joanin red wines, notably the Les Griottes. From a parcel of Syrah vines planted at an altitude of 840 feet on pebbly soil, it is very different from the other wines, which are from sandy silt. From the Côtes-du-Luberon vines, red, white, and rosé wines are made. We took special note of the unusual '95 Les Merises rosé (39 F; 50 cl), predominantly Syrah, barrel aged: vanilla, vinous, a touch of cherry-like acidity; and we enjoyed the '94 red wine (36 F), strawberries and spice bouquet, all softness and balance. Good to drink now. There is a good varietal *vins de pays* (Domaine Chancel, 26 F), Sauvignon and Syrah.

Our choice The '93 red Côtes-du-Luberon Les Griottes (56 F): mainly Syrah, with Grenache and Mourvèdre, barrel aged. Pine resin and moka, aroma less open than in the Château *cuvée*. The taste is still soft, spicy, with marked, delicate tannins and a tobacco finish. Ready to drink.

Reception Professional, by a hostess, in a beautiful tasting room with Provençal decoration.

***How to get there** (Map 11): 41km from Cavaillon, 22km from Aix. 3km from Pertuis on the road to Cavaillon (D973). The road to the domaine is indicated by arrows.*

Château Simone is the vinous memory of the tiny Palette appellation planted by Carmelite monks from Aix-en-Provence in the 16th century.

Château Simone

Owners René and Jean-François Rougier. **Address** 13590 Meyreuil - Tel. 04.42.66.92.58 Fax 04.42.66.80.77. **Open** From Monday to Saturday, 9:00-12:00 and 14:00-18:00, preferably by appointment. **Spoken** English.

Château Simone stands isolated by the pine forest on the Montaiguet hillside. The particularity of its vines, an average sixty years old, lies in their exposure due north, with seventeen hectares cascading down over innumerable terraces. A host of grape varieties today extinct in most Provençal vineyards continue to flourish along with Clairette and Ugni for white wines, and Grenache Noir, Mourvèdre, and Cinsault for the reds and rosés. All the wines are aged in old oak barrels or casks. Models unequalled in Provence, the white wines from 80% Clairette are highly distinguished, masterpieces. They can be drunk young or cellared for ten to fifteen years. The '96 Blanc de Blancs (about 98 F), its bouquet of peppermint, is deliciously basil and glazed lemons in taste, long and ethereal. The rosé (bout 85 F) is vinous, soft, slightly tannic, and smoky. The '93 red (about 102 F) offers a discreet bouquet of moist *garrigue*, mouth-filling volume; compact, velvety tannins. To be cellared.

Our choice The '94 white Palette Château Simone Grand Cru (about 115 F). Both dry and rich, full, no heaviness or unbalanced alcohol: an expression of precise maturity, with overtones of vanilla, honey, custard, interminable length on palate. Superb. And to think it's from an average vintage!

Reception Instructive, by René Rougier or his son, Jean-François, the fifth generation. You will get a better image of the long history of the famous wine by visiting the cellars with their somber, mysterious corridors dug out by monks in the 16th century. Time seems to stand still here.

How to get there *(Map 11): From Aix-en-Provence (6km), take N7 towards Fréjus. On leaving Aix, turn right towards Meyreuil, go over an old bridge; the domaine is in 2km. Signposted.*

ROUSSILLON

13
Castres
Lacrouzette
Brassac
Cambon-et-Salvergues
St-Gervais-s.-Mare
Bédarieux
Le Bez
Valdurenque
Anglès
Hérépian
Faugères
Soual
Labruguière
Mazamet
Labastide-Rouairoux
St-Pons-de-Thomières
Roquebrun
Laurens
Roujan
Dourgne
Aussillon
St-Amans-Soult
Courniou
Cessenon
Murviel-lès-B.
Rieussec
St-Chinian
Cazouls-lès-Béziers
Les Martys
Cébazan
Montblanc
Cuxac-Cabardès
Mas-Cabardès
Lespinassière
Aigues-Vives
Cruzy
Maureilhan
Béziers
Brousses-et-Villaret
Caunes-Minervois
Capestang
Peyriac-Minervois
Olonzac
Nissan-lez-E.
Sérignan
Conques-s.-O.
Vendres
Alzonne
Ginestas
Coursan
Bram
Aigues-Vives
Canal du Midi
Valras-Plag
Carcassonne
Trèbes
Narbonne
Montréal
Lézignan-Corbières
Narbonne-Plage
St-Pierre-s.-Mer
Lavalette
Capendu
Leuc
Rouffiac-d'Aude
Ferrals-les-Corb.
Gruissan
Gruissan-Plage
St-Hilaire
St-Laurent-de-la-C.
Portel
Limoux
Sigean
Aude
11
Lairière
Durban-Corbières
Port-la-Nouvelle
Ajac
Félines-Termenès
Lanet
Couiza
Arques
Mouthoumet
Villeneuve-les-Corbières
Cap Leucate
Espéraza
Tuchan
Leucate
Quillan
Soulatgé
Port-Leucate
Bugarach
Cubières-s.-Cinoble
Vingrau
Salses
St-Paul-de-Fenouillet
Port-Barcarès
Axat
Maury
St-Hippolyte
Caudiès-de-F.
Ste-Colombe-s.-Guette
Ansignan
Rivesaltes
Le Barcarès
Estagel
Bains-Escouloubre
Sournia
Baixas
Perpignan
Canet-en-R.
Mosset
Ille-s.-Têt
Millas
Canet-Plage
Toulouges
Alénya
Molitg-les-Bains
Thuir
Trouillas
St-Cyprien
Prades
Vinça
Boule-d'Amont
Fourques
Bages
Elne
Argelès-Plage
Olette
Llauro
Vernet-les-Bains
Argelès-s.-Mer
Pyrénées-Orientales
66
Port-Vendres
Mont-Louis
Le Boulou
Collioure
Banyuls-s.-Mer
Py
Céret
Arles-s.-Tech
Amélie-les-Bains-Palalda
Cap Cerbère
Cerbère
Pla-des-Hospitalets
La Jonquera
Port-Bou
Nuria
La Preste
Prats-de-Mollo
Setcasas
Capmany
Caralps
Coustouges
El Port de Llançà
Llançà
Ribes de Freser
El Port de la Selva
Camprodon
ESPAGNE
Figueres
Cadaquès
Sant Pau de Seguries
Castello d'Empuries
Roses
Castellfollit de la Roca
Sant Joan de les Abadesses
Ripoll
Besalu
Olot
Bascara
Els Llosses
Santa Pau
Sant Esteve d'en Bas
Banyoles
511
19
517
516
13
514
515
509
518
513 14
15 16
5
512
1
6
18
4
504 9 10
11 12
20
508 510
502 17
7 8
507
499 500 501
503 505 506
2 3

R O U S S I L L O N

INTRODUCTION

Situated in France's southernmost *département*, the vineyards of the Roussillon offer a variety of unusual and arresting landscapes. There are the rocky foothills of the Corbières, flat, easterly plains that disappear into the Golfe du Lion, and the spectacular Albarès mountains that plunge dramatically to the sea at the Spanish border. Everywhere the traveler is confronted by the vine, reminding him or her that although often grown with apparent nonchalance on the plains it sometimes requires laborious cultivation when the vines assault the rocky hillsides. Calcareous rock of gray-blue and striking ocher tones and brown-violet schistous rock pepper the countryside whetting the appetite for wines that one correctly imagines are as varied in nuance.

There is no wine highway with wines indicated in five languages for busloads of tourists. Instead, the Roussillon invites the traveler to cross the country to discover the tiny villages of typical Catalan architecture and wine growers that are as warm and direct as the sun which shines overhead for more than 2,500 hours a year making this the hottest region in France.

Direct selling to the public is well developed and there is every attraction in the region while searching out the treasures of *vins doux naturels* and the best reds (often reserved for export or for visionary merchants, but a few bottles are always available for the passing visitor).

VINS DOUX NATURELS: A PARTICULAR METHOD OF VINIFICATION

Exceptionally sweet, the vins doux naturels (VDN) of the Roussillon follow a particular process of production. The grapes are harvested very ripe (a minimum alcohol potential of 14.5%) and at a certain point the fermentation is stopped by the addition of a pure, neutral, grape alcohol of 96%. If this "*mutage*" occurs after the grape juice has fermented for a few days the wine will be very rich and sweet. Carried out later on the grape-pomace or marc during the period of maceration (here they speak of "*mutage sur grains*") the wines become dry or semi-sweet. The wines finish at an alcohol level of 15% to 19%.

The wines are traditionally aged, for a number of months or even years, in an oxidative environment, in oak barrels and sometimes in glass *bonbonnes* that are left exposed to the climatic elements in order to accelerate the effects of ageing. A second type of ageing, in a reductive environment, has since developed. The wine, held in vat for six to 24 months, is bottled early. This way the fruit of the young wine is preserved and the wine sold as a "rimage" or "rimatge" (meaning "age of the grape" in Catalan) and sometimes as a "vintage" (the English expression). Finally, there is an intermediate form of ageing, the rimage or vintage "*à mise tardive*," where the wine is held in vat for five years and then bottled.

ROUSSILLON APPELLATIONS

The Roussillon has nine appellations for its dry wines (red, white and rosé) and *vins doux naturels* of which Rivesaltes, Muscat-de-Rivesaltes, Maury and Banyuls represent 94% of French *VDN*.

Rivesaltes is an appellation that embraces everything. A mass of wines of no great interest, sold in supermarkets under aperitif brand names rub shoulders with nectars of 20 to 30 years of age forgotten at the back of the cellars of certain wine growers. These wines, made predominantly from Grenache (Noir, Gris and Blanc) and Macabeo and vinified as white, rosé and sometimes red wines, are commercially having a difficult time. A quarter of the 15,000 hectares of vines have been converted to Muscat-de-Rivesaltes, Côtes-du-Roussillon and Vin de Pays.

Muscat-de-Rivesaltes covers the same *terroirs* as Rivesaltes, Maury and Banyuls but is made uniquely from two varieties of the Muscat grape that are often blended together. The Muscat à Petits Grains is the most perfumed with extravagant aromas of exotic and citrus fruits, and mint and a rather fine palate. The Muscat of Alexandria is particularly enjoyable for its fullness and flavor of crystallized fruits. A good Muscat is aromatic without being excessive, with good fruit concentration on the palate but also length and freshness.

On the border with the Aude *département*, Maury covers 1,740 hectares to the north of the river Agly (communes of Maury, Tautavel, Rasiguère, Saint-Paul de Fenouillet and Lesquerde). The sweet wines of Maury are, as in Banyuls, produced from Grenache Noir (90% of plantings) grown on schistous soils. But in these foothills of the Corbières the black schistous rock is younger and the region is subjected to the influence of a more continental climate than in Banyuls. Hence the wines are deeply colored, rich in sugar content, and solidly tannic but do not, with age, attain the complexity and elegance of Banyuls. The local wine cooperative vinifies 85% of the production.

The four harbor communes of Collioures, Port-Vendres, Banyuls and Cerbère mark the Banyuls appellation. Close to the Spanish border, the schistous *terroir* rises in small terraces from sea level to 500 meters in altitude. Exposure to the sun's rays is exceptional and the wind frequent, whether from the north or the sea. The Grenache Blanc, Gris or Noir (a minimum 50% for Banyuls) vines are old (70% are over 40 years old) and have difficulty providing yields of 30 hectoliters/hectare.

Traditional Banyuls is notable for its varyingly nuanced color: brick-red, mahogany and sometimes amber, great suppleness on the palate and rich, complex aromas. The rimage or vintage wines have a purple, violet hue, intense cherry and plum aromas and a present tannic structure.

Côtes-du-Roussillon and Côtes-du-Roussillon Villages, comprising approximately

6,000 hectares in the Rivesaltes area, are the principal dry wine appellations in the Roussillon. Côtes-du-Roussillon (79% red) produces *petits vins rouges* to be drunk in the year produced as well as more ambitious, complex wines. They are produced from traditional grape varieties (Grenache Noir and Blanc, Carignan, Lladoner Pelut, Cinsault, Macabeo, Malvoisie du Roussillon) and from aromatic grape varieties that have been more recently planted (Syrah, Mourvèdre, Roussanne, Marsanne, Vermentino) in a diverse range of soils and sub-soils (limestone, clay-limestone, schists, alluvial terraces, etc). The small production of dry, white wines (5%) produced from Macabeo, Grenache Blanc, Vermentino or Rolle, Marsanne and Roussanne progresses, slowly attempting to find a path between slightly crisper wines with primary aromas and a more powerful style with a strong alcoholic content. The same can be said for the rosés but with less progresss.

The Côtes-du-Roussillon Villages (2,000 hectares) are 100% red. Four communes have the right to add their name to the Villages label: Caramany, Latour-de-France, Lesquerede and Tautavel. Except from a handful of wine growers, the appellation Villages wines are often disappointing (rather dull, dry, and hard). The Syrah already produces some remarkable wines, providing vines are planted in the appropriate soils with well selected clones, which isn't always the case.

Superimposed on to the Banyuls region, Collioure (red and rosé) is the most fashionable dry wine appellation (and therefore the most expensive) in the Roussillon. There are only 350 hectares but the volume has continued to increase. Grown on schistous soils and with a maritime influence, Grenache Noir (minimum 60%), Carignan, Cinsault, Syrah and Mourvèdre provide an expressive character. Formerly dry, the best of these red wines are today more full-bodied and fine with the aroma of ripe, red fruits and spices and a mineral nuance on the back palate. The rosés, which have a marked personality, are warm (sometimes heavy) and lightly tannic.

The Roussillon has not escaped the fashion for varietal wines, made under the vin de pays banner, which respond to an international demand and which are often more profitable for the wine growers than appellation wines. Certain wine growers have, nevertheless, rediscovered certain local varieties dismissed by the administrators. Taste some of the white vins de pays made from Grenache (Blanc and Gris) and the deliciously original dry Muscats which have explosive fruit and which deserve an appellation.

BUYING IN THE ROUSSILLON

The whites and rosés are generally available from March of the year after the vintage. Apart from certain exceptions they are sold at 20 F to 30 F and do not benefit from any ageing. The '96 vintage provided more lively, aromatic whites and rosés than is usual. The majority of red Côtes-du-Roussillon is released in the summer. Fruit-driven and with very little tannic structure, the wines are for drinking over a maximum period of two years. The Côtes-du-Roussillon Villages and Collioure aged for 12 months in the cellar are rarer but can evolve over two, three, even five to seven years for the special *cuvées* from great years.

The '96 and '95 vintages provided contrasting results. In '96 there were some very successful wines produced in the south of the *département* (Collioure) whereas elsewhere the wines had varying degrees of ripeness. It was the reverse in '95 where wine growers were happier in the north. As well, one can still find '94s and '93s, two attractive and powerful vintages. Prices for red wines from the Roussillon are extremely variable. Basic Côtes-du-Roussillon sells for around 25 F, then from between 30 F to 50 F for wines aged in oak barrel, with certain *cuvées* available in limited quantity from three or four star winemakers fetching as much as 70 - 100 F. The price scale for Collioure is more restrained but at a generally higher level (between 45 F and 70 F). In *vins doux naturels*, the '96 vintage (except for the Muscats) appears to be inferior to '95. In fact, '92 apart, the 1990s have been good for all the *VDNs*. The rimage or vintage wines, like the older wines, remain as a general rule an excellent buy, particularly in Rivesaltes where it is possible to find ten-year-old wines for less than 50 F. The same applies to the great prestige *cuvées* of Banyuls which can be acquired for less than 200 F, which is a small sum given the quality and work that goes into producing these wines.

AT TABLE WITH THE WINES OF THE ROUSSILLON

The Côtes-du-Roussillon whites and rosés are generally simple wines to be served at 10-12°C with summer cuisine. The more powerful Collioure rosé is a good match for rock fish, recipes based on anchovies and spicy dishes (tagine, paella). Spicy dishes also work with the powerful ripeness and tannins of young reds. After two or three years bottle age, Côtes-du-Roussillon, Côtes-du-Roussillon Villages or Collioure are best suited to a winter or autumnal cuisine (stewed meats, reduced sauces, salmis, civets and wild mushroom garnishes).

It is rather limiting to confine *vins doux naturels* to the rôle of aperitif as the wines also work well during and after a meal. Sacrosanct matches that are guaranteed include warm foie gras, duck cooked with orange or honey, blue cheeses (served with raisin or wallnut bread), cantal, and dry goat's cheeses. There is also a natural marriage with cakes or ice cream made with crystallized fruits, wallnuts, almonds, prunes, coffee or chocolate. The exotic notes of the Muscat respond mischievously to sweet dishes based on citrus fruits, peach, apricot, and exotic fruits. Young vintage Banyuls (served at 14°C) matches well with desserts that have a strong chocolate flavor or those based on red fruits and is doubly revealing with creamy blue cheeses like gorgonzola. Finally, when the chocolates are brought to the table and the cigars come out it is time to wisely savor the power and length on the palate of the old, sweet wines. These should be served in relatively large glasses, in small quantities as their alcohol (15% to 19%) and sugar content is strong. The young vintage wines are best consumed within a week of the bottle being opened and should be kept with the cork replaced in the bottom of the fridge. Older sweet wines, however, can be kept for up to one or two months.

ALENYA

1 - BED & BREAKFAST - **Domaine du mas Bazan**: *Annie and Paul Favier, 66200 Alénya. Tel. 04.68.22.98.26 Fax 04.68.22.97.37.* This shady Catalonian mas with its five lovely, comfortable rooms offers a truly charm-

ing stay. Good family-style cooking (Catalonian specialties with farm-grown produce), wines from the property (presented in our guide), pool on the premises, beach within five kilometers. Count on 280 F per night for a couple, breakfast included, and 100 F per head for dinner (by reservation).

BANYULS-SUR-MER

2 - HOTEL-RESTAURANT - **Hôtel Les Elmes - restaurant La Littorine**: *Plages des Elmes, 66650 Banyuls-sur-Mer. Tel. 04.68.88.03.12 Fax 04.68.88. 53.03. Closed in December and January (except for holidays) and Wednesday in low-season.* In a modern setting, currently the best restaurant on the

Côte Vermeille with a relaxing view of the little beach. The freshness of products and the power of the Catalonian region sing on your plate. Excellent offering of wines from the Roussillon, particularly from Banyuls, with some delicious old vintages. Three menus: 100 to 260 F (wine included). A la carte: around 300 F. Thirty-one well-equipped rooms (some air-conditioned) from 190 to 400 F. The owner organizes excursions in the vineyards and at sea (by reservation).

3 - RESTAURANT - **Al Fanal**: *Avenue du Fontaulé (in the port), 66650 Banyuls-sur-Mer. Tel. 04.68.88. 00.81.* For a feast of fresh fish (delivered daily from the port) accompanied by a violet sauce, served with care by Marie and Laurent Sagols. Very respectable first menu at 90 F. In summer, some tables on the terrace face the private boating port. The wine list is full of the best Roussillon wines, with a constant preference (and rightfully so) for the Banyuls and Collioures from the Rectorie estate whose aging-cellar is situated under the restaurant.

CAÏXAS

4 - BED & BREAKFAST - **Mas Saint-Jacques**: *Jane Richards and Ian Mayes, 66300 Caïxas. Tel. 04.68.38.87.83. Fax 04.68.38.87.83.* An isolated village house kept by a very considerate couple of Brittish musicians, with five simple, bright rooms. Room (2 pers.): 295 F, suite (4 pers.): 550 F. Spectacular view of the montain. Swimming pool. Meals at communal table (95 F, by reservation, apéritif,

wine and coffee included): personalized Mediterranean cuisine and a

small but excellent selection of local wines.

CARAMANY

5 - RESTAURANT - **Auberge du Grand Rocher**: *Rue Éloi Tresserres, 66720 Caramany. Tel. 04.68.84.51.58. Closed December to mid-March and Monday. Reservation are advised.* In a steep village founded on a rocky peak, this new inn offers a splendid view of the Agly dam. Five menus prepared with fresh products (75 to 150 F) are served informally by a couple who enjoys good living. Small but good selection of Côtes-du-Roussillon at less than 100 F.

CASES-DE-PENE

6 - RESTAURANT - **Le Grill du château de Jau**: *66600 Cases-de-Pène. Tel. 04.68.38.91.38. Open every day from June 15 to September 30. On reservation.* The walls of the charming castle encircle a vast and renowned viticultural estate and a contemporary art fondation (exhibitions all summer). Summer cuisine served with wine from the property. Same owners, same atmosphere as the Clos de Paulilles (see Collioure). Menu: around 145 F.

CERET

7 - HOTEL - **Les Terrasses du Soleil**: *Route de Fontfrède, 66400 Céret. Tel. 04.68.87.01.94 Fax 04.68.87.39.24. Closed from 11/1 to 2/28.* On the heights, 2 km from Picasso's beloved village, this comfortable hotel with its warm welcome offers a

perfect calm and a view of the Pyrénées. Pool. 27 rooms: 595 to 795 F.

8 - RESTAURANT - **Les Feuillants**: *1 bd La Fayette, 66400 Céret. Tel. 04.68.87.37.88. Closed Sunday evening and Monday. Reservations preferable.* The best restaurant in the Pyrénées-Orientales established in a bright, colorful private residence in the heart of the village, shaded by the plane trees. Didier Banyols tenderly prepares the regions best products to produce an ingenious, robustly fla-

vored cuisine. You'll fall for the regional menu (350 F with wine) accompanied by the finds of the enthusiastic wine waitress, Marie-Louise Banyols. With more than 200 entries from Languedoc-Roussillon, her wine list is unequalled. The other wine-producing regions are not forgotten. Reasonable prices given the high quality (several bottles at around 130 F). Brasserie menu: 130 F. Seasonal menu: 420 F. 3 luxurious rooms: 400 to 700 F reservation obligatory.

COLLIOURE

9 - BED & BREAKFAST - **Brigitte Banyuls**: *40 avenue du Miradou, 66190 Collioure. Tel. 04.68.82.12.63.* In the center of old Collioure, four independant rooms (with shower or bath and toilets), very cozy. Friendly welcome. From 170 to 220 F (low-season) and 200 to 240 F (high-season).

10 - BED & BREAKFAST - **Ermitage de la Consolation**: *CD 86, 66190 Collioure. Tel. 04.68.82.17.66. Open from Easter to Halloween.* Amidst the vineyard in the lunar landscape of Collioure's terraced hinterland, a religious site bought by Collioure families and run by their philanthropic descendants. 9 simple rooms with shower: around 200 F, breakfast included (1 night for a couple).

11 - HOTEL - **Hôtel Casa Pairal**: *66190 Collioure. Tel. 04.68.82.05.81 Fax 04.68.82.52.10.* In the heart of the city, 150 m from the port, an old Catalonian dwelling hidden at the back of a courtyard that's been converted into a charming, very comfortable, and tastefully decorated hotel. 28 air-conditioned rooms looking out on a

verdant patio (swimming pool). From 330 to 890 F (Relais du Silence).

12 - HOTEL - **Hôtel Les Templiers**: *12 quai de l'Amirauté, 66190 Collioure. Tel. 04.68.98.31.10 Fax 04.68. 98.01.24. Closed in January.* In the artist's-hotel tradition, wall-to-wall paintings (the most famous have been stolen). One gets the impression of sleeping in a museum annex. The prettiest rooms, with their traveller's comfort, look out on the port (noisy in summer). fifty-five rooms: 250 to 390 F.

ESTAGEL

13 - HOTEL-RESTAURANT - **Les Graves**: *9 bd Jean Jaurès, 66310 Estagel. Tel. 04.68.29.00.84 Fax 04.68.29.47.04.* In the heart of the village, a charming hotel restored with tasteful simplicity by new winegrowers. Simple cooking with a local inspiration. 22 rooms: 135 to 270 F. Menu: 68 to 118 F.

PERPIGNAN

14 - HOTEL-RESTAURANT - **Hôtel Villa Duflot**: *109 avenue Victor-d'Albiez, 66000 Perpignan. Tel. 04.68.56.*

67.67 Fax 04.68.56.54.05. On the outskirts of Perpignan (not very cheerful), this large new villa is set in a park. Fashionable contemporary decor, vast, well-equipped rooms looking out on the garden (pool). 24 rooms: 540 to 750 F.

15 - HOTEL-RESTAURANT - **Park Hôtel**: *18 bd J.-Bourrat. Tel. 04.68.35.14.14 Fax 04.68.35.48.18. Restaurant closed Sun.* Centrally located, comfortable hotel with an irreproachable family welcome. 67 rooms: 240 to 500 F.

16 - RESTAURANT - **Al-Tres**: *3 rue de la Poissonnerie, 66000 Perpignan. Tel. 04.68.34.88.39. Closed Sun. and Mon. noon, and Mon. evenings from October to June.* The new " in " spot in the Catalonian capital, appreciated for its Côté-Sud decor, its tapas and especially its very well-stocked cellar of Roussillon vintages. To be discovered. Menus: 65 (lunch weekdays) and 120F.

PORT-VENDRES

17 - RESTAURANT - **Ferme auberge du Clos de Paulilles**: *Baie de Paulilles, 66660 Port-Vendres. Tel. 04.68.98. 07.58. Open from 6/1 to 9/31. By reservation.* On the seaside, in a lovely viticultural property (see properties) restored in 1995. Chic, informal atmosphere and generous Catalonian cuisine. Only one menu at 160 F, good wines from the property (Collioure, Banyuls, Muscat) at will.

SAINT-CYPRIEN

18 - HOTEL-RESTAURANT - **Hôtel de l'Île de la Lagune**: *Les Capellans, boulevard de l'Almandin, 66750 Saint-Cyprien-Sud. Tel. 04.68.21.01.02 Fax 04.68.21.06.28. Closed 1/5 to 3/5.* This modern palace is preserved from the concrete invasion by the surrounding vegetation and its position facing the sea. Modern decoration, high-class, but conventional. 18 rooms and 4 suites from 575F to 1,250F. The restaurant, l'Almandin (closed Sun. evening and Mon. from October to May) is one of the best in the region, with an overtly Languedocian cuisine. Good, lengthy selection of regional wines that won't run up the bill (too much). Menus: 180 to 390 F.

TAUTAVEL

19 - RESTAURANT - **Le Petit Gris**: *Route d'Estagel, 66720 Tautavel. Tel. 04.68. 29.03.23.* Two paces from the Maury vineyards, the winegrowers, and the prehistoric site of Tautavel: a simple inn situated in a vineyard that's specialized in Catalonian grill cooking on a wood fire (cargolade, sausages and meats), very hearty. Short list of local vintages. A la carte: around 150 F.

VILLENEUVE DE LA RAHO

20 - BED & BREAKFAST - **Domaine de Val Marie**: *Jeanine Deprade, route de Montescot, 66180 Villeneuve de la Raho. Tel. 04.68.55.90.71.* One suite and one guest room (290F) with old-fashioned decor, but perfectly kept in a 19th-century family residence in the countryside. Excellent breakfast with homemade jams. Simple and warm welcome.

TO SEE

BANYULS-SUR-MER

MUSEUM - **Maillol Museum**: *Vallée de la Roume, 66650 Banyuls-sur-Mer. Tel. 04.68.88.57.11. Closed Tuesday, holidays and in December. 10/1 to 4/30 from 10 to 12 and 2 to 5; 5/2 to 9/30 from 10 to 12 and 4 to 7.* Admission: 20 F, reduced price and groups: 10 F. Between the vineyard and the green oak forest, on the small farm where Aristide Maillol (1861-1944) lived and rests: a modest museum that charmingly retraces- with photographs, lithographs and statuettes- the life of the man that dominated sculptural art in his time. The artist's most important works are on display at the Hôtel Bouchardon in Paris.

CERET

MUSEUM - **Modern art museum**: *8 bd Maréchal-Joffre, 66400 Céret. Tel. 04.68.87.27.76. Every day, except Tuesday and holidays, from 10 to 6 (7pm from July to September; open every day from May to September).*

Admission: 35 F. Collection centered on artists who have stayed in Céret: Chagall, Dali, Dufy, Gris, Maillol, Matisse, Miro, Picasso for modern art, and d'Arman, Ben, Tapiès, Viallat for contemporary art.

COLLIOURE

OUTING - **Château royal**: *66190 Collioure. Tel. 04.68.82.06.43. Every day (except holidays) from 10 to 5:15 from June to September (4:15 from October to May).* Admission: 20 F. Former residence to the kings of

Aragon and Majorca from the 13th to the 17th century. Exhibits on the graphic arts and on Catalonia's traditional commercial activities (cork, viticulture, anchovies, etc).

OUTING - **Fauvism trail**: *Mairie, 66190 Collioure. Tel. 04.68.82.05.66.* Since summer of 94, a pedestrian itinerary guides walkers through Collioure. 20 reproductions of masterworks by Derain and Matisse are placed in

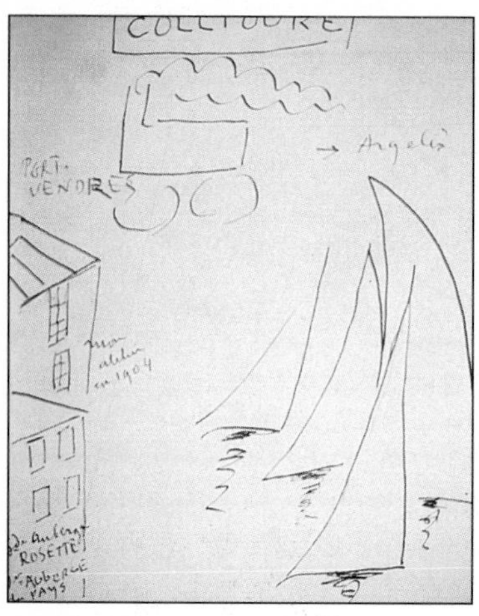

situ, in the perspective chosen by the painters. Two different ways of amiring the bell-tower, the beach or the " red roofs " of the village.

OUTING - **Vineyard route**: *Maison de la vigne et du vin de Collioure, Place du 18-Juin, 66190 Collioure. Tel. 04.68.82.49.00. Open every day from May to September (1 to 7:30pm).* Rental or purchase (50 F) of an audio-cassette for a " guided tour " by car along 12 km of mountainous road (D86), punctuated by 5 stops, to discover the history of Collioure's vineyard.

ELNE

MUSEUM - **Cloister and Historical and archeological Museum**: *66200 Elne. Tel. 04.68.22.70.90. Every day from 10 to 6:45 June to September (shorter hours in low-season).* Admission: 20 F. An archeological capital perched high on its oppidum, Elne dominates the Roussillon plain. 11th-century cathedral and cloisters in marble built from the 12th to the 14th century: a marvel of Roussillonnais art .

TAUTAVEL

MUSEUM - **European Prehistoric Center**: *66720 Tautavel. Tel. 04.68. 29.07.76 Fax 04.68.29.40.48. Open every day. From 10/1 to 3/31, from 10 to 12:30am and 2 to 6pm. From 7/1 to 8/31, from 9am to 9pm. From 9/1 to 31, from 10am to 6pm.* Admission: 35 F, children: 17 F. Presentation of Tautavel's prehistoric and paleontology collections and its famous 450,000 year old " man ". Educational and entertaining.

VITICULTURAL FETE

OCTOBER
The harvesting fête in Banuyls-sur-mer, the 3rd Sunday in October. *For information: tel. 04.68.88. 00.62.*

Jean-Paul Ramio, Manager of the Cave de l'Etoile, at the harvest.

Cave de l'Étoile

Manager Jean-Paul Ramio. **Address** 26 avenue Puig-del-Mas, 66650 Banyuls-sur-Mer - Tel. 04.68.88.00.10 Fax 04.68.88.15.10. **Open** From Monday to Friday, 8:00-12:00 and 14:00-18:00 (From Easter to Sep. 30, open until 19:00). Saturday, Sunday and national holidays, 10:00-12:30 and 15:00:19:00. **Spoken** Catalan **Credit cards** Visa, Eurocard, MasterCard.

Admired by the local population, this tiny (180 hectares) 70-year-old wine cooperative is the historical archive of Banyuls. The cellars resemble an antique shop. They are full of wrinkled, seeping barrels of various sizes from which escape the outflow of maderized (*rancio*), spice, coffee, and chocolate aromas which imbue the majority of the wines of l'Etoile. Even the rimage and vintage wines here have a slight oxidative note but this doesn't, like the Terra Vinya '91 (150 F), prevent them from ageing remarkably well. L'Etoile, however, is particularly renowned for its old Banyuls. We presently prefer the Macéré Tuilé '88 (81 F), a Banyuls for beginners which is round, soft and has a full gamut of aromas, the Grande Réserve '82 (126 F) which is amazingly young on the palate, soft and very fruity (fig jam), and the Banyuls Grand Cru Doux Paillé Hors d'Age (146 F) which has complex and never-ending flavors of honey and roasted hazelnuts.

Our choice Banyuls Select Vieux '79 (212,50 F). After ten minutes in the glass the aromas develop magnificently with notes of chocolate, fig, marmalade and vanilla which can also be found on the palate. This is dense with a long finish but not at all cloying. Empty, the glass still holds the bouquet for a good hour.

Reception Friendly. In the shop with a member of the staff used to serving tourists.

How to get there *(Map 13): Arriving from Perpignan take the sea front then turn right into Avenue Puig-del-Mas. The cellars are 50m further on.*

Over a period of 13 years Alain Soufflet has quietly developed his own style in Banyuls.

Domaine de la Casa Blanca

Owners Alain Soufflet and Laurent Escapa. **Address** 16, avenue de la Gare, 66650 Banyuls-sur-Mer - Tel. 04.68.88.12.85 Fax 04.68.88.04.08. **Open** July - Sep., every day except Sunday, 10:30-12:30 and 15:30-19:30. In low season, by appointment. **Spoken** English, Spanish. **Credit cards** Visa, Eurocard, MasterCard.

The domaine (8 hectares) is more than 100 years old but the wine has only been bottled and sold here since Alain Soufflet returned to the region in 1983. This agricultural lawyer, whose mother was from Banyuls, worked for a long time in the north of France before going into partnership with Laurent Escapa, the viticulturalist at the domaine. Responsible for vinification and commerce, Alain has quietly developed his own style of young Banyuls. Never astounding, these wines are balanced, without an excess of sugar, as demonstrated by the Tradition '94 (see our choice) or the '94 version of the Vintage (65 F) which is more elegant than the '93. In a different genre the Rancio '79 (130 F: 50 centiliters) is excellent. It has not been filtered, hence the cloudy, caramel color, and has finely oxidized notes mixed with Mocha chocolate. This is very much a wine for reflection. For Collioure take the '95 which is better than the '94 (45 F), a weak vintage.

Our choice Banyuls Tradition '94 (50 F). A blend of Grenache Noir, Gris and Blanc from vines of more than 80 years. Very aromatic (*garrigue*, pine resin, black fruits), soft on the palate with fruit and smoky flavors. The finish is tannic but not excessively so. Excellent value for money, this wine can be drunk or aged a little.

Reception Easy-going, with a "student of human nature" who is never without his pipe. In an old cellar full of barrels which gently coax the wine to the sound of *Radio France-Musique*.

How to get there *(Map 13): Arriving from Perpignan along the coast turn right before Banyuls at a corner signposted "Gare." The cellar is next to the railway station.*

A view from Mas Reig of some of the old barrels for ageing and the village of Banyuls.

Cellier des Templiers

Manager Jean-Pierre Parayre. **Address** Rue du Mas Reig, 66650 Banyuls-sur-Mer - Tel. 04.68.98.36.70 Fax 04.68.98.36.91. **Open** The *Grande Cave*, Apr. 1 - Oct. 30, every day, 9:00-19:00. The rest of the year, except Sunday and national holidays, 9:30-12: 30 and 14:00-18:00. The *cave souterraine* (Mas Reig), June 1 - Sep. 30, every day 9:00-19:00. **Spoken** English, German, Spanish **Credit cards** Visa, Eurocard, MasterCard, Amex.

The giant cooperative GICB (Groupement Interproducteur Collioure Banyuls), which produces 80% of all Collioure and 50% of all Banyuls, has as a flagship the Cellier des Templiers, which sells directly to the general public. Fourteen Banyuls and seven Collioures are produced under the direction of Jean-Pierre Campadieu, the house enologist and discreet and knowledgeable connoisseur of the *terroir.* Of the Collioures produced by Le Cellier the Mas Parer '95 (60 F) and the Château des Abelles (71 F) will not disappoint. The first is round, fruity, and to be drunk young and the second more structured and marked by the Syrah. For the Banyuls' you'll need to break the piggy bank to discover the trilogy of Grands Crus from the '82 vintage. The Président Vidal (168 F) is very coffee, caramel, crystallized orange peel and old wood with a powerful and warm (18.5%) palate. The Vivian Le Roy (169 F) is a dry Banyuls with a long brandy-like flavor.

Our choice Banyuls Grand Cru Amiral de Vilarem '82 (199 F). Aged eight years in bottle. This is semi-sweet with a diluted black coffee color and intense, jammy nose (fig, tomato). The palate is full and mellow with a long, bitter chocolate finish. It is wonderfully balanced and not at all cloying.

Reception Open to the general public with an accent on wine sales. At the Grand Cave there is a video and a visit to the imposing winemaking installations. At Mas Reig there are underground cellars dating from the 13th century.

How to get there *(Map 13): On the sea front turn right before the town hall (mairie), towards La Tour Madeloc. The Grande Cave is 1km from the center.*

Estelle Dauré and her favored Mourvèdre which marks the style of the Collioure.

Les Clos de Paulilles

Owners Estelle and Bernard Dauré. **Address** 66600 Port-Vendres - Tel. 04.68.38.90.10 Fax 04.68.38.91.33. **Open** From Easter, Saturday and Sunday; June 1 - Sep. 31, every day. **Spoken** English, Spanish. **Credit cards** Visa, Eurocard.

The largest of the private cellars in the appellation (80 ha) nestles in the Bay of Paulilles, a site listed by the *Conservatoire du Littoral*, next to a mysterious industrial wasteland owned by the Nobel company. In summer the place swings to the rhythm of a fashionable *ferme-auberge* (see hotels-restaurants in Roussillon). All this is managed by the ever-active Estelle Dauré, daughter of a celebrated Catalan family/*negociant* who also own Château de Jau in Cases-de-Pene (130 ha in appellations Muscat de Rivesaltes and Côtes-du-Roussillon Villages). The Collioure from Paulilles is constantly improving thanks, in part, to the increasing age of the Mourvèdre vines (average age 10 years) and to an adventurous ageing in oak barrels, of which one-third are renewed yearly. The vintage Banyuls is made from 100% Grenache Noir and the '95 (68 F) has plenty of charm. It has the aromas of coffee, pine resin and rich plum on the nose and is delicious on the palate. The residual sugar (115 grams/liter) will not necessarily be to everyone's taste. The Château de Jau Muscat de Rivesaltes (53 F) is one of the finest in the appellation and the Mas Christine Rivesaltes '93 (69 F) which is soft and complex shows decided improvement.

Our choice Collioure red '95 (66 F) The nose has a concentrated raisin and resinous aroma. The palate is full, flavorsome, tannic, and firm but attractive young. This is a good example of maritime Mourvèdre.

Reception A competent member of the staff looks after the cellar which is situated in the *auberge*.

How to get there *(Map 13): Arriving from Perpignan on the coast road between Port-Vendres and Banyuls. Building clearly visible on the left in the middle of the vines.*

Thierry (the winemaker, left) and Marc Parcé, the champions of Collioure and young vintage Banyuls, in the midst of pruning.

Domaine de la Rectorie

Owners Marc and Thierry Parcé. **Address** 65 avenue du Puig-del-Mas, 66650 Banyuls-sur-Mer - Tel. 04.68.88.13.45 Fax 04.68.88.18.55. **Open** All the week, by appointment only. **Spoken** English, Spanish. **Credit cards** Visa, Eurocard, MasterCard.

In 14 years, the Parcé brothers have radically rejuvenated the image of Banyuls and Collioure. Thierry, the winemaker, has brought precision and an aromatic intensity to the wines that has never been seen before. Marc, with his lively Catalan spirit, has converted a whole generation to the originality of the schist soils. The two brothers are today the masters of young vintage Banyuls and Collioure. Of the latter, Coume Pascol '95 (70 F), produced from Syrah, Grenache and Carignan matured in barrel, is a reference even in difficult years. The nose is toasted and the palate fine, spicy and showing plenty of class. The '96 will be for longer ageing. Apart from the *cuvée* Parcé Fréres there are a number of good vintage Banyuls. The *cuvée* Léon Parcé '95 (98 F), aged for a year in barrel, is always the most complex. It is very sweet and soft on the palate with a nuance somewhere between eucalyptus and concentrated fig. The lovely *cuvée* Elisabeth (80 F) produced from Grenache *noir* and *gris* and vinified as a white wine is all honey and finesse.

Our choice Always the Banyuls Parcé Frères '96 (70 F). Produced from 60% Grenache Noir this is fruitier (distinct cherry) and more lively than the '95. A curiosity wine: Vin de Pierre (90 F), aged three years in barrel without topping up. The wine is a homage to guitarist Pedro Soler and the schist soils. This sherry-like wine goes perfectly with Collioure anchovies.

Reception In an office installed in an artist's atelier at the end of the garden of the family home.

How to get there *(Map 13): Arriving from Perpignan take the road alongside the beach then turn right into Avenue Puig-del-Mas. Signposted.*

The vineyard of Collioure-Banyuls owes its perennial nature to the stubbornness of *vignerons* like Cantié-Campadieu.

Domaine La Tour Vieille

Owners Christine Campadieu and Vincent Cantié. **Address** Shop: 2 rue Berthelot, Cellar: 3 avenue du Mirador, 66190 Collioure - Tel. 04.68.82.42.20/04.68.82.44.82 Fax 04.68.82.38.42. **Open** Shop, April 1 - Sept. 30, every day 10:00-13:00 and 16:00-19:00. Cellar, in low season, by appointment. **Spoken** English, Spanish, catalan. **Credit cards** Visa, Eurocard, MasterCard, Amex.

Between Collioure and Cerbère the grape growers shape their schist combes into terraces facing the Mediterranean in the same way that others sculpt marble. Vincent Cantié, the son of a salt-curer from Collioure, is one of these sculptors of the hills. This viticultural aesthete and his partner Christine Campadieu "continue the love and spirit" of this Catalan vineyard. Their 12 hectares produce an interesting range of Collioures including the Rosé des Roches '96 (40 F), one of the best in the region, and three reds including the Puig Oriol '95 (50 F), produced from Grenache Noir (60%), Syrah and Carignan, which is dense and supple and should be good starting in October 1997. Of the Banyuls, the Vintage '94 (60 F) has intense, crunchy fruit (squashed raspberries) and velvety tannins. The Francis Cantié '93 (90 F), concentrated fig, is more powerful but retains a real elegance. As a rarity there is the Vin de Table Rancio Sec Cap de Creus (120 F) made from late-harvested Grenache (16°5) and yeasts from Vin Jaune from the Jura.

Our choice Vin de Pays white Les Canadells '96 (60 F). Produced from old vines of Grenache Gris (70%), partially barrel fermented. With the aroma of broom, fenel and citrus fruits this is a generous wine and one that proves that the grape varieties from this region can produce original wines.

Reception The competent Agnès runs the tiny shop in the center of the town.

***How to get there** (Map 13): In the center of Collioure. The shop is located in a pedestrian street behind the Hotel La Frégate.*

Monique and Bernard Saperas.

Domaine Vial-Magnères

Owners Bernard and Monique Saperas. **Address** Clos Saint-André, 14 rue Édouard Herriot, 66650 Banyuls-sur-Mer - Tel. 04.68.88.31.04 Fax 04.68.55.01.06. **Open** From spring on the "parking de la Méditerranée" (opposite at the beach), 10:00-12:30 and 15:00-19:00 or in the cellar, by appointment. **Spoken** English, Spanish.

During the week Bernard Saperas manages his food processing laboratory in Toulouges. On the weekend he relaxes at the family domaine (10 hectares) which he has improved in a spectacular way with the help of his wife's family. Trained as a chemist, this explorer of the *terroir* of Banyuls was the first, in 1986, to produce a white Banyuls Rivage from 80% Grenache Blanc vinified on lees in new oak barrels and bottled early. The success was instantly recorded. The Rivage '94 (85 F) has notes of vervain, concentrated apricot and mead and a soft, round, crisp palate. Bernard was again innnovative in launching the first dry white vin de pays in the area (*cuvée* Armen) which has become a reference for others. His interest in white wines is explained by the abundance of Grenache Blanc and Gris on the property. There are some good red Banyuls but of a lighter style. Traditionalists will appreciate El Tragou '76 (150 F), a great and powerful dry Rancio which has spent 18 years in barrel.

Our choice Banyuls Grand Cru André Magnères '88 (120 F). One of the greatest vintages in the last 20 years aged for 30 months in large barrel. The intense tertiary aromas develop on the nose while the palate remains young, fleshy, fat and long on the finish.

Reception At a stand at the port or at the cellar in an impeccably kept tasting room.

How to get there *(Map 13): Arriving from Perpignan take the sea front then turn right into Avenue Puig-del-Mas. Pass in front of the Cave de l'Etoile and take the second road on the right. There is no signpost.*

The *casot*, a traditional stone shelter in the vineyards of Banyuls.

Domaine le Casot des Mailloles

Owners Ghislaine Magnier and Alain Castex. **Address** 17, avenue Puig-del-Mas, 66650 Banyuls - Tel. 04.68.88.59.37 - 52.52 Fax 04.68.88.54.03. **Open** From Monday to Saturday, 9:30-13:00 and 16:30-20:00. In low season, preferably by appointment. **Credit cards** Visa, Eurocard, MasterCard.

Alain Castex and his companion Ghislaine Magnier have made a new start. In 1994, they abandoned the Corbières, where Alain was an experienced wine grower (Domaine des Amouriès), and set off on the road to Andalucia in Spain. En route they came across Banyuls and what a surprise. "The ancestral work on the terraces in this vineyard is astonishing," says Alain with great enthusiasm. "We are overwhelmed by the beauty that surrounds us in the vines and have difficulty returning to the village!" With the luck that befalls lovers the Castex-Magnier team unearthed 4 hectares and, at the last minute, a place to make the wine in the village, just a month before the harvest. This is the first domaine to be created in Banyuls in years. In their first vintage ('95) they experienced both success and failure. The vintage Banyuls was not great (wait for the '96) but Alain's experience with dry wines has helped score a hit with the red Collioure, Clôt de Taillelauque '95 (58 F) which is fine, fruity, spicy, and lively, and above all with the dry white vin de pays.

Our choice Vin de Pays de la Côte Vermeil Blanc du Casot '95 (54 F: 50 centiliters). Grenache Blanc, Gris, and Muscat (10%) fermented in oak barrel. This is a big wine with discreet fruit on the nose but open and opulent on the palate (13.8%). It is round with the astonishing flavor of apricots, *garrigue*, and fennel. A real delight. The '96 follows in the same footsteps.

Reception Simple and passionate. At the entrance to the tiny vinification cellar.

***How to get there** (Map 13): Arriving from Perpignan take the sea front then turn right towards the Cave de l'Etoile. The cellar is opposite the church.*

Former pharmacist, Pierre Alquier, in his cellar with traditional Catalan architecture.

Domaine Alquier

Owner Pierre Alquier. **Address** 66490 Saint-Jean-Pla-de-Corts - Tel. 04.68.83.20.66 Fax 04.68.83.55.45. **Open** In summer, every day, 8:00-20:00. In low season, Saturday morning and Monday; the rest of the week, by appointment. **Spoken** English, Spanish.

Goodbye to pharmaceutical prescriptions and hello to the vine and fresh air! Pierre Alquier, 40, a pharmacist by trade, abandoned his dispensary in 1992 to commit himself full-time to the 30 hectare family-domaine situated at the foot of the Albarès. These Pyrenean foothills provide well-drained sand and stony soils, a northerly exposure for the vineyard terraces, and benefit from a higher rainfall than on the plain. Assisted by old Grenache and Carignan, a new planting of Syrah (8 hectares), and modernized installations (destemmer and pneumatic press) that are impeccably maintained, this young domaine has successfully orientated itself towards the production of round, fruity wines that can be appreciated young. The reds have been destemmed since 1994. The white Côtes-du-Roussillon '95 (28 F) made from Macabeo (50%), Grenache Blanc and Vermentino has perfect citrus aromas and should be consumed within the year.

Our choice Côtes-de-Roussillon red '94 (28 F). A lovely Syrah-based (70%) red wine with expressive redcurrant and blackberry aromas on the nose. It has a pleasing fruitiness on the palate which is round, lightly structured, and balanced. Good price-pleasure value.

Reception In a cellar that has been recently renovated with a view over the vines and the Albères.

How to get there *(Map 13): South from Perpignan towards Le Boulou via N9 then Saint-Jean-Pla-de-Corts. Cross the village and turn left towards Maureillas. Pass the Pont du Tech and follow signs to Domaine Alquier.*

Etienne Montès, from photojournalism to the vine.

La Casenove

Owner Étienne Montès. **Address** 66300 Trouillas - Tel. 04.68.21.66.33 Fax 04.68.21.66.33. **Open** Every day 14:00-20:00, preferably by appointment. **Spoken** English, Spanish, catalan. **Credit cards** Visa, Eurocard, MasterCard.

After 15 years of photojournalism Etienne Montès has finally returned to the family domaine. The last of a long line of travelers and an associate of enologist Jean-Luc Colombo, he is now diligently exploring his *terroir* (48 ha on clay and mountain scree from the Canigou). He takes care of his old vines and successfully experiments with Syrah while maintaining small yields, picking at optimum ripeness, and instigating a long vatting time and ambitious ageing in oak barrels and vat. The white Côtes-de-Roussillon '95 (50 F) is superb. Very old Grenache, Macabeo and Tourbat provide aniseed flavors and a generous palate. The red Côtes-de-Roussillon Tradition '95 (34 F) is round and fruity with fine tannins. More complex and firm the Commandant Jaubert (see our choice) will come to maturity after four or five years. There are two very good sweet, fortified wines at La Casenove. The Rivesaltes '94 (60 F), made from Grenache Noir is not at all cloying and the Muscat de Rivesaltes '95 (50 F) is the absolute expression of pure, ripe Muscat of Alexandria (70%).

Our choice Côtes-de-Roussillon red Commandant Jaubert '94 (100 F). Produced from Syrah (80%, vines of 12 years) macerated for a month and aged in oak barrels (20%) and cement vats (for two years). The color is dense and nose intense with notes of *garrigue*, leather and very ripe fruit. Reserved, dense, and firm the palate will open out with panache over six to ten years. An exceptional wine for the vintage.

Reception Friendly. In the harvesters' dining-room.

How to get there *(Map 13): South from Perpignan towards Le Boulou-Le Perthus via N9. Turn right after 10km towards Trouillas via D612 and pass the Pont du Reart.*

André (left) and Bernard Cazes on the Rivesaltes plain.

Domaine Cazes

Owners André and Bernard Cazes. **Address** 4 rue Francisco Ferrer, 66000 Rivesaltes - Tel. 04.68.64.08.26 Fax 04.68.64.69.79. **Open** From Monday to Friday (Saturday in Summer), 9:00-12:00 and 14:00-18:00. **Spoken** English. **Credit cards** Visa, Eurocard, MasterCard.

Routine is a mystery to the Cazes brothers. Not content with being at the head of the most renowned and consistent private domaine in the Roussillon Bernard, the bubbly winemaker, and André, the traveling salesman, never stop planning and building for the future. Consequently, over the last few years, their vast vineyard of 160 hectares on the Rivesaltes plain has been increasingly planted with Syrah, Merlot, Cabernet Sauvignon and Mourvèdre to the detriment of Grenache and Carignan. Having responded to a demand for wines of simple pleasure (varietal wines, Canon du Maréchal) they are also unwavering supporters of blended wines and wines for ageing (Côtes-du-Roussillon Villages and Crédo). As for their *vins doux naturels (VDN)* these remain model wines. The Muscat de Rivesaltes '96 (53 F) has a perfect sugar-alcohol balance while the Rivesaltes Aimé Cazes '75 (165 F), made from Grenache Blanc and aged 20 years in large *foudres*, is elegant. Perhaps it is less complex than the '73 but we wouldn't want to split hairs over it!

Our choice Heads, the traditional style of the Côtes-du-Roussillon Villages '93 (42 F) made from Grenache, Syrah and Mourvèdre aged in vat which is powerful and generous with animal and crystallized fruit notes. Tails, the innovative style of the Vin de Pays Crédo '94 (52 F) produced from Merlot and Cabernet Sauvignon aged in new oak casks which is full, soft, spicy, and delicious and very much a wine of today.

Reception In the cellar opposite the offices in Rivesaltes with a competent member of the staff.

How to get there *(Map 13): From Perpignan towards Narbonne via N9, then Rivesaltes. Turn right at the statue of Maréchal Joffre and follow the signs.*

An independent cooperative providing regular quality which works directly with the consumer.

Celliers Trouillas

Manager Thierry Cazach. **Address** 1 avenue du Mas Deu, 66300 Trouillas. - Tel. 04.68.53.47.08 Fax 04.68.53.24.56. **Open** From Monday to Saturday, 8:00-12:00 and 14:00-18:00 (19:00 in summer). **Credit cards** Visa, Eurocard, MasterCard.

The originality of the Cellier Trouillas is that it sells over half its production directly to the individual consumer. Managed by a young team and solidly backed by 900 hectares of vineyard situated in the Vallée des Aspres (sandy-gravel soils) the cooperative has, over the last six years, pursued a courageous policy of selecting the best parcels in the Côtes-du-Roussillon and the area marked for *vins doux naturels*. Even if there is still plenty of room for improvement the cave is on the right track. The Côtes-du-Roussillon is vinified to provide a simple style of wine (the traditional range - red, white and rosé, 17 F) and some oaked cuvées (Réserve and Gouverneur) for ageing a short legth of time and which like the *Cuvée* du Gouverneur '91 (28,90 F) represent good price-pleasure value. One can also find treasures in the old fortified wines and always at unbeatable prices. Among others we recommend the Rivesaltes Ambré '86 (42.80), aged nine years in oak barrel which is rich with a long *rancio* finish or the Rancio '82 (40.50 F) which has little sugar and is extremely elegant.

Our choice Rivesaltes Rubis '94 (34,80 F), 100% Grenache Noir, fortified on the *marc*, and bottled six months after the harvest. Pronounced fruit character, fluid and soft, this is a novel wine. Serve fresh as an aperitif or with a chocolate cake or red fruits.

Reception Convivial. In a large, traditional cooperative cellar.

***How to get there** (Map 13): South from Perpignan towards Le Boulou-Le Perthus via N9. Turn right after 10km towards Trouillas via D612. The cave is in the village center.*

The cirque of Vingrau.

Domaine Gardiès

Owner Jean Gardiès. **Address** 1, rue Millère, 66000 Vingrau - Tel. 04.68.64.61.16 Fax 04.68.64. 69.36. **Open** Every day by appointment.

Every year for the last ten years, in the month of June, the "Saint-Bacchus," a vast tasting of the wines of Roussillon open to professionals only, takes place in Perpignan. During this vinous competition that allows new talent to be revealed we discovered the wines of Jean Gardiès. Having taken over the 45 hectare family domaine this young wine grower bottled his first wines in 1990. If his Muscat de Rivesaltes '95 (46 F) is honest but lacks a little stuffing it is the red Côtes-du Roussillon Villages aged in oak barrel (see our choice) that shows the most promise. His southern grape varieties (Syrah, Grenache Noir, Mourvèdre and Carignan) planted in the cirque of Vingrau and Espira-de-l'Agly produce wines that are deep and solid. They could perhaps have a little more concentration and polish but generally seem to be heading in the right direction. This is a domaine to follow closely.

Our choice Côtes-du-Roussillon Villages Fût de Chêne '94 (34 F). A blend of destemmed Syrah (40%), Grenache Noir, Mourvèdre and Carignan aged for a year in new oak barrels. A velvety wine with good concentration and elegant tannins. The "fashionable" barrel ageing softens the Catalan character without making the wine too heavy. A wine to appreciate over two years.

Reception Simple, in the vinification cellar which is situated in a house in the village.

How to get there *(Map 13): From Perpignan towards Narbonne via N9, then towards the autoroute péage (Perpignan Nord). At the péage roudabout towards Vingrau. The cellar (large green door) is in the rue de la Révolution, third on the right, towards Tautavel.*

Annie and Paul Favier in the dining-room of their *ferme-auberge*, a little paradise of human warmth and relaxation.

Domaine du Mas Bazan

Owners Paul and Annie Favier. **Address** 66200 Alénya - Tel. 04.68.22.98.26 Fax 04.68.22.97.37. **Open** Every day, 8:00-13:00 and 15:00-20:00. **Spoken** English, Spanish.

She was a physiotherapist for handicapped children and he a medical inspector. In 1990 Paul and Annie Favier changed hats and opened a bed and breakfast and *table d'hôtes* on the plain of Alénya. Their shady *mas*, where conviviality and the sharing of good Catalan products are of a premium, rapidly became an obligatory stop. Gradually, Paul redeveloped the 12 hectares of vines that encircle the farm in order to offer his own wine to guests and then in 1994 started selling directly to the public. Like all young domaines with youthful plantings (Syrah, Roussanne) the Mas Bazan is still searching for its true direction. Each vintage Paul makes further progress, assisted by top advisors such as Bordeaux enologist Denis Dubourdieu, who followed the white wines in '96. The Vin de Pays Chardonnay '96 that we tasted in barrel was fresh and direct and seems very promising with more individual character than the '95 (28 F). There are two red Côtes-du-Roussillons: the Tradition (see our choice) and the Fût de Chêne which was well-made in '94 (approx: 40 F). There is also a good Muscat de Rivesaltes.

Our choice Côtes-du-Roussillon red '95 (32 F), 70% Syrah, fermented and aged in vat. A very fruity, supple wine which is delightful and easy to drink young. The expression of young vines from silty-sandy soils.

Reception In the dining-room of the farm or in the shadow of two old plane trees. Sincere and friendly.

How to get there *(Map 13): From Perpignan towards Elne-Argeles via N114. Turn right after 10km towards Saleilles via D12, then Alenya via D22. The mas is on the left, 900m after passing Saleilles.*

Suzy Malet, energetic and distinguished, still 20 years old like her Rivesaltes.

Domaine Sarda-Malet

Owner Suzy and Jérôme Malet. **Address** Mas Saint-Michel 12, chemin de Sainte-Barbe, 66000 Perpignan - Tel. 04.68.56.72.38 Fax 04.68.56.47.60. **Open** From Monday to Friday, 9:00-12:00 and 14:00-18:00, wee kend by appointment. **Spoken** English, Spanish, Catalan.

Suzy and Max Malet arrived at the family property in 1982 and set about replanting the vineyard. This consists of 48 hectares of stony terraces situated in the southern fringes of Perpignan which are subject to the influence of the maritime climate. The production of the three colors of Côtes-du-Roussillon as well as the Rivesaltes is, under the direction of their son Jérôme, of consistent quality. This year we particularly liked the "white label" Côtes-du-Roussillon red '95 (approx. 29 F), dominated by the Syrah and fairly robust, representing excellent price-pleasure value. In white a new and promising barrel-fermented Côte-du-Roussillon Roussanne and Marsanne *Terroir* Mailloles (78 F) will be available from 1997 and the fat and subtle "green label" Côte-du-Roussillon '95 (50 F) remains as reliable as ever. Of the fortified wines, the Muscat de Rivesaltes '96 (58 F) is light and airy and more successful than the '95 and the Rivesaltes 20 Ans d'Age (138 F) will please lovers of wine and cigars.

Our choice Côte-du-Roussillon red "black label" '94 (48 F). Syrah, Mourvèdre and Grenache aged one year in oak barrels. Deep, dark hue, very structured on the palate but already harmonious with a superb spicy finish. As a rarity, L'Abandon '95 (approx. 80 F). Late-harvested, unfortified Malvoisie (20% potential). Vervain and acacia honey with incredible freshness for a sweet wine.

Reception Suzy Malet or her secretary receive visitors in the domaine office amid the vines.

How to get there *(Map 13): Autoroute A 9, exit Perpignan Sud. Turn right 50m after the péage and follow the signs. From Perpignan, towards Thuir. At the Maillol roundabout take péage A 9, then turn left towards the signposted route.*

Ghislaine, Gérard and "Look" Gauby in their vines at Calce.

Domaine Gauby

Owners Ghislaine and Gérard Gauby. **Address** Le Faradjal, 66600 Calce - Tel. 04.68.64.35.19 Fax 04.68.64.41.77. **Open** Every day, by appointment. **Spoken** Catalan.

Gérard Gauby is the leader of the young generation of Catalan wine growers. These are the ones who struggle to make the best of the good *terroir* on the hillsides and which push ever further the selection and expression of each parcel. If Gérard Gauby was originally recognized for his concentrated and oaky style of wines, today he has introduced more balance into the wine at the same time remaining direct and sincere in keeping with his character. The vintage '96 is a superb year for the white wines. The Muscat Sec is fine and flavorsome and the blend of old vines, Les Centenaires (76 F), explodes with fruit. The awards go to the red wines in '95 with a Syrah *cuvée*, Muntada (70% new oak barrels), that is rich, tannic, and with a rare freshness. This wine is worthy of a Côte Rôtie. The '96 (to reserve, approx. 80 F on subscription) will be less structured but of a very high quality for the vintage. The Côtes-du-Roussillon Fût de Chêne '95 (38 F) remains a sure bet. It is fruitier and easier than the Villages and will be perfect in three to four years.

Our choice The Côtes-du-Roussillon Villages Vieilles Vignes '95 (72 F) made predominantly from Grenache and Mourvèdre and aged for a year in oak barrel. The nose is still closed, the palate full, fat and generous on the attack then covered with long, spicy, complex tannins. In five to seven years it will link power and elegance.

Reception Excellent, more often than not with Ghislaine who provides warmth and simplicity. In a long tasting room decorated with photos of the *vendanges*.

How to get there *(Map 13): From Perpignan direction airport, then D12 to Baixas. From the center of Baixas direction Calce via D18. Signposted. From Estagel take the magnificent route that passes by the Col de la Dona.*

The hour of the Catalan siesta.

Domaine du Mas Crémat

Owners Catherine and Jean-Marc Jeannin-Mongeard. **Address** 66600 Espira-de-l'Agly - Tel. 04.68. 38.92.06 Fax 04.68.38.92.23. **Open** From Monday to Saturday, 8:00-12:00 and 14:00-19:00.

Arriving at this isolated *mas* (25 hectares), the most striking sight is that of the black schist that surrounds the cellar. Using this early ripening soil which has the particularity of storing heat ("Crémat" means "scorched by the sun") and which is planted with old vines, Jean-Marc Jeannin has become the champion of dry white wines in the Roussillon and has taken the first steps towards the podium for his reds. This Burgundian, who arrived in Catalonia in 1990, controls the freshness in his white wines by harvesting "according to the acidity in the grapes rather than the alcoholic content." This is proven by the elegant Côtes-du-Roussillon '95 (26 F), which will be bettered by the '96, and by the original, barrel fermented, Vin de Pays Grenache Blanc Vieilles Vignes '96 (45 F), 20 hectoliters/hectare, which is full and oaky but lively for the grape variety. In the reds, look out for the release of the sumptuous Côtes-du-Roussillon Fût de Chêne '95 (approx. 45 F). There is also a flawless Muscat de Rivesaltes (43 F).

Our choice The star of the domaine: Vin de Pays Muscat Sec '96 (30 F). A delicious, fruity aperitif which is full on the palate. "The only grape variety that is truly unique here and which nobody can copy." Equally good is the Côtes-du-Roussillon red '95 (32 F), made from Grenache Noir and Syrah aged in vat. Very wild-gamy on the nose with a palate that is dense and long with persistent notes of the schist soil. A real mouthful.

Reception Simple. By a charming couple in the new cellar created in a Catalan spirit.

How to get there *(Map 13): From Perpignan direction Narbonne, then Foix-airport. Continue to Espira-de-l'Agly and in the village turn right, direction Vingrau. The route is then signposted.*

Nadine and Jacques Sire . A parcels of their vineyard which was previously just *garrigue*. The schistous soils inspired the name of the domaine.

Domaine des Schistes

Owners Nadine and Jacques Sire. **Address** 1, avenue Jean-Lurçat, 66310 Estagel - Tel. 04.68.29.11.25 Fax 04.68.29.47.17. **Open** Every day by appointment.

The majority of this 50 hectare domaine is composed of gray (at Tautavel) and pink (at Estagel) schist soils, in particular, the parcels that Jacques Sire, an agronomic engineer, cleared from the *garrigue* with the assistance of a bulldozer and stone crusher. Only the vine, under sufferance, can take root in this dry land (the water stress can result in the loss of half the crop) which is poor in mineral and organic matter. In brief, this is a *terroir* of character for wines of substance. The tone was set from the first bottling in 1990 of robust, tannic red wine produced from Carignan grown on the hillsides, Syrah and Grenache. The Côtes-du-Roussillon Villages Les Terraces needs a minimum of two to three years ageing. In a more supple register one can exercise patience with the Vin de Pays Merlot '95 (26 F), or the fruity Côtes-du-Roussillon Villages '95 *cuvée* Tradition (32 F) from Carignan and Grenache, which represents good price-pleasure value. Of the fortified wines, the Rivesaltes (55 F) is a quality wine and all chocolate and crystallized fruits.

Our choice Côtes-du-Roussillon Villages Les Terraces '94 (40 F). A blend of Syrah (50%), Grenache Noir and Carignan, aged for a year in oak casks. Notes of black fruits, pine resin and spices. The palate is powerful, still hard (the mark of wines from young schist soils) but fatter than the '93. A wine to match with game dishes or meat in sauce.

Reception A real enthusiast, Jacques Sire normally receives visitors at the cellar (rue Victor Hugo) or occasionally at home.

How to get there *(Map 13): From Perpignan, direction Narbonne, then Rivesaltes, Espira-de-l'Agly, Case-de-Pène and Estagel. In the village the cellar is signposted on the road to Millas and Latour de France.*

The originality of *vin doux naturel* Maury is partly due to its long ageing in glass demijohns that are subject to the inclemancy of the weather.

Mas Amiel

Owners Charles and Christiane Dupuis. **Manager** Jérémie Gaïk. **Address** 66460 Maury - Tel. 04.68.29.01.02 Fax 04.68.29.17.82. **Open** June 15 - Sep. 15, every day, 9:00-12:00 and 13:00-18:00. The rest of the year, same hours, from Monday to Friday. **Spoken** English. **Credit cards** Visa, Eurocard, MasterCard.

Maury (1,700 hectares), the aristocrat of *vin doux naturel* along with Banyuls, is practically unknown to the general public. The weak rivalry between producers (one wine cooperative produces 85% of the appellation) partly explains this situation. As in Banyuls, Maury is the product of Grenache Noir cultivated on hillsides, but here planted on much younger schistous-marl soils with climatically a continental influence. The wines are well-built and rich in sugar content. The Mas Amiel (155 hectares) is a private cellar of particular note in Maury which specializes in delicious young vintage wines (see our choice). This style, however, should not detract from the Maury that is aged for a long time in the sun in glass demijohns or *bonbonnes* and then in oak barrels of various size. The 15 Ans d'Age (100 F) with dark mahogany color, chocolate and chicory nose and elegant notes of *rancio*, Mocha chocolate and fig, is representative of this style.

Our choice Maury Vintage '96 (58 F). The cave's best seller. Bottled six months after the harvest in a high necked Italian-style bottle. This is an intensely fruity (small red and black berry fruits) sweet, fortified wine, which is supple with appetizing tannins. Serve at 13°C with black chocolate desserts.

Reception In a montainous site. The new cellar is bright and spacious. Visit the high, dark cellar where the large foudres repose.

How to get there *(Map 13): From Perpignan, direction Rivesaltes, Espira-de-l'Agly, Case-de-Pène and Estagel. At the exit to Estagel, direction Maury. The route is signposted on the right by the railway bridge.*

Baixas, the leading producer of Muscat de Rivesaltes.

Cave des vignerons de Baixas

Président Augustin Toreilles. **Address** 14, avenue Maréchal-Joffre, 66390 Baixas - Tel. 04.68.64.22.37 Fax 04.68.64.26.70. **Open** From Monday to Saturday de 8:00-12:00 (Monday, 9:00) and 14:00-18:00. **Credit cards** Visa, Eurocard.

Founded in 1923, this cooperative has not ceased to modernize since. It has 430 members and accounts for 2 100 hectares of appellation controlée vineyards. The cave assumes, with justice, its rôle as the leading producer of Muscat de Rivesaltes (10% of the appellation) but also produces a volume of vin de pays, Côtes-du-Roussillon and Rivesaltes. Part of the production is commercialized under the label Dom Brial, Marie-Antoinette's monk confessor, a native of the village and, so the saying goes, a connoisseur of sweet, fortified wines. The cave also administers the Château des Pins, a beautiful Catalan building in the center of Baixas (pronounced Baichas in Catalan) which has been completely restored and whose name is given to the top of the range wines. The Côtes-du-Roussillon wines, like the Côtes-du-Roussillon Villages *cuvée* des Terres Rouges '94 (25 F), are fruity, supple and well-made. Our preference in Muscat de Rivesaltes goes without contest to the aromatic and powerful Château Les Pins '96 (55 F) and in young Rivesaltes to the Château Les Pins '94 (45 F), a promising vintage of pure fruit extract.

Our choice Rivesaltes Dom Brial Hors d'Age '73 (120 F). You should throw yourselves at the last 1 000 bottles of this excellent vintage which is playing out extra-time. Complex nose of quince, Mocha chocolate and honey. The palate is very full and fine with persistent flavors of roasted coffee and orange peel. It is still remarkably young and excellent value for money.

Reception In a modern cellar organized for direct sales (bottles and bulk).

How to get there *(Map 13): From Perpignan direction Narbonne, then airport-Rivesaltes and Baixas. The cave is clearly visible on the right at the entrance to the village.*

SAVOIE

14
Foncine-le-Bas
Bonlieu
St-Laurent-en-Grandvaux
Le Chenit
Cossonay
Oron-la-Ville
Clairvaux-les-lacs
La Tour-du-Meix
Morbier
Bois-d'Amont
Apples
Bière
Crissier
Châtel-St-Denis
Étival
La Rixouse
Morez
Les Rousses
St-Cergue
Morges
Lausanne
Vevey
Montreux
Rolle
535
536
7
6
2
Moirans-en-Montagne
St-Claude
Mijoux
Dully
Nyon
Évian-les-B.
Meillerie
Villeneuve
Lavans
Divonne
St-Gingolph
Chevenoz
Vouvry
Thonon-les-Bains
Sciez
Gex
Dortan
Les Bouchoux
Douvaine
Versoix
Abondance
Châtel
Oyonnax
Ferney-Voltaire
Monthey
Genève
St-Cergues
Boëge
Bellevaux
Avoriaz
Chézery-Forens
St-Germain-de-Joux
Les Gets
Morzine
Bonne
Collonges
St-Julien-en-G
Annemasse
St-Jeoire
Taninges
Samoëns
Bellegarde-s.-Valserine
Reignier
Bonneville
Cluses
Vallorcine
Génissiat
La Roche-s.-Foron
Scionzier
Cruseilles
Flaine
Argentière
Frangy
Oëx
Rhône
Haute-Savoie
Les Praz
Hauteville-Lompnes
9
Passy
Chamonix
10
Le Grd-Bornand
Seyssel
St-Jean-de-Sixt
Sallanches
Annecy
Combloux
Anglefort
Vallières
La Clusaz
St-Gervais-les-B.
Les Houches
Seynod
Thônes
Megève
Artemare
Menthon-St-Bernard
Sevrier
Praz-s.-Arly
Rumilly
Virieu-le-Grand
Culoz
Talloires
Flumet-Val d'Arly
Les Contamines-Montjoie
527
528
Duingt
Serraval
Albens
1
Doussard
Ugine
Faverges
Belley
Lucey
Beaufort
Lescheraines
Yenne
Aix-les-B.
Le Châtelard
8
Albertville
Bonneval
531
532
533
529
Frontenex
Le Bourget-du-Lac
Bourg-St-Maurice
La Motte-Servolex
534
Aime
Les Arcs
St-Pierre-d'Albigny
Aiguebelle
Challes-les-Eaux
526
Chambéry
Aigueblanche
4
5
Le Pont-de-B.
Montmélian
Celliees
Moutiers
La Plagne
Tignes
Rotherens
Valmorel
Bozel
Chapareillan
La Rochette
Épierre
Savoie
Les Échelles
530
Pontcharra
Courchevel
St-Laurent-du-Pont
St-Pierre-d'Entremont
3
Allevard
St-Martin-de-Belleville
Méribel-les-Allues
Pralognan-la-Vanoise
St-Étienne-de-Cuines
St-Pierre-de-Ch.
Le Touvet
Lanslebourg-Mt-Cenis
Voiron
Goncelin
St-Colomban-des-Villards
Les Ménuires
Val-Thorens
Voreppe
Termignon
St-Jean-de-Maurienne
St-Egrève
Crolles
Le Curtillard
St-Julien-Mt-Denis
Villard-Bonnot
St-Michel-de-M.
Modane
Sassenage
Domène
St-Sorlin-d'Arves
Noiray
Le Rivier
Grenoble
Valloire
Tunnel du Fréjus
Lans-en-Vercors
Échirolles
Chamrousse
L'Alpe-d'Huez
Bardonecchia
Salbertrand
Le Pont-de-Claix
Vizille
Vif
Séchilienne
Le Bourg-d'Oisans
Pont-de-l'Alp
Névache
Laffrey
Les Deux-Alpes
Chantelouve
Le Monêtier-les-Bains
Cesana-Torinese
Sestriere
Ain
01
74
73
Fier
Arc
Usses
Dranse
Bienne
N5
N9
N1
N201
N203
N205
N212
N90
N508
N516
N6
N75
N91
A40
A41
A410
A43
A430
A4
A51
D415
D470
D118
D437
D25
D436
D984C
D991
D55
D984
D903
D12
D26
D902
D907
D910
D909
D909A
D912
D3
D911
D925
D992
D10
D913
D916
D95
D94
D117
D90
D915
D525A
D523
D926
D526
D520

SAVOIE

INTRODUCTION

The wines of Savoie have the unfortunate reputation of being *après-ski* wines, those which are meant to stay in their place, wash down a *fondue*, but which are never intended to leave the confines of Savoie. It is true that Savoyard winemakers do not make a great effort to remedy the situation, assured as they are of selling almost all of their production on the spot during the vacation seasons. But while the mountains, with or without snow, are by far the main tourist attraction of the region, its wines should not be taken lightly. Their presence in the great restaurants of the region is much more than a concession to local color. And their attractive price should inspire the wine lover to explore the vineyards with interest and curiosity.

GRAPE VARIETIES

As Chasselas is limited to the banks of Lake Geneva, Jacquère is the main white grape variety, accounting for 70% of white wines produced. They are labelled with the regional Vin de Savoie appellation, which can be followed by a village name for those making the best wines, such as Abymes or Apremont. In good years, Chasselas yields a delicate, fragrant wine, low in alcohol.

The Bergeron (the local name for the Côtes-du-Rhône's Roussanne) grows only on the limestone scree of Chignin. It makes smooth, aromatic, well-structured wines. The other great grape variety is Altesse, which goes into wines called Roussette. In four wines--Marestel, Monthoux, Monterminod, Frangy--it is vinified alone, yielding varietals of great finesse, richness, and body.

The main red grape variety is the Mondeuse: tannic but fruity, it deserves to be (re)discovered. On the other hand, the other well-known vines (Chardonnay, Gamay, Pinot Noir) generally give results which are a far cry from those attained in other vineyard regions.

BUYING WINE IN SAVOIE

Often available at Christmas following the harvest, Chasselas and Jacquères wines should be drunk during the year at the peak of their freshness, and they develop quickly. If possible, it is best to buy Jacquère varietals during July and August, because the local winemakers generally bottle vat after vat, without blending. The final bottlings, from *cuvées* which are slower to open up, are usually from old vines, yielding riper, more concentrated grapes, or from more interesting *terroirs*. Bergeron and Altesse, on the contrary, can improve with bottle age. 1996 was especially favorable for these two varieties. The best Mondeuse wines can be cellared.

A TABLE WITH WINES OF SAVOIE

More or less vigorous depending on whether or not it has undergone malolactic fermentation, Chasselas is good as an apéritif or an accompaniment for grilled fish. Apart from its traditional role as an escort for *fondue* and other Savoyard cheese specialties like *tartiflette* and *raclette*, the freshness of Jacquère serves to lighten Savoyard family dishes like *matafan*, *farçon*, *diots*, and *pormonier*, which can be excessively heavy.

Smooth and sometimes marked with a touch of residual sugar, Rousette wines from the Altesse grape can be good matches for sauced fresh-water fish, particularly those from the lakes. Bergeron plays the same role, extending it to accompany white meats or fried chicken.

Cold cuts, sausages, white and especially red meat call for Mondeuse wines.

ALBERTVILLE

1 - HOTEL-RESTAURANT - **Million**: *8 place de la Liberté, 73200 Albertville. Tel. 04.79.32.25.15 Fax 04.79.32.25.36. Closed Monday and Sunday evening.* Wonderful, classic cuisine, excellent cheese-board. Good selection of local wines. Menus: 150 to 500 F. Pretty rooms: 200 to 600 F.

ANTHY-SUR-LEMAN

2 - HOTEL-RESTAURANT - **L'Auberge d'Anthy**: *74200 Anthy-sur-Léman. Tel. 04.50.70.35.00 Fax 04.50.70.40.90. Closed Monday and Tuesday except in July and August.* A few kilometers from Thonon. A friendly inn, decorated with pictures of fishermen, where lake fish is prepared with a passion (in fishing season) and the motto is " in a pig, everything's good ". Good selection of Savoyard wines. Menus: 85 to 210 F. Rooms: 235 to 309 F. Excellent breakfast.

APREMONT

3 - HOTEL - **L'Auberge Saint-Vincent**: *73190 Apremont. Tel. 04.79.28.21.85.* Menus: 50 to 175 F. A country inn established in a former storehouse that wagers strongly- and successfully- on regional dishes and wines. Simple rooms: 190 and 210 F (ask for the one looking out on Mount Granier).

CHAMBERY

4 - RESTAURANT - **L'Essentiel**: *Place de la Gare, 73000 Chambéry. Tel. 04.79.96.97.27 Fax 04.79.96.17.78. Closed Saturday noon.* Jean-Michel Bouvier's menu combines innovation, home-style dishes and revised local recipes. Attractive regional wine list (fifty entries and some old vintages in Altesse and Bergeron that allows one to discover these wines' aging

potential). Menus: 130 to 390 F.

5 - HOTEL-RESTAURANT - **Château de Candie**: *Rue du Bois-de-Candie, 73000 Chambéry. Tel. 04.79.96.63.00 Fax 04.79.96.63.10.* An old castle, superbly renovated and transformed into a palace. Remarkable decoration. Cuisine in its finishing touches

and a wine list that needs to fill out. Menus: 145 to 280 F. Very pretty rooms: 450 to 950 F.

DIVONNE-LES-BAINS

6 - HOTEL-RESTAURANT - **La Terrasse**: *Avenue des Thermes, 01220 Divonne-les-Bains. Tel. 04.50.40. 34.34 Fax 04. 50.40.34.24.* Currently being restored, the Grand Hôtel is already equipped with a tempting table thanks to the savory hadywork of Jean-Marc Delacourt. The wine list still needs to be strengthened in Savoyard and Swiss wines, but the new wine waiter has taken up the task. Menus: 280 to 395 F. A la carte: around 350 F. Lovely, comfortable rooms (750 to 1,650 F).

EVIAN

7 - HOTEL-RESTAURANT - **Café Royal**: *Domaine du Royal Club, 74500 Evian. Tel. 04.50.26.85.00 Fax 04.50.75.61.00.* In a Belle Epoque decor, a cuisine where lake and countryside come together. Attractive wine list that doesn't neglect the region. Menus: 340 to 420 F. Palatial rooms: 1,680 to 3,120 F depending on dates. Breakfast: 105 F.

GRESY-SUR-ISÈRE

8 - HOTEL-RESTAURANT - **La Tour de Pacoret**: *Montailleur, 73460 Grésy-sur-Isère. Tel. 04.79.37.91.59 Fax 04.79. 37.93.84. Hotel closed from Halloween to Easter, restaurant closed Tuesday except in July and August.* Between Albertville and Montmélian, niched in an old 14th-century watchtower. Dinner on the terrace in high-season. Rooms: 280 to 429 F. Menus: 90 (lunch) to 185 F.

MANIGOD

9 - HOTEL - **Chalets-hôtel de la Croix-**

Fry: *74230 Manigod. Tel. 04.50.44. 90.16 Fax 04.50.44.94.87.* Run by Marie-Ange Guelpa-Veyrat, Marc Veyrat's sister, this peaceful mountain stop is worth leaving the vineyard a moment for. Cuisine is traditional (featuring pormoniers, matafans and other tartiflettes), and wines on par. It's good, copious, and served in an amusing confusion of rustic furniture. Very warm welcome. For a week's stay with a large family, choose a private chalet (3,000 to 6,000 F and 6,500 to 11,000 F per week depending on size and dates). Or else there's the more classic, very comfortable hotel rooms (from 550 to 1,500 F). Full and half board available.

VEYRIER-DU-LAC

10 - HOTEL-RESTAURANT - **L'Auberge de l'Eridan**: 1*3 Vieille Route des Pensières, 74290 Veyrier-du-Lac. Tel. 04.50.60.24.00 Fax 04.50.60.23.63. Closed Monday and noon Tuesday (low-season).* 6 km from Annecy, the restaurant of one of the highest rated and most original chefs. His cuisine sculpts textures and veils itself in the robust flavors of wild mountain plants and vegetables. Menus: 365 F (lunch weekdays), 595 and 995 F. The exceptional wine list features a large selection of regional wines. Exemplary for wines, a rare find. Pharaonic rooms: 1,500 to 4,350 F.

TO SEE

THONON-LES-BAINS

OUTING - **Le château de Ripaille**: one of the region's best viticultural domains, established in an old

Carthusian monastery.

MIOLANS

OUTING - The castle dominating the vineyard was built as early as 923. The dukes of Savoie used it as a prison from the 16th to the 18th century.

Claude Marandon's tiny vineyard.

Claude Marandon

Owner Claude Marandon. **Address** 116 chemin des Moulins, 73000 Chambéry Tel. 04.79.33.13.65. **Open** By appointment. **Spoken** Anglais, German.

Before "annexing France", says Claude Marandon, the House of Savoie reigned over Jerusalem and Cyprus in the twelfth century. It is said that Anne de Lusignan, of the powerful feudal family of that era, brought back the Altesse grape variety from Cyprus. Marandon, whose kingdom is a small forty-are vineyard here, paid homage to the feudal lady by naming his Cuvée Anne de Chypre (Anne of Cyprus) after her.

This Sunday winemaker is officially a wine salesman, but we have often found him in his tiny vineyard, digging the soil and planting his vines in serried rows -9000 vines per hectare- and attaching them to winches for support on this steep escarpment. Fermenting his wines in oak, Marandon has corrected his excessively oaky wines, now blending his unique barrel and vat to make a single wine. It is typically very dry, without residual sugar, and lively: there is no malolactic fermentation. It is more or less smooth and full-bodied depending on the vintage.

Our choice The '96 Roussette de Savoie Anne de Chypre (120 F): tasted before the barrel and vat were blended. Very delicate bouquet and taste Smooth, lingering, beautiful mellow vivacity. A very elegant wine, dry, unmasked by residual sugar. Some bottle age.

Reception In the beautiful countryside.

How to get there *(Map 14): Leave Chambéry direction Albertville via N6. In Saint-Jeoire-Prieuré (8kms after Challe-les-Eaux), at the traffic light, turn left (wrong way on one-way street!) to the cellar, rue des Colombiers. If you have made an appointment, Claude Marandon will be waiting for you, pipette in hand.*

Preparing to attach the young vines.

Noël Dupasquier

Owner Noël Dupasquier. **Address** Aimavigne, 73170 Jongieux - Tel. 04.79.44.02.23 Fax 04.79.44.03.56. **Open** Saturday, 8:00-12:00 and 14:00-19:00 or by appointment. July and Aug., from Monday to Saturday, 8:00-12:00 and 15:00-20:00.

Aimavigne, "vine lover": what a charming name for a village where a winemaker does indeed love his *terroir*, which enjoys a beautiful hillside exposure and rocky, clay-limestone soil; facing due west, the vines are bathed by the setting sun until the last ray fades below the horizon. Noël Dupasquier likes wines that have matured past their "adolescence" and aged in bottle in his cellar. He is one of the rare Savoyard *vignerons* to bottle-age his wines before making them available. Apart from Roussette, the star of the cellar, you will find a '95 Jacquère (21 F): smooth, full-bodied, with a touch of gentian: It's worth tasting in order to discover an usual aspect of Savoie's predominant grape variety, but one which is often badly treated. The lovely '94 Roussette (27 F) has a delicate aroma, a fine, spicy taste, and a trace of mint at the finish. Of the reds, try the '95 Gamay (25 F), fruity and fleshy; or the '94 Pinot, with overtones of eau-de-vie cherry pits (28 F).

Our choice The '94 Roussette de Savoie Marestel (36 F). Reserved aroma but full flavor, concentrated and spicy (cumin), long. Bottle-age two years. The '95 will be very concentrated, but very little was made because of hail at the harvest.

Reception In a tasting room reminiscent of the Beaujolais for its winemaking ribaldry.

How to get there *(Map 14): From Chambéry, drive towards Bourg-en-Bresse via Le Bourget-du-Lac (N504). Immediately after leaving the Tunnel du Chat, turn right towards Jongieux (D210, then Aimavigne. The cellar is in the village, on the right, indicated by a sign.*

The Jongieux vineyards in winter, before pruning.

Edmond Jacquin et Fils

Owner Family Jacquin. **Address** 73170 Jongieux - Tel. 04.79.44.02.35 Fax 04.79.44.03.05. **Open** Saturday, 9:00-20:00 and Sunday, 9:00-12:00 or by appointment. **Spoken** English. **Credit cards** Visa, Eurocard, MasterCard.

Edmond Jacquin and his sons devote a great part of their vineyard to the Roussette grape, accounting for a third of the 19-hectare domaine, mostly planted in Marestel, one of the two Roussette appellations of the region, with that of Monthoux. His Altesse vines, the most prestigious white Savoyard grapes, with Bergeron, are planted throughout his parcels; Altesse enables wines to age... in the Jacquin's cellar: few Savoyard winemakers bottle age their wines before putting them on the market. Wines are vinified and bottled by parcel in the case of simpler wines, but there is only one bottling for the Altesse from Marestel, "in order to translate the distinctive nature of the wine." You will find an inexpensive Jacquère here (21 F; '96): well balanced, vigorous without hard edges; and Gamays, especially the delicious, concentrated Gamay which is sold towards mid-year, a practice not frequent in the region. Of the different Roussette bottlings, try the one at 30 Francs for its beautiful gold color, full body, and delicate finish. Harvested late, it has solid natural alcoholic structure (14.5%), but this is well balanced by the extract.

Our choice The '96 Roussette Maretel (37 F). Tasted before blending. The wine will be smooth and full-bodied, ample, with overtones of fruit kernels and white fruit; long and persistent. Good to drink or to cellar a short time.

Reception Excellent, in the tasting room.

How to get there *(Map 14): From Chambéry, go in the direction Bourg-en-Bresse via Le Bourget-du-Lac (N504). Immediately after leaving the Tunnel du Chat, turn right towards Jongieux (D210). In the center of Jongieux, on the right, indicated by a sign.*

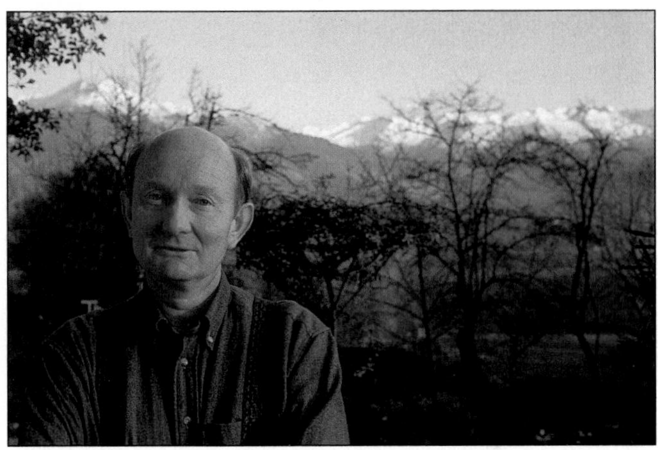

Michel Grisard.

Domaine du Prieuré Saint-Christophe

Owner Michel Grisard. **Address** 73250 Fréterive - Tel. 04.79.28.62.10 Fax 04.79.28.61.74. **Open** By appointment. **Spoken** English, Italian.

Michel Grisard is reminiscent of Gargantua's companion, Brother Jean, who knew all the good restaurants in the region. He also knows something about ageing his red wines and fermenting them in oak, which is unusual in the Savoie.

But not only do Grisard's Mondeuses wines take to oak, they cry out for it because of their concentrated extract and because their tannins require lengthy ageing, enhancing gaseous exchange and aeration. See for yourself!

Apart from his famous red wines, Michel Grisard has acquired a passion for white Altesse. His '96 Rousette, tasted at fermentation's end (in oak, with ageing on lees), promised a wine of body, structure, dense extract and volume, not dominated by its oakiness (about 60 F).

Our choice The '95 Mondeuse Prestige (about 120 F, 6 bottles maximum). Tasted before bottling. The bouquet is open, delicate; dense, tannic, but silky taste, solid backbone, with beautiful overtones of blackcurrants, long and persisent, with well integrated oaky edge. Needs bottle age. The '95 Tradition (about 60 F) is more meaty.

Reception By the impassioned and convincing winemaker.

How to get there *(Map 14): From Chambéry towards Albertville via N6. Go 20km beyond Montmélian, then turn left towards Fréterive (D201E). In the center of La Fiardière, take the road to the vineyard (very small sign).*

Mount Granier in winter.

Château de la Violette

Owner Daniel Fustinoni. **Address** 73800 Les Marches - Tel. 04.79.28.13.30 Fax 04.79.28.06.96. **Open** By appointment. **Spoken** English, Italian.

Mount Granier crashed to earth in 1248, burying 5000 people according to records of the time, but it created the turbulent *terroir* which today produces the wines of Apremont and Abymes. Planted with Jacquère, Savoie's predominant grape, the vines in good years can yield wines of delicate expression from too little sunshine. Facing what remains of Mount Granier, Daniel Fustinoni has a beautiful vineyard in which the Jacquère reigns supreme.

Apart from the traditional white Abymes and Apremonts from his cellar, you will find pleasant '96 reds for 26 francs; as well as a fruity Gamay, always in limited quantity: delightfully drinkable, with the smoky overtones often produced by the grape in Savoie; and a Mondeuse, full of fruit.

Our choice The '96 white Apremont (24 F). Slightly mineral aroma; expressive, rich, smooth taste, quite long and powerful, with vivacity that provides good balance vis à vis the slight hint of residual sugar. The '96 Abymes (22.50 F): distinctly flowery aroma, delicate on the palate. Both are good to drink now.

Reception Excellent.

How to get there *(Map 14): Coming from Chambéry via N6, turn right after Chignin direction Les Marches and Pontcharra on N90. Go 2km to Les Marches. At entrance to town, at traffic light, turn right. The domaine is immediately after the small shopping center on the left (sign).*

Pascal Quenard, the guitar-playing winemaker.

Pascal Quenard

Owners Pascal and Annick Quenard. **Address** Le Villard, les Tours 73800 Chignin - Tel. 04.79.28.09.01 Fax 04.79.28.13.53. **Open** By appointment. **Spoken** English, Italian.

In the Savoyard galaxy of Quenards, usually unrelated, Pascal, the winemaker who plays the violin and the electric guitar, is the son of famous Raymond Quenard (see Chignin-Bergeron). But he likes to make wine "my way", even though he favors malolactic fermentation, like his father.

His least expensive wines set the tempo, proving that there are no small wines, just good and bad wines. Quenard's '96 Chignins from the Jacquère grape (26 F) are bottled without blending, thus yielding variable wines depending on the age of the vines and the exposition of the parcels: wines of finesse and balance, with overtones of apricot.

Our choice The '96 Chignin from the Les Châteaux parcel (26 F). A Jacquère that stands out in a year which was not terribly favorable to Savoie's predominant grape variety. Most grapes were picked underripe, swollen with chaptalization and masked with residual sugar to conceal their greenness. This Chignin, on the contrary, is all delicacy, with a fine, flowery, rosy aroma, a quite smooth and delicate, graceful taste. Can be drunk now.

Reception Friendly.

How to get there *(Map 14): From Chambéry towards Albertville via N6. 2km after Challes-les-Eaux, turn left towards Chignin. Aim for the old towers on the hilltop, go in front of the church. The cellar is immediately after that of Raymond Quenard (large sign), but on the right.*

André (right) and Michel Quénard.

André et Michel Quénard

Owners André and Michel Quénard. **Address** Torméry, 73800 Chignin - Tel. 04.79.28.12.75 and 04.79 28 09 60 Fax 04.79.28.19.36. **Open** By appointment.

Terraced vineyards are an unusual sight in Savoie. And yet they are the only way André and Michel Quénard can plant vines on the steep slopes of their domaine.

They aim for the full expression of the *terroir*, preferring not to use artificial yeasts; smooth, full-bodied wines that come from long, slow fermentation; and relatively regular quality by means of blending vatted wines. But as is often the case in Savoie, blending and bottling are carried on throughout the year: very different wines can be found bearing the same label. Especially for their Chignin-Bergeron wines, it is thus a good idea to choose the late bottlings after Easter, which come from the oldest vines.

The Chignins from the Jacquère grape are generally lively but smooth and often rounded out with a trace of residual sugar (25 F). There will be a very beautiful *cuvée* (about 27 F), distinctly longer on the palate, with lovely fruity expressions.

Our choice The '96 Chignin-Bergeron Les Terrasses (about 40 F). A very rich wine (12.5% natural alcohol), but well balanced by the extract. The aroma is delicate and complex, the taste very fine and rich (verbena, caramel, spice, almonds), the finish very firm, sustained by crispness. Bottle age one year.

Reception By father or son, with equal enthusaism.

How to get there *(Map 14): From Chambéry towards Albertville via N6. After the fork towards Chignin, turn left towards Torméry and follow the route indicated.*

The vineyard in Tours, above the fog that covers the valley in winter.

Raymond Quenard

Owner Raymond Quenard. **Address** Le Villard, les Tours 73800 Chignin - Tel. 04.79.28.01.46 Fax 04.79.28.16.78. **Open** From Monday to Saturday, 9:00-12:00 and 14:00-18:00. **Spoken** English, Italian.

Bergeron is Savoie's most prestigious white grape along with Altesse, which produces wines called Roussette. And yet Bergeron is not particular to Savoie because it is in fact the Roussane grape from the Côtes-du-Rhône. But winemakers in Chignin have forged a fine reputation for Bergeron because it can be grown only in this commune, where it enjoys a specific appellation: the AOC Vin de Savoie Chignin-Bergeron. Like Altesse, it ages well.

Planted at the foot of the old toll towers of Chignin, some of Raymond Quenard's vines are almost a century old, yielding wines of great finesse, very dry, as opposed to many Savoyard wines with a trace (or much more than a trace) of residual sugar. Concentrated extract and malolactic fermentation account for their balance.

Our choice The '96 Chignin-Bergeron (48 F), from vines picked several times during the harvest in order to obtain grapes of optimum maturity. Tasted before blending, it already promises balance, concentration, finesse, and length. Some bottle age.

Reception Charming.

How to get there *(Map 14): From Chambéry towards Albertville via N6. 2km after Challes-les-Eaux, turn left towards Chignin. Aim for the old towers on the hilltop, go in front of the church. Take in the direction of Villard. The cellar is on the left, indicated by a large sign.*

Louis Magnin, a balance between Mondeuse and Chignin.

Louis Magnin

Owner Louis Magnin. **Address** Chemin des Buis, Arbin 73800 Montmélian - Tel. 04.79.84.12.12 Fax 04.79.84.40.92. **Open** By appointment.

Louis Magnin is not your usual Savoyard winemaker. Not just because he makes very good wines -there are others in the region- but because he has stocks of wine and thus older vintages available from the two grapes, Bergeron and Mondeuse, which he is adept at ageing. Still, he won't sell them to just anybody.

Among Magnin's recent vintages, we noted the '96 Jacquère (about 23 F), very dry, discreetly aromatic; the '96 Mondeuse (32 F), concentrated, very silky tannins; and the '95 Roussette (about 60 F). From a low yield (45 hectoliters per hectare), very ripe grapes yielding 14.5% potential alcohol and 13.5% alcohol by volume, thus a touch of residual sugar well balanced by structure and freshness, the '95 Roussette offers lovely notes of fresh almonds and full body.

Our choice The '95 Chignin-Bergeron (45 F). Deep color, delicate but still closed aroma; rich, open, round on the palate, the note of residual sugar well balanced by structure and freshness. Some bottle age. Some '94 is left (45 F): intense waxy aroma; delicate, slightly mentholated taste, but less body than the '95. Good to drink now.

Reception In the tasting/shipping room.

How to get there *(Map 14): From Chambéry towards Albertville via N6. In Montmélian, turn left directoin Arbin. At the traffic circle, turn right towards the railway track. Just before going beneath the railway bridge, turn right, and right again. The house is the the last one at the end of the Chemin des Buis, not marked.*

The fantastic world of Claude Delalex.

Domaine Delalex

Owner Claude Delalex; **Address** Hameau de Marinel 74200 Marin - Tel. 04.50.71.45.82 Fax 04.50.71.06.74. **Open** By appointment, 9:00-12:00 and 14:30-17:30 in holidays.

Marin is one of the small vineyard sites in the Haute-Savoie, with Crécy, Marignan, and Ripaille, which border on Lake Geneva and enjoy its favorable microclimate. All grow a single grape variety, the Chasselas, and all constantly ponder whether or not to practice malolactic fermentation.

Claude Delalex has made his decision: no "malo". The balance and the sensuality of his wines come from the age of the vines, an average of fifty years; and the maturity of the grapes, yielding 9.4% to 10.5% natural alcohol in 1995: enticing wines, low in alcohol, and heaven to drink. They reflect the fresco entitled *Thus Was the Lord's Vine Made*, which is displayed in his tasting room. It is the work of a retired curate uncle who spends his time sawing vine roots to create sculptures peopled by fantastic men and animals.

Delalex's cellar offers only two wines: the '95 Marin (25 F), flowery and vibrant; and a wine from selected parcels, the Clos du Pont.

Our choice The '96 Clos du Pont (31 F). Aroma still closed, taste already ample, distinctive, ripe (apricots), smooth, long, and persistent. Bottle age one year.

Reception Excellent, in the new tasting room (near the house), decorated with his uncle's sculptures.

***How to get there** (Map 14): From Thonon-les-Bains towards Evian (N5). In 3km, turn right (D61), then right again on D32 in the direction of Marin. On entering Marinel, turn right (small sign). The house is at the entrance to the village, on the left (large sign).*

In the middle of the monastery, the Château de Ripaille.

Château de Ripaille

Owner Family Necker-Engel. **Address** 74200 Thonon-les-Bains - Tel. 04.50.71.75.12 Fax 04.50. 71.72.55. **Open** From Monday to Saturday midday, 9:00-12:00 and 14:00-19:00. **Credit cards** Visa, Eurocard, MasterCard.

This domaine is in a former Carthusian monastery, shaded by century-old mulberry trees. It has been in turn a Roman villa, the hunting land of the counts of Savoie, and finally the château of Amédée VIII, Duke of Savoie, an antipope who ended his days as a simple monk. Carthusian monks lived in a string of buildings there--the blacksmith's forge, the stables--until the French Revolution.

Today, the Château de Ripaille's vines tumble down to the edge of the lake, surrounded by almond trees, cypresses, fig trees and parasol pines, which enjoy the microclimate created by the stable temperatures of Lake Geneva's waters.

The Chasselas is the only grape variety grown on the domaine, which is the sole vineyard in the Ripaille appellation. The wines are dry, without residual sugar, softened by malolactic fermentation, their crispness sustained by a trace of carbon dioxide. While wines are vinified by parcel, they are made into homogenous blends before bottling, contrary to the prevalent practice in Savoie.

Our choice The '95 Ripaille (35 F). Mellow aroma, flowery touch. Smooth, very balanced on the palate but without residual sugar, enhanced by a pleasantly bitter trace and carbon dioxide. Tasted before blending, the '96 is somewhat more flowery on the nose, very delicate on the palate, well maintained by greater acidity. Good to drink now.

Reception Don't miss a visit to the chateau, a stroll in the forest, or seeing the vines on the lake-side.

How to get there *(Map 14): In the center of Thonon-les-Bains, follow the itinerary indicated.*

SOUTH-WEST

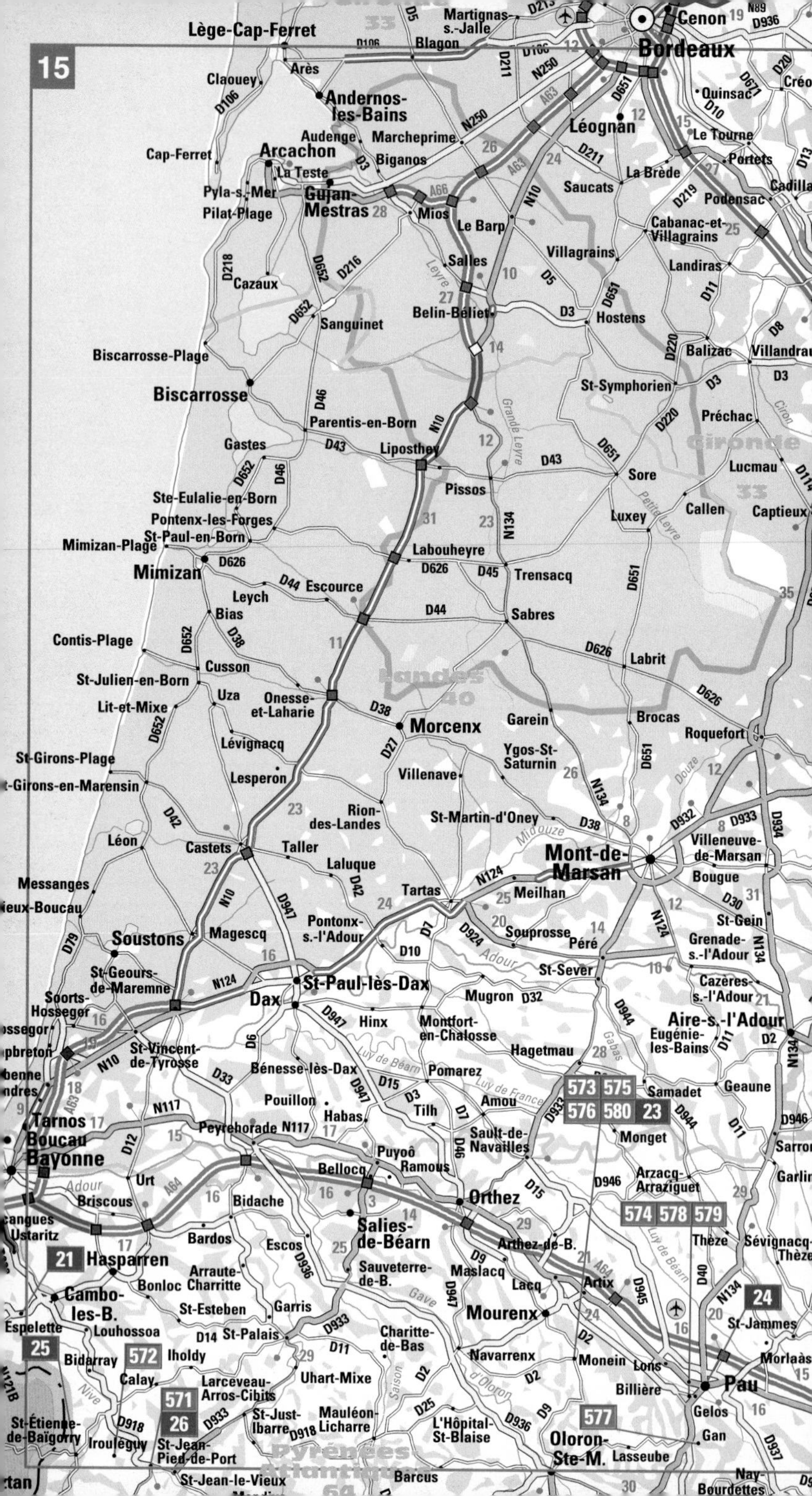
15
Lège-Cap-Ferret
Martignas-s.-Jalle
Cenon
Bordeaux
Blagon
Claouey
Arès
Andernos-les-Bains
Quinsac
Créo
Léognan
Le Tourne
Portets
Audenge
Marcheprime
Arcachon
Cap-Ferret
La Teste
Biganos
Gujan-Mestras
La Brède
Saucats
Cadillac
Pyla-s.-Mer
Pilat-Plage
Mios
Le Barp
Podensac
Cabanac-et-Villagrains
Salles
Villagrains
Landiras
Cazaux
Belin-Béliet
Hostens
Sanguinet
Balizac
Villandraut
Biscarrosse-Plage
St-Symphorien
Biscarrosse
Préchac
Parentis-en-Born
Gironde
Gastes
Liposthey
Sore
Lucmau
Pissos
Ste-Eulalie-en-Born
Pontenx-les-Forges
Luxey
Callen
Captieux
St-Paul-en-Born
Mimizan-Plage
Labouheyre
Mimizan
Trensacq
Escource
Leych
Bias
Sabres
Contis-Plage
Labrit
Cusson
St-Julien-en-Born
Uza
Onesse-et-Laharie
Landes
40
Lit-et-Mixe
Garein
Brocas
Morcenx
Roquefort
Lévignacq
Ygos-St-Saturnin
St-Girons-Plage
Villenave
Lesperon
St-Girons-en-Marensin
Rion-des-Landes
St-Martin-d'Oney
Léon
Castets
Taller
Mont-de-Marsan
Villeneuve-de-Marsan
Laluque
Bougue
Messanges
Tartas
Meilhan
Vieux-Boucau
Soustons
Magescq
Pontonx-s.-l'Adour
Souprosse
Péré
St-Gein
Grenade-s.-l'Adour
St-Geours-de-Maremne
St-Sever
Cazères-s.-l'Adour
St-Paul-lès-Dax
Soorts-Hossegor
Dax
Mugron
Hinx
Montfort-en-Chalosse
Aire-s.-l'Adour
Eugénie-les-Bains
Capbreton
St-Vincent-de-Tyrosse
Hagetmau
Bénesse-lès-Dax
Pomarez
Samadet
Geaune
Pouillon
Tilh
Amou
Tarnos
Habas
Monget
Boucau
Peyrehorade
Sault-de-Navailles
Bayonne
Puyoô
Ramous
Sarron
Urt
Bellocq
Arzacq-Arraziguet
Garlin
Briscous
Bidache
Orthez
Salies-de-Béarn
Ustaritz
Bardos
Escos
Arthez-de-B.
Thèze
Sévignacq-Thèze
Hasparren
Sauveterre-de-B.
Maslacq
Arraute-Charritte
Bonloc
Lacq
Artix
Cambo-les-B.
St-Esteben
Garris
Mourenx
St-Jammes
Espelette
Louhossoa
St-Palais
Charritte-de-Bas
Navarrenx
Monein
Lons
Morlaàs
Bidarray
Iholdy
Uhart-Mixe
Calay
Larceveau-Arros-Cibits
Billière
Pau
St-Just-Ibarre
Mauléon-Licharre
L'Hôpital-St-Blaise
Gelos
St-Étienne-de-Baïgorry
Irouléguy
St-Jean-Pied-de-Port
Oloron-Ste-M.
Gan
Lasseube
St-Jean-le-Vieux
Barcus
Nay-Bourdettes
Pyrénées-Atlantiques
64
573 575
576 580 23
574 578 579
577
21
24
25
572
571
26

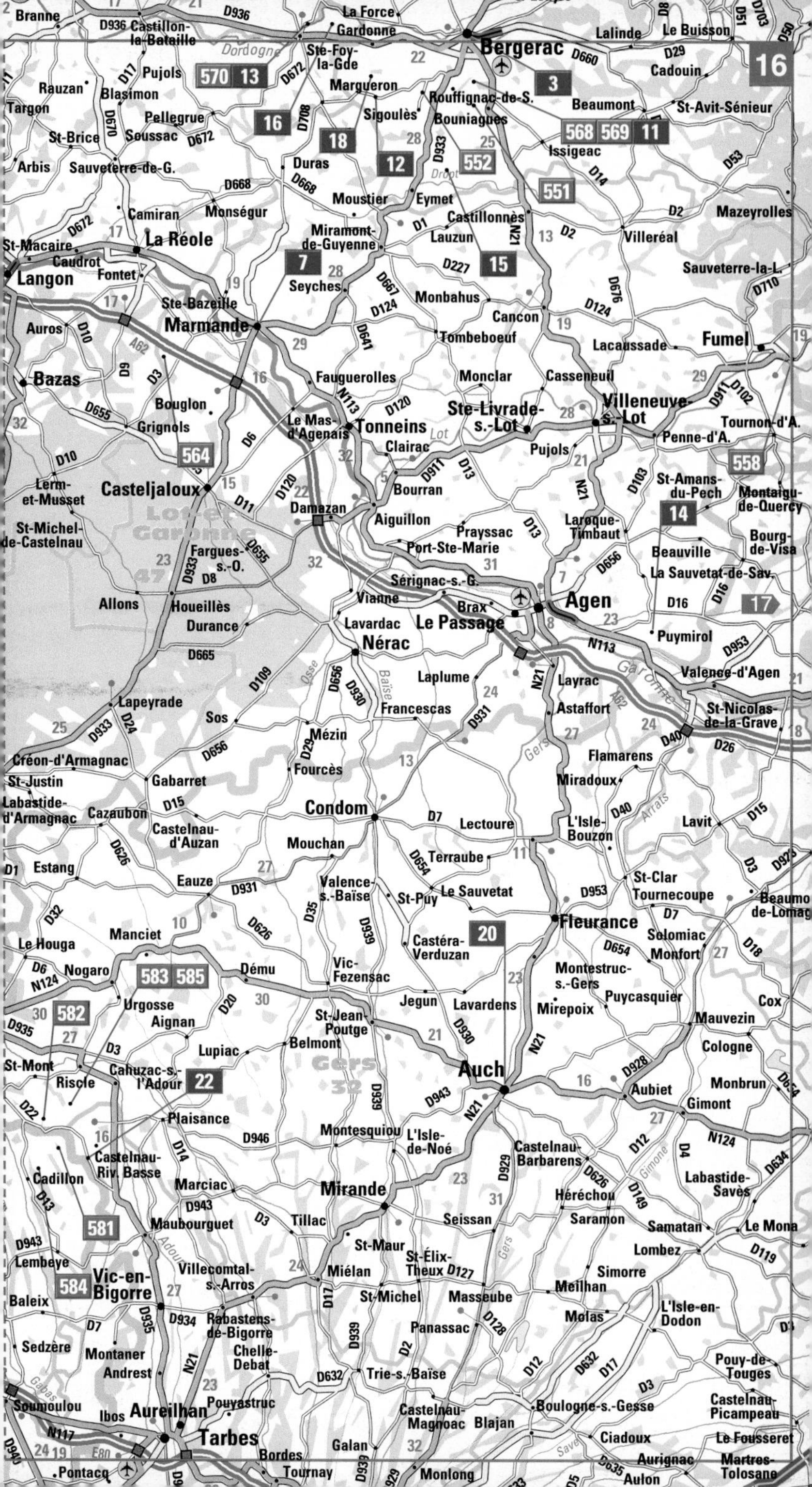
16
Branne
Castillon-la-Bataille
La Force
Gardonne
Bergerac
Lalinde
Le Buisson
Dordogne
Ste-Foy-la-Gde
Cadouin
Pujols
570
13
3
Rauzan
Blasimon
Marqueron
Rouffignac-de-S.
Beaumont
St-Avit-Sénieur
Targon
Pellegrue
16
Sigoulès
Bouniagues
568
569
11
St-Brice
Soussac
18
Issigeac
Arbis
Sauveterre-de-G.
Duras
12
552
Droot
551
Moustier
Eymet
Camiran
Monségur
Castillonnès
Mazeyrolles
La Réole
Miramont-de-Guyenne
Lauzun
Villeréal
St-Macaire
Caudrot
7
15
Langon
Fontet
Seyches
Sauveterre-la-L.
Monbahus
Ste-Bazeille
Marmande
Cancon
Auros
Tombeboeuf
Lacaussade
Fumel
Bazas
Fauguerolles
Monclar
Casseneuil
Bouglon
Ste-Livrade-s.-Lot
Villeneuve-s.-Lot
Tournon-d'A.
Grignols
Le Mas-d'Agenais
Tonneins
Lot
Clairac
Pujols
Penne-d'A.
564
558
Lerm-et-Musset
Casteljaloux
Bourran
St-Amans-du-Pech
Montaigu-de-Quercy
Damazan
Aiguillon
14
St-Michel-de-Castelnau
Lot-et-Garonne
Prayssac
Laroque-Timbaut
Bourg-de-Visa
Fargues-s.-O.
Port-Ste-Marie
Beauville
47
La Sauvetat-de-Sav.
Sérignac-s.-G.
Allons
Houeillès
Vianne
Brax
Agen
17
Durance
Lavardac
Le Passage
Nérac
Puymirol
Garonne
Laplume
Layrac
Valence-d'Agen
Lapeyrade
Francescas
Astaffort
St-Nicolas-de-la-Grave
Sos
Mézin
Gers
Flamarens
Créon-d'Armagnac
Fourcès
Miradoux
St-Justin
Gabarret
Labastide-d'Armagnac
Cazaubon
Condom
Arrats
Lavit
Castelnau-d'Auzan
Lectoure
L'Isle-Bouzon
Mouchan
Estang
Terraube
Eauze
Valence-s.-Baïse
Le Sauvetat
St-Clar
Tournecoupe
Beaumont-de-Lomagne
St-Puy
Fleurance
Manciet
Castéra-Verduzan
20
Solomiac
Le Houga
Monfort
Nogaro
583
585
Dému
Vic-Fezensac
Montestruc-s.-Gers
Urgosse
Jegun
Lavardens
Mirepoix
Puycasquier
Cox
582
Aignan
St-Jean-Poutge
Mauvezin
Lupiac
Belmont
Cologne
St-Mont
Cahuzac-s.-l'Adour
22
Gers
32
Auch
Monbrun
Riscle
Aubiet
Gimont
Plaisance
Montesquiou
L'Isle-de-Noé
Castelnau-Barbarens
Castelnau-Riv. Basse
Cadillon
Labastide-Savès
Marciac
Mirande
Héréchou
Gimone
581
Maubourguet
Tillac
Seissan
Saramon
Samatan
Le Mona
Adour
Lembeye
St-Maur
St-Élix-Theux
Lombez
Vic-en-Bigorre
584
Villecomtal-s.-Arros
Miélan
Simorre
Baleix
St-Michel
Masseube
Meilhan
Rabastens-de-Bigorre
Panassac
Molas
L'Isle-en-Dodon
Sedzère
Montaner
Chelle-Debat
Andrest
Trie-s.-Baïse
Pouy-de-Touges
Soumoulou
Ibos
Aureilhan
Pouyastruc
Castelnau-Magnoac
Blajan
Boulogne-s.-Gesse
Castelnau-Picampeau
Tarbes
Ciadoux
Le Fousseret
Gabas
Galan
Save
Aurignac
Martres-Tolosane
Pontacq
Bordes
Tournay
Monlong
Aulon

17
St-Cyprien
Sarlat-la-Canéda
D703
Souillac
Carlux
D703
Bretenoux
Frayssinhes
Sousceyrac
Carsac-Aillac
Meyronne
Calès
St-Céré
Cayrols
St-Mamet-la-Salvetat
Latronquière
Alvignac
Aynac
Cénac-et-St-Julien
D704
Payrac
Rocamadour
Gramat
D677
D653
Daglan
St-Pompont
D46
Gourdon
D673
9
10
A20
Thémines
N140
559
Le Bastit
Maurs
D60
555
560
St-Chamarand
Salviac
Labastide-Murat
D2
Assier
31
D19
St-Constant
Villefranche-du-Périgord
D673
St-Germain-du-Bel-Air
Fontanes-du-Causse
Livernon
21
N122
Bagnac-s.-Célé
D963
Cazals
Lamothe-Cassel
D653
Lot
Frayssinet-le-Gélat
17
D6
Uzech
D653
28
Célé
D19
Figeac
Capdenac-Gare
Decazeville
D660
Lauzès
N20
553
Puy-l'Évêque
Catus
6
Marcilhac-s.-Célé
Viviez
Praissac
22
22
Aubin
Firmi
D911
Cabrerets
Cajarc
Montbrun
D922
Luzech
Pradines
567
Montbazens
D5
St-Géry
Aveyron
554
Cahors
556
Lot
Lot
D24
Villeneuve
Lanuéjouls
19
D656
Sauzet
D653
Concots
D19
Rignac
D1
St-Matré
557
Villesèque
D911
Limogne-en-Quercy
Martiel
8
D653
D19
22
Bach
D911
Villefranche-de-Rouergue
4
Lalbenque
Montcuq
46
D19
27
D926
12
Colombies
D2
D953
D911
D20
D922
23
Rieupeyroux
Castelnau-Montratier
N20
Parisot
Sauvensa
Puylaroque
Montpezat-de-Quercy
D17
D19
D926
D39
La Fouillade
D997
5
20
Caylus
Montesquieu
Molières
La Salvetat-Peyralès
D905
Septfonds
D2
D20
D5
St-Antonin-Noble-Val
5
Naucelle
D957
Lafrançaise
D959
Caussade
D964
D958
Laguépie
Réalville
22
D115
Mirandol-Bourgnounac
Pampelonne
Viaur
Moissac
Aveyron
D922
Tarn-et-Garonne
565
566
D91
Monestiés
30
Tanus
82
Montricoux
Vaour
N20
N88
Castelsarrasin
D927
Negrepelisse
Vindrac-A.
1
2
Carmaux
16
25
D15
D115
563
D964
Campagnac
Blaye-les-M.
D91
D903
Montauban
14
Monclar-de-Quercy
Noailles
D922
D8
Le Verdier
Valderiès
8
Montech
D600
27
Labastide-St-Pierre
La Salvetat-Belmontet
561
562
Les Barrières
D964
Marssac-s.-Tarn
St-Juery
Larrazet
17
Albi
D999
N113
D13
D4
Villebrumier
Gaillac
12
A62
N88
Villemur-s.-Tarn
Salvagnac
N88
Verdun-s.-Garonne
26
Lisle-s.-Tarn
23
D81
21
Villefranche-d'Albigeois
A68
Cadalen
Fronton
D14
Grisolles
Tarn
D87
Teillet
Rabastens
D964
D3
Lombers
D86
30
Parisot
Ondes
D30
D630
Montdragon
Dadou
St-Sulpice
D631
Graulhet
Grenade
27
28
D631
Réalmont
D63
Cépet
Montredon-Labessonnié
Briatexte
Girou
Tarn
81
D1
27
D20
Montastruc-la-Conseillère
N112
D112
D83
Lavaur
Lévignac
Montaigut-s.-Save
Castelmaurou
Agout
21
Roquecourbe
N20
A681
St-Paul-Cap-de-Joux
Save
12
D112
D17
Blagnac
L'Union
Verfeil
Lacougotte-Cadoul
D112
L'Isle-J.
Léguevin
27
Toulouse
Balma
20
D20
Castres
N126
N124
Colomiers
N126
Puylaurens
11
Plaisancedut
8
12
D1
Valdurenque
D632
D11
Soual
23
D621
Cugnaux
26
N126
16
Castanet-Tolosan
Lanta
St-Lys
D12
Seysses
Caraman
D1
Labruguière
N20
25
D2
D622
Bragayrac
D3
32
St-Julia
Revel
Dourgne
D7
N113
St-Clar-de-Riv.
14
Muret
Montgiscard
Baziège
D25
23
D622
Rieumes
Vernet
27
Villefranche-de-Lauragais
D629
Les Martys
Haute-Garonne
Bérat
31
Cuxac-Cabardès
D28
Nailloux
29
D624
D4
Auterive
Saissac
Gratens
D622
D625
N113
23
A61
Castelnaudary
Brousses-et-Villaret
D16
St-Sulpice-s.-Lèze
N20
Cintegabelle
26
Carbonne
D7
Salles-s.-l'Hers
Villepinte
23
N117
D626
Lézat-s.-Lèze
D35
17
N113
20
24
St-Ybars
Alzonne
D624
St-Julien
D919
Saverdun
Mazères
D6
D623
14
Bram

SOUTH WEST

INTRODUCTION

From the border of the Libournais to the foothills of the Aubrac and from the Garonne to the Pyrenees, this vast region accounts for 70,000 hectares of vines scattered within a vast triangle of 450 kilometers between the Pays Basque and the Aveyron. The wines are continually improving, the prices are often reasonable and there are some wonderful country wines that are very undervalued (Cahors, Jurançon). Approaching the Pyrenees or the Aubrac the countryside becomes a revelation and the food is of a hearty nature. Is all that not good enough reason to explore these wines that speak with a flavorsome accent via a multitude of fiercely preserved local grape varieties ?

SOUTH WEST APPELLATIONS

The South West comprises all the appellations of the Midi-Pyrénées (Cahors, Côtes-de-Frontonnais, Gaillac, Madiran, Marcillac, etc) and those of Aquitaine not contained within the Bordeaux region (Bergerac, Côtes-du-Marmandais, Jurançon, Irouléguy, to cite the principal appellations). If one excludes the three appellations relative to Armagnac, the number of appellations for non-distilled wines totals 34, sometimes geographically overlapping or superimposed according to the style, color, or rules governing the production of each wine. Even the most knowledgeable wine lover cannot always find his or her way around. We'll try to make a little sense of all this without being overly simplistic but you will, however, learn what is hidden behind each label.

The Bergerac region and the vineyards of the Dordogne form the nearest zone to Bordeaux. They also have a similar oceanic climate and grape varieties: Cabernet Sauvignon, Cabernet Franc, and Merlot for the reds (with eventually a little Côt or Fer Servadou); Semillon, Sauvignon, and Muscadelle for the whites (with eventually a little Ondenc, Chenin Blanc or Ugni Blanc). There are twice as many red as white wines produced. Both red and white wines in the Bergerac appellation are dry. The appellation Côtes-de-Bergerac corresponds to wines made from lower yields (55 hectoliters/hectare for red Bergerac and 60 for white as opposed to 50 hectoliters/hectare for both red and white Côtes-de-Bergerac). The reds are, therefore, more concentrated and the white Côtes-de-Bergerac become sweet wines.

South of Bergerac is the appellation Monbazillac which can produce great sweet wines providing the wine growers harvest by hand. But too many producers here imagine that great sweet wines can be made when the grapes are harvested by machine. This certainly doesn't help the appellation to assume the level it could once again claim following the period of disaffection that hit all sweet wines. The grape varieties are the same as those for Sauternes: Semillon, Sauvignon, and Muscadelle.

The three white Montravel appellations, named after the village of Lamothe-Montravel, are located between Bergerac and Libourne. Montravel is a dry wine. Côtes-de-Montravel is a limited area producing dry or sweet wines. Haut-Montravel produces sweet wines.

The other appellations remain extremely marginal: Pécharmant for red and Rosette and Saussignac for sweet, white wines.

Marcillac, an appellation in the Aveyron above Rodez, is worth discovering for its majestic countryside and the quality wines of several wine growers. These are red and rosé, essentially produced from the Fer Servadou grape variety.

The Côtes-du-Marmandais is located in the Garonne valley, in an extension of the Entre-Deux-Mers. The grape varieties, practically the same as in Bordeaux, produce dry whites, rosés and supple reds. Further south, almost at the gates of Toulouse, the Côtes-de-Frontonnais produces reds and rosés. We prefer the wines that have a large percentage of the original grape variety, the Négrette. The others have an eye for the Bordeaux varieties without reaching the same quality of wine.

The vineyards of Cahors are situated in the "high country" on both sides of the Lot valley. The region was able to resist the lure of the Bordeaux grape varieties and keep its own original variety, the Auxerrois (at least 70% of plantings). The wines are uniquely red and tannic, but can be very fine and have the potential for long ageing.

The number of authorized grape varieties in Gaillac makes it difficult to determine a style. In white one finds Len de l'Ehl, Mauzac, Muscadelle, Ondenc, Sauvignon and Sémillon and in red Duras, Fer Servadou, Gamay, Syrah, Cabernet Sauvignon, Cabernet Franc and Merlot. The appellation produces, at one and the same time, red, white, rosé, sweet white, and sparkling wines. We, of course, prefer the wine growers who use the most original of the grape varieties in order to discover a different flavor.

At the foot of the Pyrenees, Madiran produces uniquely red wines that are robust and tannic. The spread of new techniques of vinification, however, has resulted in more finesse and ripeness in the tannins without any loss of structure. The wines of this appellation are produced from a majority of Tannat. The white wines produced in the same geographic area take the appellation Pacherenc du Vic Bilh. They are dry or sweet and produced from a range of grape varieties: Arrufiac, Gros and Petit Manseng, Courbu, Sauvignon, and Semillon. In Jurançon the wines are white, dry or sweet, and made from Gros and Petit Manseng. The Basque vineyard Irouléguy offers wines in three colors. Courbu, Gros and Petit Manseng are the white varieties while Tannat, Cabernet Sauvignon, and Cabernet Franc are used for the production of the reds and rosés.

INTRODUCTION

GRAPE VARIETIES

The Auxerrois (also known as Côt and Malbec in Bordeaux) is the red variety of Cahors. It produces wines that are original and characterful and very fine if the yields are reduced. The Fer Servadou is a red variety of which the hardness suggested by the name (*fer* = iron) applies to the wood of the plant and not the wine. It is cultivated throughout the South West but in particular in Gaillac and Madiran and produces well-colored and structured wines. The Négrette is an authentic variety limited to the appellation Côtes-du-Frontonnais. It produces light but well-colored wines that are very aromatic and which can be astonishing when the yields are low. The Tannat, the very tannic red variety, is the basis of the wines of Madiran and Irouléguy. Vinified in a modern fashion and with low yields it is capable of producing fine wines of character which can be aged.

Ondenc, the normally discredited white variety, can produce astonishing wines with a note of crystallized fruits if harvested in an over-ripe state. Proof of this can be found in the wines of Plageoles in Gaillac. The Mauzac: Gris, Rose, Vert, Roux, Jaune, and Côte de Melon is a family of its own. The Plageoles of Gaillac have eagerly preserved all these varieties with convincing results. The Len de l'Ehl (*loin de l'œil* or "far from sight" in the local language) is a characterful white variety that is rich with low acidity and again found predominantly in Gaillac.

The Petit Courbu is a white variety usually used in blends but several wine growers offer a pure version that is round and aromatic.

Finally, there are the Gros and Petit Manseng. The Gros Manseng is usually used for dry white wines while the Petit, particularly in Jurançon, produces great sweet wines thanks to its acidity.

METHODS OF VINIFICATION

The region produces sweet wines, both *moelleux* and *liquoreux* (Pacherenc du Vic Bilh and Jurançon), but also wines aged sous voile or for a long time under a veil of film-forming yeast (like Vin Jaune from the Jura or Sherry) in Gaillac. This appellation also produces sparkling wines from a single fermentation without the addition of sugar and yeasts as in Champagne. Towards the end of the alcoholic fermentation the wines are bottled and the fermentation completed in bottle producing a light sparkle. These are rare and delicious wines that are very fine.

BUYING IN THE SOUTH WEST

The appellations of this region have all experienced difficult vintages but today offer wines of good quality, particularly at the wine growers we have selected. If you like solid wines for ageing we advise Cahors. If you like to mix the discovery of wines with that of the countryside and its people we suggest Irouléguy and Marcillac. If you like sweet wines it has to be Jurançon and, for an unusual taste, the Frontonnais.

AT TABLE WITH THE WINES OF THE SOUTH WEST

Sparkling Gaillac, dry Jurançon, Montravel, dry or sweet Pacherenc du Vic Bilh all make good aperitifs.

The wines of the Frontonnais and Marmandais go well with raw vegetables or *crudités* and charcuterie and later in the meal with grilled meats.

INTRODUCTION

Irouléguy, white and rosé, also makes a good accompaniment for *crudités* and charcuterie but the white should be sampled with grilled fish. The same for white Gaillac.

Jurançon is dedicated to foie gras but if dry is a good match for grilled and marinated fish dishes.

For a great white Bergerac think of a fish dish with sauce. For a red Bergerac prepare a stew.

Madiran is a good match for *garbure* (a traditional south west stew), red meats, game and confit duck while Marcillac goes with grilled meats. Cahors needs to be matched with confit duck, red meats or game and with a meat roast for a more mature wine.

Finally, Monbazillac, sweet Gaillac or Haut-Montravel will embellish your desserts.

FROM THE GARONNE TO THE AUBRAC

ALBI

1 - RESTAURANT - **Le Jardin des Quatre Saisons**: *19 boulevard de Strasbourg, 81000 Albi. Tel. and fax 05.63.60.77.76. Closed Monday.* Refined and well-prepared seasonal cuisine. Attractive wine list. Menus: 135 and 160 F (wine included).

2 - RESTAURANT - **L'Esprit du vin**: *11 quai Choiseul, 81000 Albi. Tel. 05.63.54.60.44 Fax 05.63.54.54.79. Closed Sunday evening, Monday and from 2/15 to 2/28.* Menus: 98 to 300 F. Alongside the old city, above the Tarn, a cuisine served in vaulted dining rooms run by a man with a thirst for discovering new wines.

BERGERAC

3 - RESTAURANT - **Le Cyrano**: *2 bd Montaigne, 24100 Bergerac. Tel. 05.53.57. 02.76 Fax 05.53.57.78.15. Closed noon Saturday and Sunday and the last week in December.* An institution that isn't resting on its laurels. Good selection of regional and Bordeaux wines. Menus: 100 to 150 F.

CAHORS

4 - HOTEL-RESTAURANT - **Le Balandre**: *5 avenue Charles-de-Freycinet, 46000 Cahors. Tel. 05.65.30.01.97 Fax 05.65.22.06.40. Closed Sunday evening and Monday in low-season, noon Saturday in high-season.* Fine cuisine, always impeccable, that espouses and renews local tradition (sumptuous panaché de foies gras). Marvellous wine list, particularly for Cahors (a hundred entries from 1994 to 1949, with old Clos de Gamot). The rest of the list is as good, especially in the Loire, Alsace and Bordeaux. Dining room in art nouveau style. As for the old hotel, it got a complete make-over with lovely rooms, all of which are different. Menus: 150 (dinner), 170 (lunch), 250 and 340 F. Rooms: 280 to 850 F.

CORDES

5 - HOTEL-RESTAURANT - **Le Grand Écuyer**: *Rue Voltaire, 81170 Cordes. Tel. 05.63.53.79.50 Fax 05.63.53.79.51. Closed Monday and Tuesday lunch in low-season and from late October to mid-March.* In the old medieval residence of the counts of Toulouse. Cuisine grand style (sometimes a bit too grand). Impressive wine list (1,000 entries). Menus: 170 to 440 F. A la carte: around 450 F. Impressive rooms: 450 to 850 F.

LAMAGDELAINE

6 - RESTAURANT - **Claude Marco**: *46090 Lamagdelaine. Tel. 05.65.35.30.64*

Fax 05.65.30.31.40. Closed Sunday evening and Monday from September 15 to June 15. Closed the last week in October and from January 4 to

March 4. Dining room situated in a lovely vaulted cellar. Very subtle and light cuisine accompanied by a good choice of Cahors. Menus: 130 to 295 F.

MARMANDE

7 - RESTAURANT - **Le Trianon**: *1 rue Paul Valéry, 47200 Marmande. Tel. 05.53.20.80.94 Fax 05.53.20.80.18 Closed noon Saturday and Sunday.* The best table in town. Copious, well-prepared cuisine. Several dishes are offered in half-portions. Cellar at nice prices. Menus: 80 to 220 F.

MAUROUX

8 - HOTEL-RESTAURANT - **Le Vert**: *46700 Mauroux. Tel. 05.65.36.51.36 Fax 05.65.36.56.84.* Out in the countryside, 7 spacious, pleasant rooms arranged in an old farm: 290 to 390 F. Breakfast: 38 F. Decent restaurant, menus: 100 to 165 F. Good selection of Cahors.

MERCUÉS

9 - HOTEL-RESTAURANT - **Château de Mercués**: *46090 Mercuès. Tel. 05.65.20.00.01 Fax 05.65.20.05.72. Closed November 1 to late March.* 7 km from Cahors. Built in the 13th century, the old castle of the Bishops of Cahors is now converted into a luxurious hotel. Philippe Combet, the new chef, has revived the cuisine that playfully taunts Quercy tradition. But the wine list should be more ample. Don't forget to ask to see the splendid underground cellar. Menus: 195 to 420 F. Exceptional rooms: 700

to 1,500 F, apartments: 1,400 to 1,950 F. Sumptuous breakfasts: 80 F.

10 - BED & BREAKFAST - **Le Mas Azemar**: *Rue du Mas de Vinssou, 46090 Mercuès. Tel. and Fax 05.65.30.96.85.* An 18th-century building sumptuously restored and simply decorated. Guest rooms: 360 to 430 F, breakfast included. Meals served at communal table (170 F) and half board.

MONBAZILLAC

11 - BED & BREAKFAST - **La Rouquette**: *24240 Monbazillac. Tel. 05.53.58.*

30.60 Fax 05.53.73.20.36. Guest rooms in a lovely 18th and 19th-cen-

tury house. Two pretty rooms overlook the Monbazillac vineyard. From 300 to 500 F, breakfast included.

MONESTIER

12 - HOTEL-RESTAURANT - **Château des Vigiers**: *24240 Monestier. Tel. 05.53.61.50.00 Fax 05.53.61.50.20 e-mail: Vigiers@Calvanet, web - http://www.vigiers.com. Hotel closed in January and February.* A superb castle rebuilt from its ruins and richly decorated. Pool, golf course. Menu " Le Chai ": from 98 F. A la carte: around 300 F. Rooms: from 650 F depending on dates. Breakfast: 80 F.

PORT SAINTE FOY

13 - BED & BREAKFAST - **Château La Ressaudie**: *Jean Rebeyrolle, 33220 Port Sainte-Foy-et-Ponchapt. Tel. 05.53. 58.42.82.* 3 guest rooms in a viticultural estate in the heart of the Montravel landscape. Rooms: 210 F. Breakfast: 30 F.

PUYMIROL

14 - HOTEL-RESTAURANT - **L'Aubergade**: *52 rue Royale, 47270 Puymirol. Tel. 05.53.95.31.46 Fax 05.53.95.33.80. Closed Monday in high-season.* A legendary table brilliantly orchestrated by Michel Trama, with a sumptuous wine list for Sud-Ouest and Bordeaux. Menus: 280 to 680 F. Rooms: 750 to 1,410 F.

RAZAC D'EYMET

15 - HOTEL-RESTAURANT - **La Petite Auberge**: *24500 Razac d'Eymet. Tel. 05.53.24.69.27 Fax 05.53.61.02.63.* Near Bergerac, a charming little country hotel, open year-round. Rooms: 180 to 375 F. Nicely priced restaurant.

SAINT-AVIT-SAINT-NAZAIRE

16 - BED & BREAKFAST - **Château du Bru**: *Josette and Guy Duchant, 33220 Saint-Avit-Saint-Nazaire. Tel. 05.57. 46.12.71 Fax 05.57.46.10.64.* Two comfortable and well-equipped rural vacation houses (6 and 7 pers.) run by Bordeaux producers. Per week: 1,800 F (low-season, not during vacations), 2,000 F (June and September) or 3,000 F (July and August).

SAINT-MEDARD

17 - RESTAURANT - **Le Gindreau**: *46150 Saint-Médard. Tel. 05.65.36.22.27 Fax 05.65.36.24.54. Closed Sunday evening in low-season and Monday, and from mid-November to mid-December.* A memorable Falstaffian wine waiter and homemade cuisine. In summer, the terrace under the chestnut trees is irresistible. Attractive wine list with 80 perfectly chosen Cahors, classed by village, with old vintages. Menus: 160 to 450 F (wine included).

SAUSSIGNAC

18 - RESTAURANT - **Le relais de Saussignac**: *24240 Saussignac. Tel. 05.53.27.92.08 Fax 05.53.27.96.57. Closed 2 weeks in November and from 1/20 to 3/1. Closed Sunday evening and Monday from 11/1 to 3/31.* A good country inn serving from the Périgourdin repertory. The Saussignac (a small sweet wine appellation in the Bergerac area) is, of course, given the honors. Menus: 65 (lunch weekdays) to 180 F.

TOUZAC

19 - HOTEL - **Hostellerie de la Source bleue**: *46700 Touzac. Tel. 05.65.36.52.01 Fax 05.65.24.65.69. Closed January to late March.* On the bank of the Lot, hidden among the bamboo, these three mills (11th, 12th and 13th centuries) were the residence of

Marguerite Moreno. Lovely setting, pleasant rooms from 300 to 460 F. Breakfast: 35 F.

FROM THE GARONNE TO THE PYRENEES

AUCH

20 - HOTEL-RESTAURANT - **André Daguin**: *2 place de la Libération, 32003 Auch. Tel. 05.62.61.71.71/05.62.61.71.84 Fax 05.62.61.71.81. Restaurant closed Sunday evening*

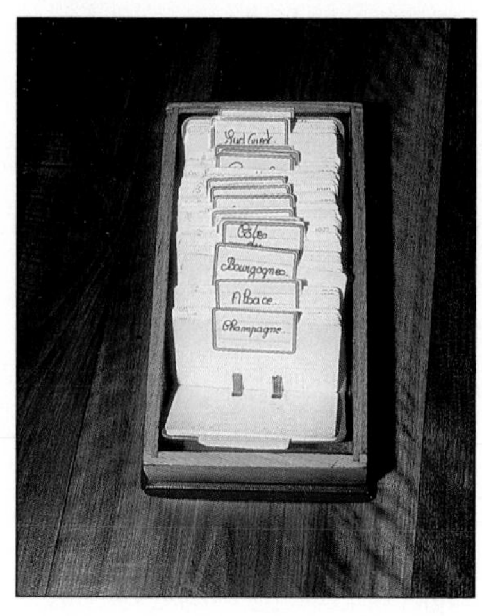

and Monday (except summer and holidays). Menus: 185 and 505 F (goose and duck dishes). Rooms: 290 to 970 F. Sumptuous breakfasts. Daguin is entirely devoted to the region, with his soups, pâtés and salted meats, his variations on magret and foie gras, his ode to simmering... Marvellous southwestern wine list.

ESPELETTE

21 - RESTAURANT - **Euzkadi**: *Rue principale. Tel. 05.59.93.91.88 Fax 05.59.93.90.19. Closed Monday year-round, Tuesday from 9/15 to 6/15. Annual closing from 11/5 to 12/15.* Basque cuisine (in Basque on the menu), robust and delicious. Selection of wines from Irouléguy. Menus: 85 to 165 F.

MADIRAN

22 - HOTEL-RESTAURANT - **Le Prieuré**: *65700 Madiran. Tel. 05.62.31.92.50 Fax*

05.62.31.90.66. Closed Sunday evening and Monday in low-season, and the first 3 weeks in January. In a former Benedictine convent. Good wine list, nearly exhaustive in the appellation. Menus: 95 to 165 F. Very simple rooms in the former cells: 290 F.

MONEIN

23 - HOTEL-RESTAURANT - **L'Estaminet**: *17 place Henri Lacabanne, 64360 Monein. Tel. 05.59.21.30.18 Fax 05.59.21.49.00.* A pleasant village inn with a good selection of Jurançon. Menus: 80 to 140 F. Simple but pleasant rooms: 210 F.

PAU

24 - RESTAURANT - **Pierre**: *16 rue Louis-Barthou, 64000 Pau. Tel. 05.59.27. 76.86 Fax 05.59.27.08.14. Closed Saturday noon and Sunday, and the last 2 weeks in February.* Regional tradition in its flavors and colors. A la carte: around 300 F.

SAINT-ÉTIENNE-DE-BAIGORRY

25 - HOTEL-RESTAURANT - **Arcé**: *64430 Saint-Etienne-de-Baigorry. Tel. 05. 59.37.40.14 Fax 05.59.37.40.20. Closed from mid-November to mid-March.* Shaded terrace on the river.

Traditional cuisine. Good wine list. Menus: 110 to 215 F. Quiet rooms: 350 to 715 F.

SAINT-JEAN-PIED-DE-PORT

26 - HOTEL-RESTAURANT - **Les Pyrénées**: *64220 Saint-Jean-Pied-de-Port. Tel. 05.59.37.01.01 Fax 05.59.37.18.97. Closed Tuesday (low-season) and from late November to late January except for Christmas vacation.* Rich, tender cuisine. Attractive wine list (France and Spain) with a notable collection of old sweet Jurançons. Menus: 230 to 500 F. Rooms: 540 to 880 F. Breakfast: 85 F.

TOULOUSE

27 - RESTAURANT - **Les Jardins de l'Opéra**: *1 place du Capitole, 31000 Toulouse. Tel. 05.61.23.07.76 Fax 05.61.23.63.00. Closed Sunday, the first week in January and 3 weeks in August.* Lovely decor, fine table with colorful cuisine. Very attractive wine list. Menus: 200 to 540 F.

TO SEE

BERGERAC

MUSEUM - **Wine and water transport Museum**: *5 rue conférence, 24100 Bergerac. Tel. 05.53.57.80.92. Open Tuesday-Friday from 10 to 12 and 2 to 5:30, Sat. from 10 to 12 h, Sunday from 2:30 to 6:30pm.* In a lovely 18th-century complex, an 18th-century fermenting room, a collection of agricultural tools used in the vineyards and cooper's tools. The second floor is devoted to inland water navigation and wine transportation.

MONBAZILLAC

OUTING - The castle dominating the vineyard houses a museum of popular arts and traditions and a beautiful collection of wine bottles.

GAILLAC

MUSEUM - **The vineyard museum**.

CROUSEILLES

OUTING - The Romanesque church surrounded by vineyards.

IROULEGUY

OUTING - The village at the foot of the mountains and its old cemetery with vertical and round grave stones bearing mysterious engravings.

MADIRAN

OUTING - In the chapel on the left: freizes with horizontal grape clusters.

MAUMUSSON-LAGUIAN

OUTING - The garden devoted to celebrating the grape vine and wine around the world.

ORTHEZ

OUTING - The decanter factory.

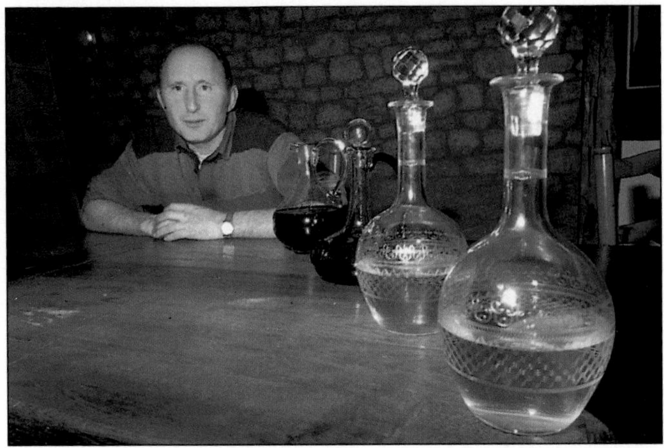

Luc de Conti.

Château Tour des Gendres

Owner Family de Conti. **Supervisor** Luc de Conti. **Address** Les Gendres, 24240 Ribagnac - Tel. 05.53.57.12.43 Fax 05.53.58 89.49. **Open** From Monday to Saturday midday, 9:00-12:30 and 14:00-17:00. **Spoken** English **Credit Cards** Visa, Eurocard, MasterCard.

Luc de Conti is not one to rest on his laurels. Each year offers new surprises and wines that are made with greater precision. Today, the whites are sumptuous and have great expression on the palate. This is obtained by the extended task of stirring the lees, as for the Cuvée des Conti '96 (30 F), a pure Semillon aged on lees, which has marvelous ripeness, weight and finesse. The reds have also benefited from slow lees contact. The Cabernet Sauvignon has increased in the blend and the wines have gained in structure and elegance. The red Bergerac Moulin des Dames '95 (approx. 75 F), tasted during maturation, has undergone malolactic fermentation in barrel and gained a remarkably mellow feel. The black fruit and toasted notes combine well together and the palate is fine, full, and fruity with firm, silky tannins. The '96, which is stuffed with fruit and spicy notes, appears to have amazing finesse, weight and length. This is our top recommendation in Bergerac.

Our choice Bergerac Moulin des Dames white '96 (approx. 50 F). Very expressive nose of white fruits (peach), brioche, and honey. The palate is full, fruity, and fat with a richness added by the alcohol but supported by the extract. Elegant oak and plenty of length. Age a while.

Reception With a passion that is rapidly communicated. An attractive *gîte* is presently being restored.

How to get there *(Map 16): Leave Bergerac direction Agen via N21. Turn left at Bouniagues (10km) between the post office and bakery, then follow signs.*

Laurent de Bosredon.

Château Bélingard

Owner Family de Bosredon **Supervisor** Laurent de Bosredon **Address** 24240 Pomport - Tel. 05.53.58.28.03 Fax 05.53.58.38.39 **Open** From Monday to Friday, 8:00-18:00, Saturday (in hight season) by appointment.

This is a large domaine geared towards the production of Monbazillac and dry white wines using an important percentage of Muscadelle for its lightness and elegance. However, the reds are not without interest, the '95, in particular, the regular *cuvée* (26 F) for its fruitiness and the *cuvée* Prestige (49 F), tasted during maturation, for the density and finesse of the extract and the aromatic ripeness.

The dry white '96s, tasted during maturation, promise to be as good as their reputation. The Première Cuvée (25 F) combines Semillon, Sauvignon and Muscadelle to produce a wine that is full but fine, precise and long, lively, and fruity. The Blanche de Bosredon (38 F) was vinified in oak with the lees stirred. The nose is elegantly oaky, the palate rich on attack, fine, fruity with more presence and length than the '95.

Our choice The Monbazillacs, tasted during maturation, but with a promising future in store. The Premier '95 (49 F) is fine and fruity, well-balanced, and fresh. The Blanche de Bosredon is a more ambitious wine. The deep color indicates the ripeness of the vintage. The nose is rich and intense and the palate very concentrated, fine, and balanced. The Premier is ready for drinking while the Blanche de Bosredon should be aged.

Reception Attentive. In a large tasting room.

How to get there *(Map 16): Leave Bergerac direction Mont de Marsan. Turn right at the top of the hill towards Pomport. Follow the signs.*

Château du Cayrou nestles in a beautiful park.

Château du Cayrou & Clos de Gamot

Owner Family Jouffreau. **Address** Clos de Gamot, 46220 Prayssac. **Open** Everyday, 9:00-19:00. Château du Cayrou. **Address** 46700 Puy l'Évêque - Tel. 05.65.22.40.26 Fax 05.65.22.45.44. **Open** 10:00-12:00 and 14:00-19:00 from Monday to Saturday, May - end Oct. In winter, visit in Clos de Gamot **Spoken** English, Spanish, German.

The Clos de Gamut seems firmly rooted to the soil with the oldest of its Auxerrois vines reaching 110 years in 1995. The soils are worked and plowed, the grapes hand harvested, and the wines aged in large wooden *foudres* to produce wines of character which are not inclined to give of themselves in youth. One can, however, profit from this situation as their are eight vintages of Château du Cayrou available. We particularly liked Château du Cayrou '90 (38 F) for its aromas of chocolate powder; the '89 (40 F) for the fruit and concentration; the '85 (57 F) for the complexity of the nose, the firm, fine thread, the richness, and the complex notes (leather, plum but also raspberry and violet); the '82 (69 F) for the great structure, finesse, and persistence. Of Clos de Gamot, taste the '92 (43 F) for its finesse and length but above all, in the same vintage, the Cuvée Vignes Centenaires (only in magnum: 140 F) for the rich, chewy style.

Our choice Clos de Gamot '94 (41 F) For its fruity nose, concentrated palate, extract, well-knit and concentrated tannins, power, and lovely smoky finish. To keep.

Reception At the Clos de Gamut don't miss the gallery of paintings tracing the history of the Jouffreau family back to the 13th century. Château du Cayrou is surrounded by a beautiful park.

How to get there *(Map 17): From Cahors direction Puy l'Evêque via D911. Clos de Gamot is in Prayssac and Château du Cayrou in Puy l'Evêque. Signposted.*

The cedar tree of Cèdre.

Château du Cèdre

Owners Charles Verhaeghe and sons. **Address** Bru, 46700 Vire-sur-Lot - Tel. 05.65.36.53.87 Fax 05.65.24.64.36. **Open** From Monday to Saturday, 9:00-18:00, everyday in summer. **Spoken** English **Credit cards** Visa, Eurocard, MasterCard.

Half the vineyard is located on clay-limestone soils (the "*tran*") which produce light but fleshy wines and the other half on clay-sandy soils, with plenty of large stones or *galets*, which produce much richer wines. The two *cuvées* from this domine are a blend of both *terroirs*, the Prestige benefiting from the oldest vines (a blend of Tannat and Auxerrois) while the *cuvée* Domaine is a blend of younger Auxerrois and Merlot.

The wines, certainly the Prestige, are heavily extracted but maintain finesse, flesh, and a certain roundness. The Prestige is aged in oak barrels, of which one third are renewed yearly, and the other *cuvée* in large wooden *foudres.*

The Domaine '95 (34 F) has an intense nose, concentrated palate with lively tannins and a hint of good quality oak. Normally there is no oak flavor in this *cuvée* but the frost and the reduced harvest "liberated" some oak casks.

Our choice Château du Cèdre Prestige '95 (54 F). The nose is still slightly oaky, mixed with notes of violet and fruit. The palate is very dense, well structured with flesh and silky tannins. This is a wine to age. A superb *cuvée* Vieilles Vignes d'Auxerrois (approx. 100 F) will be released in mid-1998 which is fine, aromatic, silky, delicious, and very persistent. To be reserved.

Reception In a tiny cellar more often than not with Pascal, the son who is the winemaker. The other son, Jean-Marc, is normally in the vineyard.

How to get there *(Map 17): From Cahors drive towards Puy l'Evêque via D911. Turn left having crossed the river Lot, in the direction of Mauroux, Tournon d'Agenais via D5. The cave is signposted on the right.*

The château dates from 1780 but has vestiges of the 13th and 14th centuries.

Château Gautoul

Owner Alain Senderens. **Address** 46700 Puy l'Évêque - Tel. 05.65.30.84.17 Fax 05.65.30.85.17. **Open** From Monday to Friday, 9:00-12:00 and 14:00-18:00. **Spoken** English. **Credit cards** Visa, Eurocard, MasterCard, Amex.

Installed since 1992, Alain Senderens, the proprietor-chef of the restaurant Lucas-Carton in Paris, has thrown himself into wine with the same passion he shows for his cuisine. He is ambitious (he wants to find the true identity of the Auxerrois), extreme (he has created a splendid new barrel cellar) but at the same time modest (he has done numerous vinification and ageing trials). Generally impetuous, he has been obliged to learn a new set of rules in order to let time go by and remain patient. "For the first time in my life I'd like to gain a year every year," he says in order to see the results of his work.

Generally speaking, three *cuvées* are produced. The Petit Château '96 (34 F) is round and fruity; the *cuvée* Chatenet where the fruit blends with the finesse of the tannins and the wine can be drunk rapidly - the '94 (53 F) is fleshy, fruity, endowed with fine tannins and stretches like a cat - and the *cuvée* Prestige (only produced in good vintages).

Our choice Cuvée Château '94 (88 F). Dark, bright hue. The nose is slightly oaky, and very ripe. The palate is elegant and concentrated with fine, silky tannins, an aromatic note of licorice and delicately smoky on the finish. Long and persistent. The '95 and '96, tasted during maturation, will be very fine. To keep.

Reception Beautiful modern room for tasting. Don't forget to see the barrel cellar.

How to get there *(Map 17): From Cahors to Puy l'Evêque via D911. Turn left having crossed the river Lot, towards Mauroux and Tournon d'Agenais via D5. The domaine is signposted on the left.*

The open spaces of Haute-Serre.

Château Haute-Serre et Château de Mercuès

Head winemaker Bertrand-Gabriel Vigouroux. **Address** Haute-Serre, 46230 Cieurac. **Open** Everyday, 9:00-12:00 and 13:30-18:00. Mercuès, 46090 Mercuès - Tel. 05.65.20.80.80 Fax 05.65.20.80.81. **Open** Every day, 9:00-12:00 and 13:30-18:00, Easter - Nov. 1, the rest of the year by appointment. **Spoken** English. **Credit cards** All major.

Other than their important activity as *negociants*, Georges Vigouroux and his sons manage several domaines and own two, Mercuès and Haute-Serre. The important percentage of Merlot in the wines of Mercuès produces wines that are powerful but round, which open up rapidly. The '94 (45 F) is fine, quite ample, square with a distinct note of elegant oak. The wines of Haute-Serre, produced from a vineyard that lies in a single unit on stony, clay-limestone soils, take longer to mature. The '94 (41 F) has an attractive, curranty nose, full, concentrated palate, weight, spicy notes (cinnamon), and plenty of finesse.

Our choice The '90s. The Haute-Serre (66 F) has a fine, spicy nose with just a touch of fig, full, ripe palate with spicy, smoky notes, good length, and elegance. Château de Mercuès (68 F) has a squarer, more powerful style.To cellar.

Reception At Mercuès don't forget to visit the barrel cellar (in season). If possible go to Haute-Serre for the beautiful countryside. Wines are on sale at the *negociant* house Atrium (road to Toulouse). Open all day in season, 7:30-12:30 and 14:00-19:00.

How to get there *(Map 17): For Mercuès leave Cahors towards Puy l'Evêque. Turn right in the village. Signpost. For Haute-Serre leave Cahors towards Montauban via N20 and turn left opposite the aerodrome. Route signposted.*

Pigeon houses punctuate the countryside. That of Lagrazette is one of the most beautiful.

Château Lagrezette

Owner Alain-Dominique Perrin. **Cellarmaster** Vincent Dols. **Address** 46140 Caillac - Tel. 05.65.20.07.42 Fax 05.65.20.06.95. **Open** Every day, 9:00-19:00. **Spoken** English. **Credit cards** Visa, Eurocard, MasterCard.

In 1980, Alain-Dominique Perrin, President of Cartier, bought this large domaine of 53 hectares, a part of which encircles the 15th and 16th century château and pigeon house. These are visible from the road that passes above the cellar. Vinified until 1991 at the cooperative, the wines are now made in a modern, functional cellar, at a sunken level near the château. Depending on the vintage, three or four blends are made, all red and all subject to varying methods of maturation.The Moulin is usually supple and fruity. The Cuvée de Printemps '96 (36 F) has benefited from modern methods of vinification and is round and seductive. The '95 (41 F), aged in seasoned barrels preserves the fruit but is a little more austere. The *cuvée* Château '95 (75 F), aged for a long time in new oak barrel, needs time to let the oak integrate but the concentrated fruit extract is not overwhelmed and the tannins are fine. The finish is long. In certain vintages the *cuvée* Dame d'Honneur is produced but always seems dominated by the wood.

Our choice The *cuvée* Chevaliers '94 (52 F), also aged in new oak casks but for a shorter length of time, has absorbed the wood intelligently. The palate is concentrated and tannic but remains elegant. A wine to age a little longer.

Reception In a sales and tasting room, with the chance of a glimpse of the beautiful barrel celar.

How to get there *(Map 17): From Cahors towards Puy l'Evèque via D911. Turn left at the entrance to Mercuès, towards Douelle via D12 and follow the signs.*

The doggerel of grandfather Serougne.

Château Lamartine

Owner Alain Gayraud. **Address** 46700 Soturac - Tel. 05.65.36.54.14 Fax 05.65.24.65.31. **Open** From Monday to Saturday, 9:00-12:00 30 and 14:00-19:00, Sunday by appointment. **Spoken** English. **Credit cards** Visa, Eurocard, MasterCard.

"Pur, de bonne famille/d'Auxerrois et cépages du cru/Comme de la jolie fille/On désire ma vertu...." (Pure, from a good family/From the Auxerrois and other varieties of the *cru/* Like a pretty girl/They covet my virtue.) The doggerel of grandfather Edouard Serougne greets you at the entrance to this unusual domaine. Why is it so unusual? First, because the grapes ripen early here, an enormous benefit in difficult years. This is due to the southerly exposure and because the domaine is located at the furthest point west of the appellation and therefore benefits from an Atlantic influence. Second, because Alain Gayraud loves the Tannat, a grape variety that has been marginalized in the appellation to the benefit of Merlot. Using the Tannat he produces vigorous wines with plenty of weight and flesh, above all in the *cuvée* Particulière where 20% is used to give structure to the traditional Auxerrois. The basic *cuvée* is a wine that conforms more to general rules. The '95 (32 F) is supple on attack, fleshy, with tannins that are present on the finish. It needs a little more time.

Our choice Cuvée Particulière '95 (54 F). Good, dense color with a present, tannic extract which is fine and well knit. The oak is still a little dominant. The wine finishes powerfully. It needs to be aged to mature and lengthen. The '94 (54 F) shows well from a difficult vintage, the wine being generally softer, with more emphasis given to the aromatic expression.

Reception Passionate. At the cellar.

How to get there *(Map 16): From Cahors towards Puy l'Evêque and Fumel via D911. The cave is signposted on the right 5km after Fumel and a little before Soturac.*

The 11th century cellars.

Domaines Rigal

Owners Franck and Jacques Rigal. **Address** Château Saint-Didier-Parnac, 46140 Parnac - Tel. 05.65.30.70.10 Fax 05.65.20.16.24. **Open** From Monday to Saturday, 8:00-12:00 and 14:00-18:00. **Spoken** English. **Credit cards** Visa, Eurocard, MasterCard.

This *negociant* house, a specialist in the sale of South West wines bottled at the property, is also the owner of three domaines. Château de Grezels is characterized by the important percentage of Merlot in the blend (30%) providing supple, fruity wines from which we've selected the '94 (30 F) for its ripe fruit and freshness. Château Saint-Didier, where the visits take place, is marked by the Auxerrois (80%). The '94 (27 F) has plenty of color and is ripe on the nose (red fruits), explosive on the palate (black currant, spices), long, and balanced. The '95 will be fuller on the palate with very round tannins, fruit and well integrated oak.

The Prieuré de Cenac is the most consistent of the wines, particularly brilliant in the great vintages if given time to allow the structure and oak influence (half the production is aged in new oak barrels) to soften.

Our choice Prieuré de Cenac. The '94 (38 F) has a deep color, fine extract, fruit lifted by spicy, smoky notes, and plenty of length and persistence. The '95 will have the same seductive aromas with a more concentrated palate. Being a little more austere it will need longer ageing.

Reception Don't miss the two vaulted barrel ageing cellars. They date from the 11th century and hold 1,400 barrels.

How to get there *(Map 17): From Cahors towards Puy l'Evêque. Turn left at the entrance to Mercuès, in the direction of Douelle via D8. Pass this village and continue towards Parnac and signs to Château Saint-Didier.*

Jean-Luc Baldès.

Clos Triguedina

Owner Jean-Luc Baldès. **Address** 46700 Puy l'Évêque - Tel. 05.65.21.30.81 Fax 05.65.21.39.28. **Open** From Monday to Friday, 9:30-12:00 and 14:00-18:00, Saturday and Sunday by appointment. **Spoken** English, Spanish. **Credit cards** Visa, Eurocard, MasterCard.

The name of the domaine is itself an invitation to the gourmand as it comes from "*Me trigue dina*" or "I can't wait for dinner." Spread throughout the different *terroirs* of the appellation, the vineyard provides access to a varying palette of expressions. The vines are often very old and planted at a high density. Clos Triguedina, the regular *cuvée*, is a blend of 70% Auxerrois, 20% Merlot, and 10% Tannat with a third each of the production aged in *foudres*, vat, and one-year-old oak barrels. The *cuvée* Probus is produced from 50-year-old Auxerrois vines that resisted the frost in 1956 and is aged in new oak barrels. The Clos Triguedina '94 (46 F) has intense, licorice notes and fine tannins. The Clos '93 (48 F) is less concentrated but has plenty of elegance while the '90 (65 F) has lots of body and weight but fine tannins. Older vintages are available but the recent vintages have gained in fruit extract, finesse and harmony.

Our choice The *cuvée* Prince Probus. The '94 (70 F) is beginning to mellow and the finish is really elegant. The tannins demand a little more patience. The '95 (73 F) is very concentrated and full with notes of spice and eucalyptus. To age.

Reception Friendly and competent. At the cellar.

How to get there *(Map 17): From Cahors towards Puy l'Evêque via D911. Turn left having crossed the river Lot, towards Mauroux, Tournon d'Agenais via D5. The domaine is signposted on the right after 2km.*

The rather kitschy Château Bellevue La Fôret.

Château Bellevue La Forêt

Supervisor Patrick Germain. **Address** 31620 Fronton - Tel. 05.61.82.43.21 Fax 05.61.82.39.70. **Open** From Monday to Saturday, 9:00-12:00 and 14:00-18:00. **Spoken** English. **Credit cards** Visa, Eurocard, MasterCard.

This is a large domaine of 115 hectares situated not far from Toulouse, on the road to Moissac, which has preserved an identity by replanting the Négrette, a grape variety which is unique to the region. The name is derived from the dark color of the grape's skin. The Négrette represents half the plantings in the vineyard the rest comprising a cocktail of Syrah, Cabernet Franc, and Cabernet Sauvignon. Patrick Germain, whose grandparents hail from the Ardèche and Burgundy, knows what cross-breeding is all about. We prefer the lighter, fruitier wines which are easy to drink young from this domaine. The others tend to cast a longing eye at Bordeaux by leaning deliberately towards the Cabernets and by accentuating the passage through oak. The Cuvée Or '94 (30,35 F) is the exception to the rule remaining fresh although marked by the Cabernet. On the other hand the *cuvée* Château '95 (25,20 F) preserves the originality of the Négrette and its immediate fruitiness and uses the Syrah and Cabernet for a little structure. This provides a good compromise beween the immediate pleasure of the fruit and the potential to age the wine a little.

Our choice Ce Vin '95 (30,35 F). A voluntarily mysterious name to describe a wine made from pure Négrette which has a delicate nose, tender palate, light tannic structure and which is very fruity (raspberry) with slightly smoky notes.

Reception In a vast space with contemporary paintings.

How to get there *(Map 17): From the center of Fronton drive towards Grisolles and follow the signs. The château is on the right.*

Training for the launch of the *cuvée* Don Quichotte.

Château Le Roc

Supervisors Jean-Luc and Frédéric Ribes. **Address** 31620 Fronton - Tel. 05.61.82.93.90 Fax 05.61.82.72.38. **Open** By appointment. **Spoken** English, German.

In 1990, four young associates, Frédéric Ribes, his wife, his brother and a friend, took over this 18-hectare domaine from old Ribes, a legendary figure in Fronton. The Négrette, a grape variety unknown outside the appellation, remains the principal variety (50%) complemented by Syrah, Cabernet Franc and Sauvignon and Côt. The vines are relatively old, the soils partially worked or sown with grass seed and natural yeasts used for the fermentation. In other words the domaine is worked in a simple, open manner. Apart from a really easy-drinking rosé '96 (20 F), which is also rich and vinous, there is a red *cuvée* Classique '96 (22 F) which is round and fruity and red *cuvée* Réserve '96 (approx. 34 F, available March '98) which is full and complex with soft, silky tannins. If you insist a little there is also a delicious *cuvée* of pure Négrette to taste which is dense and firmly knit but which is not for sale as it is reserved for the pleasure of the *vigneron* and his friends. In the vineyard this is called a *cuvée PMG ("pour ma gueule"* or only for me!).

Our choice Cuvée Don Quichotte '95 (45 F). We leave the explanation of the name to the owners! A blend of Négrette and Syrah which produces an intensely fine aroma and delicious, full palate with very silky tannins. The oak is well integrated, the finish beautifully long and the wine fruity and fresh.

Reception Could not be more informal. In the cellar surrounded by the vats.

How to get there *(Map 17): On the right at the entrance to Fronton having arriving from the direction of Toulouse.*

Ancient Persian ceramic tiles decorate the cellar.

Château Saint louis

Owner Alain Mahmoudi. **Address** 82370 Labastide Saint-Pierre - Tel. 05.63.30.13.13 Fax 05.63.30.11.42. **Open** By appointment.

"Renounce,/ renounce everything/ in this world:/fortune, power, honors/...Hold on without fear/to the delicious golden wine./It's the only way/to save yourself." Never before has this poem by Omar Khayyam been so applicable to a given situation. Alain Mahmoudi is actually Persian. Having arrived in France to study and having earned a degree in nuclear physics (specializing in radiology) he took a mild interest in his father-in-law's distillery before being hit by the bug of viticulture and vinification. His new life confirmed by studies in enology, he set about restructuring the domaine and improving the quality of the wines.It's not surprising then that the arches of the cellar have the look of Andalucia and that the ceramic Roses of Esfahan stand guard over the barrel cellar.

All vintages since 1991 are still for sale. We prefer the '92 (25 F) which has attractive fruit and which is just beginning to evolve and the '94 (22 F) which has a ripe but discreet nose, supple and fruity palate still teased by the tannins.

Our choice Red '95 (25 F). Bright color, delicious palate which starts with a light touch of vanilla and finishes spicier. The extract is soft, the tannins silky and the finish long. To drink.

Reception A tasting room in the middle of vines with a view over the barrel cellar is nearing completion.

How to get there *(Map 17): From Toulouse towards Montauban via D13. 10km from Fronton in the center of Labastide Saint-Pierre pass the Arbeau distillery and turn left following the tiny signs.*

The Beaulieu château, a 14th century country-house.

Château de Beaulieu

Owners Robert and Agnès Schulte. **Address** 47180 Saint-Sauveur de Meilhan - Tel. 05.53. 94.30.40 and 05.53.94.29.29 Fax 05.53.94.30.40. **Open** By appointment. **Spoken** English, German, Spanish.

Robert Schulte, a specialist in food product marketing in the United States (!) then an organizational consultant (!!) and his wife Agnès settled here in what they initially considered the perfect holiday home. When the vineyard came up for sale they couldn't resist the temptation. Consequently, the wine bug took hold. The Schultes' are not looking any the worse for it ! Even better, they are producing some wonderful wines from the 31 hectares which surround the gravelly hill crowned by the château, a spledid 14th century Gascon country-house.

The vineyard is relatively old, dominated with the Bordeaux grape varieties of Merlot, Cabernet Franc and Cabernet Sauvignon but with a hint of the local South West given by the Auxerrois and Abouriou varieties. Syrah is also present as a guest star. The wines are supple but well formed, balanced, and the oak ageing, which is skillfully applied, doesn't over-power the fruit. The construction of a vinification cellar at the château should enable the domaine to progress even further.

Our choice The '94 (33 F) for its open, fruity nose and palate which is soft on attack, characterful, and enjoys a supple tannic structure.

Reception In the cellar, or for groups, in a beautiful room in the château.

How to get there *(Map 16): From Marmande towards Grignols via D3. Turn right in front of the war memorial in the center of Cocumont direction Saint-Sauveur. Turn right at the crossroads at the bottom of the hill. The château is visible at 200m.*

Patrice Lescarret.

Domaine de Causse-Marines

Owner Patrice Lescarret. **Address** 81140 Vieux - Tel. 05.63.33.98.30 Fax 05.63.33.96.23. **Open** By appointment. **Spoken** English.

This newcomer to the appellation, installed since 1993, has more than one thing in common with the great old timer Robert Plageoles. They both have the same love of the soil, neglected grape varieties, the purety of the fruit, and experimenting as well as a desire to do better.

In 1996 we much prefer the white (38 F) to the red wines. The dry white Les Greilles, produced from Muscadelle, Len de l'El and Mauzac, has a bright, golden color. The nose is intense (dried fruits, spring flowers) and the palate teasingly sharp. The *cuvée* Mauzac, a dry white made from 90% Mauzac Vert and 10% Mauzac Rose, has a pale yellow hue with green flecks. The nose is also mischievous (apple, aniseed) but the palate is generously fleshy with a long fennel and bread-crust finish.

Our choice Grain de Folie '96 (49 F: 50 centiliters). A sweet wine which merits its name. The grape by grape harvest included seven passages through the vines and finished on 18 December. The blend of Mauzac, Muscadelle and Len d'El provides a full, rich, crystallized fruit wine which is well balanced with good acidity. The nose is very fine, the palate unctuous with notes of hay, spice, honey, and resin. To drink through gourmandise or age wisely.

Reception Passionate. In a tiny cellar. The brochure and technical notes for visitors are extremely well conceived.

How to get there *(Map 17): From Gaillac towards Cordes via D922. Turn left at Cahuzac direction Vieux via D1 and follow the signposted itinerary.*

Robert (right) and Bernard Plageoles.

Domaine Plageoles

Owners Robert and Bernard Plageoles. **Address** Domaine des Tres Cantous, 81140 Cahuzac sur Vere - Tel. 05.63.33.90.40 Fax 05.63.33.95.64. **Open** From Monday to Saturday, 8:00-12:00 and 14:00-19:00, Sunday by appointment.

In another life Robert Plageoles must have been a gardener in the Garden of Eden. There is nobody who pays as much attention to the plant life, to the point of preserving and replanting seven of the local grape varieties (Mauzac Gris, Rose, Vert, Roux, Jaune, Côte de Melon and Noir).

Apart from a full, spicy, sparkling Mauzac (44 F), the domaine produced some wonderful wines in '96. Of the dry wines the Mauzac Vert (33 F) has a note of lime tree, a lively but full palate with a gentle finish. The sweet Mauzac Roux (38 F) has a honey and fenel palate with plenty of volume and weight (known here as "*ventru*"). The sweet Ondenc (50 F: 50 centiliters) is full of aromatic notes of white fruits (peach), likewise the Muscadelle (50 F: 50 centiliters).

The Vin de Voile '87 (150 F) , aged for a long time under a veil of film-forming yeast in the same way that Vin Jaune or Sherry is matured, is a full, powerful wine with plenty of presence on the palate and a note of green walnut.

Our choice Vin d'Autan (160 F: 50 centiliters). From the name of an autumn wind, produced from the Ondenc grape variety. Very concentrated with a note of dried fig on the nose. The palate has notes of quince, honey, and spice (cinnamon).

Reception Perfect, but take your time. The wines and the Plageoles (father and son) demand it. Anybody in a hurry will more than likely be shown the door even more rapidly.

How to get there *(Map17): From Gaillac towards Cordes. The domaine is on the right at the entrance to Cahuzac. Signposted.*

Until 1979, Philippe Teulier harvested with the *carredjadou*, a basket for carrying up to 35 kilos of grapes on the head.

Domaine du Cros

Owner Philippe Teulier. **Address** 12390 Goutrens - Tel. 05.65.72.71.77 Fax 05.65.72.68.80. **Open** Every day, 8:00-12:00 and 13:00-19:00.

Philippe Teulier's great-grandfather settled on the Haut du Coteau when the appellation comprised 3,000 hectares and supplied the mineworkers of Decazeville and Carmaux with wine. There are now only 950 hectares. The grape variety is the Fer (so called because of the hard nature of the wood of the vine and not the tannins) known locally as the Mansois. The domaine consists of 20 hectares planted on the mountain escarpment. The *cuvée* Lo Sang del Païs '95 (25 F) is crisp and fruity with notes of hay and aromatic herbs.

Our choice Red cuvée Spéciale '94 (37 F). This deeply colored wine with a clean, fine aroma is made from grapes from 50 and 90 year-old vines. The palate is meaty, solid, tannic without being hard, crisp with a long fruitiness and menthol finish. To drink in a year. The '95 will be more concentrated but still as silky.

Reception Excellent. Apart from the wines, the hilly countryside and the villages constructed from red sandstone are also worth discovering. For lovers of local history there is a remarkable monograph that can be found in the bookshops of Marcillac entitled ("*Le Vignoble de Marcillac, une Oasis de Pampres au coeur du pays vert*" par J.M. Cosson and C. Bex du Beffroi, 21 rue du Pont de Fer, 12100 Millau).

How to get there *(Map 17): From Rodez to Decazeville (N140). In Nuces, on left to Clairvaux. In the center of the village, at the fountain turn on left towards Goutrens (4km). At the top on right to the cellar.*

Dominique Vidal

Château Fonmourgues

Owner Dominique Vidal. **Address** 24240 Monbazillac - Tel. 05.53.63.02.79 Fax 05.53.27.20.32. **Open** By appointment. **Spoken** English.

Dominique Vidal is not a clown. At least it was not that long ago he could be found under the "big top" he had erected to vinify the wines. Plumber and electrician by necessity, he handles the vinification, ageing of the wines and construction of his cellar all at the same time. He set up here in 1994 having been his father's tenant farmer, the winemaker at Château La Borderie, and then a *negociant.*

The vineyard nurtures its old vines (the youngest were replanted in 1957 after the frost) and there are some large parcels planted in 1947. The shaky nature of the installations belies the rigor of the winemaking. The grapes are harvested by hand, the red and white wines fermented without the addition of cultured yeasts, the red Côtes-de-Bergerac is aged in wood and the dry white wine fermented in new oak barrels.

There is a good dry white Bergerac '96 (22 F) which is crisp and full and a red Côtes-de-Bergerac '95 (33 F) which is black, dense and meaty on the palate and endowed with round tannins and a well integrated oakiness.

Our choice Monbazillac '94 (limited stock). The palate is subtle and balanced with good botrytis notes. The finish is superb with a lingering taste of dried apricots.The '95 (40 F) mixes notes of citrus fruits and mint. The extract is dense and silky. Age a little.

Reception Passionate.

How to get there *(Map 16): From Bergerac towards Mont de Marsan. Turn left just after the Monbazillac cooperative and pass Château La Borderie. Fonmourgues is a little farther on (first house on the right without signpost).*

Armand Vidal, the reference for Monbazillac.

Château La Borderie et Château Treuil de Nailhac

Owner Armand Vidal. **Address** 24240 Monbazillac - Tel. 05.53.57.00.36 Fax 05.53.63.00.94. **Open** From Monday to Friday, 8:00-12:00 and 14:00-18:00, Saturday by appointment. **Spoken** English. **Credit cards** Visa, Eurocard, MasterCard.

Situated on the hillsides of Monbazillac with a northerly exposure, the vineyards of Armand Vidal are more suited to the production of white wines than red although the rustic but fruity Côtes-de-Bergerac '94 (approx. 31 F) is not without charm. Of the dry whites, there is, in the years it is made, a curious *cuvée* of 100% Muscadelle (approx. 30 F) whose tender qualities attracted us in '92 and '93. Otherwise (in white), choose Château La Borderie '95 (25 F) for its notes of dried fruits and toast or the Treuil '96 (25 F), a mischievous Sauvignon.

Recent vintages offered at the cellar have not been favorable for the production of great sweet wines. The Monbazillac '94 (72 F) is certainly accented towards fruity.

The *cuvée Sélectionée* '93 (76 F) is more complex with an opulent nose and notes of orange blossom and a lively, crystallized fruit palate.

The domaine regularly offers older vintages for sale. At present the Château Treuil de Nailhac '86 (70 F) is being offered. The palate has maintained a good acidity which lifts the notes of toast and crystallized fruits.

Our choice Château La Borderie Monbazillac '91 (80 F). Having survived the frost (the production fell to 7 hectoliters/hectare) the wine has a fine nose with a hint of praline, a creamy, long palate, well balanced by the acidity, and a toasted note on the finish. To drink or age a little.

Reception Good.

How to get there *(Map 16): From Bergerac towards Mont de Marsan. The property is on the left just after the Monbazillac cooperative.*

Daniel Hecquet with *pipette* in hand.

Château Puy-Servain et Château Calabre

Supervisor Daniel Hecquet. **Address** 33220 Port Sainte-Foy et Ponchapt - Tel. 05.53.24.77.27 Fax 05.53.58.37.43. **Open** From Monday to Friday, 8:00-12:00 and 14:00-18:00, Saturday and Sunday by appointment. **Spoken** English.

On the plateau of Montravel, Daniel Hecquet now puts into practice the advice he once gave to the *vignerons* of the appellation as enologist for the local promotional body. Of the two wines we preferred the Puy-Servain range. The grapes are hand harvested and sorted, the white wines held on lees and the reds matured in oak casks. The wines are, therefore, elegant, direct, and rich and only in need of a great vintage (1995) to be really formidable. Of the range of wines from Château Calabre, which have an easier style, we preferred the fruity red '95 (31,55 F) and the soft, white '96 (26,30 F). Lovers of sweet wine should not miss the Château Puy-Servain Haut-Montravel '95 (66,80 F: 50 centiliters) with its intense, crystallized fruit nose and full, rich (*pain d'épice*) palate. "A great, big teddy bear," says Daniel Hecquet amusingly.

Our choice Château Puy-Servain Terrement Montravel white '96 (34,70 F). Fine, expressive nose dominated by the notes of exotic fruits (pineapple). The palate is fine, elegant and flavorsome with notes of exotic fruits, almond and spice. The finish is lifted and persistent. To drink.

Reception Excellent.

How to get there *(Map 16): From Bordeaux towards Libourne, Castillon, Sainte-Foy la Grande. Arriving at Sainte-Foy la Grande turn left at the roundabout direction Port Sainte-Foy/Le Fleix then 200m further on turn left towards Le Fleix. Continue straight on towards Montpon. Climb the hill. After approximately 5km turn right towards Le Fleix. The route is signposted from here.*

The barrel cellar.

Domaine Brana

Owners Adrienne and Jean Brana. **Address** 3bis Avenue du Jaï-Alaï, 64220 Saint-Jean Pied de Port - Tel. 05.59.37.00.44 Fax 05.59.37.14.28. **Open** 10:00-12:00 and 14:30-18:30. Everyday in July and Aug., from Monday to Friday, June 15 - Sep. 15. The rest of the year by appointment, on request to visit the cellar. **Spoken** Spanish, English.

Like contemplating the frescos in the Sistine Chapel, there is a risk of getting a crick in the neck looking at the vines of the Domaine Brana. The head has to be tilted completely backwards as the slope is 80% sheer and formed more like a wall. "Brana has taken root by clutching at the mountain," says the inscription in Basque on the lintel of the cellar. The Branas decided to attack the vine in 1985, remodeling a superb site on the mountain of Aradoy, building terraces and laying out 70 kilometers of slopes, 1,5 to 4 meters high. Other than the white there is a Domaine red '95 (65 F) which puts the emphasis on the Cabernets, in particular, Cabernet Franc. The nose is seductive, the palate flavorsome, fruity and covered with silky tannins.

Our choice Domaine white '96 (60 F). The Petit Courbu (60%) grape variety provides a mineral edge, the Gros Manseng (40%) agreeable notes of exotic fruits (pineapple, lichee) and toasted almonds, and the Petit Manseng a lively freshness. With its aromatic nose (butter, citrus fruits) and crisp finish this is a truly delicious wine. To drink.

Reception Superb cellar at the foot of the vertiginous vineyard. Intelligent slide show, which is rare. Buying wine, however, is complicated. The wines are available for purchase between May and October. The fruit brandies (another of the family activities) are remarkable.

How to get there *(Map 15): On the left, exiting from Saint-Jean Pied de Port towards Oloron.*

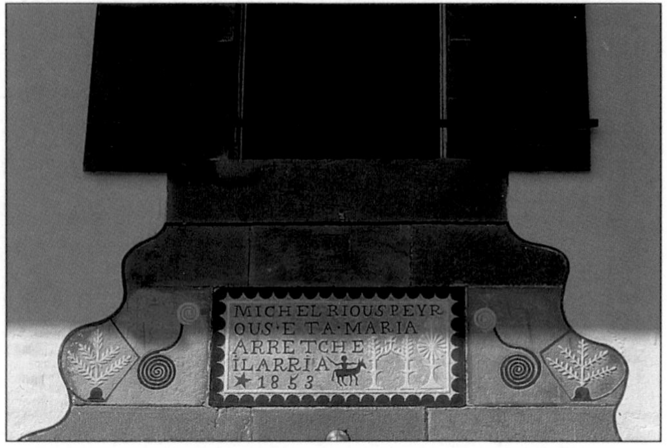

The intriguing decoration on a lintel.

Domaine Ilarria

Owner Family Espil. **Address** 64220 Irouléguy - Tel. and Fax 05.59.37.23.38. **Open** 9:30-12:30 and 13:30-19:30 in July and Aug., by appointment the rest of the year. **Spoken** Spanish, English. **Credit cards** Visa, Eurocard, MasterCard.

Peio Espil has returned from far afield. In Ethiopia and Somalia he looked after refugees and in the Seychelles worked on village development sites. He is now managing the 30 hectare family domaine which is planted to a high density with an equal percentage of Cabernet and Tannat. He is also clearing Iri Larrea or "the heath" (where virtually no living culture can survive as the land is so poor) and planting the vine following the slope or contour-lines so as not to upset the natural balance of the soil with terraces. He also practices an organic form of viticulture. The grapes are hand harvested, destemmed, *pigé* by foot and the wine macerated for a length of time that varies according to the vintage. Whether for red wines or rosés the grapes undergo a cold pre-fermentation maceration to increase the aromatic content.

Among the '96s (38 F) there is a delicious rosé, produced by direct pressing of the grapes, which has smoky, strawberry notes and a supple, ripe, fruity, fine red.

Our choice Cuvée Bixintxo (Vincent in Basque) red '95. A pure Tannat aged in oak casks. After a little time in the glass the nose becomes very floral (iris). The palate is fruity (black cherry, grape) and spicy with silky tannins and delicious extract. The wine can be aged a little.

Reception Very open and attentive. Don't forget to see the curious round tombstones in the old cemetery of Irouléguy.

How to get there *(Map 15): From Saint-Jean-Pied-de-Port towards Saint-Etienne de Baigorry as far as Irouléguy. Signposted on the right from the entrance to the village.*

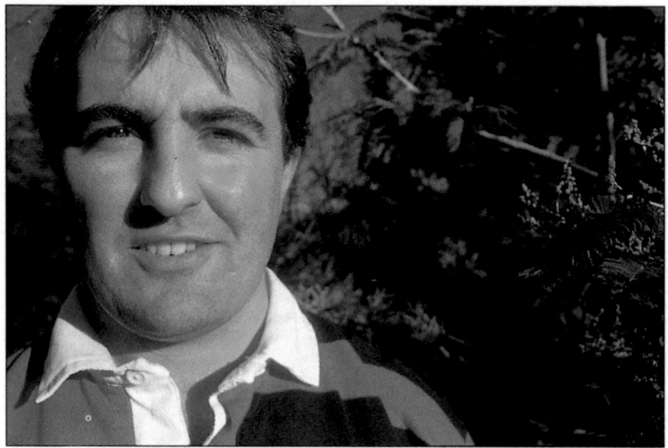

Pascal Labasse.

Domaine Bellegarde

Supervisor Pascal Labasse. **Address** 64360 Monein - Tel. 05.59.21.33.17 Fax 05.59.21.44.40. **Open** From Monday to Friday, 9:00-12:00 and 14:00-18:00. **Credit cards** Visa, Eurocard, MasterCard.

André Labasse transported his grapes to the local cooperative until 1986 when he decided to vinify and bottle his own wines. His son Pascal has since developed an interesting style of vinification and barrel ageing which preserves the fruit at the same time as consolidating the extract and substance of the wine. This provides wines that are both accessible when young and have the property to age. The dry whites, often forgotten in the appellation to the benefit of the sweet wines, are particularly well made here and worthy of note.

In Jurançon sec, we liked the '96 (35 F), made from Gros Manseng, which is agreeably rustic and pure like gold. The barrel fermented *cuvée* '96 (approx. 48 F), produced from old vines, needs to age a little to allow the oak influence to subside but has plenty of fruit. The sweet white '96 (49 F) appears round and flattering but we preferred the other two *cuvées*. The *cuvée* Thibault '95 (74 F) is exotic and rich but well balanced.

Our choice Jurançon *moelleux cuvée* Sélection '93 (230 F). Produced from a particularly smart parcel of low yielding Petit Manseng. The nose is fine and fruity, the palate fine, balanced, powerful, long with crystallized fruit richness, and a quince jelly finish. A powerful, well-structured wine, thanks to a good acidity, that should age well.

Reception In a tiny section of the barrel cellar.

How to get there *(Map 15): From Jurançon towards Laroin, Tarsacq, Abos to Monein via D2. Exit Monein towards Oloron. Take the first road on the right and follow the signposts.*

Jean-Pierre Bousquet and Jean, his father, study the evolution of their barrels.

Domaine Bousquet

Owner Jean-Pierre Bousquet. **Address** Saint-Faust, 64110 Jurançon - Tel. 05.59.83.05.56. **Open** From Monday to Saturday, 9:00-12:00 and 14:00-19:00.

First there was the grandfather Jean, then the father, also Jean, and now the son, Jean-Pierre. They all have in common a feeling for sweet wines, 95% of the production at the cellar, and a passion for the Petit Manseng. If you look hard you won't find more than 300 vines of Gros Manseng. These are used exclusively for the production of the dry whites. The wines here are treated like pedigree cats. All that's asked of them is that they express their *terroir.* They are fermented with natural yeasts in old 600 liter Martinique rum barrels, aged on fine lees for three years and bottled without any fining or filtering. In other words they follow the "ABC's" of vinification. The wine is bottled barrel by barrel without any prior blending so there can be a substantial variation from one bottling to the next. It's the price one has to pay for an authentic form of viticulture which should not be judged as being completely out-of-date. Four people work for a month to selectively hand-harvest the 2.7 hectares. Those who have tasted the wines of Bousquet, however, rapidly become disciples.

Our choice Jurançon *moelleux*'94 (50 F). The nose has a note of vervain, the palate, which is rich with a soft but dense extract, a note of mandarin orange, an acidity swathed in the glycerol of the wine and a remarkable balance between the alcohol, sugar and acidity. A wine to age.

Reception Older vintages are always available.

How to get there *(Map 15): From Jurançon towards Laroin via D2. Turn left towards Saint-Faust-le-Bas via D502 and continue 3km. Turn right at the signpost.*

Georges Bru-Baché, the guardian angel of the domaine.

Domaine Bru-Baché

Owner Claude Loustalot. **Address** Rue Barada, 64360 Monein - Tel. 05.59.21.36.34 Fax 05.59.21.32.67. **Open** From Monday to Friday, 9:00-12:00 and 14:00-18:00 (Saturday by appointment). **Spoken** English.

Georges Bru-Baché has handed over the reins to his nephew, Claude Loustalot. There has never been a more harmonious exchange. The Jurançon *sec* Cuvée des Casterrasses '94 (approx. 50 F) is ripe, powerful, and concentrated. The '95 will be richer and finer still. The Jurançon *moelleux* Cuvée des Casterrasses '95 (60 F) is still a little teasing and reserved on the nose but should follow the same evolution as previous vintages passing from floral to lightly honeyed notes. For the moment, the palate, which is full and long, is very expressive. If you want a real treat choose the Eminence '95 (250 F) which was harvested with an alcohol potential of 21%. The wine has a beautiful golden hue, an intense nose of crystallized fruits, and a powerful, full, rich, toasted palate with notes of dried apricots and crystallized pineapple. It's a wine made robust by the alcohol (14.3%) which balances the residual sugar (approx. 110 grams/liter) and which is refined by the acidity. All this confirms the Petit Manseng as a truly great variety for sweet wines, of the same class as the Chenin Blanc from the Loire and the Riesling from Alsace and Germany.

Our choice Jurançon *moelleux* Cuvée Quintessence '94 (95 F). The wine has a hint of mint on the nose, and fine, aromatic palate (dried fruits, crystallized fruits). Age in order to see a greater explosion of flavor. The '95 is richer in color (riper maturity) with a crystallized fruit nose and lovely rich, full palate with extraordinary persistence.

Reception Perfect. Attractive barrel cellar.

How to get there *(Map 15): From Jurançon towards Laroin, Tarsacq and Abos via D2. The cellar is on the right at the entrance to Monein. Signposted.*

Henri Ramonteu.

Domaine Cauhapé

Supervisor Henri Ramonteu. **Address** 64360 Monein - Tel. 05.59.21.33.02 Fax 05.59.21.41.82. **Open** By appointment. **Spoken** English, Spanish. **Credit cards** Visa, Eurocard, MasterCard.

When it comes to the vine Henri Ramonteu is a late-comer and completely self-taught. An artisan driven by his own intuition, he has turned viticulture into a real art.

The sweet wines here are beyond measure. The Vendanges du 2 Novembre '95 (90 F) is like velvet with its soft attack on the palate before giving a glimpse of its power, volume and structure. The Noblesse du Temps '94 is a more subtle style of wine with plenty of finesse. The Quintessence du Petit Manseng '93 (500 F, sold only by the bottle), from a yield of 7 hectoliters/hectare hence the price, is monumental for its concentration and for its extreme finesse.

Our choice If you take for granted that the sweet wines are the most fabulous at the domaine it is also worth exploring the dry wines. The Sève d'Automme '95 (60 F), a Gros Manseng of which one third has been vinified in oak barrel, is anything but "Gros" with its delicate nose and well-formed palate. The Noblesse du Petit Manseng '92 (120) is an equally tempting dry white wine with an overripe nose (quince pâté) and unctuous palate with dry notes of tabacco and lichen which improves as it persists.

Reception Henri Ramonteu is as exuberant as his wines. Don't miss the old half-timbered cellar.

How to get there *(Map 15): From Jurançon towards Laroin, Tarsacq and Abos via D2. Exit from Monein towards Navarrenx. Turn left after 4km towards Cardesse. The route is signposted.*

The tiny details of decoration hidden in the park at Château Jolys are like the eggs that are left to be discovered in the garden at Easter.

Château Jolys

Owner Family Latrille. **Address** 64290 Gan - Tel. 05.59.21.72.79 Fax 05.59.21.55.61. **Open** From Monday to Saturday morning, 8:30-12:30 and 13:30-17:30. **Spoken** English.

Arriving from Algeria in 1961, the Latrille family settled in a large domaine of 36 hectares where the vineyard had been uprooted. Planting started in 1964 with a slight preference for the Gros Manseng over the Petit Manseng in order to make Jurançon sec. Bottling at the domaine started in 1983. The domaine specializes in the production of young, fresh-styled dry and sweet white wines that are instantly attractive. They are wines to drink rapidly to benefit from the immediate pleasure of the fruit.

The Jurançon sec is always soft and full (due to the malolactic fermentation taking place) with a nose that is at the same time floral (honeysuckle, jasmin) and fruity (grape, citrus fruits), a palate characterized by warmer notes (milk caramel) and good length ('95: 29 F). The sweet wines run along the same lines, being light and fresh, very floral with a hint of honey ('96: 39 F). The Vendanges Tardives '94 (145 F) doesn't vary from the general house style even if the notes of overripeness are more marked.

Our choice Jurançon *moelleux* Cuvée Jean '95 (59 F). Forward nose, fine palate (honey, pineapple, apricot and dried fruits) in a light, fresh style with good persistence. Drink as an aperitif.

Reception Don't forget to see the beautiful 18th century wooden beams in the barrel cellar.

How to get there *(Map 15): From Jurançon towards Oloron. Near the Auberge du Rousset turn right. At the top of the hill turn left towards Chapelle Rousse and follow the signs.*

Here they still use the traditional method of attaching the vine to the wire with a willow shoot.

Clos Lapeyre

Supervisor Jean-Bernard Larrieu. **Address** Chapelle de Rousse 64110 Jurançon - Tel. 05.59. 21.50.80 Fax 05.59.21.51.83. **Open** From Monday to Saturday 10:00-12:00 and 14:00-18:00, Sunday by appointment. **Spoken** Espagnol.

This is a beautiful vineyard that nestles in a sloping mountain hollow, arranged in terraces, at the highest point in the appellation. It is dotted with thickets of willow and benefits from some very old vines. Following selective hand picking the grapes are pressed and the juice fermented and matured in oak barrels (80% new for the *cuvée* Sélection) on lees which adds plenty of flesh and weight to both the dry and sweet wines.

Of the sweet wines we prefer the '96 (54 F) where the Gros Manseng continues the old tradition of the appellation. The first approach is a little rough in texture but this is quickly overcome by the weight and flesh and aromatic note of exotic fruits. The *cuvée* Sélection '96 (89 F) extracts its finesse, balance and above all its weight from the Petit Manseng. The finish is lively and clean with toasted, apricot notes.

Our choice The various dry wines. The Jurançon sec '96 (41 F) for the ripe, spicy nose and fine, lifted palate with a fleshiness that comes from the ageing on lees. The *cuvée* Vitalge Vielh '95 (56 F) for the delicately powdery and spicy nose with notes of white fruits and honey and the fine, delicate palate where the weight and density are highlighted by a lively acidity. To drink.

Reception Beautiful barrel cellar and collection of old implements. The domaine also offers farm products from local artisan friends (honey, foie gras, preserves).

How to get there *(Map 15): From Jurançon towards Oloron. Turn right near the Auberge du Rousset, climb the hill and follow the signs.*

A typical Jurançon vineyard with the vines trained high.

Clos Thou

Owner Henri Lapouble-Laplace. **Address** Chemin Larredya, 64110 Jurançon - Tel. and fax 05.59. 06.08.60. **Open** From Monday to Saturday, 9:00-12:00 and 13:30-19:00.

From earliest days Henri and his father Raoul were partisans of Petit Manseng. The virtues of this variety for the production of sweet wines can now be discovered throughout the appellation, so they can be proud of their vineyard which was planted in 1974 with 70% Petit Manseng and are now old vines. Another unusual thing about this tiny domaine (5.3 hectares planted of which 4 hectares are in production) is the important percentage of Petit Courbu (50%) used in the dry white wines. This gives them a distinct, round, mineral style, as found in the '96 (35 F). The Jurançon *moelleux* '96 (approx. 45 F), produced from Gros Manseng, is a jolly, fat, round wine which is a little more lively than in the two previous vintages. The Délice de Thou '95 (70 F, limited quantity) is a sweet wine which combines the roundness of the Petit Courbu with the finesse and liveliness of the Petit Manseng.

Our choice Jurançon *moelleux* Suprême de Thou. The '95 (90 F) is delightful for its finesse and purity on the nose, generosity, power and sweetness on a lively palate and notes of white fruits and spice on the finish. The '96 (approx. 70 F) will be crisp but fleshy, spicy and raisined. If there is still some of the '94 75 F) don't hesitate as it is concentrated and filled with notes of crystallized fruits. To drink or cellar.

Reception Excellent and attentive. In a little tasting room installed in the oldest part of the house.

How to get there *(Map 15): From Jurançon towards Oloron. Turn right near the Auberge du Rousset, climb the hill and follow the signs.*

Charles Hours.

Clos Uroulat

Owner Charles Hours. **Address** 64360 Monein - Tel. 05.59.21.46.19 Fax 05.59.21.46.90. **Open** By appointment. **Spoken** English, Spanish.

Come here in the evening when the sun stes over the Pyrenees. The Clos Uroulat ("the chestnut") is no longer the prickly husk of a chestnut but a gentle universe. Charles Hours has chosen simplicity (or rigor ?) by proposing only two *cuvées*, one dry and the other sweet. Since he enjoys eating he gives preference to the structure of his wines and is wary of deceptive seasoning. Since 1989 the wines have been vinified in wood without the oak overpowering them. They are subtle in style and demand a certain concentration to be appreciated. The Jurançon *moelleux* '95 (70 F) is raisined and fruityCome here in the evening when the sun sets over the Pyrenees. The on the nose with spicy notes. The palate is fresh, elegant, long, and persistent with notes of white fruits. In an appellation better known for its sweet wines, the dry white wines are particularly worth discovering here. They are full, elegant and reserve a number of surprises for those who are patient.

Our choice Jurançon *sec* Cuvée Marie '95 (45 F). The wine is aromatically very fine with notes of honey and hazelnut on the nose. The palate is clean, and elegant with a little well-placed weight. Seductive, it is full of promises that will be kept. It will evolve on drier notes like the '92 (vervain, lichen, lime-tree). Age a little.

Reception Simple. At the cellar.

How to get there *(Map 15): From Jurançon towards Laroin, Tarsacq, Abos and Monein via D2. From the center of Monein towards Navarrenx (2km).Turn left at the first crossroads, climb the hill and follow the signs.*

The château, presently being restored.

Château d'Aydie

Owner Family Laplace. **Address** 64330 Aydie - Tel. 05.59.04.03.96 Fax 05.59.04.01.53. **Open** Every day, 8:00-12:00 and 14:00-20:00 – E-mail: Pierre.Laplace@wanadoo.fr. **Spoken** English, Spanish. **Credit cards** Visa, Eurocard, MasterCard.

A large domaine of 45 hectares which, although far from science fiction, is approaching a return to the future. This means a return to using traditional methods of viticulture and harvesting (reasoned treatment against fungal diseases and parasites, harvesting by hand for the Tannat and white varieties, long period of maceration with *pigeage*) in order to produce great wines. The red wines are aged in oak barrels (new oak and 14 months maturation for the Château, seasoned oak and six to eight months for the *cuvée* Odé d'Aydie). The emphasis for the sweet wines is placed on the Petit Manseng, the best grape variety in the region. They are aged on lees which are regularly stirred (barrel fermentation in new oak for the Château, vat and seasoned oak for the *cuvée* Fleury Laplace). Apart from our choice the reds are particularly successful. The Fleury Laplace '95 (28 F) is supple and fruity. The Frédéric Laplace '94 (36 F) is powerful and concentrated. The Château d'Aydie '94 (52 F) is rigorous and full. Of the sweet wines take the Pacherenc du Vic-Bilh Château '95 (46 F: 50 cent.) for its exotic nose, weight on the palate and lively finish.

Our choice Madiran *cuvée* Château '95 (55 F). The nose is open and ripe with notes of coffee. The palate is elegant and silky with notes of black fruits, and a fine and well-integrated oakiness. The '96, tasted during maturation, will perhaps be superior due to its weight.

Reception Good. At the cellar.

***How to get there** (Map 16): From Madiran towards Riscle via D164. Turn left after 2km towards Garlin and Aydie via D548. The cellar is on the left a little after the château. Signposted.*

Didier Barré.

Domaine Berthoumieu

Owner Didier Barré. **Address** 32400 Viella - Tel. 05.62.69.74.05 Fax 05.62.69.80.64. **Open** From Monday to Saturday, 9:00-12:00 and 14:00-18:00.

There have been vine-growers here since 1850 and the oldest vines date from the beginning of the century. This was still perhaps a little too young for Didier Barré's father, Louis, who placed his prestige *cuvée* under the patronage of Charles de Batz. "Who was Charles de Batz ?" I hear you ask. He was d'Artagnan and the wines he evokes carry themselves well in a fight.

The domaine produced two lovely sweet wines in '95. The Charles de Batz (43 F), harvested in November, is all spice and fruit (medlar, peach) on the nose with an elegant, toasted palate which has a hint of honey and a crisp finish. The Symphonie d'Automne (46,50 F: 50 centiliters) was harvested in December. The nose is intense (concentrated pineapple, white peach), and the palate full. The wine needs to age a little longer to allow the oak, which is still present, to mellow.

Our choice Madiran Charles de Batz '94 (48 F). The nose has notes of black fruits and new leather with a hint of vanilla. The palate is full, the structure powerful and robust with plenty of depth and length. The tannins are present but the wine is not hard. The '95 promises to be the same style with fine, dense, extract and silky tannins. To age at least five years.

Reception Attentive. Pretty little barrel cellar.

***How to get there** (Map 16): From Madiran towards Maumusson-Laguian via Viella. Turn right 1km before the village (signposted) and follow the signs.*

The old convent of Maumusson.

Domaine Capmartin

Owner Guy Capmartin. **Address** Le Couvent, 32400 Maumusson-Laguian - Tel. 05.62.69.87.88 Fax 05.62.69.83.07. **Open** From Monday to Saturday, 9:00-13:00 and 14:00-19:00.

In 1986 Guy Capmartin settled here on 7.5 hectares of vineyard planted mainly (80%) with red grape varieties. Through long maceration (up to a month) and fermentation at high temperatures he produces robust, tannic wines but always with fine extract.

The '94 Madirans are presently on sale while the '95s are still maturing. We preferred the 95s, which are fuller and rounder, for earlier drinking, allowing the '94s time to age. There will also be some good '96s with the same weight and fullness as the '95s but with a little less concentration. The dry, white Pacherenc du Vic-Bilh '95 (approx. 20 F) is fruity and long. The '96 will be richer and livelier. In Madiran, the Tradition '94 (19 F) is spicy and tannic, the '95 round and fruity. The Vieilles Vignes (produced to 70% from Tannat vines that survived phylloxera and Cabernet) is dense and tannic but with full, ripe tannins (28 F). Of the sweet wines there is an exotic, balanced '96 (44 F)

Our choice Madiran Cuvée du Couvent '94 (37 F). Produced from 90% Tannat and aged in oak barrels (half new and half one year). The nose is very toasted, still marked by the oak ageing, but the fruit is present. The palate is concentrated, fine, and tannic without being dry. The wine needs to age longer. The '95 will be along the same lines.

Reception Good. In a small cellar.

How to get there *(Map 16): From Madiran towards Riscle via D164. Turn left after 7km towards Maumusson via D136. The cellar is in the village on the right just before the church.*

Alain Oulié.

Domaine du Crampilh

Supervisor Alain Oulié. **Address** 64350 Aurions-Idernes - Tel. 05.59.04.00.63 Fax 05.59.04.04.97. **Open** From Monday to Friday, 8:00-12:00 and 14:00-18:00.

The Oulié family have kept the tradition of mixed farming. While Alain and one of his sons, Bruno, look after the vines and the cellar the other son, Eric, cultivates cereal crops. The family remains attached to traditional viticulture and the Tannat grape variety that represents 55% of the plantings at the 28 hectare domaine. A third is used in the basic wine but the Tannat is unblended in the *cuvée* Baron, which is aged in new oak barrels, and which is tannic and requires a certain amount of ageing. The basic *cuvée* '94 (30 F) is round and fruity on the attack but still a little severe on the finish. The '95 will be more flattering on the palate.

The dry white wines, which are full with notes of roasted almonds, are conspicuous for the dominance of the Arrufiac grape variety in the blend. In the sweet *moelleux* style there is an attractive '95 (45 F: 50 centiliters) with exotic nose, lightly oaked but fleshy palate, and good length with notes of dried fruits.

Our choice Madiran Vieilles Vignes '90 (40 F). This is a Tannat which has had time to age and the tannins to mellow. The nose evokes moist earth but the structure is still vigorous. On the palate there are some amazing notes of ground coffee which owe nothing to the oak ageing. This is a balanced wine with loads of crunchy extract which can be drunk now.

Reception Good. In a building surrounded by vines.

How to get there *(Map 16): Leave Madiran following the signs for the Cave de Crouseilles. Turn right at the bottom of the hill towards Arrosès and Aurions-Idernes then follow the signs.*

The old game of *quilles* (skittles) at Château Bouscassé.

Château Montus et Château Bouscassé

Supervisor Alain Brumont. **Cellarmaster** Alain Dutilh. **Address** 32400 Maumusson-Laguian - Tel. 05.62.69.74.67 Fax 05.62.69.70.46. **Open** From Monday to Saturday, 8:00-12:00 and 14:00-18:00. **Spoken** English, German. **Credit cards** Visa, Eurocard, MasterCard.

Alain Brumont is playing at being Pharaoh and at the moment is building an immense cellar at Montus. But he is not yet ready to be embalmed or to fall asleep at the pyramid of his success. The same passion for wine still flows through his veins. The range of wines is extremely varied, from dry white Pacherenc du Vic-Bilh to red Madiran, not forgetting the *moelleux.* They all merit interest. The '95s are particularly successful. Even Château Bouscassé, often austere, has a velvety touch in the *cuvée* Classique (42 F) and is fruity and smoky on the nose and silky and delicious on the palate. The Vieilles Vignes (74 F) is fine, fruity, and very long and elegant with beautifully mellow oak. Of the dry white wines, choose the Pacherenc du Vic-Bilh '95 (62 F), a wine made entirely from Petit Courbu with plenty of form and charm and a fullness and freshness that makes it deliciously exotic. From the different *moelleux* choose the *cuvée* Frimaire '95 (183 F: 50 centiliters) for its fullness, notes of crystallized fruits and above all its balance. With 13°5 alcohol and 110 grams/liter of sugar the wine remains light and fine.

Our choice Madiran Château Montus Prestige '95 (110 F). For the very ripe, fine, elegant nose and the opulent, satiny palate that mixes black fruits with coffee. To age.

Reception Presently at Château Bouscassé. Don't forget to see the *quillet* (skittle-room) and the barrel cellar (2,800 barrels). When the new barrel cellar at Château Montus is finished it will hold 3,500 barrels !

How to get there *(Map 16): From Madiran towards Riscle via D164. Turn left after 7km towards Maumusson via D136 and follow the signs.*

LOIRE VALLEY

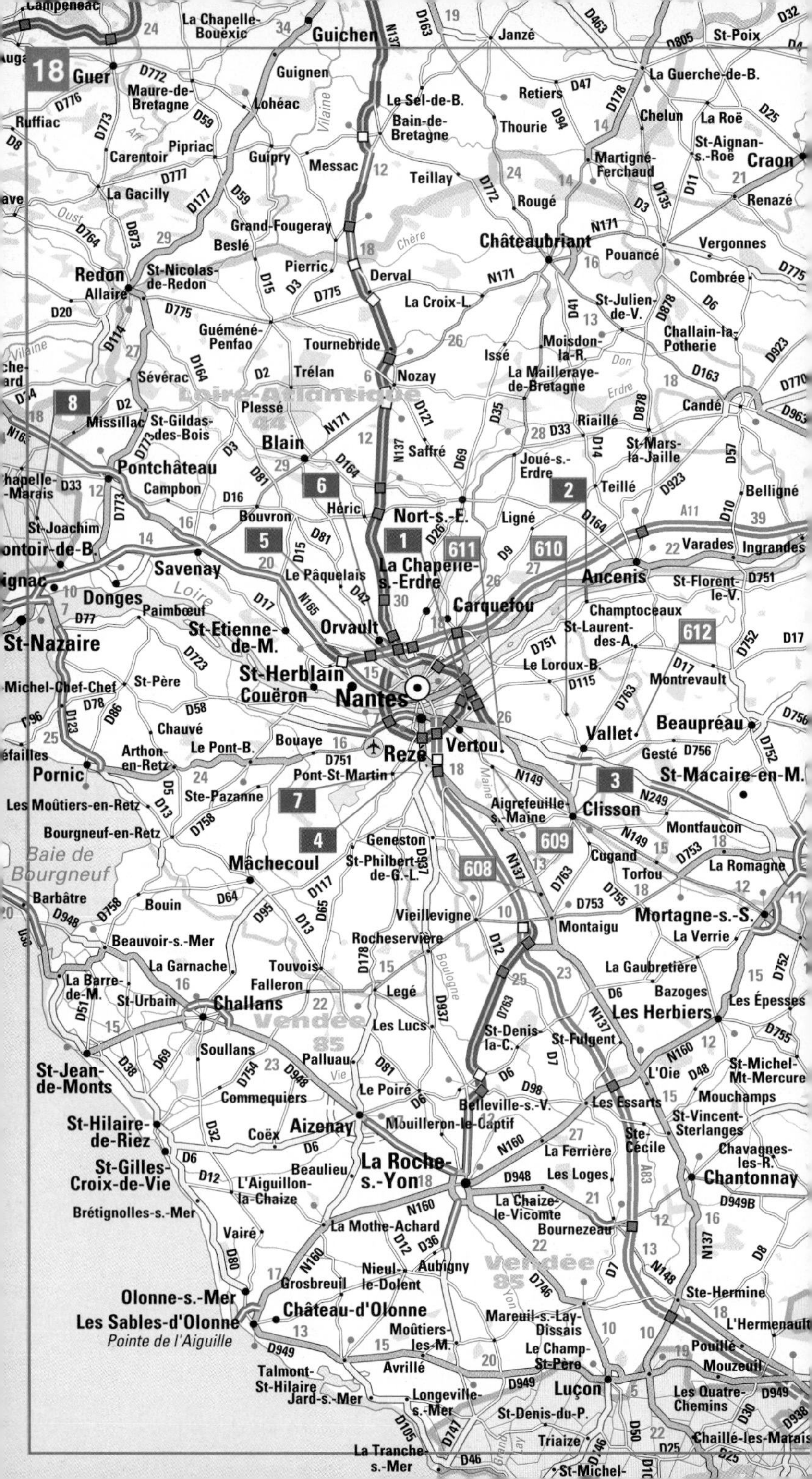

18
Campeneac
La Chapelle-Bouëxic
Guichen
Janzé
St-Poix
Guer
Maure-de-Bretagne
Guignen
Lohéac
Le Sel-de-B.
Bain-de-Bretagne
Retiers
La Guerche-de-B.
Chelun
La Roë
Ruffiac
Thourie
St-Aignan-s.-Roë
Carentoir
Pipriac
Guipry
Messac
Martigné-Ferchaud
Craon
Teillay
La Gacilly
Rougé
Renazé
Grand-Fougeray
Besié
Châteaubriant
Pouancé
Vergonnes
Redon
St-Nicolas-de-Redon
Pierric
Derval
Combrée
Allaire
La Croix-L.
St-Julien-de-V.
Challain-la-Potherie
Guémené-Penfao
Tournebride
Moisdon-la-R.
Issé
La Meilleraye-de-Bretagne
Sévérac
Trélan
Nozay
Candé
Loire-Atlantique
44
8
Missillac
St-Gildas-des-Bois
Plessé
Riaillé
Blain
Saffré
St-Mars-la-Jaille
Pontchâteau
Joué-s.-Erdre
Teillé
Belligné
Chapelle-Marais
Campbon
6
2
Héric
Nort-s.-E.
Ligné
St-Joachim
Bouvron
A11
Varades
Ingrandes
Montoir-de-B.
5
1
611
610
Savenay
La Chapelle-s.-Erdre
Ancenis
St-Florent-le-V.
Donges
Le Pâquelais
Carquefou
St-Nazaire
Paimbœuf
Champtoceaux
St-Etienne-de-M.
Orvault
St-Laurent-des-A.
612
St-Herblain
Le Loroux-B.
Montrevault
Michel-Chef-Chef
St-Père
Couëron
Nantes
Chauvé
Vallet
Beaupréau
Pornic
Arthon-en-Retz
Le Pont-B.
Bouaye
Rezé
Vertou
Geste
St-Macaire-en-M.
Pont-St-Martin
3
Les Moûtiers-en-Retz
Ste-Pazanne
7
Aigrefeuille-s.-Maine
Clisson
Montfaucon
Bourgneuf-en-Retz
4
Geneston
609
Baie de Bourgneuf
Machecoul
St-Philbert-de-G.-L.
608
Cugand
Torfou
La Romagne
Barbâtre
Bouin
Vieillevigne
Mortagne-s.-S.
Montaigu
Beauvoir-s.-Mer
Rocheservière
La Verrie
La Garnache
Touvois
La Gaubretière
La Barre-de-M.
Falleron
Bazoges
St-Urbain
Challans
Legé
Les Herbiers
Les Épesses
Vendée
85
Les Lucs
St-Denis-la-C.
St-Fulgent
Soullans
Palluau
St-Michel-Mt-Mercure
St-Jean-de-Monts
L'Oie
Mouchamps
Le Poiré
Commequiers
Belleville-s.-V.
Les Essarts
St-Hilaire-de-Riez
Aizenay
Mouilleron-le-Captif
St-Vincent-Sterlanges
Coëx
Ste-Cécile
La Ferrière
Chavagnes-les-R.
St-Gilles-Croix-de-Vie
Beaulieu
La Roche-s.-Yon
Les Loges
Chantonnay
L'Aiguillon-la-Chaize
La Chaize-le-Vicomte
Brétignolles-s.-Mer
La Mothe-Achard
Bournezeau
Vairé
Aubigny
Olonne-s.-Mer
Grosbreuil
Nieul-le-Dolent
Ste-Hermine
Les Sables-d'Olonne
Château-d'Olonne
Mareuil-s.-Lay-Dissais
L'Hermenault
Pointe de l'Aiguille
Moûtiers-les-M.
Le Champ-St-Père
Pouillé
Talmont-St-Hilaire
Avrillé
Mouzeuil
Jard-s.-Mer
Longeville-s.-Mer
Luçon
Les Quatre-Chemins
St-Denis-du-P.
Triaize
Chaillé-les-Marais
La Tranche-s.-Mer
St-Michel-
Vilaine
Loire
Oust
Chère
Erdre
Don
Maine
Boulogne
Vie
Yon
Lay

Vaiges
St-Denis-d'Orques
Coulaines
Le Mans
Champagné
19
Entrammes
Cossé-le-Vivien
Brûlon
Loué
Coulans-s.-Gée
Allonnes
Meslay-du-Maine
Chemiré-le-G.
Parigné-l'Evêque
Quelaines
Auvers-le-H.
Arnage
Mayenne
Bouessay
La Suze-s.-S.
Mulsanne
Bazouges
Grez-en-Bouère
Solesmes
St-Mars-d'O.
Château-Gontier
Sablé-s.-S.
Malicorne-s.-Sarthe
Cérans-F.
Chemazé
Bierné
Ecommoy
Sarthe
La Fontaine-St-M.
Daon
Miré
Précigné
Pontvallain
Jupilles
Segré
Mayet
Châteauneuf-s.-Sarthe
19
Daumeray
La Flèche
Clermont-Créans
Château-du-Loir
Oudon
Champigné
Durtal
Le Lion-d'Angers
Loir
Le Lude
Clefs
Vern-d'A.
Tiercé
Seiches
Chevіré-le-Rouge
Le Louroux-Béconnais
Montreuil-Juigné
Briollay
615
Baugé
Bécon-les-Granits
Jarzé
Avrillé
Baune
Noyant
Château-la-Vallière
St-Barthélemy-d'Anjou
Beaufort-en-V.
Mouliherne
Breil
Angers
Trélazé
Rillé
St-Georges
Les Ponts-de-Cé
Cléré-les-Pins
Montjean
Chalonnes
Brissac-Quincé
Longué-Jumelles
Les Rosiers
Gizeux
La Pommeraye
Beaulieu
Gennes
Authion
St-Martin-de-la-Place
Langeais
N.-D.-d'Allençon
Allonnes
Restigné
Thouarcé
Milly
Bourgueil
Maine-et-Loire
Chemillé
Saumur
Azay-le-R.
Jallais
Martigné-Briand
Doué-la-F.
Avoine
Vihiers
Le Puy-Notre-Dame
Fontevraud-l'Abbé
Chinon
Trémentines
Montreuil-Bellay
L'Ile-Bouchard
Vezins
Roiffé
Nuaillé
Cléré-s.-Layon
Layon
Cholet
St-Pierre-à-Champ
Les Trois-Moûtiers
Champigny-s.-V.
Maulévrier
Richelieu
Argenton-Château
Thouars
Loudun
Les Aubiers
Pas-de-Jeu
Mauléon
Moûtiers-s/s-Argenton
Argent
Martaizé
Jaulnay
Deux-Sèvres
79
La Butte
Moncontour
Leigné
St-Varent
Orches
St-Jouin-de-Marnes
Bressuire
Sossais
Pouzauges
Cerizay
Airvault
Boussais
Chiché
La Forêt-s.-Sèvre
La Grimaudière
Lencloître
Chanteloup
St-Loup-Lamairé
Mirebeau
Amailloux
Moncoutant
Vendeuvre-du-Poitou
Mouilleron-en-P.
St-Pierre-du-Chemin
Clessé
Thénezay
Vouzailles
La Châtaigneraie
Neuvy-Bouin
Jaunay-Clan
Neuville-de-P.
Thouet
La Ferrière-en-P.
Parthenay
Villiers
L'Absie
Loge-Fougereuse
Secondigny
Vouillé
Buxerolles
Poitiers
Vasles
Fenioux
Fontenay-le-Comte
Vausseroux
Benassay
Coulonges-s.-l'Autize
Mazières-en-Gâtine
St-Benoît
St-Julien-l'Ars
Champdeniers-St-Denis
Ménigoute
St-Hilaire-des-Loges
Sanxay
La Villedieu-du-Clain
Fleuré
Villiers-en-Plaine
Jazeneuil
St-Maixent-l'Ecole
Lusignan
Pamproux
Vivonne

20

Connerre D302 Vibraye D117 D921 St-Agil Droué D141 D15 Châteaudun D923 Lutz-en-Dunois Patay D3 Sougy D5

Lavaré 28

Berfay Loire 18 11

32 Cloyes-s.-le-Loir Prénouvellon St-Péravy-la-Colombe D955

N157 D1 Mondoubleau N10 La Ferté-Villeneuil D2

D34 15 D921 24 D924 Charsonville 17

St-Calais 20 Binas Ingré

Tresson Épuisay Les Fontaines Morée La Chapel St-M.

D13 Savigny-s.-B. 16 N157 13 N157 Ouzouer-le-Marché

Le Grand-Lucé Bessé-s.-Br. D5 652 19 St-Léonard-en-B. D104 15

St-Pierre-du-Lorouër 654 D9 17 Cravant Cléry-St-André 20

D303 La Bonaventure Oucques

Pont-s.-B. Troo Vendôme D917 D110 Marchenoir Meung-s.-L 20

653 Beaugency

Loir Montoire-s.-le-Loir D917 D957 Selommes 644 29 Lailly-en-Val D11

La Chartre-s.-le-Loir N10 Pontijou 17

D108 26 Champigny-en-B. 645 23 Loire

D11 D62 D29 D47 D9 28 Mer St-Laurent-N.

Chemillé-s.-Dême 662 663 664 St-Amand-Longpré 17 Ligny-le-R. D61

N138 665 666 Loir-et-Cher Gombergean 20 La Ferté-St-Cyr

D2 La Ferrière Villechauve A10 31 41 N152

Beaumont-la-Ronce D766 Château-Renault 18 Herbault Blois Chambord Dhuizon La Marolle-en-S.

28 D47 D766 17 Vineuil

D68 42 Neuvy D925

20 Neuillé-Pont-P. 43 N10 27 30 661 646 16 5 Bracieux D13 D923

12 44 40 Beuvron Neung-s.-B.

30 E05 Onzain 15 Cour-Cheverny D119 D922

D959 D29 Monnaie 660 D31 N152 17 D13

La Membrolle-s.-C. 35 23 Chaumont-s.-L. D956

D751 D764 658 Contres Mur-de-Sologne Millança

Fondettes Tours 27 24

St-Pierre-des-C. Amboise D30 17 14

Joué-lès-T. Montlouis D61 D114 Pontlevoy D675 Chémery D765 Romorantin-Lanthenay

Villandry Chambray Chenonceaux Montrichard

6 N143 21 St-Romain-s.-Cher 659 Sauldre

14 Bléré N76 16 16 D724 Villefranch

Indre 38 Montbazon Cormery N76 12 Selles-s.-C. 17

D57 Indre-et-Loire D58 D31 D764 St-Aignan D35

25 St-Branchs Rochette 656 Céré D17 Chabris D51

34 N10 37 Le Liège 15 D4

A10 26 22 Genillé D89 D81 D675 D37 Nahon D25 D922

St-Épain 655 657 D58 Lucay-le-Mâle Valençay D68

Manthelan Loches D960 Poulaines

Ste-Maure-de-Touraine D760 D9 D11 D15 D956 Graça

Indre D960

D50 D31 Loché-s.-Indrois Ecueillé A20

Vienne 19 D59 D675 D8 21 Vatan

Verneuil-s.-Indre

La Celle-St-Avant Ligueil D59

D750 D31 Ferrière-Larçon 31 23 Moulins-s.-Céphon D926

Les Ormes

30 Creuse Descartes Châtillon-s.-I. Levroux 30

Vellèches D58 Pellevoisin Brion

N10 D60 D50 D41 St-Flovier Indre D11

Dangé-St-Romain Le Grand-Pressigny 36 D926 D8

N143 N20 Neuvy-Pailloux

15 D975 Villiers 23 19

Barrou D750 Buzançais N143 22 D956 A20

Châtellerault D725 Preuilly-s.-Claise Azay-le-F. Mézières-en-B. D926 Déols N151

Coussay St-Michel-en-Brenne Villedieu-s.-Indre Châteauroux Vo

D14 Yzeures-s.-Creuse

La Roche-Posay Vendœuvres D925

D749 D5 D6 D17 D11 N20 15

D14 Lureuil Méobecq

D3 Pleumartin D6 D975 Le Poinçonnet

Vouneuil-s.-V. Douadic Migné Lothiers Arthon

Bonneuil-Matours Nuret-le-Ferron 27 Bouzanne

D749 La Puye D2 Fontgombault D27 N151 D990

D1 Ruffec N151 24

Vienne D5 10 Bouesse Neuvy-St-Sépulchre

86 Le Blanc 30 D927 St-Gaultier

Lavoux 19 17 N151 17 21

Chauvigny St-Savin D975 Bélâbre Argenton-s.-C.

D54 D11 D10 Cluis

Valdivienne Leignes-s.-F. Anglin Prissac D1

Jouhet

D749 D5 La Trimouille 22 Orsennes D990

18 Montmorillon D121 D36

St-Laurent-le-Jourdes Lussac-les-Châteaux D727 Tilly Chaillac Eguzon

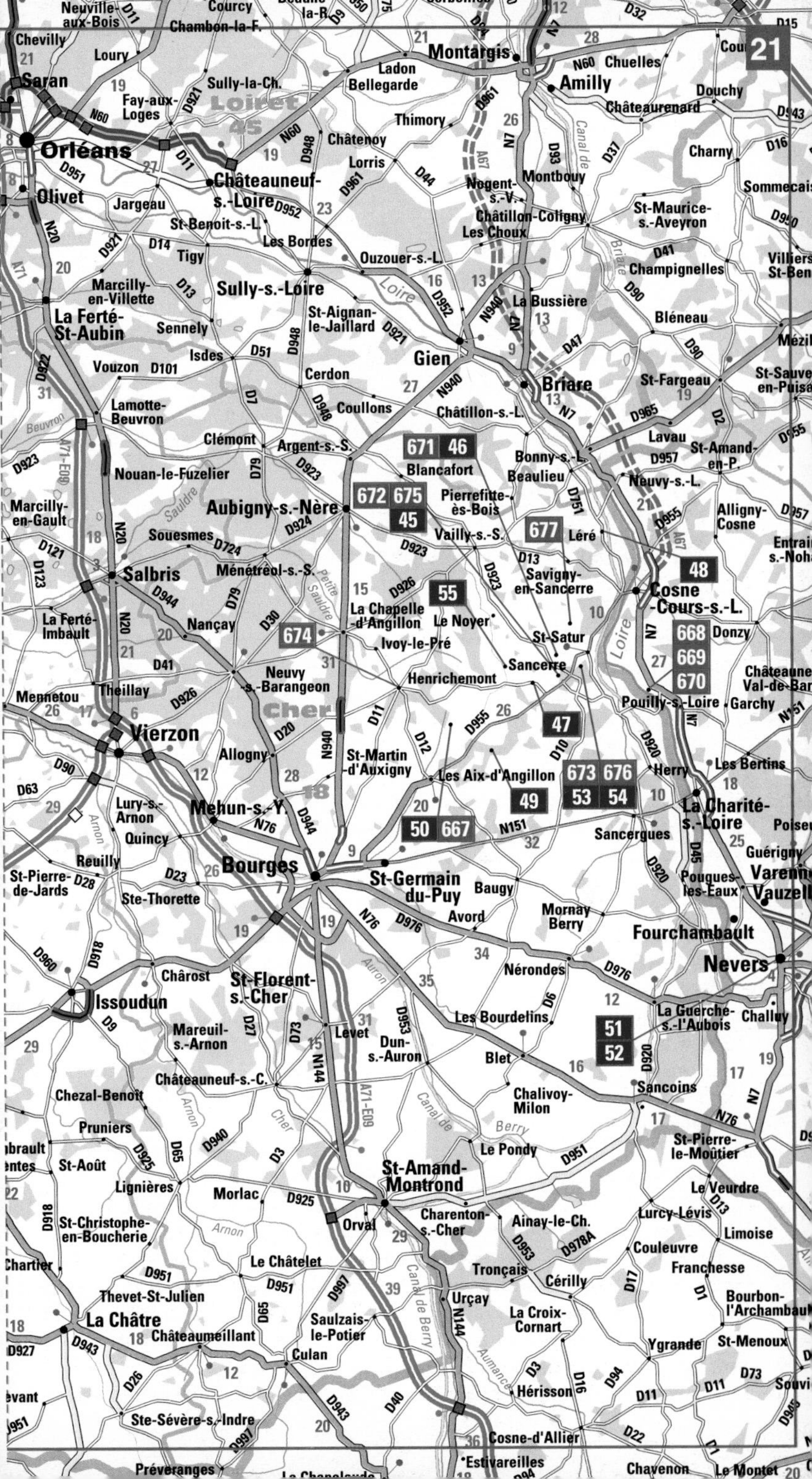

21
Neuville-aux-Bois
Courcy
Beaune-la-R.
Corbeilles
Chambon-la-F.
Chevilly
Loury
Montargis
Ladon
Bellegarde
Chuelles
Amilly
Douchy
Saran
Sully-la-Ch.
Fay-aux-Loges
Loiret
45
Thimory
Châteaurenard
Orléans
Châtenoy
Lorris
Charny
Olivet
Jargeau
Châteauneuf-s.-Loire
Nogent-s.-V.
Montbouy
Sommecaise
St-Benoit-s.-L.
Les Bordes
Châtillon-Coligny
Les Choux
St-Maurice-s.-Aveyron
Tigy
Ouzouer-s.-L.
Champignelles
Villiers-St-Benoît
Marcilly-en-Villette
Sully-s.-Loire
Loire
La Bussière
La Ferté-St-Aubin
St-Aignan-le-Jaillard
Bléneau
Sennely
Isdes
Gien
Mézilles
Vouzon
Cerdon
Briare
St-Fargeau
St-Sauveur-en-Puisaye
Lamotte-Beuvron
Coullons
Châtillon-s.-L.
Beuvron
Clémont
Argent-s.-S.
Lavau
St-Amand-en-P.
Blancafort
Bonny-s.-L.
Nouan-le-Fuzelier
Beaulieu
Neuvy-s.-L.
Marcilly-en-Gault
Aubigny-s.-Nère
Pierrefitte-ès-Bois
Alligny-Cosne
Sauldre
Vailly-s.-S.
Léré
Entrains-s.-Nohain
Souesmes
Salbris
Ménétréol-s.-S.
Petite Sauldre
Savigny-en-Sancerre
Cosne-Cours-s.-L.
La Chapelle-d'Angillon
Le Noyer
La Ferté-Imbault
Nançay
Ivoy-le-Pré
St-Satur
Donzy
Neuvy-s.-Barangeon
Henrichemont
Sancerre
Loire
Châteauneuf-Val-de-Bargis
Mennetou
Theillay
Pouilly-s.-Loire
Garchy
Cher
Vierzon
Allogny
St-Martin-d'Auxigny
Les Aix-d'Angillon
Herry
Les Bertins
18
Lury-s.-Arnon
Mehun-s.-Y.
La Charité-s.-Loire
Arnon
Quincy
Sancergues
Poiseux
Reuilly
Bourges
Guérigny
St-Pierre-de-Jards
St-Germain-du-Puy
Baugy
Pougues-les-Eaux
Varennes-Vauzelles
Ste-Thorette
Avord
Mornay-Berry
Fourchambault
Nérondes
Nevers
Chârost
St-Florent-s.-Cher
Auron
Issoudun
La Guerche-s.-l'Aubois
Challuy
Mareuil-s.-Arnon
Les Bourdelins
Levet
Dun-s.-Auron
Blet
Châteauneuf-s.-C.
Sancoins
Chezal-Benoît
Chalivoy-Milon
Arnon
Cher
Canal de Berry
Pruniers
St-Pierre-le-Moûtier
St-Août
Le Pondy
St-Amand-Montrond
Lignières
Le Veurdre
Morlac
St-Christophe-en-Boucherie
Orval
Charenton-s.-Cher
Ainay-le-Ch.
Lurcy-Lévis
Limoise
Arnon
Couleuvre
Le Châtelet
Tronçais
Franchesse
Cérilly
Thevet-St-Julien
Urçay
Bourbon-l'Archambault
La Châtre
Saulzais-le-Potier
La Croix-Cornart
Châteaumeillant
Ygrande
St-Menoux
Culan
Canal de Berry
Aumance
Hérisson
Souvigny
Ste-Sévère-s.-Indre
Cosne-d'Allier
Préveranges
Estivareilles
Chavenon
Le Montet

LOIRE VALLEY

INTRODUCTION

Of the groups of travelers in the Loire one can distinguish *homo touristicus* and *homo vinus* by the respective movement of their noses. The former points his towards turrets, buttresses and the machicolations of the numerous monumental châteaux which stand out as landmarks along the banks of the Loire and in the history of France. Contrary to this, *homo vinus* passes the day with his nose inclined over a glass of wine either pale in color like the face of a princess from Muscadet, golden like the throne of a Valois from Layon or purple like the robes of a cardinal from Chinon. Each has his own journey of discovery. Sometimes, *touristicus* turns into *vinus* (or vice versa), proof of total allegiance to the region. Through impromptu excursions on weekends or repeated detours when taking a holiday break it is easy to become more and more curious and enamored with this noble realm.

In the Central Loire, a countryside of calcareous valleys, the leading vineyards of Pouilly-Fumé (right bank) and Sancerre (left bank) fight a Sauvignon duel witnessed by Menetou-Salon, Reuilly and Quincy. Between the Loire and Cher rivers, Touraine combines lifestyle with the pleasures of life. Its three colors of wine are stamped with the Loire's saintly trinity : freshness, fruitiness and delicacy, with prices as sweet as the air of this garden of France. Further west, between the Loire and the Vienne, in the footsteps of the giant Gargantua, there is a desire to shout, like Rabelais' hero, "*A boyre ! A boyre ! A boyre !*" ("A drink ! A drink ! A drink !"), the other trinity of the Loire. The first ray of sunshine reveals the pale colored stones of Saumur. Homo vinus knows that this calcareous rock, normally called chalk, tuffeau or tufa, provides the originality in the local wines. It is in this same soft tufa that surrounds the town that the vine plunges its roots and draws substance. In caves now transformed into cellars for ageing, this same nutritive Turonienne chalk which shapes the habitat and personality of the *crus* also increases the freshness and natural finesse of the wines. Beyond Angers, Anjou leaves Savennières to watch over the river from the right bank in order to better distance itself from the Loire and extend its red and, in particular, its sweet white vineyards as far as the sources of the Layon. Before leaving the waters of the Loire to their oceanic destiny there is one final stop in the Pays Nantais, a region of windmills without sails and rounded hills lashed by sea breezes where Muscadet, a white wine as crystal clear as the soils, is given life.

LOIRE VALLEY APPELLATIONS

The Loire Valley comprises, from west to east, four large vineyard areas: Muscadet, Anjou-Saumur, Touraine, and the Central Loire. In these northern limits for vine cultivation the region displays a staggering diversity of wines. There are 65 appellations located on a range of soils (from the schistous soils of Anjou to the sandy soils of the Sologne, not to mention the calcareous tufa of Saumur and Vouvray) with a particularly favorable climate. With a plentiful supply of localized climates these *terroirs* are attractive to a large number of grape varieties (more often than not vinified on their own) producing an extensive palette of wines. The white varieties include Melon, Chenin Blanc, Sauvignon, and Chardonnay while the reds and rosés are produced from Cabernet Franc, Pinot Noir, Gamay, Côt, Cabernet Sauvignon, and Grolleau.

The Cher is the kingdom of Sauvignon but with two capitals, Sancerre and Pouilly (where it has been given the bizarre name Fumé). The soils of the two appellations are a mix of kimmeridgian clay ("*les terres blanches*"), calcareous limestone ("*les caillottes*") and flinty-clay ("*les chailloux*"). The wines, full-bodied from the kimmeridgian clay, softer from the limestone and crisp and incisive from the flinty-clay are usually blended together and their individual styles rarely isolated. In the region of Pouilly-Fumé the Chasselas vine can still be found (formerly more planted than the Sauvignon) and produces the wine that takes the appellation Pouilly-sur-Loire. For its part, Sancerre continues to vinify the Pinot Noir (previously dominant) but the majority of these red wines do not deserve their reputation.

The vineyards of the appellation Touraine extend along the valleys of the Loire, Indre and Cher. The majority of red wines are produced from the Gamay grape, as in the Beaujolais, and sometimes from a happy blend of Gamay, Cabernet Franc or Côt. The whites are mainly Sauvignon and rarely from Chenin Blanc. Certain *terroirs* have obtained the Villages appellation. Touraine-Mesland, between Blois and Amboise, is essentially red and ages well. Touraine-Amboise also produces mainly red wines but with an easier, fruity, *primeur* character. Touraine-Azay-le-Rideau produces some good whites based on Chenin Blanc and a dainty, thirst-quenching rosé from Grolleau. Some vines still survive at Valençay, near the Cher, and south of Blois, Cheverney (red, white, and rosé) and Cour-Cheverny (only white) are two reborn appellations. The white Cheverny, produced from Sauvignon and Chardonnay, is lively, fine and to drink young. The Cour-Cheverny, produced from the Romorantin, a grape variety unknown elsewhere, is generally dry, fairly full with good length on the palate.

A few kilometers upstream towards Tours, Vouvray (right bank) and Montlouis (left bank) produce a staggering panoply of still (*sec*, *demi-sec*, and *moelleux*) and sparkling (*mousseux* and *pétillant*) white wines made from Chenin Blanc. Sometimes jolly (warm years), sometimes austere, the Pineau de la Loire, as it is known here, plays a timeless symphony for the taste buds.

In the historic triangle of Touraine's red appellations (Chinon, Bourgueil, Saint-Nicolas-de-Bourgueil) one encounters wines produced from Cabernet Franc, also

known as the Breton, which vary according to the *terroir.* Near the banks of the river and its tributaries the alluvial soils constitute an "easy" *terroir* of sand and gravel favorable to young vines which express themselves rapidly and in a flattering manner with lots of fruit and little tannin. A notch above are the classic clay-limestone hillsides. Sometimes gently sloping, sometimes abrupt, they provide the wines with a more serious, marked character. Finally, the longer ageing, tannic reds are produced on the calcareous plateau above (known as tuffeau or tufa).
Anjou-Saumur also cultivates the art of diversity with white, red, rosé, with or without bubbles, and from very dry to sweet *liquoreux.* The two most interesting categories are the reds and sweet whites. Among the four sweet white wines produced from late harvested Chenin Blanc, Coteaux-du-Layon, the most widespread, has seen a spectacular increase in the level of quality since the end of the 1980s. Bonnezeaux and Quarts-de-Chaume play their rôle as *Grands Crus* in a more timid fashion. As for the Coteaux-de-l'Aubance, it produces fine, aromatic *moelleux.* The originality of Anjou is partly derived from its schistous soils which provide a mineral taste for the whites and for the reds (Anjou, Anjou-Villages), produced from Cabernet Franc, plenty of structure and good ageing potential (two to eight years). The Saumur chalk, also known as tufa, supplies more fruitiness and finesse to the wines without harming the potential for ageing. The best example, when made correctly, is Saumur-Champigny and in white the delicious Saumur and Coteaux-de-Saumur (*moelleux*) which have incomparable breed. Since the 19th century Saumur has also acquired a strong reputation for the production of sparkling wines.
In the vineyards of the Pays Nantais the three Muscadet appellations are characterized by their soils: Muscadet de Sèvre & Maine (gneiss, granite), Muscadet des Coteaux-de-la-Loire (schist), and Muscadet (silt and sand). Here, the wine carries the name of the grape variety, Muscadet or "Melon de Bourgogne," under the direct influence of the Atlantic Ocean (40 kilometers away). The Coteaux-de-la-Loire is often more full-bodied and drier than the Sèvre & Maine which is finer, matures well in bottle and when aged "*sur lie*" (on its lees) conserves a seductive bouquet and freshness. (Note : A fourth appellation, Muscadet Côtes de Grand Lieu, has recently been added.)

BUYING IN THE LOIRE VALLEY

In Sancerre and Pouilly Fumé, the simple Sauvignons aged in vat and bottled in spring for drinking in the summer, exist alongside wines that have been aged for a year, sometimes in barrel, produced from the oldest vines and which have a real complexity. The second style of wine evolves remarkably well over a period of ten years. Menetou-Salon, Reuilly, and Quincy are destined for rapid consumption.
In general, the wines from Touraine are to be bought within a year and consumed within two. The wines from Cheverny, produced from Romorantin, are agreeable young but come into their own, in the good vintages, after a short period of ageing (four to six years). Vouvray and Montlouis, in their youthful stage, seduce with the aromas of fresh fruits and flowers and trees of the region, then evolve to attain their apogee after ten to 25 years with smoky, earthy notes, sometimes truffle, but always with a hint of fruit and *confit.* Chinon, Bourgueil, and Saint-Nicolas-de-Bourgueil (the softest of the three) produced from young vines on gravel soils and vinified in vat for a fruity, easy-drinking style should be consumed young. It's bet-

ter to cellar the old vines (*vieilles vignes* is often mentioned on the label) which have generally been aged for a year in barrel and which are better appreciated with between three and 15 years bottle age.

Saumur-Champigny is a double faceted red wine. On the one hand it can be flattering, fruity, and with little tannic structure (hence its commercial success) and on the other it can be produced as a wine with good ageing potential (ten years). At Saumur one can also find some very good dry whites that are crisp and floral but where the best only really reveal themselves after ten years bottle age. Still relatively unknown, white and red (Villages for ageing) Anjou are rapidly gaining in quality and sell for between 25 F and 30 F. Between 70 F and 120 F the Coteaux-du-Layon produces sweet wines that offer superb price-pleasure value.

As for Muscadet, the wines are surprising in their youth and capable of ageing and the prices remain attractive.

Direct sales from the property are practiced by just about all the wine growers in the Loire. But be careful, these are small properties with a limited output. One vintage chases another and the good wines are often taken before the end of the year. The '95 and '96, actually on sale, are two excellent vintages. Depending on the domaine, there are soft wines, often very ripe, to drink young as well as wines to age (particularly in '96) which should be drunk after ten years for the best reds and beyond 25 years for the sweet.

AT TABLE WITH THE WINES OF THE LOIRE VALLEY

Simple fruity wines match simple, sincere dishes. The Gamays and Cabernets from Touraine work with pan-fried or grilled red meats. Avoid dishes that are too spicy. Dry (*sec*) or semi-sweet (*demi-sec*) white wines produced from Chenin Blanc go remarkably well with charcuterie (*rillon, rillette, andouillette*) and river fish. Those made from Sauvignon go with goat cheeses. If you don't want the aggressiveness of too many bubbles in your aperitif choose a fruity, thirst-quenching Vouvray *pétillant* where the pressure is less than in wines produced by the "méthode traditionnelle" like Crémant de Loire.

The sweet wines (*moelleux*) of Vouvray, Montlouis, Coteaux-du-Layon or Jasnières have all the qualities necessary to be the guideline for a meal of foie gras, roast fowl (the marriage with the crispy part of the skin is divine), roquefort (or any other creamy blue cheese), and *tarte tatin* (caramelized upside-down apple pie). Remember a young Montlouis or Coteaux-de-l'Aubance for fruit tarts or exotic desserts (made with ginger or other spices). An old vintage (Vouvray, Coteaux-du-Layon, Quarts-de-Chaume, Bonnezeaux) is marvelous with roast capon, roast pork with prunes or quail with grapes. We prefer to reserve young dry wines (Anjou, Saumur, Savennières) for fine fish (salmon, sandre, turbot) and crustaceans. With the most noble seafish dishes (lobster, scallops) you can't do better than a ten-year-old Savennières or more modestly a dry Anjou of four to five years.

MUSCADET

BASSE-GOULAINE

1 - RESTAURANT - **Villa Mon Rêve**: *Route des bords de Loire, 44115 Basse-Goulaine. Tel. 02.40.03.55.50 Fax 02.40.06.05.41.* The charm of Gérard Ryngel's cuisine lies in the dexterity with which he rejuvenates regional classics. Sumptuous list of Muscadet with some old vintages reaching back to 1947 and tasting, by the glass, of every year since 1982. Menus: 148 to 240 F.

CHAMPTOCEAUX

2 - RESTAURANT - **Les Jardins de la Forge**: *1 place des Piliers, 49270 Champtoceaux. Tel. 02.40.83.56.23 Fax 02.40.83.59.80. Closed Sun. and Mon. evenings, Tues. and Wed.* An old building that got a serious face-lift. Classic cuisine, excellent products. Attractive wine list. Menus: 160 to 405 F. A la carte: around 350 F.

CLISSON

3 - RESTAURANT - **La Bonne Auberge**: *1 rue Olivier de Clisson, 44190 Clisson. Tel. 02.40.54.01.90 Fax 02.40.54.08.48. Closed Sun. evening and Mon.* Cuisine harmonizing the flavors of products, seasonings and sauces. Impeccable service. Remarkable wine list in the Loire offering the renowned and the lesser known. Menus: 98 (lunch weekdays) to 430 F. A la carte: around 350 F

LES SORINIÈRES

4 - HOTEL-RESTAURANT - **Abbaye de Villeneuve - Restaurant l'Épicurien**: *Route de la Roche-sur-Yon, 44840 Les Sorinières. Tel. 02.40.04.40.25 Fax 02.40.31.28.45.* 18th-century buildings set in a park. Large rooms with antique furniture (450 to 1245 F). The restaurant tingles taste

buds in the monks' former library. The wine list favors Burgudy and Bordeaux over local wines. Menus: 140 to 440 F. A la carte: around 270 F.

NANTES

5 - HOTEL - **Hôtel La Pérouse**: *3 allée Duquesne, 44000 Nantes. Tel. 02.40.89.75.00 Fax 02.40.89.76.00.* A modern hotel designed by the architect Jean-Michel Wilmotte. Sober and unadorned. Rooms: 410 to 495 F. Breakfast: 50 F.

ORVAULT

6 - HOTEL-RESTAURANT - **Le domaine d'Orvault**: *Chemin du Marais-du-Cens, 44700 Orvault. Tel. 02.40.76.84.02 Fax 02.40.76.04.21. Closed noon Mon., school vacation in February.* A veritable profusion from the cuisine to the dining room to the wine cellar. The wine list plays the classics. Menus: 165 to 350 F. A la carte: around 400 F. Comfortable rooms ornately decorated, from 430 to 750 F.

PONT SAINT-MARTIN

7 - HOTEL - **Château du Plessis**: *44860 Pont-Saint-Martin. Tel. 02.40.26. 81.72 Fax 02.40.32.76.67 web: http://wwwchâteaux-france.com /~plessis.* Superb 14th-century residence with a lovely rose garden. Guest rooms (breakfast included): 600 to 800 F (1,000 to 1,200 F for 2 nights). Meals: 250 to 350 F (in all).

SAINT-JOACHIM

8 - HOTEL-RESTAURANT - **L'Auberge du Parc**: *162 Île de Fedrun, 44720 Saint-Joachim. Tel. 02.40.88.53.01 Fax 02.40.91.67.44. Closed from January 2 to February 15.* In the heart of the Brière, a bit far from the vineyard. But the cuisine, fine and inventive, and favoured by an attractive, intelligent wine list, is worth the detour. After lunch, embark (out in the garden) on a discovery of the Brière marsh by boat. Four pretty rooms (300F) in a tastefully renovated old house. Menus: 150 to 215F.

TO SEE

LE PALLET

MUSEUM - **Nantais vineyard Museum**: *82 rue Pierre Abélard, 44330 Le Pallet. Tel. 02.40.80.90.13 Fax 02.40.80. 49.81. Every day, May 1 to September 30 from 10:30 to 1 and from 2:30 to 7pm. October 1 to April 30, from 2:30 to 6pm.* Guided tour the first Sunday of each month at 4pm and every Sunday from May to September. Tasting on request (12 F). Admission: 25 F, children: 15 F.

SAINT-FIACRE-SUR-MAINE

OUTING - The cellar with sculpted

beams in the **château de Chasseloir**. Sculptures jeeringly depict vices and virtues.

A N J O U   S A U M U R

ANGERS

9 - HOTEL - **Hôtel du Mail**: *8 rue des Ursules, 49000 Angers. Tel. 02.41. 88.56.22 Fax 02.41.86.91.20.* The

welcome is curteous in this private residence in the city's center. Very quiet, with 27 recently refurbished rooms (150 to 300 F). Nice prices.

10 - RESTAURANT - **Le Relais**: *9 rue de la gare, 49100 Angers. Tel. 02.41.88. 45.51 Fax 02.41.24.75.20. Closed Sunday evening and Monday.* Genuine, high-quality cuisine (a lot of seafood) at good prices. The wine list at heavenly prices is worth the stop. 4 menus: 67 to 169 F.

11 - HOTEL-RESTAURANT - **Hôtel d'Anjou - Restaurant La Salamandre**: *1 bd du Maréchal-Foch, 49100 Angers. Restaurant Tel. 02.41.88.99.55. Hôtel Tel. 02.41.88.24.82 Fax 02.41.87.22.21. Restaurant closed Sunday.* Provincial palace with vast, elegantly decorated and recently refurbished rooms. Its restaurant is one of the best tables in Angers. Menus: 130 (lunch) to 210 F. 53 rooms: 360 to 660 F. Breakfast: 60 F.

12 - HOTEL-RESTAURANT - **Pavillon Le Quéré**: *3 bd du Maréchal-Foch, 49100 Angers. Tel. 02.41.20.00.20 Fax 02.41.20.06.20. Restaurant closed Sunday evening and Monday Reservation preferable.* A completely restored 19th-century private residence. Original fine cuisine by one of Robuchon's disciples. Very attractive wine list in the Loire. Menus: 170 to 460 F. A la carte: around 400 F. 10 perfectly comfortable rooms: 450 to 1,200 F. Breakfast: 60 F.

BEHUARD

13 - RESTAURANT - **Les Tonnelles**: *49170 Behuard. Tel. 02.41.72.21.50 Fax 02.41.72.81.10. Closed from January to 2/14; Sunday evening and Monday. In November, December and the last 2 weeks in February, open weekends and by reservation.* A heartwarming stop on an island on the Loire. This restaurant offers an arbor (reserve in summer), an excellent Anjou wine list (30 Anjous and Layons from 150 to 250 F, with some old vintages). Contemporary cuisine with careful attention paid to sauces. Menu dégustation: 285 F with wines. Irreproachable lunch menu: 120 F, except Sun. A la carte: around 230 F.

FONTEVRAUD-L'ABBAYE

14 - HOTEL-RESTAURANT - **Le prieuré Saint-Lazare**: *49590 Fontevraud-l'Abbaye. Tel. 02.41.51.73.16.* Menus: 98 to 265 F. Rooms: 290 to 470 F. Breakfast-buffet: 55 F. The restaurant is situated in the ancient cloisters around the garden. Cuisine is good, but not exceptional. The Loire valley is well represented on the wine list with fifty entries. Pleasant monastic rooms and a lovely bar.

15 - RESTAURANT - **La Licorne**: *Allée Sainte-Catherine, 49590 Fontevraud-l'Abbaye. Tel. 02.41.51.72.49 Fax 02.41.51.70.40. Closed Sunday evening and Monday and from Christmas to early January.* Lovely house, good welcome, fine cuisine with subtly prepared, flavorful dishes. Splendid wine list (thirty-seven pages!), perfectly organized, full of great vintages, where you'll find the crème de la crème in the region. Large selection of half bottles and magnums. Menus: 110 (weekdays) to 350 F. A la carte: around 300 F.

16 - BED & BREAKFAST - **Le domaine de Mestre**: *Mestré, 49590 Fontevraud-l'Abbaye. Tel. 02.41.51.75.87/02.41.51.72.32.* Rooms: 325 F. Excellent breakfast: 35 F. Dining by reserva-

tion: 140 F. 12 guest rooms on one of the Fontevraud abbey's old agricultural properties. The welcome is reserved, singles for one person are very small and walls are thin. Those looking out on the little park, on the other hand, are lovely and spacious.

LES ROSIERS-SUR-LOIRE

17 - RESTAURANT - **Auberge Jeanne de Laval**: *54 rue Nationale, 49350 Les Rosiers-sur-Loire. Tel. 02.41.51.80.17 Fax 02.41.38.04.18. Restaurant closed Monday from October to April.* Elegant setting, inventive cuisine based on regional products. Large selection of Anjou and Touraine wines, with some old vintages. Menus: 180 to 400 F. A la carte: around 300 F.

SAINT-LAMBERT DES LEVEES

18 - BED & BREAKFAST - **La Croix de la Voulte**: *Route de Boumois, 49400 Saint-Lambert des Levées. Tel. 02.41.38.46.66.* Rooms: 330 to 430 F. Good breakfast: 35 F. 4 guest rooms in a former royal hunting lodge built from the 15th to the late 17th centuries. Rooms are spacious and remarkably decorated, not overdone. Excellent welcome.

SAINT-SYLVAIN-D'ANJOU

19 - RESTAURANT - **Auberge d'Éventard**: *Jean-Pierre Maussion, Route de Paris, 49480 Saint-Sylvain-d'Anjou. Tel. 02.41.43.74.25 Fax 02.41.34.89.20. Closed Sunday evening and Monday.* Near Angers' parc des expositions, warm welcome, and a guenuine and unfaltering cuisine by Jean-Pierre Mausson (variations on Anjou pigeon) who excels in sauces. Attractive list of Anjou wines. Attentive service. Menus: 165 to 385 F. A la carte: around 350 F.

SAUMUR

20 - HOTEL - **Hôtel Anne d'Anjou**: *33 quai Mayaud, 49400 Saumur. Tel. 02.41.67.30.30 Fax 02.41.67.51.00. Closed from December 23 to January 4.* On the banks of the Loire, a building classified as a historical monument with 45 ornately decorated rooms, some of which look out on the castle (lit up at night). From 280 to 550 F.

21 - BED & BREAKFAST - **Château de Baulieu**: *Route de Chinon, 49400 Saumur. Tel. 02.41.67.69.51 Fax 02.41. 50.42.68.* Rooms: 230 and 380 F. Good breakfast: 35 F. Dining by reservation: 200 F (grill-cooking in summer: 120 F). Six guest rooms

in a small 18th-century castle with an old-fashioned charm. Pleasant park and heated pool.

22 - RESTAURANT - **Le Relais**: *31 quai Mayaud, 49400 Saumur. Tel. 02.41. 67.75.20. Open every day.* Menus: 100, 120 and 180 F. An enticing table and above all a sumptuous wine list, perfectly organized. 25 are served by the glass. Attractive selection of Loire with all the great vintages of recent years. Marvellous list of whiskies. It's possible to taste wines without dining.

TO SEE

LA HERPINIERE

OUTING - The mill, above a troglodytic cellar, surrounded by vineyards.

FONTEVRAUD

OUTING - Within the abbey's walls, don't miss the ancient Romanesque

kitchens and their admirable roof-chimneys.

MONTREUIL-BELLAY

OUTING - The castle (13th and 15th centuries) is a remarkable exemple of fortified architecture. It contains an impressive medieval kitchen. *Open from 4/1 to 11/1. Closed Tuesday except in July and August. Torch-lit tours Tuesday and Thursday by reservation. Tel. 02.41.52.33.06.*

PARNAY

OUTING - Don't miss the vineyard of Father Cristal, a winegrower who lived from 1837 to 1931. A series of parallel walls divide the vineyard. The grape vines are at the north end

and pass through the wall to find a southern exposure. That way they keep their feet cool, and their heads in the sun...

SAINT-LAMBERT-DU-LATTAY

MUSEUM - **Anjou Wine and Vineyard Museum**: *Place des Vignerons, 49750 Saint-Lambert-du-Lattay. Tel. 02.41.78.42.75. Open in April, May, June, September and October, Tuesday-Sunday from 10 to 12 and 2:30 to 6:30, and in July and August every day from 10 to 6:30.* Lively and instructive. Audiovisual showing, walking path for observing the vineyard. Adults: 24 F, children: 14 F, groups: 17 F.

SAUMUR

OUTING - **Saumur House of Wine**: *25 rue Beaurepaire, 49400 Saumur. Tel. 02.41.51.16.40. Open Monday to Saturday (except Monday from October to May and holidays) from 9 to 12:30 and from 2 to 6:30.* Tasting cellar not to be missed during a short stay in the Saumur region. Brochures, tasting and sales on the premises.

TURQUANT

OUTING - **Troglodytic site of the Grande Vigolle, owned by the Filliatreau estates**: *49730 Turquant. Tours and tasting every day from 10 to 6, from Easter to 11/1 and by reservation the rest of the year.* The

site is exceptional. Property of the Filliatreau estate, one can also taste the wines of this good winegrower-wholesaler.

TOURAINE

AMBOISE

23 - HOTEL-RESTAURANT - **Le Choiseul**: *36 quai Charles Guinot, 37400 Amboise. Tel. 02.47.30.45.45 Fax 02.47.30.46.10.* A lovely spot where the visit to the troglodytic storerooms

is not to be missed. Rooms: 480 to 1,040 F and 600 to 1,300 F depending on dates. Apartments: 1,120 to 1,360 F and 1,400 to 1,700 F depending on dates. Menus: 270 to 440 F, featuring regional culinary traditions. The menu offers half-portions.

Attractive, well-chosen wine list covering a large part of the Loire, with some good vintages.

BOURGUEIL

24 - RESTAURANT - **Auberge de Touvois**: *Route de Gizeux, 37140 Bourgueil. Tel. 02.47.97.88.81. Fax 02.47.97. 82.34. Closed Sunday evening and Monday.* A good inn devoted to regional wines (organization of tastings). Menus: 85 to 190F.

25 - BED & BREAKFAST - **Le Moulin bleu**: *37140 Bourgueil. Tel. 02.47.97. 73.13. Fax 02.47.97.79.66. Restaurant closed Tuesday evening and Wednesday.* One guest room next to the mill that looks out on the vineyard. 220 F (breakfast included). Classic dining in a dining room under the mill with menus from 85 to 195 F.

CHINON

26 - HOTEL - **Hôtel Diderot**: *4 rue Buffon, 37500 Chinon. Tel. 02.47.93.*

18.87 Fax 02.47.93.37.10. Open year-round. A charming and simply comfortable house whose rooms are currently being renovated. 28 rooms: 250 to 400 F.

27 - RESTAURANT - **Au Plaisir Gourmand**: *2 rue Parmentier, 37500 Chinon. Tel. 02.47.93.20.48 Fax 02.47.93.06.66. Closed Sunday evening and Monday, as well as in February.* Lovely dining room, and generous and precise cooking. The best Chinons are on the list. Menus: 175 to 340 F. A la carte: around 300 F.

CHOUZE-SUR-LOIRE

28 - BED & BREAKFAST - **Château des Réaux**: *37140 Chouzé-sur-Loire. Tel. 02.47.95.14.40 Fax 02.47.95. 18.34.*

A few kilometers from Bourgueil: one of the first Renaissance châteaux, residence of Gédéon Tallemant des Réaux. Lovely rooms, all different, restored over the last 20 years by the proprietor. The only disadvantage: the proximity of the train tracks, discreet but audible. From 400 to 1,100 F. Breakfast: 55 F. Meals: 250 F, but unremarkable wines.

COUR-CHEVERNY

29 - BED & BREAKFAST - **Le Béguinage**: *41700 Cour-Cheverny. Tel. 02.54.79. 29.92 Fax 02.54.79.94.59.* Large park and 6 vast guest rooms in the old, well-restored house. 290 to 360 F (250 F low-season), breakfast included.

JOUÉ-LES-TOURS

30 - RESTAURANT - **Le Noble Joué**: *86 bd*

de Chinon, 37300 Joué-les-Tours. Tel. 02.47.53.57.97 Fax 02.47.53. 24.17. Closed Sunday and Monday evening and in August. Bistro kept by a connoisseur of Touraine wines. Menus: 70 to 130 F. A la carte: around 120 F.

LE PETIT-PRESSIGNY

31 - RESTAURANT - **La Promenade**: *37350 Le Petit-Pressigny. Tel. 47.94.93.52 Fax 47.91.06.03 Closed Sunday evening and Monday and 3 weeks in January, 2 weeks in September/ October.* It's worth taking this side trip out of the vineyard to discover Jacky Dallais' cuisine and passion for vegetables. An exemplary wine list. Menus: 120 (except Sat. evening and Sun.) to 360 F.

L'ÎLE-BOUCHARD

32 - RESTAURANT - **Auberge de l'Île**: *37220 L'Île-Bouchard. Tel. 02.47.58. 51.07. Closed Sunday evening, Monday and in January.* On an island in the Vienne, 16 km east of Chinon, this respectable establishment concocts a pleasing traditional cuisine that's open to innovation. The cellar, though not exhaustive, is remarkable for its choices in red Loire wines and for its reasonable prices. 5 menus: 98 to 280 F. A la carte: around 300 F.

MARÇAY

33 - HOTEL-RESTAURANT - **Château de Marçay**: *37500 Marçay. Tel. 02.47.93. 03.47 Fax 02.47.93.45.33. Closed from 1/30 to 3/17.* A 15th-century feudal castle, terrace facing the park. Long wine list with over 500 entries. It's the " who's who " among the Loire valley's best. Menus: 150 to 385 F. Rooms: 495 to 1,660 F. Breakfast: 90 F.

MONTBAZON

34 - HOTEL-RESTAURANT - **Le Château d'Artigny**: *32 route de Monts. Tel. 02.47.34.30.30 Fax 02.47.34.30.39. Closed from late November to mid-January.* Majestic Loire valley wine list. Menus: 290 to 450 F. Rooms: 680 to 1,340 or 850 to 1,670 F depending on dates.

NOIZAY

35 - HOTEL-RESTAURANT - **Château de Noizay**: R*oute de Chançay, 37210 Noizay. Tel. 02.47.52.11.01 Fax 02.47. 52.04.64. Closed from 1/5 to 3/15.* Attractive wine list in the Loire. Menus: 150 to 360 F. Rooms: 650 to 1,300 F. Breakfast: 85 F.

PANZOULT

36 - BED & BREAKFAST - **Domaine de Beauséjour**: *37220 Panzoult. Tel. 02.47.58.64.64 Fax 02.47.95.27.13.*

On a viticultural property, 4 pretty rooms and a large, perfectly calm vacation house. Pool. Rooms: 450 F for 2 persons, house: 2,500 F to 1,800 F per week.

RESTIGNE

37 - BED & BREAKFAST - **Château Louy**: *37140 Restigné. Tel. 02.47.96.95.22.* A vast guest room in the annex of a

17th-century house. Great welcome. 290 F.

ROCHECORBON

38 - HOTEL-RESTAURANT - **Domaine des Hautes Roches**: *86 quai de la Loire. Tel. 02.47.52.88.88 Fax 02.47.52. 81.30. Closed from late January to mid-March.* A unique hotel: some of the vast rooms are troglodytic (carved into the rock). Fine table with an attractive wine list in the Loire. Menus: 150 (lunch weekdays) to 355 F. A la carte: around 400 F. 11 rooms: 600 to 1,350 F. Breakfast: 85 F.

SAINT-NICOLAS-DE-BOURGUEIL

39 - BED & BREAKFAST - **Manoir du Port Guyet**: *37140 Saint-Nicolas-de-Bourgueil. Tel. 02.47.97.82.20 Fax 02.47.97.98.98. Closed from November to March.* 3 rooms in a lovely house where Ronsard wrote his

poems, restored and classed as an historic monument. Rooms: 550 to 750 F.

SAINT-OUEN-LES-VIGNES

40 - RESTAURANT - **L'Aubinière**: *Rue Jules Gauthier, 37530 Saint-Ouen-les-Vignes. Tel. 02.47.30.15.29 Fax 02.47.30.02.44. Closed Tuesday evening and Wednesday, from November to 4/15, Sunday evening and from mid-February to mid-March.* Menus: 98 (weekdays and lunch) to 380 F. If you can put up with the often too loud music and the " cozy " decor, it's worth coming a few kilometers out from Amboise for the merry cuisine, fine and subtle, but flavorful. An attractive wine list in the Loire, with all of our favorites from Montlouis and Vouvray. Only one regret: the vintages are a bit too young.

SAINT-PATRICE

41 - HOTEL-RESTAURANT - **Château de Rochecotte**: *37130 Saint-Patrice. Tel. 02.47.96.16.16 Fax 02.47.96.90.59.* Talleyrand's last home, niched in a large park. Rooms overlooking the park that tastefully bring together old and modern furniture, from 580 to 950 F. Sumptuous dining room, fine dining and a good selection of regional wines. Menus: 195 to 295 F.

TOURS

42 - RESTAURANT - **Jean Bardet**: *7 rue Groison, 37100 Tours. Tel. 02.47.41.41.11 Fax 02.47.51.68.72. Closed Sunday evening and Monday in low-season.* The cuisine often depends on the chef's mood, and can make for a grand evening or offer a pinch of disappointment. Staggering wine list in the Loire with nearly 150 entries. Less prestigious appellations have not been looked down upon. The Montlouis and even more so the Vouvray have caught the owner's eye, and that of the wine waiter. Menus: 250 (splendid all-vegetable menu) to 750 F. Appetizing truffle menu when in season: around 800 F. Decoration of the rooms is often overly ornate, but they are comfortable: 500 to 1,900 F.

43 - RESTAURANT - **Le Charolais, chez Jean Michel**: *123 rue Colbert, 37000 Tours. Tel. 02.47.20.80.20 Fax 02.47.66.66.25. Closed Sunday and Monday lunchtime.* Excellent wine-bistro offering the classics and some finds, reasonable prices, service by the glass. Loire wines are held in honor, but the rest of France is present as well with some lovely bottles. Good bistro-style cuisine. Menu: 70 F. (lunch). A la carte: around 150 F.

44 - RESTAURANT - **La Roche Le Roy**: *55 route de Saint-Avertin, 37200 Tours. Tel. 02.47.27.22.00 Fax 02.47.28.08.39. Closed Saturday lunchtime, Sunday evening and Monday.* In a Renaissance manor, a serious offering of regional wines at smart prices. Menus: 160 (noon) to 350 F. A la carte: around 350 F.

TO SEE

ROCHECORBON

OUTING - **Cellar art**: *Domaine Bourillons-Dorléan, Rue Vaufoynard, 37210 Rochecorbon. Tel. 02.47.52.57.58. Open from May 1 to October 31.* Admission: 35 F. In a cellar: sculptures of bacchic scenes evoking the birth of wine, carved in the calcareous tufa by young artists. Wine tasting.

SEUILLY

MUSEUM - **La Devinière**: *37500 Seuilly. Tel. 02.47.95.91.18 Fax 02.47.95.91.18. Every day except 1/1 and 12/25, from 9 to 12 and 2 to 5 (to 6pm from 3/15 to 4/30). 5/1 to 9/30, from 10 to 7.* François Rabelais' birth house with museum visit. Admission: 23 F.

TOURS

MUSEUM - **Touraine Wine Museum**: *16 rue Nationale, 37000 Tours. Tel. 02.47.61.07.93. Every day (except Tues.) from 9 to 12 and 2 to 6. Closing possible in January and February: ask.* Wonderful collection of objects in an 18th-century cellar.

C E N T R E

BUÉ

45 - RESTAURANT - **Le Caveau**: *18300 Bué. Tel. 02.48.54.22.08. Closed Thursday and Wednesday evening.* Bar on the ground floor where Bué winegrowers are among the regulars, a convivial restaurant on the first floor with simple and generous cooking. The Sancerre is king of the wine list (70 to 110 F) but there are some great surprises. Don't hesitate to ask for the owner's advice, not all of his wines are listed. Menus: 78 to 128 F.

CHAVIGNOL

46 - RESTAURANT - **La Côte des Monts-Damnés**: *Tel. 02.48.54.01.72 Fax 02.48.54.14.24. Closed Sunday evening and Monday. Closed in February.* Large selection of Sancerres favoring local vintners (the chef is the son of Jean-Marie Bourgeois, of the estate of the same name) and particularly those wines from the slopes of Monts damnés. Good choice of old vintages. Ten wines served by the glass. Menus: 98 to 245 F.

CRÉZANCY

47 - BED & BREAKFAST - **Manoir de Vauvredon**: *Le Briou, 18300 Crézancy. Tel. 02.48.79.00.29.* Large, pretty guest rooms in a completely restored manor. Excellent welcome. Four rooms at 250 and 350 F (breakfast included) and a vacation house at 1,500 F (high-season) or 1,250 F (low-season), plus taxes.

LÉRÉ

48 - HOTEL-RESTAURANT - **Le Lion d'Or**: *1 rue de la Judelle, 18240 Léré. Tel. 02.48.72.60.12 Fax 02.48.72.56.18.* Twenty kilometers north of Sancerre. Attractive wine list for white Sancerre (forty-four entries) and Pouilly (twenty-onr entries), with some old vintages (year by year for Cotat, in Sancerre, reaching back to 1983). The fact that only regulars are served from the reserve explains

why it's not among the properties we present, although it's the appellation's best producer. Menus: 95 to 295 F. A la carte: around 250 F. Pleasant mansarded rooms: 240 F. Breakfast: 35 F.

MONTIGNY

49 - BED & BREAKFAST - **Ferme de la Reculée**: *18250 Montigny. Tel. 02.48.69.59.18 Fax 02.48.69.52.51.* Two paces from Henry Natter's property, five pretty guest rooms (choose

those on the second floor) at 260 F (breakfast included). Meals: 90 F.

MOROGUES

50 - RESTAURANT - **Auberge de la Ferme des Pellets**: *18220 Morogues. Tel. 02.48.26.90.68. Open every day from 6/15 to 9/15, closed Tuesday and Wednesday from 9/15 to 6/15.* The table offers a variety of excellent homemade crottin de Chavignol (which can be found in the best cheese stores). Menu: 60 F weekdays. A la carte: around 85 F.

NEVERS

51 - RESTAURANT - **Les Jardins de la Porte-du-Croux**: *17 rue de la Porte-du-Croux, 58000 Nevers. Tel. 03.86.57.12.71 Fax 03.86.38.08.80. Closed Sunday evening and Monday.* A jaunt out of the vineyard that's justified by a wine list cataloguing Loire valley appellations only: they are all present, vins de pays included, with their best producers. A true reference. Menus: 118 to 230 F. A la carte: around 280 F.

52 - RESTAURANT - **Jean-Michel Couron**: *21 rue Saint-Étienne, 58000 Nevers. Tel. 03.86.61.19.28 Fax 03.86.36.02.96. Closed Sunday evening and Monday, but open holidays.* A former understudy to Michel Bras, who has kept the passion for flavors while equalizing their force and subtlety. The selection of wines is limited but good. Many wines offered by the glass, including some bearing prestigious labels; it's even possible to taste some Grands Crus by the glass. Remarkable selection of rare coffees. Menus: 109 to 230 F.

SANCERRE

53 - RESTAURANT - **La Tour**: *31 place de la Halle, 18300 Sancerre. Tel. 02.48.54.00.81 Fax 02.48.78.01.54.* An exemplary list of Sancerres (70 whites, 55 reds), classed by communes and presented by an enthusiastic and competent wine waiter. Menus: 75 to 250 F. A la carte: around 300 F.

54 - RESTAURANT - **La Pomme d'Or**: *Place de la Mairie, 18300 Sancerre. Tel. 02.48.54.13.30. Closed Monday and Wednesday evening.* A short but well-chosen wine list, containing notably some old vintages from the Cotat property. Menus: 78 to 220 F.

SENS-BEAUJEU

55 - BED & BREAKFAST - **Château de Beaujeu**: *18300 Sens-Beaujeu. Tel. 02.48.79.07.95 Fax 02.48.79.05.07.* A few kilometers from Sancerre, a 16th-century castle with an Empire-period make-over. Two pretty guest rooms, one of which is perfect for a romantic stay, at 550 and 650 F.

TO SEE

CHAVIGNOL

OUTING - To better admire Sancerre. Sales of the famous goat cheese in several cheese shops. We suggest going to the Dubois-Boulay cheese shop, *187300 Chavignol. Tel. 02.48.54. 15.69. From 7:30 to 12 and from 2 to 6:30. Closed from 11/11 to mid-February Saturday afternoon and Sunday.*

Part of the collection of old viticultural implements found and restored at the domaine.

Château de la Preuille

Owners Philippe and Christian Dumortier. **Address** 85600 Saint-Hilaire de Loulay - Tel. 02.51.46.32.32 Fax 02.51.46.48.98. **Open** From Tuesday to Saturday, 10:00-12:00 and 14:00-17:30, Sunday and Monday by appointment. **Credit Cards** Visa, Eurocard, MasterCard.

"The granite makes the wine weep." The Dumortier brothers have this simple saying to describe, on the one hand, the particular *terroir* of their domaine, and on the other, the tiny yields they obtain from their 50-year-old vines. The grapes are hand harvested and fermented with natural yeasts. The wines do not have the right to the prestigious appellation Muscadet de Sèvre-et-Maine but La Preuille's simple Muscadet-sur-Lie can better more honored wines. As an appetizer we chose the Gros-Plant (31 F). The '95 is powerful and concentrated and the '91 mature, persistent and complex (chalky, honey, hazelnut). It's worth noting that for a purchase of 24 bottles of the '96 Muscadet one can obtain six of the '89 and discover the possibilities of aged Muscadet. The nose is intense and the palate ample (tea, lime-tree, quince), long, fresh, and fruity. If you are persuasive you might obtain some of the '86 which is robust and very long with notes of vervain and plum.

Our choice Muscadet-sur-Lie Tête de Cuvée '96 (39,70 F). The nose is still discreet and slightly mineral. The palate is full and complex mixing mineral and floral (acacia) notes and there is a long, persistent finish. Age for two or three years.

Reception Very attentive, by the cellar master's wife. Don't forget to see the museum of old viticultural implements or the glass-bottomed barrel which shows the ageing of the wine on lees.

How to get there *(Map 18): From Nantes towards Montaigu via N137. Turn left 4km after Remouillé towards La Preuille and follow the road to the château. The cellar is on the left.*

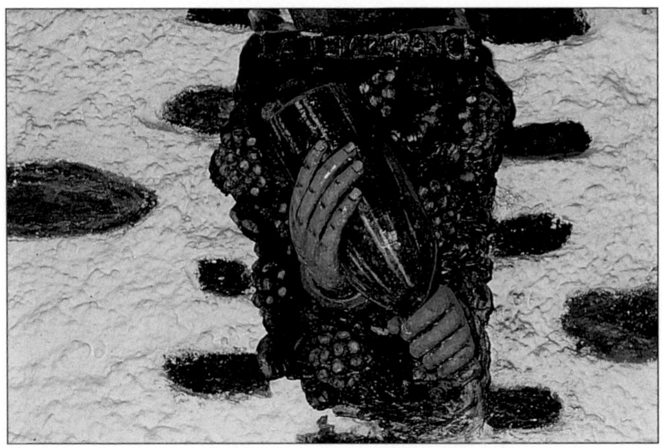

One of the sculptures at the cellar of Château du Chasseloir.

Vignobles Chéreau-Carré

Owner Family Chéreau-Carré. **Address** Château de Chasseloir, 44690 Saint-Fiacre-sur-Maine - Tel. 02.40.54.81.15 Fax 02.40.54.81.70. **Open** From Monday to Saturday, 8:00-18:00. **Spoken** English, German. **Cedit Cards** Visa, Eurocard, MasterCard.

This reputable négociant also possesses a number of domaines of which we particularly liked Châteaux de Chasseloir and du Coing. The first produces subtle, minerally wines and the latter precocious, floral wines that have an astonishing ability to age.

Château du Coing '95 (41,60 F), with its concentration and length, is a delightful success in a vintage that was not always easy. The '96 (tasted from various vats but not yet assembled) will be richer, fuller and more persistent. Thanks to the cellar master, Claude Charrier, who insists on ageing the great wines, it is still possible to find a little of the Château du Coing '89 (52,95 F). The nose is still cautious but the palate more expressive and fine mixing toasted aromas (peanut) with white truffle. This perfectly balanced wine is still crisp and fresh.

Our choice Château du Coing *cuvée* Comte de Saint-Hubert '95 (52,10 F). Chosen for its deep, dense extract, balance and great length. This wine is far from reaching its true potential and needs to be aged further. The Château du Coing *cuvée* Saint-Hilaire '93 (44,50 F) is a good example of a more mature wine. The nose is fine and soft. The palate clean and full. The wine is beginning to evolve (caramel, peach kernel, lichen) but still has great freshness. The finish is unctuous with a hint of honey.

Reception Don't miss a visit to the beautiful cellar of Château de Chasseloir with its sculptures illustrating vice and virtue.

How to get there *(Map 18): From Nantes towards Clisson via D59. Turn right 1km after Saint-Fiacre (signposted) for the domaine.*

The mare Fillette who has the responsibility for tilling the soil at this organically run domaine.

Domaine de l'Écu

Owner Guy Bossard. **Address** La Bretonnière, 44430 Le Landreau - Tel. 02.40.06.40.91 Fax 02.40.06.46.79. **Open** By appointment.

There is an indispensable figure at the domaine responsible for cultivating the soil. Fillette is her name and she's a mare. The domaine is run on organic lines with the tilling of the soil done by horse. The vinification, using natural yeasts, is left to her brilliant assistant, Guy Bossard.

He is now oriented towards the expression of each of the soils in a different *cuvée*. These are presently represented by the '96 vintage which was bottled during the course of 1997. The wines from granite soils produce the *cuvée* Hermine d'Or, those from southwest facing, hard, gneiss slopes the Clos du Bien-Aimé and the Vieilles Vignes du Clos de l'Ecu is derived from the same sub-soils but with a lighter top soil and southerly exposure.

Our choice Muscadet de Sèvre-et-Maine Hermine d'Or '96 (approx. 29 F). A mischievous *cuvée*, due to the acidity, but tender, due to the roundness and maturity. The grapes were picked at a natural 12.3%. The nose is extremely pure, the palate ample and soft, the finish long and persistent. To drink or age a little.

Reception Excellent. In a beautiful cellar.

How to get there *(Map 18): From Nantes towards Cholet via N249. At Vallet towards Loroux-Bottereau via D37. Turn left at Le Landreau, in front of the church, towards the agricultural college. The cellar is just before the college on the right. Signposted.*

The different terroirs of Muscadet.

Domaine de la Louvetrie

Owner Joseph Landron. **Address** les Brandières, 44690 La Haye-Fouassière - Tel. 02.40.54.83.27 Fax 02.40.54.89.82. **Open** By appointment. **Spoken** English. **Cedit Cards** Visa, Eurocard, MasterCard.

The little glass of Muscadet here is replaced by a large glass of amphibolites or a finger of orthogneiss. Joseph Landron has a passion for *terroirs.* They are all there in wooden boxes, ready to be rolled around the fingers of the demonstrator. For each type of soil there corresponds a different style of vinification and ageing *sur lie* and a different date of bottling to underline the vivacity of the amphibolites or the richness and fleshiness of the clay-sand soils.

Apart from the Hermine d'Or '95 (for its delicacy and finesse) we preferred the '96s. The *cuvée* Amphibolite Nature (23 F), a natural 11%, is tender while the Domaine de la Louvetrie (25 F), produced from older vines but the same *terroir*, is round and delicious. Both are for immediate drinking. The *cuvée* Hermine d'Or '96 (29 F) is produced from sandstone soils. The nose is open with a note of white fruits and the palate persistent with a note of pear.

Our choice Muscadet de Sèvre-et-Maine Fief du Breil '96 (41 F, available from 1998). The fruit in the other *cuvées* is replaced here by drier aromatic notes (almond, fruit kernel) with the wine showing more power. To age a little. The same *cuvée* but aged in oak barrel (48 F) amplifies the potential. There is power, weight, concentration, and persistence with lovely dried orange notes. The oak, still very present, demands that the wine be aged much longer for better harmony.

Reception Passionate. In a large cellar.

How to get there *(Map 18): From Nantes towards Clisson via N149. At Haye-Fouassière follow the direction Maison des Vins and then the signs.*

Bernard Couillaud, without his brothers.

Domaine de la Ragotière

Owners Couillaud's brothers **Address** 44330 La Regrippière - Tel. 02.40.33.60.56 Fax 02.40.33.61.89. **Open** From Monday to Saturday, 8:00-12:00 and 14:00-18:00. **Spoken** English.

The 25 hectare domaine lies in one single unit but the variation of *terroirs* (clay soils to the north of the domaine and flinty to the south) allows for the intricate blending of the more robust wines from clay soils with the more elegant from flinty soils.

The wines are both ready for early drinking and adaptable for longer ageing like the '89 (36 F) which is still available from the château. It stayed for four years on lees. The nose is slightly evolved but remains fine. The palate is fine, soft, full and very ripe (a natural 11°7 at the harvest) with spicy notes (nutmeg, cedar) and a touch of toast and vervain. It remains fresh and long. The wine is worth trying in order to discover the unimagined potential that Muscadet has for ageing. When the stock of bottles has run out you will still be able to find it in magnum.

Our choice Muscadet de Sèvre-et-Maine La Ragotière '96 (approx. 26 F). Tasted from various *cuves* but not yet assembled. The wine has a richness of extract, powerful expression and perfect balance. A ripe but lively, well-balanced wine that can be drunk or aged a little.

Reception In the cellar or, for groups, in the 15th century chapel.

How to get there *(Map 18): From Nantes towards Vallet via N249. In front of the church take the exit Beaupreau via D756. Turn left after 800m on to D116. Turn right at the third crossroads, then first on the left, then first on the right and follow the signs.*

Mark Angeli. " The domaine is seven years old which is the age of reason, but not for me who despairs of finding it one day..."

Domaine de la Sansonnière

Owner Mark Angeli. **Address** La Sansonnière, 49380 Thouarcé Tel. 02.41.54.08.08 or 06.07.75.12.08 Fax 02.41.54.08.08. **Open** Saturday morning, by appointment.

Installed since 1990 on a property of seven hectares in the appellations Anjou, Coteaux-du-Layon and Bonnezeaux, Mark Angeli fights all the excesses of modern agriculture. Adept at biodynamics (tilling the soil by horse, homeopathic treatment of the vine with vegetal and mineral substances and respect of astral influences), he uses minimal amounts of sulfur (difficult adjustment for the *liquoreux*) and doesn't chaptalize. This trouble-maker pushes his research for authenticity to the point of planting mixed and ungrafted grape varieties at a very high density. He uses an old vertical press and does *pigeage* in open wooden vats. Whether or not one agrees with Mark in his ecological stance one has to admit that after a few errors his wines today have a veritable openness and harmony. We were very taken by the reds. The Gamay Les Sables (35 F) has a Pinot (cherry, violet) nose, is firm and concentrated and can be kept three or four years. The Anjou Les Gélinettes (40 F) has a nose of crystallized black fruits and spice and is powerful with soft tannins. The white Anjou Les Fourchades '96 (55 F, *en primeur*) is rich and minerally and should be aged three years.

Our choice Bonnezeaux Coteau du Houet '96 (145 F, en primeur). Pure Chenin Blanc (15 hectoliters/hectare) harvested at 19°5 potential. The opposite extreme from a big *liqoreux*, this wine shows elegance and finesse at the same time preserving a powerful richness.

Reception By an admirer of the pianist Martial Solal who is timid, passionate and militant. There is an excellent organic wheat flour for sale.

How to get there *(Map 19): 28km south of Angers. The domaine is on the outskirts of Thouarcé on the road to Martigné-Briand.*

Christian Papin, ambassador for the Anjou-Villages of Brissac.

Domaine de Haute-Perche

Owners Agnès and Christian Papin. **Address** 9 chemin de la Godelière, 49610 Saint-Melaine-sur-Aubance - Tel. 02.41.57.75.65 Fax 02.41.57.75.42. **Open** From Monday to Saturday, 9:00-12:00 and 14:00-18:00. **Credit cards** Visa.

At the southern gates of Angers, Saint-Melaine-sur-Aubance figures as one of the communes which will, in the future, obtain the appellation Brissac Anjou-Villages. Christian Papin (32 hectares of vineyard), along with the Lebretons, Daviau and Richou, is one of the safe bets in this region which already has the appellation Coteaux-de-l'Aubance designated for its sweet (*moelleux*) white wines. His Anjou-Villages (aged in vat) is regularly among the list of top wines at tastings, particularly competitions for the wines of Brissac. He demonstrates a rigorous method of working established with the assistance of enologist Didier Coutenceau. The Anjou-Villages '96 appears to have plenty of charm due to the perfect ripeness of the Cabernet Sauvignon. The simple red Anjou '96 (25,50 F), a pure Cabernet Franc, is soft and lively and delicious young. The style of the Coteaux-de-l'Aubance veers towards the crisp and fine as illustrated by the '96 (42 F) which is lively with a light sweetness and notes of grapefruit and menthol. It makes the perfect aperitif.

Our choice In 1996 the Anjou Gamays are excellent and that of Christian Papin is a real treat (25,50 F). It is ripe and peppery, very concentrated, almost southern in style, with plenty of flesh and fruit. The Anjou-Villages '95 (34 F) has more power and structure but has been rounded out by the ageing process. To drink or keep.

Reception Warm, with Christian Papin or one of the staff in a well organized cellar.

How to get there *(Map 19): 10km from Angers towards Cholet-Niort then Brissac. Having crossed over the bridge that spans the highway turn right and follow the signs.*

Victor Lebreton (left), the winemaker, and his brother Vincent, responsible for the vineyard.

Domaine de Montgilet

Owners Victor and Vincent Lebreton. **Address** Domaine de Montgilet, 49610 Juigné-sur-Loire - Tel. 02.41.91.90.48 Fax 02.41.54.64.25. **Open** From Monday to Saturday, 9:00-12:00 and 14:00-19:00. Sunday by appointment.

The Lebreton brothers are well situated at the top of two major appellations, Anjou-Villages (red) and Coteaux-de-l'Aubance (sweet white), where they cultivate 32 hectares, 15 of which are located on the typical slate-y, schistous soils of the Anjou region. The yields are small, the different parcels of vines selectively treated, the grapes sorted at the harvest and gently pressed (vertical press since 1996) and the wines aged in oak barrels. These are some of the elements that have led to the success of this domaine. The Anjou '96 (27 F), 90% Cabernet Franc, has a full black currant nose and with its exuberant extract can be appreciated young. The Anjou-Villages '96 (35 F), produced from Cabernet Sauvignon and Franc, is more rigid, powerful and tannic (cold pre-fermentation maceration). This is a wine to be cellared like the lovely '95 which will open up in four to five years.

Our choice The club of five Coteaux-de-l'Aubance from the '95 and '96 vintages. A *Crescendo* towards power and sweetness: The *cuvée* Générique '96 (40 F) is fruity, elegant and lightly sweet, ideal as an aperitif. The Trois Schistes '95 (90 F) is rich with a varietal expression The Terteraux '95 (120 F: 50 centiliters) has raisined notes and a complex mineral flavor. The '96 (100 F: 50 centiliters) is even more mineral. The Clos des Huttières '95 (160 F: 50 centiliters) has a rich *liqueur* and is dense, firm and massive. The '96 (120 F: 50 centiliters) has more botrytis but is less impressive. Finally, the Clos Prieur '96 (160 F: 50 centiliters) is extremely rich and dense with great length on the palate. To age of course.

Reception Family atmosphere. In a small cellar.

How to get there *(Map 19): 10km from Angers towards Cholet-Niort then Brissac. Having crossed over the bridge that spans the highway turn left towards Juigné-sur-Loire.*

Didier Richou (pruning) and his younger brother Damien look after 36 hectares.

Domaine Richou

Owners Didier and Damien Richou. **Address** Chauvigné, 49610 Mozé-sur-Louet - Tel. 02.41.78.72.13 Fax 02.41.78.76.05. **Open** From Monday to Saturday, 9:00-12:00 and 14:00-19:00. **Spoken** English. **Credit cards** Visa, Eurocard, MasterCard.

The Richou vineyard is divided and formed by the rivers Louet, Aubance and Loire. It is situated to the southwest of Angers in the *Anjou noir* on a range of varying schist soils. Installed since 1979 on the domaine created by his grandfather and father, Didier Richou, assisted by his younger brother Damien, manages a large cellar where the full gamut of Anjou wines can be found. This ranges from still to sparkling, dry to sweet and fruity to the more structured. They are all of consistently good quality. We particularly liked the new dry white Anjou Clos de Rogerie '96, a pure Chenin Blanc planted on rhyolite soils, which is ripe, full, powerful, very dry with crystallized fruit flavors. Of the early drinking red wines the Anjou Gamay Les Chateliers '96 (24 F) is delicious, very fruity and generous and the Anjou Cabernet '96 (25 F) is equally fruity with supple tannins and an acidulous finish. The Anjou-Villages '95 (32 F) has vanilla and spicy notes, is well-structured with quality tannins and should start opening out in 1998. The '96 is very successful but with more finesse.

Our choice Coteaux-de-l'Aubance *moelleux* Les Trois Demoiselles '96 (95 F). A pure Chenin Blanc barrel fermented and aged (12% and 120 grams/liter residual sugar). Aromas of tobacco, mint, vanilla and crystallized citrus fruits with a fine, open, long, and flavorsome palate. To drink or age.

Reception Family atmosphere, convivial and instructive vis-à-vis the *terroirs.* Around a large table in the cellar.

How to get there *(Map 19): 20km from Angers towards Cholet via N160. Turn right after 10km towards Denée. The domaine is on the left before Denée.*

Gilles Musset, in the western reaches of Anjou.

Domaine Musset-Roullier

Owners Gilles Musset and Serge Roullier. **Address** Le Pélican, 49620 La Pommeraye - Tel. 02.41.39.05.71 Fax 02.41.77.75.76. **Open** From Mon. to Sat., 9:00-12:00, 14:00-19:00, by appointment.

In 1994, Gilles Musset and Serge Roullier entered into a partnership to create a 30-hectare domaine near the banks of the Loire at Montjean and La Pommeraye in the western limits of Anjou. This is no longer the Coteaux-du-Layon region but the Coteaux-de-la-Loire where the terrain is particularly varied. Thanks to an extremely healthy harvest in 1996 Serge and Gilles have sparklingly confirmed the potential of their domaine for both red (superb, see our choice) and white wines. Of the latter in '96, there is the first attempt at a dry Anjou vinified in barrel (approx. 40 F) which is powerful and generous and worth following in the future. The Coteaux-de-la-Loire '96 (30 F) is a lightly sweet white *moelleux* which is fresh and well-balanced with aromas of cloves mint, and grapefruit. It makes the perfect festive aperitif. For more concentration choose the Sélection de Grains Nobles '95 (110 F: 50 centiliters) with its concentrated notes of honey and apricot jam, full palate and fresh finish.

Our choice The two Anjou-Villages '96. 100% Cabernet Franc harvested at the beginning of November, macerated for a long period, and aged in vat. The Cuvée Classique from soils of schist and faluns has crystallized cherry and smoky notes and a round, full, deep, generous palate. The Cuvée du Petit Clos (approx. 40 F) from 35-year-old vines grown on schist and quartz soils, is even more concentrated on the palate, suave, dense and voluptuous. The prices are extremely reasonable and the wines absolutely worth discovering.

Reception Attentive. In a small, improvised corner in the large and recently constructed vinification cellar.

How to get there *(Map 19): 30km southwest of Angers. The cellar is beside the road from Monjean-sur-Loire to La Pommeraye. Signposted.*

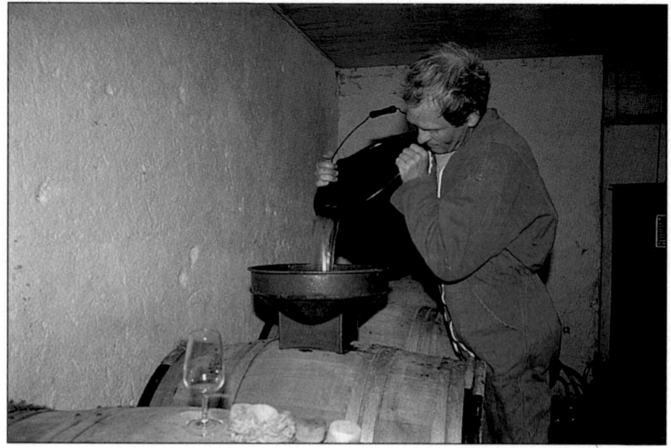

Patrick Baudoin puts into barrel his first Coteaux-du-Layon juices in 1995.

Domaine de La Cour d'Ardenay

Owner Patrick Baudouin. **Address** La Cour d'Ardenay, 49290 Chaudefonds-sur-Layon - Tel. and Fax 02.41.78.66.04. **Open** From Monday to Saturday, by appointment. **Spoken** German.

Among the new wave of producers of great *moelleux* in the Coteaux-du-Layon, those who selectively harvest and refuse to chaptalize (Delesvaux, Pithon and followers), the former bookseller, Patrick Baudouin, plays the rôle of the "intellectual," having changed from white pages to green leaves with almost insolent success. From his Ardenay vineyard (7.5 ha) he extracts a nectar which derives its concentration (without being deprived of elegance) from an almost unprofitably severe selection of the grapes. The production in 1996, moreover, was particularly small (rich but marked by a good acidity) and was distributed between three *cuvées*. These include the Saint-Aubin Les Bruandières (78 F), 17% potential and harvested at the end of the period of selective harvesting before the rain, which is the easiest to taste and purchase, and the *cuvées* Maria Juby and Après Minuit (see our choice). Patrick also produces a red Anjou-Villages ('95: 35 F) which has firm, angular tannins and which needs cellaring for four or five years (decant two hours before serving).

Our choice Maria Juby (165 F 50 centiliters), 24% potential. This is the wine we preferred. It has notes of crystallized citrus fruits and is extremely well-balanced. Apres Minuit (450 F: 50 centiliters, 600 bottles available). It took eight people four days, harvesting grape by grape, to produce two barrels with a potential of 30%. This is a concentrate of botrytized grapes which is extremely rich. For the collector of great *liquoreux*.

Reception Improvised but always passionate in a tiny vinification cellar.

How to get there *(Map 19): At Saint-Lambert-du-Lattay towards Saint-Laurent. Turn right after 7km towards Chaudefonds, then Ardenay. In the center of the hamlet.*

Philippe Delesvaux harvested one hectoliter/hectare for his *cuvée* Anthologie.

Domaine Philippe Delesvaux

Owners Catherine and Philippe Delesvaux. **Address** Les Essards, La Haie-Longue, 49190 Saint-Aubin-de-Luigné - Tel. 02.41.78.18.71 Fax 02.41.78.68.06. **Open** From Monday to Saturday by appointment. **Spoken** English, German.

The chapter on great sweet wines in any specialist wine book is about to become obsolete. This is due to a group of crazy young producers, including Philippe Delesvaux, who set out to reconquer the *terroir* of the Coteaux-du-Layon, and today produce great *liquoreux.* Originally from Savoie but an Anjou vintner since 1983, Philippe cultivates 14,5 ha, of which 10.5 ha Chenin Blanc, at Saint-Aubin and Chaudefonds. An opponent of heavy yields, the lack of selective harvesting, and over-chaptalization, this wine grower translates his words into deeds. The '96 equals the success of '95 but in a different style. There is less botrytis but more intensity and elegance and just as much concentration (the entire harvest was brought in before the November rain).The Saint-Aubin (50 F) is soft and long with quince pâté richness and a clean finish. The Moque (80 F) is amber-colored, concentrated, sweet and finishes with finesse.

Our choice Coteaux-du-Layon Sélection de Grains Nobles '96 (170 F: 50 centiliters), 23% potential. This is a very rich wine but less fleshy and fresher than the '95. It recalls the sugar-acid balance of the '94. To drink over the next 20 years. For collectors of exceptional wines Anthologie (500 F: 50 centiliters) is a fabulous sweet wine (30% potential, 1 hectoliter/hectare). "As expensive as Yquem but better," they say ironically here.

Reception "In an architecturally modern cellar," says Philippe. Translated this means a shed in the middle of the vines. The show is in the glass and Philippe's enthusiasm.

How to get there *(Map 19): 22km southwest of Angers. At Rochefort-sur-Loire towards Chalonnes by the river road. Turn right at the hamlet La Haie-Longue towards Les Essards. The cellar is in the middle of the vines.*

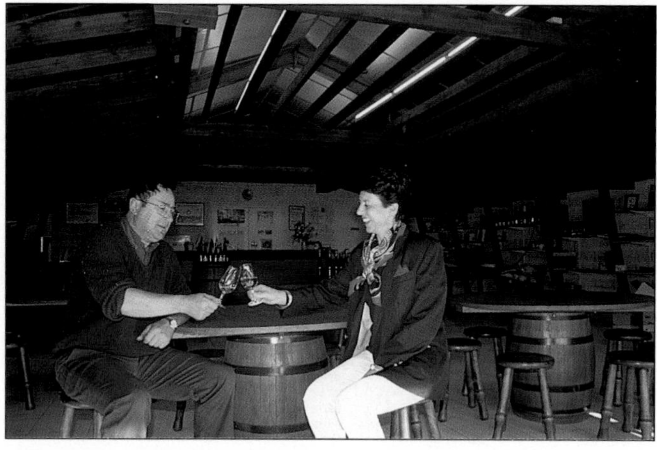

The Aguilas are always attentive to their customers.

Domaine Gaudard

Owner Pierre Aguilas. **Address** La Brosse, route de Saint-Aubin, 49290 Chaudefonds-sur-Layon - Tel. 02.41.78.10.68 Fax 02.41.78.67.72. **Open** From Monday to Saturday, 9:00-12:00 and 14:00-19:00. Sunday by appointment. **Credit cards** Visa, Eurocard, MasterCard.

Pierre Aguilas is the link between two generations of Anjou wine growers. A committed wine grower himself (we've lost count of the number of presidencies he holds and the number of trade associations and committees he attends), he listens to and supports the young turks who are fighting for a more natural Coteaux-du-Layon as well as staying in contact with the older generation, those for which tradition means over-chaptalization. However, this Bordelais of Spanish origin with a military background, chose which side he was on at the end of the 1980s when he turned to small yields and selective harvesting for his sweet wines. One only needs to taste his range of Coteaux-du-Layon to be convinced. The Varennes '96 (38 F) is light and easy, the Saint-Lambert '96 (52 F) big and imposing and the Sélection Or (75 F) richer and more elegant. There are still some of the '95s available including the Sélection Or (150 F), a sweet nectar of crystallized fruits. The 24-hectare domaine also produces some good dry wines including a Rosé de Loire (24.50 F) and a Cabernet d'Anjou (26.50 F) which we preferred in 1996.

Our choice Coteaux-du-Layon Chaume '96 (130 F). Produced from a new parcel of 25 ares at a potential of 25%. Beautiful amber-colored hue and a full, powerful, unctuous palate which is amazingly long on the finish. A really great wine to keep 20 years.

Reception Considerate. In a spacious tasting room with plenty of tables allowing for access of groups.

How to get there *(Map 19): 33km southwest of Angers. At Saint-Aubin towards Chaudefonds. Turn left after 4km and follow the road which runs alongside the Layon. Signposted.*

Family portrait.

Domaine Ogereau

Owner Vincent and Catherine Ogereau. **Address** 44, rue de la Belle Angevine, 49750 Saint-Lambert-du-Lattay - Tel. 02.41.78.30.53 Fax 02.41.78.43.55. **Open** From Monday to Saturday, 9:00-12:00 and 14:00-19:00.

A charismatic figure in Anjou, Vincent Ogereau took over from his father who had launched the domaine (22 hectares) on the road to quality and direct sales to the public. With the assistance of enologist Didier Coutenceau he produces fruity, full, aromatic rosés and white wines in a modern fashion and fights against rusticity in the reds. The red Anjou (25.50 F) is acidulous and round with an aroma of blackberry jam and can be appreciated young. The Anjou-Villages, 70% Cabernet Franc, appears rounder and more supple than the '95 (34 F). It was aged for 18 months and has a dense extract and pronounced taste of black currants and should be cellared for a while. Congratulations on the white Anjou Prestige '96 (45 F), a pure Chenin Blanc vinified in barrel, which is a powerful, dry wine with the complex flavors of a sweet wine. In Coteaux-du-Layon Saint-Lambert, the balance of the Prestige '96 (70 F) is remarkable. The Clos des Bonnes Blanches '96 (142 F: 50 centiliters), 12% and 170 grams/liter of sugar, is velvety and fat with a honeyed subtlety. The *terroir* is still relatively discreet due to the youthful age of the vines.

Our choice Each year Vincent successfully produces a delicious semi-sweet rosé Cabernet d'Anjou. The '96 (22 F) which is extremely fruity (crushed strawberries), gently sweet, fresh, and elegant will be sold out by the end of 1997 but you can take a bet on the '97 without hesitation.

Reception More often than not in a good-humored, attentive way by Catherine in a small tasting room.

How to get there *(Map 19): 29km southwest of Angers towards Cholet via N160. On the right at the exit to Saint-Lambert-du-Lattay towards Cholet.*

In beautiful surroundings, seductive wines and a warm welcome.

Château de Passavant

Owners Families David-Lecomte. **Address** Route de Tancoigné, 49560 Passavant-sur-Layon - Tel. 02.41.59.53.96 Fax 02.41.59.57.91. **Open** From Monday to Friday, 8:00-12:00 and 14:00-19:00, weekend by appointment. **Spoken** English.

Passavant, located a few kilometers from Gérard Depardieu's château (Tigné), is a real medieval château (13th century tower) and formerly a defensive site for the southern part of Anjou. The château and vineyard (60 hectares) has been in the hands of the family of the present owners since 1900. Jean and Noëlle David (in semi-retirement as there is always something that needs doing at such a property), who made a name for the wines of Passavant, have passed the baton to their children Claire and François (a talented young winemaker) and to their son-in-law Olivier Lecomte who looks after the commercial and viticultural side of the venture. At this southern frontier of Haut-Layon the red Anjou-Villages have plenty of character, solid tannins and demand at least four years to settle down. The Coteaux-du-Layons' are not opulent but naturally fine, direct and very agreeable.

Our choice There are two. The dry, white Anjou '96 (25 F), made from pure Chenin Blanc, is powerful and full with crystallized citrus fruit and spicy flavors. The sweet Coteaux-du-Layon Grains Nobles '95 (110 F) is clean and open with notes of tobacco, lime tree, crystallized mandarin orange, and citronella and remains amazingly fresh despite the 125 grams/liter of sugar. To drink or keep.

Reception Excellent, whichever member of the family, in the vinification cellar. Visits to the château (by request). Parking possible for a camping trailer for one night.

How to get there *(Map 19): 42km south of Angers passing by Brissac, Thouarcé, Matigné, Tigné and Tancoigné. The cellar is at the entrance to Passavant. The château overhangs the Layon.*

The Pithon family, fishing in their own river.

Domaine Jo Pithon

Owners Isabelle and Jo Pithon. **Address** 3, chemin du Moulin, 49750 Saint-Lambert-du-Lattay - Tel. 02.41.78.40.91 Fax 02.41.78.46.37. **Open** From Monday to Saturday, 8:00-12:00 and 14:00-18:00, by appointment.

With his solid build and banter of a street marketeer, Jo Pithon, son of a school-teacher and grandson of a wine grower, has imposed his own style. In 1991 the frost stripped his vineyard of 14 hectares. He kept only 4.5 hectares of Chenin Blanc (6 hectares today) and set his sights on producing wines from grapes extremely selectively chosen (*tris*) and vinified in oak barrels. Since 1992 his success in Coteaux-du-Layon has been masterful. If the richness of certain *cuvées* destabilizes some wine tasters, his fans are numerous, which explains the sales en *primeur* (March to June) and the prices which are at the same level as the greatest sweet wines. The '96s, tasted at the end of fermentation, have given the best of themselves in Saint-Aubin and Bealieu. The simple Coteaux-du-Layon Saint-Aubin (78 F) is deliciously fruity and very present on the palate. The Beaulieu (78 F) gains in finesse. The four Sélections de Grains Nobles are of a very high quality level, less powerful than in '95 with an average potential of 22%, but 30% for the Clos des Bonnes Blanches Ambroisie (380 F: 50 centiliters). In 1997 the Chaumes (45 ares) and Quarts-de-Chaume (75 ares) arrived on the scene.

Our choice Coteaux-du-Layon Beaulieu Les Ortinières SGN '96 (195 F). A wonderful concentration of liqueur but subtle, elegant and minerally. A great wine.

Reception In the barrel cellar, with the gift of gab and good humour of a couple who never take themselves seriously.

How to get there *(Map 19): 30km southwest of Angers. Leave Saint-Lambert-du-Lattay towards Cholet and take the first road on the left : Chemin les Grandes-Tailles.*

Michel Robineau and his noble rotted Chenin Blanc which produces the Coteaux-du-Layon.

Domaine Michel Robineau

Owners Michel and Martine Robineau. **Address** 16 rue Rabelais, 49750 Saint-Lambert du Lattay - Tel. 02.41.78.34.67. **Open** From Monday to Saturday, by appointment.

Michel Robineau set up his tiny cellar in Saint-Lambert in 1993 after having worked for five years for Jo Pithon (see previous entry). With his wife Martine, he cultivates 8 hectares (3.5 hectares of Coteaux-du-Layon) and during the harvest pursues a course of extremely selective picking (*tris*) in order to extract the absolute quintessence of the grape. The vinification is conscientious but we would like to see the maturation followed in a greater percentage of new oak barrels in order to complement the quality of the juice. This is particularly so for the Coteaux-du-Layon Sélection de Grains Nobles (see our choice). However, we shouldn't be too exacting with this retiring young couple who still sell a percentage of their wines in bag-in-box and are present at markets and fairs in order to establish a list of customers. Taking into account the work involved and the quality of the wines the price of their Coteaux-du-Layon is very reasonable. The Coteaux-du-Layon Saint-Lambert '96 (39 F), 18.8% potential, has the aroma of crystallized citrus fruits and ripe apples, a little iodized, and a savoury palate.

Our choice Coteaux-du-Layon Saint-Lambert Grains Nobles '96 (76 F) with 205 grams/liter of residual sugar. Caramel color with aromas of apricot jam, quince and crystallized apples, the wine has a rich, sweet, powerful, full *liqueur,* still a little massive but with good acidity on the finish. The price is not the only positive point.

Reception In the middle of the barrels and vats with a reserved and earthy couple.

How to get there *(Map 19): 29km southwest of Angers. Arriving at Saint-Lambert-du-Lattay from Angers via N160 take the tiny road on the left, 100m before the church. The cellar is on the right.*

"Winegrower artisan, partisan of the *terroir*," says Claude Papin of himself.

Château Pierre-Bise

Owners Joëlle and Claude Papin. **Address** 49750 Beaulieu-sur-Layon - Tel. 02.41.78.31.44 Fax 02.41.78.41.24. **Open** From Mon. to Sat., 9:00-12:00 and 14:00-19:00. Sun. by appointment.

Guru of the Anjou *terroir* with 24 years winemaking experience, Claude Papin clears and analyzes the soils with the patience of an entomologist and speaks about them with the conviction of a preacher. "When I taste a good wine blind, I need to feel where it comes from, where it has its roots," he exclaims. This dedication has pushed him to produce a staggering range of eight Coteaux-du-Layon corresponding to the particular village and soil represented on his 42 hectares of vines. This logic indicates faultless work in the vineyard, an "organic" tendency and refined vinification (no chaptalization or addition of cultured yeasts). There is not one wine that leaves you indifferent; the problem is making the choice. Do you prefer the full, rich, generous style of the Coteaux-du-Layon Beaulieu L'Anclaie '95 (70 F: 50 centiliters) or the toasted, crystallized fruit character of the Les Rouannières (80 F: 50 centiliters)? Even the Anjou Gamay '95 has an original spicy, crystallized fruit flavor. The white Anjou Haut de la Garde '95 (35 F), the Savennières Coulaines '95 (49 F) and the red Anjou-Villages (33 F) are also worth investigating.

Our choice Coteaux-du-Layon Beaulieu '96 (42 F). Fresh and pure, this is really excellent value. In a fuller style and for long ageing choose the Coteaux-du-Layon Chaume '95 (90 F: 50 centiliters) and the Quarts-de-Chaume '95 (165 F: 50 centiliters) which is fluid, elegant and exquisitely textured.

Reception Pedagogical and wordy with Claude or with more reserve but equal competence with Joëlle.

How to get there *(Map 19): 28km southwest of Angers. On the N160 at the level of Beaulieu-sur-Layon go in the direction Rochefort-sur-Loire via D54. Turn left after 1km towards Pierre-Bise. In the center of the hamlet.*

The Baumard vines in Quarts-de-Chaume.

Domaine des Baumard

Owners Family Baumard. **Supervisor** Florent Baumard. **Address** 8, rue de l'Abbaye, 49190 Rochefort-sur-Loire - Tel. 02.41.78.70.03 Fax 02.41.78.83.82. **Open** From Monday to Friday, 10:00-12:00 and 14:00-18:00, Saturday by appointment, closed Dec. 20 - Dec. 31. **Spoken** English.

The Baumards have a foot on each bank of the river Loire. They have 15 hectares on the right bank at Savennières and 25 hectares at their left bank fief of Rochefort, of which 6 hectares are at Quarts-de-Chaume, spectacularly located on terraces next to the Layon. The Baumards' genealogical line can be traced back to 1634, and it is Jean Baumard who was responsible for the present form of the domaine. A partisan of wide planting and high trellising, seeding between the rows alternated with working the soil, he has now passed the baton to his son Florent, a fine technician and curious and unblinkered wine grower. The wines are vinified with due attention to hygene, to avoid oxydation of the white wines (80% of the production), and without barrels as Florent wants to make wines that are consumed in a balanced state. There is a lovely Savennières '95 (64 F), at the same time dry and unctuous but still closed and a powerful Coteaux-du-Layon Le Paon '95 (65 F). The domaine also makes excellent Crémant de Loire (39-45 F).

Our choice Savennières Clos du Papillon '95 (70 F). Chosen for its power, length and mineral finish on the palate which only this *terroir* and Chenin Blanc can produce. To keep. To accompany lobster and sea-urchins. The Quarts-de-Chaume has a long finish and crystallized citrus fruits and honeyed flavors. It takes the place as father of the family.

Reception Professional and attentive, in a brightly lit room in the 17th century manor house, with a magnificent fresco on the wall dating from 1730.

How to get there *(Map 19): On the N160 on the Beaulieu level, towards Rochefort-sur-Loire via D54. Little road on the left opposite the church in Rochefort. At 50m.*

Supported by the best wine growers in the region, Francis Poirel has quietly entered their limited circle.

Château de Suronde

Owners Francis Poirel. **Address** 49190 Rochefort-sur-Loire - Tel. 02.41.78.66.37 Fax 02.41.78.68.90. **Open** From Monday to Friday, by appointment. **Spoken** English.

You doubtless don't know Francis Poirel. It's not too surprising as this apprentice-vintner, 46, produced his first vintage in 1995. The first part of his adult life, Francis, the grandson of a wine grower from the Côtes-de-Toul, worked as a representative for a Breton fishery. Then, deciding to do "what he really wanted," he bought Suronde in August 1995. The domaine consists of 5 ha in Quarts-de-Chaume (ex-property Laffourcade), one of the two sweet *Grands Crus* in the region. The vines are situated on magnificent southeast and southwest facing slopes overhanging the right bank of the river Layon but are old and have been little maintained or weeded. Francis is now working the soil, reducing yields (10 hl/ha in 1995) and selectively (*tris*) harvesting. In the cellar the grapes are vertically pressed, the juice naturally settled and neither enzymes nor yeasts added. The wines are not chaptalized and are fermented and aged in oak barrels (18 - 20 months). The *terroir* is evident. Hats off to Francis.

Our choice Quarts-de-Chaume '95 (130 F: 50 cl.) 12% and 120 grams/liter residual sugar. On the attack, the pureness, finesse and floral notes typical of this sweet wine are very marked. The sugar-acid balance and persistence are excellent. A wine of undeniable class. You should also try to obtain one of the 800 bottles of Victor et Joseph (320 F: 50 cl.) 11°5 and 240 grams/liter residual sugar. Very fat, rich, and complex with crystallized fruit notes and destined for a long life due to the mellow acidity.

Reception By Francis, a *bon vivant* who is passionate about his new vocation.

How to get there *(Map 19): On the N160 on the Beaulieu level, towards Rochefort-sur-Loire via D54. Turn left after 5km, then left again opposite the large aerial towards Chaume-et-Suronde.*

Joël Lévi has deep cellars hewn from the tufa soil where he ages his own Saumur Brut.

Domaine de la Paleine

Owners Anne-Marie and Joël Lévi. **Address** 9 rue de la Paleine, 49260 Le Puy-Notre-Dame - Tel. 02.41.52.21.24 Fax 02.41.52.21.66. **Open** From Monday to Saturday, 8:00-12:00 and 14:00-18 :00. Sunday and national holidays by appointment. **Spoken** English.

Parisian Joël Lévi sold his bill-posting business at the end of the 1980s to settle in 1991 in Saumur at Puy-Notre-Dame. At 54, this former advertising agent with no attachment to the region or the world of wine, except as a true wine lover, fell for this beautiful property studded with immense underground cellars hewn from the tufa and possessing 35 hectares producing red, white and sparkling Saumur. He experienced the difficult path of an apprentice wine grower on a property which, until his arrival, had never bottled its own wines. "I invested a lot in winemaking equipment and took the advice of a well-known enologist in the region. It proved more expensive and complicated than I thought but I don't regret a thing." The proof is that the wines rapidly became the standard in the commune and the appellation. Joël Lévi ages his own sparkling wines in his own cellars. The Saumur Brut (38 F) which is now on sale has plenty of finesse and loads of character. A wine to look out for.

Our choice Saumur Réserve red '96 (26 F). For a gentle price, this wine, from a very good vintage in the appellation, offers fruit, fine tannins, and immediate pleasure. To drink. For a more serious but equally agreeable wine choose the '95 (33,60 F) for its smoky notes.

Reception In a simple tasting room. Vists to the undergroud cellars by appointment.

How to get there *(Map 19): 26km south of Saumur. Leaving Puy-Notre-Dame, on the road to Doué-la-Fontaine.*

Yves Drouineau.

Domaine Les Baumiers

Owner Yves Drouineau. **Address** 3 rue Morains, 49400 Dampierre Tel. 02.41.51.14.02 Fax 02.41. 50.32.00. **Open** By appointment.

Along with the stars of an appellation one often finds discreet young vintners. Yves Drouineau is one of them. In 1991 he took over the domaine which he'd managed with his father since 1980. The domaine, with vines spread throughout the appellation, has an important production of white wines which is unusual in the region. Winegrowers have consistently been pulling up Chenin Blanc vines to replace them with Cabernet Franc, known here, as in Touraine, as Breton. The origin of the name is believed to come from Father Breton, one of Richelieu's administrators and a member of the clergy at Fontevraud, who could have been responsible for the spread of this Bordeaux variety throughout the region. Alternatively, it could have been because the wines and grape varieties of Aquitaine transited through Brittany ports before flowing down the Loire river. Other than the dry white wine (in fact a "*sec tendre*" or "tender dry" as they say in Vouvray to indicate the tiny amount of residual sugar) the domaine offers a lovely sweet white wine which is very *liquoreux* in style. The '95 (approx. 50 F: 50 centiliters) had an alcohol potential of 19°5 which balanced out at 12°8 with 110 grams/liter of residual sugar. The marked acidity maintains a fresh, lively presence and prolongs the note of crystallized citrus fruits. There is also a good Saumur-Champigny '95 (32 F) with an upright, tannic palate but plenty of fleshy fruit.

Our choice Saumur white '95 (24 F). Rich and full, produced by selective harvesting (*tris*) with a point of residual sugar which gives the wine a certain tender appeal. To drink.

Reception Available and very open.

How to get there *(Map 19): The cellar is on the right in the center of Dampierre.*

A château made from tufa rock typical of the Saumur region which can be admired when visiting Langlois-Château.

Langlois-Château

CEO Michel Villedey. **Address** Route de Gennes, 49400 Saint-Hilaire Saint-Florent - Tel. 02.41.40.21.40 Fax 02.41.40.21.49. **Open** April 1 - Oct. 30, everyday, 10:00-12:30 and 14:30-18:00. The rest of the year, closed Monday and Tuesday. **Spoken** English, German. **Credit cards** Visa, Eurocard, MasterCard.

A serious establishment which has chosen to produce Crémant de Loire and not sparkling Saumur. "The rules for the production of Crémant are more strict, nearer to Champagne when it comes to pressing the grapes and notably in the ageing of the bottle," explains the Managing Director Michel Villeday. In fact, all the grapes for Langlois-Château's sparkling wines come from around Saumur and in the Crémant category we class it among the best. The wines include the simple Crémant (48 F) which is beautifully ripe, the long and evolved Crémant Réserve '92 (59 F), and the Cuvée Quadrille (84 F) which has notes of honey and pollen. However, Langlois-Château possess other treasures which are representative of this diverse viticultural region including the crisp, white Saumur '95 (29 F), the smoky red Vieilles Vignes (56 F), Saumur-Champigny, Chinon, Sancerre, and Muscadet.

Our choice Saumur Vieilles Vignes white '95 (56 F). 100% Chenin Blanc vinified and aged in barrel with the malolactic fermentation completed. A dry, white wine with a bread aroma on the nose and a buttery, unctuous palate with good freshness. A well-balanced wine which will evolve successfully over the next four or five years.

Reception More oriented towards individual visits than the other houses in Saumur, with visits to the vineyards that overlook Saumur, weather permitting.

How to get there *(Map 19): 3km northwest of Saumur. From the center of Saumur run along the left bank of the Loire towards Saint-Hilaire Saint-Florent, then Gennes. The entrance to the cellars is on the left.*

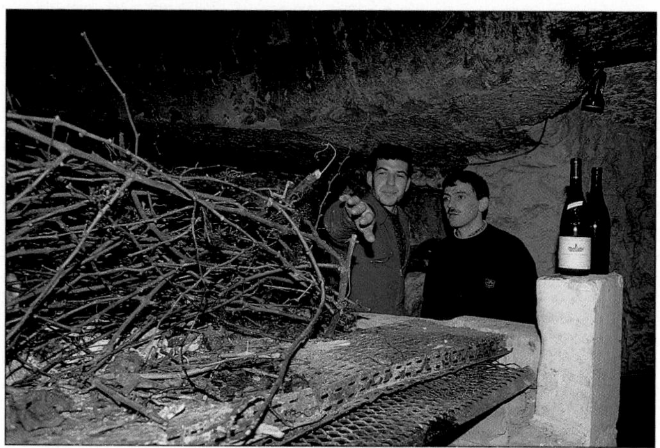

Patric Rétif (right) and his brother-in-law Denis Rétiveau light a fire in the old underground family cellar.

Domaine de Champs Fleuris

Owners Patrice Rétif and Denis Rétiveau. **Address** Rue des Martyrs, 49730 Turquant - Tel. 02.41. 38.10.92/02.41.51.48.97 Fax 02.41.51.75.33. **Open** By appointment.

Largely unappreciated, the dry, white wines of Saumur, produced from Chenin Blanc, at present offer excellent price-pleasure value. Lively and floral in their youth, they demonstrate their limestone origins with a mineral accent and a variety of notes like fern, mushroom and green apple. Turquant, a commune of "La Cote" by the Loire, possesses an excellent reputation for these dry, white wines.

Installed at his parents-in-law's domaine, Patrice Rétif, a former biology student, assisted in the vines by his brother-in-law Denis Rétiveau, produced one of the best white wines in the region in '95. He also makes good Saumur-Champigny, with wines that are lively and solid, marked by the *terroir* of La Cote, that need a minimum of two or three years ageing. There were two good *cuvées* in '95, the Vieilles Vignes (approx. 35 F) and Caudalies (approx. 45 F) which is spicy, tasteful, and long.

Our choice The white '95s. The dry (26,50 F) is ripe and complex (fruit kernel, white fruits,almond), full and powerful but linear thanks to the natural acidity of the Chenin, with a long finish. To drink. The *moelleux* (70 F: 50 centiliters) is very botrytized, with an ample palate, complex sweetness sharpened by the acidity. To age a little.

Reception With courtesy at the vinification cellar but you must ask to visit the spectacular old cellars excavated under the vines.

How to get there *(Map 19): 11km southeast of Saumur, towards Montsoreau via D947, along the left bank of the Loire. Climb to the top of Turquant. Domaine sign-posted.*

Philippe Vatan.

Château du Hureau

Owner Philippe Vatan. **Address** 49400 Dampierre-sur-Loire - Tel. 02.41.67.60.40 Fax 02.41.50.43.35. **Open** From Monday to Friday, 9:00-12:00 and 14:00-18:00 (and Saturday afternoon from May to Aug.). **Spoken** English. **Credit cards** Visa, Eurocard, MasterCard.

Château du Hureau, a beautiful tufa and slate building clinging to the hillsides of the Loire, dominates the river. This is the fief of the Vatan family. Since the end of the 1980s, the wines of Hureau have, under the guidance of Philippe Vatan, shown an increase in quality. This has been due to a stricter selection by parcel, a sorting of the harvest (picked at a better level of maturity) and a studied improvement in the barrel ageing. In Saumur-Champigny choose the '95s: the Grande Cuvée (approx. 42 F) for its depth, *gourmandise*, and "entertaining" pleasure, as Philippe Vatan says, or the cuvée Lisagathe (approx. 60 F). This wine is very structured, ample and ripe, direct and square in the style of the '90 but needs a little time. In principle there is also a non-filtered version of the Lisagathe which has to be tasted. The '94s need more time.

Our choice The '95 whites. The dry (50 F) for its ripe, concentrated nose, bouquet of aromas (flowers, pear, fruit kernel), and length. The *moelleux* (120 F) for the concentration on the palate, finesse, length, and crystallized citrus fruit finish. Both need to be aged a little.

Reception Good, at the entrance to a vast cellar hewn from the tufa.

How to get there *(Map 19): 4km east of Saumur, towards Montsoreau via D947, along the left bank of the Loire. The château is on the right overlooking the Loire in Dampierre.*

The Foucault "dream team": Charlie (left) "the town-councillor for Chacé," his son Antoine and Nadi.

Clos Rougeard

Owners Jean-Louis (Charlie) and Bernard (Nadi) Foucault. **Address** 15 rue de l'Église, 49400 Chacé - Tel. 02.41.52.92.65 Fax 02.41.52.98.34. **Open** From Monday to Saturday, by appointment only.

If you ask the Foucault brothers what their secret is for making great Saumur-Champigny they reply: "We harvest the grapes, press them, and put the wine in barrel, *voilà*!" So what really makes the quality of Clos Rougeard? The 8 hectares of Cabernet Franc are situated on the best limestone-clay soils in the appellation. The parcels at Les Poyeux and Le Bourg (75-year-old vines) are low yielding (approx. 30 hectoliters/hectare) and never treated with chemical fertilizers. In their rock-hewn cellar Charlie and Nadi Foucault handle the barrel ageing to perfection. They work in a traditional manner so as to mature the wines gracefully while adding an oaky edge. The ageing extends over a period of 12, 18, and sometimes more than 24 months for the *cuvée* Le Bourg. Following this any character-stripping filtration is totally unneccessary. Unfortunately, the demand for the wines is strong so there is little for sale at the property.

Our choice Saumur-Champigny Les Poyeux '94 (approx. 65 F by reservation). Sixty percent of the harvest was hit by frost but what remains is superb. Nose of fresh tobacco and ripe fruit, the palate is firmly structured with silky tannins and elegant oak, providing a long finish. The wine will be perfect with another three years' bottle age.

Reception Hewn from the rock and decorated with coins, the Ali Baba cellar provides a memorable visit where time is of no consequence.

How to get there *(Map 19): 6km south of Saumur via D93 to Varrains. A grey gate in the village.*

Jean-Pierre Chevallier.

Château de Villeneuve

Owner Jean-Pierre Chevallier. **Address** 3 rue Jean-Brevet, 49400 Souzay-Champigny - Tel. 02.41.51.14.04 Fax 02.41.50.58.24. **Open** From Monday to Saturday, 9:00-12:00 and 14:00-18:00. **Spoken** English. **Credit cards** Visa, Eurocard, MasterCard, Amex.

Jean-Pierre Chevallier, enologist, has managed the family domaine of 20 hectares for the last 13 years. This rigorous wine grower has dramatically improved the cultivation of his vines and hence the quality of the grapes and the wines. The Villeneuve Cabernet Franc planted on a turonien soil, produces a deeply colored, solid Saumur-Champigny which is closed when young and which requires three years bottle age. This can be certified by the *cuvée* Grand Clos '95 (approx. 80 F), tasted during maturation, which is concentrated and silky but which should open in time. The domaine's basic *cuvée* (35 F : '96) is fruity and more readily accessible but without any loss of extract and equally concentrated and silky. Villeneuve also possesses a great *terroir* for white Saumur. The *cuvée* Les Cormiers '96 (approx. 60 F) is very full, structured by the alcohol but well-rounded by the fleshy extract, fine and complex. The Coteaux-de-Saumur *moelleux* is excellent but rare. If there is any don't hesitate.

Our choice Saumur-Champigny Vieilles Vignes '95 (45 F). Deep, dark, brilliant hue, fine and concentrated, very ripe, with silky tannins. A delicious wine, balanced and very long, superb. To age a while.

Reception Perfect, in the cellar opposite the château.

How to get there *(Map 19): 8km southeast of Saumur, towards Montsoreau via D947, along the left bank of the Loire. At Souzay follow the signs which climb to the right of the château.*

An invitation to visit with the gate open and vines running up to the château.

Château de Chaintres

Owner Gaël de Tigny. **Manager** Krishna Lester. **Address** Chaintres, 49400 Saumur - Tel. 02.41.52.90.54 Fax 02.41.52.99.92. **Open** From Monday to Friday, 8:00-12:00 and 14:00-18:00. Saturday and Sunday by appointment. **Spoken** English. **Credit cards** Visa, Eurocard, MasterCard.

The origins of the Logis de Chaintres can be traced as far back as the 16th century. In the 17th century the property passed into the hands of the Oratorian monks who were attached to the Abbey of Fontevrault. Circled by a wall and practically in one single unit of 16 hectares, the property has clearly been in decline, in terms of the quality of the wines, over the last decade. However, recent tastings show that this trend has been reversed with good but light-styled wines being produced that are not lacking in quality, particularly in the good vintages. Krishna Lester, the former capitain of a cruise-barge and English by birth (his father was fascinated by Indian culture, hence the first name) now manages the estate for the owners. The work practices at Chaintres : relatively old Cabernet Franc vines (average 30-35 years but certain 90 years), working of the soils with experiments in seeding between the rows, restriction of yields, harvesting by hand and destemming the grapes and a relatively long period of maceration during vinification, show that the domaine has now chosen a more rigorous path.

Our choice Saumur-Champigny '95 (38,50 F). The nose is clean and fresh. The palate full and dense with silky, ripe tannins. This is a lively, delicious wine that is long and fresh. The '96 will be dense, rich and round.

Reception Very open to visitors with a touch of British humor if you happen on the manager, Krishna Lester.

How to get there *(Map 19): From Saumur towards Brézé via D93. Turn left after Varrains towards Chaintres. The château is in the center of the village. Large gate.*

Thierry Germain.

Domaine des Roches-Neuves

Owners Marie and Thierry Germain. **Address** 56 bd Saint-Vincent, 49400 Varrains - Tel. 02.41.52.94.02 Fax 02.41.52.49.30. **Open** By appointment.

Thierry Germain, 28, should logically be whiling away his days in Bordeaux, content to be the heir to a large viticultural estate. However, this energetic vintner chose to leave the family domaines in Bourg and Blaye and in 1993 settled, with his wife Marie, in Saumur. In a matter of only three years, Thierry has become a native of Saumur, recognized and appreciated as one of the best wine growers in the appellation. Taking over Roches-Neuves (18 hectares) did not mean that success was guaranteed from the outset. The domaine already had a sound reputation and many awaited with interest Thierry's first offerings. Few were disappointed.

Four *cuvées* were produced in '96. The Clos Prieur (40 F) is structured but fruity and supple. The Terres Chaudes (60 F) is powerful and full on the palate with clean, direct acidity and tannins which need to mellow a little. The *cuvée* Jeanne (approx. 65 F) is fine and expressive on the nose (plum) with tannins as soft as a baby's skin (Jeanne is Marie and Thierry's daughter).

Our choice Saumur-Champigny La Marginale '95 (approx. 100 F). Tasted from different barrels during maturation. From yields of 25 hectoliters/hectare and 60-year-old vines, this wine underwent a period of 35 days maceration including 18 days alcoholic fermentation. Extremely ripe (13.8% natural) with spicy aromas and loads of finesse. A wine not to miss that needs ageing.

Reception Dynamic and enthusiastic, in the wine storehouse, with either Thierry or Marie.

How to get there *(Map 19): 4km south of Saumur alongside the four lane highway (D93) that runs through Varrains. Signposted.*

Pierre Gauthier and his mass selection vine plants.

Domaine du Bel Air

Owner Pierre Gauthier. **Adresse** La Motte, 37140 Benais - Tel. 02.47.97.41.06 Fax 02.47.97.47.07. **Open** Every day by appointment.

Pierre Gauthier admits that vinification was never his strong point. However, he has been a conscientious vine-grower for 18 years, and is captivated by his 100% Cabernet Franc vineyard in Bourgueil which he tends like a garden (he propagates his own vine plants by mass selection and plows the soil.) Until recently he bottled very little wine, preferring to sell in volume to the *negociants.* This explains why in 1995 enologist Denis Duveau offered to look after the vinification of his wines. Far from being an unknown figure in the region Duveau was, until 1993, the intrepid owner of the Domaine des Roches-Neuves in Saumur-Champigny. Now a consultant enologist he dreamed of returning to work in his native Loire. The Duveau imprint can be seen in the late harvesting, long period of maceration ("things I never dared do," confides Pierre), and above all in the adventurous ageing in new 500 liter oak barrels. The first trials in 1995 were continued in 1996.

Our choice Bourgueil Clos Sénéchal '96 (75 F). A selection from 60-year-old vines. Deep purple hue, expressive black fruit and toasted nose, dense, fine extract with crushed raspberry flavor. Deep, elegant style. Reserve the Grand Mont '96 (approx. 100 F) which is concentrated, full and powerful with superbly elegant fruit.

Reception Generous and rustic, at the domaine. If possible, ask Pierre for a visit to his vast underground cellar, 1km from the house.

How to get there *(Map 19): From Tours towards Langeais via N152, then Saint-Patrice and Ingrandes via D35. Turn right near Restigné, just before the petrol station to the right, towards La Motte. Cellar on the right with no signposting.*

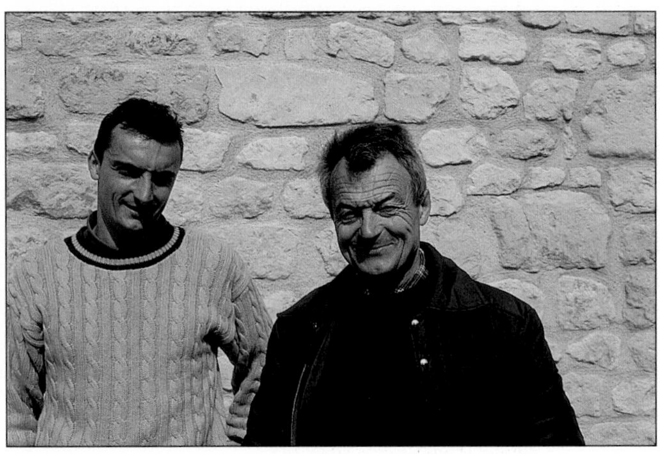

Marc Delaunay and his son, François.

Domaine de la Lande

Owners Marc and François Delaunay. **Address** La Lande, 37140 Bourgueil - Tel. 02.47.97.80.73 Fax 02.47.97.95.65. **Open** By appointment.

Assisted by his son François, Marc Delaunay cultivates 14 hectares of vines, 11 hectares of which are in Bourgueil. " Eighty percent are on the hillside, above the road that passes in front of the house," he specifies. The Delaunays are serious craftsmen, advocates of hand harvesting (except the 1.5 hectares in Chinon which are too far away), separate vinification for each parcel of land, and the moderate use of oak barrels for ageing (on the condition that the wines preserve the fruit and, therefore, never for more than ten months). Following several cheerless vintages the wines are now displaying an open smile. The Saint-Nicolas-de-Bourgueil '96 (33 F) is round, fluid and fruity with a light and tender tannic structure. The Chinon '95 (32 F), from sandy soils close to the Loire, is very aromatic (strawberry, plum), round, and full. It's a festive wine that gives instant pleasure. In Bourgueil, the Domaine '96 (32 F) has an expressive aromatic fruitiness (crushed black currant and raspberry). The Les Pins '96 (34 F), from sandy, stony soils is more vigorous and direct. The Les Graviers '95 (35 F) is marked by jammy, spicy flavors and a mellow tannic structure.

Our choice Bourgueil Prestige '95 (42 F). Aged eight months in oak barrels. Deep color, the nose is lightly gamy but dominated by very ripe, small, red-berry fruits. These aromas reappear on the palate which is full and velvety with a firm finish. To drink or age ten years.

Reception Excellent, in a small room in the house reserved for visitors.

How to get there *(Map 19): From Tours towards Langeais via N152, then Saint-Patrice and Ingrandes and finally Restigné and Bourgueil via D35. Turn right 1km after Bourgueil, at the restaurant La Lande, towards Moulin Bleu. The cellar is immediately on the right at the stop sign.*

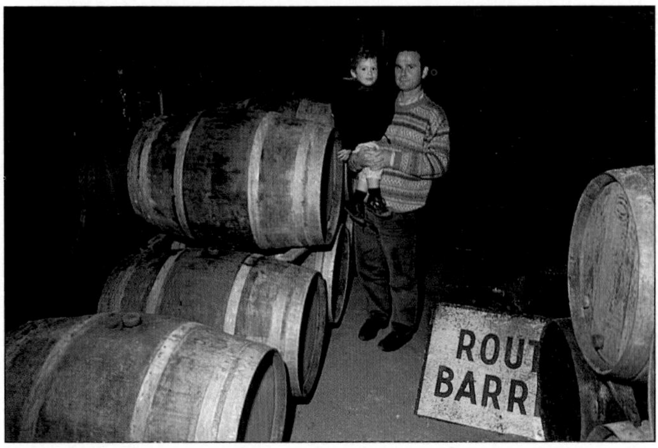

Family portrait: Pierre Breton, his son and the wine.

Domaine Catherine et Pierre Breton

Owners Catherine and Pierre Breton. **Address** Les Galichets, 8 route du Peu Muleau, 37140 Restigné - Tel. 02.47.97.30.41 Fax 02.47.97.46.49. **Open** By appointment. **Spoken** English.

What a great name for a wine grower in Touraine as Breton is none other than the local name for Cabernet Franc. Installed since 1982 and benefiting from old vines (average age 40 years) Pierre Breton is a man of perpetual motion. Having just established an organic culture at the domaine he has now passed on to the biodynamic system with complete working of the soil, hand harvesting, natural yeasts, little or no sulfur and no filtration. These distortions of modern viticulture have resulted in wines with a purity of fruit that are fine, frank on the palate, and remarkably digestible (a note for thirsty drinkers). The Bourgueil Trinch '96 (36 F) shows a profusion of fruit. Les Galichets '96 (45 F) offers a purée of fruits and is supple finishing on a crisp, vigorous note. The Chinon Les Beaumont '96 (approx. 45 F) is balanced between the notes of crystallized prune, the gras and the silky extract.

Our choice Bourgueil Les Perrières '95 (65 F). From vines that are more than 70-years-old, aged 18 months in oak barrels. The power of the wine is linked to the finesse of the tannins and the ripe, spicy flavors. It will close up for a while before opening out again with panache.

Reception On our last visit, Pierre had just left for Belgium to get chocolates for the children. A commendable act on the eve of Easter. In the absence of the boss Catherine briskly leads the tasting.

How to get there *(Map 19): From Tours towards Langeais via N152, then Saint-Patrice, Ingrandes and Restigné via D35. Turn right at the signpost. The cellar is on the right. New signpost.*

Pierre-Jacquet Druet, fascinated by long ageing Bourgueil.

Domaine Pierre-Jacques Druet

Owners Martine and Pierre-Jacques Druet. **Address** Le Pied-Fourrier, hameau de la Croix-Rouge, 37140 Benais - Tel. 02.47.97.37.34 Fax 02.47.97.46.40. **Open** From Monday to Saturday, by appointment only.

Old (40-50 years) and very old (over 80 years) Cabernet Franc, low yields, late harvesting and a relatively short vatting period but with high temperatures and significant *pigeage*, these are the tools Pierre-Jacquet Druet uses to make wines. “I’m looking for the nobility of the tannins,” says this wine grower who learned his trade in Bordeaux. Installed in Bourgueil for the last 17 years, he is fascinated with long ageing red wines, those which leave an impression long after our stay on earth. The ageing of the wines (12-24 months) takes place in 700 liter oak barrels. Apart from the Bourgueil Les Cent Boisselé (’96: 41 F, half fruit, half floral, very fresh and long) and in a lesser way the Chinon Clos de Danzay (’95: 44 F, quite powerful, spicy with settled tannins) the wines of Druet defy time with their dense color and intense extract. The Vaumoreau ’90, for instance, stayed four years in barrel and is just now beginning to open out with a chocolate note, mellow structure and great complexity. The Vaumoreau ’96, similar to the ’90, is for sale *en primeur*, to be available in 1999.

Our choice The ‘93s actually on sale are dense, concentrated but very closed. The Bourgueils Vaumoreau (90 F) and Grand Mont (60 F) will open up in 2000 and 2003. The 95’s which follow are riper.

Reception By Pierre-Jacques or his wife Martine. For those passionate about wine.

How to get there *(Map 19): From Tours towards Langeais via N152, then Saint-Patrice, Ingrandes and Restigné via D35. Turn right at the level of Restigné into Benais and continue towards La Croix-Rouge. The domaine is on the left.*

Thierry Boucard and the *Miroir de la Chanteleuserie.*

Domaine de la Chanteleuserie

Owner Thierry Boucard. **Address** 37140 Benais - Tel. 02.47.97.30.20 Fax 02.47.97.46.73. **Open** From Monday to Saturday, by appointment. **Credit cards** Visa, Eurocard, MasterCard.

The domaine mixes tradition (pigeage in open-top wooden vats) with modernity (stainless steel vats) depending on the origin of the parcels of vines and the style of the vintage. Moïse Boucard swears by the old chestnut Port barrels to age his wine (the bulk wines are always aged in them). His son Thierry, at the domaine since 1985, prefers new 500 liter oak barrels. The vines in appellation Bourgueil (18 hectares), which are machine harvested, are located at Benais on clay-limestone soils that have a reputation for producing solid wines, particularly in the zone known as Beauvais. The '93 (35 F) has fine tannins but has closed up again and needs a little patience. The Vieilles Vignes '95 (35 F) is more supple but with slightly drier tannins. The Saint-Nicolas-de-Bourgueil Irène '96 (28 F) is simple, fruity, and easy drinking.

Our choice Bourgueil Alouette '96 (28 F). A spring-time wine that is round, fruity, fleshy, delicious, and to be drunk now. For longer ageing, the Bourgueil '95 (35 F) has black fruit notes and the marked flavor of bellpepper and moist earth.

Reception Good, in a tasting room opened in 1991.

How to get there *(Map 19): From Tours towards Langeais via N152, then Saint-Patrice, Ingrandes and Restigné via D35. Turn right at the level of Restigné, before the petrol station on the right, for 1km. Large signpost on the wall of the domaine.*

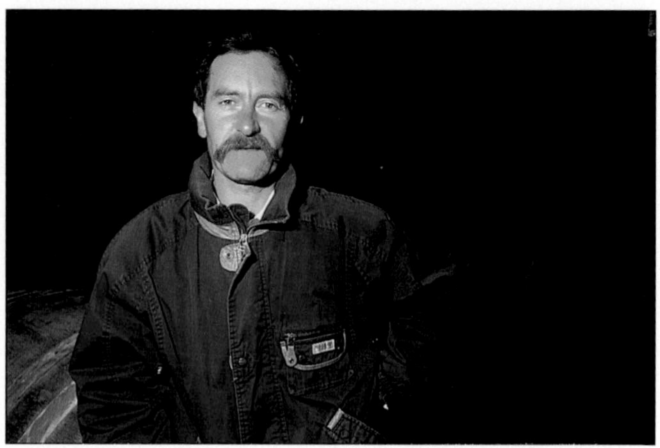

Yannick Amirault.

Yannick Amirault

Owner Nicole and Yannick Amirault. **Address** La Coudraye 37140 Bourgueil - Tel. 02.47.97.78.07 Fax 02.47.97.94.78. **Open** From Monday to Satuturday, 9:00-12:00 and 14:00-18:00, by appointment.

While Saint-Nicolas-de-Bourgueil, and to a lesser extent Bourgueil, traverse a rather uninspiring period (too many wine growers sleeping on their laurels), the wines of Yannick Amirault have never been so good. There are few domaines that can offer such satisfaction at the end of a tasting of so many different *cuvées*. To say that '95 and '96 are successful is an understatement. The Amirault style is one of intensely colored wines that are deep and structured but silky. Among the three Saint-Nicolas-de-Bourgueils, La Source '96 (36 F) is a drinkable, fruit delicacy, and Les Malgagnes '95 (50 F) a concentrated wine that will make a great bottle beyond the year 2000. Of the Bourgueils (four reds), Les Quartiers '95 (40 F), which is marked by the clay-limestone soils, is still a little austere and needs time, like Le Grand Clos '95 (46 F), which is dense, firm and velvety with notes of spices and blackberry jam. In 1996 Yannick returned to plowing the soil and vinified a percentage of the wines with a minimum of sulfur.

Our choice Saint-Nicolas-de-Bourgueil Les Graviers Vieilles Vignes '96 (42 F). Blackcurrant and raspberry, tender, ripe, delicious, and rich. One of the best in the appellation. The Bourgueil La Petite Cave '95 (60 F) is a wine to age but how can one resist its deep, rich (spices, plum, ripe cherry) nose, soft, sweet palate, and deliciously velvety texture and flavor? What a dilemma.

Reception Passionate by Yannick, more reserved but with equal attention by Nicole, in a room of their recently-built house.

How to get there *(Map 19): From Tours towards Langeais via N152, then Saint-Patrice, Ingrandes and Restigné via D35. Turn right 1km after Bourgueil, by the restaurant La Lande, towards Moulin Bleu. 500m on the right.*

Joël Taluau: "... imprison the maximum fruit and pleasure."

Domaine Joël Taluau

Owners Clarisse and Joël Taluau. **Address** Chevrette, 37140 Saint-Nicolas de Bourgueil - Tel. 02.47.97.78.79 Fax 02.47.97.95.60.

In a region where the term "vieilles vignes" (old vines) is usually abused Joël Taluau (16.5 hectares in Saint-Nicolas-de-Bourgueil) is one of the rare wine growers to attach the inscription "jeunes vignes" (young vines) to one of his *cuvées*. "Just like man, the vine does stupid things up to the age of 20, from 20 to 40 it gets wiser and after that it's a question of philosophy," he says. His wines are orientated towards the fruit (there is no barrel ageing) and usually vigorous in youth indicating that they are not necessarily for early drinking. Both the *cuvées* Domaine and the Vieilles Vignes need a certain amount of time. However, the Jeunes Vignes '96 (33 F), a fruit purée which is acidulous, round and endowed with soft tannins can be consumed now. The Domaine '95 (39 F), for which a second bottling was made at the end of 1997, has more concentration, ripeness, and flavor. To drink or age.

Our choice Saint-Nicolas-de-Bourgueil Vieilles Vignes '95 (46 F). Bright red hue, the nose is ripe and slightly peppery with the aroma of raspberry jam while the palate is full, round and generous with plenty of liveliness on the finish. To drink or age four or five years. The '96 (available spring 1998) is equally attractive.

Reception Well organized, in a room reserved for visitors.

How to get there *(Map 19): From Tours towards Langeais via N152, then Saint-Patrice, Ingrandes and Restigné via D35. Turn right 1km after Bourgueil, by the restaurant La Lande, towards Moulin Bleu. Turn left at the stop sign and follow the signs.*

Michel Gendrier, more white than red.

Domaine des Huards

Owners Jocelyne and Michel Gendrier. **Address** Les Huards, 41700 Cour-Cheverny - Tel. 02.54.79.97.90 Fax 02.54.79.26.82. **Open** From Monday to Saturday, 8:00-12:30 and 14:00-19:00 **Credit Cards** Visa, Eurocard, MasterCard.

Contrary to the other domaines in the appellation, the Domaine des Huards, with its calcium soils, produces more white wines than red. There are two *cuvées* of red. Le Pressoir, made only in good vintages, is produced from 80% Pinot Noir and 20% Gamay and is generous and robust. The *cuvée* Domaine des Huards is based on the Gamay grape (60%). In the whites, choose the Cheverny '95 (24 F) for its orange peel nose and crisp palate or the *cuvée* La Haute-Pinglerie '95, produced from vines grown on a more clay-based soil, for its expressive palate which verges towards a nuance of almond and fruit kernel. We preferred the wines produced from the Romorantin grape variety. The '95 (25 F) has an intensely mineral nose (damp chalk), fleshy palate, fine "legs," and notes of plum and fruit kernel and plenty of length and persistence.

Our choice Cour-Cheverny Vieilles Vignes Cuvée François 1er white '93 (28 F). The Romorantin vines are aged between 50-70 years, the oldest being planted in 1922 on clay-limestone soils. The nose is intense, mineral, the palate crunchy with notes of tobacco, fresh straw and spices. It's a wine that is long and persistent to drink now. The '95 (approx. 30 F), available from Easter 1998, has an exotic nose with a fleshy, full-bodied palate which is flavorsome and has plenty of extract. To age a little.

Reception Warm, in the tasting room.

How to get there *(Map 20): Leave Cour-Cheverny towards Blois via D765. Turn right after the gendarmerie and follow the Gendrier signposts.*

Philippe Loquineau, the king of Romorantin.

Domaine de la Plante-d'or

Owner Philippe Loquineau. **Address** La Demalerie, 41700 Cheverny - Tel. 02.54.44.23.09 Fax 02.54.44.22.16. **Open** By appointment. **Spoken** English. **Credit cards** Visa, Eurocard, MasterCard.

The "*plant d'or*" or golden plant is the lupin. According to old texts on the subject studied by Philippe Loquineau: "Only the yellow lupin prospered on our soils." These are poor soils favorable to the vine. Philippe Loquineau runs a domaine of 20 hectares, the vines planted on sandy-clay soils (in the Cheverny region) and several parcels of clay-limestone (at Cormeray). The white Cheverny '95 (30 F) , a blend of 80% Sauvignon Blanc and 20% Chardonnay, provides a discreet, floral nose and a fine, fresh palate which mixes the aromas of plum and fruit kernel. However, it is the Romorantin, the white grape variety particular to the appellation Cour-Cheverny, that justly inspires curiosity. It was imported from Burgundy by François 1er who planted 80 000 vines near his hunting lodge in Romorantin, hence the name. Like the Melon de Bourgogne, the grape variety of Muscadet that also derives from Burgundy, it is a much traveled variety that has only found success away from its origins.

Our choice Cour-Cheverny '95 (30 F). 100% Romorantin. The attack is very mineral evolving towards floral notes.The palate is expressive and fleshy with aromatic notes of honey and dried fruits (almond) crowned by a crisp and persistent finish. To drink.

Reception In a perfectly-restored farm typical of the Sologne region.

***How to get there** (Map 20): Opposite Château de Cheverny take the lefthand road running alongside the railing as far as the wayside cross then towards Fougères-Château du Breuil via D52. Turn left after 2,5km and follow the signs. The cellar is on the left.*

A domaine that champions non-conformist wines.

Clos du Tue-Bœuf

Owners Thierry and Jean-Marie Puzelat. **Address** 6 route de Seur, 41120 Les Montils - Tel. 02.54.44.05.16 Fax 02.54.44.13.37. **Open** By appointment. **Spoken** English.

This is a domaine that makes us rock and roll, not only because the group, Les Garçons Bouchers, take regular inspiration from it, but because the brothers Puzelat perform an amazing juggling act with the wines of the region. They prefer to declare their wines as vin de pays or even vin de table rather than give up winemaking without sulfur and with extremely ripe grapes (14.10% natural for the white Cheverny '96). They also propagate vines by mass selection from old plants, preserve the traditional grape varieties (Meslier, Menu Pineau) and age their wines for a long time on lees. This domaine is definitely outside the norms of the region. Among the palate of wines to discover, without any set priority, we liked the Sauvignon Vieilles Vignes '96 (35 F) for its expressiveness and smoky notes, the white Cheverny '96 (32 F) for its fruit, the white Touraine Brin de Chèvre (30 F), produced from Menu Pineau, for its musky notes, the red Cheverny La Gravotte '96 (39 F) for its finesse, and the red Cheverny La Caillère '96 (29 F) for the fleshy extract.

Our choice Chardonnay Vin de Pays '96 (45 F). Produced from a tiny yield (18 hectoliters/hectare) and very powerful (15.5% natural). This is simply a monster. The palate is very rich and powerful but fine and delicate with a well-endowed structure, length, persistence and musky notes. To drink.

Reception In an attractive tasting room that mixes old work implements and modern paintings.

How to get there *(Map20): From Cheverny towards Amboise via D77 passing by Cellettes and Seur. The cellar is on the right at the entrance to Montils. Signpost.*

Proudly hoisted, the colors of a new star in Chinon.

Domaine Philippe Alliet

Owner Philippe Alliet. **Address** L'Ouche Mondé, 37500 Cravant - Tel. and Fax 02.47.93.17.62. **Open** By appointment.

Philippe Alliet created his domaine in 1985 by grouping together family land, which he qualifies as "an average *terroir*," made up of sand and gravel soils. "It took time to tame the vines which had been saturated in chemicals," he acknowledges. The turn in quality came between 1990 and 1992 with the land ploughed, the number of buds on the vine reduced and minimum yields for a Chinon (38 hl/ha) introduced. The vatting period and *pigeage* have been lengthened and the barrel has become a key element (malolactic fermentation in oak barrel). Three-quarters of the production goes towards the Chinon Tradition with the young vines of 13-25 years aged in seasoned oak barrels. The '96 (38 F), harvested at the beginning of October, provides a supple, fleshy extract with a mix of fruity (blackberry, black currant) and floral notes and fine tannins. In spring 1998 Philippe will release his first Coteaux de Noiré '96 (approx. 60 F, to reserve as quantities are limited) produced this time from a great *terroir.* The vines have a southerly exposure and are located at Chinon near the celebrated Chêne Vert and Clos de l'Olive. Tasted during maturation, the wine appears majestic, very rich and velvety with long ageing potential.

Our choice Chinon Vieilles Vignes '96 (48 F, to reserve, available March 1998). From vines of 40-50 years. Aged 100% in seasoned oak barrels. A deeply-colored wine with very ripe extract but good acidity, beautifully structured with long ageing potential.

Reception Discreet, around a small bistro table, in the dispatch area or in the small vinification cellar.

How to get there *(Map 19): From Chinon towards Cravant via D21. Turn left in front of the church, then first on the left after 500m, then first on the right. The cellar is signposted on the left.*

The Grézeaux vineyard in the autumn.

Domaine Bernard Baudry

Owners Henriette and Bernard Baudry. **Address** 13, coteau de Sonnay, 37500 Cravant - Tel. 02.47.93.15.79 Fax 02.47.98.44.44. **Open** By appointment. **Spoken** English.

The originality of Bernard Baudry's domaine is based on the fact that the majority of his 27 hectares are located on rather light soils. From these he produces remarkably concentrated wines assisted by selective picking of each parcel, reasonable yields and intelligent maturation in oak barrels (*cuvée* Les Grézeaux). Bernard, however, is a far-sighted wine grower who doesn't cease to pose questions, increasing the number of experiments at each vintage. In '96, for instance, he returned to harvesting by hand for all the red wines. The Les Granges '96 (37 F), from young vines, has fine extract and is supple, long and delicious when young. The Domaine '95 (42 F), vinified and aged in vat, is on another level in terms of structure and ripeness. It is round on the palate and marked by the ripeness of the grapes with stewed fruit consistency and soft tannins.

Our choice Chinon Les Grézeaux '95 (52 F), aged in oak barrels and produced from old vines located opposite the cellar planted on gravel soils with a clay sub-soil. A wine which has volume and ripeness with a powerful but velvety extract and long, spicy finish. To drink with great pleasure or to age.

Reception Passionate, with Bernard or his wife Henriette, in their charming, classic, stone house which backs on to the Coteaux de Sonnay where the cellars have been excavated.

How to get there *(Map 19): From Chinon towards Cravant-les-Coteaux via D21. The cellar is on the left at Sonnay, 1km before Cravant. Signpost.*

Jean-Christophe Pelletier, the aspiration of Chinon.

Domaine des Beguineries

Owner Jean-Christophe Pelletier. **Address** Saint-Louans, 37500 Chinon - Tel. 06.08.92.88.17 - Tel. and Fax 02.47.93.04.30. **Open** Every day, by appointment.

Jean-Christophe Pelletier, 31, has been installed at his own eight-hectare domaine since 1995. In all, he cultivates 16 hectares, including the family vines, and looks after the vineyard at Château de Saint-Louans. During a vast blind tasting of 150 Chinons, his Vieilles Vignes '95 (34 F), aged in vat and oak barrels, excited us with its deep, dark hue, ripeness, fruit, and density. His vineyard is located at Saint-Louans (very fruity wines) and at Les Beguineries. He works the soil, harvests by hand, and vinifies the old and young vines separately. His first Cuvée du Terroir '96 (29 F) is aromatic (cherry, black currant) and has plenty of color and structure for an early drinking, spring *cuvée.* Until recently Jean-Christophe bottled very little wine but sold in bulk at a very good price to the best negociant in Chinon.

Our choice Chinon Vieilles Vignes '96 (32,50 F). The first bottling (September '97) will be a blend of vat-aged and barrel-aged wines. It has a pronounced fruit character (blackberry, cherry), a full, fleshy palate and soft but present tannins. To drink or age. There will be a second bottling (Prestige: 35 F) at the beginning of 1998 from wines aged 100% in oak casks.

Reception By Christophe or his parents, in an agricultural building, with boots off! During our last visit Christophe talked of obtaining a new cellar to receive visitors.

How to get there *(Map 19): From Beaumont towards Chinon via D749. Turn left before entering Chinon towards Saint-Louans, climb the slope for 300m and turn left again. Running alongside the park of the château, the road to the domaine is 50m along on the right. There is a shed covered with sheet-metal.*

Serge Sourdais, "a devotee of separate vinification."

Le Logis de la Bouchardière

Owners Serge and Bruno Sourdais. **Address** 37500 Cravant-les-Coteaux - Tel. 02.47.93.04.27 Fax 02.47.93.38.52. **Open** From Monday to Saturday, 8:00-12:00 and 14:00-18:30.

This large domaine of 42 hectares is spread throughout Chinon, Cravant and Panzoult with a quarter of the vineyard planted on sand and gravel soils, three-quarters on clay-silica hillsides and plateau and a tiny parcel on clay-limestone (Les Cornuelles). Each parcel (machine harvested) is vinified separately. "I am a devotee of separate vinification," says Serge Sourdais who with his son Bruno (the sixth generation) manages the property and presides over the Chinon wine growers association. During vinification the temperatures for fermentation are adjusted to produce densely colored wines that are intensely aromatic. All the wines are aged in wood, either *foudres* or barrels. The *cuvée* Sourdais-Taveau '96 (25 F), produced from a portion of young vines, has the pronounced aroma of crushed black currants, humus, and fruit concentrate and is round on the palate. La Bouchardière '96 (29 F) has a more solid pair of shoulders but at the same time remains approachable when young. Les Clos and Les Cornuelles, selections according to *terroir* and old vines, are concentrated, long ageing wines in '95 and '96.

Our choice Chinon Les Clos '95 (33 F), deep hue, very ripe on the nose with ample, suave fruit that has not been over extracted and an attractive peppery finish. A lovely wine to keep or to drink. Les Cornuelles '95 (45 F) is at this stage closed and austere. Make an appointment with this wine in another five years.

Reception Family atmosphere, brisk, in a large tasting room with rustic decor next to the barrel cellar.

How to get there *(Map 19): From Chinon towards Cravant-les-Coteaux via D21. Turn left 2km before Cravant, at Narçay, and follow the signs.*

Jean, Marie-Claire and Christophe Baudry.

Domaine de la Perrière

Owners Christophe, Jean and Marie-Claire Baudry. **Address** 37500 Cravant - Tel. 02.47.93.15.99 Fax 02.47.98.34.57. **Open** From Monday to Saturday midday, 9:00-12:00 and 14:00-19:00, by appointment. Saturday afternoon and Sunday morning. **Credit cards** Visa, Eurocard, MasterCard.

This very old domaine of 40 hectares, practically in one single unit except for the vines at Les Grézeaux, is located on a homogeneous, free-draining *terroir* of gravel terraces. It is, therefore, the age of the vines that differentiates the various *cuvées*. The young vines are aged in vat, the *cuvée* Domaine in old *foudres* and the Vieilles Vignes partially in seasoned oak barrels. The Domaine '96 (32 F) has a bright red hue, an intense black currant aroma, and is fleshy, tender and delicious. The '95 (30 F), like all the wines from gravel soils after bottling, is more closed but without fault, and will help bridge the gap before the arrival of the rather firm and dense Vieilles Vignes '95 (42 F). It's also worth noting that La Perrière produces an excellent Chinon rosé (26 F) every year which is round and fruity and available from the spring.

Our choice In '96 Christophe Baudry pushed a little further than usual the ripeness and extraction of the fruit. He was right to do so as the *cuvée* Vieilles Vignes (42 F) is better than the '90 with greater density, flesh, and softness in the tannins. The wine is a real delight.

Reception Excellent, usually with Christophe's mother, Marie-Claire, in a beautiful tasting room.

How to get there *(Map 19): From Chinon towards Cravant-les-Coteaux via D21. The cellar is on the left at Sonnay, 1km before Cravant.*

Patrice Colin, an eighth generation wine grower.

Domaine Patrice Colin

Owner Patrice Colin. **Address** 5 impasse de la Gaudetterie, 41100 Thoré-la-Rochette. - Tel. 02.54.72.80.73 Fax 02.54.72.75.54. **Open** From Monday to Saturday, 9:00-12:00 and 14:00-19:00.

Alongside the prestigious appellations, Touraine offers a number of appellations of lesser reputation that are even on occasion totally obscure. However, the conscientiousness of several wine growers has resulted in a number of wines worth discovering, particularly as the prices are more than reasonable. Profiting from the experience of eight generations of wine growers Patrice Colin also benefits from some very old vines. The Pineau d'Aunis is over 100 years and the Chenin Blanc will soon have a healthy 80 years. It's the wines produced from this last variety that we prefer but one can also select from the reds without any problem. They are generally lively and supple with a rustic texture and peppery notes when produced from the Pineau d'Aunis (also known as Chenin Noir) like the well-defined Les Marnières '96 (25 F). The *cuvée* Pierre-François Colin (19 F), produced from Gamay, Pinot Noir and Pineau d'Aunis, is daintier and more fluid, providing easy pleasure for all.

Our choice To drink young: The dry white *cuvée* Silex '96 (20 F), pure Chenin Blanc, acidulous fruit with a touch of mineral, lively on the palate. The Vieilles Vignes '96 (25 F), still dry and pure Chenin Blanc, has more depth and ripeness but is still crisp and long with a citrus fruit finish. To drink over the next five years: the Vieille Vigne BR 163 '96 (35 F) is a selection of Chenin Blanc, harvested at 13°8 natural, which has 8 grams/liter residual sugar. Subtle and fresh, this is truly an original wine.

Reception Friendly. Different regional products are for sale at the cellar.

How to get there *(Map 20): From Vendôme towards Montoire-sur-le-Loir via D917. Turn right after 8km towards Thoré-la-Rochette via D82. The cellar is in the center of the village, on the right. Signpost.*

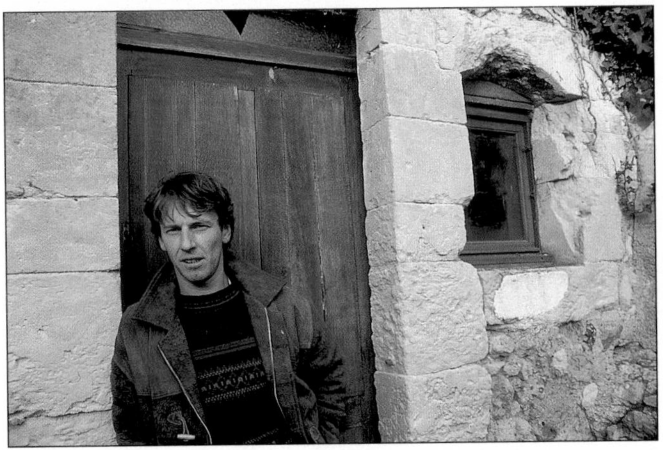

Nicolas Renard, the "Martian" of Jasnières.

Domaine Renard-Potaire

Owner Nicolas Renard. **Address** Cellar: La Borde Gaudin 72240 Marçon. Home: La Pointe 72240 Marçon - Tel. 02.43.79.90.59 Fax 02.43.79.25.08. **Open** Every day, by appointment. **Spoken** English.

With his concern for late harvesting and plowing the soils and phobia of sulfur during vinification, Nicolas Renard appears like a being from outer space in Jasnières. This young wine grower, who worked for the *Office National des Fôrets*, is not one to follow the crowd. In 1996, while the majority applied for a reduction in the minimum level of alcohol for the appellation, this madcap was requesting a dispensation for overstepping the limit, and this of course without any chaptalization (as in the previous six years). This brazen vintner even harvested the equivalent of a barrel at 23% natural in '96, "just to prove that we can harvest really ripe here." Tasted before bottling the '95s are all thrilling wines. Les Molières (42 F), the driest, is fine and direct with a hint of honey. Les Molières *Demi-sec* (52 F) has a toasted nose and is round and fluid. The Saint-Jacques (59 F) is fleshy and expressive while Les Vignes sous les Bois (45 F) is more mineral.

Our choice Jasnières Les Jasnières '95 (82 F). 60 and 80-year-old vines harvested in mid-November at 13°7. Honey-gold hue, this wine has to be aerated in order to release the complex aromas and elegant mineral and crystallized fruit flavors. Superb.

Reception Passionate and warm, in the long cellar hewn from the rock.

How to get there *(Map 20): From Vendôme towards La Chartre-sur-le-Loir via D917, then towards Marçon. Turn left before Marçon for 150m, then climb to the right for 200m. The entrance to the cellar is hidden by the vegetation. There is no signpost.*

Joël Gigou, a wine grower with "bottle."

Domaine Joël Gigou

Owner Joël Gigou. **Address** 4 rue des Caves, 72340 La Chartre-sur-le-Loir - Tel. 02.43.44.48.72 Fax 02.43.44.42.15. **Open** By appointment. **Credit cards** Visa, Eurocard, MasterCard.

Joël Gigou is the star of Jasnières, the tiny appellation in the Sarthe producing white wines from Chenin Blanc, and of rare Coteaux-du-Loir (Chenin and Pineau d'Aunis). He works with passion and self-confidence. In 1995, he took over the old vines that belonged to Jean-Baptiste Pinon, his rival in terms of quality. He was excited by the '96 vintage which was particularly good for the reds. The Pineau d'Aunis is peppery and fruity (cherry). "It was harvested at 13.5% which is rare," explains Joël. The Gamay and rosé are equally as good while the white wines are as good as ever. The Jasnières L'Aillerie '96 (37 F) is round, lemony and fruity and can be appreciated young. The late harvest Sélection de Raisins Nobles '96 (80 F) appears as promising as the '95, with toasted, crystallized citrus fruit flavors and an elegant finish.

Our choice Jasnières Clos Saint-Jacques '96 (47 F). A fine, direct, lengthy white wine marked by notes of silex and a hint of menthol. To drink or age. A rarity : Coteaux-du-Loir Oppus '96 (75 F, to reserve), produced from Chenin Blanc affected by oidium, harvested at 18% natural and at 17 hectoliters/hectare. Concentrated and mineral.

Reception Good. Don't refuse an invitation to visit the cellar located a little further away. It is made up of tiny recesses coated with a fungus which gives the walls a lovely red color.

How to get there *(Map 20): From Vendôme towards La Chartre-sur-le-Loir via D917, then the D305. At La Chartre towards Tours. Turn left after crossing the Loire towards Tréhet via D154. The rue des Caves is on the right.*

François Chidaine, "*vigneron paysan*" and proud of it.

François Chidaine

Owner François Chidaine. **Address** 5, Grande Rue, Husseau, 37270 Montlouis-sur-Loire - Tel. 02.47.45.19.14 Fax 02.47.45.19.08. **Open** By appointment.

François Chidaine has had the words "*vigneron paysan*" (wine grower-countryman) embroidered on his work jacket in the same way as restaurant chefs. This he did after a "mild fit of temper" in order to assert his intention "to be completely involved in his land and vines" and due to the pride in a status he had for a long time refused. If anyone reproaches him for the intransigence of the newly converted then they should also congratulate him on his exacting labor: total working of the soils, no cultured yeasts, and the refusal to deacidify or manipulate the wines in order that they remain true to the vintage. He started with a small surface area, only 30 ares, then expanded (although more often as tenant than owner) on to the best parcels with silica soils (Clos du Breuil, Clos du Renard), saving from being uprooted the old vines planted at the beginning of the century. There is a lovely dry white, Clos du Breuil '95 (35 F) which is fine and linear and a *demi-sec*, Les Tuffeaux '95 (38 F) which is mild and floral. Les Lys are the *moelleux* and without any doubt we preferred the '90 (1464 F for a case of 12 bottles). The nose is riper and more expressive than in the '89 vintage with a note of quince. The palate is rich, raisined by botrytis, fine and elegant, long and persistent.

Our choice Montlouis *demi-sec* Clos Habert '95 (42 F) for the finesse of the nose, the dense, present palate, the soft, sweet extract, good sugar-acid balance and long, crisp finish. To age a while.

Reception Passionate, at the vinification cellar.

How to get there *(Map 20): From Tours towards Amboise via D751. Turn right 4km after Montlouis (signpost) and enter the hamlet. The cellar is on the right.*

Saint-Vincent stands vigil over the tasting room at the domaine.

Domaine Delétang

Owner Olivier Delétang. **Address** 19 rue d'Amboise, 37270 Saint-Martin-Le-Beau - Tel. 02.47.50.67.25 Fax 02.47.50.26.46. **Open** From Monday to Friday, 9:00-12:00 and 13:30-18:30, Saturday and Sunday by appointment. **Spoken** English. **Credit cards** Visa, Eurocard, MasterCard.

The wines of Montlouis were for a long time sold under the name Vouvray. A "Vouvray from Montlouis" was the expression which the wine growers of Vouvray fought against in court for nearly 20 years. Like its rival, Montlouis produces a range of different wines from the Chenin Blanc, from dry to *moelleux.* In dry (sec), the Domaine '95 (37 F) is fine on the nose with a long, expressive palate. The *demi-sec* Les Bâtisses '95 (42 F) is fruitier and more pleasing, but delicate and balanced (the '96 will be fleshier). The *moelleux* that are actually for sale are very different. The Domaine '95 (50 F) is floral (acacia) and fruity (fig) on the nose with a very elegant palate with a hint of date. The Grande Réserve '95 (120 F) is very raisined. The Petits Boulay Grande Réserve *moelleux* '90 (140 F) is already a very seductive wine with fruity nose (white peach), toasted palate, great finesse and astonishing persistence.

Our choice Montlouis *moelleux* Les Bâtisses '90 (95 F). For its delicate nose of fresh mushrooms, quince and clementines, and the fresh, full, toasted palate which has plenty of botrytis and which finishes on a note of Mocha coffee. To keep.

Reception In an attractive corner for tasting in the cellar.

How to get there *(Map 20): From Tours towards Chenonceaux via D140. Turn left after 18km in to the center of Saint-Martin-le-Beau. The cellar is 100m further, on the left. Sign.*

Jacky Blot surveys the fermentations in his cellar.

Domaine de la Taille-aux-Loups

Owner Jacky Blot. **Address** 8 rue des Aîtres, Husseau, 37270 Montlouis - Tel. 02.47.45.11.11 Fax 02.47.45.11.14. **Open** Everyday, 9:00-19:00. **Spoken** English, German, Spanish. **Credit cards** Visa, Eurocard, MasterCard.

Since settling in Montlouis in 1989, Jacky Blot has become one of the wine growers helping to restore the appellation. He is a devotee of selective harvesting (*tris*), a perfectionist (sorting table placed in the vines, transport of the juice that has escaped during the picking in water-tight bottles), and a "modernist" (vinification in relatively new oak). His Chenin Blanc, whether dry or *moelleux*, has a particular style. Through blending he avoids the production of "monster" wines that are very rich and instead aims for delicacy and elegance. The dry wines are really dry and the demi-secs only slightly sweet. Of the dry wines we liked the '95 (45 F) for its weight but the wood needs time to mellow out. In the *demi-secs*, the '90 (75 F) is powerfully expressive and the '96 (60 F) has astonishing aromas of red fruits. There is an excellent range of *moelleux* including the '90 (100 F) which is extremely linear despite the sugar (40 grams/liter) and which has an exotic nose (crystallized pineapple) and botrytized, Mocha chocolate palate. The Cuvée des Loups '90 (160 F) has a long, complex palate (milk coffee, date, plum). If you want a treat don't forget the sparkling *naturel, non dosé* which is extremely tasty.

Our choice Montlouis *moelleux* '89 (80 F). The nose is fine, botrytised and toasted. The palate is fine, full and very long with notes of dried fruits lifted by a crisp, acid finish.

Reception Perfect. Don't miss an invitation to visit the well-arranged vinification cellar hewn from the tufa rock.

How to get there *(Map 20): From Tours towards Amboise via D751. Turn right 4km after Montlouis towards Husseau. Climb the Grand-Rue, then the rue des Aîtres. The cellar is on the right. Signposted.*

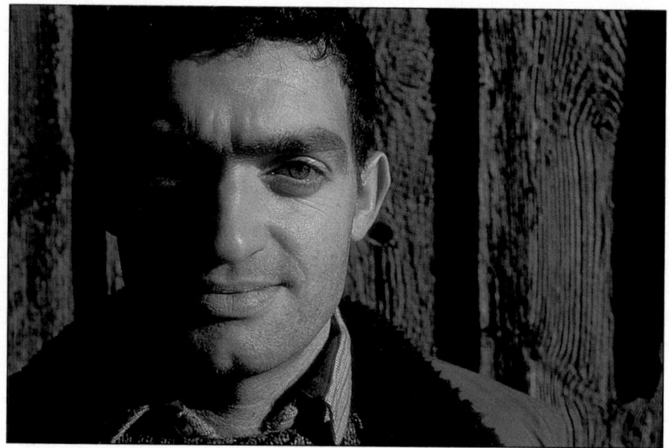

Thierry Michaud is an enthusiast of Sauvignons "with substance."

Domaine Michaud

Owners Thierry and Dorothée Michaud. **Address** Les Martinières, 41140 Noyers-sur-Cher - Tel. 02.54.32.47.23 Fax 02.54.75.39.19. **Open** By appointment. **Spoken** English.

This was a wonderful little discovery, brought back in our nets from an expedition in 1996. The prices are negligible but the wines made with great care. Thierry Michaud preserves the old vines, even the more marginal grape varieties planted by his father, vinifies by *terroir* before blending the different *cuvées,* does very little or no chaptalization, and doesn't use cultured yeasts. He seeks, among the rather lax attitude towards yields in the region, to produce Sauvignons "with substance." His Touraine '96 (20 F) was harvested at 13% natural and is, therefore, round and rich (with a point of unintentional sweetness), floral on the nose and ripe, fruity, expressive, and long on the palate. In red, look out for the Cabernet '96 (19 F) or the Gamay '96 (19 F) for their fruit, the Côt (Malbec) '96 (20 F) for its attractive notes of plum compote and above all the Touraine '96 (20 F), a blend of Gamay, Cabernet Franc and Côt for its plum and raisin nose, crisp, fine palate and good length.

Our choice Touraine rosé Cuvée Gris des Faiteaux '96 (20 F). A Pinot Gris planted by his father "to be conspicuously different". A well-balanced wine, fixed by its robust alcoholic structure (13°2 natural) and the color provided by light skin contact. Loads of flesh, finesse and attractive notes of apricot with a delicious fruit kernel finish and plenty of length. To drink.

Reception Attentive.

How to get there *(Map 20): From Tours towards Romorantin and Vierzon via N76. Turn right 5km after Noyers-sur-Cher towards Les Martinières. The cellar is in the center of the village.*

Illustration and support for Fié Gris and its mineral taste.

Jacky Preys et Fils

Owner Jacky Preys. **Address** Le Bois Pontois, 41130 Meusnes - Tel. 02.54.71.00.34 Fax 02.54.71.34.91. **Open** Everyday, 8:00-20:00, Sunday morning until 12:00.

Jacky Preys and his son Pascal have two passions. The first is the Fié Gris or "Surin du Poitou " grape variety, an ancestor of Sauvignon Blanc with a pink skin and white juice. The second is white silica soils. In fact, the domaine proudly announces that the wines are "*produits sur la pierre à fusil*," or "products of the flinty soils." A tasting goes well with the retelling of the story of the *caillouteux*, flintcutters for lighters and guns, and the quality of their products. The white flint from Meusnes could fire off, so they say, at least 30 shots from a harquebus gun while their opponents brown or black stones ceased firing after the eighth spark. The stones were in such demand that in order to baffle thieves they were sent secretively in small casks of wine! Among the numerous red wines offered by this domaine we liked the Touraine Vieille Tradition (19 F), a blend of Gamay, Cabernet and Côt, for its earthiness.

Our choice Touraine white '95 (28 F). This is the famous Fié Gris. It has an intense boxwood and smoky nose, very fleshy, round palate with an intense aromatic expression that mixes smoke and boxwood with mineral notes. Astonishing. To drink.

Reception Voluble, in a corner of the dispatch area.

How to get there *(Map 20): From Tours towards Romorantin via N76 and Chenonceaux, Montrichard and Saint-Aignan. At Saint-Aignan towards Selles via D17 for 10km. Turn right in the center of Meusnes towards Bois-Pontois and follow sign "Route du vignoble." The cellar is signposted.*

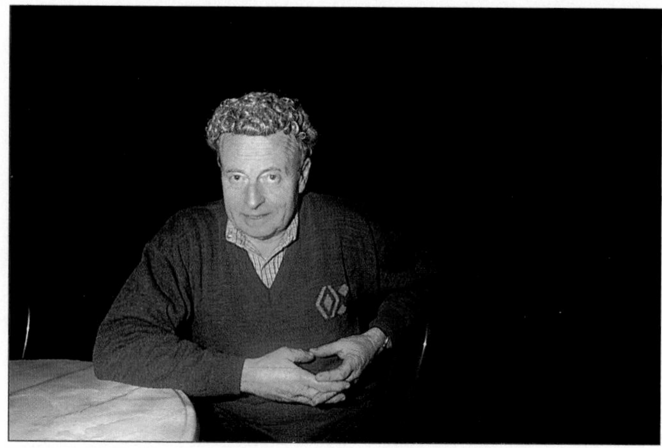

François Girault, a fan of meaty wines.

Clos de la Briderie

Owners Jeannine and François Girault. **Address** 7 quai des violettes, 37400 Amboise - Tel. 02.47.57.07.71 Fax 02.47.57.65.70. **Open** From Monday to Friday, 8:00-12:00 and 14:00-17:30, Saturday and Sunday by appointment. **Credit cards** Visa, Eurocard, MasterCard.

Like son, like father ! François Girault, the father, followed the example of his son Vincent (Château Gaillard) and four years ago converted his nine hectare domaine to the biodynamic system of cultivation. The vineyard, which exists as one single unit, is managed in an exemplary way. The dead vine plants are replaced progressively without uprooting the whole parcel, even if the difference in maturity means harvesting twice over. Contrary to the rest of the appellation which largely gives preference to the Gamay, the red wines of Clos de la Briderie blend this variety with Cabernet Franc and Côt which provides a meatier style of wine that can age a little. The white Touraine-Mesland Vieilles Vignes '95 (32 F) has a nose marked by the Chenin Blanc (80% and 20% Chardonnay), and a fine fleshy, persistent palate with a note of roasted almonds. Stocks of this wine may have run out in 1997. The '96, tasted when only a provisional blend, will be the same style of wine with the Chardonnay, which is now vinified in oak, well-integrated.

Our choice Touraine-Mesland Vieilles Vignes red '95 (32 F). A blend of a third each of old Gamay (30-40 years), Cabernet Franc (15 years) and Côt (10 years). It has a delicious, aromatic bouquet of red fruits with a hint of pepper. The palate is fine, ripe, well-formed, and teasing with a point of Côt. The '96, tasted when only a provisional blend, will be spicy and a little more structured. Age for a year.

Reception Excellent, in a corner of the cellar hewn from the tufa rock.

How to get there *(Map 20): Follow the quay alongside the Loire in Amboise towards Blois. The cellar is located 1km after the château, on the right. Sign.*

Vincent Girault, a follower of biodynamics.

Château Gaillard

Owner Vincent Girault. **Address** 41150 Mesland - Tel. 02.54.70.25.47 Fax 02.54.70.22.56. **Open** By appointment. **Spoken** English. **Credit cards** Visa, Eurocard, MasterCard.

Vincent Girault loves the idea that people come to buy his wines without him actively promoting them and that his customers compensate his efforts. These include a conversion to biodynamic cultivation six years ago, the progressive abandonment of mechanical harvesting to concentrate on selective harvesting, the discovery of the equation between each *terroir* and the different grape varieties (early ripening Gamay on sandy soils and later ripening Cabernet Franc, Côt and Chenin Blanc on clay and silica), the blending of different parcels and grape varieties and reducing yields. In just a few years the red wines have incontestably gained in flesh and flavor and the whites in complexity. There is a good *non dosé* Crémant (35 F) with fine bead, Chenin nose with notes of honey and fruit kernel, and ripe, fruity palate. Other wines of interest include the white Touraine-Mesland '95 (28 F) which is lively and lemony but rich, a Gris (28 F) with present acidity and an expressive, chewy red Touraine-Mesland Vieilles Vignes '95 (33 F).

Our choice Touraine-Mesland red '96 (28 F) for its fresh, lightly spicy nose, and ripe, meaty palate which is still a little tannic but will soften in a while.

Reception Cordial, around a barrel, in a corner of the cellar, soon to be converted into a tasting area.

How to get there *(Map 20): From Blois towards Tours via N152 on the right bank of the Loire. Turn right after 32km towards Onzain. In the village towards Mesland via D1. The cellar is on the right, in the first house on entering Mesland. Sign.*

The new tasting room hewn from the tufa rock.

Domaine des Aubuisières

Owner Bernard Fouquet. **Address** 30 rue de la Vallée de Nouy, 37210 Vouvray - Tel. 02.47.52.61.55/67.82 Fax 02.47.52.67.81. **Open** By appointment. **Spoken** English.

"Each harvest starts with a big clean up," says Bernard Fouquet. He isn't the *mère Denis* of Vouvray but simply a winemaker who is skilful with barrels and a maniac for hygene. In this way, his seasoned barrels, purchased in Sauternes, will be fresh and clean but coated with a gloss from the west of the Garonne. "Sauvignon and Semillon provide a bed for the Chenin." He likes everything well organized. The domaine's 20 hectares are entirely worked and some parcels seeded between the rows. In dry Vouvray, the Marigny '95 (41 F) offers a mineral nose and fine, delicate palate which finishes with a hint of apricot and which is lively without being hard. The acidity is well balanced by the ripeness. The '96 is very long and persistent with more of an almond aroma. In *demi-sec* it's best to wait for the '96s (approx. 40 F) which will be a little more concentrated and either fine and elegant (*cuvée* Les Girardières) or with more character, power and unctuosity (*cuvée* Le Bouchet). Of the *moelleux*, keep an eye on the '96s for their volume, in particular, the Plan de Jean with its attractive aroma of roasted almonds.

Our choice Vouvray Les Marigny *moelleux* '95 (130 F). Full color, persistent on the nose (mango) and palate, fruity with well-integrated oak. The '96 will be exceptional, very rich, mixing fruit and mineral, with a powerful *liqueur* (160 grams/liter of residual sugar) balanced by the acidity. To age.

Reception Attentive and friendly.

How to get there *(Map 20): From the center of Vouvray follow the route de Monnaie, then turn right in the direction of the Valléé de Nouy. The cellar is on the left. Sign.*

The entrance to the cellars of the Clos Baudoin and labeling of the sparkling wines during the summer.

Clos Baudoin

Owner Prince Poniatowski. **Address** Vallée de Nouy, 37210 Vouvray - Tel. 02.47.52.71.02 Fax 02.47.52.60.94. **Open** From Monday to Friday, 8:30-12:00 and 13:30-19:30, weekend by appointment. **Spoken** English. **Credit cards** Visa, Eurocard, MasterCard.

The production at this domaine revolves around three labels: Clos Baudoin, the original domaine, Clos de l'Avenir and Aigle Blanc which represents all the parcels outside the two *clos*. Philippe Poniatowski claims to make "a wine typical of the year," including the lesser vintages, and is generally reluctant to chaptalize his wines. According to the vintage the wines are either dry (sec), "*sec tendre*," in other words softened by a hint of residual sugar, or *moelleux*. One can also find these three qualities in the same vintage, corresponding to grapes picked at different times during the harvest period. There is nothing simple in Vouvray and the domaine now offers 22 references from ten different vintages! Of the dry wines we chose the Aigle Blanc '88 and '86 (37 F) for their mineral notes and preserved vigor which maintains a balance as they mature. Apart from our choice in the *moelleux*, one can also hesitate between the Aigle Blanc '89 (61 F) with its seductive aroma (smoky on the nose, caramel on the palate) and the '90 (47 F) if you prefer a well-constituted, structured wine (wrapped in extract and finesse).

Our choice Vouvray Clos Baudoin Grand *Moelleux* '89 (152,50 F). A fine, open, very ripe nose. Clean attack on the palate (blanched almonds), very long, lengthened by the ripe acidity and mineral notes. To age.

Reception Very good, by the owner or one of the cellar staff.

How to get there *(map 20): In Vouvray take the route de Monnaie, then turn right in the direction of the Vallée de Nouy. The cellar is on the left.*

Château Gaudrelle, twenty Michelin stars.

Château Gaudrelle

Owner Armand Monmousseau. **Address** 87 route de Monnaie, 37210 Vouvray - Tel. 02.47.52.67.50 Fax 02.47.52.67.98. **Open** From Tuesday to Saturday, 9:00-12:00 and 14:00-17:00. **Spoken** English.

Carrying the name of the "king" of sparkling wines (Monmousseau) is not always easy. Alexandre, however, is making a name for the 14 hectares of Château Gaudrelle and displays, like so many decorations, the stars from the Michelin guide (15 restaurants with a total of 20 stars) who have placed this rather special Vouvray on their wine lists. The wines are, in effect, generally low in alcohol, even though the grapes are late harvested with plenty of botrytis. The residual sugar is, therefore, appreciable and the wines need to be aged for a fair length of time for everything to blend together.

Our choice Vouvray Réserve Personnelle '90 (150 F: 50 centiliters) Our choice from last year continues to progress. An astonishing wine for its structure which puts one in mind of the great German sweet wines (little alcohol, plenty of sugar). It has, in effect, a balance of 10% alcohol for 238 grams/liter of residual sugar ! It's the intense, but good acidity that holds the wine together giving it grip, elegance and balance. The color is very deep, the nose ripe and intense (dried fruits, dried flowers). The palate is very rich and concentrated with notes of dried apricot, quince, caramel, and a toasted impression due to the high level of botrytis (95%). A monumental wine and, of course, to keep.

Reception Friendly, even if direct selling is not one of the domaine's priorities.

How to get there *(Map 20): Leave Vouvray by the route de Monnaie. The domaine is on the right on arrival on the plateau. Sign.*

The "*gueules-bées*" for transporting grapes to the domaine.

Domaine Huet

Supervisor Noël Pinguet. **Address** 11-13 rue de la Croix-Buisée, BP 34, 37210 Vouvray - Tel. 02.47.52.78.87 Fax 02.47.52.66.51. **Ventes** From Monday to Saturday, 9:00-12:00 and 14:00-18:00, by appointment. **Spoken** English. **Credit cards** Visa, Eurocard, MasterCard.

This is a large and exemplary domaine that is biodynamically cultivated with, of course, a total working of the soils and the use of natural yeasts for the fermentations. Among the dry wines we appreciated Le Haut-Lieu '93 (53 F) for its power and notes of stock and quince. In *demi-sec*, we enjoyed the Clos du Bourg '92 (56 F) for its licorice notes and length and above all Le Mont '93 55 F) which is more austere than the precedent but ample and forward with a sumptuous aromatic finish. In *moelleux,* the '90s are more approachable than the '89s. Of the latter choose Le Haut-Lieu (82 F) for its elegance and notes of walnut and citrus fruits as well as the Clos du Bourg "*1er tries*" for its superb palate (toast, dried apricot). In '90, the remarkable Le Mont "*1er tries*" (180 F) has a bread-crust note on the nose, full and very fine (toast, apricot, fig) palate and long, persitent caramel finish.

Our choice Vouvray Le Mont sec '95 (58 F). The nose is still reserved but already fine. The palate is full, fine and unctuous with notes of fresh almonds. Very persistent. Wait a while.

Reception Excellent. All the wines on the price list can be tasted and old vintages purchased (*demi-sec* : '69, '64, 61, 57, 52 ; *moelleux* : 71, 64, 59, 53, 47) from 120 - 600 F as an addition to an order placed from the regular price-list.

How to get there *(Map 20): From the center of Vouvray take the route de la Monnaie, then on the right the route de Vernou via D46. Pass in front of the town hall and the church, then on the left take the rue de la Croix Buisée. The cellar is clearly indicated on the right.*

At dusk, the last day of harvesting botrytized grapes in mid-November.

Clos Naudin

Owner Philippe Foreau. **Address** 14 rue de la Croix Buisée, 37210 Vouvray - Tel. 02.47.52.71.46 Fax 02.47.52.73.81. **Open** From Monday to Saturday, 8:30-12:00 and 14:00-18:30, by appointment.

Philippe Foreau today lives a passion that was born some 12 years ago when he was given the responsibility for choosing, from the cellar, the wines for important family meals. A tasting in his company is constantly sprinkled with suggestions for food-wine combinations. In the dry wines, we enjoyed the '91 (50 F) for the palate (honey, pollen) and the '88 (55 F), which is again on sale, for its vivacity and mineral and menthol notes. In *demi-sec*, we appreciated the '94 (47 F) for its peppery and exotic nose and fruity, powerful, long palate and above all the '96 (approx. 57 F) for the citrus fruit aroma and balance. From fish cooked in foil to grilled red mullet, not forgetting Dublin Bay prawns, Philippe Foreau will have a pertinent culinary suggestion to make as he is more concerned with the alcohol-sugar-acid balance than the aromatic combination.

Our choice Vouvray Réserve *moelleux* '95 (136 F). 6 600 bottles to be grabbed for the sumptuous nose (crystallized pineapple, toast, butter), and dense, full, fine, round (toast, plum, pineapple, currants, rum, crystallized angelica) palate. A delicate wine (despite the 120 grams/liter residual sugar) that passes by notes of chocolate and dried fruits before finishing on prune.

Reception Perfect, attentive, in a room decorated with some rather fine black and white photos.

How to get there *(Map 20): From the center of Vouvray take the route de Monnaie, then turn right towards Vernou via D46. Pass in front of the town hall and church then on the left take the rue de la Croix Buisée. The cellar is on the left. Signposted.*

The cellar that was built in the 1970s.

Domaine Henry Pellé

Owner Family Pellé. **Address** Morogues 18220 Les Aix-d'Angillon - Tel. 02.48.64.42.48 Fax 02.48.64.36.88. **Open** Everyday, 9:00-12:00 and 14:00-18:00, except Sunday and national holidays.

Menetou-Salon is an expanding appellation of more than 350 hectares (there were only 20 hectares at the end of the 1950s) situated a few kilometers southwest of Sancerre. Appreciated in the region of Bourges for many years the wines, like those of its more famous neighbor, are available in three colors : Sauvignon for the whites and Pinot Noir for the reds and rosés. Without the vivacity, depth and mineral quality of the great Sancerres, the Menetous, which can generally be drunk young (they are bottled at Easter), offer a roundness and fruity charm that is there own personal character. The pioneer Henry Pellé embodies the success of this appellation with 40 hectares of Menetou completed by 10 hectares of Sancerre on La Croix-au-Garde at Montigny. Since the death of his son Eric in 1995, he has entrusted the vinification to the young enologist Julien Zernott. The latter did not fail his task in 1996, notably regarding the red '96 which is well-made and fresh with pepper and raspberry notes.

Our choice The two selections of parcels of white Menetou-Salon in '96. The Clos Ratier (approx. 45 F) which, despite the youthful age of the vines, offers a good mineral character and clean, dry flavors and the Clos des Blanchais (approx. 42 F) which is rounder and more flattering with lovely ripe fruit.

Reception Good, at the tasting room adjoining the cellar, where one can taste the complete range of wines.

How to get there *(Map 21): From Sancerre towards Bourges via D955, then right towards Morogues. Turn left at the stop sign in the village. The cellar is 200m on the right.*

Michelle and Jean-Michel Masson Blondelet.

Domaine Masson-Blondelet

Owners Jean-Michel and Michelle Masson-Blondelet. **Address** 1 rue de Paris, 58150 Pouilly-sur-Loire - Tel. 03.86.39.00.34 and 03.86.39.04.61. **Open** By appointment. **Spoken** English. **Credit Cards** Visa, Eurocard, MasterCard.

This 18-hectare domaine has an "all-embracing" approach with vines in Sancerre, Pouilly-sur-Loire (wines made from Chasselas) and Pouilly-Fumé. To commence the festivities we recommend the early drinking Pouilly-sur-Loire '96 (38 F) which is aromatic with a taste of almonds and fresh grapes, well-rounded, and short on the finish. In an easy style the Sancerre Thauvenay '96 (48 F) offers varietal character with a fine extract. More serious without being sorrowful, the Pouilly-Fumé Les Angelots '96 (50 F) is a chubby, well-rounded wine to be drunk young. Still in Pouilly-Fumé we reach another level with the *cuvée* Tradition Cullus '95 (96 F) produced from a selection of old vines and partially vinified in oak barrels. The quality of the fruit extract is so generous that it already overcomes the wood, developing spicy, crystallized fruit flavors. A wine to age.

Our choice Pouilly-Fumé Villa Paulus '96 (50 F). The ripe, full extract provides more distinction than in the *cuvée* Les Angelots. It's fuller on the palate with a long finish highlighted by fresh, mineral notes. To drink or age a little.

Reception Excellent, in the sales area, with either Jean-Michelle or his wife Michelle.

How to get there *(Map 21): From Cosne towards Nevers via N7. Turn right after 13km towards Pouilly. The cellar is on the right at the entrance to the village, 100m after the passage under the railway bridge.*

Thierry Redde harvesting in Pouilly-Fumé on 4 November 1997.

Domaine Michel Redde

Owner Thierry Redde. **Address** La Moynerie, 58150 Pouilly-sur-Loire - Tel. 03.86.39.14.72 Fax 03.86.39.04.36. **Open** From Monday to Friday, 8:30-18:30, Saturday and Sunday by appointment. **Spoken** English. **Credit Cards** Visa, Eurocard, MasterCard.

The cellar next to the highway might arouse suspicions in those who imagine that all good winemakers are lost in the depths of the countryside. Wrong, for here you can find one of the greatest special *cuvées* in the appellation. One of the great figures of the region, Michel Redde, departed this earth to harvest the vines of his maker in February 1997. His son, Thierry, adhering to his father's philosophy, prefers wines that are sapy and full, aged for a lengthy period on lees and which blend the different *terroirs* of the appellation. The Chasselas (that Thierry replanted), elsewhere vinified as an easy drinking wine, is here luxuriously aged in barrel for the *cuvée* Gustave Daudin '95. Rich and very oaky it's a confusing wine which doesn't have us entirely convinced. The Pouilly-Fumé La Moynerie '95 (54 F) is fine, vigorous, balanced, and to drink over two years.

Our choice The Redde family have adopted a Latin motto, "recta facere more majorum" (to do well with respect to old traditions) in order to baptize their prestige *cuvée* Majorum. This is a selection from old vines (approximately 40 years) planted on flinty and calcareous soils. The '93 (96 F) is complex with a lightly honeyed nose, and delivers a fine elegant, velvety extract with notes of lime-tree and vervain rather than fruit. There are still several older vintages available by the bottle.

Reception In a small sales cellar with rustic decor next to the highway.

How to get there *(Map 21): From Cosne towards Nevers via N7. The cellar is on the right, next to the highway, 4km after Maltaverne.*

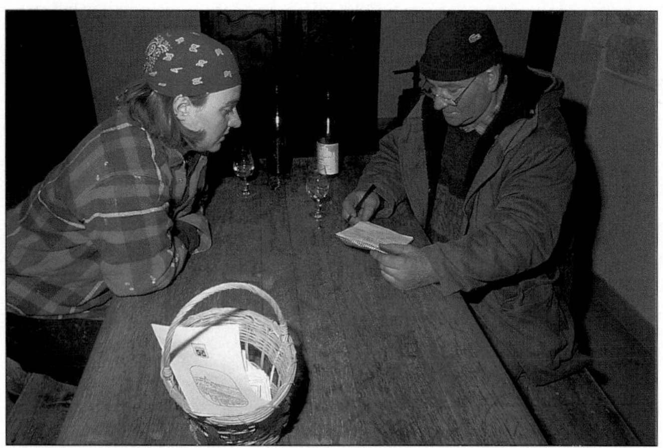

Serge and Valérie calculate their blends.

Domaine Serge Dagueneau & Filles

Owners Serge, Florence and Valérie Dagueneau. **Address** Les Berthiers, 58150 Pouilly-sur-Loire - Tel. 03.86.39.11.18 Fax 03.86.39.05.32. **Open** From Monday to Friday, 8:00-12:00 and 14:00-18:00, weekend by appointment. **Spoken** English.

"Serge Dagueneau et ses filles, vignerons," announces the sign in bold letters on the front of the cellar. The girls in question, Florence and Valérie Dagueneau, are not just there for decoration but help their father run the domaine. "Black currant leaf is not my style," says Serge Dagueneau, who is as distrustful of Sauvignons which explode with aroma three months after the harvest and collapse in the same length of time as he is of phylloxera. Eighty percent of his vineyard is located on white calcareous soils, which demand that the wines are aged for a long time. He leaves the wines to age on their lees in order that they obtain the roudness of which he is so fond. He even provokes the malolactic fermentation in the prestige *cuvée* Le Clos des Chaudoux (our choice). The Pouilly-Fumé '96 (50 F) is fat and powerful but without any loss of its mineral character. A lovely wine.

Our choice The Pouilly-sur-Loire from old Chasselas vines is a great speciality at this domaine. The '96 (35 F) is very aromatic, full of fruit, round, and crunchy like ripe grapes. This time from old Sauvignon vines, the Pouilly-Fumé Clos de Chaudoux '95 (80 F) is still firm but offers great potential. It is rich, full and long on the palate and would be perfect with a poulard in cream sauce. "Anyone who drinks that with oysters I'll give a kick in the pants ....!" Serge has given due warning.

Reception Good-natured, in a cellar where several old photos retrace the family history and where Léontine has the place of honor.

How to get there *(Map 21): From Cosnes towards Nevers via N7. Turn left 4km after Maltaverne near Michel Redde's cellar towards Les Berthiers. The cellar is in the center of the village on the left.*

The Côte des Monts-Damnés.

Maison Henri Bourgeois

Owner Family Bourgeois. **Responsable** Jean-Marie Bourgeois. **Address** 18300 Chavignol - Tel. 02.48.78.53.20 Fax 02.48.54.14.24. **Open** From Monday to Saturday, 9:00-12:00 and 14:00-18:00, Sunday 10:30-12:00 and 15:00-19:00, except Sunday, Jan. and Feb. **Spoken** English. **Credit Cards** Visa, Eurocard, MasterCard.

This is a well-known domaine and quality *negociant* with plenty of experience. Ten generations have succeeded one after the other augmenting little by little the vineyard area. Starting with two hectares in 1950, there are now 60 comprising around 100 parcels spread throughout nine communes, principally in Sancerre (a large part in Saint-Satur), plus a small part in Pouilly. La Demoiselle de Bourgeois is justly a fine, linear Pouilly which lacked a little ripeness in '95 (72 F) and which is more marked by the kimmeridgian clay *terroir* in '96. In white Sancerre, the Grande Réserve '96 (49 F) is the house's "fighting arm," says Arnaud Bourgeois, Henri's grandson. It is very grapefruity, full, and round and drinks well now. With reference to the Monts-Damnés, the famous hillslope in Chavigny so named because of the slope and the difficulty it poses for working the vine, the MD '95 (61 F), which is not produced uniquely from grapes grown on the slope, seduces with its aromatic finesse and crystalline palate. The same applies to the '96.

Our choice Sancerre La Bourgeoise Vieilles Vignes '95 white (72 F). A Sancerre which is always generous and which in a very ripe vintage like 1995 is soft and open without any loss of subtlety. The '96 which follows will gain in elegance.

Reception In a small cellar oriented towards sales. Groups are received in a beautiful underground cellar (by appointment).

How to get there *(Map 21): From Sancerre towards Chavignol via D923. Traverse the village. The cellar is on the left.*

Gilles Crochet climbs out of the vat he has just cleaned.

Domaine Lucien Crochet

Owner Family Crochet. **Address** Place de l'église, 18300 Bué - Tel. 02.48.54.08.10 Fax 02.48.54.27.66. **Open** From Monday to Friday, 9:00-12:30 and 14:00-18:00, Saturday by appointment. **Spoken** English. **Credit Cards** Visa, Eurocard, MasterCard.

This is a large domaine of 35 hectares spread over the *terroirs* of Chêne-Marchand at Bué and La Croix-du-Roy at Crézancy. Lucien Crochet also has the statute of négociant for buying in grapes. In the good years the red wines are aromatic (crystallized cherry) with a concentration and a finesse of tannins that is unusual in Sancerre. It's the mark of an outstanding *terroir* that appears in the La Croix-du-Roy '95 (approx. 58 F) which is full and ripe or the Prestige '95 (approx. 105 F) which has a noble extract but is still dominated by the oak. This is a great wine to drink or to keep. The '96s also inspire the same confidence. The white Sancerres in '95 were round and flattering whereas the '96s have a more minerally expression and great length. The Chêne-Marchand '96 (approx. 56 F), which had rather knotted aromas when last tasted, releases a very ripe, flavorful extract on the palate and has a long, chalky finish.

Our choice Sancerre Prestige white '95 (100 F). This is always by far the most opulent wine as much for the extrovert aromas as the full, generous palate. However, it is never unbalanced thanks to a good acidity that lightens the finish. A great Sancerre to drink or to keep.

Reception Good, in a large tasting room, but essentially sales driven.

How to get there *(Map 21): From Sancerre towards Bourges via D955. Turn right after 4km towards Bué. Traverse the village. The cellar is on the left at the top of the church square.*

Alphonse Mellot with Alphonse "junior" and Yquem the dog.

Domaine de la Moussière

Owner Alphonse Mellot. **Address** 3 rue Porte-César, 18300 Sancerre - Tel. 02.48.54.07.41 Fax 02.48.54.07.62. **Open** Everyday, 8:00-12:00 and 14:30-19:00 at the shop, (in the central Square); From Friday to Monday (same hours) Nov. - March. By appointment to visit the cellars. **Credit Cards** Visa, Eurocard, MasterCard.

It's possible to be a *negociant* and manage an exemplary domaine. It's possible to own a large 50 hectare vineyard and persist in harvesting by hand. It's possible to be covered in eulogies and continue to be innovative. As an example have "cigars" constructed. These are long, wooden barrels, inspired by Port pipes, which increase the surface area of the wine in contact with the lees. As a further example there is the application of *micro-bullage*, a system for oxygenating the wine during fermentation and maturation. It's possible to be an important *negociant* but also a connoisseur and supporter of the smaller wine growers in the appellation. The Mellots consistently demonstrate all this.Their Sancerre Domaine de la Moussière '96 (49 F) is marked by the aromas and flavors of citrus fruits and is present, lively and persistent on the palate. The prestige *cuvée* Edmond '95 (102 F) is always rich and ripe and at the same time dry and suave with an oaky nuance. This is a great wine to age. The '90 is just beginning to open out.

Our choice "The reds were never my passion," admits Alphonse. However, since his son "junior," who likes this color, has taken the vinification in hand the reds have taken off. The new *cuvée* Génération XIX '95 (80 F) is a real Pinot Noir, with fine, dense tannins and a structure for ageing. The '96 appears even deeper.

Reception Don't miss visiting the beautiful cellars.

How to get there *(Map 21): In the center of Sancerre. The shop is next to the restaurant La Tour. The cellars are just behind.*

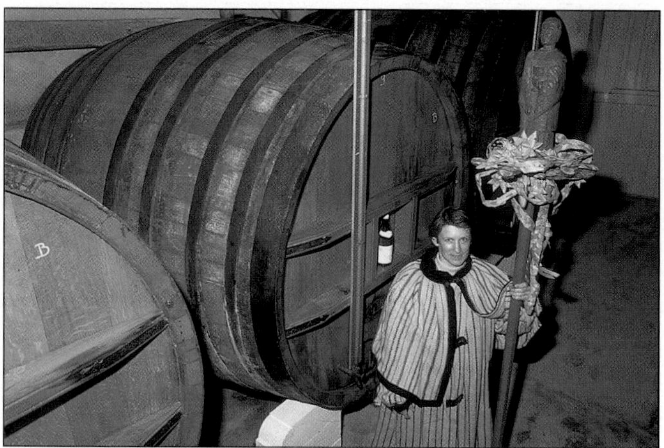

Cécile Natter wearing the *limousine*, the shepherd's coat worn by her *confrérie.*

Domaine Natter

Owners Henri and Cécile Natter. **Address** Montigny, 18250 Henrichemont - Tel. 02.48.69.58.85 Fax 02.48.69.51.34. **Open** By appointment. **Spoken** English.

In 1975 Henri and Cécile Natter settled a stone's throw from Menetou-Salon in the western extremity of the appellation, until then abandoned little by little to the benefit of the historical fiefs of Sancerre, Bué and Chavignol. The clay soils produce powerful wines which are compact and vigorous in youth. However, long ageing in large *foudres* allows them time to mellow. The *cuvée* Domaine is produced from vines planted by the Natters (approximately 20 years old). The '95 (44,50 F) provides lovely peppery aromas that are far removed from the varietal aromas of the Sauvignon, a round, citrus fruit palate that is well-balanced but powerful. The *cuvée* François de la Grange, a selection of old vines that have been rented (between 50 and 60 years) ages remarkably well (there are always two or three old vintages for sale). The rosé '95 (44,50 F) has a peach kernel nuance and is slightly smoky. It is present on the palate with a roundness accentuated by a hint of residual sugar. In red, the '95 (45 F) is structured, powerful and to be enjoyed starting in 1998.

Our choice Sancerre François de la Grange white '95 (58 F). The wine has a complex nose that mixes the notes of very ripe Sauvignon with a touch of chalky mineral. The palate is full, round and almost unctuous without having fully developed its potential. To taste from 1998-1999.

Reception By a couple that are calm and gentle, like the environment, with plenty of care.

How to get there *(Map 21): From Sancerre towards Bourges via D955. Turn left after 16km towards Montigny via D93. The cellar is on the right of the church square.*

"Saint Vincent".

Domaine Vincent Pinard

Owners Vincent and Cosette Pinard. **Address** 42 rue Saint-Vincent, 18300 Bué - Tel. 02.48. 54.33.89 Fax 02.48.54.13.96. **Open** By appointment.

Vincent and Cosette Pinard stopped using the vineyard names on their wine labels in 1989, despite possessing some very good parcels of vines on the calcium soils of Bué, in particular, at two notable sites, Grand Chemarin and Chêne-Marchand. Instead, they decided to work on the notion of blending. Their wines are always well-built, even in difficult years, with plenty of finesse and good density thanks to a partial vinification in oak barrel and an ageing on lees. The two excellent vintages '95 and '96, are presently for sale. The white Sancerre *cuvée* Florès '96 (44 F) is elegant on the palate with flavors of peach kernel and a finish that is clean and direct. The wine can be drunk now. Vincent also owns some good terroirs for red wines and in '95 produced, for the first time, a *cuvée* Vieilles Vignes (56 F) which is well-structured and which can age for three years. A name for this wine had not been found on our last visit.

Our choice Two white '95 Sancerres with different characters. The Nuance (56 F) is a blend of wines from vat and barrel, combining the richness from the barrel with the vigor and directness of the wine vinified in vat. The freshness and fullness compliment each other on the finish. The *cuvée* Harmonie (92 F) was vinified and aged in 100% new oak barrels. If the nose is still marked by the oak the palate is more harmonious with the ripe fruit evident and just a note of toast. This is a great wine that should be aged five or six years.

Reception Excellent, in the cellar under a recently built house.

How to get there *(Map 21): From Sancerre towards Bourges via D955. Turn right after 4km towards Bué. The cellar is on the left at the entrance to the village. Signposted.*

Pierre Prieur and Thierry, one of his sons.

Domaine de Saint-Pierre

Owners Pierre, Bruno and Thierry Prieur. **Address** Verdigny 18300 Sancerre - Tel. 02.48.79.31.70 Fax 02.48.79.38.87. **Open** From Monday to Saturday, 9:00-12:00 and 14:00-18:00, Sunday by appointment. **Spoken** English. **Credit Cards** Visa, Eurocard, MasterCard.

The Prieur family work 16 hectares of vineyard composed of 30 parcels (in six communes) spread throughout the three classic terroirs of Sancerre. Half are located on stony, calcareous soils known as *caillotes* (very fruity wines), 40% on white soils or "*grosses terres*," a clay-limestone base (full-bodied, rich wines), and 10% on flinty soils (firm, minerally, aromatic wines). Pierre Prieur works with his two sons, Bruno and Thierry. We particularly enjoyed the white Sancerre '96 (44 F) which had an underlined ripeness (a note of crystallized fruits) and which was round and fleshy on the attack with a dry finish. We also liked the red Sancerre Classique '96 (44 F) which had black fruit notes and which is extremely supple. It will be drinking well from 1998. This is a serious domaine.

Our choice Sancerre Cuvée Maréchal Prieur red '95 (approx. 70 F). This is a Pinot Noir with a strawberry and plum nose that is also slightly gamy and with the flavor of spice and crystallized red fruits on the palate which is rich and persistent. It's worth remembering that before phylloxera, Sancerre produced a majority of red wines and not without reason in terms of quality. If there are still some bottles of the '93 don't hesitate as it tastes wonderful.

Reception Professional within a family atmosphere, in a small well-maintained tasting room.

How to get there *(Map 21): From Sancerre, turn left at the entrance to Saint-Satur towards Verdigny and Sury-en-Vaux, then left again towards Verdigny. Cross the village. The cellar is on the left. Sign.*

Pascal and Nicolas Reverdy, in the front row for Sancerre.

Domaine Pascal et Nicolas Reverdy

Owner Pascal and Nicolas Reverdy. **Address** Maimbray 18300 Sury-en-Vaux - Tel. 02.48.79.37.31 Fax 02.48.79.41.48. **Open** Everyday, by appointment.

Rugby and wine are the two passions of brothers Pascal, 31, and Nicolas, 27, Reverdy. Both obsessions can be played out in Sancerre, one at the local rugby club and the other at their ten hectare vineyard at Maimbray in the commune of Sury-en-Vaux. A part of their vineyard can be seen on the beautiful hillside of Saint-Romble which overlooks the courtyard of the cellar. They took over the family domaine five years ago on the retirement of their parents. Solicited by the best *negociant* in the region (they only bottle a third of their production), the go-ahead brothers are equipped with a pneumatic press to gently press the grapes which are hand harvested. The red Sancerre '96 (38 F) is seductively fruity (raspberry) with a hint of pepper and round, well-structured palate. Look out for the release of the white Sancerre Fût de Chêne '96. Tasted during maturation it appears well-made and generous.

Our choice Sancerre white '96 (39.50 F). A selection from old vines harvested at 13% natural. This is a rich, ample wine with ripe Sauvignon flavors and full, clean finish. Excellent price-pleasure value.

Reception Passionate and direct, in a stone tasting room, more often than not with Nicolas.

How to get there *(Map 21): From Sancerre, turn left at the entrance to Saint-Satur towards Sury-en-Vaux. Turn left in Sury towards Les Maimbray. The cellar is on the left in the hamlet.*

NORTHERN RHONE

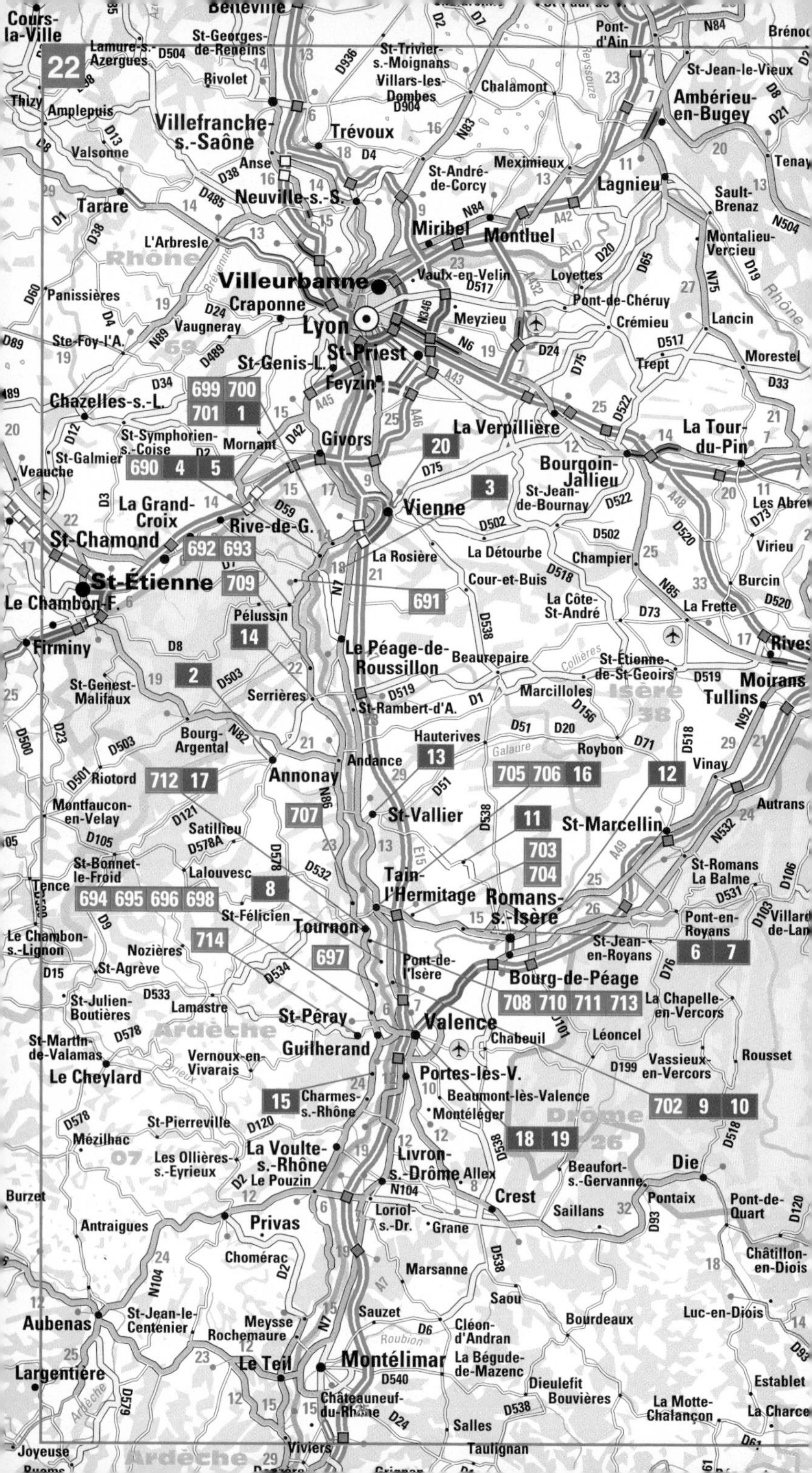
22
Cours-la-Ville
Lamure-s.-Azergues
St-Georges-de-Reneins
St-Trivier-s.-Moignans
Villars-les-Dombes
Pont-d'Ain
Brénod
St-Jean-le-Vieux
Ambérieu-en-Bugey
Thizy
Amplepuis
Rivolet
Villefranche-s.-Saône
Chalamont
Trévoux
Valsonne
Anse
St-André-de-Corcy
Meximieux
Lagnieu
Tenay
Sault-Brenaz
Tarare
Neuville-s.-S.
Miribel
Montluel
Montalieu-Vercieu
L'Arbresle
Rhône
Villeurbanne
Vaulx-en-Velin
Loyettes
Panissières
Craponne
Pont-de-Chéruy
Lyon
Meyzieu
Crémieu
Lancin
Vaugneray
Ste-Foy-l'A.
St-Priest
Trept
Morestel
St-Genis-L.
Feyzin
699
700
701
1
Chazelles-s.-L.
La Verpillière
La Tour-du-Pin
St-Symphorien-s.-Coise
Mornant
Givors
20
St-Galmier
690
4
5
Veauche
Bourgoin-Jallieu
3
St-Jean-de-Bournay
Vienne
Les Abrets
La Grand-Croix
Rive-de-G.
St-Chamond
692
693
La Rosière
La Détourbe
Champier
Virieu
St-Étienne
709
Cour-et-Buis
Burcin
Le Chambon-F.
691
La Côte-St-André
La Frette
Pélussin
14
Rives
Firminy
Le Péage-de-Roussillon
Beaurepaire
St-Étienne-de-St-Geoirs
Moirans
St-Genest-Malifaux
2
Serrières
Marcilloles
Isère
38
Tullins
St-Rambert-d'A.
Bourg-Argental
Hauterives
13
Roybon
Vinay
Andance
Riotord
712
17
Annonay
705
706
16
12
Montfaucon-en-Velay
707
St-Vallier
11
St-Marcellin
Autrans
Satillieu
703
704
St-Bonnet-le-Froid
Lalouvesc
8
Tain-l'Hermitage
St-Romans
La Balme
Tence
694
695
696
698
Romans-s.-Isère
St-Félicien
Tournon
Pont-en-Royans
Villard-de-Lans
Le Chambon-s.-Lignon
714
St-Jean-en-Royans
6
7
Nozières
697
Pont-de-l'Isère
St-Agrève
Bourg-de-Péage
St-Julien-Boutières
Lamastre
708
710
711
713
La Chapelle-en-Vercors
St-Péray
Valence
St-Martin-de-Valamas
Ardèche
Chabeuil
Léoncel
Guilherand
Vernoux-en-Vivarais
Rousset
Vassieux-en-Vercors
Le Cheylard
Portes-lès-V.
15
Charmes-s.-Rhône
Beaumont-lès-Valence
702
9
10
Montéléger
Drôme
St-Pierreville
18
19
26
Mézilhac
La Voulte-s.-Rhône
Livron-s.-Drôme
Allex
07
Les Ollières-s.-Eyrieux
Beaufort-s.-Gervanne
Die
Le Pouzin
Crest
Burzet
Pontaix
Pont-de-Quart
Saillans
Privas
Loriol-s.-Dr.
Antraigues
Grane
Châtillon-en-Diois
Chomérac
Marsanne
Saou
Aubenas
St-Jean-le-Centenier
Meysse
Sauzet
Cléon-d'Andran
Bourdeaux
Luc-en-Diois
Rochemaure
Largentière
Le Teil
Montélimar
La Bégude-de-Mazenc
Dieulefit
Establet
Bouvières
Châteauneuf-du-Rhône
La Motte-Chalançon
La Charce
Salles
Joyeuse
Viviers
Taulignan
Ardèche

INTRODUCTION

From Vienne to Valence the villages are often gray and dour and the region offers few attractions to the tourist. On the other hand the majority of the vineyards are a wonderful sight : the steep escarpments of Condrieu and Côte-Rôtie, the monumental hill of Hermitage, and the secret cirque of Cornas. Roads suitable for motor vehicles provide access to these vineyards enabling the traveler to understand the hard physical labor required to tear these great wines from the granite soils (and consequently the price of this hard work).

Before leading you on a trip down the Rhône Valley there is a specific point to be made. Two of the best winemakers in the region, Chave (wine grower) and Guigal (wine grower and negociant) do not sell directly to the public and, therefore, are not included in this guide. But if you should find their wines at a wine merchant (for example in Tain l'Hermitage) or in a good restaurant, leap on Chave's Hermitage or Guigal's Côte-Rôtie as they are the great standards of the region.

NORTHERN RHÔNE APPELLATIONS

The number of grape varieties being limited, it is essentially the various terroirs and exposures that explain the difference from one appellation to the next. Other variations are brought by the guiding hand of the wine grower. From north to south, these are the various appellations:

Côte-Rôtie (right bank). Produced uniquely in red (Syrah) this is a powerful but supple wine that is also aromatic and full-bodied. The prices are high and the wine growers often out of stock.

Condrieu (right bank). This is exclusively a white wine (Viognier). The vineyard is going through a period of renaissance, the wines extremely in demand and the prices are, therefore, flying.

Château-Grillet (right bank). Also exclusively a white wine (Viognier), this is a mini-cru which is the monopoly of one domaine. The vineyard is wonderful but the rather limited production is not at the level of its true potential. We have not, therefore, retained this wine.

Saint-Joseph (right bank). The appellation extends over 80 kilometers and pro-

duces both red (Syrah) and white (Marsanne, Roussanne) wines.
Cornas (right bank). Uniquely a red (Syrah) wine that is full-bodied, fleshy and ripe (the soils are earlier ripening than in the neighboring appellations).
Saint-Péray (right bank). Only white (Marsanne, Roussanne) wines are produced in this appellation. It is also the only appellation to offer sparkling wines, some of which are remarkable.
Crozes-Hermitage (left bank). White (Marsanne, Roussanne) and, in particular, red (Syrah) wines are produced in this extensive appellation where the light soils provide supple, aromatic wines.
Hermitage (left bank). This appellation produces both white (Marsanne, Roussanne) and red (Syrah) wines. It is the leading appellation in the region producing long ageing wines. The underestimated whites are a real discovery but need ageing in order to reveal all their secrets.

GRAPE VARIETIES
Contrary to the Southern Rhône which has a multiple number of grape varieties (is it the exhuberance of the south?), the north has a limited choice. The Syrah is the only red grape variety and there are just three white : Viognier, Marsanne and Roussanne (this last rare variety is slightly the southerner of the region).
The reputation of the Syrah (high and justified) is inversely proportional to its expansion (feeble). It only represents 2% of French red varieties. It's origins remain mysterious. For some it originates in Persia, from the town of Shiraz, and was introduced along the Rhone corridor by the Phoenicians. For others it comes from Syria and arrived at the time of the Roman invasion.
In the past it was considered as a "vin médecin" and used, in a hidden manner, to boost the color and body of the more anemic wines from Bordeaux.
This was known as "hermitager," in a reference to the Hermitage. Since then Syrah has advanced in its own right and not just in the Rhone, in particular, in the Languedoc-Roussillon.
The Viognier produces very aromatic white wines that are full-bodied but fresh. It is unique in the appellations Condrieu and Château-Grillet and is certainly the most limited grape variety in the world. Ten years ago there were only 32 hectares in the world (source: Wines, Grapes, Vines, Jancis Robinson). Of course, there are diverging theories about its origins. Perhaps it was brought by the Greeks at the same time as the Syrah? Or perhaps it came from Dalmatia, brought by the Emporer Probus who gave the Gauls the liberty to cultivate the vine (after Domitian had imposed the pulling up of practically all the vineyard area in Gaul in order not to cast a shadow over Roman viticulture).
The Viognier has certainly made progress since, notably due to the return to production of the Condrieu vineyard, at one time within two fingers of disappearing as the conditions of cultivation are difficult and the cost of production high on the sheer slopes. Elsewhere the Viognier legally has a very particular status. It can be blended, up to 20% (much less in reality), with Syrah grapes during fermentation in the neighboring appellation of Côte-Rôtie to bring roundness to the wine and complexity of aroma to the palate. It's new fashionable image has led to it being planted in the south of France but except for two Southern Rhône domaines the results have not attained the grandeur of its origins.

INTRODUCTION

The Marsanne is the largely dominant variety for the white wines of the region. With its strong personality it produces colored, structured, aromatic wines that are fleshy but firm. Having been more successful than its predecessor this variety is now being planted all over the south of France.

Like the Viognier, the Marsanne has a privileged position allowing it, with the Roussanne, to be used in the red wines of the region (a maximum 10% for Saint-Joseph and 15% for Hermitage and Crozes-Hermitage). This privilege, however, is rarely used as the large demand for white wines in these appellations means they reserve the total production of these two varieties.

The Roussanne, a sumptuous grape variety due to its finesse, palette of aromas, structure, and ageing potential, is also a low-yielding, fragile variety which explains why the Marsanne is often preferred. Several wine growers in the region happily continue to play the gallant knight. It is above all in Savoie that the Roussanne has gained a noble status under the name of Bergeron in the appellation Chignin-Bergeron.

METHODS OF VINIFICATION

Apart from the sparkling wines from Saint-Péray, some wine growers offer sweet (moelleux) wines from Condrieu as well as Vin de Paille (produced by the same method as in the Jura).

BUYING IN THE NORTHERN RHÔNE

The stocks being rare, the vintages offered are generally recent. This is not a problem for the wine lover as the '95 and '96 vintages are vastly superior to '92 and '93, and even '94. If you have a good cellar we encourage you to discover the whites by leaving them to age.

AT TABLE WITH THE WINES OF THE NORTHERN RHÔNE

Try the full-bodied whites (Hermitage) with strong flavored foods, even spicy, or with more complex dishes that mix flavors (duck with peach) or with crustaceans (lobster). The aromatic whites (Condrieu) will accept spicy dishes as long as they are not too seasoned.

Light reds (Saint-Joseph, Crozes-Hermitage) will accompany meat terrines. Slightly more robust reds are a match for organ meats (kidneys with certain Saint-Josephs), and soft white meats (pork and Saint-Joseph). Poultry with red meat (duck, pigeon), and game demand more powerful wines (Cornas, Côte-Rôtie, Hermitage) that have reached maturity.

We have tasted numerous wines of the region at table. Here are a few precise suggestions :

Rabbit liver terrine in large pieces: Côte-Rôtie of average age.

Crustaceans with a cream sauce (lobster or freshwater crayfish) : mature white Hermitage but still with a good acidic structure.

Red mullet with a red wine sauce (careful with the reduction as this accentuates the acidity of the sauce) : young Côte-Rôtie. Grilled we would rather serve the dish with a young white Hermitage.

Poached turbot accompanied by a sauce made from the ink of cuttlefish and a touch of vinegar : young red Hermitage that is not too tannic (the vinegar accentuates the tannins).

Sea bream : very young white Hermitage.
Raw truffles : mature white Hermitage.
Cold poulard stuffed with foie gras : young white Hermitage.
Veal cutlet cooked rare with crystallized onions : mature white Hermitage.
Veal liver (in thick slices to preserve the sweetness) : mature Côte-Rôtie.
Pan-fried foie gras : slightly mature white Hermitage.
Veal sweetbreads : great red Hermitage fully mature.
Poultry in a cream sauce : red Crozes-Hermitage.
Spicy chicken : young and fleshy Côte-Rôtie.
Best end of lamb : great red Hermitage of average age.
Rib of beef : powerful Cornas or Côte-Rôtie (the '96s).
Cheese : a slightly evolved white Hermitage is marvelous with roquefort. Young red and white Crozes-Hermitage are a match for goats cheeses that are not fully matured.

AMPUIS

1 - RESTAURANT - **Le Côte-Rôtie**: *18 Les Allées, 69420 Ampuis. Tel. 04.74.56. 12.05 Fax 04.74.56.00.20. Closed late August and the first week in*

September and in January. Lunch under the trees in fine weather. A wine list celebrating the Rhône, with 44 Côtes-Rôties. Menus only: 160 (lunch weekdays) to 310 F.

ANNONAY

2 - RESTAURANT - **Marc et Christine**: *29 avenue Seguin, 07100 Annonay. Tel. 04.75.33.46.97 Fax 04.75.32. 30.00. Closed Sunday evening and Monday.* Eleven kilometers west of Serrières. Fine traditional cuisine with local products, notably the different varieties of potatos and cheeses. Menus: 100 to 285 F. Superb wine list with over 500 entries. One hundred Côtes-du-Rhône, with white wines a bit underrepresented. The selection of growers is unsurprising, but offers interesting vintage years.

CHONAS-L'AMBALLAN

3 - RESTAURANT - **Domaine de Clairefontaine**: *Chemin des Fontanettes, 38121 Chonas-l'Amballan. Tel. 04.74.58.81.52 Fax 04.74.58.80.93. Closed Sunday evening and Monday.* On the right bank of the Rhône, facing Condrieu: a large, impressive, but gloomily decorated house. You'll be cheered up though by the cuisine and the wine list containing a great selection of Condrieu and Côte-Rôtie: 55 entries for whites, 150 for reds, some lovely old vintages. Menus: 150 to 380 F. A la carte: around 350 F.

CONDRIEU

4 - HOTEL-RESTAURANT - **Hôtel Beau Rivage**: *69420 Condrieu. Tel. 04.74.59.52.24 Fax 04.74.59.59.36. Open year-round.* Splendid wine list (150 Côtes-du-Rhône, wide selection from great years, several old vintages at moderate prices). Menus: 195 (lunch) to 600 F. A la carte: around

450 F. Old-fashioned but comfortable rooms (550 to 850 F).

5 - RESTAURANT - **La Reclusière**: *39 Grande-Rue, 69420 Condrieu. Tel. and Fax 04.74.56.67.27. Closed*

Sunday evening, Monday, 2 weeks in February and one in August. Home-style cooking. Menus: 75 (lunch weekdays), 90 and 150 F. Some lovely wines from the region and elsewhere at moderate prices.

GRANGES-LES-BEAUMONT

6 - RESTAURANT - **Les Cèdres**: *26600 Granges-les-Beaumont. Tel. 04.75. 71.50.67 Fax 04.75.71.64.39. Closed Monday and Thursday evening.* Between Tain and Romans. Classic, well-prepared cuisine. Attractive wine list with a good selection of Rhône appellations and many vintages, but prices can be excessive. Menus: 260 (lunch) to 430 F.

7 - HOTEL-RESTAURANT - **Les Vieilles Granges**: *26600 Granges-les-Beaumont. Tel. 04.75.71.50.43/04.75.71. 62.83 Fax 04.75.71.59.79. Restaurant by reservation, but closed Sunday evening and Monday.* Pretty, simple, bright rooms on the bank of the Isère. Excellent welcome. Rooms: 240 to 320 F. Very good family-style cooking and a nice selection of wines (130 entries from the Rhône, with several old vintages, including some '90s). Menus: 90 to 180 F.

LA ROCHE-DE-GLUN

8 - RESTAURANT - **Gilbert et Charlette - Auberge du Rhône**: *Quai Saint-Georges, 26600 La Roche-de-Glun Tel. 04.75.84.60.45. Closed December to March and Wednesday from September to December and March to June.* For a fried fish feast on the terrace of this charming guinguette. Menus: 95 (except lunch Sun.), 135 and 165 F. A la carte: around 150 F.

PONT-DE-L'ISÈRE

9 - HOTEL-RESTAURANT - **Michel Chabran**: *26600 Pont-de-l'Isère. Tel. 04.75. 84.60.09 Fax 04.75.84.59.65.* Nine kilometers au north of Valence. Lovely contemporary decor, flavorful and talented cooking, impeccable service. A pleasure. Sumptuous wine list (just over 200 perfectly chosen references in the Rhône valley, well-classed and presented, with some old and great vintages). Among the strong points, the best in red and white Hermitage, with 93 entries, and, for amateurs of anniversaries, a list of old vintages from 1973 back to 1936 from the different appellations. Menus: 215 (lunch, wine included) to 495 F. A la carte: around 700 F. 12 comfortable rooms (390 to 690 F). Remarkable breakfast: 80 F.

10 - RESTAURANT - **Chalaye**: *17 rue du 16 August 1944, 26600 Pont-de-l'Isère. Tel. 04.75.84.59.40 Fax 04.75.84. 76.36.* Menus: 165 to 260 F. The cuisine plays the classic repertory with an American twist (the chef worked for a long time in the US). Lovely summer terrace. Good wine list.

SAINT-DONAT-SUR-L'HERBASSE

11 - HOTEL-RESTAURANT - **Chartron**: *1 avenue Gambetta, 26260 Saint-Donat-sur-l'Herbasse. Tel. 04.75. 45.11.82 Fax 04.75.45.01.36. Closed Monday evening from September to June and Tuesday year-round.* Fif-

teen kilometers northeast of Tain-l'Hermitage. The cuisine is classic and refined, perfectly prepared. Good selection of Côtes-du-Rhône at reasonable prices. Menus: 120 (weekdays), 160 and 480 F. A la carte: around 300 F. 7 quiet, well-equipped rooms: 320 to 350 F.

SAINT-PAUL-LÉS-ROMANS

12 - RESTAURANT - **La Malle-Poste**: *RN92, 26750 Saint-Paul-lés-Romans. Tel. 04.75.45.35.43 Fax 04.75.71.40.48. Closed Sunday evening and Monday.* Thirty kilometers east of Tain-l'Hermitage. Provence-inspired cooking. The wine list is well stocked with regional wines (especially Rhône nord). Menus: 185 to 350 F. A la carte: around 350 F.

SAINT-VALLIER

13 - HOTEL-RESTAURANT - **Hôtel Terminus - Restaurant Lecomte**: *116 avenue Jean-Jaurès, 26240 Saint-Vallier. Tel. 04.75.23.01.12 Fax 04.75.23.38.85. Closed Sunday evening and Monday.* Innovative cuisine based on regional products. Attractive wine list, with half bottles. A hundred entries from Côtes-du-Rhône in good vintage years. Smart prices, for the hotel's simple, comfortable rooms as well. Menus: 160 (lunch weekdays) to 420 F. A la carte: around 350 F. 10 rooms: 300 to 380 F.

SERRIERES

14 - HOTEL-RESTAURANT - **Schaeffer**: *Quai Jules-Roche, 07340 Serrières. Tel. 04.75.34.00.07 Fax 04.75.34.08.79. Open every day in July and August. The rest of the year, closed Sunday. evening and Monday.* Great cooking, particularly fond of sharp seasonings and flavors. Menus: 120 to 440 F. A la carte: around 400 F. Lots of game in season (woodpigeon, grouse, partridge, hare, pheasant, wild rabbit, roe deer…) Around 130 well-chosen Côtes-du-Rhône on the wine list. 12 comfortable rooms: 290 to 330 F. Breakfast: 42 F.

SOYONS

15 - HOTEL-RESTAURANT - **La Musardière**: *RN86, 07130 Soyons. Tel. 04.75.60.83.55 Fax 04.75.60.85.21.* Eight kilometers south of Saint-Péray. Pretty rooms and apartments in a park with 100 year old trees, from 420 to 2,000 F. Menus: 120 to 290 F. Aside from the menu offering generous and tasty Ardéchois cuisine, some amusing thematic menus for all-mushroom or all-crustacean monomaniacs. Short selection of wines that could be longer, and better.

TAIN L'HERMITAGE

16 - RESTAURANT - **Restaurant Rive gauche**: *17 rue Joseph Péala, 26600 Tain l'Hermitage. Tel. and Fax 04.75.07.05.90. Closed Sunday. evening and Monday.* Menu-carte: 235 F. A new establishment that's off to a good start with its savory cuisine and great wine list (strangely classed by owner). The choices are excellent, and offer a chance to discover lesser known wines. The list should make more room for older vintages. The restaurant also offers tea and cigar lists.

TOURNON

17 - RESTAURANT - **Le Chaudron**: *7 rue Saint-Antoine, 07300 Tournon. Tel. 04.75.08.17.90. Closed Thursday evening and Sunday.* Perfectly respectable cooking, but one comes here above all for the wine list with its eighty well-chosen entries from Côtes-du-Rhône. Terrace in summer. Menus: 110 to 190 F.

VALENCE

18 - HOTEL-RESTAURANT - **Pic**: *285 avenue Victor-Hugo, 26000 Valence. Tel. 04.75.44.15.32 Fax 04.75.40.96.03. Restaurant closed Sunday evening.* The table has been scorned and celebrated, but the fabulous wine list offers the crème de la crème of

French production. Menus: 290 (lunch) to 960 F. A la carte: around 800 F. Twelve rooms and three apartments: 750 to 1,500 F. Breakfast: 120 F. The bistro that just opened attracts all of Valence in droves and it's often impossible to get a table.

19 - RESTAURANT - **Le Bistrot des clercs**: *26000 Valence. Tel. 04.75.55.55.15 Fax 04.75.43.64.85. Open every day except Sunday.* Decor recreates an old bistro, good, often revised home-style cuisine. Menus: 59 to 135 F. A la carte: around 140 F. Very good selection of wines (by the glass, carafe or bottle) made by the former Chabran wine waiter.

VIENNE

20 - HOTEL-RESTAURANT - **La Pyramide**: *14 boulevard Fernand-Point, 38200 Vienne. Tel. 04.74.53.01.96 Fax 04.74.85. 69.73. Closed Wednesday and Thursday lunchtime (except from June 15 to September 15).* Rooms: 650 to 1350 F. Menus: 430 to 630 F. A la carte: around 500 F. The legacy of Fernand Point modernized with loads of color and flavor. Service is strict, but above all neither stilted nor intimidating. Sumptuous Rhône Valley wine list with 200 perfectly chosen and aged wines from the region. The wine waiter gives wise advice.

TO SEE

CHAMPAGNE

OUTING - Saint-Pierre's church, with a fortress look, displays sculpted harvesting scenes on the façade, a Last Supper on the lintel.

CHATILLON-EN-DIOIS

OUTING - The little vineyard train.

CONDRIEU

OUTING - Discovery trails (particularly J. J. Rousseau's botanical trail) run through the vineyard, which is terraced with short retaining walls (chaillets).

OUTING - On the Romanesque lintel of the (Gothic) church, a lovely Last Supper.

COTE-ROTIE

OUTING - You can wander through the steep flanks of the vineyard, even by car. Note the special training: each vine-stock is tied to a prop, then joined to another in such a way that they form an upside-down V, to resist the wind.

DIE

MUSEUM - Die's Clairette Museum.

SAINT-DESIRAT

MUSEUM - **The Still Museum**: *07340 Saint-Désirat. Tel. 04.75.34.23.11 Fax 04.75.34.28.81. Open weekdays from 8 to 12 and 2 to 6:30; weekends from 10 to 12 and 2 to 7.* Mannequins recreate local life with the itinerant distillers. Lovely collection of shiny copper stills. Eau-de-vie tasting. Free visit and tasting.

TAIN L'HERMITAGE

OUTING - One can drive up to the little chapel dominating the Hermitage hill.

VERIN

OUTING - Leave the N86 and go up towards Saint-Michel-sur-Rhône to admire the Château-Grillet appellation's terraces (one single property of 3 ha).

VIENNE

MUSEUM - **In the lapidary museum**: a statue of Tutela (the godess who protects agriculture and the household) bearing a bunch of grapes on her shoulder.

VITICULTURAL FESTIVITIES

FEBRUARY
Tain l'Hermitage: the region's most important wine fair, third weekend of the month.

SEPTEMBER
Saint-Péray: wine fair, the first Sunday of the month.
Tain l'Hermitage: harvest festival, the third weekend of the month.

OCTOBER
Crozes: winegrowers fête, the last Sunday of the month.

NOVEMBER
Mercurol: white wine festival, on the 9th and 10th.

DECEMBER
Cornas: wine fair, the first weekend of the month.

The work of trimming the vine or *rognage* (known here as "*émoucher*") on the Coteau du Vernon.

Georges Vernay

Supervisor Georges Vernay. **Address** 1 route nationale, 69420 Condrieu - Tel. 04.74.59.52.22 Fax 04.74.56.60.98. **Open** From Monday to Saturday, 9:00-12:00 and 14:30:19:00. **Spoken** English, Italian. **Credit cards** Visa, Eurocard, MasterCard.

Georges Vernay declares that he is happy to do as he wants: Use grapes from the lower slopes of the mythical Coteau de Vernon in the generic Condrieu or declassify his young vines to Vin de Pays status. At the price at which Condrieu sells his wine this is a brave act. But Georges Vernay is courageous by nature. When he created his domaine in 1953 nobody would have put a dime on the future of Viognier. However, he had faith, and not that which moves mountains (he is happy to have taken a gamble on these incredibly precipitous slopes) but that which gives the energy to accept them as they are and work them. The wines are always characterized by the fruit, which is accentuated by some skin contact during the vinification. Each *cuvée* has its own unique character. The Condrieu '95 (approx. 120 F) is fruity with a linear structure whereas the *cuvée* Les Chaillées de l'Enfer '94 (approx. 150 F) is fuller and more powerful with mineral and floral notes and great persistence.

Our choice Condrieu Coteau du Vernon '95 (approx. 180 F, sales limited to 6 bottles). The nose has the aroma of white fruits. The palate is delicate and lacy with a linear structure which is noticeable for its elegance rather than power but leaves a firm impression. The oak is discreet and of good quality. To drink.

Reception In an attractive tasting room around an old winch press that has been converted into a bar. The tasting (50 F for three AOC wines) is charged if not followed by a purchase.

How to get there *(Map 22): From Vienne towards Valence via N86 to 5km south of Ampuis. The cellar is on the left at the entrance to Condrieu, indicated by a large sign.*

François Villard, cook then butcher and finally vintner.

François Villard

Owner François Villard. **Address** Montjoux, 42410 Saint-Michel sur Rhône - Tel. 04.74.53.11.25 Fax 04.74.53.38.32. **Open** By appointment.

François Villard sold 400 bottles in 1991, 700 in 1992, 1,500 in 1993, 5,000 in 1994 and produced 9,500 in 1996. The rise in success has been rapid and has already led to his wines being placed in some of France's top restaurants (La Pyramide in Vienne, Laurent and Gagnaire in Paris).

Having tried cooking, then the butcher's trade and studies as a sommelier, he is now firmly fixed as a wine grower. He has rented (on *fermage*) parcels of magnificently exposed old vines that their owners, now retired but without successors, feared would return to the wilderness. He has cleared land, abandoned because of the difficulty of working it, and replanted at a high density. He has set his standards high and selectively harvests, with several passages through the vines if necessary, conducts long fermentations in recently seasoned oak barrels, and ages the wines on lees that are continuously stirred (*batonnage*).

Our choice Condrieu Coteaux de Poncins '95 (130 F). Produced from vines at Saint-Michel. The nose is ripe the palate very full, fine, minerally and still austere. The finish is lifted and fresh. If the wine is no longer available François Villard will give you a tasting of and take reservations for the '96 which appears to be a great vintage.

Reception Passionate. In a completely new cellar.

How to get there *(Map 21): 15km south of Vienne towards Valence via N86. Turn right at Vérin, after Condrieu, towards Saint-Michel-sur-Rhône. Pass in front of the church. At the fork take the lefthand road towards Pelussin and pass in front of the cross. The cellar is immediately on the right.*

The harvest ritual : Yves Cuilleron lets his beard grow and adopts an elfin air.

Yves Cuilleron

Owner Yves Cuilleron. **Address** RN86 Verlieu 42410 Chavanay - Tel. 04.74.87.02.37 Fax 04.74.87.05.62. **Open** From Monday to Saturday, 8:00-12:00 and 13:30-19:00. **Spoken** English. **Credit cards** Visa, Eurocard, MasterCard.

Yves Cuilleron took over his uncle Antoine's vines in 1986 which enabled him to benefit from old vines right from the beginning. The domaine is divided between the appellations Saint-Joseph (8 hectares) and Condrieu (8 hectares), with just a seasoning of Côte-Rôtie (1.5 hectares). The wines are solidly constructed but always very fine.

You can purchase, between November and January, the latest vintage *en primeur* at 15% below the eventual sales price. The red Saint-Josephs from the '95 vintage, *cuvée* Pierres Sèches (approx. 49 F) and *cuvée* Amarybelle (approx. 65 F), tasted from barrel before the final blend, appear exceptional with plenty of flesh and silky tannins. The Côte-Rôtie Coteau de Bassenon '95 (approx. 98 F) is long and full of finesse. In white the prestige *cuvée* Saint-Joseph Le Bois Lombard '96 (approx. 65 F) already combines richness and maturity.

Our choice Condrieu Vieilles Vignes Les Chaillets '95 (approx. 150 F). The nose is very ripe, the palate full and fleshy with notes of fruit kernel and a long, persistent finish. The '96, tasted during maturation, is particularly powerful, endowed with a fine, ripe, concentrated extract.

Reception Competent and attentive on the part of Yves's sister, who usually runs the tasting room.

How to get there *(Map 22): 15km south of Vienne towards Valence via N86. The cellar is in the center of Verlieu, on the right just after the church. Sign.*

André Perret, the occasional provider of an exceptional wine for the celebration of mass.

André Perret

Owner André Perret. **Address** Verlieu, 42410 Chavanay - Tel. 04.74.87.24.74 Fax 04.74.87.05.26. **Open** By appointment. **Spoken** English, German.

The local village priest is a happy man. He often "procures" a bottle of André Perret's Condrieu to help celebrate Mass. The angels find their "part" and their wings hum a little more sweetly. The customers, on the other hand, have often a long way to go to find a bottle. The wines are more sought after than a place in paradise.

The domaine produces Saint-Joseph and Condrieu. The former is representative of the northern part of the appellation where the granite soils produce wines that are immediately seductive with plenty of suppleness and aromatic expression. The red Saint-Joseph '95 (40 F) is powerful and spicy while the *cuvée* Les Grisières '95 (50 F) is silky and extraordinarily concentrated. The white Saint-Joseph '95 is completely seductive with its ripe nose and fine, fleshy palate which evokes the flavor of ripe apricots. The Condrieu '95 (90 F) is fleshy and harmonious while the Condrieu Clos Chanson from the same vintage (100 F) is fuller and more intense.

Our choice Condrieu Coteau de Chéry '95 (110 F). The nose is sweet like brioche, the palate creamy and balanced with persistent notes of apricot. Wait a year. The '96 will be even more exhilerating. André Perret's wines tend to run out quickly but it is possible to reserve them with confidence in both great and average years.

Reception In the new cellar. For passionate wine lovers André Perret often finds a marvellous old bottle to discover.

How to get there *(Map 22): 15km south of Vienne via N86. In the center of Verlieu, on the right just before the church.*

The Ruchets vineyard.

Jean-Luc Colombo

Owners Jean-Luc and Anne Colombo. **Address** Rue Pied-la-Vigne, 07130 Cornas - Tel. 04.75. 40.24.47 Fax 04.75.40.16.49. **Visite** By appointment. **Spoken** English.

Jean-Luc Colombo belies the proverb that shoemakers are the worst shod people. A well-known enologist who consults to some of the best producers in the region and elsewhere (he can be found as far afield as the Roussillon), he preaches by example at his own 5,5 hectare domaine and cellar. Here, he harvests at optimum ripeness, destems the grapes and ages the wines in 225 liter oak barrels and not *foudres.*

The Cornas Terres Brûlées '94 (110 F) is a blend of grapes from eight parcels. The nose is open and fruity, the palate fine with soft tannins and plenty of finesse and concentration.

Our choice Cornas Les Ruchets '94 (165). Produced from old vines aged from 80 to 100 years. Certain vines only give parsimoniously 200 grams of grapes and the total yield is never more than 15 hectoliters/hectare. The nose is still closed but the palate speaks for it with fine extract, toasted notes and plenty of length. It is one of the great successes of a difficult vintage. To keep. The '95 (185 F), tasted from barrel, will clearly be superior with very fine tannins, and plenty of flesh. The special *cuvée* La Louvée (185 F) will mark the '94 vintage, as the '95, with its very ripe, well-built, driven palate.

Reception In the beautiful barrel cellar.

How to get there *(Map 22): From Valence towards Vienne via N86 and Saint-Péray. Turn left at the exit to Cornas, climb the rue Pied-la-Vigne and enquire at the enology laboratory on the right.*

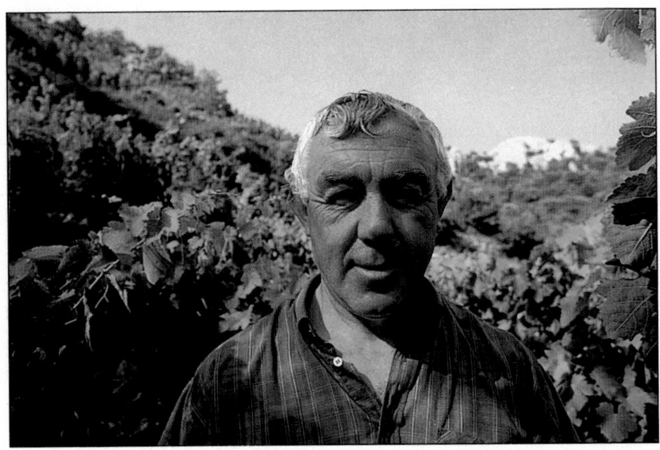

Jean Lionnet in his cormas vines.

Jean Lionnet

Owner Jean Lionnet. **Address** 48 rue Pied-la-Vigne, 07130 Cornas - Tel. 04.75.40.36.01 Fax 04.75. 81.00.62. **Open** By appointment. **Spoken** English, German.

Red or white? The choice isn't easy, for Jean Lionnet is rightly known for his red wines of Cornas which combine extract (a long vatting time for the destemmed grapes) with fruit (final blend with wines aged only in vats). But he also offers a rather attractive white wine from the appellation Saint-Péray. The '95 (45 F) blends Marsanne and Roussanne (20%) to produce a wine with an intense, floral aroma, and fleshy palate which is less oaky than usual. Very ripe and soft, the wine gives Saint-Péray a fine, round image, even good natured.

In the reds, there is a Côtes-du-Rhône, Cornas and Cornas *cuvée* Rochepertuis. The Côtes-du-Rhône '95 (35 F) is spicy, delicious, ample on the palate with freshness and aromatic notes of dried fruits. It can be drunk now but has some ageing potential. The '94 (60 F) Cornas has an aroma of figs and fresh, open palate. The Cornas *cuvée* Rochepertuis is produced from old vines grown on the most granite-based soils with reduced yields. It is unusual for not having a limited production and in fact represents a third of the output at this domaine.

Our choice Cornas *cuvée* Rochepertuis '94 (75 F). The nose is still closed but the palate already fine and elegant with a fleshiness unusual for this vintage. To age a while. The '93 (60 F) can also be reinstated. This is a harmonious wine from an average year which can be drunk now for its secondary aromas.

Reception Attentive, straightforwardly jovial with Jean, in the cellar.

How to get there *(Map 22): From Valence towards Vienne via N86 and Saint-Péray. Turn left at the exit to Cornas turn left. Signposted.*

Robert Michel oversees the ageing of his Cornas.

Robert Michel

Owner Robert Michel. **Address** 19 Grande-Rue, 07130 Cornas - Tel. 04.75.40.38.70 Fax 04.75.40.58.57. **Open** By appointment. **Spoken** English. **Credit cards** Visa, Eurocard, MasterCard.

Robert Michel is as well known for his traditionally tannic, long-ageing wines as Auguste Clape but since 1993 he has been destemming certain of his *cuvées* in order to soften them. The *cuvée* La Geynale, however, continues the house style. The wine is vinified in open-top vat without the addition of yeasts, the color and tannins heavily extracted, new oak banned for the ageing and the richness of the extract preserved by the absence of filtration.

The '94 Cornas' are evolving quickly and should be drunk over the next three years. On the other hand, the '95s can be aged and are clearly finer and more elegant. In the more supple style the Cuvée des Coteaux (approx. 85 F) is fruity and concentrated.

Our choice Cornas *cuvée* La Geynale '95 (approx. 130 F). Produced from old vines in the La Geynale (broom) parcel. The nose is still reserved, but allows the aroma of fresh fruits to filter through with just a hint of chocolate. The palate is concentrated, with tight-knit but well-enveloped tannins and a strong, fleshy sensation. The wine manifestly hasn't reached its true potential and needs at least another five years before it reveals its true character. It will, however, like previous vintages, close up again before reviving in a bouquet of secondary aromas.

Reception Simple, among the barrels.

How to get there *(Map 22): From Valence towards Vienne via N86 and Saint-Péray. Turn right at the exit to Cornas and climb the rue Pied-la-Vigne, then the Grand-Rue. The cellar is on the left, indicated by a small sign.*

The steeps slopes of Royes.

Domaine Courbis

Owners Maurice and Dominique Courbis. **Address** 07130 Châteaubourg - Tel. 04.75.40.32.12 Fax 04.75.40.25.39. **Open** By appointment. **Spoken** English. **Credit cards** Visa, Eurocard, MasterCard.

When the locals speak of "*rognon*" (kidney) they are not referring to a gourmet dish or a medical operation. Instead, they are talking of Châteaubourg's limestone outcrop, at the junction between the appellations Cornas and Saint-Joseph, which is conspicuous for its existence amidst this granitic terrain. Here, the white wines of Saint-Joseph, which are in the minority, have a particular allure. Of the red wines, we especially liked the Domaine des Royes Saint-Joseph '95 (72 F). The nose is still a little reserved with notes of black fruits but the palate is full and concentrated with well-integrated wood and the finish is fresh and long.

The Courbis family also have two small pearls in the appellation Cornas: the *cuvée* Champelrose '95 (85 F) with its rich suave palate is already very drinkable and the *cuvée* Sabarote '94 (105 F) which has a ripe, toasted nose and silky tannins with a note of dried raisins but needs to age a little longer.

Our choice Saint-Joseph white '95 (52 F). The nose is minerally but rounded out by a light oak influence. The palate is full and very fleshy with notes of plum, white fruits and peach kernel. The finish is lifted and persistent. This is a lovely wine which has more flesh and finesse than the '94 and where the blend of wines half vinified in vat and half in new oak barrels on lees is well-balanced.

Reception Without any fuss, at the cellar.

How to get there *(Map 22): 8km south of Tournon via N86. On the right at the entrance to Châteaubourg. The cellar is indicated by a large sign and the route signposted.*

Auguste Clape and his son Pierre-Marie.

Auguste Clape

Owners Auguste and Pierre-Marie Clape. **Address** RN86, 07130 Cornas - Tel. 04.75.40.33.64 Fax 04.75.81.01.98. **Spoken** English. **Open** By appointment.

This is a tiny domaine with vines on the best exposed granite slopes in the appellation and in the *quartier* (the name here for a *cru*) Reynard where the granite is mixed with limestone. The vines have an average age of 60 years. The grapes, which are harvested when very ripe, are neither destemmed nor have cultured yeasts added. The fermentations take place in open-top vats with *pigeage* and pumping over (*remontage*). The extraction of color and tannins is optimal. The ageing takes place in old *foudres* which provide the character of the cellar. The wines are blended at the end of fermentation continuing, year in, year out, the house style which is one of concentration, richness and maturity. There is a lovely white Saint-Péray ('95: 50 F, limited stocks), produced from old vines, which is floral on the nose and mineral on the plate but round and fleshy with a lifted finish. The reds, though, are the domaine's forte including the Côtes-du-Rhône ('95: 45 F, limited stocks) which is powerful and concentrated on the palate with a spicy finish.

Our choice Cornas '95 (120 F). Tasted in a provisional blend. The fruit is deliciously crunchy (black currant), the extract concentrated, tannins ripe and full, and the palate a mix of power, finesse and persistent fruit. A wine of great character to be aged.

Reception In a corner of the dispatch room or among the old foudres. Sales are usually limited to a carton of six bottles!

How to get there *(Map 22): From Valence towards Vienne via N86. The cellar is in the middle of Cornas, on the right next to the highway, opposite the restaurant Ollier.*

A blue square on a blue background. It's not a painting by Malevitch but an indicator for crop spraying (against disease) by helicopter.

Jean-Michel Gerin

Owner Jean-Michel Gerin. **Address** 19 rue de Montmain, Verenay, 69420 Ampuis. 04.74.56.16.56 Fax 04.74.56.11.37. **Open** By appointment. **Spoken** English. **Credit cards** Visa, Eurocard, MasterCard.

In another life Jean-Michel Gerin could have been a railway signalman. The selection at harvest is as precise as operating the signals. During the picking he has to sort the grapes several times over to be sure to obtain perfectly healthy berries that can endure a long period of maceration without producing any unwanted flavors. The grapes must also support high temperatures for maximum extraction and in order to attain a range of particular aromas. "I'm looking for pronounced aromas like undergrowth, game, and fruits macerated in alcohol, supported by plenty of dense extract," says Jean-Michel. Each *cuvée* is aged and fashioned in a particular way by adjusting the oak influence so as not to overpower the fruit or lose the freshness of the wine.

The Côte-Rôtie Champin le Seigneur '95 (approx. 100 F), barrel tasted before the final blend, is notable for the flavorsome palate, softness and fleshiness. The tannins are full and ripe, the oak elegant, and the finish fresh. Choose the fruity, balanced Côtes-du-Rhône for drinking now. In white there is an attractive Condrieu Coteau de la Loye '95 which is fleshy, long and persistent.

Our choice Côte-Rôtie Grandes Places '95 (approx. 160 F). Barrel tasted before the final blend. Dark color, intense, toasted nose, full, concentrated palate with velvety tannins. Very long on the finish. To wait for impatiently!

Reception Perfect, in a large tasting room.

How to get there *(Map 22): From Vienne towards Valence via N86. Turn right at the sign in the center of Verenay, then left.*

Jean-Paul, Jean-Luc and Joseph Jamet.

Domaine Jamet

Owners Jean-Paul and Jean-Luc Jamet. **Address** Le Vallin, 69420 Ampuis - Tel. 04.74.56.12.57. Fax 04.74.56.02.15. **Open** By appointment.

The two brothers took over the family domaine in 1986 and are quietly in the process of establishing a place among the top names in the appellation.

The grapes are painstakingly sorted at the harvest, left on the stems, vinified with natural yeasts and given a fairly long period of maceration. The extraction of color and tannins is at an optimum at this domaine. The tight-knit extract is then softened by a long maturation in oak (nearly two years), with a small proportion of new oak barrels (roughly 20%).

The wines are regularly distinguished by a powerful aromatic expression and persistence of fruit. The Côte-Rôtie '94 (105 F) is typical of the style. Tasted after a recent bottling and, therefore, still a little shaken up, the nose already shows a certain maturity and the palate is frank and honest with ripe fruit and a tannic structure softened by a discreet oak influence. For instant pleasure the Côtes-du-Rhône (32.50 F) is more than adequately fruity.

Our choice Côte-Rôtie Côte Brune '94 (140 F). The nose is ripe with the aroma of red fruits (bilberry). The palate is full and robust with attractive silky tannins and plenty of persistence. There are still bottles of the '88 (180 F) and '89 (170 F) vintages for sale.

Reception Simple but attentive, in the old cellar (often with the father Joseph, an inexhaustible story-teller) or the new vinification cellar.

How to get there *(Map 22): From Vienne towards Valence via N86. Turn right in the center of Ampuis towards Vallin, climb the slope and follow the signposted route for 4km. The cellar is on the right.*

After fermentation the grape skins are extracted from the vat for pressing.

Clusel-Roch

Owners Gilbert Clusel and Brigitte Roch. **Address** 15 route du Lacat, Verenay 69420 Ampuis - Tel. 04.74.56.15.95 Fax 04.74.56.19.74. **Open** By appointment. **Spoken** English, German.

Gilbert Clusel and Brigitte Roch cultivate a tiny vineyard of three hectares of which 70 ares are located on the excellent Grandes Places site (which they share with their accomplice Jean-Michel Gerin) with a magnificent exposure on the schist soils of the Coteau de Verenay. The carefully nurtured vines have attained the half-century. A walk here at midday when the sun is at its zenith will make you understand how the appellation got its name. Côte-Rôtie means "roasted slope" and you will probably be cooked to a turn!

The grapes are not destemmed and the fruit extract is particularly dense and tight-knit. A short vatting-time, however, preserves the aromas. Wood ageing is necessary to polish the tannins which are very present when the wine is young. The percentage of new oak barrels is moderated according to the *cuvée* (approximately 15% for the *cuvée* Classique and up to 50% for Les Grandes Places).

The domaine also produces a tiny quantity of excellent Condrieu which is delicate and fruity, often peppery, and always concentrated ('95 : approx. 120 F).

Our choice Côte-Rôtie Les Grandes Places '94 (150 F) The nose is still reserved but the palate is fine and rich with silky tannins, a smoky hint and well-integrated oak. It's a wine to age alongside the characterful Côte-Rôtie *cuvée* Classique '94 (98 F) which explodes with fruit and which has an already mellow oaky presence.

Reception Passionate, in the cellar among the barrels.

***How to get there** (Map 22): From Vienne towards Valence via N86. Turn right at the sign in the center of Verenay and continue 300m past Gerin's cellar.*

Laurent Combier.

Domaine Combier

Owner Family Combier. **Winemaker** Laurent Combier. **Address** RN7, 26600 Pont de l'Isère - Tel. 04.75.84.61.56 Fax 04.75.84.53.43. **Open** May - Sept., from Monday to Saturday, 9:00-12:00 and 14:00-19:00; Oct. - end April, Friday and Saturday, 9:00-12:00 and 14:00-19:00, the rest of the week, by appointment.

Laurent Combier started winemaking in 1990 with the benefit of grapes from old vines that his father, predominantly a fruit farmer, had previously taken to the local wine cooperative. The wines from this domaine are very good in hot years, the fully ripe grapes harmonizing particularly well with the sophisticated maturation where oak barrels play an integral part. The domaine also produces one of the rarely attractive white wines in the appellation. The '95 (48 F) has a rich, fleshy, lemony nose which accompanies a full, fresh, expressive palate.

Our choice If your visit falls at the right time of the year (December 1 to 25) the choice has to be the Crozes-Hermitage *cuvée* Clos des Grives, selected from low-yielding vines and aged 50% in new oak barrels and 50% in one-year-old barrels. The '95, already out of stock, was concentrated and ripe and as tasty as you could wish. The '96 should have the same well-marked qualities. In the absence of the Clos des Grives the regular red Crozes-Hermitage '95 (45 F), which is more readily available throughout the year, should provide happy consolation. It gambols on the fruit with a slightly smoky lift, unravels a tightly-knit extract, demonstrates fine, full tannins and finally settles with a fruity and persistent finish. To drink now.

Reception In the large tasting room, created from nothing like the rest of the cellar by Laurent Combier.

How to get there *(Map 22): From Tain-l'Hermitage towards Pont-de-l'Isère via N7. The cellar is located on the left, alongside the highway, a little before Pont-de-l'Isère.*

The old bread oven in the tasting room.

Château de Curson

Supervisor Etienne Pochon. **Address** 26600 Chanos-Curson - Tel. 04.75.07.34.60 Fax 04.75.07.30.27. **Open** July - Sept., every afternoon except Sunday, Oct. - June, Friday and Saturday afternoon and by appointment the rest of the week. **Spoken** English. **Credit cards** Visa, Eurocard, MasterCard.

Etienne Pochon, the young rebel of the appellation, presides from a partially restored 16th century château surrounded by walls made from round stones typical of the region. Certain fellow wine growers regard him with suspicion as his methods of vinification have shaken-up some of the diehard habits of the appellation. For the reds, the extra-ripe grapes are entirely destemmed. For the white wines, the grapes are destemmed and given skin contact before being fermented (for the *cuvée* Château) in new oak barrels with lees stirring. The *cuvée* Domaine is vinified and aged in vat to provide more immediately fruity wines. The white Crozes-Hermitage Domaine '96 (39 F) is more lively than usual (the wine did not undergo malolactic fermentation). The white Château '96 (65 F) is marked by a significant percentage of Roussanne (one-third). The nose is lightly oaky, the palate fine, fairly fleshy, and lifted but the wine needs a little more time to allow the wood to mellow out. The red Crozes-Hermitage Domaine '96 (39 F) is round and balanced with silky tannins and an attractive aromatic note of dried figs.

Our choice Crozes-Hermitage Château red '96 (65 F). Tasted before the final blend the wine appears ripe and dense, very aromatic, long and, above all, endowed with a beautiful velvety extract on the palate. To drink.

Reception The tasting room shelters the old bread oven.

How to get there *(Map 22): From Tain-l'Hermitage towards Romans via D532. The domaine is on the left at the entrance to Curson. Signposted.*

The best white *terroir* in Crozes-Hermitage.

Domaine des Entrefaux

Owners Charles and François Tardy, Bernard Ange. **Address** Quartier de la Beaume, 26600 Chanos-Curson - Tel. 04.75.07.33.38 Fax 04.75.07.35.27. **Open** From Monday to Saturday, 8:00-12:00 and 14:00-19:00. **Credit cards** Visa, Eurocard, MasterCard.

In the region they speak of Tardy and Ange with reference to the brothers-in-law, Charles and Bernard, and François, Charles's son. This trio have established a justifiable reputation for their white wines (20% of the production) with the help of an exceptional *terroir.* There are two cuvées for both the red and white wines. The *cuvée* Domaine (41 F) is fruit driven with, in the '95 white, a note of apricot , and in the '94 red, a hint of pepper. Both have plenty of fleshy fruit. The *cuvée* Dessus des Entrefaux (57 F) is a more structured wine. The red '95 shows good color, a supple palate and a hint of oak which doesn't overpower the evident ripe fruit.

Our choice Crozes-Hermitage Dessus des Entrefaux white '95 (57 F). The wine is produced from grapes from old vines grown on the Coteaux de Mercurol and in particular on the Coteau des Pends which had a certain reputation well before the creation of the appellation Crozes-Hermitage. In the 1930s the white wines from here sold at the same price as white Hermitage! The *terroir* is very calcareous, covered in stones or *galets* and exposed to the south. The blend holds scrupulously to an even percentage of Marsanne and Roussanne. The nose is extremely ripe with a clean note of apricots. The palate is very fine and aromatic (fresh, blanched almonds) and finishes on a note of crystallized fruits. To drink.

Reception In a bright, modern tasting room decorated with old documents (wine labels, catalogues).

How to get there *(Map 22): From Tain towards Romans via D532 for 4km. At the church of Chanos follow the signs to the left. The cellar is on the high ground dominating the vineyard.*

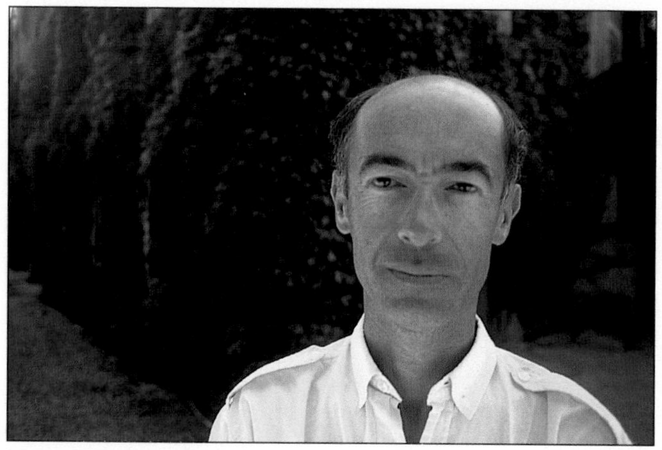

Marc Sorrel slips discreetly among the greats of Hermitage.

Marc Sorrel

Owner Marc Sorrel. **Address** 128 bis avenue Jean-Jaurès, 26600 Tain-l'Hermitage - Tel. 04.75.07.10.07 or 04.75.08.47.16 Fax 04.75.08.75.88. **Open** By appointment. **Spoken** English.

Readers with memories of their youth may remember an album called "*Croguphan*" where from cuttings of parts of known beasts one could create fantastic animals. Marc Sorrel has transposed this idea to the world of wine to fashion his red Hermitage "Gréal" by using a contraction of "Méal" and "Greffieux," two *terroirs* in Hermitage that are blended in this *cuvée*. It's the only fantasy permitted by this reserved wine grower.

The character of the wines is marked by their ripeness, alcoholic constitution and density of extract (the whites are fined but not filtered, the reds neither fined nor filtered). Be careful not to forget the Crozes-Hermitage, particularly the white wine. The '95 (approx. 48 F), fermented in seasoned oak and aged on lees, is very ripe (12.5% natural), golden, with a powerful floral nose (lime-tree, jasmin) and an unctuous, concentrated, characterful palate. The wine can be aged a little without problem.

Our choice Hermitage Les Rocoules white '95 (approx. 100 F). Tasted before the final blend. Very robust (13°5 natural), this is, however, a misleadingly tough constitution as the extract is soft. The nose mixes smokiness with wax and the palate is very full, powerful, and still slightly marked by the oak. The fruit, though, is still very present, lifted by a hint of spice. To keep.

Reception In the tasting room with a view of the cellar.

How to get there *(Map 22): In the center of Tain-l'Hermitage, on the left just after the Tournon bridge when heading north.*

The chapel that dominates the Hermitage vineyard.

M. Chapoutier

Supervisors Marc et Michel Chapoutier **Address** 18, avenue du docteur Paul Durand, 26600 Tain-l'Hermitage - Tel. 04.75.08.28.65 Fax 04.75.08.81.70 – web: www.chapoutier.com **Open** Every day. **Spoken** English, German. **Credit cards** Visa, Eurocard, MasterCard.

This house combines the activity of *negociant* with the management of a large vineyard (more than 80 hectares) centered on Hermitage but present in other appellations. The vines are cultivated biodynamically, the yields restricted, and the old vines painstakingly preserved. The wines, aged in oak barrels, are characterised by their ripeness, concentration, finesse and strong aromatic expression. In white, we enjoyed the Crozes-Hermitage Meysonniers '95 (52 F) for the fleshiness that surrounds the structure, the Saint-Joseph Deschant '96 (67 F) for the ripe nose and creamy palate and the Hermitage Chantalouette '93 (133 F) for its honeyed notes and the '94 (approx. 147 F) for its power.

In red, we were easily seduced by the Cornas '95 (90 F), a monumental wine with concentration and firm expression, the Crozes-Hermitage Les Varonniers '95 (200 F) for its finesse and the Saint-Joseph Granits '95 (200 F) for its smoky notes and silky texture.

Our choice Hermitage La Sizeranne red '94 (162 F) for the finesse of the extract, the note of ripe, red prunes, the length and persistence and the '91 (158 F) for its fullness and smoky notes. If you have to break the piggy bank it would be for the red Hermitage Pavillon '94 (572 F) whose dense, velvety extract lifts it to the summit of the appellation.

Reception Good, in a new tasting room.

How to get there *(Map 22): In the center of Tain-l'Hermitage. Take the road to the railway station.*

The collection of Rhône grape varieties.

Maison Delas

Head Winemaker François Chamboissier and Jacques Grange; **Address** 07300 Saint-Jean-de Muzols - Tel. 04.75.08.60.30 Fax 04.75.08.53.67. **Open** Every day, 9:30-12:00 and 14:30-18:30. **Spoken** English. **Credit cards** Visa, Eurocard, MasterCard.

Having been taken over by a champagne house this old negociant company has made discreet but steady progress. Delas has consequential vineyard holdings in Hermitage (12 hectares), Saint-Joseph and Côte-Rôtie. A change in techniques of vinification with total destemming for the red wines, partial fermentation in oak for the whites, ageing in recent or new oak barrels for the reds and the absence of filtration for the best *cuvées* has improved the majority of the wines. In the '95 vintage we particularly liked the white wines. The Crozes-Hermitage Les Launes (42.20 F) has a floral nose and expressive, apricot flavored palate. The Saint-Joseph Sainte-Epine (80,90 F) has a ripe, vigorous palate and the Condrieu Clos Boucher (146,40 F) a complex nose and full, fine extract.

In the reds choose from the '91 and '94 vintages. The Côte-Rôtie Seigneur de Maugiron '91 (132.70 F) is a powerful wine with plenty of finesse and a note of prune on the palate. It still needs a little time. The Crozes-Hermitage *cuvée* Tour d'Albon (56.70 F) is fruity and fresh with smoky notes.

Our choice Hermitage Les Bessards red '94 (approx. 245 F). Chosen for its depth of aroma on the nose, density on the palate and the finesse and ripeness. The tannins are fine and the oak well-integrated. This is a solid wine with rich, concentrated extract but which is characterised by its finesse. To age.

Reception Don't miss the collection of Rhône grape varieties.

How to get there *(Map 22): From Tournon towards Vienne via N86 for 3km. Turn left at the sign in Saint-Jean-de-Muzols, just after the railway bridge, and follow the D238 to the cellar.*

René Despeisse, the *régisseur.*

Clos de l'Arbalestrier

Owner Family Florentin. **Address** 32 avenue du Saint-Joseph, 07300 Mauves - Tel. 04.75.08.60.97 Fax 04.75.08.60.96. **Open** By appointment.

The domaine consists of four walled-in hectares at the foot of the slopes with an unusually high percentage of white varieties (a quarter of the plantings). Of these, the Roussanne finds equal status with the usually more dominant Marsanne. Dominique Florentin continues the tradition of his forefathers. The soil is tilled by horse (Bichette), the old vines pruned short to reduce yields (30 hectoliters/hectare) and the wine aged for a long time without the addition of sulfur or, prior to bottling, filtration. The vinification in seasoned *foudres* for the whites and the reds, the latter destemmed and pigés, provides deliciously rich, concentrated wines which are only sold after a long period of ageing. The wines, therefore, are very particular, for having been vinified and aged in a very traditional manner the accent is placed on the structure and the extract rather than youthful aromas. These are wines for the palate and the dinner table rather than the nose. The white Saint-Joseph '94 (approx. 55 F) is marked by the Roussanne which provides a solidly structured, powerful palate with a hint of honey. The red Saint-Joseph '92 (approx. 52 F), tasted before the final blend, appears very soft with plenty of finesse.

Our choice Saint-Joseph red '90 (55 F) for its aromatic notes of cedar and tobacco and for the tannins which have had time to learn a few good manners.

Reception Among the old *foudres*, with Monsieur and Madame Despeisse, the winemaker and historical memory of the domaine.

How to get there *(Map 22): North of Valence towards Tournon via N86. The cellar is on the right at the entrance to Mauves (on a dangerous bend with no visibility).*

Louis Chèze.

Louis Chèze

Owner Louis Chèze. **Address** Pangon, 07340 Limony - Tel. 04.75.34.02.88 Fax 04.75.34.13.25. **Open** By appointment. **Spoken** English. **Credit cards** Visa, Eurocard, MasterCard.

Recently installed, Louis Chèze hedges against his young vines by renting old vines which he uses for his prestige *cuvée* Caroline. The reds are destemmed and aged in barrel. The whites are partially fermented in oak and then blended with wines vinified in vat. In all cases the oak influence is dominated by the ripeness and power of the wine. This can be seen in the white Saint-Joseph '95 (46 F), tasted before the final blend, which is fleshy and well-constituted with a lovely note of Williams pears. For early drinking in red choose the cuvée Rô-Rez '94 (46 F) for its fruit and delicious, ripe palate and long, elegant finish.

Our choice Saint-Joseph *cuvée* Caroline '94 (60 F) Bright, dark hue, very ripe nose, palate full and concentrated with the freshness of the *terroirs* from the north of the appellation. The extract is fine, the oak well-integrated and matured with a little bottle age. Preferably to drink in two or three years. The '95 is more concentrated with the same quality of extract and silky tannins. The '96 appears to have astonishing color, finesse and concentration.

Reception Excellent, in a granite cellar. Ask to see the barrel cellar which has been attractively restored.

How to get there *(Map 22): 23km south of Vienne towards Valence via N86. Turn right in the center of Limony (small sign) towards the plateau, crossing the orchards to Pangon. The cellar is on the right at the exit to this tiny village.*

The Coursodon vineyard, a tiny corner of paradise.

Pierre Coursodon

Owner Pierre Coursodon. **Address** 3 place du Marché, 07300 Mauves - Tel. 04.75.08.18.29 Fax 04.75.08.75.72. **Open** From Monday to Saturday, 8:00-12:00 and 14:00-18:00. **Spoken** English. **Credit cards** Visa, Eurocard, MasterCard.

Pierre Coursodon produces a number of different *cuvées* from his large 12-hectare vineyard, situated at Tournon and Saint-Jean-de-Muzols on the well-known *terroir* of Sainte-Epine. Each cuvée has its own character but they all have a powerful aromatic expression. This, however, doesn't prevent the palate from being concentrated and balanced. There are two white wines produced from the Marsanne variety. The first is aged in vat. The nose of the '95 (52 F) is still closed but the palate is crisp and lively. The second, the *cuvée* Paradis Saint-Pierre, is vinified in two or three-year-old oak casks. The '95 (64 F) has a toasted nose, full, fleshy palate and an equally vigorous finish. There are three red wines. The regular cuvée ('95: 51 F) is fruity and round, the *cuvée* l'Olivaie powerful and the third, the Paradis Saint-Pierre, which undergoes a long period of maceration, more tannic but well polished by a maturation in seasoned oak. The '94 (68 F), produced from tiny yields (20 hectoliters/hectare), is fleshy with a present tannic structure, but without any aggressivity. The '95 (66 F) will be superior. The domaine also has a number of older vintages which are available on demand.

Our choice Saint-Joseph *cuvée* l'Olivaie red '94 (68 F). The nose is very forward. The palate is well-constructed, clean and powerful and doesn't deceive the promise of the first aromatic impression finishing with good length and freshness. The wine needs a little time before drinking but is also capable of longer ageing.

Reception In a tasting room.

How to get there *(Map 22): From Valence towards Vienne via N86. The cellar is on the market place in the center of Mauves.*

Jean Gonon.

Domaine Pierre Gonon

Owner Family Gonon. **Address** 11 rue des Launays, 07300 Mauves - Tel. 04.75.08.07.95 Fax 04.75.08.65.21. **Open** By appointment. **Spoken** English.

It's impossible to visit here without an appointment as Pierre and Jean Gonon are more often than not up in the vines that cling to the hillsides. They rightly believe that the work of a wine grower consists firstly of "producing beautiful grapes," and that the work in the cellar must be "kept simple."

Simple but effective is what they mean. The white wines are fermented with natural yeasts in seasoned oak and are aged on lees which are regularly stirred, which is what produces the fleshiness. The reds are partly destemmed, fermented with natural yeasts and *pigés* to obtain good extraction. The domaine is conspicuous for its significant percentage of white wines (1.5 hectares out of the 6 hectares presently in production) and the importance of Roussanne (one-third of the white vines) which provides a different style of wine to the Marsanne and plenty of fullness of body. If there is any white wine left when you visit don't hesitate. The Saint-Joseph les Oliviers '95 (58 F) is floral on the nose, fleshy and round on the palate with a note of mandarin orange and hint of oak.

Our choice Saint-Joseph red '95 (53 F). Often more available. Tasted before the final blend. A very ripe wine with more of a note of plums (*quetsche*) than violets and black currant, the traditional aromas of the wines from this appellation. It's a square-built, spontaneous wine, harmonious from birth with the potential for long ageing and an interesting evolution.

Reception In one of the two cellars.

How to get there *(Map 22): From Valence towards Vienne via N86. Turn left at the entrance to Mauves, in front of the War Memorial, into the rue de la Claustre then follow the road to the right as far as the little square near the church. Signposted.*

The vines of the Hospice: you need a ladder to get up there!

Jean-Louis Grippat

Owner Jean-Louis Grippat. **Address** La sauva, 07300 Tournon - Tel. 04.75.08.15.51 Fax 04.75.07.00.97. **Open** By appointment.

Standing in the center of Tournon and raising one's head towards the statue which caps the roof of the Hospice, one can imagine a green flag held in her hand which becomes clearly detatched on the granite cliffs. These are the 100-year-old vines that Jean-Louis Grippat cultivates *en fermage* (via a rental agreement). To say that they are inaccessible is not quite an exaggeration. In the absence of a path or stairs the vines can only be worked by using a ladder!

The wines of Jean-Louis Grippat are, however, more accessible but with just as much character. Full-bodied, tannic, and vinified in a traditional manner (frequent *pigeage*), they have become more readily accessible since the introduction of destemming in 1995. Like the red Hermitage les Murets '95 (approx. 105 F) these are delicious wines. Tasted before the final blend, this wine is packed with fruit and finesse. The white Hermitage '94 (approx. 87 F) loses nothing in comparison with its fleshiness and notes of plum.

Our choice Saint-Joseph Vignes de l'Hospice red '95 (approx. 90 F, sales allocated). A tiny yield (30 hectoliters/hectare) from 100-year-old vines has produced a wine of tight-knit but fine extract with dense, silky tannins. To keep. If there is none available the regular red Saint-Joseph (approx. 52 F) is a very safe bet. Tasted before the final blend, the different elements competed with fruit and finesse. To drink or age a little.

Reception Good, by a member of the family, all equally passionate and competent.

How to get there *(Map 22): On the right, at the exit to Tournon, towards Valence via N86.*

The vines of the "*berceau*" in the heart of the appellation Saint-Joseph.

Bernard Gripa

Owner Bernard Gripa. **Address** 5 avenue Ozier, 07300 Mauves - Tel. 04.75.08.14.96 Fax 04.75.07.06.81. **Open** From Monday to Saturday, 9:00-12:00 and 14:00-19:00, by appointment.

The vines are very well exposed on the hillside which gave its name to the appellation, hence the name "*Berceau*" (cradle) to identify the best *cuvées*. The old vines are planted at a high density (8 000 vines/hectare) and the grapes vinified in a traditional manner (no destemming, *pigeage*) to provide maximum extract. Although concentrated this extract is always silky even in difficult years. The reds are usually in heavy demand and are often snatched up as early as the spring. If it is still available choose the red Saint-Joseph *cuvée* Berceau '95 (84 F). Tasted during blending, the wine already promises plenty of extract on the palate. Wrongly neglected, the white wines are more easily obtainable.

The white Saint-Joseph '95 (56 F) has a mineral nose and fleshy, powerful palate with notes of broom and fruit kernel. The *cuvée* Vielles Vignes Berceau (84 F) is even more unctuous with a slight but well-integrated note of quality oak.

Our choice Saint-Péray '95 (48 F) For its floral nose (iris), fleshy, powerful palate with notes of bread-crust and caramel and delicious acidulous finish with aromas that veer more towards white fruits and plum. The final is long, persistent and still lively. The wine can be aged a while to allow the structure and bouquet to develop.

Reception At the cellar, passionate and attentive.

How to get there *(Map 22): From Valence towards Vienne via N86. The cellar is on the right in the center of Mauves, indicated by a sign.*

The shears, ready to top and trim ("*émoucher*") the vines.

Domaine du Biguet

Owner Jean-Louis Thiers. **Address** Le Biguet, Toulaud, 07130 Saint-Péray - Tel. 04.75.40.49.44 Fax 04.75.40.33.03. **Open** By appointment.

Standing in ruins (but what allure!) the Château de Crusol can no longer protect its flock from the urban advance of the suburbs of Valence nor from the disaffection for sparkling wines other than Champagne. However, since the beginning of the 19th century a number of wine growers in Saint-Péray have persisted in the production of a rather distinct sparkling wine made from the Marsanne grape variety with an occasional addition of Roussanne. This wine has a unique taste developed by the granite soils. Wagner, they say, was excessively fond of it.

Jean-Louis Thiers also produces a still wine from his oldest Marsanne vines grown on clay-limestone soils. The '94 (36 F) has a delicately floral nose with a palate that veers more towards vervain and almond. The '95 is fuller in style. Both are to drink now.

Our choice Saint-Péray sparkling Brut (approx. 40 F). The wine sold in 1997 was based on the '94 vintage with just a touch of the '93 (10%). The nose is powerful, with toasted notes, followed by an expressive palate which is long and fine and which has an orange peel aroma. The bead and mousse are fine. The wine is powerful without being heavy and to drink now.

Reception In a bright, simple cellar decorated with a "*ventadou*", an old instrument for blowing the (wheat) grain and separating it from the husk.

How to get there *(Map 22): Leave Valence from the north towards Vienne. At the entrance to Saint-Péray towards Lamastre via D533, then towards Toulaud via D279 for 2km. Turn right towards Biguet via C4 and follow the signs for 2km to the property.*

SOUTHERN RHONE

23
Charmes-s.-Rhône
Beaumont-lès-Valence
Montéléger
Drôme 26
St-Pierreville
La Voulte-s.-Rhône
Les Ollières-s.-Eyrieux
Le Pouzin
Livron-s.-Drôme
Allex
Crest
Beaufort-s.-Gervanne
Die
Saillans
Pontaix
Pont-de-Quart
Antraigues
Privas
Loriol-s.-Dr.
Grane
Chomérac
Marsanne
Châtillon-en-Diois
Saou
Aubenas
St-Jean-le-Centenier
Meysse
Rochemaure
Sauzet
Cléon-d'Andran
Bourdeaux
Luc-en-Diois
Le Teil
Montélimar
La Bégude-de-Mazenc
Dieulefit
Bouvières
Largentière
Châteauneuf-du-Rhône
Salles
Taulignan
La Motte-Chalançon
La Charce
Establet
Ardèche
Viviers
Donzère
Grignan
Joyeuse
Ruoms
Rémuzat
Rosans
St-Remèze
Les Pilles
La Maison-Neuve
Vallon-Pont-d'Arc
Bourg-St-Andéol
Pierrelatte
Valréas
Nyons
Verclause
St-Paul-Trois-Ch.
Mirabel-aux-Baronnies
Drôme
St-Martin-d'A.
Suze-la-Rousse
Barjac
Laval-St-R.
Pont-St-Esprit
Bollène
Tulette
Buis-les-Baronnies
Ste-Cécile-les-V.
Vaison-la-Romaine
Mollans
St-Léger-du-V.
St-Laurent-de-Carnols
Mondragon
Sérignan
Malaucène
Bagnols-s.-Cèze
Vacqueyras
Lussan
Orange
Bédoin
Vaucluse 84
Sault
Seynes
Cavillargues
Jonquières
Mormoiro
Connaux
Courthézon
Gard
Châteauneuf-du-P.
Foissac
Pouzilhac
Roquemaure
Monteux
Carpentras
Monieux
St-Christol
Bédarrides
Uzès
Sorgues
Entraigues
Pernes-les-Font.
Villeneuve-lès-A.
St-Saturnin-d'Apt
Fontaine-de-Vaucluse
St-Chaptes
Avignon
Le Pontet
L'Isle-s.-la-Sorgue
Rustrel
Remoulins
Le Thor
La Calmette
Aramon
Caumont
Apt
Marguerittes
Châteaurenard
Le Coustellet
Nîmes
Jonquières
Maillane
Cavaillon
Robion
Bonnieux
St-Rémy-de-Prov
Plan-d'Orgon
Beaucaire
Tarascon
Lauris
St-Étienne-du-Grès
Orgon
Ansouis
Bellegarde
Cadenet
Vergèze
Fontvieille
Maussane-les-A.
Eyguières
Sénas
Mallemort
Fourques
Vauvert
Arles
Mouriès
Rognes
Salon-de-P.
Lambesc
Pélissanne
St-Cannat
St-Gilles
Le Merle
Durance
St-Martin-de-Crau
Albaron
La Fare-les-Oliviers
Éguilles
Miramas
Mas-Thibert
Aix-en-Provence
Sylvéréal
St-Chamas
Istres
Rognac
Vitrolles
Bouches-du-Rhône 13
Berre-l'Ét.
Gardanne
Marignane
Canal d'Arles à Port-de-Bouc
Stes-Maries-de-la-Mer
Fos-s.-M.
Port-de-Bouc
Septèmes-les-Vallons
Salin-de-Giraud
Martigues
Allauch
Lavéra
Port-St-Louis-du-Rhône
Golfe de Fos
Pointe de Beauduc ou du Sablon
Carro
Carry-le-Rouet
Marseille
Cap Couronne
Ile Pomègues
Cap Croisette

SOUTHERN RHONE

INTRODUCTION

In as much as the Northern Rhône clings to the river, following its course from on high to avoid occasional angry outbursts, so the Southern Rhône spreads comfortably away from it. The river is soon no more than a vague point of reference. The left bank becomes the main focus of attention and eyes are raised towards the mountains of the Dentelles de Montmirail as one follows the route from the Côtes-du-Rhône Villages to the *crus*, Séguret to Gigondas, and towards Mount Ventoux when surveying the extraordinary stony (*galets*) plateau of the vineyards of Châteauneuf-du-Pape. Everything is on a larger scale : the sky, the surface area of the appellations, the size of the properties, and the number of grape varieties used to make the wines.

In particular, the region takes on an aspect of the Midi. The villages have an ocher color and shelter under plane-trees and under the umbrella of wine. Whereas the region around Valence still hesitates between fruit trees and the vine, the south has largely chosen the vine, planting it on the best *terroirs,* using it to decorate houses, and lecturing on it at the university dedicated to wine at Suze-la-Rousse.

If, in addition, you like olives (those of Nyons near the appellation Vinsobres), old buildings (Château de Grignan, the sumptuous dwelling of the Marquise de Sévigné near Tricastin), Roman remains (Vaison-la-Romaine near Séguret) or beautiful villages (Séguret), the region will be a delight. If you only have time for one expedition then wander through the vineyards of Châteauneuf-du-Pape. In a single glance you will fall in love with this spectacular region with its stony ground, the Ventoux, and because it doesn't let us forget the Rhône.

Southern Rhône Appellations

Whereas it's easy to find one's way in the Northern Rhône with the *crus* ranged successively in order, it is more difficult to come to grips with the south and its overlapping generic appellations and specific *crus*.

The Côtes-du-Rhône is an enormous appellation, on the same scale as the region, with 44,000 hectares producing 2.3 million hectoliters of wine. The appellation covers six *départements* (Gard, Ardèche, Drôme, Vaucluse, Loire, and Rhône) and

163 communes. In the second largest regional appellation, after Bordeaux, one can find some real pearls hidden in the haystack and sometimes a little manure !
Within the ocean of Côtes-du-Rhône there are 77 communes which having gained a certain esteem and having conformed to stricter quality regulations benefit from the appellation Côtes-du-Rhône Villages which covers approximately 4,000 hectares. Among these, 16 have been singled out for distinction and can add their names to the label. In the Gard we found some attractive wines in the appellations Laudun and Saint-Gervais; in the Vaucluse in the villages of Sablet, Séguret, Rasteau, and certainly Cairanne which merits extensive exploration. In the Drôme, Valréas and Vinsobres are easily the best.
Thereafter, there are a certain number of *crus* of uneven quality including Costières-de-Nîmes, Coteaux-du-Tricastin, and Côtes-du-Ventoux where one can find some interesting wines but where the average quality level is no better than simple Côtes-du-Rhône. Tavel is uniquely a rosé, the appellation proclaiming that it is the capital of this style of wine despite the fact that the quality is very irregular. The same applies in Lirac and in Vacqueyras although in each of these appellations we have chosen a few wine growers that are well above the average level. In the region there is also plenty of vins de pays, some of which is truly remarkable.
Finally, Gigondas and Châteauneuf-du-Pape are the two leading lights of the region. They have a very good average-quality level and regularly produce exceptional wines.
It's worth noting that apart from Tavel which is dedicated to the production of rosé all these appellations produce wines in three colors (red, white and rosé).

Grape varieties
The appellation Châteauneuf-du-Pape flaunts the fact that 13 different grape varieties are authorized for the red and white wines : Grenache Noir, Syrah, Mourvèdre, Picpoul (without specifying whether it is Noir, Gris or Blanc!), Terret Noir, Counoise, Muscardin, Vaccarèse, Picardin, Cinsault, Clairette, Roussanne, and Bourboulenc, even if in reality far fewer are used. The other appellations use a percentage of these varieties or have added others : Carignan, Grenache Blanc, Picpoul Blanc, Ugni Blanc, Marsanne, Viognier (Coteaux-du-Tricastin), Camarèse (in the "Villages" rosés), Grenache Gris (in Rasteau), Pascal Blanc (in the Côtes-du-Ventoux), Clairette Rose, Calitor (Tavel), etc.
In every case, the decree that governs each appellation fixes the minimum and maximum number of varieties and their varying percentages. In a land of blending and cross-breeding, the appellations of the Southern Rhône each knit a personalized sweater. The wines have multiple character with style due as much to the hand of the wine grower as the *terroir* and grape varieties. Certain ones, however, are still considered stars. The Syrah in red, and Viognier, Marsanne, and Roussanne in white are presented in the chapter on the Northern Rhône. The following are the other principal varieties:
The Grenache Noir is to the south what the Syrah is to the north. Originally from Spain (where it glories in Vega Sicilia) it passed to the Languedoc-Roussillon region before spreading throughout Provence. Rich in sugar and, therefore, high in potential alcohol and low in acidity it produces opulent wines as seen in Châteauneuf-du-Pape.

INTRODUCTION

The Mourvèdre is a red variety that probably also originated from Spain. Opinion varies as to as to the exact place of origin, possibly Murviedro near Valencia or Mataro near Barcelona. It contributes, in particular, to the glory of Bandol. Tannic and with a higher acidity than the Grenache Noir, it provides backbone when blended with this variety.

The red variety Counoise, habitually discredited but praised to the skies by certain wine growers, seems to be coming back in to favor. The wines made from pure Counoise by Doctor Parcé (appellation Collioure in the Roussillon) prove correct the supporters of this variety but here it is only found in blends and then only in homeopathic quantities. The Cinsault, a red variety more often than not vinified as a rosé, is used in blends for its fruit rather than tannic structure. The Carignan, another variety originating from Spain (the region of Carinena in Aragon), is the most planted grape variety in the world and perhaps the most denigrated of French red varieties (it was over-yielded and served for a long time as the base wine for vin de table from the Midi). In reality it reveals unsuspecting virtues if the yields are restrained and the vines old.

The other grape varieties, although marginal, add their touch to the blend : vigor and aroma from the Terret Noir, tannin and peppery notes from the Vaccarèse, and perfum and lightness of body from the Muscardin.

Methods of vinification

The wines of the region are all dry except for Rasteau which also makes a *vin doux naturel* (see the chapter on the Roussillon) produced from Grenache and Beaumes-de-Venise which also produces a *vin doux naturel* based on Muscat à Petits Grains.

Buying in the Northern Rhône

The wines on sale at present are generally the ‘94s and ‘95s which are generally superior to the preceding vintages. Lovers of wines from this region should, therefore, secure supplies as the ’96 vintage appears inferior to the ’95. Enthusiasts of older wines will certainly look to Châteauneuf-du-Pape, an appellation which still offers the exceptional ’89 and ’90 vintages and some older wines, the best of which we have noted. Have confidence and follow us through the appellations without any notion of hierarchy (vins de pays, generic Côtes-du-Rhône) as there are some marvelous wines to discover at very sweet prices.

At table with the wines of the Southern Rhône

With such a range of wines it is difficult to give advice on wine and food matches except for certain general ideas : light white wines with grilled poultry; light red wines with charcuterie ; full bodied, fruity wines (Côtes-du-Rhône and Village) with hot and cold stews (*daube*), poulty in sauce, organ meats, rib of beef or a more exotic cuisine ; powerful, tannic wines (Châteauneuf-du-Pape, Gigondas) with game.

Here are some of the matches we were able to come up with:

Gazpacho: Tavel.

Truffle *chausson*: mature Gigondas.

Hot truffles: mature Châteauneuf-du-Pape, with tertiary aromas.

Sausage and boiled potatoes: young Gigondas.

Veal heart: young Châteauneuf-du-Pape.
Confit (duck or goose): Côtes-du-Rhône.
Rib roast of veal *à la provençale*: powerful Gigondas.
Pigeon and duck: young Châteauneuf-du-Pape.
Duck with spices: generous, velvety, aromatic Châteauneuf-du-Pape ('89 or '90 vintages).
Roast duckling : young and tannic Gigondas.
Hare *à la royale*: mature, structured, great Châteauneuf-du-Pape (Beaucastel or La Gardine where one can find old vintages).
Meat and vegetable stew (*potée*) : Coteaux-du-Tricastin.
Shoulder of lamb : fine Gigondas from a great vintage (Cayron).
Stew (*daube*) : great, mature Gigondas (Goubert '85).

AVIGNON

1 - RESTAURANT - **La Cuisine de Reine**: *Le Cloître des Arts, 83 rue Joseph Vernet, 84000 Avignon. Tel. 04.90. 85.99.04. Closed Sunday and Monday evening.* Ancient cloisters, a former private residence that was long shut down, and where one now finds exhibition rooms, a bookshop, a tea room and a restaurant run by Reine Samut of Lourmarin. Attractive, well-chosen wine list at moderate prices. Menu: 90 (lunch) and 145 F (dinner). Brunch at lunchtime on Saturday.

2 - RESTAURANT - **Christian Étienne**: *10-12 rue Mons (place du Palais-des-Papes), 84000 Avignon. Tel. 04.90. 86.16.50 Fax 04.90.86.67.09. Closed Saturday lunchtime year-round and Sunday except in July.* Lovely 14th-century frescoes. An innovative, colorful cuisine (surprising all-tomato menu). Very attractive wine list. Menus: 160 (lunch weekdays) to 480 F. A la carte: around 500 F.

3 - RESTAURANT - **Les Domaines**: *28 place de l'Horloge, 84000 Avignon. Tel. 04.90.82.58.86 Fax 04.90.86.26.31.* Bistro cooking and a very attractive list with the best Rhône valley wines, full of finds, many served by the glass. A la carte: around 200 F.

4 - HOTEL - **Hôtel de la Mirande**: *4 place de la Mirande, 84000 Avignon. Tel. 04.90.85.93.93 Fax 04.90. 86.26.85.* Lovely 16th-century house with silk curtains, tapestries, period furniture and valuable objects. Rooms: 1,700 to 2,100 F. Breakfast: 95 F.

5 - HOTEL-RESTAURANT - **Cloître Saint-Louis**: *20 rue du Portail-Boquier, 84000 Avignon. Tel. 04.90.27.55.55 Fax 04.90.82.24.01. Hotel open year-round. Restaurant closed in February.* Rooms: 450 to 950 F and 575 to 1145 F depending on dates. Menus: 99 to 190 F. Breakfast (a disaster): 65-70 F. A lovely hotel established in the former Jesuit novitiate that harmonizes old stones and ascetic, modern decorating in its spacious rooms. Average table, but good selection of wines.

BAGNOLS-SUR-CEZE

6 - HOTEL-RESTAURANT - **Château de Montcaud et les Jardins de Montcaud**: *Hameau de Combes-Sabran, 30200 Bagnols-sur-cèze. Tel. 04.66.89.*

60.60 Fax 04.66.89.45.04. Closed from January to March. A few kilometers from Orange, a beautiful house in the middle of a park. Flavorful southern cooking and a wine list generously welcoming Rhône wines with a hundred entries, well-classed and generally well-chosen, recent vintages. Menus: 250 to 420 F. A la carte: around 320 F. Weekdays and for lunch, the " bistro under the chestnut trees " formula with reduced menus at 145 and 185 F. Rooms: 750 to 2,400 F and from 950 to 2,900 F depending on dates. Excellent breakfast: 100 F.

CAIRANNE

7 - BED & BREAKFAST - **La Maison vigneronne**: *84290 Cairanne. Tel. 04.90.30.77.57.* Two pretty, simple

rooms in a house in the village center. 180 and 230 F, breakfast included. In the joint-run shop one can find Corinne Couturier and Marcel Richaud's wines, as well as those of their friends from other regions.

8 - BED & BREAKFAST - **Le Moulin Agapê**: *84290 Cairanne. Tel. 04.90.30.77.04.* Currently being restored, this old mill offers perfectly quiet guest rooms from 270 to 570 F (2 to 5 pers.). Communal table by reservation: 100 F (total). Reduced prices for children.

CARPENTRAS

9 - RESTAURANT - **Le Vert Galant**: *12 rue de Clapies, 84200 Carpentras. Tel. 04.90.67.15.50. Closed Saturday lunchtime, Sunday and 3 weeks in August.* Market-based cuisine with excellent products. Menus: 130 (lunch weekdays), 210 and 290 F. Good wine list.

CHÂTEAUNEUF-DU-PAPE

10 - HOTEL-RESTAURANT - **La Sommellerie**: *84230 Châteauneuf-du-Pape. Tel. 04.90.83.50.00 Fax 04.90.83.51.85. Closed Sunday evening and Monday from Halloween to Easter.* 2 km from Châteauneuf on the Roquemaure route. A lovely mas amidst the grapevines. Very fine, flavorful cuisine. Attractive wine list with over 150 entries from Châteauneuf-du-Pape, many old vintages. Good selection from the other appellations. Menus: 170 to 360 F. Rooms: 400 to 890 F.

CRILLON-LE-BRAVE

11 - HOTEL-RESTAURANT - **Hostellerie de Crillon-le-Brave**: *Place de l'Église, 84410 Crillon-le-Brave. Tel. 04.90. 65.61.61 Fax 04.90.65.62.86. Closed Tuesday evenings in March.* Between Malaucène and Carpentras. Terrace in summer, vaulted dining room with chimney in winter. Good regional cuisine. Lovely view of Mount Ventoux. Menus: 250 to 340 F. A la carte: around 350 F. Rooms: 750 to 1,690 F and apartments: 1450 to 2,400 F. Breakfast: 80 F.

ENTRECHAUX

12 - HOTEL - **La Manescale**: *Route de Faucon (D205), 84340 Entrechaux.*

Tel. 04.90.46.03.80 Fax 04.90.46. 03.89. A former sheepfold transformed into a hotel with pleasant rooms from 450 to 950 F. Breakfast: 75 F.

GIGONDAS

13 - RESTAURANT - **L'Oustalet**: *Place de la Mairie, 84190 Gigondas. Tel. 04.90. 65.85.30. Closed Sunday evenings and Monday (except festival).* Menus: 73 and 110 (lunch); à la carte: 45 to 100 F. Menu-carte: 165 (evening and Sun.); à la carte 53 to 100 F. Genuine cuisine, flavorful and elegant. Unfortunately, after ordering, cooking and service are slow to follow. Afternoon snacks and light meals. Good wine list, especially for Gigondas.

GRIGNAN

14 - HOTEL - **Manoir de La Roseraie**:

Route de Valréas, 26230 Grignan. Tel. 04.75.46.58.15 Fax 04.75.46. 91.55. Two paces from the castle of Madame de Sévigné, a beautiful house, restored in Provençal style. Rooms: 680 to 1650 F. Breakfast: 90 F.

LA BAUME DE TRANSIT

15 - BED & BREAKFAST - **Domaine de Saint-Luc**: *26790 La Baume de Transit. Tel. 04.75.98.11.51 Fax 04.75.98. 19.22.* Guest rooms in a lovely 18th-century farm run by one of the best Tricastin growers (360 F, breakfast included). In the evening, meals at a communal table (135 F) that deserve their good reputation. Pool.

LA GARDE-ADHEMAR

16 - RESTAURANT - **Le Logis de L'Escalin**: *26700 La Garde-Adhémar. Tel. 04.75.04.41.32 Fax 04.75. 04.40.05.* Menus: 105 to 340 F. At the foot of the beautiful old village, a savory cuisine to be enjoyed if one doesn't get turned off by the complicated

jumble of menus offered. Attractive wine list (120 entries from the Rhône) well chosen and presented, though with some errors. Large selection of half bottles.

LE PONTET

17 - HOTEL-RESTAURANT - **Auberge de Cassagne**: *450 allée de Cassagne, 84130 Le Pontet-Avignon. Tel. 04.90.31. 04.18 Fax 04.90.32.25.09.* Very pretty rooms decorated with Provençal furniture and apartments from 420 to 1780 F. Breakfast: 95 F. Menus: 230 to 460 F. 5 km northeast of Avignon. A lovely, shaded house in unattractive surroundings. Pleasant terrace in summer. Creative cooking, with a Provençal accent. Superb selection of well-presented wines (650 entries, the best Rhône wines, no weak spots in other regions, and a selection of half bottles). Abundant selection of whiskies and true, fine Cognacs.

MERINDOL LES OLIVIERS

18 - RESTAURANT - **Auberge de la Gloriette**: *26170 Mérindol les Oliviers. Tel. 04.75.28.71.08.* Among the olive trees, facing the Ventoux, this restaurant-bakery run by cat-lovers keeps

guest rooms, from 250 to 300 F (200 to 250 F, low-season), one of which, very pretty, is all white. The table, simple but tasty, offers a menu at 95 F. The short wine list could be better organized, but the bottles are well chosen.

MONDRAGON

19 - HOTEL-RESTAURANT - **La Beaugravière**: *N7, 84430 Mondragon. Tel. 04.90. 40.82.54 Fax 04.90.40.91.01. Closed Sunday evenings and Monday in low-season, and from September 15 to 30.* The best cellar in the whole Rhône valley (with old collector's vintages). Very good cuisine, rich and savory. Menus: 135 to 395 F (wine included). A la carte: around 350 F. Truffle menu when in season: 395 and 670 F. 3 rooms: 265 to 345 F. Breakfast: 40 F.

ROCHEGUDE

20 - HOTEL-RESTAURANT - **Château de Rochegude**: *Tel. 04.75.97.21.10 Fax 04.75.04.89.87. Closed from January 15 to mid-March.* All that's missing in this medieval kitsch work of art are the ghosts. Good table but unimaginitive wine list. Menus: 200 (lunch) to 490 F. A la carte: around 450 F. 3 apartments and 26 rooms: 650 to 1700 F.

SAINT-PAUL-TROIS-CHÂTEAUX

21 - RESTAURANT - **L'Esplan**: *Place de l'Esplan, 26130 Saint-Paul-Trois-Châteaux. Tel. 04.75.96.64.64 Fax 04.75.04.92.36. Restaurant closed Sun. evenings (except October 15 to April 15) and from December 20 to January 5.* A splendid building that

offers a maze of terraces and patios decorated with comtemporary precision. Good cuisine and an irreproachable wine list. Menus: 98 to 198 F (good truffle menu from December 1 to March 31).

SÉGURET

22 - HOTEL-RESTAURANT - **Domaine de Cabasse**: *Route de Sablet, 84110 Séguret. Tel. 04.90.46.91.12 Fax 04.90.46.94.01. Closed November 2 to Easter.* In one of the appellation's best viticultural estates, a good hotel-restaurant at the foot of the historic village of Séguret. The wine list favors some very good wines from the property. Menus: 91 and 163 F. Rooms: 350 to 650 F. Breakfast: 60 F

23 - BED & BREAKFAST - **Domaine Saint-Jean**: *Chemin Montvert - L'Esclade, 84110 Séguret. Tel. 04.90.46. 91.76.* 1 very pretty guest room and 2 suites,

perfectly decorated. Beautiful park behind the house (lawn, ornemental lake, fountain, trees and hidden spots where one can relax alone). Rooms: 480 to 550 F, (sumptuous) breakfast included .

SUZE-LA-ROUSSE

24 - BED & BREAKFAST - **La Poupaille**: *26790 Suze-la-Rousse. Tel. 04.75.04. 83.99.* A comfortable, quiet Bed & Breakfast with a kind welcome. Five rooms: 250 F, breakfast included. Good communal dining: 100 F by reservation.

VAISON-LA-ROMAINE

25 - BED & BREAKFAST - **Hostellerie le Beffroi**: *Rue de l'Évêché, Cité médiévale, 84110 Vaison-la-Romaine. Tel. 04.90.36.04.71 Fax 04.90.36.24.78.*

Closed November 10 to December 20 and February 15 to March 20. One of the most beautiful buildings in the city, dating from the 16th century. Lovely view from certain rooms, from 450 to 655 F. Breakfast: 50 F.

26 - RESTAURANT - **Le Brin d'Olivier**: *4 rue du Ventoux, 84110 Vaison-la-romaine. Tel. 04.90.28.74.79. Closed Wednesday and Saturday lunchtime and late June to early July, and late November to mid-December.* A small, new restaurant, brightly decorated. Exciting cuisine and good selection of wines. To be discovered. Menus: 70 (lunch except Sun.) to 180 F, truffle menu: 300 F.

27 - RESTAURANT - **Le Moulin à huile**: *1 quai maréchal Foch, route de Malaucène. Tel. 04.90.36.20.67 Fax*

04.90.36.20.20. Closed Sunday evenings and Monday in low-season. Menus: 150 F (except weekends and holidays). Menu-carte: 240 F. Very fine Provençal cuisine. Pleasant terrace. Decent wine list.

28 - HOTEL-RESTAURANT - **La Fête en Provence**: *Haute ville, 84110 Vaison-la-Romaine. Tel. 04.90.36.36.43.* Handsome studio-apartments: 300, 450 and 600 F. Menus: 100 (lunch) and 150 F. La Fête is a splendid restored house in old Vaison. Pert cuisine and an attractive wine list featuring the Rhône valley. Excellent welcome.

VALAURIE

29 - HOTEL-RESTAURANT - **La Table de Nicole**: *Les Petites-Condamines, 26230 Valaurie. Tel. 04.75.98.52.03 Fax 04.75.98.58.45.* A hotel-restaurant with a homemade flair. Fifteen house appetizers and a plat du jour. Truffles play the lead role when in season. Well-stocked cellar. Menu: 145 F (wine included). Rooms: 340 to 520 F. Truffle discovery days and cooking lessons from December to March.

30 - HOTEL-RESTAURANT - **Valle Auréa**: *Route de Grignan, 26230 Valaurie. Tel. 04.75.98.56.40 and 04.75.97.25.00 Fax 04.75.98.59.59. Closed Sunday evenings and Monday except from June to September.* Rooms: 435 to 595 F Breakfast: 65 F. Menus: 158 and 199 F. A la carte: around 250 F. A lovely, quiet house. Cuisine is classic, the wine list is short but well-chosen.

VALRÉAS

31 - BED & BREAKFAST - **Domaine des Grands Devers**: *84600 Valréas. Tel. 04.90.35.15.98 Fax 04.90.37.49.56.* Pleasant guest rooms kept by one of the best winegrowers in the region at 270 F, memorable breakfast included.

32 - RESTAURANT - **La Ferme du Champ-Rond**: *Chemin des Anthelmes, 84600 Valréas. Tel. 04.90.37.31.68. Closed Sunday evenings, Monday and in February.* Menus: 85 to 168 F. Excellent table with good products and an exemplary welcome. Very good selection of local wines.

VILLEDIEU

33 - BED & BREAKFAST - **Ferme fortifiée de la Baude**: *84110 Villedieu. Tel. 04.90.28.95.18 Fax 04.90.28.91.05.*

Three rooms and two very well-equipped duplexes in an old, tastefully restored fortified farm. Tennis courts and pool. Rooms: 520 F, duplex for 4 persons: 850 F. Communal dining in the evening by reservation: 135 F, wine and coffee included.

VILLENEUVE-LÈS-AVIGNON

34 - RESTAURANT - **Aubertin**: *1 rue de*

l'Hôpital, 30400 Villeneuve-lès-Avignon. Tel. 04.90.25.94.84 Fax 04.90.26.30.71. Closed Sunday evenings and Monday, except in July and August. Light, savory cuisine, excellent products. Attractive selection of Rhône valley wines. Menus: 100 (lunch weekdays), 160 and 240 F. A la carte: around 350 F.

35 - HOTEL-RESTAURANT - **Le Prieuré**: *7 place du Chapitre. Tel. 04.90.15.90.15 Fax 04.90.25.45.39. Closed early November to early March.* Menus: 200 to 460 F A la carte: around 450 F. Pretty rooms: 550 to 1,800 F. Breakfast: 80 F. Lovely park. Swimming pool. Colorful and flavorful Mediteranean cooking that hasn't forgotten traditional bourgeois cuisine. Very attractive wine

list with forty great Châteauneuf-du-Pape in excellent, often old vintages. Large selection for the rest of the Rhône and the other wine-growing regions. Good offerings in half bottles.

VIOLÉS

36 - HOTEL-RESTAURANT - **Mas de Bouvau**: *Route de Cairanne, 84150 Violès. Tel. 04.90.70.94.08 Fax 04.90.70.95.99. Closed Sunday evenings and Monday (except holidays) and from November 20 to 28, from December 20 to 30 and 2 weeks for February vacation.* Shaded terrace. Good, simple regional cuisine. Short wine list, but well-chosen among the neighboring villages. Fifty entries from 70 to 170 F. Menus: 130 to 260 F. 4 small rooms: 280 to 490 F. Breakfast: 45 F.

37 - BED & BREAKFAST - **La Farigoule**: *Le plan de Dieu, 84150 Violès. Tel. 04.90.70.91.78. Closed November to late March.* Pretty guest rooms from 270 to 330 F, (excellent) breakfast included, with a pleasant garden.

TO SEE

BOUCHET

OUTING - In the Tricastin, the Cistertian abbey has become a wine cooperative. Visit the cellar.

CHATEAUNEUF-DU-PAPE

OUTING - Ruins surrounded by vineyards .

MUSEUM - **Winegrower's tools Museum**: *Caves Brotte - Père Anselme, 84230 Châteauneuf-du-Pape. Tel. 04.90.83.70.07 Fax 04.90.83.74.34. Open every day from 9 to 12am and 2 to 6pm.* Wonderful collection of old tools.

RASTEAU

MUSEUM - **Winegrower's Museum**: *Domaine de Beaurenard, 84110 Rasteau. Tel. 04.90.46.11.75. Open Easter to late September from 2 to 6pm (from 10am in July and August).* Lovely collections of old tools and bottles.

SAINT-RESTITUT

OUTING - **The cathedral cellar of the Cellier des Dauphins**: *Le Belvédère, 26130 Saint-Restitut. Tel. 04.75.04. 95.87.* The old white stone quarries of Tricastin transformed into an aging cellar by this large cooperative. Visit by train.

SEGURET

OUTING - A beautiful medieval village overlooking the vineyards.

SUZE-LA-ROUSSE

OUTING - **Wine University**: *Le Château, 26790 Suze-la-Rousse. Tel. 04.75. 97.21.30 Fax 04.75.98.24.20. Open Monday-Friday from 8am to 6pm.* The beautiful castle can be visited afternoons every day except Tuesday. Closed in November.

FETES

MAY

Vaison-la-Romaine: wine festival at the beginning of the month. *For information: 04.90.36.02.11.*

JULY

Vacqueyras: wine festival in mid-month.

Cairanne: wine festival at the end of the month.

AUGUST

Rasteau: night-time festival of the vin doux naturel in mid-month. *For information: 04.90.46.10.47.*

Carpentras: Flavors of Provence festival, the weekend of the 15th. *For information: 04.90.62.54.36.*

Séguret: wine festival, the third Sunday of the month.

Châteauneuf-du-Pape: ripening festival at the beginning of the month. *For information: 04.90.83.77.81.*

NOVEMBER

Richerenches: truffle market Wed. mornings through March.

Carpentras: truffle market Friday mornings through March.

Vaison-la-Romaine: gourmet days and Côtes-du-Rhône Primeur festival in mid-month. *For information: 04.90.36.02.11.*

Avignon: first tasting of the vins primeurs, the third Thursday of the month. *For information: 04.90.27.24.00.*

DECEMBER

Séguret: Provençal winegrower's festival shortly before Christmas. *For information: 04.90.46.91.08.*

The barrel cellar.

Château de Beaucastel

Owners Jean-Pierre and François Perrin. **Adresse** 84350 Courthézon - Tel. 04.90.70.41.00 Fax 04.90.70.41.19. **Oupen** In the morning only by appointment. **Spoken** English, German. **Credit Cards** Visa, Eurocard, MasterCard.

The domaine comprises 100 hectares, of which 70 hectares are in Châteauneuf-du-Pape on the Courthézon plateau. In red, the Mourvèdre is planted in equal proportion with the Grenache (30%) while the Syrah (10%) ties with the Counoise, a more often than not mythical grape variety that is rarely planted in the region. The same singularity applies to the whites with a crushing proportion of Roussanne (80%). In the search for wines of character the Perrins give total priority to the soils ("a nutritious support and not simply a physical support") by working them. In white, choose without any hesitation the *cuvée* Vieilles Vignes '95 (210 F), a pure Roussanne produced from 70-year-old vines, for its deep color, fruity nose, and full, fine palate. If the 6 000 bottles of this *cuvée* are out of stock or the price (due to tiny yields) makes you hesitate, the Châteauneuf-du-Pape Tradition '94 (125 F) provides excellent consolation. The palate takes its ease with notes of ripe apricot and spice, a fleshy texture and great persistence. For a relaxed evening meal the red Côtes-du-Rhône Coudoulet '95 (59 F) is powerful and rich and the white (72 F) fine and fleshy.

Our choice Châteauneuf-du-Pape red '94 (125 F). The first nose is reserved before opening out (with aeration) to lovely ripe fruit notes. The palate is full, supported by fine tannins and refreshed by the fruit. The finale is clean, lifted and long. To keep.

Reception Excellent, in the tasting room.

How to get there *(Map 23): From Orange towards Avignon by the N7. Just before Courthézon exit towards Beaucastel following the signposted route.*

La Gardine and its tower *cuvier.*

Château de la Gardine

Owners Maxime and Patrick Brunel. **Address** Route de Roquemaure, 84230 Châteauneuf-du-Pape - Tel. 04.90.83.73.20 Fax 04.90.83.77.24. **Open** From Monday to Friday, 9:00-12:00 and 13:00-18:30. **Spoken** English. **Credit cards** Visa, Eurocard, MasterCard.

La Gardine has 55 hectares in one single unit but on varying soils. The important percentage of Syrah and Mourvèdre produces wines that are more stream-lined than classic Châteauneuf-du-Pape. They are, however, concentrated, thanks to the *pigeage,* but with very fine extract due in part to the partial destemming and to the quality of the extraction. The '90 (127 F) provides a good example with its velvety texture. The wines can be aged or consumed reasonably rapidly.

The prestige *cuvée* Génération, aged for a long time, often sharper, always seems to gain freshness and fruit with age. The '89 (250 F) offers a monumental palate, square and structured but with fine tannins and notes of fig and prune. To age a little longer.

In white, the Roussanne plays an important part in the blend. It is particularly assertive in the *cuvée* Vieilles Vignes '92 (185 F) vinified in new oak with lees stirring. The nose is floral (iris), the palate ample, powerful and persistent with a note of hazelnuts.

Our choice Châteauneuf-du-Pape Génération red '90 (250 F). For its deep color, ripe nose, full, powerful fine palate with notes of black fruits and tobacco. Resist the temptation to drink now and keep the wine a little longer.

Reception Excellent, in the tasting room.

How to get there *(Map 23): From Châteauneuf-du-Pape towards Roquemaure via D17. The château is indicated on the right after 1km.*

Aimé and Christophe Sabon.

Domaine de la Janasse

Owners Aimé and Christophe Sabon. **Address** 27 chemin du Moulin, 84350 Courthézon - Tel. 04.90.70.86.29 Fax 04.90.70.75.93. **Open** From Monday to Saturday, 8:00-12:00 and 14:00-20:00, Sunday by appointment. **Spoken** English. **Credit cards** Visa, Eurocard, MasterCard.

Aimé loves the vine. Accompanying him on a tour of the vineyard is a rare pleasure. He points out the old vines bent by the wind, the line of trees over which the birds loom during the hunting season and the nuances in each *terroir.* Aimé is a quality deliveryman whose luxery is to provide his son, Christophe, the best quality grapes possible.

The red Châteauneuf-du-Pape *cuvée* Chaupin '95 (approx. 95 F) was tasted in a provisional blend. Produced from pure Grenache from 80-year-old vines, the wine has a robust palate without showing it and is tannic, elegant and silky with the astonishing nuance of Pinot Noir!

Other than the Châteauneufs, the domaine also produces some interesting red Côtes-du-Rhône. The *cuvée* Les Garrigues '95 (approx. 60 F) has very fine and dense extract, a light and fruity (black fruits, raisins) palate and a massive alcoholic structure perfectly hidden under the flesh.

Our choice Châteauneuf-du-Pape Vieilles Vignes red '95 (approx. 130 F). Produced essentially from very old, 80 to more than 100 year- old, Grenache from different *terroirs.* The nose is intense, the palate opulent with extremely fine tannins. Well-constituted and ample, the structure is coated with a very fine extract. This is a wine with muscle, but the muscles are slender. The finish is powerful without being heavy. To age if one can be patient.

Reception Friendly, in a corner of the cellar.

How to get there *(Map 23): From Orange towards Avignon via N7. Head for the center of Courthézon then follow the signposted route.*

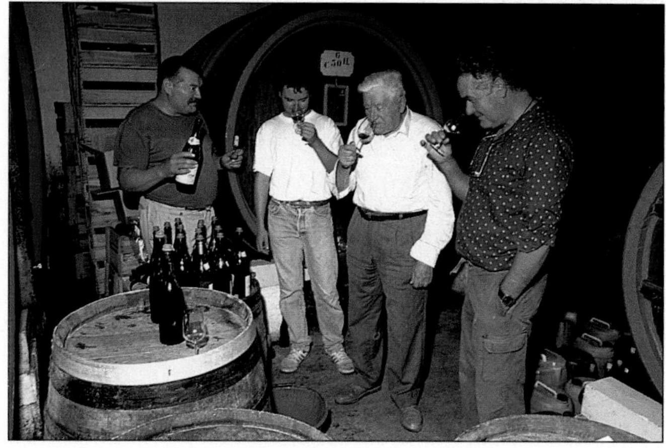

Family tasting around the "Papet."

Clos du Mont-Olivet

Owner Family Sabon. **Address** 15 avenue Saint-Joseph, 84230 Châteauneuf-du-Pape - Tel. 04.90.83.72.46 Fax 04.90.83.51.75. **Open** By appointment.

The Sabon brothers look for power and structure in their Grenache-dominated wines. The white wines are fine, floral, agreeable and very expressive like the Côtes-du-Rhône '95 and '96, produced from Clairette Rose, which is lively and alert. However, we particularly liked the red Châteauneufs which need time to age and mature thus providing attractive notes of truffle and game (venison). A number of older vintages are available to pass the time while waiting for the tannic, thick-set '95 (50 F). The '94 (50 F) has a smoky nose and full-bodied palate, the '93 (52 F) is supple, dominated by black fruits, and astonishing for the vintage, the '92 (54 F) is supple with notes of licorice, the '91 (56 F) still tannic but beginning to evolve with a body that holds the promise of the nose and the '87 (64 F) is supple but still upright.

Our choice Châteauneuf-du-Pape Cuvée du Papet red '90 (160 F). This astonishing wine is produced from very ripe, low yielding old vines. The nose is one of jam and warm bread, the palate is extremely concentrated with enough extract to bite into ("you can cut it into slices on the palate," says one of the Sabons') and notes of dried figs, aromatic herbs and spices. Finesse, flesh, balance and complexity complement the alcoholic structure. To drink but it can of course be aged.

Reception A descent into the cellar leaves a memory that remains engraved in the mind forever, particularly when the "Papet" is present.

How to get there *(Map 23): At the foot of the château ruins, on the road to Roquemaure.*

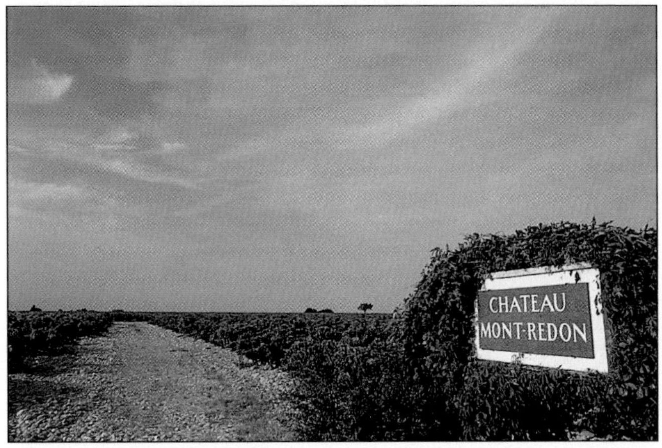

The vineyard of Mont-Redon on the high terraces of Châteauneuf.

Château Mont-Redon

Owners Family Abeille and family Fabre. **Address** 84230 Châteauneuf-du-Pape - Tel. 04.90.83.72.75 Fax 04.90.83.77.20. **Open** Every day, 8:00-19:30 except Wednesday, 8:00-12:00 and 14:00-18:00. Mid Jan. - Mid Feb., open on from Monday to Friday only (same hours). **Credit cards** Visa, Eurocard, MasterCard.

This domaine of 95 hectares on the stony (*galet*) plateau is undergoing a complete revival. Experiments are being carried out with seeding between the rows of vines, *pigeage* implemented for greater extraction, and according to the *cuvée*, a mix of barrels (*foudres*, seasoned oak, new oak) used for the ageing of the wines. These are extremely tannic and robust, often awkward in their youth, and need long ageing before they become of interest. Apart from the supple, fruity red Côtes-du-Rhône '95 (35 F) there are various vintages of Châteauneuf-du-Pape available at the domaine. The '85 (115 F) is ready to drink and has notes of Mocha coffee; the '89 (79 F) is powerful, tannic, and very spicy, the '93 (69 F) balanced, harmonious, and particularly long for this disastrous vintage. Available from 1998, the '95 (approx. 68 F) appears balanced, endowed with very fine extract, and full, ripe tannins.

The whites, never available for long, are mischievous with their notes of citrus fruits (grapefruit, lemon) and marry well with food.

Our choice Châteauneuf-du-Pape '90 (76 F). In the great years, Mont-Redon opens out, with a few years bottle age, exploding with abundance and fruit (Burlat cherries, fig, prune). The wine is balanced and fleshy with fine tannins, power, and length. To drink or age.

Reception Very good. Don't forget to take a walk in the vineyard which is renowned for its stony (round galets) soils.

How to get there *(Map 23): North of Châteauneuf towards Orange via D68.*

Under lock and key, the reserves of the great restaurants.

Château La Nerthe

Owner Family Richard. **Manager** Alain Dugas. **Address** Route de Sorgues 84230 Châteauneuf-du-Pape - Tel. 04.90.83.70.11 Fax 04.90.83.79.69. **Open** Every day, 9:00-12:00 and 14:00-18:00. **Spoken** English. **Credit cards** Visa, Eurocard, MasterCard.

This is a domaine that is on its way up. It's notable for the importance given to Syrah and Mourvèdre, which outweigh the Grenache in certain red *cuvées*, and for the high percentage of Roussanne in the whites.

The improvements made in the reds led us to prefer recent vintages, even the minor years. We appreciated the Cuvée des Cadettes '93 (145 F) for its aroma of dried prunes, fullness, freshness, and smoky notes on the palate as well as the '91 (85 F) which has a large percentage of Mourvèdre in the blend and which is even more explosive than last year. The wine takes flight, led by its smoky aroma and fleshy palate with a note of crystallized orange. Here is a "tip." There is still a little '90 in stock which has the flavor of coffee and tapenade on the palate. You just need to be a little persuasive !

Our choice The whites. The '95 (90 F) for its powerful palate and hint of honey and, above all, the '91 (92 F) for its intense floral nose, creamy palate with notes of almond and spice, and persistence with notes of zest of crystallized citrus fruits (lemon, grapefruit). If the Cuvée Clos de Beauvoir is still available don't hesitate, particularly for the '93 (145 F), which is fleshy, fine and has a long, explosive finish. All these wines can be either consumed or aged.

Reception Perfect, in an ultra-modern tasting room. Don't forget to ask to see the collection of old bottles and the barrel cellar which is shown to good advantage. One part dates from 1560 and another from the 18th century, built with crossed ribbing.

How to get there *(Map 23): From Châteauneuf-du-Pape towards Sorgues via D17. The château is signposted on the left.*

Paul Avril and his son Vincent.

Clos des Papes

Owner Paul Avril. **Address** 13 avenue Pierre de Luxembourg, 84230 Châteauneuf-du-Pape - Tel. 04.90.83.70.13 Fax 04.90.83.50.87. **Open** From Monday to Friday, 8:00-12:00 and 14:00-18:00. **Spoken** English, Italian. **Credit cards** Visa, Eurocard, MasterCard.

This 32 hectare domaine has a significant percentage of Mourvèdre (20%) with Syrah (10%) as the guest star. The vineyard is broken up into 18 different parcels producing a staggered ripening of the grapes which permits the blending of the various red *terroirs.* The relatively high fermentation temperatures for maximum extraction and long period of maceration produce wines that are very dense and tannic and which need to be aged to acquire real body and soul.

The white wines are well represented at this domaine (10% of the production) and small lots of older vintages are regularly released for sale. The '87 (146 F) is becoming clearly mineral and the '88 (140 F) needs to be decanted to release its power and toasted aroma. Whatever else, don't miss out on the '89 (134 F) for its almond, toast, and mineral nose and waxy, honeyed palate. Purchase the '95 (89 F) for its power, concentration, and aromatic bouquet (almond, dried apricot) and watch it mature with age.

Our choice Châteauneuf-du-Pape red '95 (85 F). Produced from a balance of Mourvèdre and Grenache, this wine combines opulence and rigor and preserves the extract (small yield, fining but no filtration) to envelop, with fine tannins, the strong alcoholic structure (14% natural). The palate is ripe, open without being shapeless, and has a keen acidity which ensures freshness and a lively aspect. The bouquet is aromatic with a mix of tobacco, plum, and prune. To keep.

Reception In a cellar that has been attacked by racodium celarae, a fungus which pads the walls.

How to get there *(Map 23): The cellar is on the left leaving Châteauneuf towards Avignon.*

The *terroir* of round stones or *galets*.

Domaine du Vieux-Télégraphe

Owners Henri Brunier and sons. **Address** 3 route de Châteauneuf, 84370 Bédarrides - Tel. 04.90.33.00.31 Fax 04.90.33.18.47. **Open** From Monday to Friday, 8:00-12:00 and 13:30-18:00 (2nd cellar at the Domaine Laroquette: 2, avenue L. Pasteur in Chateauneuf same hours). **Spoken** English. **Credit cards** Visa, Eurocard, MasterCard.

Daniel and Frédéric are the sons at this domaine, the latter responsible for the vinification and vineyard. He insists he'll stay there "day and night," to survey this vast area of stony (*galets*) ground. The cellar created by Henri Brunier is a model of logic and simplicity. Everything works by gravity without any mechanical manipulation avoiding damage to the grapes or a loss of fruit and freshness due to oxidation. The appellation prides itself on the multiplicity of grape varieties. The domaine (70 hectares on the plateau with an average age of 40 years for the vines with some attaining the century) has chosen simplicity: In this papal realm, the Bruniers swear by the trinity of Grenache (70%), Syrah and Mourvèdre, perfect ripeness ("when the Grenache becomes fig-like") and lucidity in their work methods. This means no destemming, no addition of cultured yeasts, no fining or filtering but plenty of racking. The red wine maintains a savory grain which rolls off the tongue. The *cuvée* Roquette '95 speaks with an accent.

Our choice Châteauneuf-du-Pape red '95 (99 F, limited to six bottles). Great finesse of extract, a light grain characteristic of the domaine, plenty of concentration, strong notes of spice. A wine structured by the Syrah and Mourvèdre with a powerful, tannic palate that becomes a little more friendly with aeration. It needs obligatory ageing.

Reception Good, at the cellar.

How to get there *(Map 23): From Avignon towards Bédarrides via N7. Turn left towards Châteauneuf. The cellar is 500m on the right.*

The sundial which serves as a symbol for the domaine.

Château Mourgues du Grès

Owner François Collard. **Address** 30300 Beaucaire - Tel. 04.66.59.46.10 Fax 04.66.59.34.21. **Open** By appointment. **Spoken** English.

The domaine, acquired by François and Anne Collard in 1989, takes its name from the fact that, until the Revolution, the farmhouse or *mas* was owned by the Ursulines. "*Mourgues*" means "nun" in Provençal and the "*grès*" or sandstone terroir is indicative of the round stones or *galets* typical of the appellation. "*Sine sole nihil*" (nothing without the sun) is the motto engraved on the sun-dial in the courtyard of the *mas*.

The wines are generally ripe, clean and fruity with spicy notes and a light grain in the regular *cuvée* ('95 : 25 F) and the same spiciness but more power in the cuvée Terre d'Argence. The name of this *cuvée* is taken, according to local history, from an old hamlet where particularly bright foliage grew. It's a selection of old parcels planted 30 years ago on the territory of the Bishop of Arles, with a dominance of Syrah.

Our choice Costières de Nîmes Terre d'Argence red '95 (33 F). A very ripe nose and powerful, spicy palate with a note of fig. The extract is fine and has flesh and silky tannins. A lovely, long, balanced wine which gives one the impression of biting into the flesh of the fruit. The '96, tasted during fermentation, should at least be at the same level. To drink for the fruit.

Reception Excellent, generally with Anne Collard, in a corner of the beautiful hall which is presently being restored.

How to get there *(Map 23): From Avignon towards Tarascon via N570 then Beaucaire. Take the direction Saint-Gilles via D38. Turn right after 6km and follow the signposted route.*

Vinification the Roman way.

Mas des Tourelles

Owner Hervé Durand. **Address** 4294 route de Bellegarde, 30300 Beaucaire - Tel. 04.66.59.19.72 Fax 04.66.59.50.80. **Open** April 1 - Nov. 1, every day 14:00-18:00; in July and Aug., 10:00-12:00 and 14:00-19:00; the rest of the year, saturday 14:00-18:00. **Spoken** English, Spanish. **Credit cards** Visa, Eurocard, MasterCard.

Hervé Durand was grabbed by a profitable commercial idea when he discovered that his domaine was situated on the site of an old Roman villa and a studio where a revolutionary style of amphora was made (their light weight and straw covering made them easier for transport). He has since devoted himself to the revival of Roman-styled wines.

With Caton and Columelle as reference books and the CNRS as consultant enologist the whole site has been turned back 2,000 years. A Roman press and cellar have been constructed and the archeological objects excavated from the villa put on display.

Our choice The vintage 2748 (1995 according to our calendar) of Turriculae (70 F). Produced according to the latin texts of the Roman author Columelle. This is a dry, white wine, richly colored, with clean notes of walnuts (the Romans didn't use sulfur to fight oxidation). During the fermentation fenugrec, a leguminous plant found in the Mediterranean basin, and sea water which has been boiled and reduced are added. As an aperitif we preferred the Mulsum (65 F), a red wine in which honey and aromatic herbs have macerated after the fermentation. Bizarre, these Romans!

Reception Don't forget to visit the site (approx. 25 F/hour). The domaine also offers an interesting pamphlet on the origins of the production of wine in the Roman era (30 F).

How to get there *(Map 23): From Avignon towards Tarascon via N570 then Beaucaire. Drive in the direction of Saint-Gilles via D38. Turn right after 4km.*

Bread and wine: The domaine also offers bed and breakfast and *table d'hôtes.*

Domaine Saint-Luc

Owners Éliane and Ludovic Cornillon. **Address** 26790 La Beaume-de-Transit - Tel. 04.75.98.11.51 Fax 04.75.98.19.22. **Open** By appointment. **Spoken** English.

Formerly a hairdresser, Ludovic Cornillon was lured to the vine by marriage, arriving at the domaine with "his tiny suitcase and kneading-trough." A fountain-maker and grave-digger, he has done everthing he can to get the domaine going. "My heart is in Tricastin," he says. His heart and his word for he is unfailing in the defense of his wine (and for "his wine" read the whole appellation). In particular, he has succeeded in the exploit of uniting what seemed to be the two irreconcilable poles of the appellation: a fruity wine and a tannic wine, thanks to a long period of maceration with destemmed grapes. The wines have grip and amiability at the same time. There is also a red *cuvée* produced from Syrah and aged in oak casks. The '95 (approx. 43 F) is powerful, dense and black (color and aromas of black currant) with a balanced amount of oak. To age a little.

Our choice Coteaux du Tricastin red '95 (29 F). Produced from Grenache but refined by a good percentage of Syrah (30%). An attractive, dark hue, fine and reserved nose, a very ripe palate with the flavor of red fruits, well structured with a fine grain and silky tannins. The wine is fleshy and elegant. To drink.

Reception In a beautifully restored farm dating from 1789. The domaine also offers bed and breakfast (360 F). The gently priced *table d'hôtes* (135 F per person, evenings) in a family atmosphere has a good reputation.

How to get there *(Map 23): South of Montélimar towards Bollène via N7. 10km after Donzère towards Suze via D59. Turn left 4km after Saint-Paul towards La-Beaume-de-Transit, then right towards Saint-Turquoit via D117. Signpost on the right after 1km.*

The wide open spaces of Tricastin.

Domaine du vieux Micocoulier

Owners Jean and Georges Vergobbi. **Address** Quartier Le Logis de Berre, 26290 Les Granges-Gontardes - Tel. 04.75.04.02.72 and 04.75.98.58.40 Fax 04.75.04.41.81. **Open** From Monday to Saturday, 9:30-12:00 and 14:30-19:00, Sunday by appointment. **Spoken** English.

Arriving from North Africa in 1966, Jean and Georges Vergobbi took three years to clear this superb domaine of 120 hectares, in one single unit, using pick and shovel to remove the *garrigue*. The stony soils (*galets*) and primarily Grenache (65%) and Syrah (25%) blend produce ripe, robust wines which have a high degree of alcohol and strong tannic structure despite the short maceration period. They need to be sought out in the hot years to see them at their best; without the alcoholic structure they dry out quickly.

It's useless to try and find the old *micocoulier* (nettle tree) which gave its name to the domaine for having lavished a protective shadow over it for 150 years, resisting the mistral, until it collapsed on June 29, 1995, beaten by a tiny breeze.

Our choice Coteaux du Tricastin red '93 (22 F). A success for this vintage in the Rhône Valley, but a wine that is not typical of the house style. It is lighter in alcohol (only 13%!) and is extract but well-balanced with plenty of fruit and good length and persistence. To drink. The '94 is more typical of the wines of this domaine being heady, square, ripe, and dense. To choose without any hesitation.

Reception Colorful, in the bowels of the cellar.

How to get there *(Map 23): 16km south of Montélimar towards Donzère via N7, then towards Bollène via D541.Turn left after 3km towards Granges Gontardes and Grignan. Turn left at the roundabout situated 700m before Granges and follow the signs.*

The 100-year-old vines of Philippe Laurent, a lover of Grenache.

Domaine Gramenon

Owner Philippe Laurent. **Address** 26770 Montbrison/Lez - Tel. 04.75.53.57.08 Fax 04.75.53.68.92 **Open** By appointment. **Spoken** English.

Philippe Laurent set up shop in 1979 when he bought some Grenache vines that were more than 100-years-old, destined to be pulled up because of lack of productivity. Their average yield is 14 hectoliters/hectare. On the other hand they offer some incomparably fine fruit.

In white, don't forget the Clairette '95 (approx. 28 F), which spent 18 months on lees, for its flesh and freshness. However, the main attraction at this domaine is the *crème*, the Cuvée des Ceps Centenaires and, when it is available, the *crème de la crème*, a non-sulfured selection of the predecessor, affectionally christened La Mémé.

Our choice Côtes-du-Rhône *cuvée* La Mémé red '95 (approx. 95 F). A pure Grenache whose light color is misleading. The nose is explosive, the attack on the palate very supple, all the better for warming the place of a tight-knit but silky extract. From there on in the rest is easy, just let yourself go along on the long and persistent finale. La Mémé is an assertive wine.The '96 version (95 F), tasted before the final blend, is even more colored and certainly more concentrated, promising some very happy evenings. Heavenly *Mémés* ! To drink.

Reception Talkative. Above all, don't refuse to be taken to the beautiful cellar hewn from the limestone rock (here it's called the safre).

How to get there *(Map 23): From Grignan (east of Donzère) towards Taulignan then Montbrison via D14. Turn right at the entrance to Montbrison-Centre towards Valréas (signpost). After 2km climb to the left (signposted).*

Ouahi and Rémy Klein.

Domaine de la Réméjeanne

Owners Ouahi and Rémy Klein. **Address** Cadignac 30200 Sabran - Tel. 04.66.89.44.51 Fax 04.66.89.64.22. **Open** 9:00-12:00 and 13:30-18:00. **Spoken** English, German.

This is a domaine after our own hearts with a generous welcome and well-made wines at very reasonable prices. Here you can find a ripe and lively white (96: 29 F), a powerful but delicious rosé, perfect for summer meals (96: 29 F) and a red wine (the *cuvée* des Arbousiers '95, 28 F, which is ripe and fruity with pretty tannins and finesse). They are, however, far from being *petits vins.*

The cultivation of the vineyard and the vinification reaches the same standards as more well-known estates. Seeding between the rows limits the yields, the grapes are hand-harvested and a selection by parcel is made for each type of wine. *Pigeage* is practiced in the new wooden vats to increase extraction and finally the maturation is precisely executed. The *cuvée* Les Eglantiers, made from Syrah, is aged in seasoned oak and the other wines in vat.

The white wines (Viognier, Roussanne, Marsanne, Bourboulenc, Ugni Blanc and Clairette) occupy an important position at this domaine. In red, the Syrah is used as a support for the charms of the Grenache (one-third in the *cuvées* Arbousiers and Genévriers or on its own (*cuvée* Les Eglantiers, of which the '95, approx. 55 F, has plenty of flesh).

Our choice Côtes-du-Rhône *cuvée* Les Genévriers red '95 (37 F). For the brilliant, dark hue, ripe nose, fleshy, powerful palate and fine tannins. To drink.

Reception In a tiny corner of the cellar, next to the stocks of bottles and the oak barrels.

How to get there *(Map 23): from Bagnols/Cèze (on the right bank of the Rhône, opposite Orange) towards Alès via D6. Turn left after 3km towards Cadignac via D274 and Colombier, following the signs.*

Château Saint-Estève d'Uchaux.

Château Saint-Estève d'Uchaux

Supervisor Marc Français. **Address** 84100 Uchaux - Tel. 04.90.40.62.38 Fax 04.90.40.63.49. **Open** From Monday bis Saturday, 9:00-12:00 and 14:00-18:00, Sunday in July and Aug. **Spoken** English. **Credit cards** Visa, Eurocard, MasterCard.

This is a large (230 hectares, of which 60 hectares are vineyard) and beautiful domaine acquired in 1952 by Gérard Français, who introduced bottling at the property in 1961. Marc Français took over in 1973. The wines always have plenty of flesh and finesse throughout the range of *cuvées*. The *cuvée* Friande ('96: 27 F), based on Cinsault, is always deliciously supple and fruity.

In red, we liked the *cuvée* Tradition '95 (36 F) which is produced mainly from Grenache. The power of the vintage combines fruit (cherry) and finesse. Even better is the Côtes-du-Rhône Villages Grande Réserve '94 (44 F) which has an intense nose (licorice), fruity palate, solid structure, and silky tannins with the agreeable sensation of biting into the flesh of the fruit. The domaine also offers a white wine with delicate nose, lively, fleshy palate with a note of peach kernel and, in particular, a full-bodied, fleshy rosé ('95: 37 F) which is long and persistent.

Our choice Côtes-du-Rhône Vieilles Vignes red '94 (44 F), (66 F). The nose is intense (black currant), the palate big and powerful, very aromatic with flesh and an agreeable grain. The oak is well integrated and the finish long and persistent. To drink or age a little.

Reception In a large, spacious tasting room.

How to get there *(Map 23): From Orange towards Nyons via D976. Turn left at the entrance to Sérignan towards Piolenc, pass to the right of the church and take D172. The château is on the right, visible from a distance.*

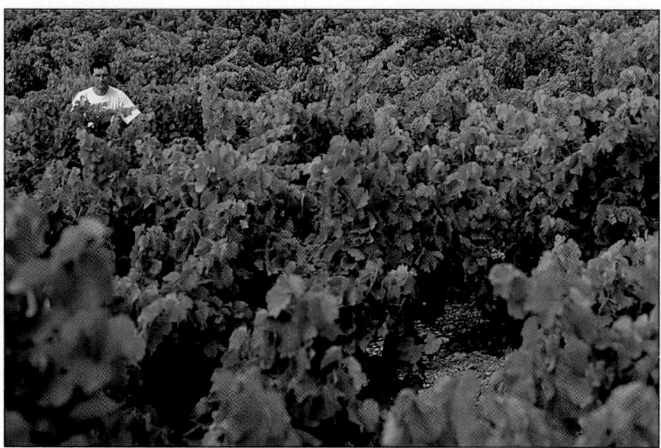

Frédéric Alary in the vines at Haut-Coustias.

Domaine de l'Oratoire Saint-Martin

Owners Frédéric and François Alary. **Address** Route de Saint-Romain, 84290 Cairanne - Tel. 04.90.30.82.07 Fax 04.90.30.74.27. **Open** From Monday bis Saturday, 9:00-12:00 and 14:00-19:00. **Credit cards** Visa, Eurocard, MasterCard.

The wines of this domaine are concentrated due to the *pigeage* but the extract remains silky thanks to the destemming of the grapes. We preferred the *cuvées* of Cairanne. The Réserve des Seigneurs '95 (approx. 34 F) is improved by the Mourvèdre and has a very fine, full palate which is cushioned by silky tannins, stuffed with aromatic notes of black fruits, and is long and persistent. One can alternatively opt for the *cuvée* Prestige (46 F) with it's rich, well-structured palate. The Côtes-du-Rhône Cairanne *cuvée* Haut-Coustias '95 (approx. 55 F), tasted from a provisional blend, merits the oak ageing for the Mourvèdre and Syrah, while the Grenache, with it's delicious, full, fleshy palate and dense, silky tannins is aged in vat. (To keep). In a region with a reputation for its red wines the surprise is in the whites.

Our choice Côtes-du-Rhône Cairanne *cuvée* Haut-Coustias white '95 (approx. 52 F). The Marsanne (75%) largely dominates in this wine with an addition of Muscat, Viognier and Clairette. The total blend is aged in oak (but well-integrated oak). The nose is a basket of fruits with a slight emphasis of Muscat. The palate has wonderfully ripe, elegant, exotic notes (pineapple, pear). The strong alcoholic structure is invisible as the wine is balanced and fresh. To drink.

Reception Very attentive, in a tiny tasting room.

How to get there *(Map 23): From Bollène (south of Montélimar) towards Carpentras via D8 passing by Rochegude and Sainte-Cécile. Turn left towards the old town in Cairanne and follow the signposted route.*

Treading (pigeage) the new harvest.

Domaine Richaud

Owner Marcel Richaud. **Address** Route de Rasteau - Tel. 04.90.30.85.25 Fax 04.90.30.71.12. **Open** From Monday bis Saturday midday, 9:00-12:00 and 14:00-18:00. **Spoken** English. **Credit cards** Visa, Eurocard, MasterCard.

Marcel Richaud reckoned, not so long ago, that he would never get things perfectly right. Now he thinks it will take 30 years. Here is a word of advice. Take the train while it's moving as the present wines are as good as plenty of other wines that have "arrived." If he likes to highlight the "wild" side of the Mourvèdre he also knows how to control it by using the old vines, tiny yields, the complicity of the Syrah and Grenache, and the quality of the extracted tannins. The prices are beyond imagination.

The domaine is regularly cleared of stock, but whatever the vintage, enjoyment can be found in all the *cuvées.* For instance, the white Cairanne (40 F) is full and fresh, the red Vin de Pays (16 F) quaffable, and the red Côtes-du-Rhone (25 F) spicy. Among the "more expensive" *cuvées* which disappear at a slower rate don't miss the red Côtes-du-Rhône Cairanne '96 (35 F) for it's concentration, finesse and delicious appeal.

Our choice Côtes-du-Rhône Cairanne Cuvée l'Ebrascade red '96 (45 F). For its ripeness, supple palate with fine, concentrated extract and its persistence. To age a while.

Reception Reserved. In case of closure or on weekends the wines of Marcel Richaud and those of his friends are on sale in the village square at the *Maison Vigneronne*, which also provides bed and breakfast accommodation.

How to get there *(Map 23): From Bollène (south of Montélimar) towards Carpentras via D8 passing by Rochegude and Sainte-Cécile. Exit from Cairanne direction Rasteau and turn left after 1,5km.*

The village of Cairanne seen from Corinne Couturier's vines.

Domaine Rabasse-Charavin

Owner Corinne Couturier. **Address** Quartier La Font-d'Estevenas, 84290 Cairanne - Tel. 04.90.30.70.05 Fax 04.90.30.74.42. **Open** From Monday to Friday, 8:00-11:30 and 14:00-18:00. Saturday morning, 8:00-11:30. **Credit cards** Visa, Eurocard, MasterCard.

Do you prefer Mourvèdre? Choose the Rasteau. Or perhaps you appreciate Syrah? Then take the Cairanne. Both have good fruit in common but also a certain grip. The majority of the wines, from highest to lowest prices, are worth investigating. For red wines that are fruit driven choose the fine and spicy (bayleaf) Côtes-du-Rhône *cuvée* Laure-Olivier '96 (29.50 F) or the supple, fruity Cairanne '96 (34 F). For a wine that has the same seductive aromas but which demonstrates structure and extract, the powerful and concentrated Rasteau '95 (34 F) fits the bill. Older vintages ('87, '88, '89) are available in boxes of three, one per vintage for the Cairanne (135 F). In Magnum, the '89 Cairanne and Rasteau (110 F), the pure Syrah (150 F) and the Cairanne *cuvée* Estevenas (150 F) are all available.

Our choice Côtes-du-Rhone Cairanne cuvée Estevenas red '95 (55,50). This very aromatic wine is produced from old vines of Grenache and Syrah. The Syrah at present shows to advantage but will soon soften under the opulent influence of the Grenache. The fruit extract is delicious, silky and very fine. To keep.

Reception In a tiny tasting room. In case of closure or on weekends the wines of Corinne Couturier and those of her friends are on sale in the village square at the *Maison Vigneronne*, which also provides bed and breakfast accommodation.

How to get there *(Map 23): From Bollène (south of Montélimar) direction Carpentras via D8 passing by Rochegude and Sainte-Cécile. Exit from Cairanne direction Vaison. The cellar is signposted at 800m on the left.*

Bird lover Luc Pélaquié.

Domaine Pélaquié

Owners Luc and Bénédicte Pélaquié. **Address** 7 rue du Vernet, 30290 Saint-Victor-la-Coste - Tel. 04.66.50.06.04 Fax 04.66.50.33.32. **Open** From Monday bis Saturday midday, 9:00-12:00 and 14:00-18:00, Saturday afternoon and Sunday morning by appointment. **Credit cards** Visa, Eurocard, MasterCard.

The white wines produced from sandy-clay soils are particularly successful, especially when the Clairette is late harvested. Luc Pélaquié prefers white wines that are round and fleshy which only a ripe harvest, around the end of October, can produce. The quality of the wines is always, therefore, dependent on the late-season weather conditions. If the sky remains blue then Luc Pélaquié is happy to wait. The white wines here are notable for their freshness and finesse, qualities that are not always current in the Southern Rhône. The reds have a smoky note which often evokes a nuance of Lapsang tea. The red Laudun '94 (29 F) is powerful and tannic with smoky, cherry-stone notes. The '95, with a marked Syrah character, is delicious and fine. The '94 and '95 Liracs (31 F) are spicy and have a slightly finer grain.

Our choice The white Laudun. They argue over it, worse still fight over it, so you have to get here before the harvest to acquire the wine. The '95 (33 F) is a clever mix of grape varieties where the Viognier gives serious support to the Clairette. The nose is ripe and intense but very fresh. The palate is incisive with a hint of hazelnut. The wine is very long and persistent. The '96 should be at the same level. To drink.

Reception In the tasting room, with a corner devoted to the protection of birds of prey.

How to get there *(Map 23): From Bagnols/Cèze (on the right bank of the Rhône opposite Orange) direction south via N86. Turn left at Connaux direction Saint-Victor and follow the signposted route to the center of Palus.*

An eternal supporter of Olympique de Marseille.

Domaine de la Soumade

Owner André Roméro. **Address** Route d'Orange, 84110 Rasteau - Tel. 04.90.46.11.26 Fax 04.90.46.11.69. **Open** From Monday bis Saturday, 8:00-11:30 and 14:00-18:00.

André Roméro is a man of outspoken loyalty. When there is only one supporter left of the soccer team Olympique de Marseille it will probably be André Roméro. His wines have the same honesty. They are muscular like a goal scorer and elegant like a winger.

You'll score precious points by picking the Côtes-du-Rhône '95 (70 F) for its power and finesse. Syrah and Viognier (20%) are blended and aged in oak with lees stirring. The methods of trainer Roméro are atypical but the results are astonishing. For the after-game party we suggest opening, on the sidelines, the fortified *vin doux naturel (VDN)* Rasteau '95 (65 F) for its delicious appeal, finesse, and notes of fig and raisins.

Our choice Côtes-du-Rhône Rasteau *cuvée* Prestige '94 (50 F). For its open nose and powerful, meaty, tannic palate. The '95 (65 F) is even better with more flesh, deliciously crunchy fruit, subtle but present tannins, and a muscly but sinewy and invisible alcoholic structure. Definitely to be chosen for the first team (but to keep).

Reception A special reward for fans of Olympique de Marseille but everyone else is welcome (even fans of Paris Saint-Germain !).

How to get there *(Map 23): From Bollène (south of Montélimar) towards Vaison via D4 passing by Rochegude, Sainte-Cécile and Cairanne. At the roundabout exiting from Cairanne towards Rasteau via D69. The cellar is signposted on the right before entering Rasteau.*

Sablet seen from the vines of Piaugier.

Domaine du Piaugier

Owners Sophie and Jean-Marc Autran. **Address** 84110 Sablet - Tel. 04.90.46.96.49 Fax 04.90.46.99.48. **Open** By appointment. **Spoken** English.

Jean-Marc Autran settled at this 25-hectare domaine in 1985. There are 18 hectares in appellation Côtes-du-Rhône Sablet, 3.5 in Gigondas and the rest in generic Côtes-du-Rhône. The parcels of this broken up vineyard are vinified separately in accordance with the *terroirs* and not blended. There are three distinct *cuvées*: Montmartel for the gravel soils on the hillsides, Briguières for the more clay-based soils and the *cuvée* Tenébi produced from some of the Briguières but with a blend of Grenache and Counoise whereas the two other *cuvées* are a blend of Grenache and Mourvèdre. The long period of maceration produces wines to age which are very concentrated but with a fine extract and very expressive aromas. The wines are clean, direct and pleasant without being easy.

The white Sablet '95 (40 F), vinified in oak, is fleshy and *gourmand* while the red '95 (38 F) is already drinkable. The Sablet Briguières '95 (42 F) is linear, the Tenébi '95 (42 F) round. The Gigondas '95 (approx. 46 F) is remarkable, concentrated, fine and exploding with fruit.

Our choice Côtes-du-Rhône Sablet Montmartel red '95 (42 F). Produced from old vines (40 years) of Grenache, the fruit of which is given vigor by a good dose of Mourvèdre (20%). The wine has power but the palate is fine and linear and already open and expressive. To keep a little longer.

Reception In the new vinification cellar while the new tasting room is being built.

How to get there *(Map 23): From Bollène (south of Montélimar) direction Vaison via D8 passing by Sainte-Cécile and Cairanne. Turn left 8km after Cairanne via D977 then right in the direction of Sablet. The cellar is on the main road behind the post office.*

A small part of Bernard Chamfort's collection of old winemaking implements.

Domaine de Verquière

Owner Bernard Chamfort. **Address** 84110 Sablet - Tel. 04.90.46.90.11 Fax 04.90.46.99.69. **Open** From Monday bis Saturday, 8:30-12:00 and 14:00-18:00. **Spoken** English. **Credit cards** Visa, Eurocard, MasterCard.

The domaine consists of 40 hectares mainly in appellation Côtes-du-Rhône, but also with vines in Sablet, Rasteau and Vacqueyras. The wines are tannic, robust and warm with the fullness of Grenache refined by an important percentage of Syrah (15 to 20%). Wisdom is acquired during the period of maturation. The reds need some bottle age to discipline the different elements.

For those who enjoy fruit-driven wines the white Côtes-du-Rhône and the rosé (approx. 26 F) are ideal. For those who take their pleasure more seriously the answer is the red Côtes-du-Rhône '96 (26 F) which is deliciously silky with notes of raisins or the Côtes-du-Rhône Rasteau '95 (approx. 29 F) with a supple, delicious palate. Still more serious is the Vacqueyras '95 (approx. 34 F) with an intense nose of fruit compote and red fruits and a palate which the Grenache has endowed with gamy notes, flesh and round tannins. The domaine also produces an attractive fortified *vin doux naturel* Rasteau (46 F) with expressive aromas of bitter almonds and coffee and a good sugar-alcohol balance.

Our choice Côtes-du-Rhône Sablet red '90 (41 F). Our pick from last year is still available and is evolving well. The palate is improving, gaining notes of undergrowth, but remains fresh and persistent. Still to keep.

Reception Excellent, in the tasting room which is decorated with old winemaking implements.

How to get there *(Map 23): From Bollène (south of Montélimar) towards Vaison via D8 passing by Sainte-Cécile and Cairanne. Turn left 8km after Cairanne via D977 then right towards Sablet. The cellar is on the right of the main road as it climbs. Signposted.*

Christian Bonfils, very Grenache.

Domaine de Boissan

Owner Christian Bonfils. **Address** 3 rue de Saint André, 84110 Sablet - Tel. 04.90.46.93.30 Fax 04.90.46.99.46. **Open** By appointment. **Spoken** English.

Christian Bonfils doesn't like "alien wines." "Each wine should have a place and stay in its place," he says, adding, "supple, fruity, summer wines from the Côtes-du-Rhône and Côtes-du-Ventoux, elegance and finesse from the Côtes-du-Rhône Sablet produced from Syrah grown on sandy soils, more full-bodied, spicy wines from Vacqueyras and wines with a more solid, fleshy extract to match with the winter cuisine of Gigondas." This is a domaine in the process of transformation which is making regular process. The vineyard is now more thoroughly cultivated (partial working of the soil, increase in the density of plantings) and the vinification handled more specifically (selection of vats, longer period of maceration). The wines, still with a notable Grenache influence, have a particularly well preserved fruitiness thanks to a winemaker whose obsession, not always shared in the region, is to fully ripen the Grenache. Among the numerous wines at the domaine we enjoyed two made from pure Grenache: the supple, aromatic Côtes-du-Ventoux '95 (20 F) and the Côtes-du-Rhône '95 (25 F) which has an acidity rare for the Grenache. The Vacqueyras '95 (39 F), also very Grenache but lengthened by a hint of Mourvèdre, was appealing. It has plenty of flesh, fullness, and a long finish.

Our choice Côtes-du-Rhône Sablet red '95 (33 F). The first bottling of this wine produced a supple, fruity version, the second (mid-1997) a fuller, more structured wine with dense but well polished tannins. To drink but the second bottling can be aged a while.

Reception Good, at the cellar.

How to get there *(Map 23): From Vaison-la-Romaine to Sablet. Drive towards Gigondas. Signpost on the right when exiting from Sablet.*

Ageing in bottle.

Domaine Sainte-Anne

Supervisors Jean and Alain Steinmaier. **Address** Les Cellettes, Saint-Gervais, 30200 Bagnols/Cèze - Tel. 04.66.82.77.41 Fax 04.66.82.74.57. **Open** From Monday bis Saturday, 9:00-11:00 and 14:00-18:00. **Credit cards** Visa, Eurocard, MasterCard.

Thanks to the policy of holding bottles in stock, this domaine offers older vintages that are mature and ready for drinking. The wines are always fleshy, fine, and well-made. They usually improve with some aeration before drinking. Be careful, as well, of the ungrateful age. These wines are best drunk young or after three years. The white wines are lovely with a rich, fleshy Viognier '96 (70 F) and persistent, powerful, fleshy Côtes-du-Rhône Villages '96 (35 F). The red wines based on Grenache are fruity but rarely available (Côtes-du-Rhône: 28 F). The Côtes-du-Rhône Villages '96 (35 F) is particularly full and structured. The older vintages, from '93 to '88, are also available in the *cuvées* Côtes-du-Rhône Villages Notre-Dame, Côtes-du-Rhône Saint-Gervais and the pure Syrah. We particularly liked the Côtes-du-Rhône Saint-Gervais '90 (80 F) for its silky palate and the Notre-Dame '90 (75 F) for the power. Older vintages ('83, 85, and '86 depending on the cuvée) are on allocated sale.

Our choice Côtes-du-Rhône Villages cuvée Notre-Dame des Cellettes red '94 (45 F). Produced from the oldest Grenache, Syrah and Mourvèdre. The color is bright, the nose and palate very fine. To keep a little while longer.

Reception In an attractive cellar for ageing the wines in bottle that was formerly a silkworm house.

How to get there *(Map 23): From Bagnols-sur-Cèze (on the right bank of the Rhône opposite Orange) to Saint-Gervais via D980. Turn right in the center of the village towards Cellettes. The cellar is on the right after 3km.*

The old village of Séguret, a must for visiting.

Domaine de Cabasse

Owners Alfred and Antoinette Haeni. **Address** 84110 Séguret - Tel. 04.90.46.91.12 Fax 04.90.46.94.01. **Open** In Summer, everyday, 8:00-12:00 and 14:00-18:00; in winter from Monday to Friday, 8:00-12:00 and 14:00-19:00. **Spoken** German, English. **Credit cards** Visa, Eurocard, MasterCard.

Alfred Haeni, of Swiss origin and formerly an agronomist, settled here in 1990. He had thought of going to Bordeaux but stopped en route, having fallen for this vineyard and its view of the beautiful old village of Séguret. He acquired this domaine in just one day, a month before the harvest. There is sometimes an exception to the rule that the Swiss are slow-mannered! Apart from some attractive labels the wines are notable for their light but lively style with a dominance of Grenache which explodes in a vintage like 1995. The regular red Côtes-du-Rhône Séguret '95 (34 F) is supple and fruity but the interest is really in the top *cuvées.* The red Côtes-du-Rhône Séguret Casa Bassa '94 (55 F) is an equal blend of Syrah and Grenache. The color is dark and the palate fleshy, fruity, juicy, and deliciously dense. However, the wine needs to age a little longer to allow the oak, still dominant, to become a little more subdued. The production of Gigondas is almost negligible.

Our choice Côtes-du-Rhône Séguret Garnacho '94 (45 F). Garnacho is an old name for Grenache, the grape variety that dominates this *cuvée.* The spicy palate is very fine with a slightly tannic character. The '95 has a little more flesh and fullness.

Reception In the tasting room. The domaine also has a comfortable hotel at the foot of the vines with a clear view of the old village of Séguret.

How to get there *(Map 23): Bollène (south of Montélimar) towards Vaison via Sainte-Cécile and Cairanne (D8 then D977). Pass by Sablet. The domaine is on the right at the entrance to Séguret.*

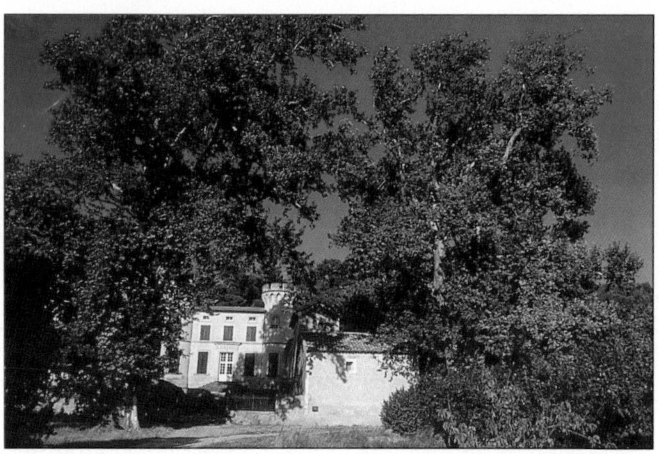

Some astonishing vins de pays to discover.

Château des Tours

Owner Emmanuel Reynaud. **Address** Quartiers des Sablons, 84260 Sarrians-Parisi - Tel. 04.90.65.41.75 Fax 04.90.65.38.46. **Open** From Monday bis Saturday, 9:00-19:00, Sunday by appointment. **Spoken** English.

Emmanuel Reynaud has made wine here since 1989. He immediately set high standards in the vineyard and the cellar. The soils are worked, the grapes harvested by hand and the wines vinified with natural yeasts, even to finish the wine. "I find it absorbing when a wine takes two years to finish fermenting its sugar," he says. He vinifies by grape variety and parcel and in the important parcels by the type of soil.

The red Vacqueyras '93 (53 F) is very Grenache with a deliciously full palate, fine tannins and beautiful spicy, smoky bouquet. The '94 (60 F), tasted from vat, is silky and full. Don't forget the vins de pays either (under the label Domaine, approx. 22 F). The white is powerful and concentrated and the red spicy and smoky.

Our choice White Côtes-du-Rhônes. The '93 (approx. 30 F) is an incredibly fleshy wine lightened by a note of Clairette. The white Grenache was harvested extremely ripe, rarely under 14%. The wine has a bouquet of spices, aromatic wood (cedar) and a hint of honey. The Réserve '92 (approx. 34 F) is a full-blown Grenache with power and concentration and smoky, quince and tobacco notes. The Réserve '94 (approx. 32 F) has amazing fleshiness, a very fine (almond), lifted palate and resin and honey finish. These wines can be drunk or aged a while.

Reception In a small sales-tasting area at the cellar.

How to get there *(Map 23): From Carpentras towards Orange via D950. Turn right 2km from the center of Sarrians towards Sablons then left towards the school. On the right after the school.*

Renée and René, a good blend.

Domaine des Grands Devers

Owners Renée and René Sinard. **Address** 84600 Valréas - Tel. 04.90.35.15.98 Fax 04.90.37.49.56. **Open** By appointment. **Credit cards** Visa, Eurocard, MasterCard.

"Quand le vin coule dans le bonhomme, sagesse passe dans le bonhomme." (When wine flows into man, wisdom seeps into man.) The Sinards have adopted this maxim, attributed to Jacob Cars, a 17th century Dutch poet, which embellishes their cellar. Does their wisdom have other origins ?

The wines are frank and assume a certain style without the sophistication of ageing in wood. It would be wrong to think of them as rustic as the level of the yields and the old vines produce a velvety palate.

A crisp, fresh white wine (approx. 35 F) and various reds are produced at the domaine. The majority offer a Grenache fruitiness. The Côtes-du-Rhône '95 (22 F) is supple and fresh and the Côtes-du-Rhône Enclave des Papes '94 (30 F) really delicious. The Syrah provides more structure in certain *cuvées* like the Côtes-du-Rhône Valréas but needs a warmer year than '94 to really open out. This cuvée needs to be seen again in the '95 vintage but from the good years we recall a fine, full-bodied wine.

Our choice Côtes-du-Rhône Syrah '93 (38 F). Impressive on the palate with fine extract, suppleness, and notes of cassis. Fruity and elegant, the wine is drinkable now but can also be aged.

Reception Heart in hand. In the new tasting room set up in an old cellar which is very cold. The domaine also offers bed and breakfast accommodation in 4 rooms (270 F) with an unforgetable breakfast.

How to get there *(Map 23): From Bollène towards Nyons via D9 and Suze, Tulette and Visan. Turn right 5km after Visan towards Saint-Maurice and follow the signs.*

Valérie Chaume-Arnaud.

Domaine Chaume-Arnaud

Owners Valérie and Philippe Chaume-Arnaud. **Address** 26110 Vinsobres - Tel. 04.75.27.66.85 Fax 04.75.27.69.66. **Open** By appointment. **Spoken** German.

Melons or vines? This was the question posed to Valérie Chaume-Arnaud when she took on her parents' various agricultural activities. She decided on the vine and started in 1987 by renting from her parents. “At first, because of the wish to work the soil, the desire to make wine came later,” she says. Before starting on her own she got a solid grounding at other domaines, in particular, Château Mont-Redon in Châteauneuf-du-Pape.

The vineyard is thoroughly worked with due respect for her capital of old vines (Grenache and Syrah, but also Carignan and Cinsault). Valérie prefers to work hard at nurturing her Carignan and Cinsault vines, today wrongly considered unworthy, rather than replanting them with other varieties.

The harvest is hand picked and the grapes for Côtes-du-Rhône destemmed as well as those for the Syrah destined for the Côtes-du-Rhône Vinsobres. The wines, therefore, gain a supple, silky texture without damaging the structure. The Côtes-du-Rhône ’95 is delicious, round, ample and fruity.

Our choice Côtes-du-Rhône Vinsobres red ’95 (approx. 32 F). A little more marked by the influence of the Grenache than usual (75% rather than 60%). The nose is intense, the palate ripe and explosive with plenty of flesh. The tannins are silky providing a good structure lengthened by the freshness of a crisp acidity. The wine has lovely notes of stewed fruit. To drink.

Reception Very good and easy going, in the modest vinification cellar.

How to get there *(Map 23): From Bollène towards Nyons via D94 passing by Suze, Tulette and Saint-Maurice. The cellar is signposted on the right just before Vinsobres.*

Hubert Valayer.

Domaine de Deurre

Owner Family Valayer. **Address** 26110 Vinsobres - Tel. 04.75.27.62.66 Fax 04.75.27.67.24. **Open** By appointment. **Spoken** English. **Credit cards** Visa, Eurocard, MasterCard.

Since 1987, Hubert Valayer, recently joined by his brother Denis, has offered very ripe, linear wines with a pronounced acidity and freshness. The domaine has one foot in the appellation Côtes-du-Rhône Vinsobres and the other in the neighboring appellation, Côtes-du-Rhône Saint-Maurice. The old vines are carefully protected by working the soils and the red grapes sorted and destemmed. This produces deliciously supple wines that are rapidly accessible. However, this seductive quality should not hide their innate character nor their potential, at least in the good years, to age.

Among the different wines produced at the domaine the reds are of most interest even if the white and rosé are of good quality. The Côtes-du-Rhône '95 (24 F) has a controlled exhuberance while the Côtes-du-Rhône Saint-Mauric '95 (30 F), from sandier soils than those of Vinsobres, is fine and fruity with a light smokiness on the finish.

Our choice Côtes-du-Rhône Vinsobres red '95 (32 F). The wine is a blend of Grenache, Syrah and Mourvèdre but the Grenache is very present on the nose with its maturity and ripe notes of red fruits and spice. The palate, also very full and ripe, is marked by a note of black currant. The tight-knit tannins are silky, the final clean, direct, and incisive. To drink.

Reception Excellent, in a small tasting room.

How to get there *(Map 23): From Bollène towards Nyons via D94 passing by Suze, Tulette and Saint-Maurice. The cellar is signposted on the right just before Vinsobres and after the Domaine Chaume-Arnaud.*

Denis Vinson: serious, generous wines.

Domaine du Moulin

Owner Denis Vinson. **Address** 26110 Vinsobres - Tel. 04.75.27.65.59 Fax 04.75.27.63.92. **Open** From Monday bis Sunday morning, 8:00-12:00 and 13:30-19:00. **Spoken** English.

When the easterly wind, the Pontias, blows the cellar is bathed in the odor of lavendar from the local distillery. Denis Vinson works in a traditional manner: the vines trained in gobelet style, the soil partially worked, no destemming or addition of cultured yeasts, and *pigeage* practiced to obtain good extraction. The wines have plenty of presence but also plenty of finesse.

There is an attractive choice of white wines in '95 with the floral, fresh regular *cuvée* (22 F) or the Côtes-du-Rhône Vinsobres (32 F) with its powerful nose and fruity palate (apricot, pineapple). The reds, firm and upright, are clearly in the style of the village (Vinsobres). The Côtes-du-Rhône '95 (22 F) is flatteringly intense and mature on the nose with notes of red fruits, likewise on the palate (spice, licorice) which finishes long and persistent with a light smoky note. The Côtes-du-Rhône Vinsobres *cuvée* Charles Joseph '90 (48 F), an equal blend of Syrah and Grenache, needs a little more time for the oak to become more subdued but the nose is intense (tobacco, red fruits) and the palate ample.

Our choice Côtes-du-Rhône Vinsobres red '94 (30 F). Produced from the oldest Grenache vines (70%) and Syrah. Bright, red hue. The nose is ripe and lightly toasted. The palate is ample, structured and fruity. The tannins are present but agreeable and the oak already mellow. To drink.

Reception In a small tasting area in the vinification cellar.

How to get there *(Map 23): From Bollène towards Nyons via D94 passing by Suze, Tulette and Saint-Maurice. Turn left 5km after Saint-Maurice towards Vinsobres via D190. The cellar is directly on the right. Sign.*

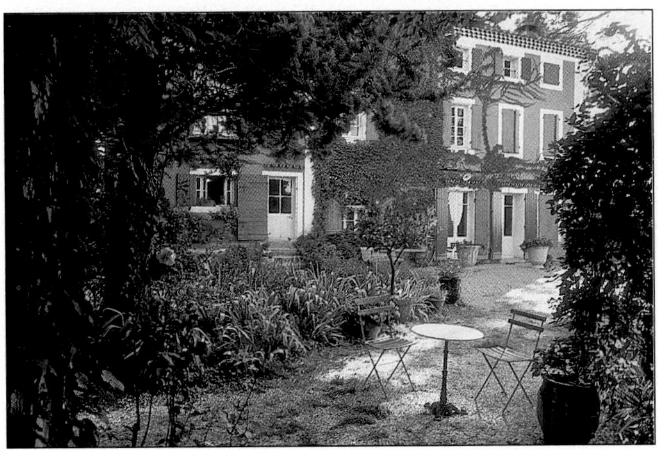

In the right season the tasting can take place in the garden.

Domaine de Fondrèche

Owners Nanou Barthélémy and Sébastien Vincenti. **Address** 84380 Mazan - Tel. 04.90.69.61.42 Fax 04.90.69.61.18. **Open** From Monday to Friday, 8:00-12:00 and 14:00-19:00, Saturday and Sunday by appointment. **Spoken** English.

Nanou, a trained biologist, took over this domaine in 1991. Sébastien, her son, arrived in 1993, drawn to wine by his step-father's work as a printer of wine labels. She reigns in the vines while he chose the cellar.

In small quantities and at less than 30 F there are some attractive whites and rosés. The white '95 has a particularly intense nose (flowers and yellow fruits) and is ample and fleshy on the palate while the rosé '95 is fleshy. But the best in '95 are the red wines. The *cuvée* Persia (39 F) is a pure Syrah aged in new or recent oak barrels. Inky, black hue, the nose has a violet and licorice aroma while the palate is full, round and fresh. This is a Syrah that is more elegant than powerful, more in the style of a Côte-Rôtie than a Châteauneuf-du-Pape. We are reacquainted with the Grenache in the cuvée Nadal (old Grenache vines that are more than 40-years-old blended with Syrah aged in seasoned oak barrels) where the wine reaffirms its power at the same time as keeping an attractive aroma of raisins and roasted almonds.

Our choice Côtes-du-Ventoux red '95 (26 F). Based on Grenache with a complement of Syrah, Cinsault and Carignan. The nose is intense, ripe and peppery. The palate solid and squarely built with plenty of stuffing (neither fined nor filtered) but very elegant and expressive, aromatic (plum, black cherry) with attractive tannins. A long and persistent wine. To drink.

Reception In the right season tastings can take place in the attractive garden.

How to get there *(Map 23): From Carpentras towards Bédoin via D974. The domaine is signposted on the right after 6,4km.*

An old spring at the domaine.

Château Pesquié

Owners Édith and Paul Chaudière. **Address** 84570 Mormoiron - Tel. 04.90.61.94.08 Fax 04.90.61.94.13. **Open** Every day, 10:00-12:00 and 14:00-18:00. **Spoken** English, German, Spanish. **Credit cards** Visa, Eurocard, MasterCard.

The Ventoux has often been a judge for the Tour de France. This domaine, which regroups a number of properties, crosses the appellation's finish line clearly in front. This is partly because the place and the cellars are very beautiful and partly because the wines, from the most simple to the most ambitious, race to the front.

Breaking free, the Château Pesquié rosé (approx. 26.45 F) wins the prize for fruit. In the pursuing group, in red, the Hauts du Parandier '94 (18,80 F) *cuvée "non filtrée"* (in fact lightly filtered) gains for its intense nose and the power on the palate while the Château Pesquié '93 (44,20 F) from the Syrah team takes honors for the intense nose and powerful palate. With plenty of extract the wines need to be kept. If you want to enjoy their youthful fruit serve them with rich dishes. The wines will react well.

Our choice Château Pesquié Moutié red '94 (26,45 F). Driven by its two legs (Grenache and Syrah), the wine has an intense nose (blackberry), a palate which is supple on attack but which quickly becomes full-bodied and tannic (but the tannins are not hard), and notes of leather with a hint of game.

Reception Don't miss seeing the very beautiful barrel cellar.

How to get there *(Map 23): East of Carpentras towards Sault via D942. Turn left towards Mormoiron (don't enter the village) 5km after Mazan. The domaine is a little further on the left, towards Flassan via D184.*

Michel Faraud.

Domaine du Cayron

Owner Michel Faraud. **Address** 84190 Gigondas - Tel. 04.90.65.87.46 Fax 04.90.65.88.81. **Open** Everyday, 9:00-12:00 and 14:00-19:00. **Spoken** English. **Credit cards** Visa, Eurocard, MasterCard.

Michel Faraud calmly runs the 15-hectare domaine that he inherited. The vineyard is spread throughout the *terroir* of Gigondas, from the Dentelles de Montmirail to the *garrigue*, with the old vines attaining an average age of 40 years and among those some that have reached 70 years. The Grenache dominates (70%) but a hint of Cinsault (15%) is added to provide suppleness while the same percentage of Syrah brings a touch of vivacity. The grapes are hand-harvested and sorted, not destemmed, and never have cultured yeasts added (Michel Faraud underlines the word "never"). There is no temperature control during fermentation and the wines are not chaptalized nor fined nor filtered.

"The wine makes itself," he says. However, one can sense that what seems to be the law of least effort is not that which spares the worry. After fermentation in vat the wines are aged in old *foudres*. The whole harvest is blended to obtain a uniform wine but there are different bottlings "in order for the wine to remain in wood for as long as possible."

Our choice Gigondas '93 (47 F). The color is still dark but bright, the nose intense, the palate full and powerful. The extract is thick but fine, the final long and persistent. It's better to wait a little longer for this wine but it is already accessible.

Reception Good, without fuss, in a corner of the old cellar.

How to get there *(Map 23): From Vaison-la-Romaine towards Orange via Séguret and Sablet. The cellar is signposted on the left in the center of Gigondas when climbing towards the main square.*

Bernadette and André Richard.

Domaine de la Tourade

Owners André and Bernadette Richard. **Address** Route de Bollène, 84190 Gigondas - Tel. 04.90.70.91.09 Fax 04.90.70.96.31. **Open** Every day 9:00-19:00. **Spoken** English, Spanish. **Credit cards** Visa, Eurocard, MasterCard.

Don't count on André Richard or his wife selling you a translucent Gigondas (or Vacqueyras, the other wine from this domaine). They prefer that their wines are solidly and comfortably rolled in Grenache. For them a Grenache "becomes good at 13.5% to 14%." Their wines are, therefore, only truly expressive in sunny years. If the alcoholic structure is powerful, however, it remains well disguised as the extract is concentrated, in particular, in the Gigondas *cuvée* Font des Aïeux, produced from old vines grown on the hillsides in the well-known zone, les Pallières.

The domaine is worked in a traditional manner with partial tilling of the soil, harvesting by hand, no destemming or introduction of cultured yeasts, ageing in *foudres*, and no fining nor filtering. These methods produce opulent wines that are tannic without being hard which play more on power than finesse but where the extract, at least in the hot years, is very rich and sweet. Apart from our choice taste the Gigondas '94 (approx. 45 F) for its intense black cherry aroma and fine, concentrated palate and the heady, full Vacqueyras '94 (approx. 38 F).

Our choice Gigondas *cuvée* Font des Aïeux '94 (approx. 55 F). Dark but bright red hue. The nose is intense (black fruits, black currant), the palate powerful and full, sweet, with strong aromas (smoky, leather, prune). Long and persistent. To keep a little.

Reception Good, in the tasting room.

***How to get there** (Map 23): Leave Gigondas towards Bollène via D8. The cellar is a large, modern construction on the left.*

The coat of arms adopted by the domaine.

Domaine Les Goubert

Owners Jean-Pierre and Mireille Cartier. **Address** 84190 Gigondas - Tel. 04.90.65.86.38 Fax 04.90.65.81.52. **Open** From Monday bis Saturday, 9:00-12:00 and 14:00-19:00, Sunday by appointment. **Spoken** English. **Credit cards** Visa, Eurocard, MasterCard.

There was no red wine made in '92, nor white in '94. The Cartiers must have had an allegory of extreme care represented on their coat of arms. Despite a short vatting time the wines are powerful and very concentrated. The extract, however, is always silky, the aromatics ripe and fresh.

Don't miss out on the delicate and fresh white Côtes-du-Rhône Sablet ('96: 38 F) or the simple red Côtes-du-Rhône ('96: 26 F) which is long but remains upright with fine quality tannins and enveloped in fruit and smoky aromas. The regular *cuvée* of Gigondas should also not be missed. Even in a difficult year like '94, and in a lighter style than usual, it unravels a pleasurable smoky swirl. If they are still available don't refuse a taste of the Beaumes-de-Venise '94 (approx. 34 F) for its perfumed nose and palate which runs away with finesse and roundness by unfolding a delicious and explosive extract, or the Viognier (62 F) for its delicacy and notes of white fruits.

Our choice Gigondas cuvée Florence (89 F). The '93 is ripe, fruity (black currant), with plenty of extract (neither fined nor filtered), and very long. This wine needs to be kept 5 to 10 years to become fully harmonious.

Reception Generally by Mireille Cartier, in an attractive but simple tasting room.

How to get there *(Map 23): southwest of Vaison via Séguret and Sablet. Turn right when level with Gigondas and follow the signposted route.*

The wines for ageing are well-guarded!

Château d'Aquéria

Supervisors Vincent and Bruno de Bez. **Address** 30126 Tavel - Tel. 04.66.50.04.56 Fax 04.66.50.18.46. **Open** From May bis Oct. every day, 8:00-13:00 and 14:00-19:00. **Spoken** English, Spanish. **Credit cards** Visa, Eurocard, MasterCard.

The billboards scattered throughout the commune unceasingly repeat that Tavel is France's number one rosé. The appellation is so sure of this that it produces neither white nor red. The rosé in question is special in that it is vinified like a red, but with a shorter vatting time, providing plenty of extract, a robust body and deep color. The average quality of the wines of this appellation is, however, inferior to its claims. Also one needs to be cautious about the choice.
The Château d'Aquéria Tavel '95 (43 F) has a deep color, fruity nose, round and fruity palate which is strongly structured by the well-disguised alcohol content. It's a robust and very persistent wine to drink with food.

The domaine also produces an attractive white Lirac. The '95 (47 F) shows well with a fine, fruity palate (almond, peach kernel).

Our choice Lirac red '94 (40 F). For its very ripe, spicy nose, powerful palate, silky tannins, and good length. The '95 (approx. 43 F) is better by a short head. There is the same power and finesse but the extract is more tight-knit and the aroma more licorice than fruity. To drink, but these wines, kept under the right conditions, are capable of an astonishing evolution.

Reception In the brand new tasting room with a view of the cellar.

How to get there *(Map 23): From Avignon towards Nîmes and A9 via N580. At the roundabout before the autoroute towards Nîmes via D976. The château is at 300m.*

The *scourtins* (woven rope filters) used in old vertical presses.

Domaine de la Fourmone

Owners Marie-Thérèse and Roger Combe. **Address** 84190 Vacqueyras - Tel. 04.90.65.86.05 Fax 04.90.65.87.84. **Open** Every day, 9:00-12:00 and 14:00-18:00. **Spoken** English, German. **Credit cards** Visa, Eurocard, MasterCard.

"Traditional vinification ...", proclaims the domaine's brochure. Following in her father Roger's footsteps, Marie-Thérèse Combe is not yet ready to yield to the call of high technology. Having been hand-harvested and fermented without being destemmed nor with the addition of cultured yeasts, the grapes are pressed in old vertical presses similar to those used in Champagne. Free-run and pressed wines are then always blended. This produces very round, fleshy wines in a ripe, well-extracted blend where the dominant Grenache makes a clear statement. This variety represents 80% of the blend to which Syrah and Mourvèdre are not just added randomly but provide a certain finesse, rigor and vivacity.

The domaine also produces Gigondas but we prefer the different *cuvées* of Vacqueyras. The white (38 F) is always fleshy, fine and long but the reds are of most interest. The *cuvée* Trésor du Poète '95 (36 F), tasted before bottling, should confirm its power and finesse.

All the wines need some aeration to really give of themselves.

Our choice Vacqueyras *cuvée* Cep d'Or red '94 (48 F). Produced from old Grenache vines, this wine offers an intense, ripe, fruity nose and full, structured palate. The extract is fine. There is plenty of freshness, balance, length and persistence. To keep a little. The '95 should be sumptuous.

Reception Excellent, in the tasting room, normally with a member of the Combe family.

How to get there *(Map 23): At the exit to Vacqueyras on the Carpentras-Bollène road. Route indicated and large signpost on the right.*

Each bottle is wrapped in tissue paper.

Domaine Clos des Cazeaux

Owners Maurice and Jean-Michel Archimbaud-Vache. **Address** 84190 Vacqueyras - Tel. 04.90.65.85.83 Fax 04.90.65.83.94. **Open** From Monday bis Saturday, 9:00-12:00 and 14:00-18:30.

Every year each *cuvée* is made from the same parcels of vines and same varieties to retain a distinct character. From Vacqueyras, the *cuvée* Saint-Roch is made from 65% Grenache and 30% Syrah and the Cuvée des Templiers from 75% Syrah and the rest Grenache. In Gigondas, the *cuvée* La Tour Sarrasine is made from 80% Grenache and 20% Mourvèdre. In Vacqueyras Saint-Roch, choose the '93 (36 F) for its fine, ripe nose and delicious, upright palate which explodes with youthful vigor, fine tannins, flesh, and good length. There are some wonderful Gigondas of which we preferred the '94 (44 F) for its concentration, finesse and full tannins (it still needs to be kept), the '93 (46 F) for its finesse and spicy finish and, in particular, the '90 (60 F, sales of one bottle only) for its structure, vivacity and raisin-like aroma. Other vintages available in Gigondas range from '92 to '89 (sales allocated, 44 F to 60 F).

Our choice Vacqueyras Cuvée des Templiers '94 (38 F). For its toasted nose and dense palate with tight-knit but polished tannins. It's a wine whose weight is balanced by length and persistence. To keep.

Reception In an old farm that once belonged to the Knights Templar, more often than not with Lucette Vache, mother of Jean-Michel, the winemaker. Each bottle from each *cuvée* is carefully wrapped in tissue paper of a specific color and placed in the old wooden tubs or cornues used for the harvest.

How to get there *(Map 23): From Carpentras towards Bollène via D7 for 12km. Enter Vacqueyras and follow the route indicated from the first road on the left.*

The domaine took its name from the old mulberry trees.

Domaine des Amouriers

Owner Jocelyn Chudzikiewicz. **Address** Les Garrigues de l'Étang, 84260 Sarrians - Tel. 04.90.65.83.22 Fax 04.90.65.84.13. **Open** By appointment. **Spoken** English.

The domaine has an excellent blue clay *terroir* with plenty of round stones or *galets*, smaller in size than those that made the name of Châteauneuf-du-Pape. Grenache accounts for half the domaine (10 hectares in AOC and 12 in vin de pays), often with old vines on mass selection, with Syrah lending a helping hand. The soil is partially worked and the grapes hand-harvested to produce solid wines that are tannic without being hard but that need to be aged.

The domaine produces a range of wines without a false note among them. The red Côtes-du-Rhône '95 (31 F) is delicious with notes of black fruits and an attractive tannic character. The Vacqueyras *cuvée* Signature '95 (approx. 46 F) has red fruit aromas, an ample, fleshy palate, tight-knit tannins, velvety texture and plenty of length. Don't underestimate the vins de pays. The red Val des Deux Rivières (18 F!) is fruity, quaffable and at an amazing price. It is made from more than 50-year-old Cinsault and should be tasted by all those who otherwise abuse this grape variety.

Our choice Vacqueyras les Genestes '95 (approx. 49 F). Solidly based on Grenache and Syrah (60% and 40%) this is an ample wine with lovely tannins which has a balanced ripeness and freshness and which is voluptuously long. To wait a little.

Reception Open and passionate.

How to get there *(Map 23): From Orange towards Carpentras via N7 then D950. Turn left at Sarrians towards Vacqueyras, then immediately left for 7km towards Les Garrigues de l'Etang. The domaine is on the left.*

INDEX BY VINEYARDS

A

B

C

D

E

F

G

H

I

J

K

L

M

N

O

P

Q

R

S

T

U

V

W

Z

INDEX BY OWNERS

A

B

C

D

E

F

G

H

I

J

K

L

M

N

O

P

Q

R

S

T

V

PHOTOGRAPHIC CREDITS

Photographs were taken by Antoine Gerbelle and Dominique Couvreur, except for those on the following pages:

- 154, 185, 188, 203, 206: © Éric Planchard.
- 199, 408, 411: © Didier Matal.
- 172: © Zapa Bordeaux/D. Le Lann.
- 503: © J.-M. Goyhenex.
- 175: © Scope/Michel Guillard.
- 202: © Fabrice Leseigneur.
- 272: © J.-P. Muzard.
- 407: © Alain Rival.
- 505, 510, 518: © Raymond Roig.
- 508: © Georges Bartli.
- 621: © Patrick Joly.
- 669: © D. Beauvois.
- Front cover: © François Tissier.

Fodor's RIVAGES
HOTELS AND
COUNTRY INNS
of Character and Charm
IN FRANCE
• WITH COLOR MAPS AND PHOTOS •

Fodor's RIVAGES
BED AND
BREAKFASTS
of Character and Charm
IN FRANCE
• WITH COLOR MAPS AND PHOTOS •

Fodor's RIVAGES
HOTELS AND
COUNTRY INNS
of Character and Charm
IN ITALY
• WITH COLOR MAPS AND PHOTOS •

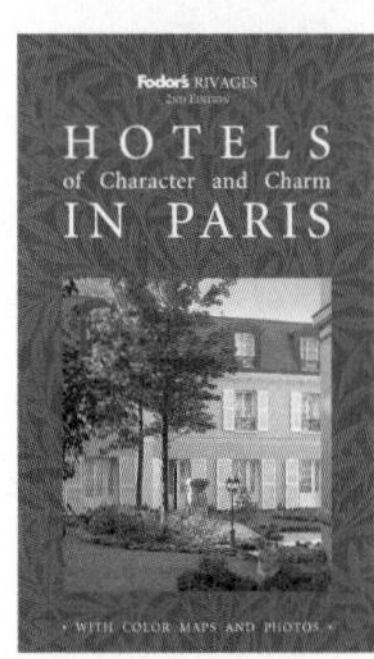
Fodor's RIVAGES
HOTELS
of Character and Charm
IN PARIS
• WITH COLOR MAPS AND PHOTOS •

Fodor's RIVAGES
HOTELS
of Character and Charm
IN SPAIN
• WITH COLOR MAPS AND PHOTOS •

Fodor's RIVAGES
HOTELS
of Character and Charm in
PORTUGAL
• WITH COLOR MAPS AND PHOTOS •

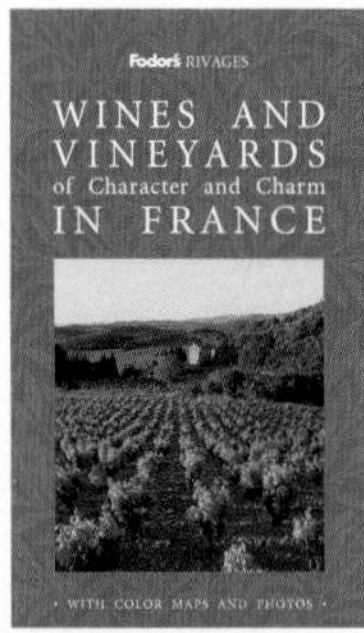
Fodor's RIVAGES
WINES AND
VINEYARDS
of Character and Charm
IN FRANCE
• WITH COLOR MAPS AND PHOTOS •